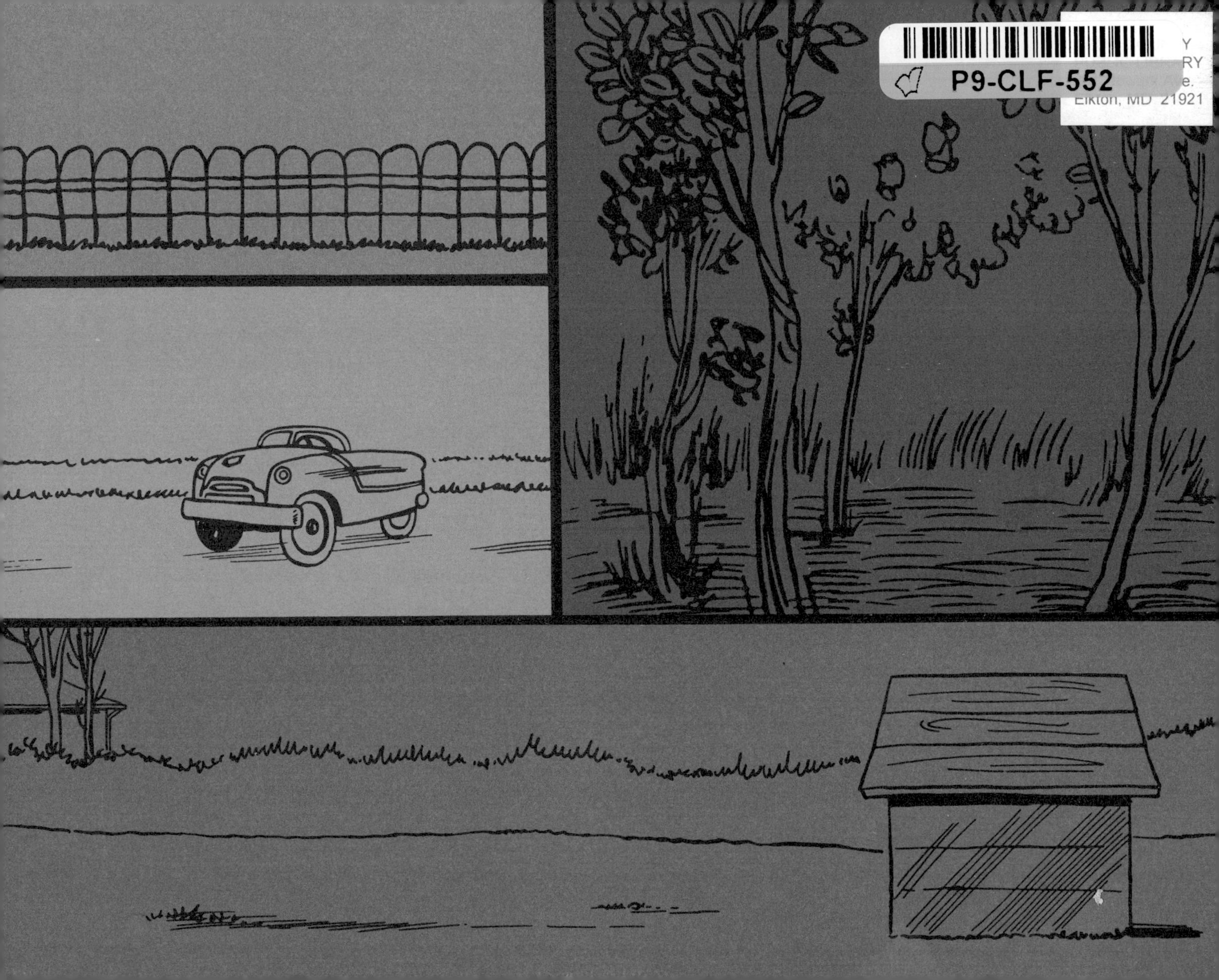

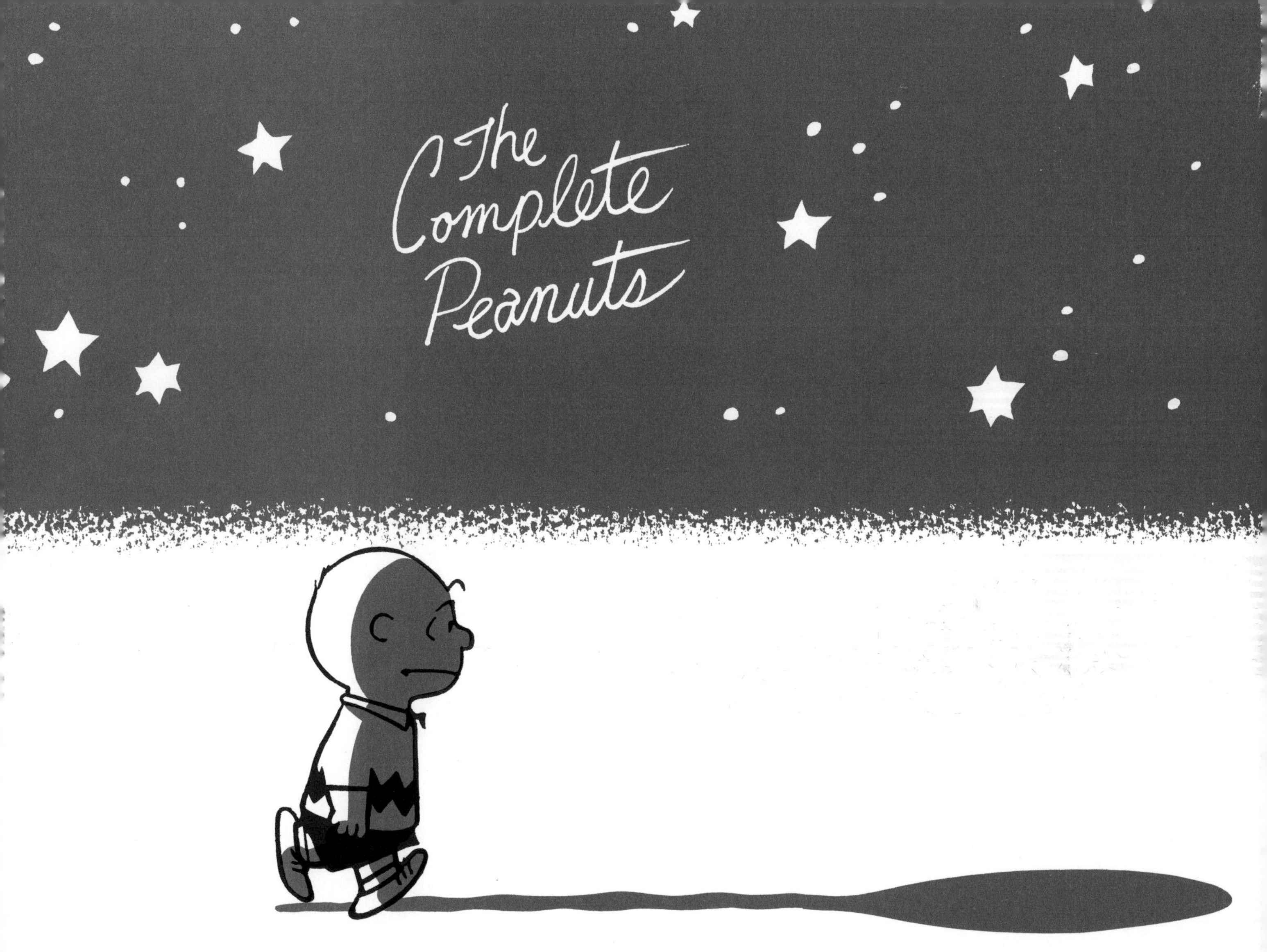
The Complete Peanuts

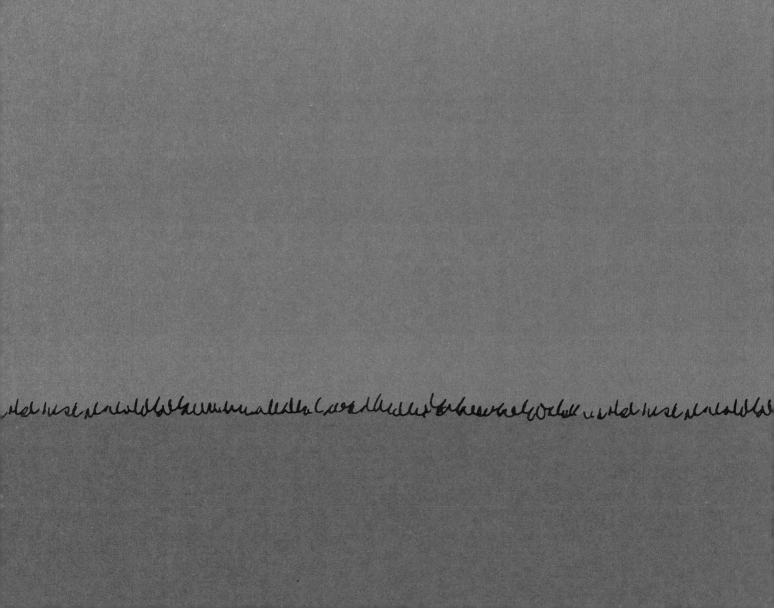

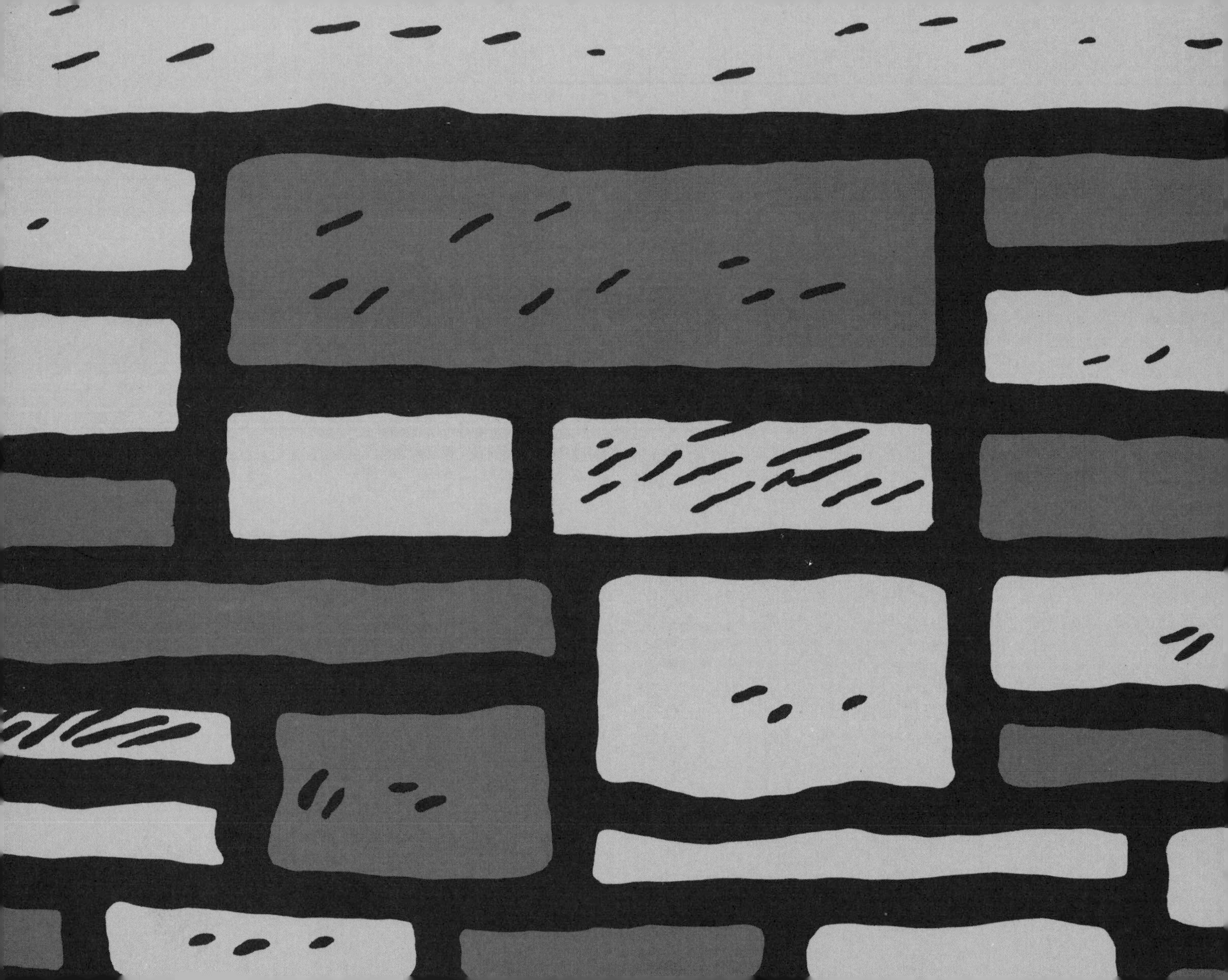

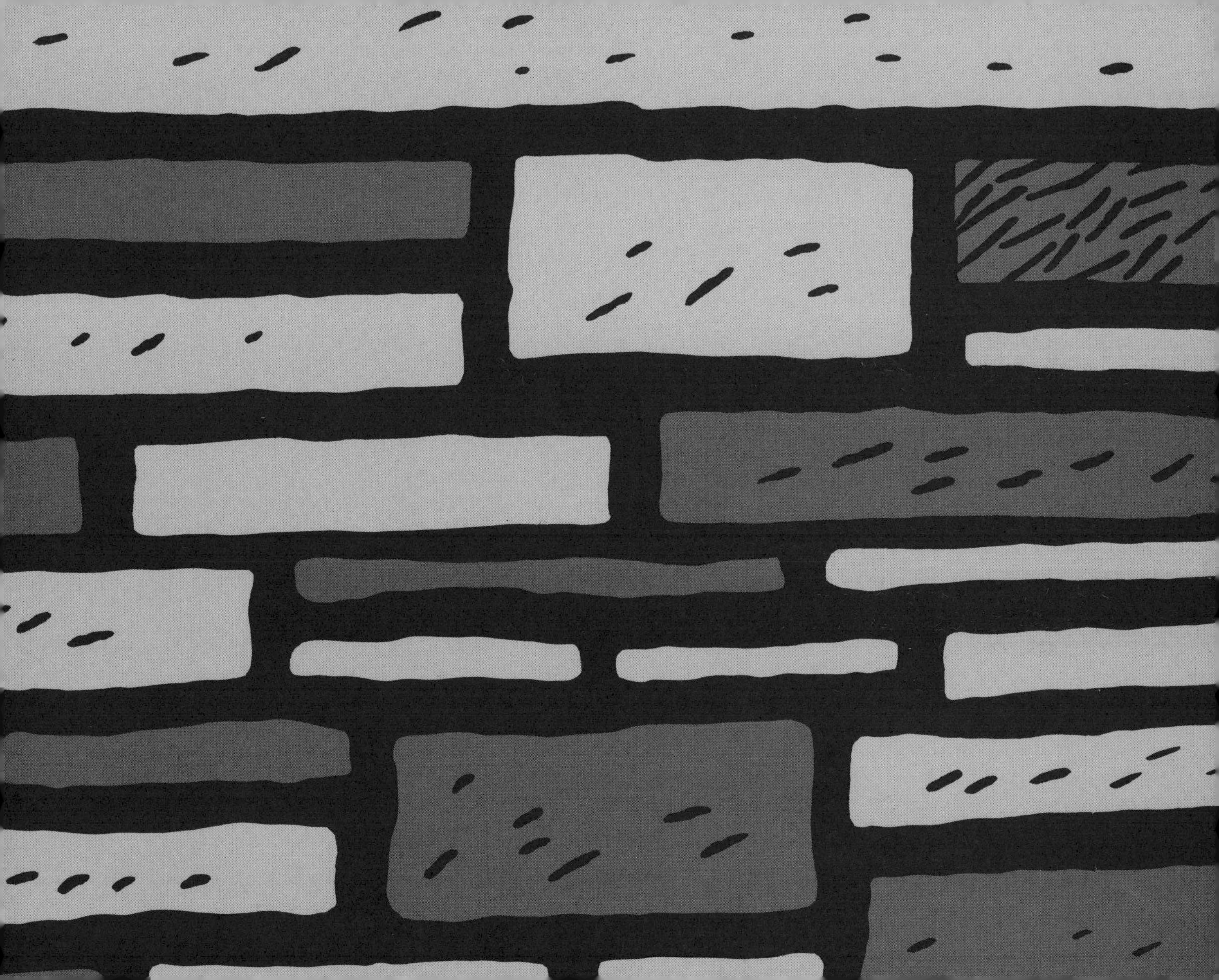

THE COMPLETE PEANUTS
by Charles M. Schulz
published by
Fantagraphics Books

Editor: Gary Groth
Designer: Seth
Production Manager: Kim Thompson
Production, assembly, and restoration: Paul Baresh and Adam Grano
Archival and production assistance: Nat Gertler,
Carys Kresny, Marcie Lee, and Linda McCurdy
Promotion: Eric Reynolds
Publishers: Gary Groth & Kim Thompson

Special thanks to Jeannie Schulz, without whom
this project would not have come to fruition.
Thanks to Timothy Chow, and to
Charles M. Schulz Creative Associates,
especially Paige Braddock and Kim Towner.
Thanks for special support from United Media.

Fantagraphics Books, 7563 Lake City Way, Seattle, WA 98115, USA. For a free full-color catalogue of
comics, call 1-800-657-1100. Our books may be viewed on our web site at www.fantagraphics.com.

Distributed to the book trade by:
USA: W.W. Norton and Company, Inc.
500 Fifth Avenue, New York, NY 10010
212-354-5500
Order Department: 800-233-4830
CANADA: Raincoast Books
9050 Shaugnessy Street, Vancouver, British Columbia V6P 6E5
Customer Service: 800-663-5714

ISBN 1-56097-670-5   First printing: September 2005   Printed in China

CHARLES M. SCHULZ

THE COMPLETE PEANUTS

1957 TO 1958

"SOMETIMES I THINK MY
SOUL IS FULL OF WEEDS!"

FANTAGRAPHICS BOOKS

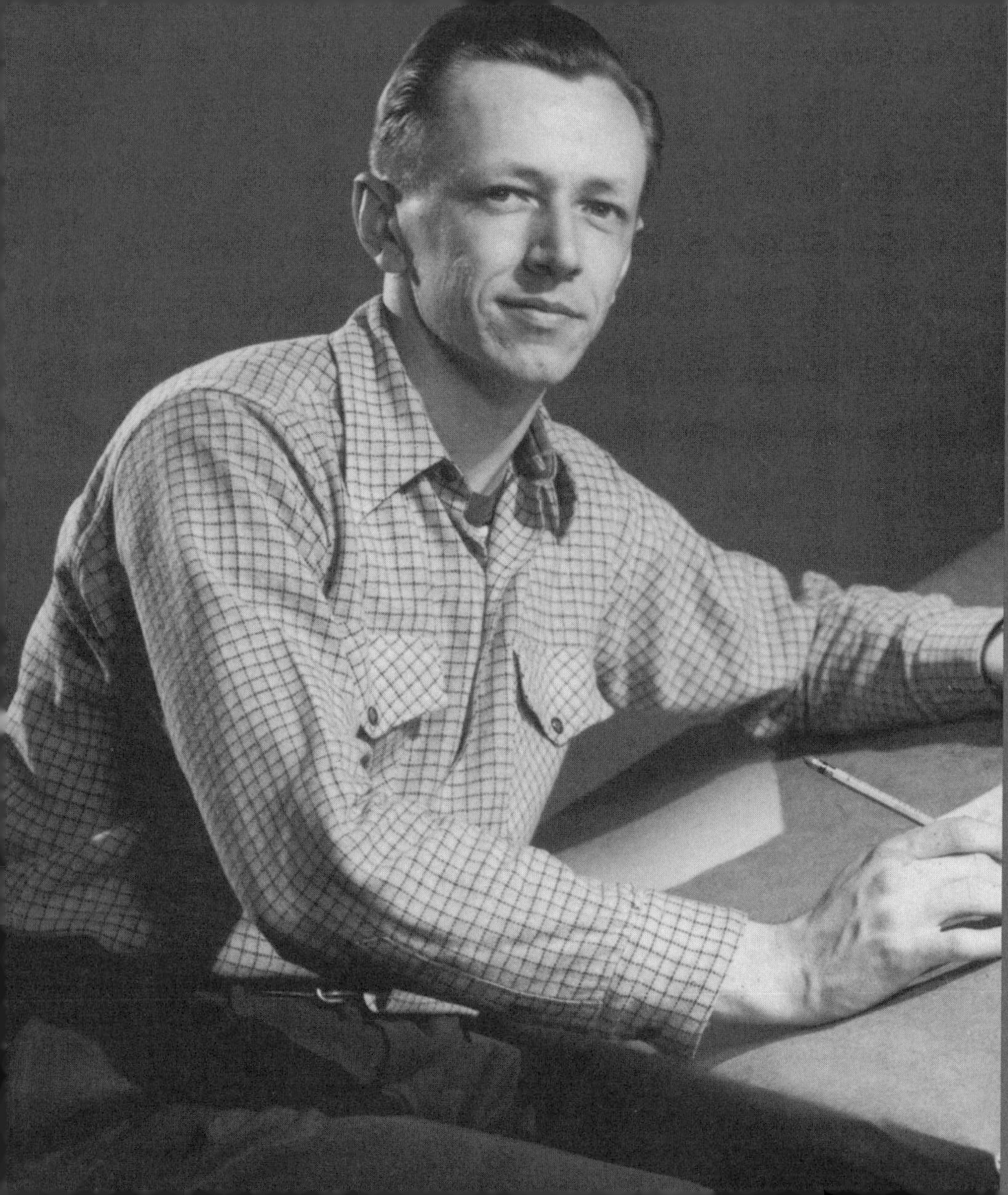

Charles Schulz
circa 1950.

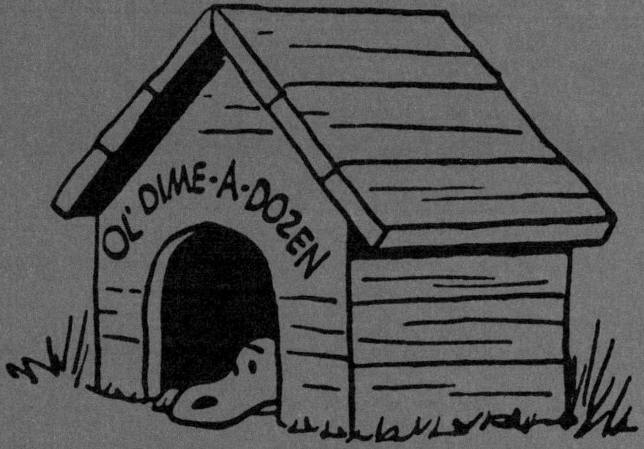
OL' DIME-A-DOZEN

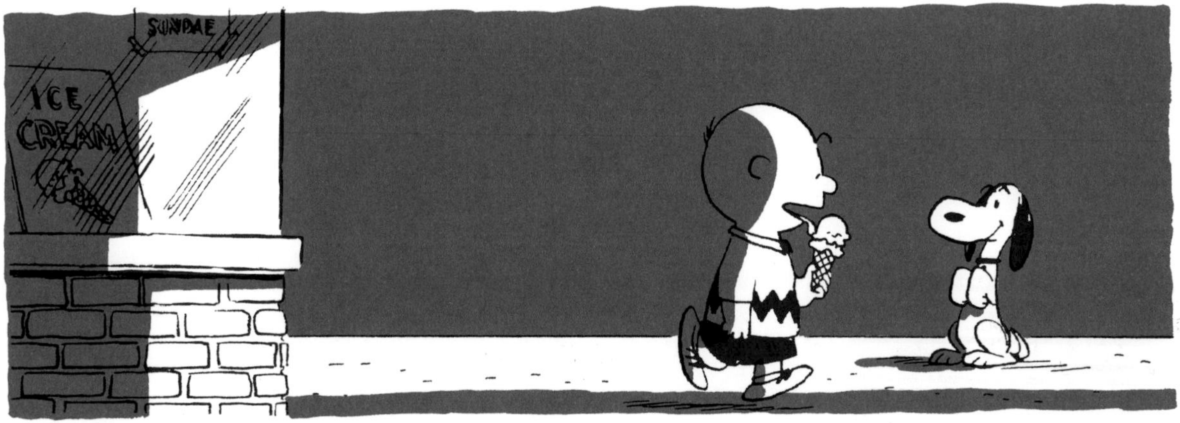
SUNDAE
ICE CREAM

FOREWORD by JONATHAN FRANZEN

Was Charles Schulz's comic genius the product of his psychic wounds? Certainly the Schulz depicted in Rheta Grimsley Johnson's authorized biography, *Good Grief* (1989), was a mass of resentments and phobias that seemed attributable, in turn, to emotional traumas in his youth: his unpopularity at school, his skinniness and pimples, the rejection of his drawings by his high school year book, the death of his mother on the eve of his induction into the army, the little red-haired girl's rejection of his marriage proposal, and so on. The man who became the best-loved artist on the planet was increasingly prone to attacks of depression and bitter loneliness. ("Just the mention of a hotel makes me turn cold," he told Grimsley.) Although he left his native Minnesota, he replicated its comforts in California, building himself an ice rink whose snack bar was called "The Warm Puppy." By the 1970s, he was reluctant even to get on an airplane unless someone from his family was with him. Here — the armchair psychologist might think — was a classic instance of the pathology that produces great art: wounded by adolescent traumas, our hero took permanent refuge in the childhood world of *Peanuts*.

But what if Schulz had chosen to become a toy salesman, rather than an artist? Would he still have lived such a withdrawn and emotionally turbulent life? I suspect not. I suspect that Schulz the toy salesman would have gutted his way through a normal life the same way he'd gutted out his military service. He would have done whatever it took to support his family — begged a Valium prescription from his doctor, had a few drinks at the hotel bar.

Schulz wasn't an artist because he suffered. He suffered because he was an artist. To keep choosing art over the comforts of a normal life — to grind out a strip every day for fifty years; to pay the very steep psychic price for this — is the opposite of damaged. It's the sort of choice that only a tower of strength and sanity can make. The reason that Schulz's early sorrows look like "sources" of his later brilliance is that he had the talent and resilience to find humor in them. Almost every young person experiences sorrows. What's distinctive about Schulz's childhood is not his suffering but the fact that he loved comics from an early age, had a gift for drawing, and was the only child of good parents.

This is not to say that the depressive and failure-ridden Charlie Brown, the selfish and sadistic Lucy,

the philosophizing oddball Linus, and the obsessive Schroeder (whose Beethoven-sized ambitions are realized on a one-octave toy piano) aren't all avatars of Schulz. But his true alter ego is clearly Snoopy: the protean trickster whose freedom is founded on his confidence that he's lovable at heart, the quick-change artist who, for the sheer joy of it, can become a helicopter or a hockey player or Head Beagle and then again, in a flash, before his virtuosity has a chance to alienate you or diminish you, be the eager little dog who just wants dinner.

On page 183 of the current volume you will find a strip in which Snoopy grabs Linus's blanket in his teeth, swings Linus round and round in the air, sends him flying skyward, and reflects: "I'm the first dog ever to launch a human being!" This strip probably refers to the Russian space dog Laika, who was launched in November 1957, but it could also serve as a description of the volume as a whole. In the 1960s, *Peanuts* would break free of gravity altogether — achieve a degree of popularity for which there was not remotely any precedent, abandon all pretense of depicting realistic children and animals, and attain the stylistic escape-velocity at which an artist is no longer shadowed by any precursor but himself. What launched the strip to such heights was, above all, the character of Snoopy. The years 1957 and 1958, which this volume covers, find Snoopy being transformed from a cartoon dog into the I-am-what-I-am of later years. These are the years when his snout reaches maximum extension, double or triple its original length. He still sheds fur, fetches balls, chases birds, and licks people for no reason; but now, for the first time, he does things that aren't conceivably doglike; he stands on Schroeder's piano and plays a violin; he suits up for baseball. Meanwhile, the children's personalities are settling into their now-familiar contours, and Schulz is developing the longer narrative sequences and archetypal gags (Linus's blanket, Charlie Brown's kite, Lucy's competition with Beethoven, Charlie Brown's "pencil pal," the baseball sequences) that characterize his breakthrough work.

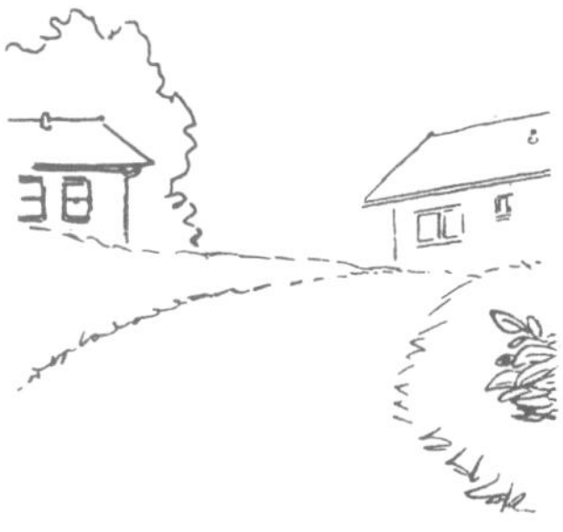

One long-running gag, given treatment in multiple strips for the first time in 1958, is Charlie Brown's yearly failure to get any valentines. In *Peanuts, A Golden Celebration*, published shortly before his death, Schulz told a Valentine's story from his own childhood. When he was in first grade, his mother helped him get valentines for everybody in his class, so that nobody would be offended by not getting one; but he felt too shy to put them in the box at the front of the classroom, and so he took them all home again to his mother. At first glance, Schulz's story recalls a strip on page 97 of this volume: Charlie Brown peers over a fence at a swimming pool full of happy kids, then he goes home and sits by himself in a bucket of water. But Schulz, unlike Charlie Brown, had a mother on duty — a mother to whom he chose to give his whole basket of valentines.

A child deeply scarred by a failure to get valentines would probably not grow up to draw lovable strips about the pain of never getting valentines. (A child like that — one thinks of R. Crumb — might instead draw a valentine box that morphs into a female body part that devours his valentines and then devours him, too.) Beneath the conventional narrative of Schulz's childhood failures is the story of a happy young man oversupplied with parental love. His little family's closeness gave him strength; its closedness probably helped estrange him from the world. Love feeding art feeding estrangement feeding forgiveness: the gifts Schulz was given became his gift to us.

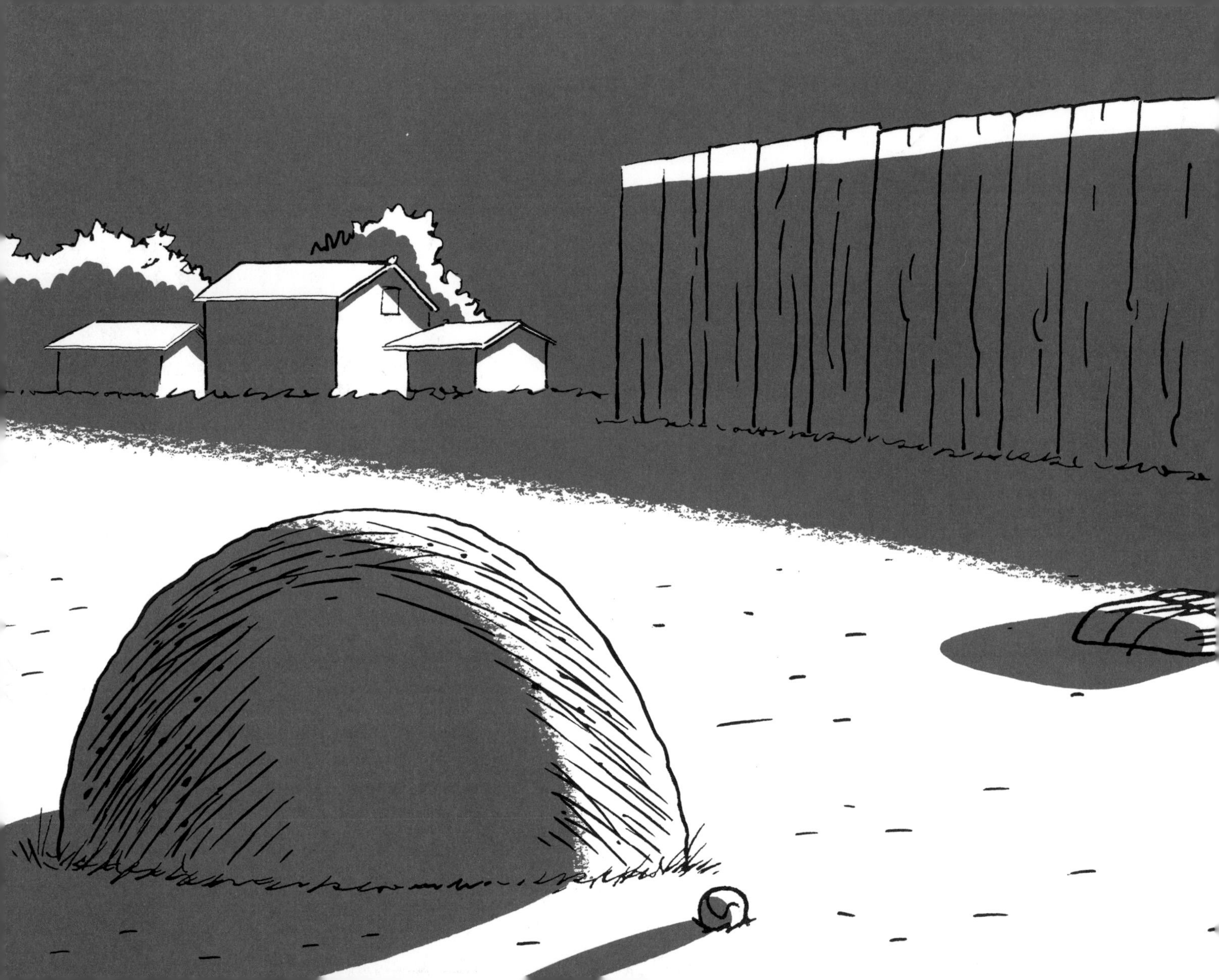

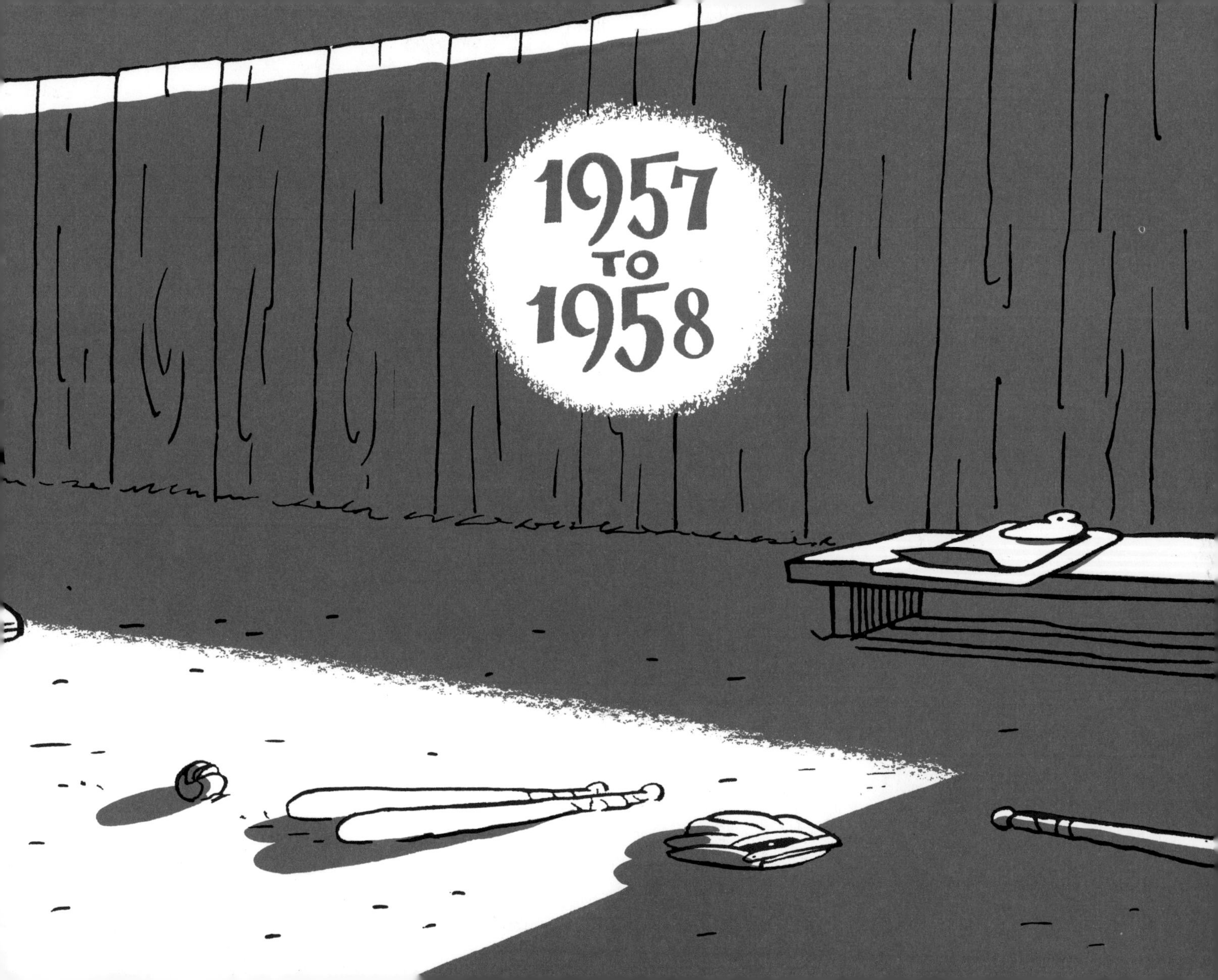
1957
TO
1958

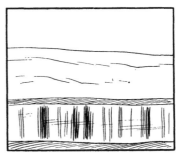

1-1

SCHULZ

I'D LIKE TO BE ABLE TO FEEL THAT I'M NEEDED..

DON'T FORGET, CHARLIE BROWN, THAT PEOPLE WHO ARE REALLY NEEDED ARE ASKED TO DO A LOT OF DIFFERENT THINGS...

UH, HUH...

WELL, I'D LIKE TO FEEL NEEDED, AND YET NOT HAVE TO **DO** ANYTHING

1-2

SCHULZ

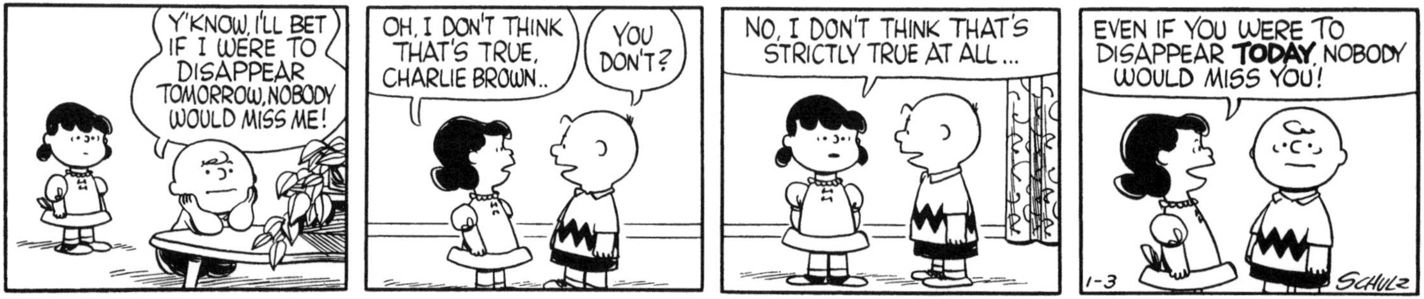
Y'KNOW, I'LL BET IF I WERE TO DISAPPEAR TOMORROW, NOBODY WOULD MISS ME!
OH, I DON'T THINK THAT'S TRUE, CHARLIE BROWN..
YOU DON'T?
NO, I DON'T THINK THAT'S STRICTLY TRUE AT ALL...
EVEN IF YOU WERE TO DISAPPEAR **TODAY**, NOBODY WOULD MISS YOU!
1-3
SCHULZ

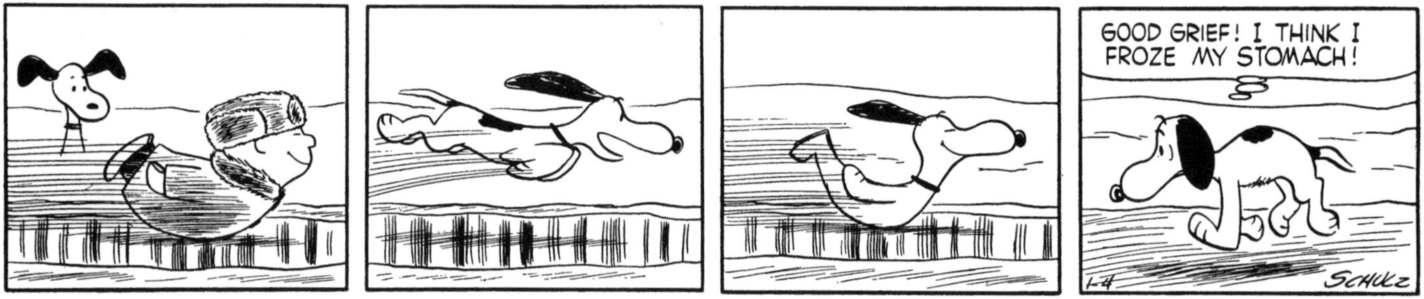
GOOD GRIEF! I THINK I FROZE MY STOMACH!
1-4
SCHULZ

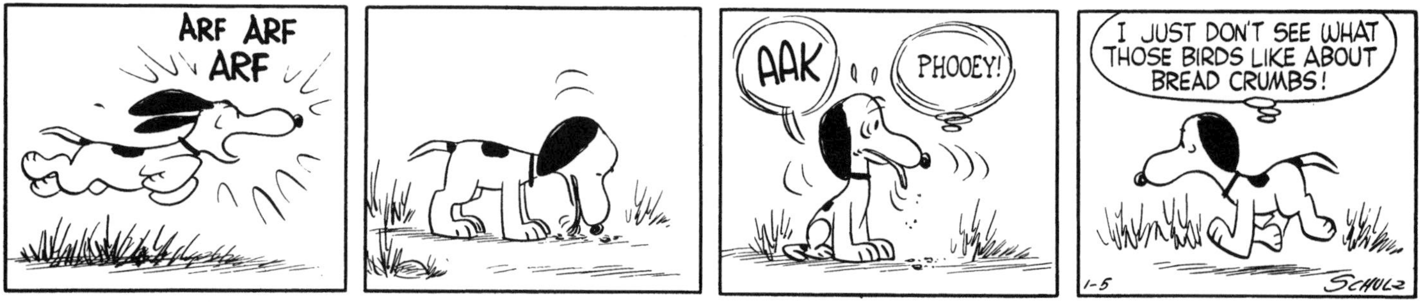
ARF ARF ARF
AAK
PHOOEY!
I JUST DON'T SEE WHAT THOSE BIRDS LIKE ABOUT BREAD CRUMBS!
1-5
SCHULZ

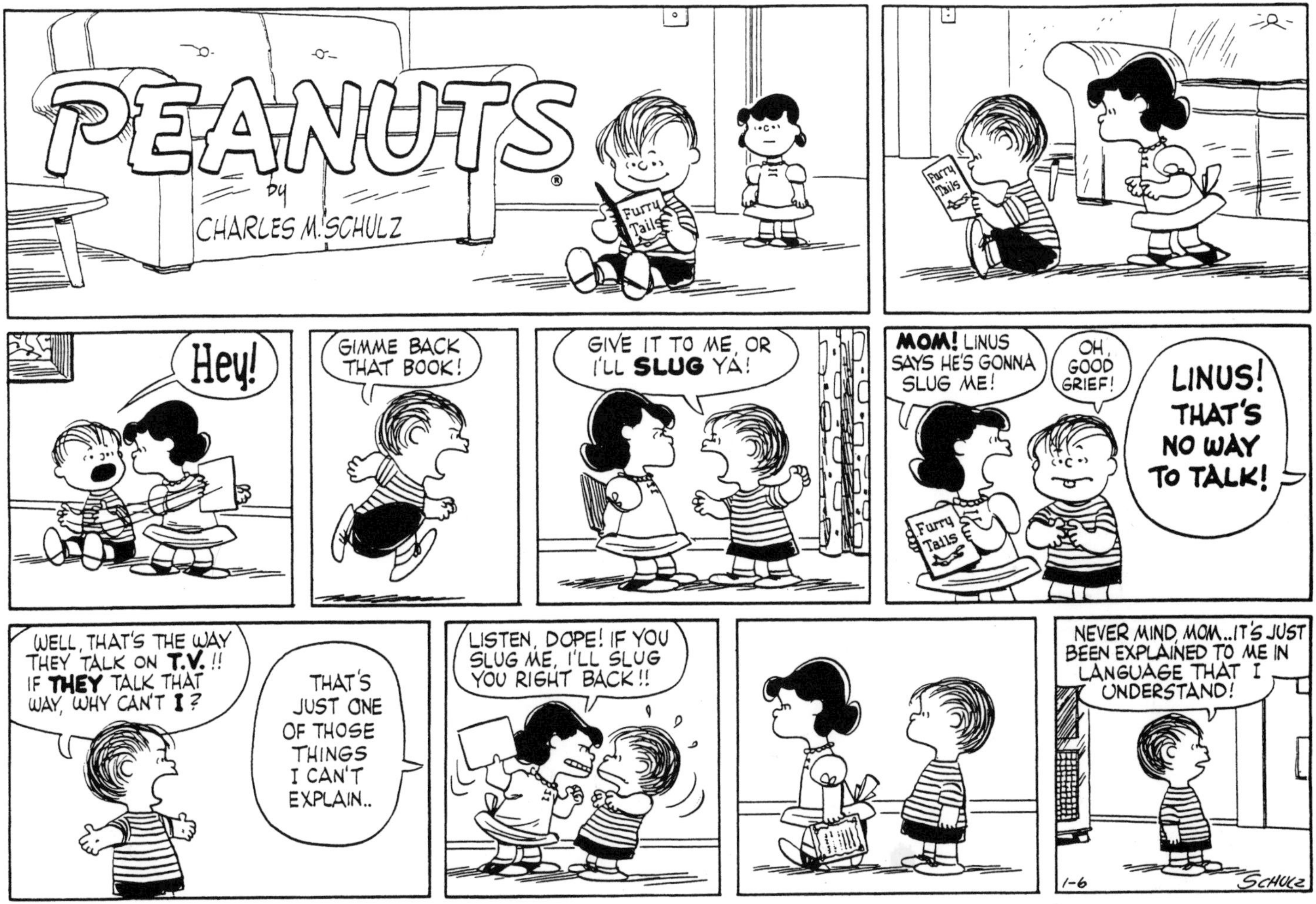
PEANUTS
by
CHARLES M. SCHULZ
Furry Tails
Hey!
GIMME BACK THAT BOOK!
GIVE IT TO ME, OR I'LL **SLUG** YA!
MOM! LINUS SAYS HE'S GONNA SLUG ME!
OH, GOOD GRIEF!
LINUS! THAT'S NO WAY TO TALK!
WELL, THAT'S THE WAY THEY TALK ON **T.V.**!! IF **THEY** TALK THAT WAY, WHY CAN'T **I**?
THAT'S JUST ONE OF THOSE THINGS I CAN'T EXPLAIN..
LISTEN, DOPE! IF YOU SLUG ME, I'LL SLUG YOU RIGHT BACK!!
NEVER MIND, MOM..IT'S JUST BEEN EXPLAINED TO ME IN LANGUAGE THAT I UNDERSTAND!
1-6
SCHULZ

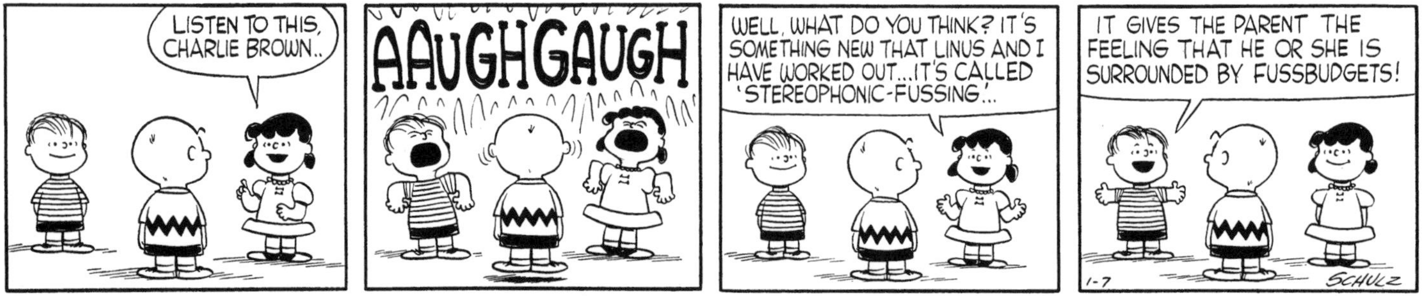
LISTEN TO THIS, CHARLIE BROWN..
AAUGHGAUGH
WELL, WHAT DO YOU THINK? IT'S SOMETHING NEW THAT LINUS AND I HAVE WORKED OUT...IT'S CALLED 'STEREOPHONIC-FUSSING'...
IT GIVES THE PARENT THE FEELING THAT HE OR SHE IS SURROUNDED BY FUSSBUDGETS!
1-7
SCHULZ

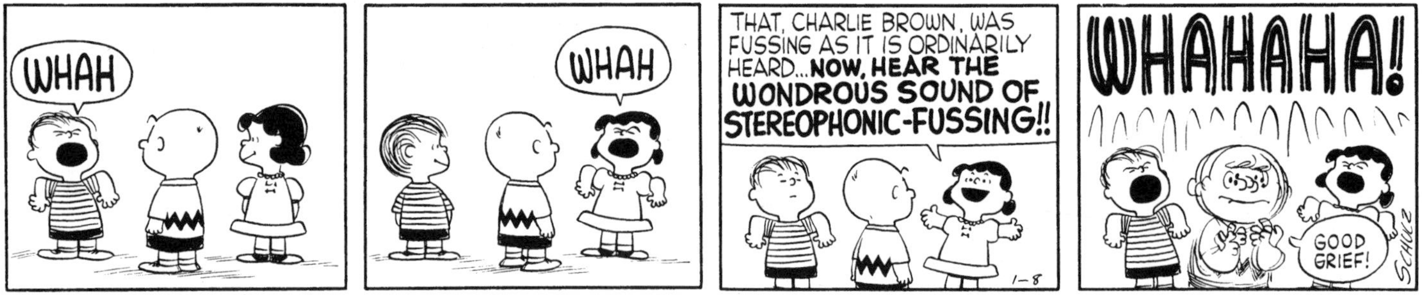
WHAH
WHAH
THAT, CHARLIE BROWN, WAS FUSSING AS IT IS ORDINARILY HEARD...NOW, HEAR THE WONDROUS SOUND OF STEREOPHONIC-FUSSING!!
1-8
WHAHAHA!
GOOD GRIEF!
SCHULZ

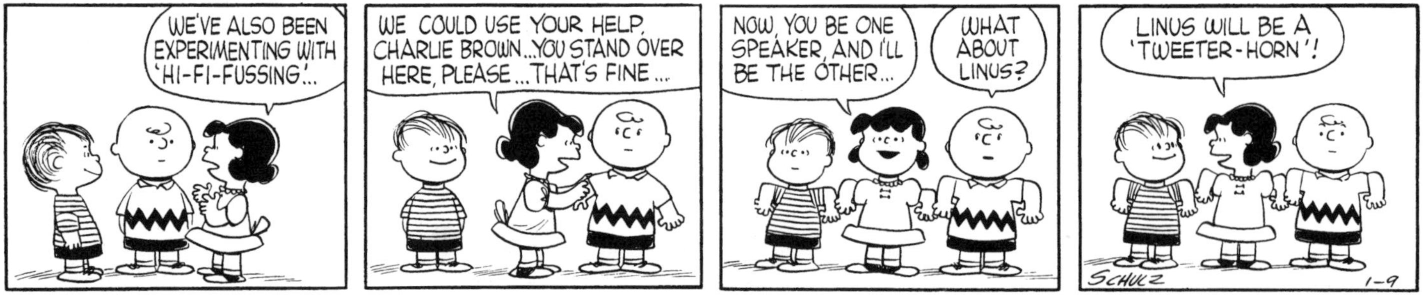
WE'VE ALSO BEEN EXPERIMENTING WITH 'HI-FI-FUSSING'...
WE COULD USE YOUR HELP, CHARLIE BROWN...YOU STAND OVER HERE, PLEASE...THAT'S FINE...
NOW, YOU BE ONE SPEAKER, AND I'LL BE THE OTHER...
WHAT ABOUT LINUS?
LINUS WILL BE A 'TWEETER-HORN'!
SCHULZ
1-9

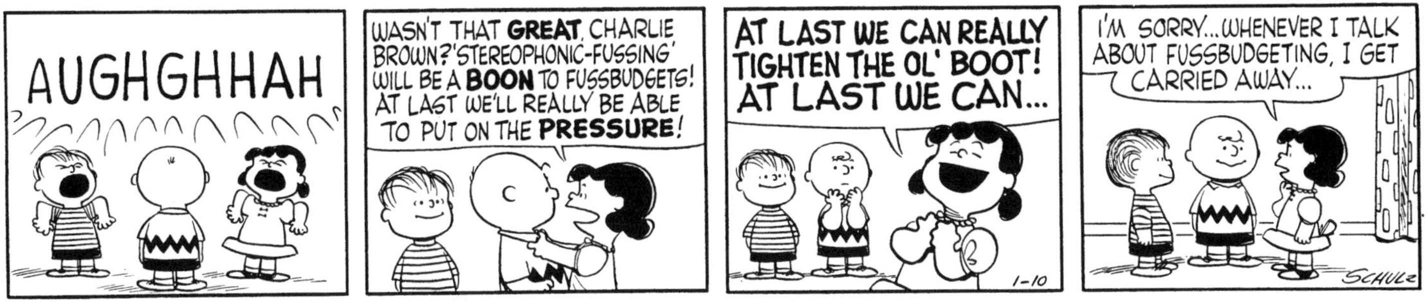
AUGHGHHAH
WASN'T THAT GREAT, CHARLIE BROWN? 'STEREOPHONIC-FUSSING' WILL BE A BOON TO FUSSBUDGETS! AT LAST WE'LL REALLY BE ABLE TO PUT ON THE PRESSURE!
AT LAST WE CAN REALLY TIGHTEN THE OL' BOOT! AT LAST WE CAN...
I'M SORRY...WHENEVER I TALK ABOUT FUSSBUDGETING, I GET CARRIED AWAY...
1-10
SCHULZ

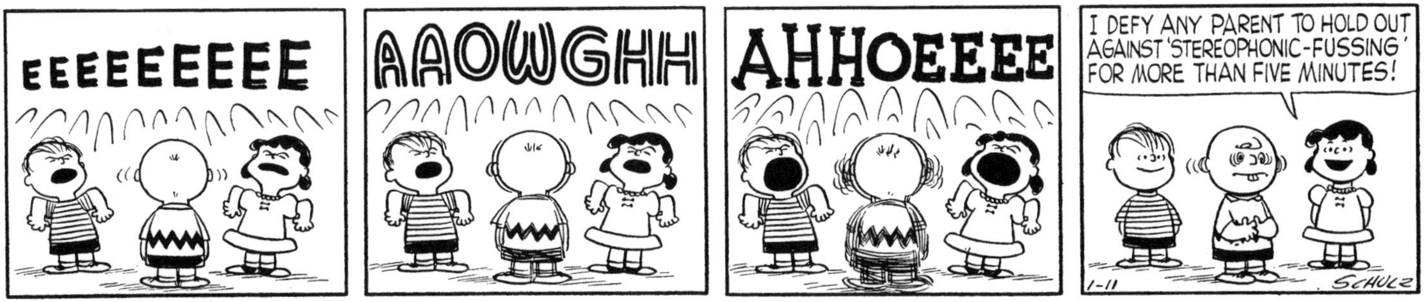
EEEEEEEEE
AAOWGHH
AHHOEEEE
I DEFY ANY PARENT TO HOLD OUT AGAINST 'STEREOPHONIC-FUSSING' FOR MORE THAN FIVE MINUTES!
1-11
SCHULZ

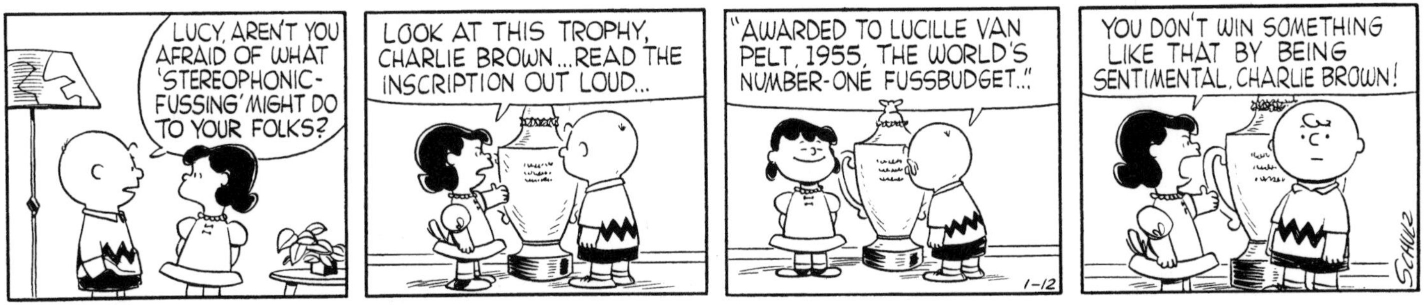
LUCY, AREN'T YOU AFRAID OF WHAT 'STEREOPHONIC-FUSSING' MIGHT DO TO YOUR FOLKS?
LOOK AT THIS TROPHY, CHARLIE BROWN...READ THE INSCRIPTION OUT LOUD...
"AWARDED TO LUCILLE VAN PELT, 1955, THE WORLD'S NUMBER-ONE FUSSBUDGET..."
1-12
YOU DON'T WIN SOMETHING LIKE THAT BY BEING SENTIMENTAL, CHARLIE BROWN!
SCHULZ

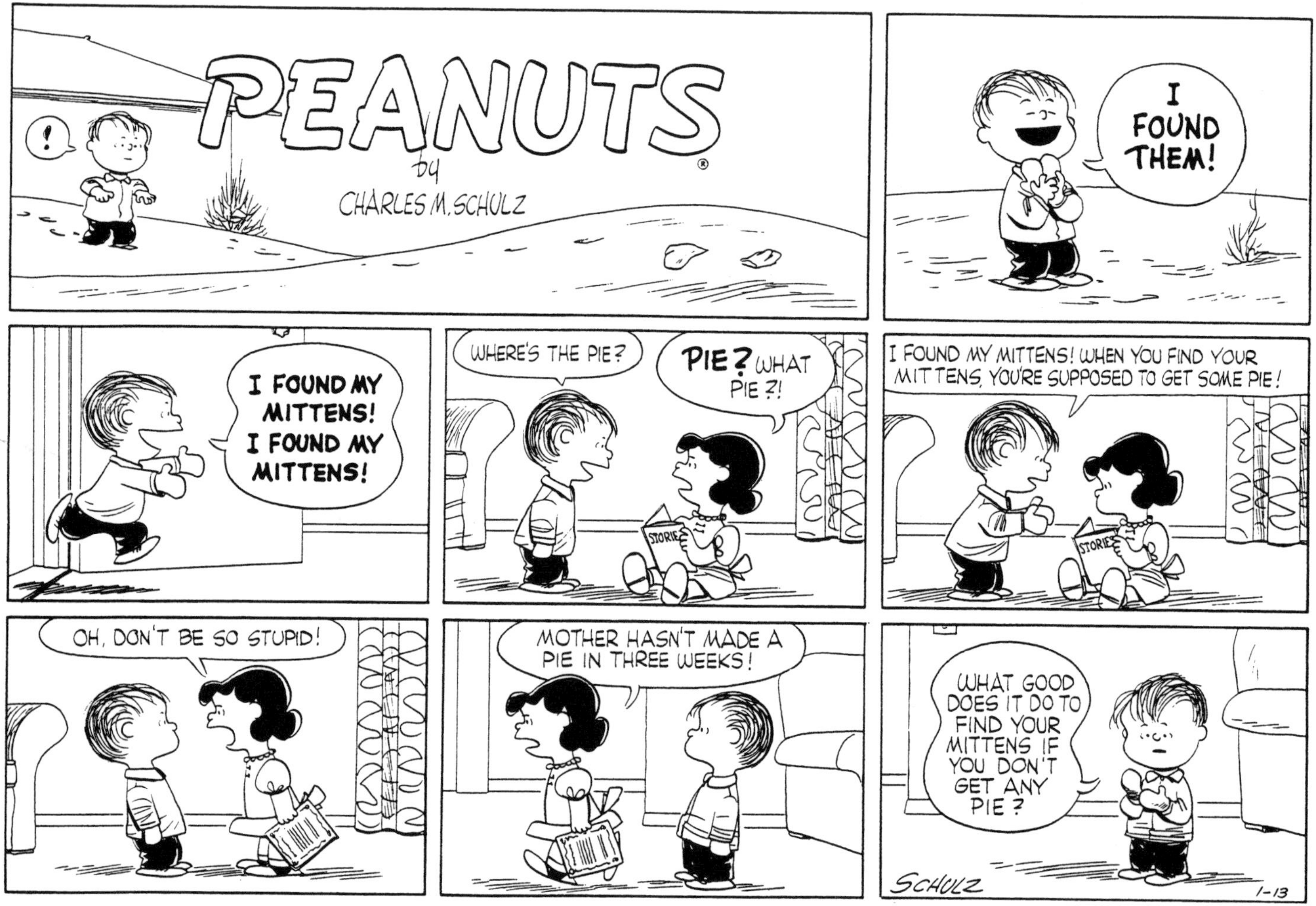
PEANUTS
by CHARLES M. SCHULZ
!
I FOUND THEM!
I FOUND MY MITTENS! I FOUND MY MITTENS!
WHERE'S THE PIE?
PIE? WHAT PIE?!
STORIES
I FOUND MY MITTENS! WHEN YOU FIND YOUR MITTENS, YOU'RE SUPPOSED TO GET SOME PIE!
STORIES
OH, DON'T BE SO STUPID!
MOTHER HASN'T MADE A PIE IN THREE WEEKS!
WHAT GOOD DOES IT DO TO FIND YOUR MITTENS IF YOU DON'T GET ANY PIE?
SCHULZ
1-13

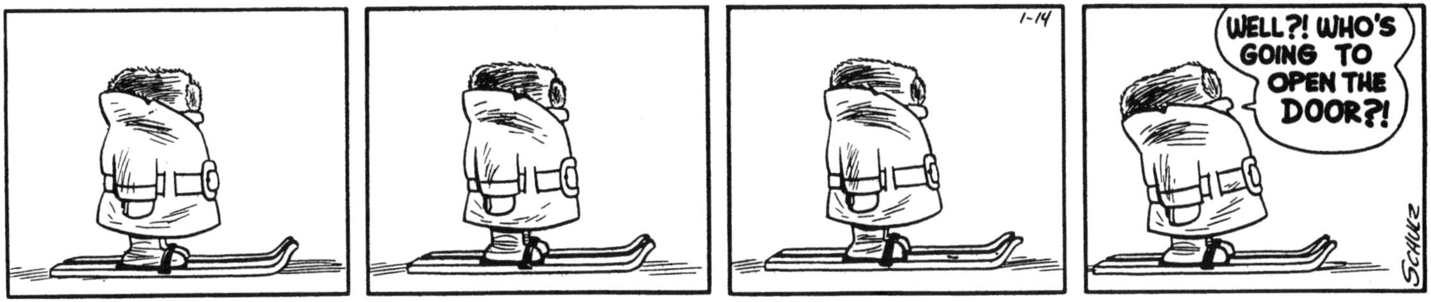
1-14
WELL?! WHO'S GOING TO OPEN THE DOOR?!
SCHULZ

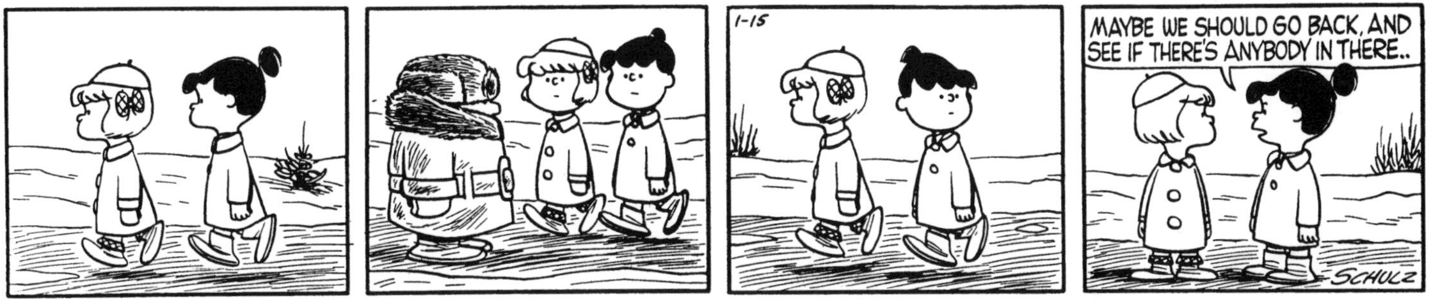
1-15
MAYBE WE SHOULD GO BACK, AND SEE IF THERE'S ANYBODY IN THERE..
SCHULZ

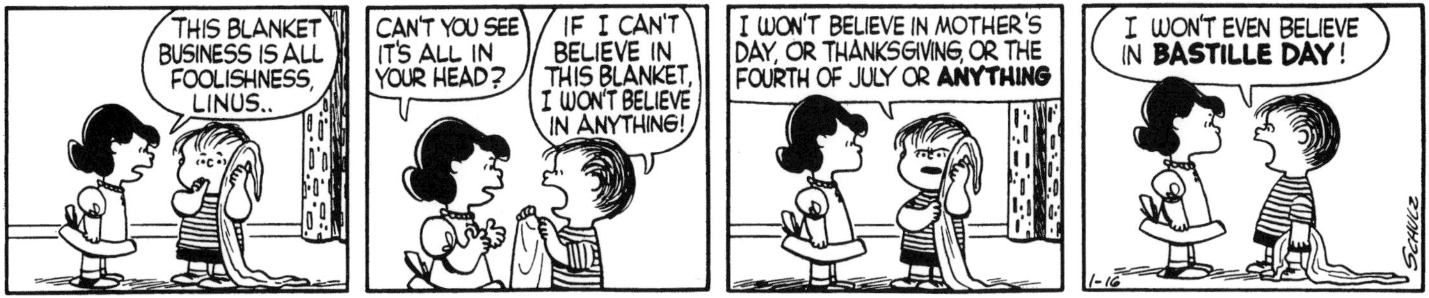
THIS BLANKET BUSINESS IS ALL FOOLISHNESS, LINUS..
CAN'T YOU SEE IT'S ALL IN YOUR HEAD?
IF I CAN'T BELIEVE IN THIS BLANKET, I WON'T BELIEVE IN ANYTHING!
I WON'T BELIEVE IN MOTHER'S DAY, OR THANKSGIVING, OR THE FOURTH OF JULY OR ANYTHING
I WON'T EVEN BELIEVE IN BASTILLE DAY!
SCHULZ
1-16

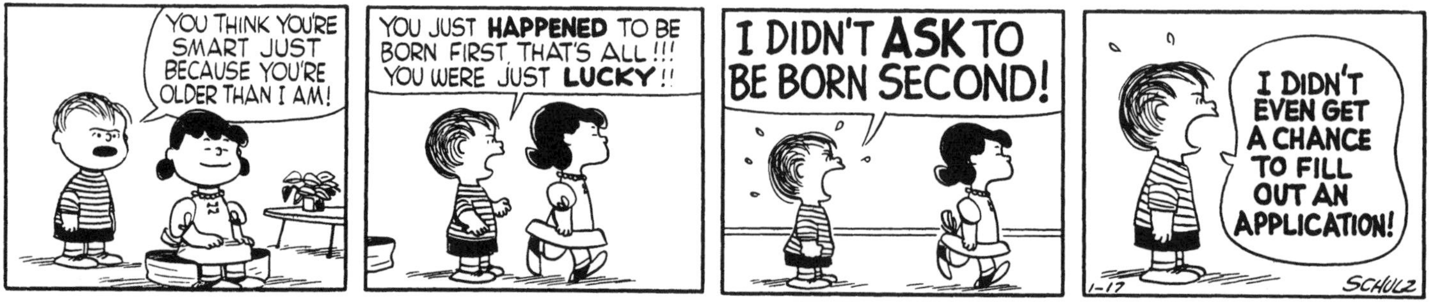
YOU THINK YOU'RE SMART JUST BECAUSE YOU'RE OLDER THAN I AM!
YOU JUST **HAPPENED** TO BE BORN FIRST, THAT'S ALL!!! YOU WERE JUST **LUCKY**!!
I DIDN'T **ASK** TO BE BORN SECOND!
I DIDN'T EVEN GET A CHANCE TO FILL OUT AN APPLICATION!
1-17
SCHULZ

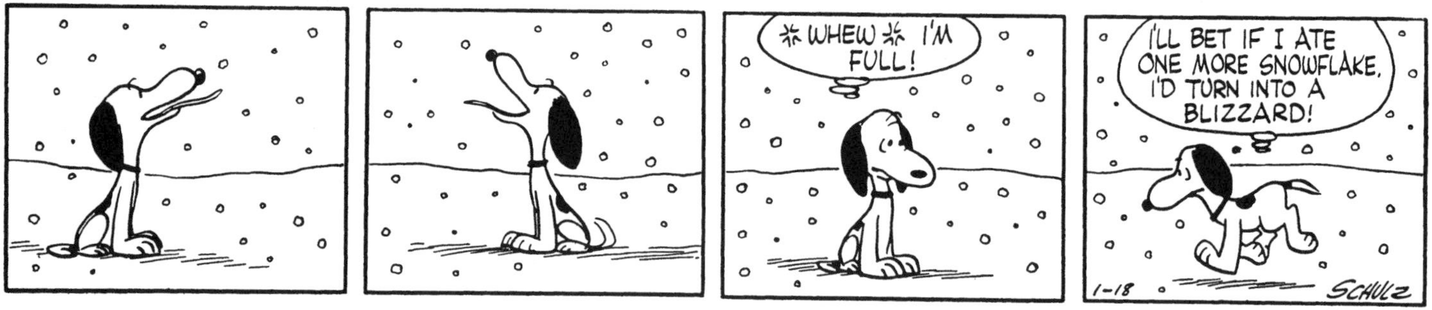
WHEW I'M FULL!
I'LL BET IF I ATE ONE MORE SNOWFLAKE, I'D TURN INTO A BLIZZARD!
1-18
SCHULZ

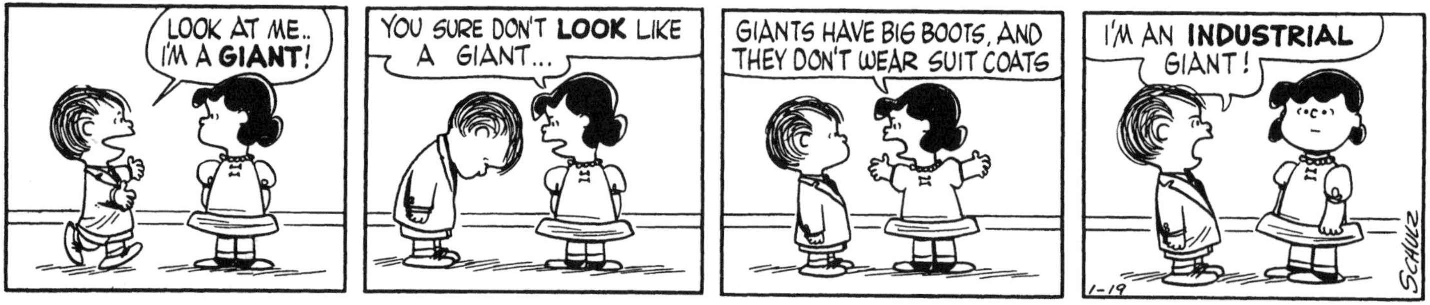
LOOK AT ME.. I'M A **GIANT**!
YOU SURE DON'T **LOOK** LIKE A GIANT...
GIANTS HAVE BIG BOOTS, AND THEY DON'T WEAR SUIT COATS
I'M AN **INDUSTRIAL** GIANT!
1-19
SCHULZ

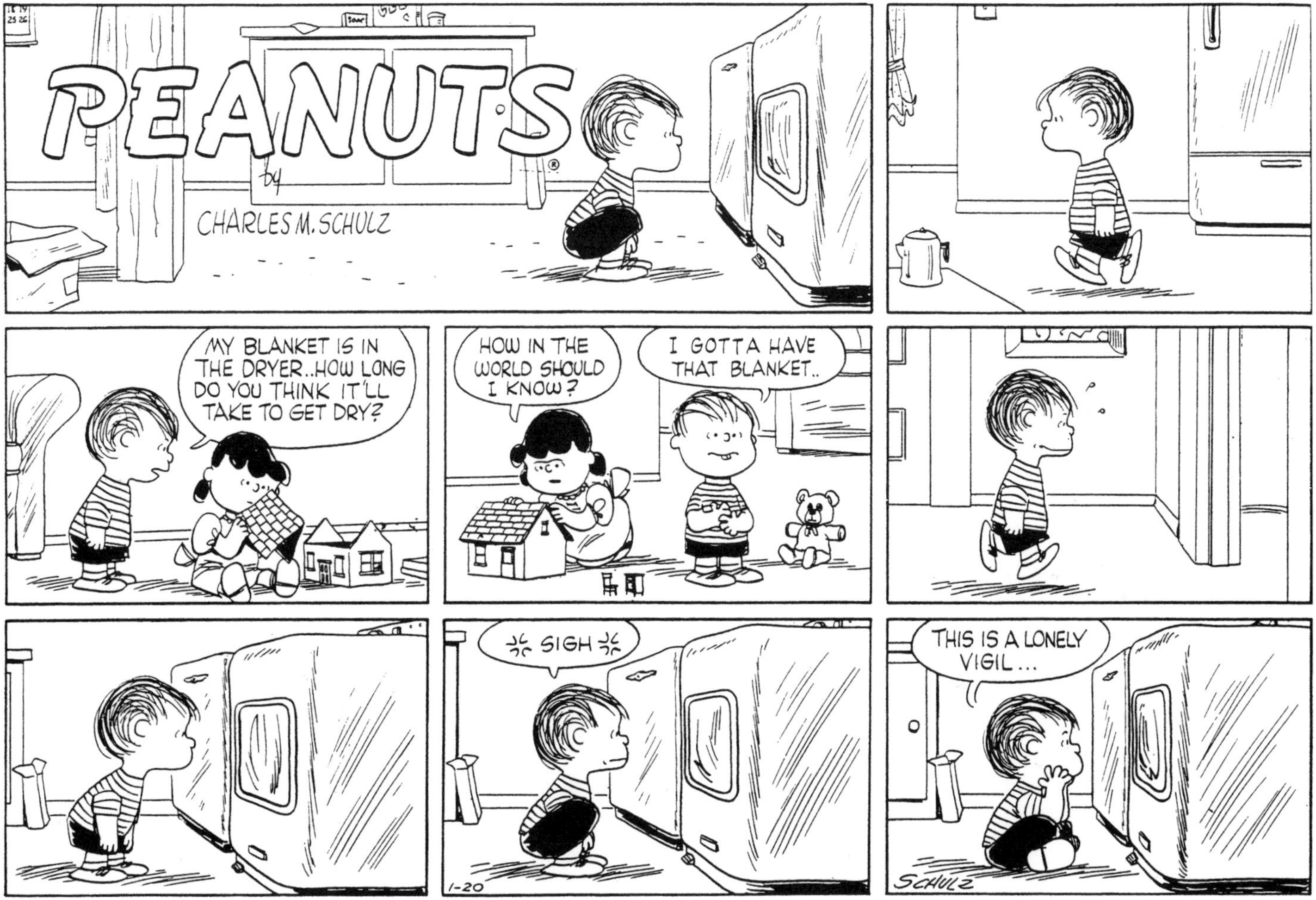
PEANUTS
by
CHARLES M. SCHULZ
MY BLANKET IS IN THE DRYER..HOW LONG DO YOU THINK IT'LL TAKE TO GET DRY?
HOW IN THE WORLD SHOULD I KNOW?
I GOTTA HAVE THAT BLANKET..
SIGH
THIS IS A LONELY VIGIL...
1-20
SCHULZ

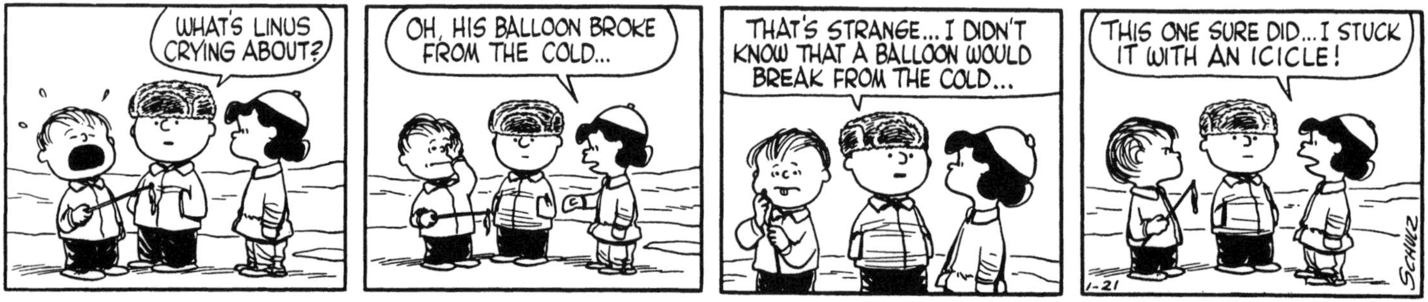
WHAT'S LINUS CRYING ABOUT?
OH, HIS BALLOON BROKE FROM THE COLD...
THAT'S STRANGE... I DIDN'T KNOW THAT A BALLOON WOULD BREAK FROM THE COLD...
THIS ONE SURE DID... I STUCK IT WITH AN ICICLE!
1-21
SCHULZ

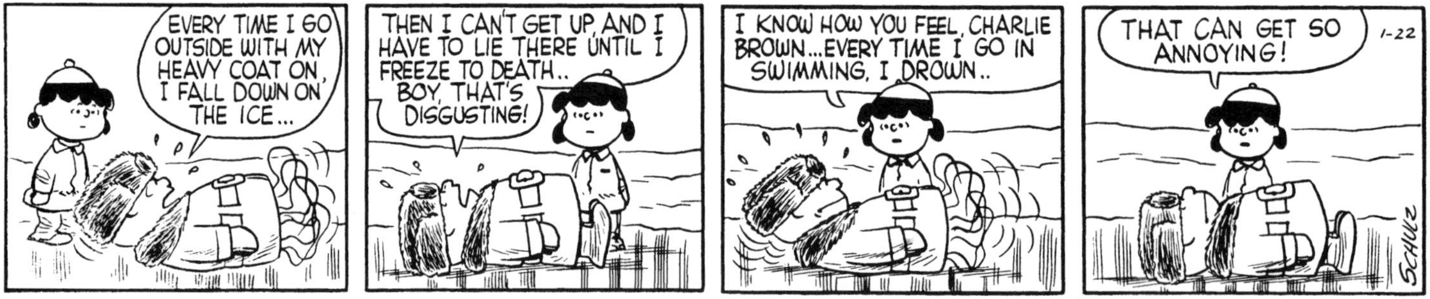
EVERY TIME I GO OUTSIDE WITH MY HEAVY COAT ON, I FALL DOWN ON THE ICE...
THEN I CAN'T GET UP, AND I HAVE TO LIE THERE UNTIL I FREEZE TO DEATH..
BOY, THAT'S DISGUSTING!
I KNOW HOW YOU FEEL, CHARLIE BROWN... EVERY TIME I GO IN SWIMMING, I DROWN..
THAT CAN GET SO ANNOYING!
1-22
SCHULZ

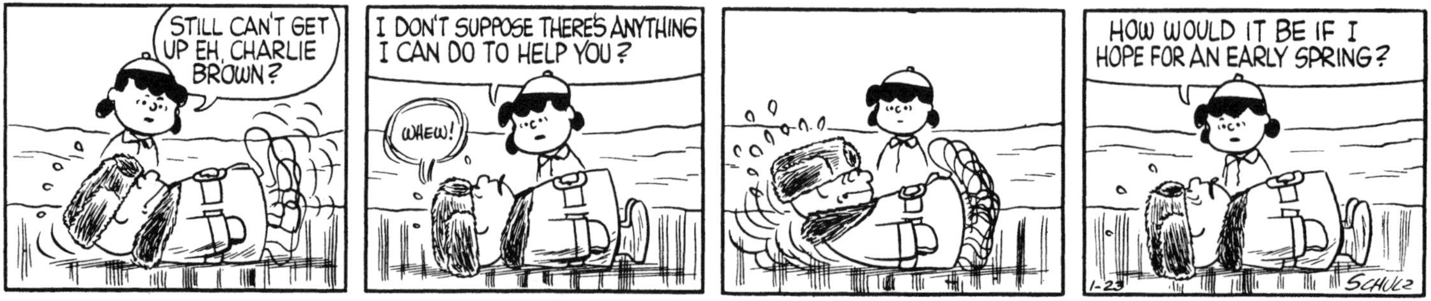
STILL CAN'T GET UP EH, CHARLIE BROWN?
I DON'T SUPPOSE THERE'S ANYTHING I CAN DO TO HELP YOU?
WHEW!
HOW WOULD IT BE IF I HOPE FOR AN EARLY SPRING?
1-23
SCHULZ

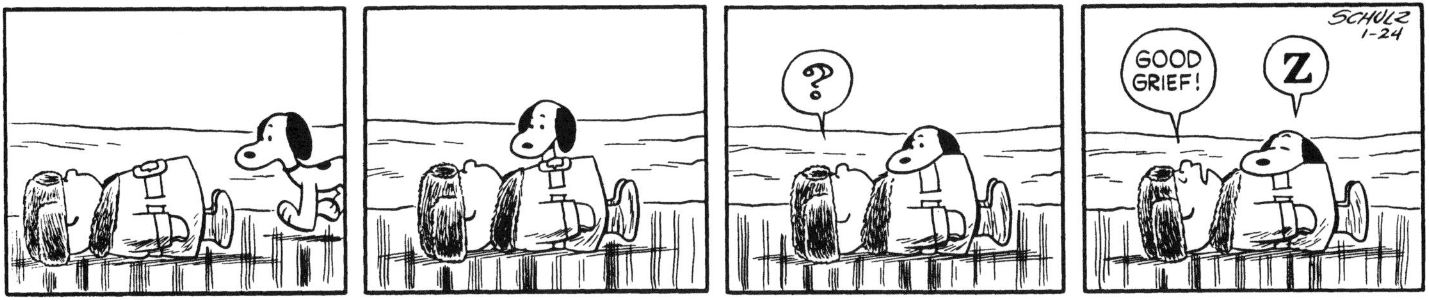
SCHULZ 1-24
?
GOOD GRIEF!
Z

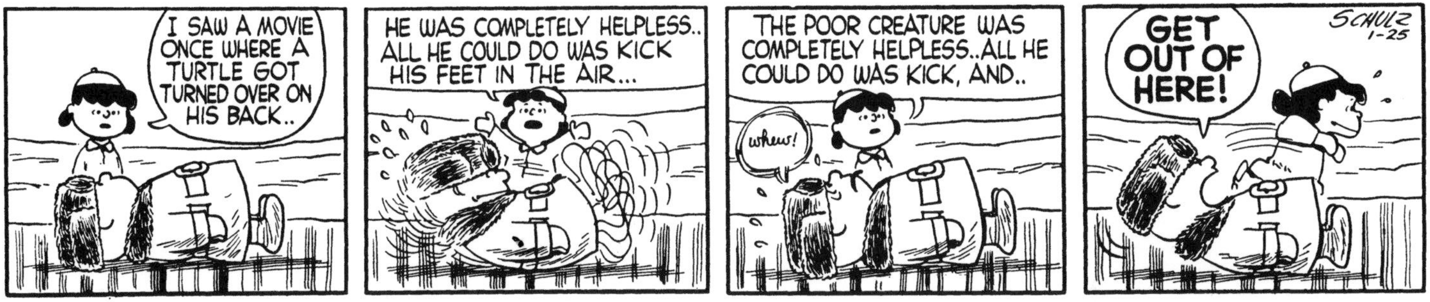
I SAW A MOVIE ONCE WHERE A TURTLE GOT TURNED OVER ON HIS BACK..
HE WAS COMPLETELY HELPLESS.. ALL HE COULD DO WAS KICK HIS FEET IN THE AIR...
THE POOR CREATURE WAS COMPLETELY HELPLESS..ALL HE COULD DO WAS KICK, AND..
whew!
SCHULZ 1-25
GET OUT OF HERE!

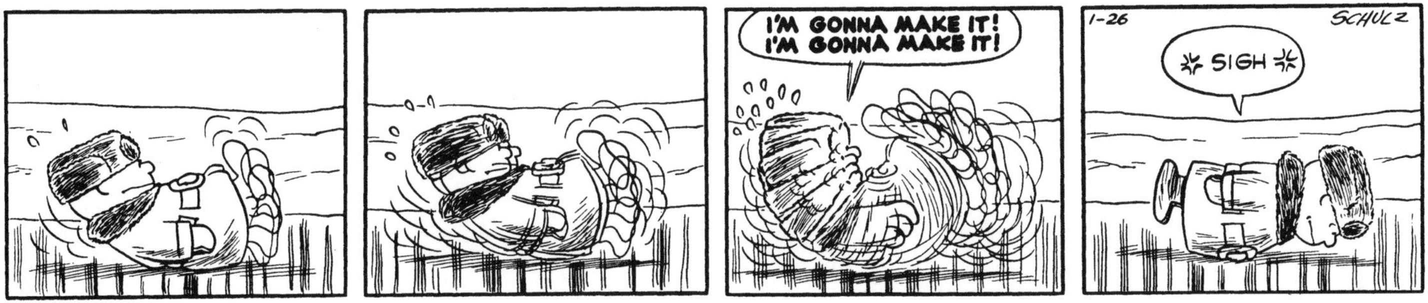
I'M GONNA MAKE IT! I'M GONNA MAKE IT!
1-26
SCHULZ
SIGH

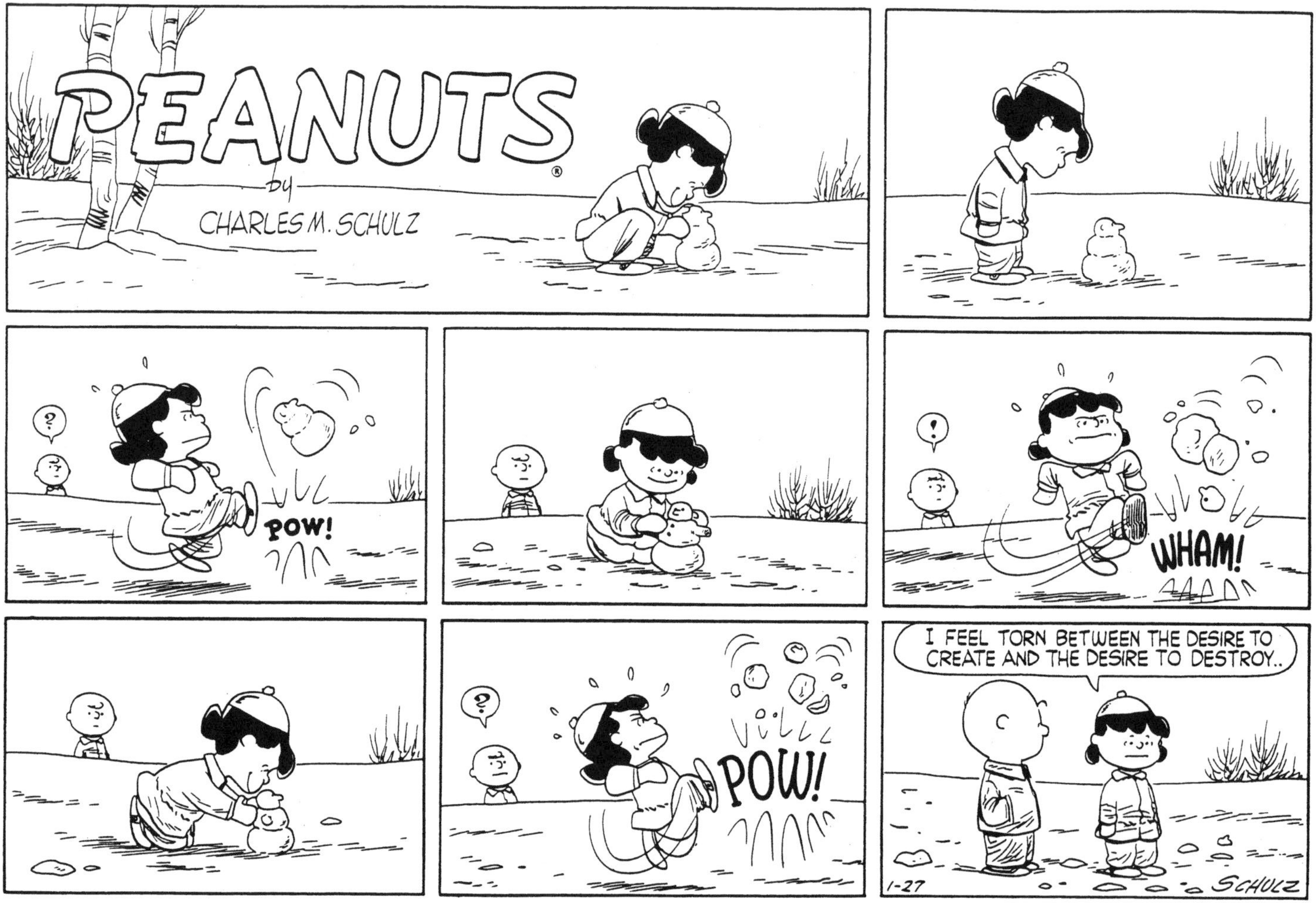
PEANUTS
by
CHARLES M. SCHULZ
?
POW!
!
WHAM!
?
POW!
I FEEL TORN BETWEEN THE DESIRE TO CREATE AND THE DESIRE TO DESTROY..
1-27
SCHULZ

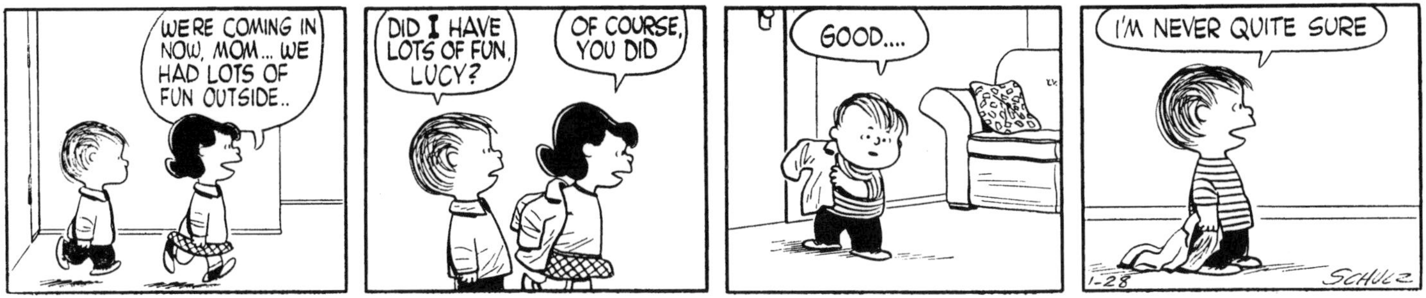
WERE COMING IN NOW, MOM... WE HAD LOTS OF FUN OUTSIDE..
DID I HAVE LOTS OF FUN, LUCY?
OF COURSE, YOU DID
GOOD....
I'M NEVER QUITE SURE
1-28
SCHULZ

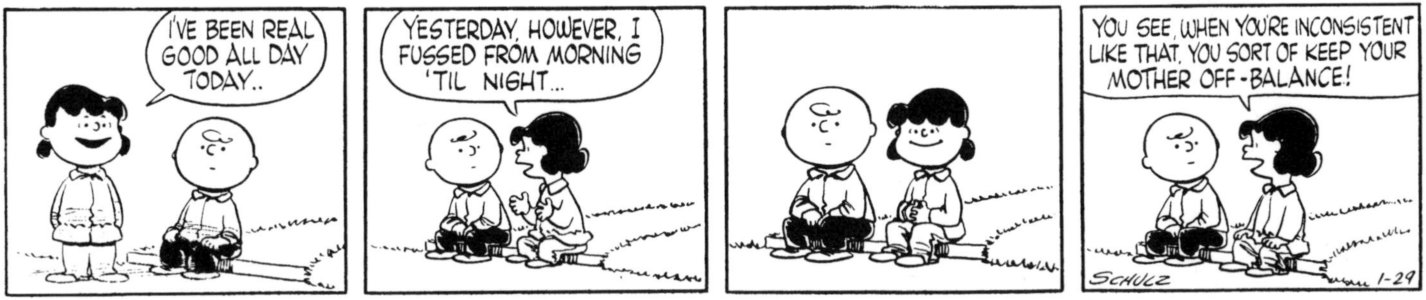
I'VE BEEN REAL GOOD ALL DAY TODAY..
YESTERDAY, HOWEVER, I FUSSED FROM MORNING 'TIL NIGHT...
YOU SEE, WHEN YOU'RE INCONSISTENT LIKE THAT, YOU SORT OF KEEP YOUR MOTHER OFF-BALANCE!
SCHULZ
1-29

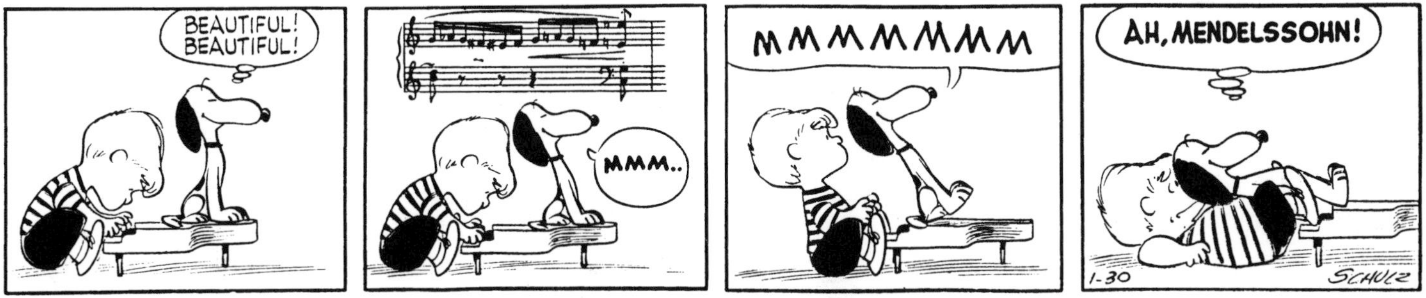
BEAUTIFUL! BEAUTIFUL!
MMM..
MMMMMMMM
AH, MENDELSSOHN!
1-30
SCHULZ

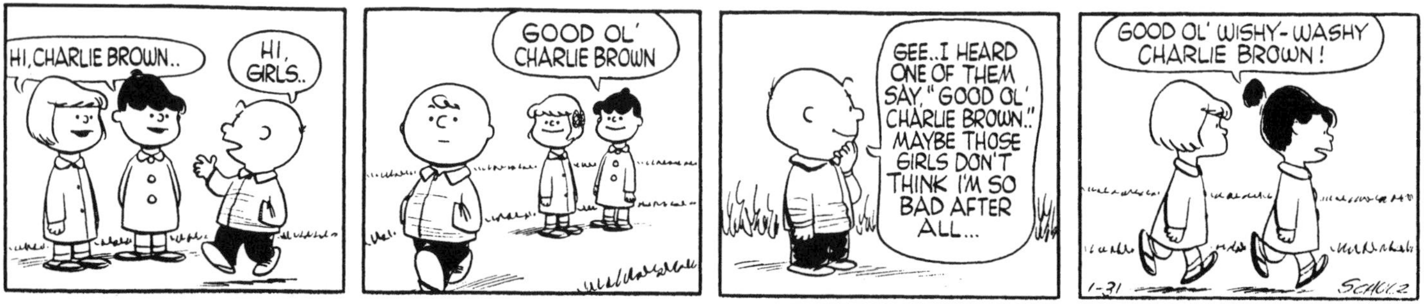
HI, CHARLIE BROWN..
HI, GIRLS..
GOOD OL' CHARLIE BROWN
GEE..I HEARD ONE OF THEM SAY, "GOOD OL' CHARLIE BROWN.." MAYBE THOSE GIRLS DON'T THINK I'M SO BAD AFTER ALL...
GOOD OL' WISHY-WASHY CHARLIE BROWN!
1-31
SCHULZ

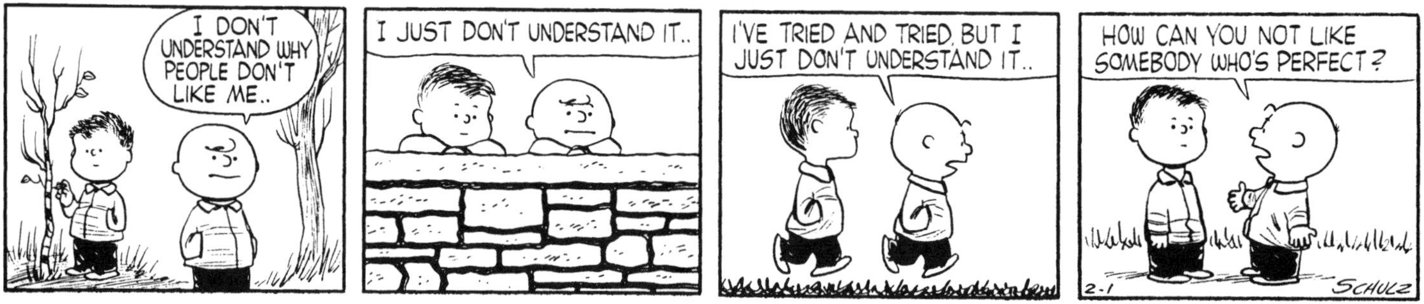
I DON'T UNDERSTAND WHY PEOPLE DON'T LIKE ME..
I JUST DON'T UNDERSTAND IT..
I'VE TRIED AND TRIED, BUT I JUST DON'T UNDERSTAND IT..
HOW CAN YOU NOT LIKE SOMEBODY WHO'S PERFECT?
2-1
SCHULZ

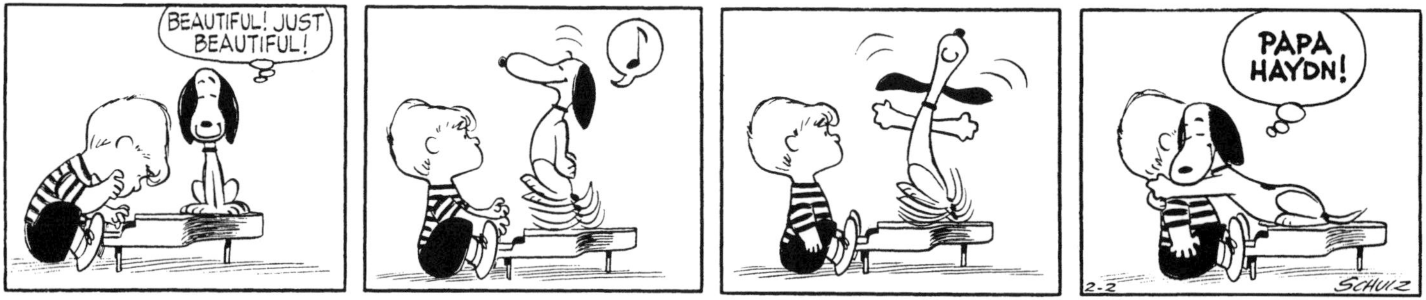
BEAUTIFUL! JUST BEAUTIFUL!
PAPA HAYDN!
2-2
SCHULZ

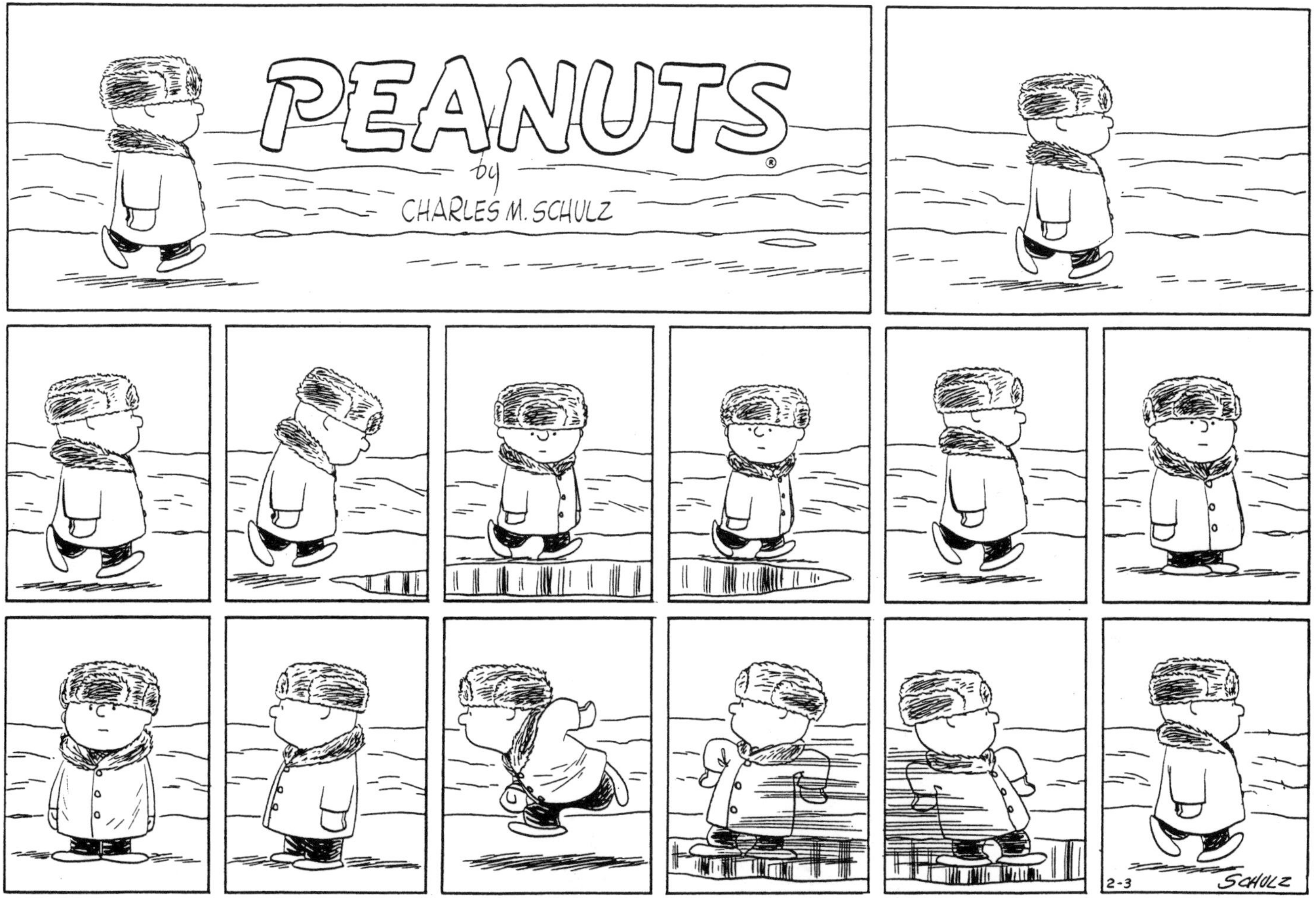
PEANUTS
by
CHARLES M. SCHULZ
2-3
SCHULZ

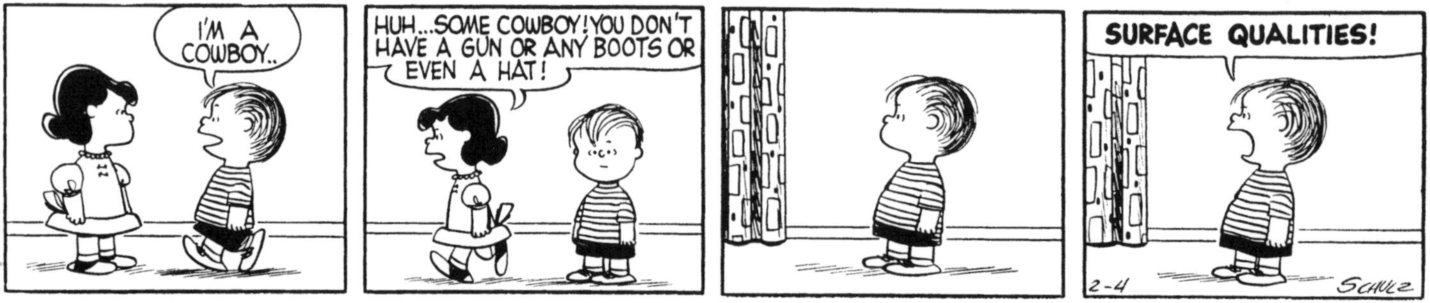
I'M A COWBOY..
HUH...SOME COWBOY! YOU DON'T HAVE A GUN OR ANY BOOTS OR EVEN A HAT!
SURFACE QUALITIES!
2-4
SCHULZ

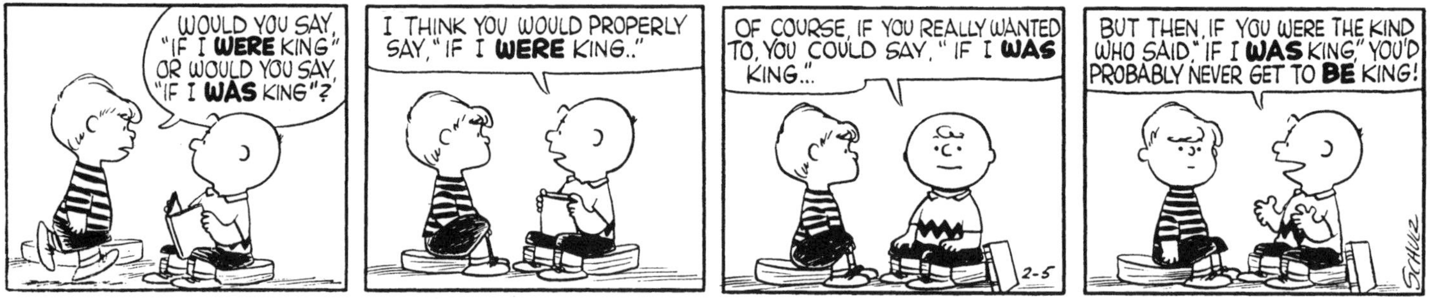
WOULD YOU SAY, "IF I WERE KING" OR WOULD YOU SAY, "IF I WAS KING"?
I THINK YOU WOULD PROPERLY SAY, "IF I WERE KING.."
OF COURSE, IF YOU REALLY WANTED TO, YOU COULD SAY, "IF I WAS KING.."
2-5
BUT THEN, IF YOU WERE THE KIND WHO SAID "IF I WAS KING," YOU'D PROBABLY NEVER GET TO BE KING!
SCHULZ

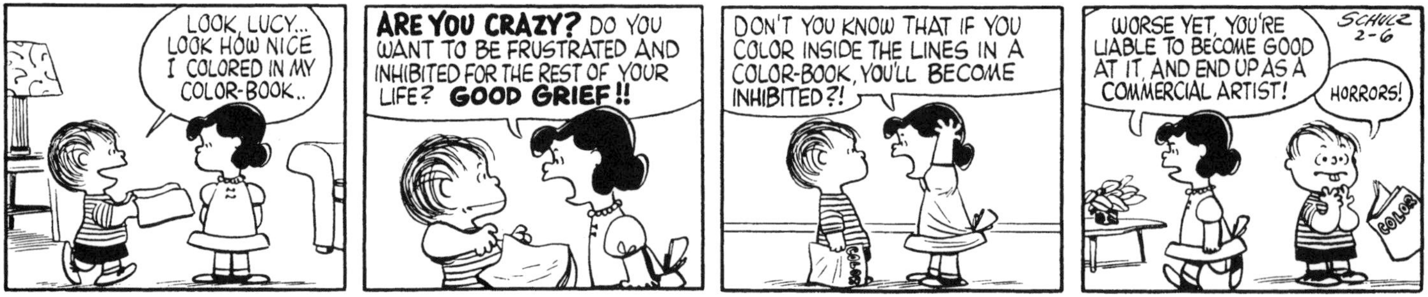
LOOK, LUCY... LOOK HOW NICE I COLORED IN MY COLOR-BOOK..
ARE YOU CRAZY? DO YOU WANT TO BE FRUSTRATED AND INHIBITED FOR THE REST OF YOUR LIFE? GOOD GRIEF!!
DON'T YOU KNOW THAT IF YOU COLOR INSIDE THE LINES IN A COLOR-BOOK, YOU'LL BECOME INHIBITED?!
SCHULZ 2-6
WORSE YET, YOU'RE LIABLE TO BECOME GOOD AT IT, AND END UP AS A COMMERCIAL ARTIST!
HORRORS!
COLOR

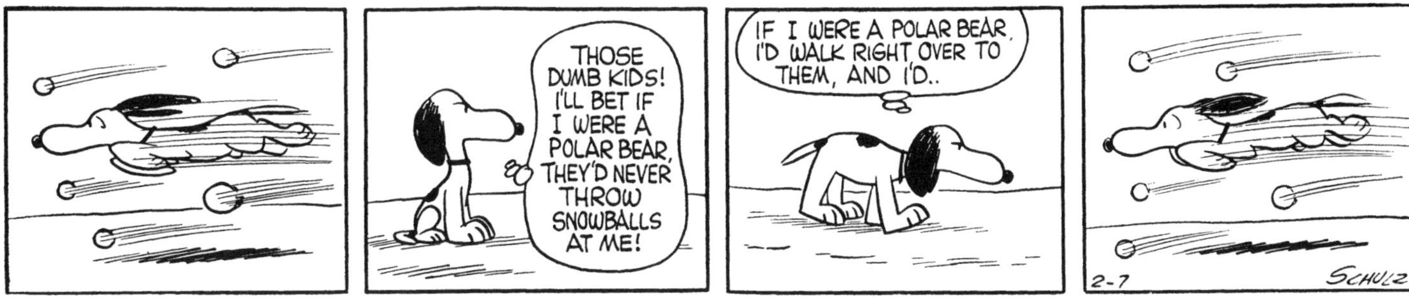
THOSE DUMB KIDS! I'LL BET IF I WERE A POLAR BEAR, THEY'D NEVER THROW SNOWBALLS AT ME!
IF I WERE A POLAR BEAR, I'D WALK RIGHT OVER TO THEM, AND I'D..
2-7
SCHULZ

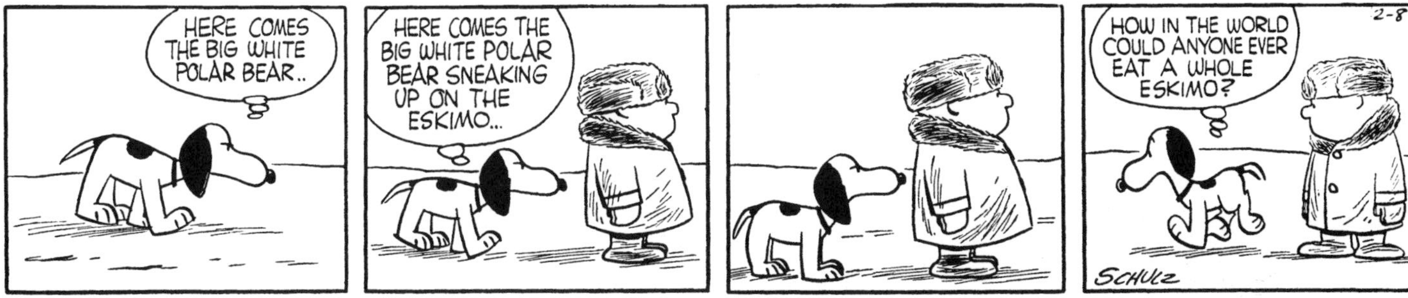
HERE COMES THE BIG WHITE POLAR BEAR..
HERE COMES THE BIG WHITE POLAR BEAR SNEAKING UP ON THE ESKIMO...
HOW IN THE WORLD COULD ANYONE EVER EAT A WHOLE ESKIMO?
2-8
SCHULZ

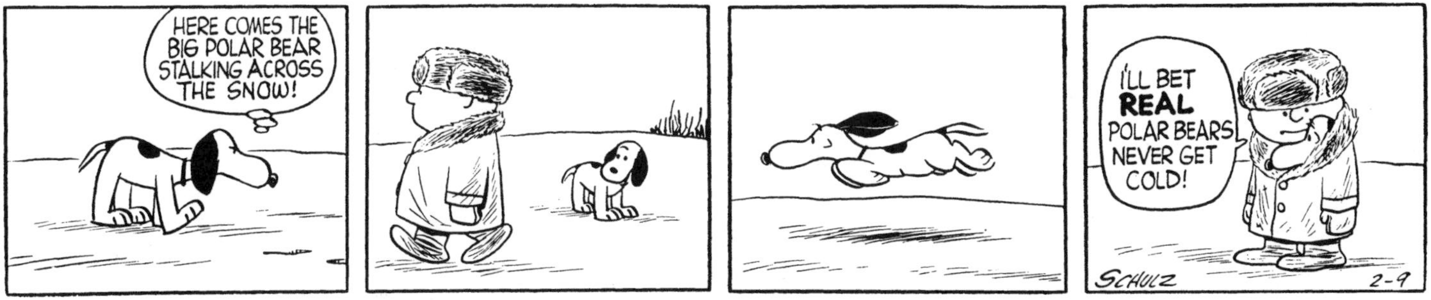
HERE COMES THE BIG POLAR BEAR STALKING ACROSS THE SNOW!
I'LL BET **REAL** POLAR BEARS NEVER GET COLD!
SCHULZ
2-9

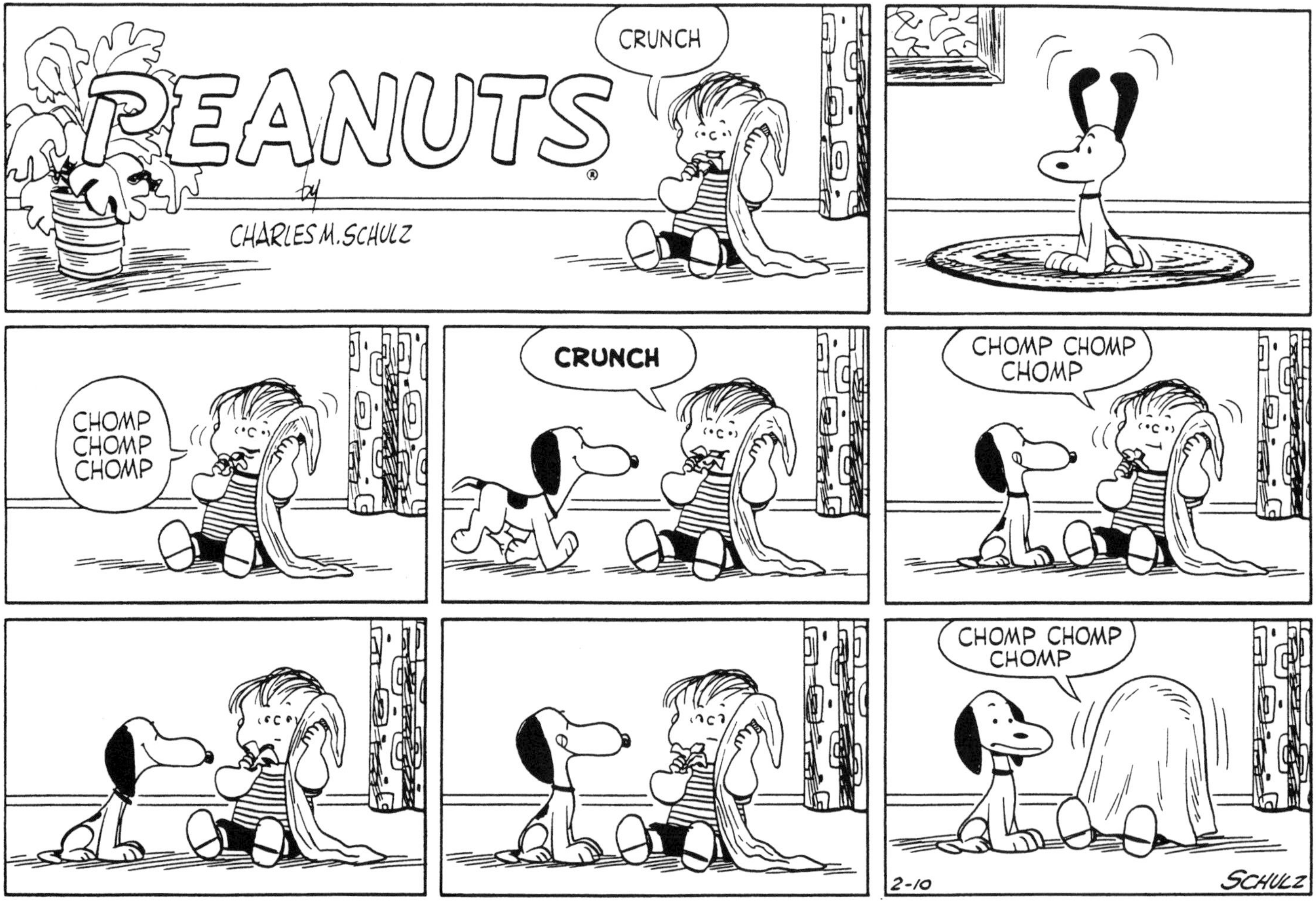
PEANUTS
by
CHARLES M. SCHULZ
CRUNCH
CHOMP
CHOMP
CHOMP
CRUNCH
CHOMP CHOMP
CHOMP
CHOMP CHOMP
CHOMP
2-10
SCHULZ

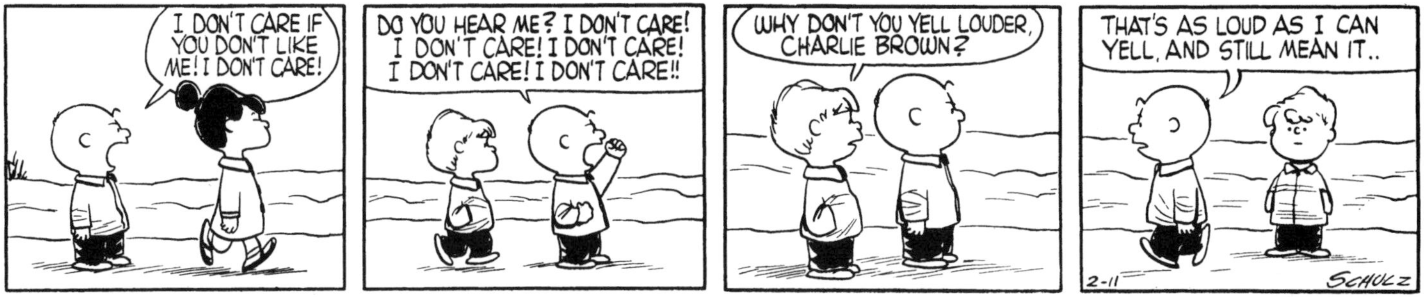
I DON'T CARE IF YOU DON'T LIKE ME! I DON'T CARE!
DO YOU HEAR ME? I DON'T CARE! I DON'T CARE! I DON'T CARE! I DON'T CARE! I DON'T CARE!!
WHY DON'T YOU YELL LOUDER, CHARLIE BROWN?
THAT'S AS LOUD AS I CAN YELL, AND STILL MEAN IT..
2-11
SCHULZ

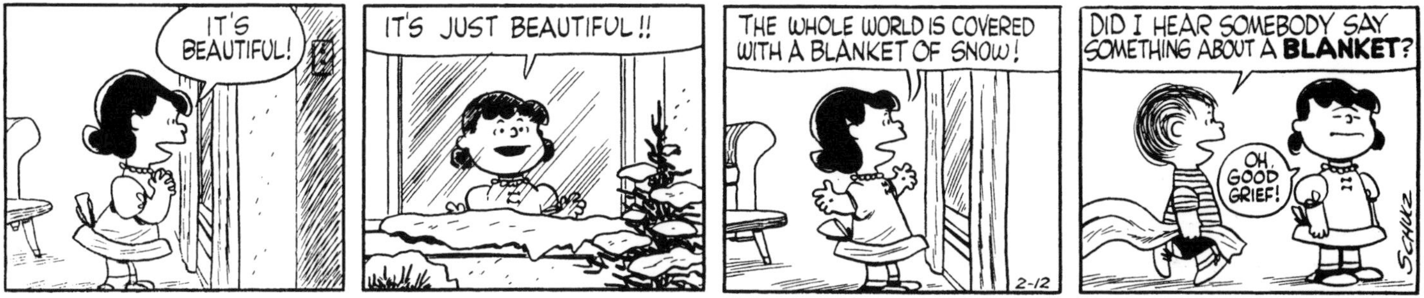
IT'S BEAUTIFUL!
IT'S JUST BEAUTIFUL!!
THE WHOLE WORLD IS COVERED WITH A BLANKET OF SNOW!
2-12
DID I HEAR SOMEBODY SAY SOMETHING ABOUT A **BLANKET**?
OH, GOOD GRIEF!
SCHULZ

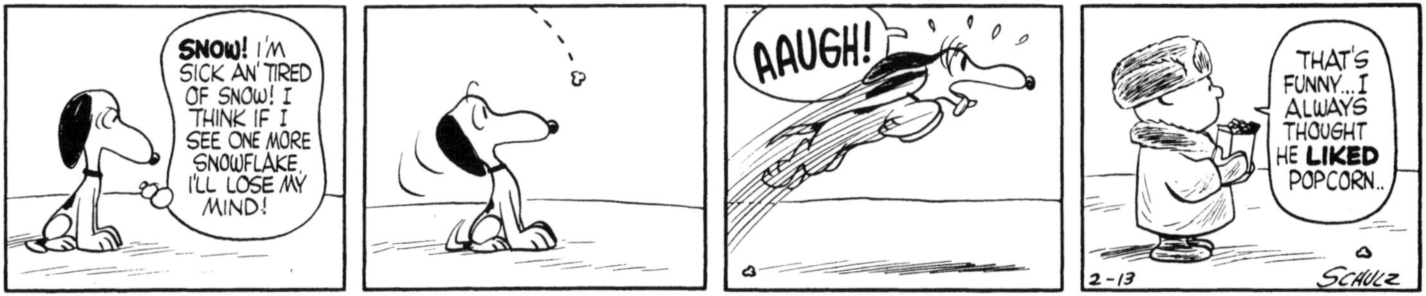
SNOW! I'M SICK AN' TIRED OF SNOW! I THINK IF I SEE ONE MORE SNOWFLAKE, I'LL LOSE MY MIND!
AAUGH!
THAT'S FUNNY... I ALWAYS THOUGHT HE **LIKED** POPCORN..
2-13
SCHULZ

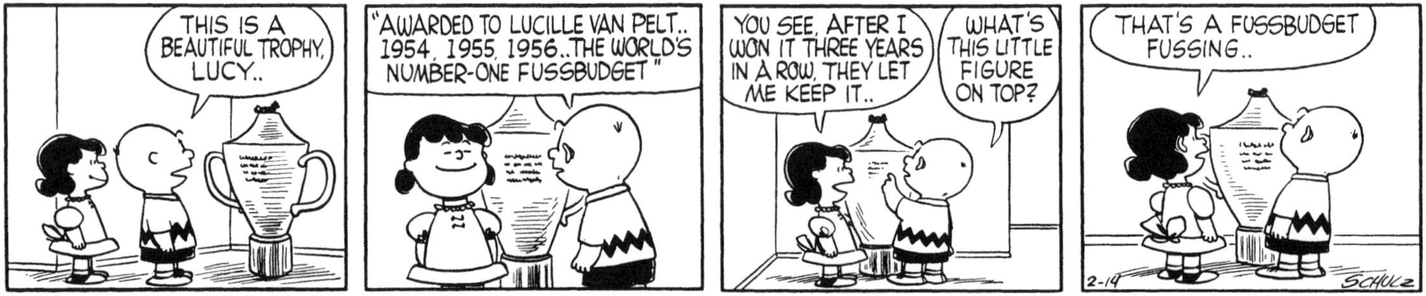
THIS IS A BEAUTIFUL TROPHY, LUCY..
"AWARDED TO LUCILLE VAN PELT.. 1954, 1955, 1956..THE WORLD'S NUMBER-ONE FUSSBUDGET"
YOU SEE, AFTER I WON IT THREE YEARS IN A ROW, THEY LET ME KEEP IT..
WHAT'S THIS LITTLE FIGURE ON TOP?
THAT'S A FUSSBUDGET FUSSING..
2-14
SCHULZ

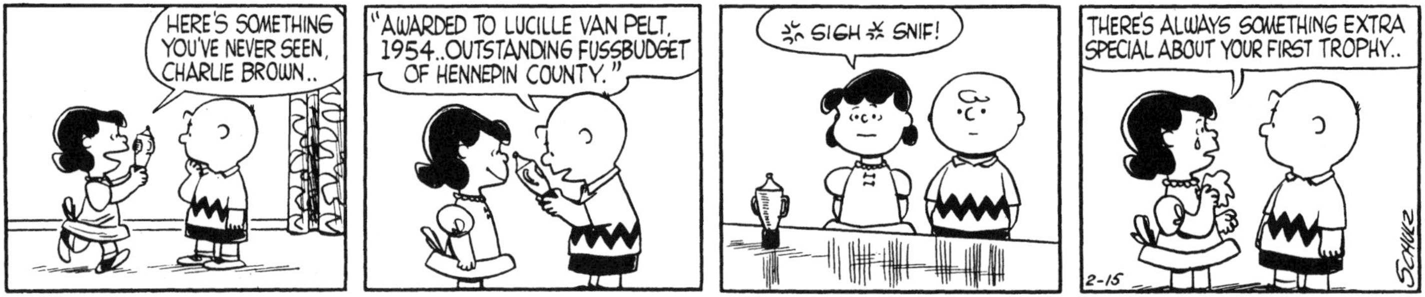
HERE'S SOMETHING YOU'VE NEVER SEEN, CHARLIE BROWN..
"AWARDED TO LUCILLE VAN PELT, 1954..OUTSTANDING FUSSBUDGET OF HENNEPIN COUNTY."
SIGH SNIF!
THERE'S ALWAYS SOMETHING EXTRA SPECIAL ABOUT YOUR FIRST TROPHY..
2-15
SCHULZ

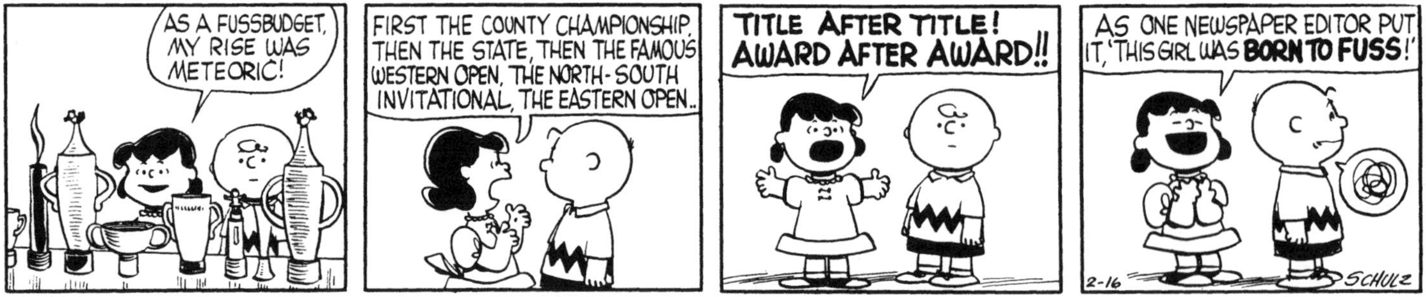
AS A FUSSBUDGET, MY RISE WAS METEORIC!
FIRST THE COUNTY CHAMPIONSHIP, THEN THE STATE, THEN THE FAMOUS WESTERN OPEN, THE NORTH-SOUTH INVITATIONAL, THE EASTERN OPEN..
TITLE AFTER TITLE! AWARD AFTER AWARD!!
AS ONE NEWSPAPER EDITOR PUT IT, 'THIS GIRL WAS BORN TO FUSS!'
2-16
SCHULZ

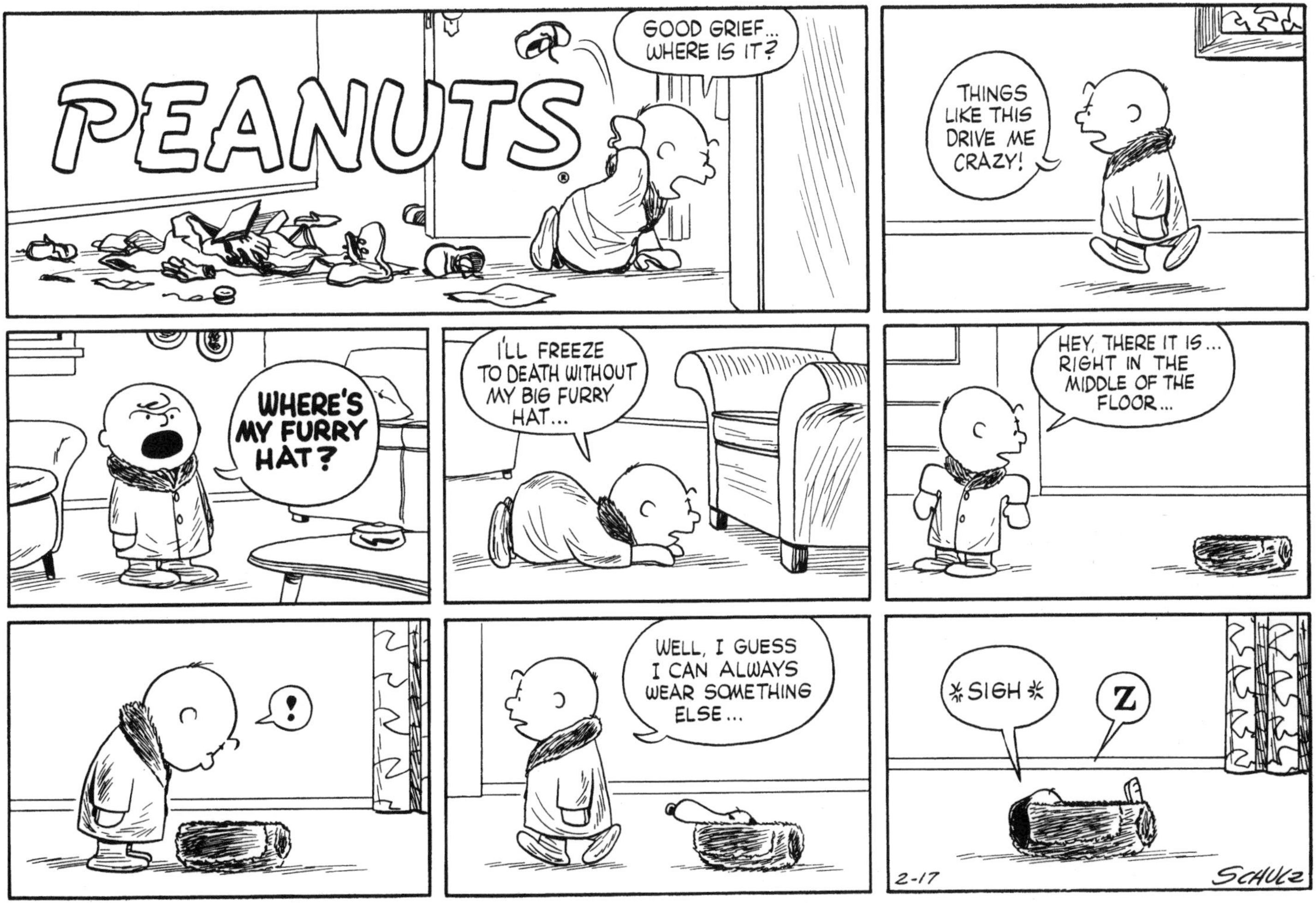
PEANUTS®
GOOD GRIEF... WHERE IS IT?
THINGS LIKE THIS DRIVE ME CRAZY!
WHERE'S MY FURRY HAT?
I'LL FREEZE TO DEATH WITHOUT MY BIG FURRY HAT...
HEY, THERE IT IS... RIGHT IN THE MIDDLE OF THE FLOOR...
!
WELL, I GUESS I CAN ALWAYS WEAR SOMETHING ELSE...
SIGH
Z
2-17
SCHULZ

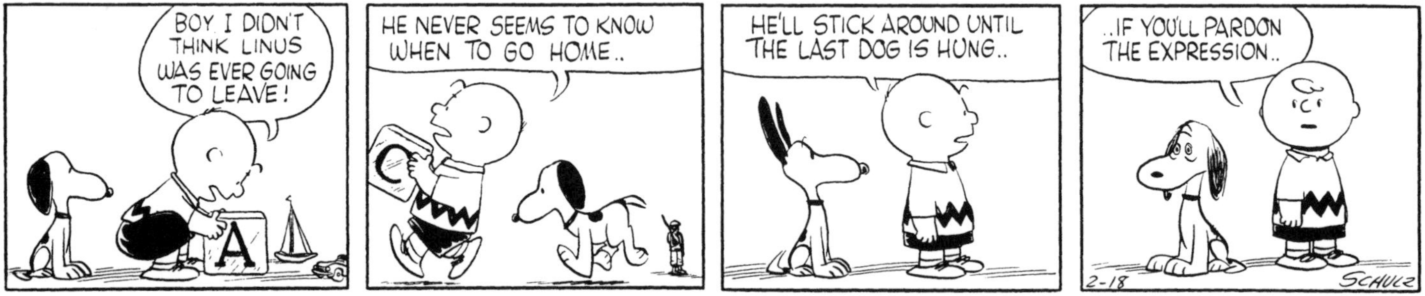
BOY, I DIDN'T THINK LINUS WAS EVER GOING TO LEAVE!
HE NEVER SEEMS TO KNOW WHEN TO GO HOME..
HE'LL STICK AROUND UNTIL THE LAST DOG IS HUNG..
..IF YOU'LL PARDON THE EXPRESSION..
2-18
SCHULZ

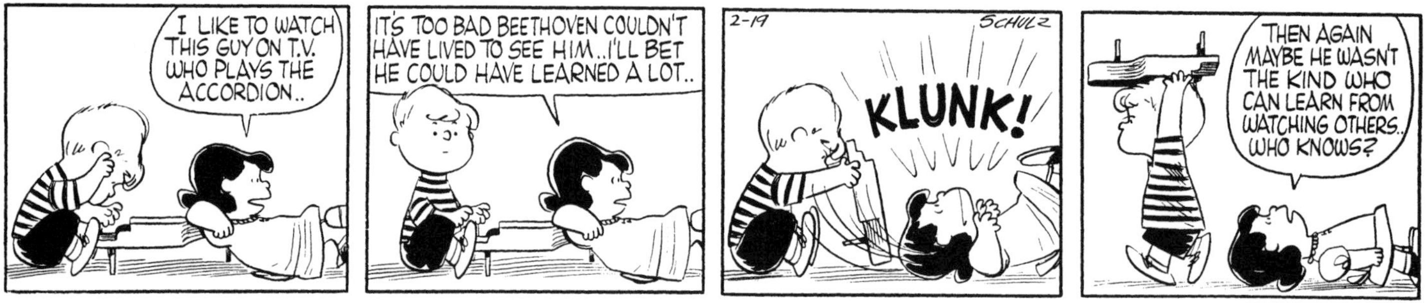
I LIKE TO WATCH THIS GUY ON T.V. WHO PLAYS THE ACCORDION..
IT'S TOO BAD BEETHOVEN COULDN'T HAVE LIVED TO SEE HIM..I'LL BET HE COULD HAVE LEARNED A LOT..
2-19
SCHULZ
KLUNK!
THEN AGAIN MAYBE HE WASN'T THE KIND WHO CAN LEARN FROM WATCHING OTHERS.. WHO KNOWS?

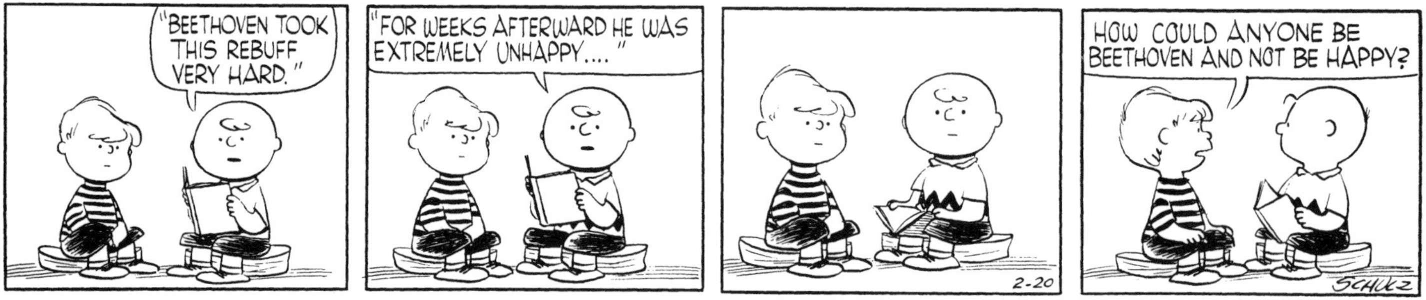
"BEETHOVEN TOOK THIS REBUFF VERY HARD."
"FOR WEEKS AFTERWARD HE WAS EXTREMELY UNHAPPY...."
2-20
HOW COULD ANYONE BE BEETHOVEN AND NOT BE HAPPY?
SCHULZ

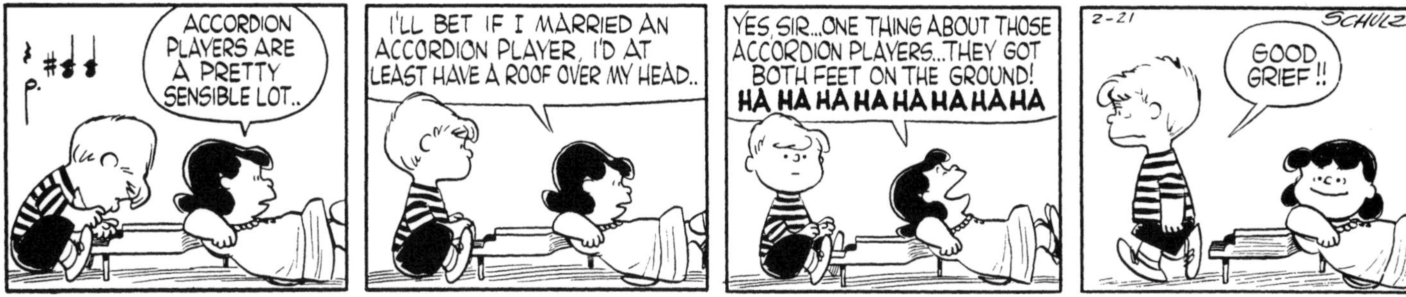
ACCORDION PLAYERS ARE A PRETTY SENSIBLE LOT..
I'LL BET IF I MARRIED AN ACCORDION PLAYER, I'D AT LEAST HAVE A ROOF OVER MY HEAD..
YES, SIR...ONE THING ABOUT THOSE ACCORDION PLAYERS...THEY GOT BOTH FEET ON THE GROUND! HA HA HA HA HA HA HA HA
2-21
SCHULZ
GOOD GRIEF!!

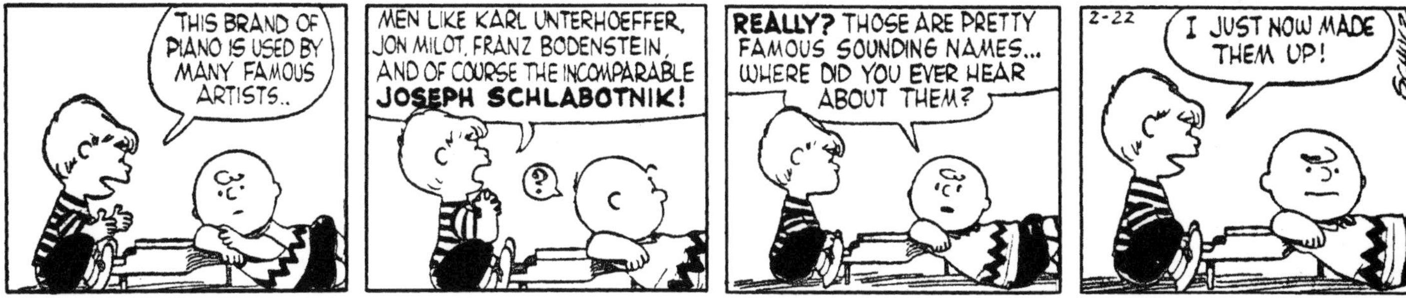
THIS BRAND OF PIANO IS USED BY MANY FAMOUS ARTISTS..
MEN LIKE KARL UNTERHOEFFER, JON MILOT, FRANZ BODENSTEIN, AND OF COURSE THE INCOMPARABLE JOSEPH SCHLABOTNIK!
?
REALLY? THOSE ARE PRETTY FAMOUS SOUNDING NAMES... WHERE DID YOU EVER HEAR ABOUT THEM?
2-22
I JUST NOW MADE THEM UP!
SCHULZ

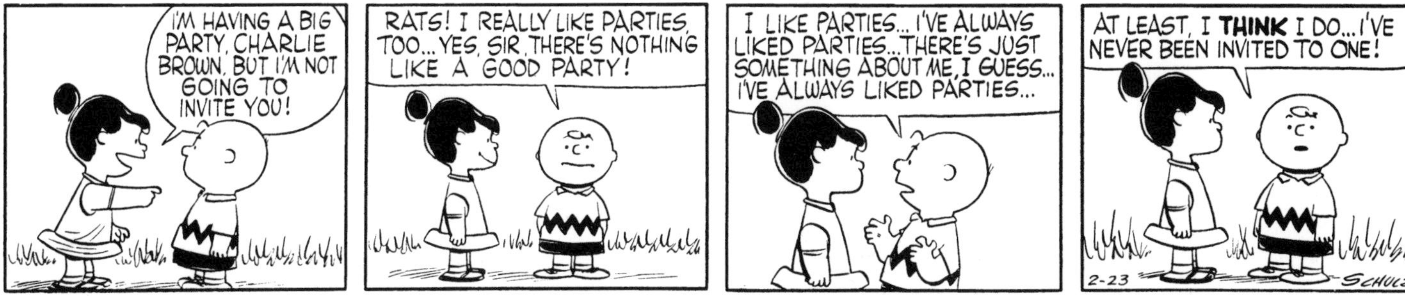
I'M HAVING A BIG PARTY, CHARLIE BROWN, BUT I'M NOT GOING TO INVITE YOU!
RATS! I REALLY LIKE PARTIES, TOO...YES, SIR, THERE'S NOTHING LIKE A GOOD PARTY!
I LIKE PARTIES... I'VE ALWAYS LIKED PARTIES...THERE'S JUST SOMETHING ABOUT ME, I GUESS... I'VE ALWAYS LIKED PARTIES...
AT LEAST, I THINK I DO...I'VE NEVER BEEN INVITED TO ONE!
2-23
SCHULZ

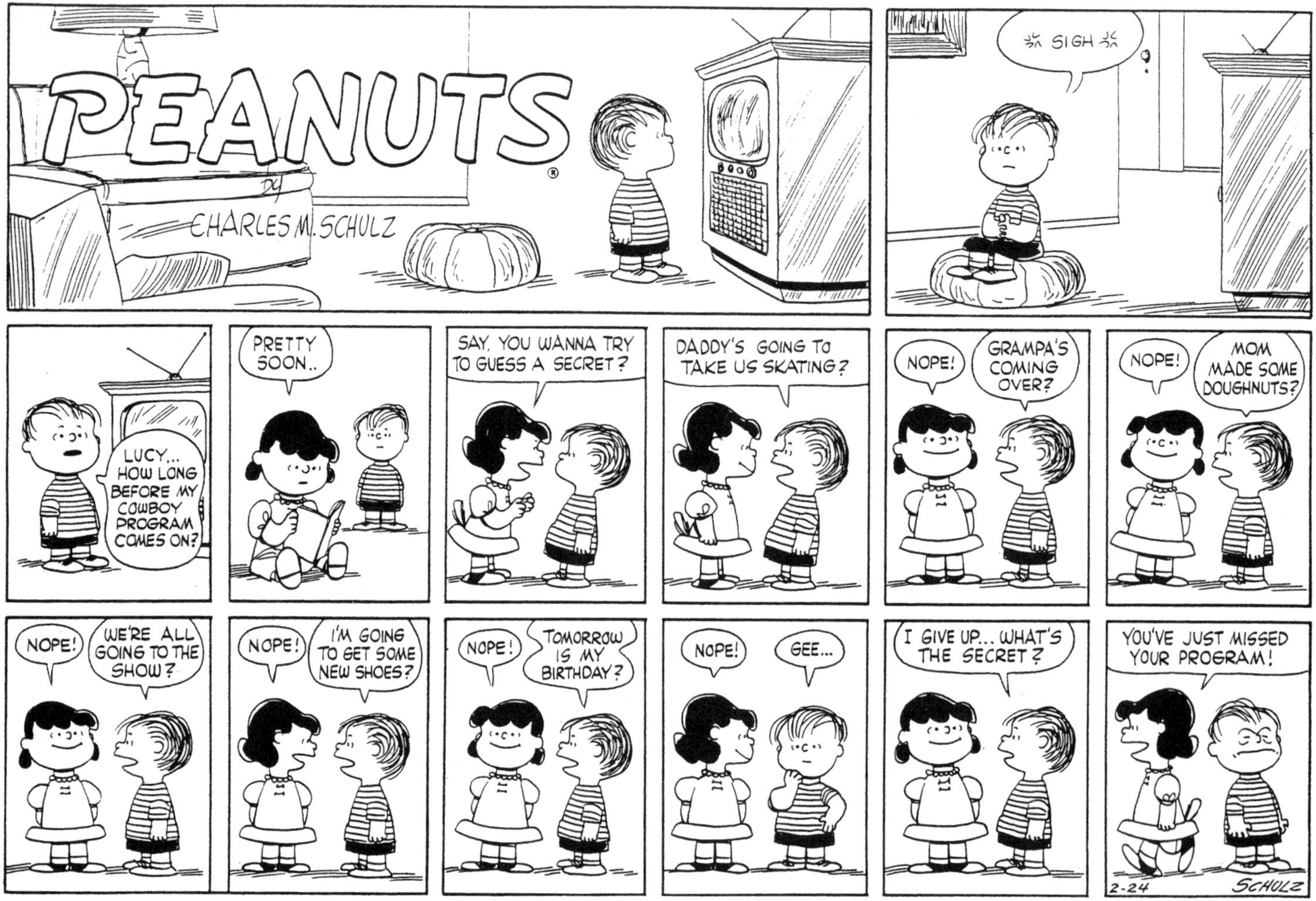
PEANUTS
by CHARLES M. SCHULZ
SIGH
LUCY... HOW LONG BEFORE MY COWBOY PROGRAM COMES ON?
PRETTY SOON..
SAY, YOU WANNA TRY TO GUESS A SECRET?
DADDY'S GOING TO TAKE US SKATING?
NOPE!
GRAMPA'S COMING OVER?
NOPE!
MOM MADE SOME DOUGHNUTS?
NOPE!
WE'RE ALL GOING TO THE SHOW?
NOPE!
I'M GOING TO GET SOME NEW SHOES?
NOPE!
TOMORROW IS MY BIRTHDAY?
NOPE!
GEE...
I GIVE UP... WHAT'S THE SECRET?
YOU'VE JUST MISSED YOUR PROGRAM!
2-24
SCHULZ

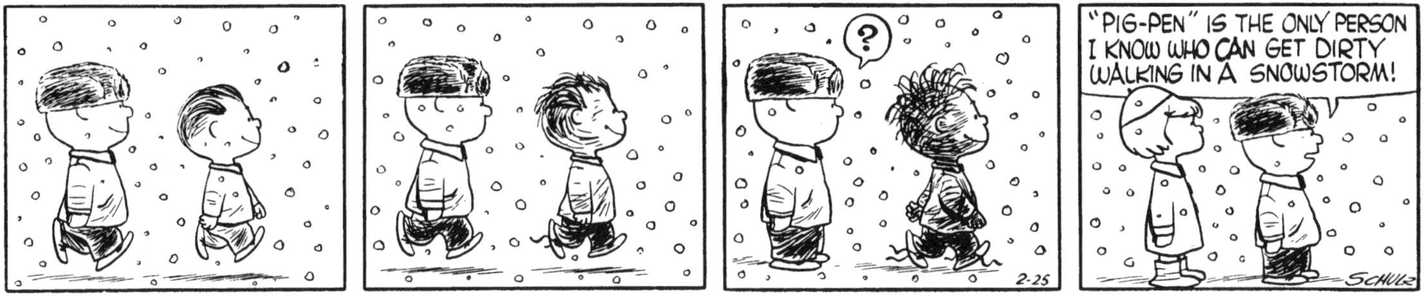
?
"PIG-PEN" IS THE ONLY PERSON I KNOW WHO CAN GET DIRTY WALKING IN A SNOWSTORM!
2-25
SCHULZ

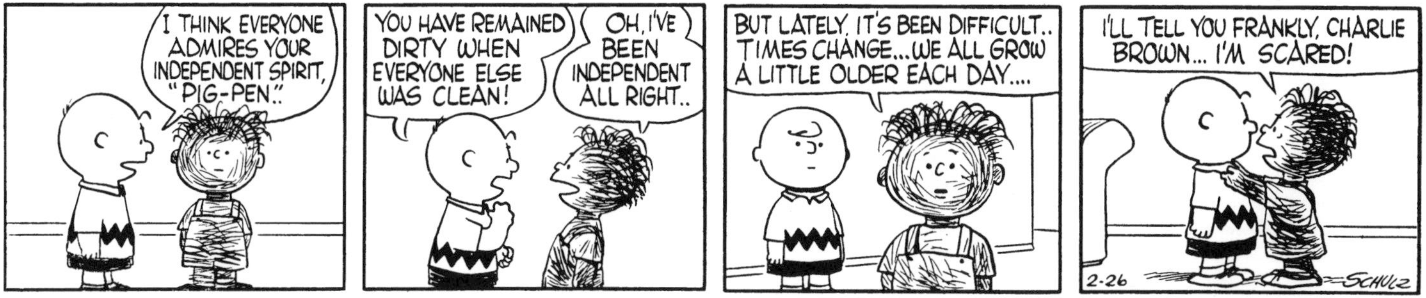
I THINK EVERYONE ADMIRES YOUR INDEPENDENT SPIRIT, "PIG-PEN."
YOU HAVE REMAINED DIRTY WHEN EVERYONE ELSE WAS CLEAN!
OH, I'VE BEEN INDEPENDENT ALL RIGHT..
BUT LATELY, IT'S BEEN DIFFICULT.. TIMES CHANGE...WE ALL GROW A LITTLE OLDER EACH DAY....
I'LL TELL YOU FRANKLY, CHARLIE BROWN... I'M SCARED!
2-26
SCHULZ

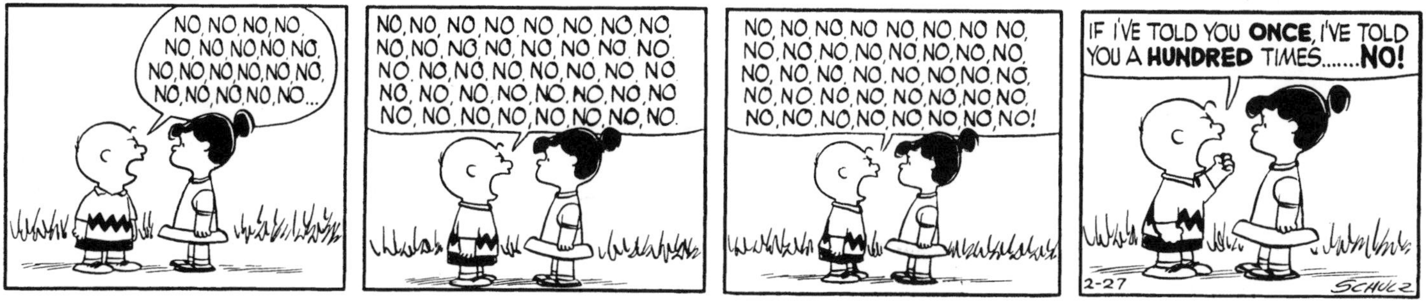
NO, NO, NO, NO, NO, NO, NO, NO, NO, NO, NO, NO, NO, NO, NO, NO, NO, NO, NO, NO, NO, NO...
NO, NO, NO, NO, NO, NO, NO, NO, NO, NO, NO, NO, NO, NO, NO, NO, NO, NO, NO, NO, NO, NO, NO, NO, NO, NO, NO, NO, NO, NO, NO, NO, NO, NO, NO, NO, NO, NO, NO, NO, NO, NO, NO, NO, NO, NO, NO, NO.
NO, NO, NO, NO, NO, NO, NO, NO, NO, NO, NO, NO, NO, NO, NO, NO, NO, NO, NO, NO, NO, NO, NO, NO, NO, NO, NO, NO, NO, NO, NO, NO, NO, NO, NO, NO, NO, NO, NO, NO, NO, NO, NO, NO, NO, NO, NO, NO!
IF I'VE TOLD YOU ONCE, I'VE TOLD YOU A HUNDRED TIMES.......NO!
2-27
SCHULZ

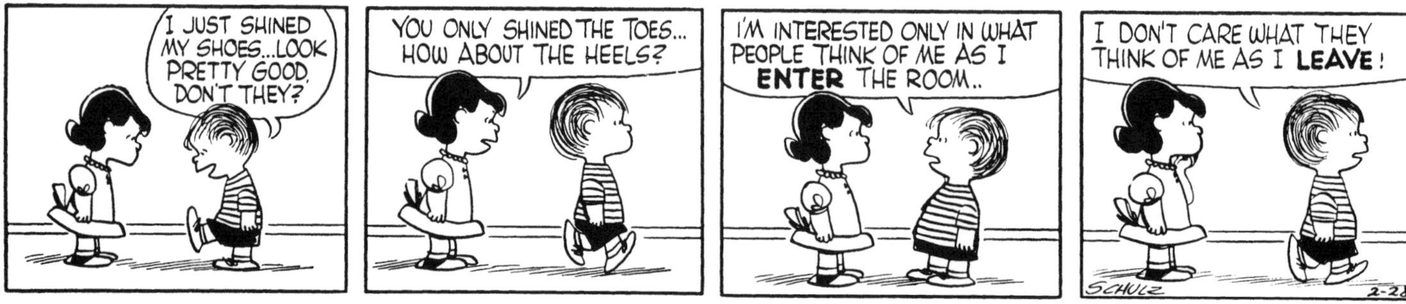
I JUST SHINED MY SHOES...LOOK PRETTY GOOD, DON'T THEY?
YOU ONLY SHINED THE TOES... HOW ABOUT THE HEELS?
I'M INTERESTED ONLY IN WHAT PEOPLE THINK OF ME AS I **ENTER** THE ROOM..
I DON'T CARE WHAT THEY THINK OF ME AS I **LEAVE**!
SCHULZ
2-28

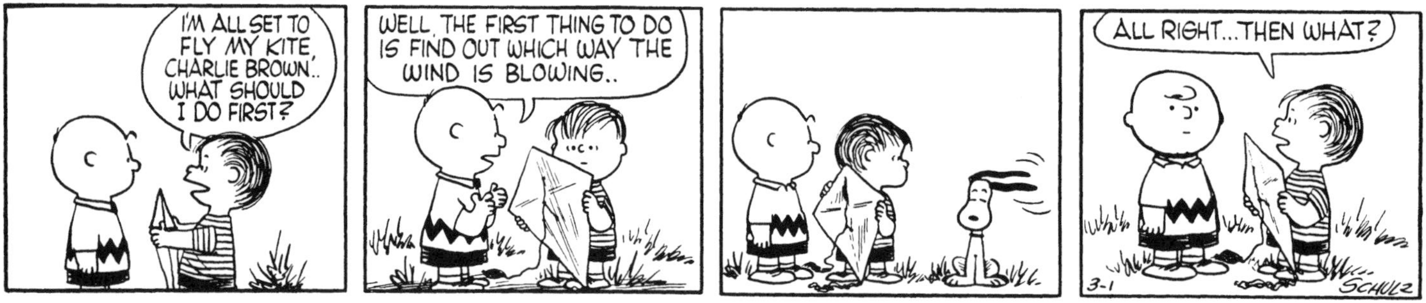
I'M ALL SET TO FLY MY KITE, CHARLIE BROWN.. WHAT SHOULD I DO FIRST?
WELL, THE FIRST THING TO DO IS FIND OUT WHICH WAY THE WIND IS BLOWING..
ALL RIGHT...THEN WHAT?
3-1
SCHULZ

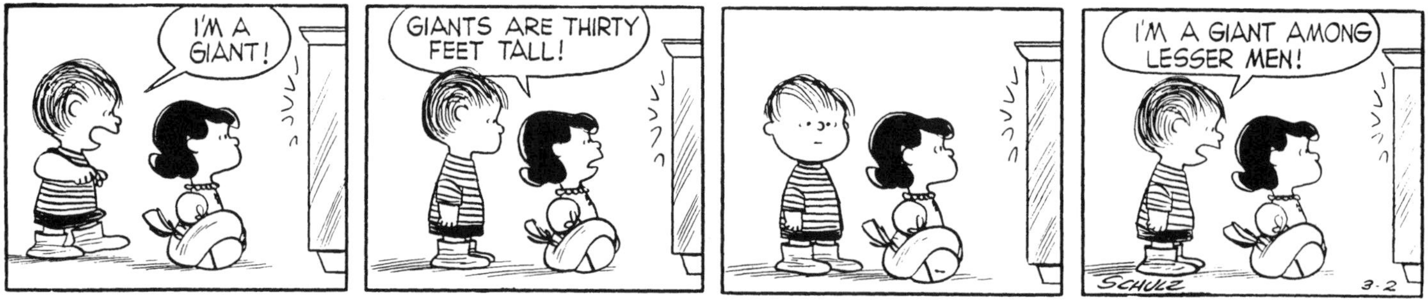
I'M A GIANT!
GIANTS ARE THIRTY FEET TALL!
I'M A GIANT AMONG LESSER MEN!
SCHULZ
3-2

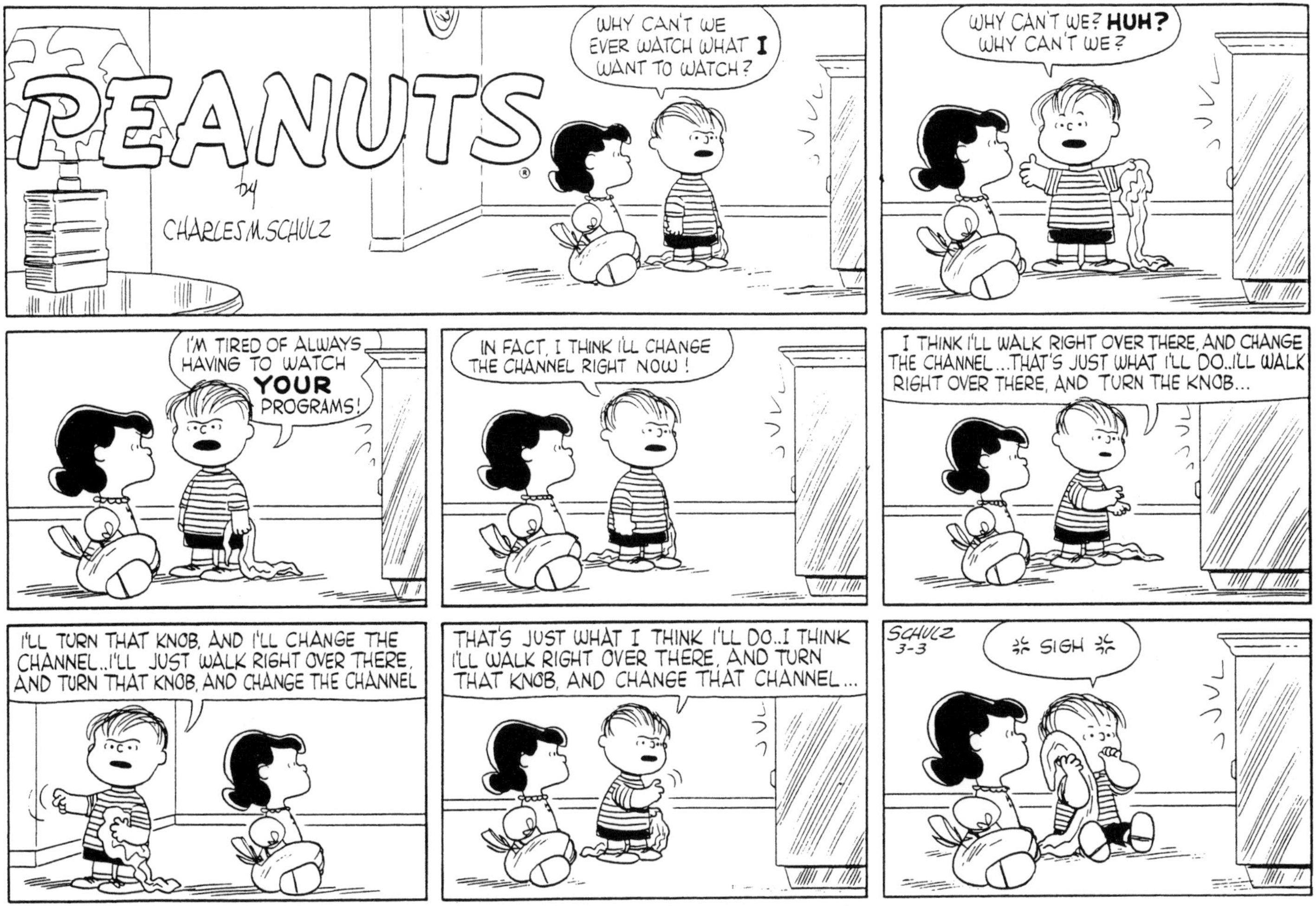
PEANUTS
by CHARLES M. SCHULZ
WHY CAN'T WE EVER WATCH WHAT I WANT TO WATCH?
WHY CAN'T WE? HUH? WHY CAN'T WE?
I'M TIRED OF ALWAYS HAVING TO WATCH YOUR PROGRAMS!
IN FACT, I THINK I'LL CHANGE THE CHANNEL RIGHT NOW!
I THINK I'LL WALK RIGHT OVER THERE, AND CHANGE THE CHANNEL...THAT'S JUST WHAT I'LL DO..I'LL WALK RIGHT OVER THERE, AND TURN THE KNOB...
I'LL TURN THAT KNOB, AND I'LL CHANGE THE CHANNEL..I'LL JUST WALK RIGHT OVER THERE, AND TURN THAT KNOB, AND CHANGE THE CHANNEL
THAT'S JUST WHAT I THINK I'LL DO..I THINK I'LL WALK RIGHT OVER THERE, AND TURN THAT KNOB, AND CHANGE THAT CHANNEL...
SCHULZ 3-3
SIGH

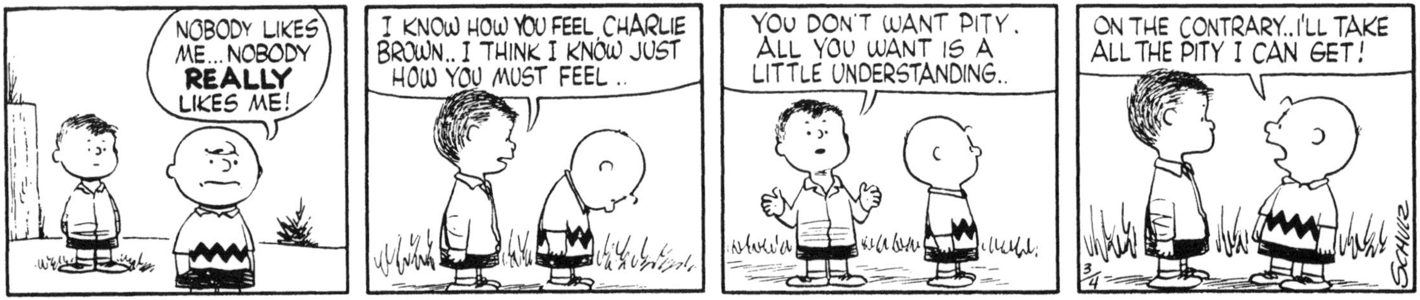
NOBODY LIKES ME... NOBODY **REALLY** LIKES ME!
I KNOW HOW YOU FEEL, CHARLIE BROWN.. I THINK I KNOW JUST HOW YOU MUST FEEL..
YOU DON'T WANT PITY. ALL YOU WANT IS A LITTLE UNDERSTANDING..
ON THE CONTRARY..I'LL TAKE ALL THE PITY I CAN GET!
3/4
SCHULZ

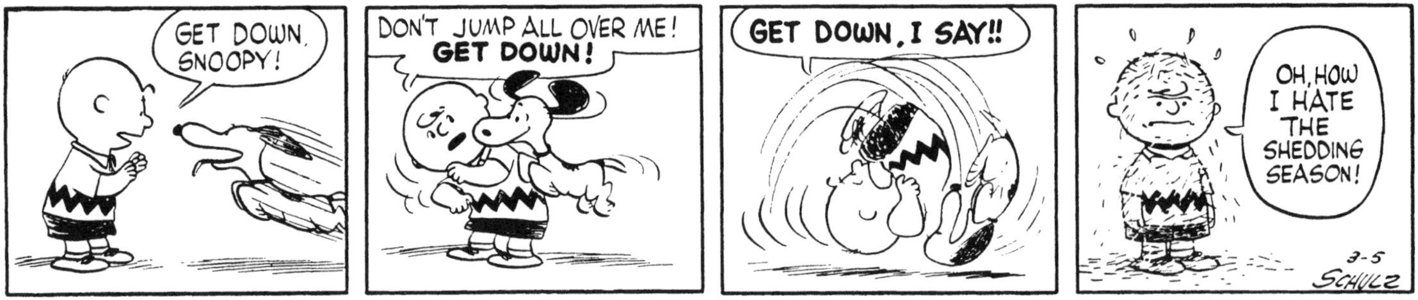
GET DOWN, SNOOPY!
DON'T JUMP ALL OVER ME! **GET DOWN!**
GET DOWN, I SAY!!
OH, HOW I HATE THE SHEDDING SEASON!
3-5
SCHULZ

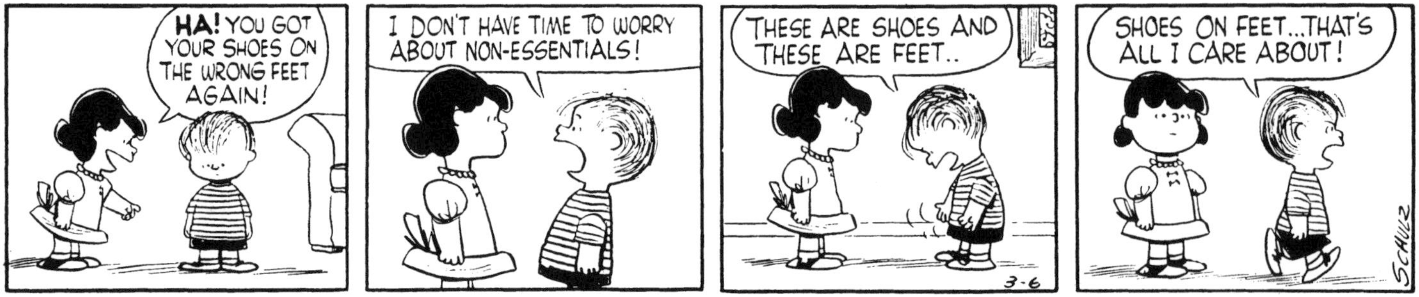
HA! YOU GOT YOUR SHOES ON THE WRONG FEET AGAIN!
I DON'T HAVE TIME TO WORRY ABOUT NON-ESSENTIALS!
THESE ARE SHOES AND THESE ARE FEET..
SHOES ON FEET...THAT'S ALL I CARE ABOUT!
3-6
SCHULZ

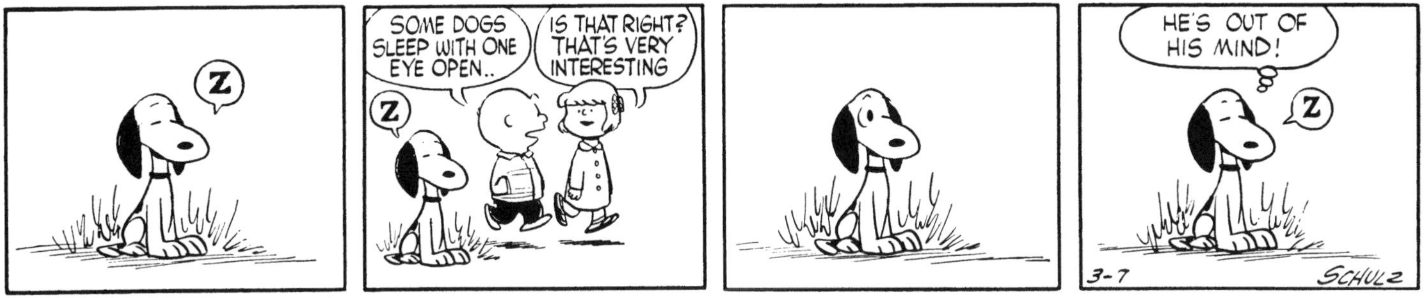
SOME DOGS SLEEP WITH ONE EYE OPEN..
IS THAT RIGHT? THAT'S VERY INTERESTING
HE'S OUT OF HIS MIND!
3-7
SCHULZ

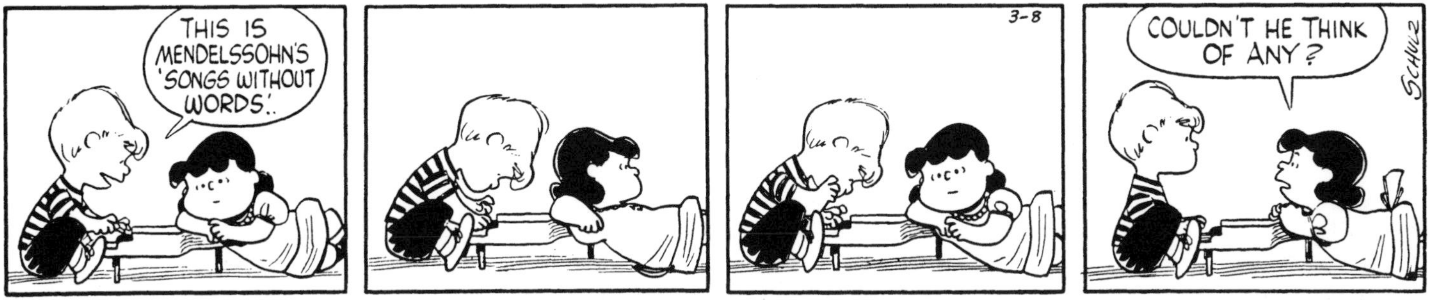
THIS IS MENDELSSOHN'S 'SONGS WITHOUT WORDS'..
3-8
COULDN'T HE THINK OF ANY?
SCHULZ

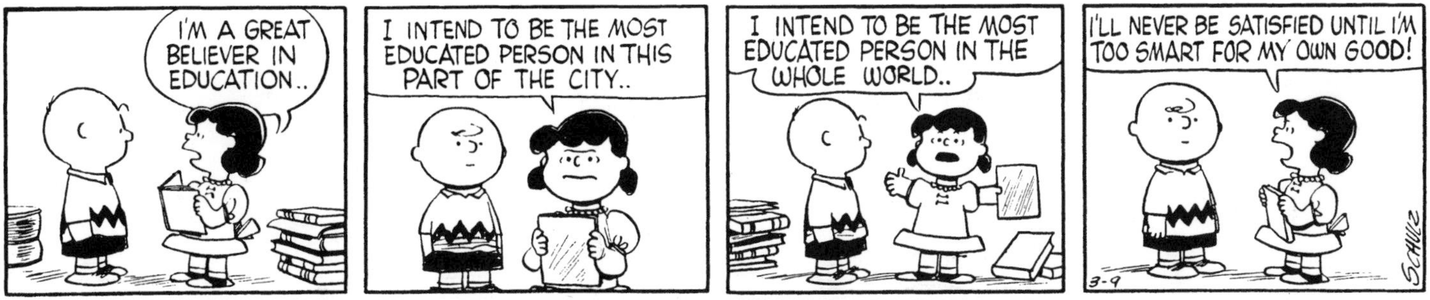
I'M A GREAT BELIEVER IN EDUCATION..
I INTEND TO BE THE MOST EDUCATED PERSON IN THIS PART OF THE CITY..
I INTEND TO BE THE MOST EDUCATED PERSON IN THE WHOLE WORLD..
I'LL NEVER BE SATISFIED UNTIL I'M TOO SMART FOR MY OWN GOOD!
3-9
SCHULZ

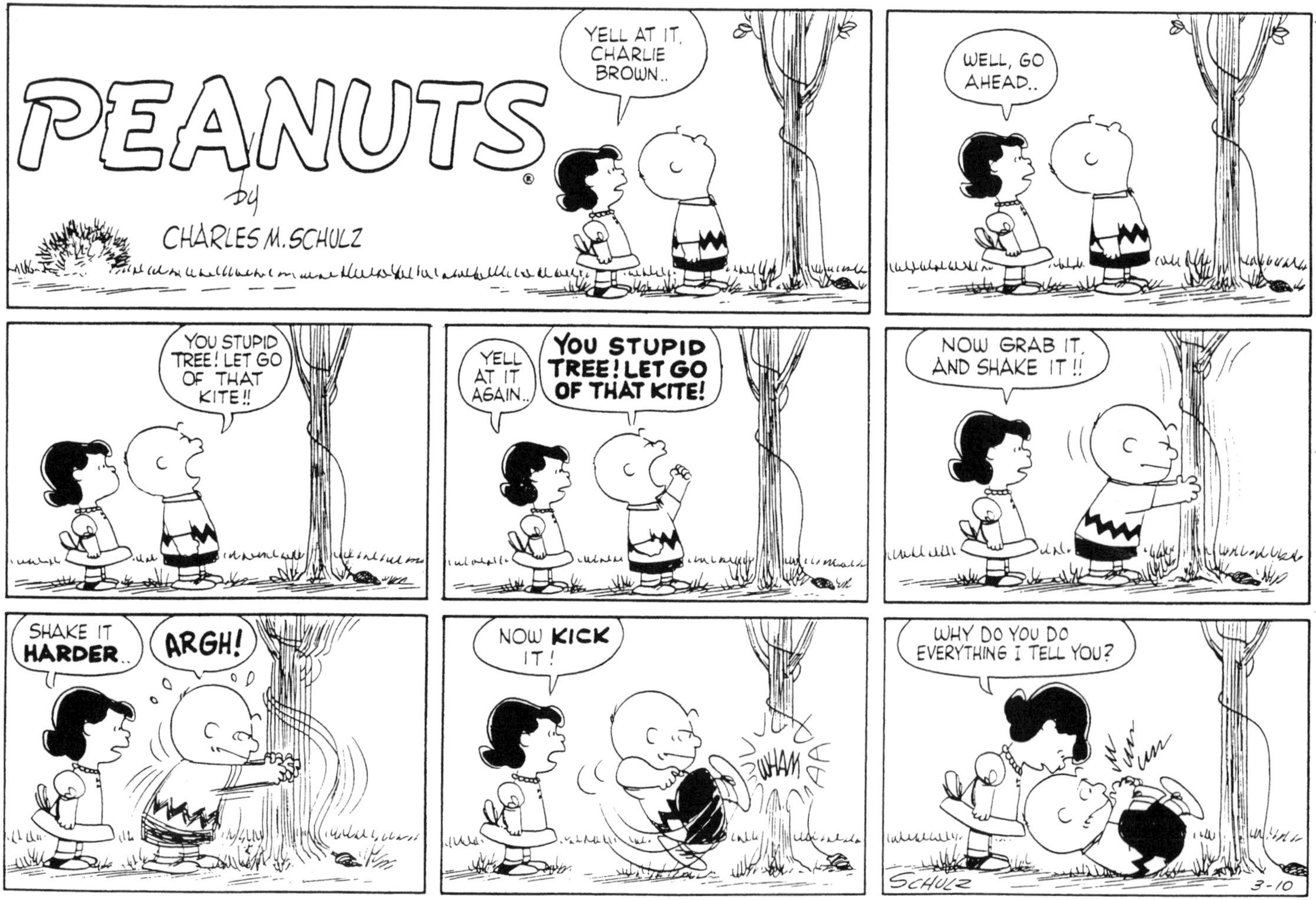
PEANUTS®
by CHARLES M. SCHULZ
YELL AT IT, CHARLIE BROWN..
WELL, GO AHEAD..
YOU STUPID TREE! LET GO OF THAT KITE!!
YELL AT IT AGAIN..
YOU STUPID TREE! LET GO OF THAT KITE!
NOW GRAB IT AND SHAKE IT!!
SHAKE IT HARDER..
ARGH!
NOW KICK IT!
WHAM
WHY DO YOU DO EVERYTHING I TELL YOU?
SCHULZ
3-10

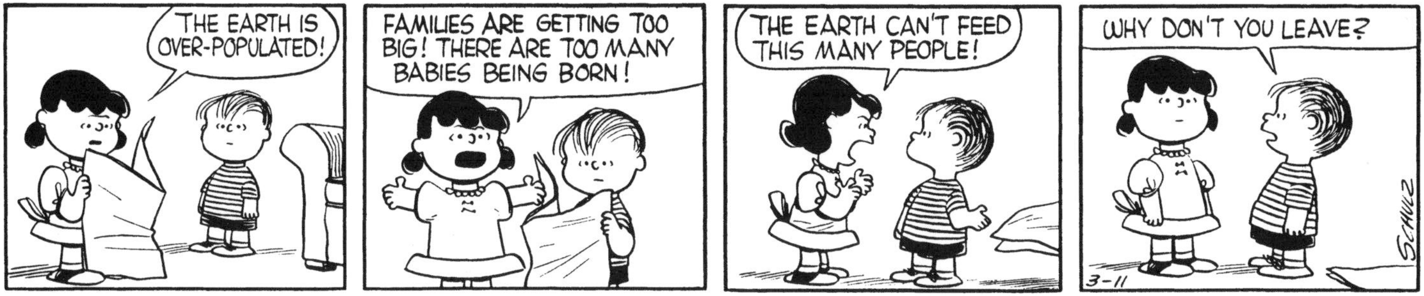
THE EARTH IS OVER-POPULATED!
FAMILIES ARE GETTING TOO BIG! THERE ARE TOO MANY BABIES BEING BORN!
THE EARTH CAN'T FEED THIS MANY PEOPLE!
WHY DON'T YOU LEAVE?
SCHULZ
3-11

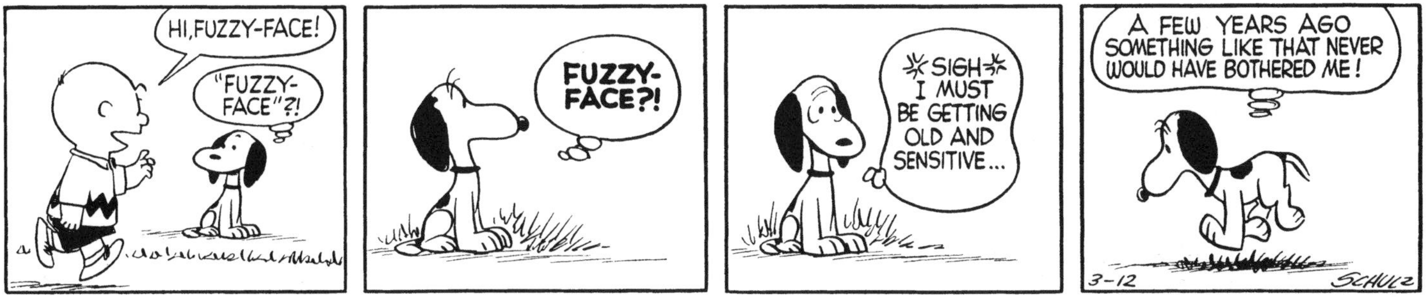
HI, FUZZY-FACE!
"FUZZY-FACE"?!
FUZZY-FACE?!
SIGH I MUST BE GETTING OLD AND SENSITIVE...
A FEW YEARS AGO SOMETHING LIKE THAT NEVER WOULD HAVE BOTHERED ME!
3-12
SCHULZ

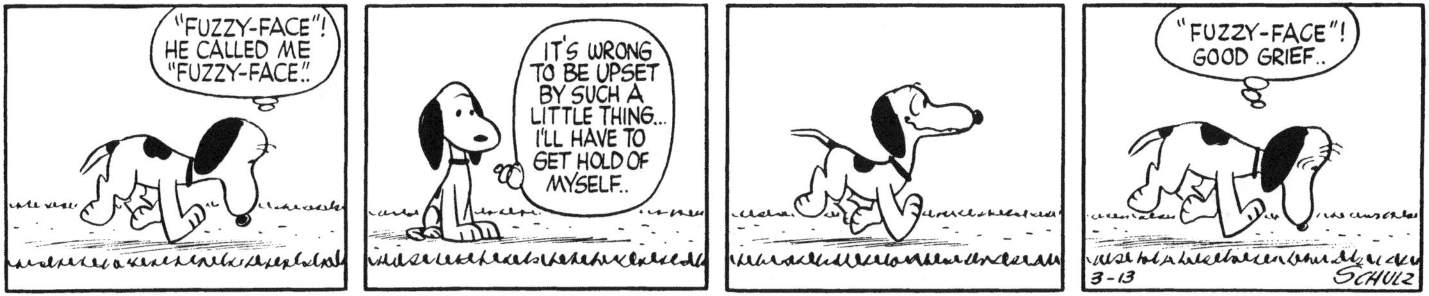
"FUZZY-FACE"! HE CALLED ME "FUZZY-FACE"..
IT'S WRONG TO BE UPSET BY SUCH A LITTLE THING... I'LL HAVE TO GET HOLD OF MYSELF..
"FUZZY-FACE"! GOOD GRIEF..
3-13
SCHULZ

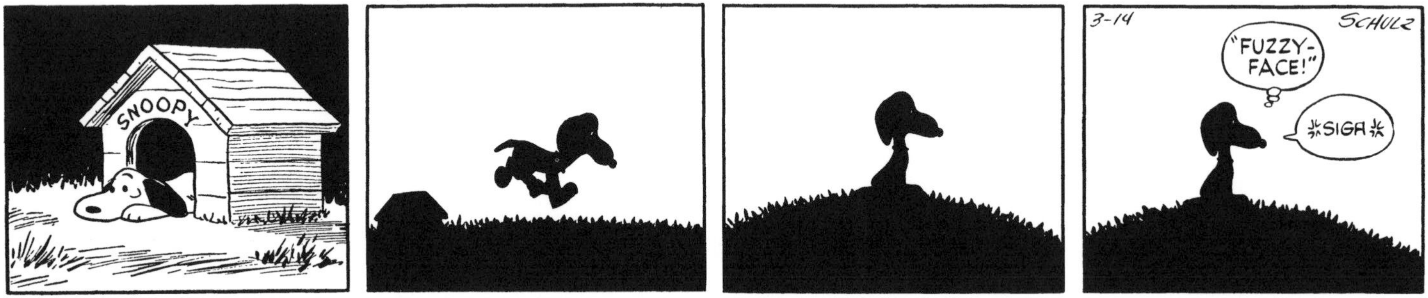
SNOOPY
3-14
SCHULZ
"FUZZY-FACE!"
SIGH

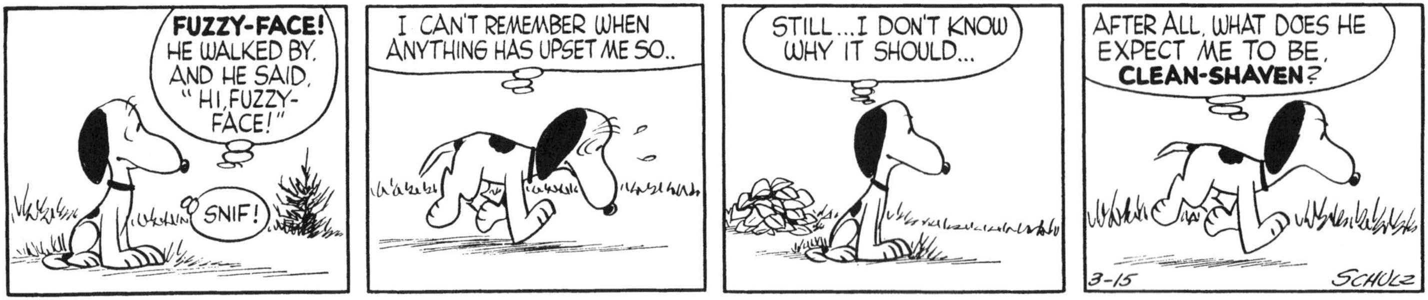
FUZZY-FACE! HE WALKED BY, AND HE SAID, "HI, FUZZY-FACE!"
SNIF!
I CAN'T REMEMBER WHEN ANYTHING HAS UPSET ME SO..
STILL...I DON'T KNOW WHY IT SHOULD...
AFTER ALL, WHAT DOES HE EXPECT ME TO BE, CLEAN-SHAVEN?
3-15
SCHULZ

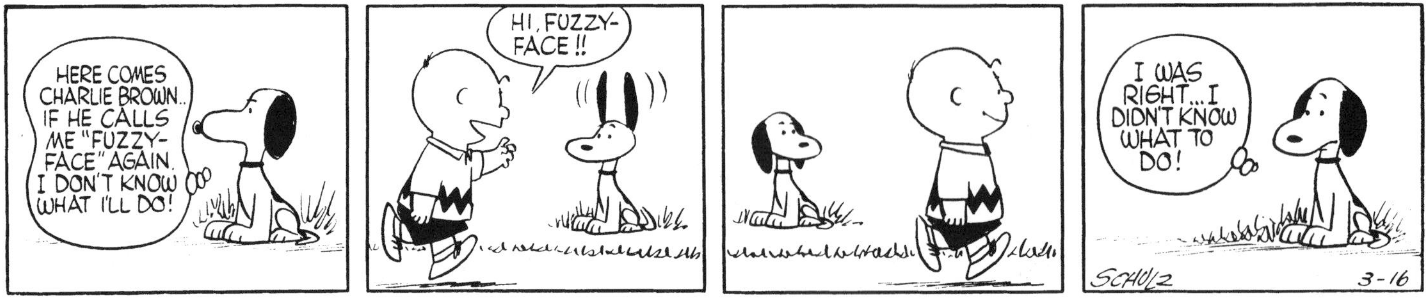
HERE COMES CHARLIE BROWN.. IF HE CALLS ME "FUZZY-FACE" AGAIN, I DON'T KNOW WHAT I'LL DO!
HI, FUZZY-FACE !!
I WAS RIGHT...I DIDN'T KNOW WHAT TO DO!
SCHULZ
3-16

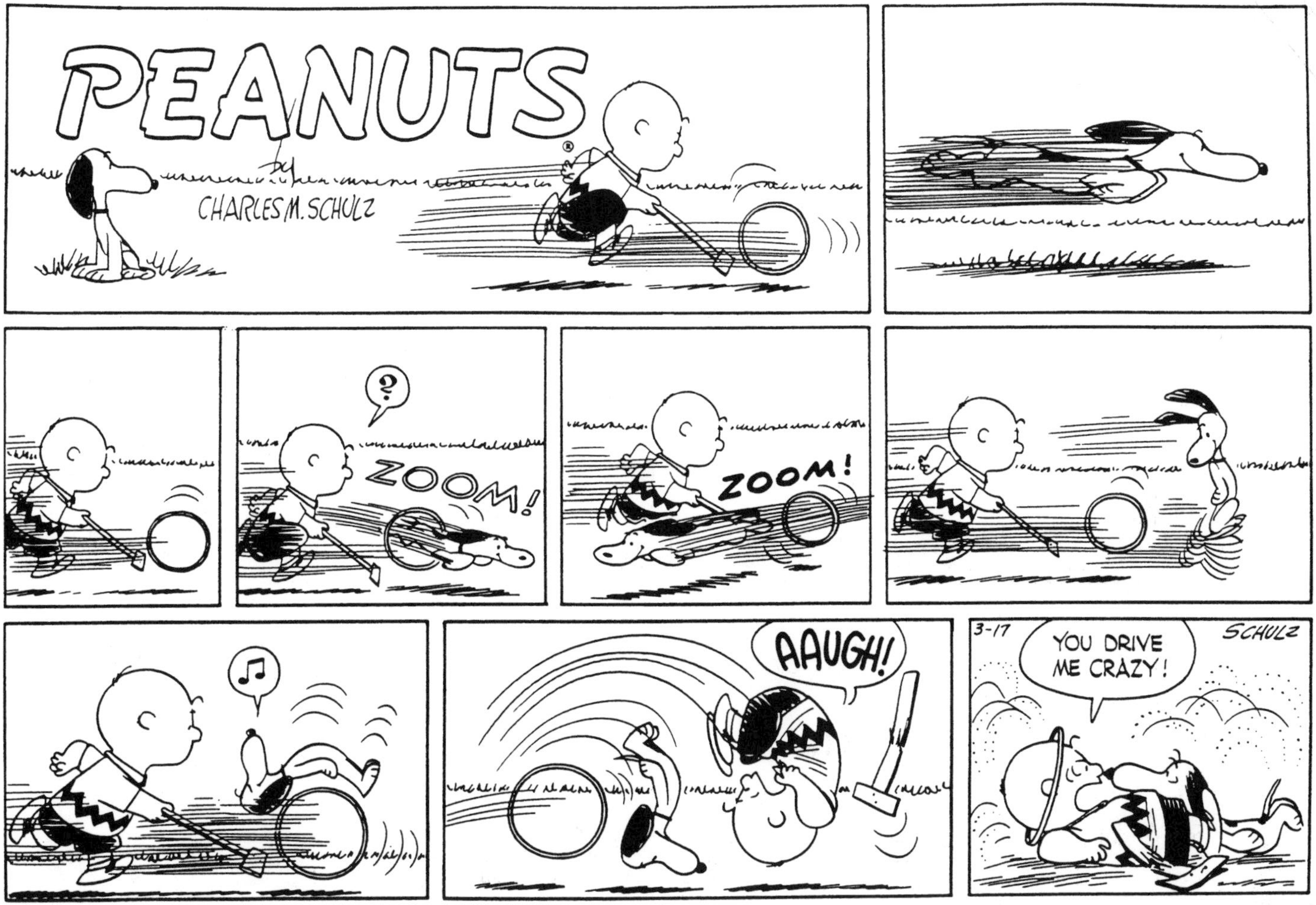
PEANUTS
CHARLES M. SCHULZ
?
ZOOM!
ZOOM!
AAUGH!
3-17
SCHULZ
YOU DRIVE ME CRAZY!

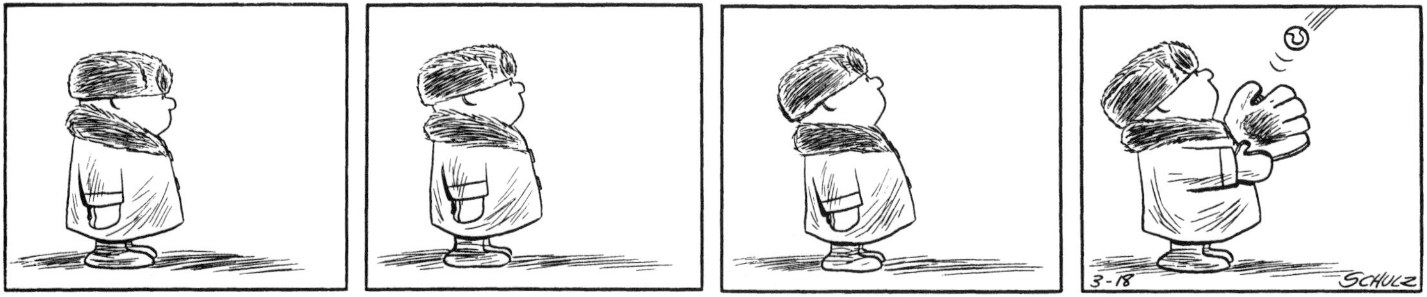
3-18
SCHULZ

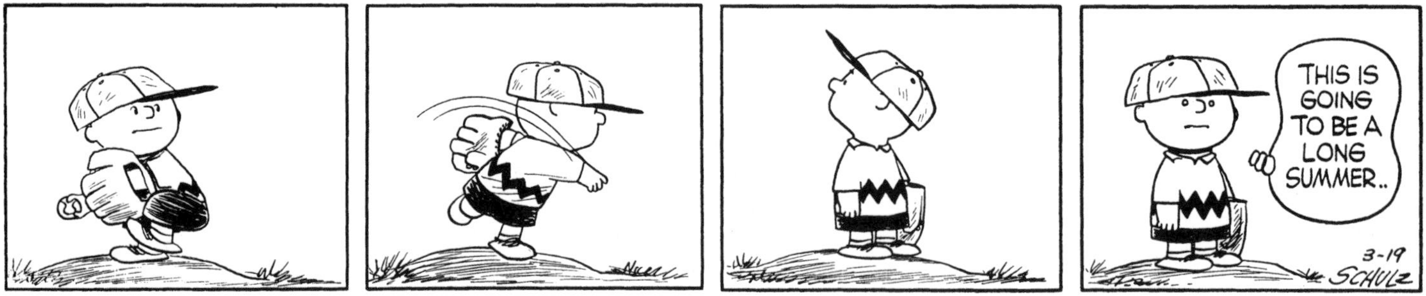
THIS IS GOING TO BE A LONG SUMMER..
3-19
SCHULZ

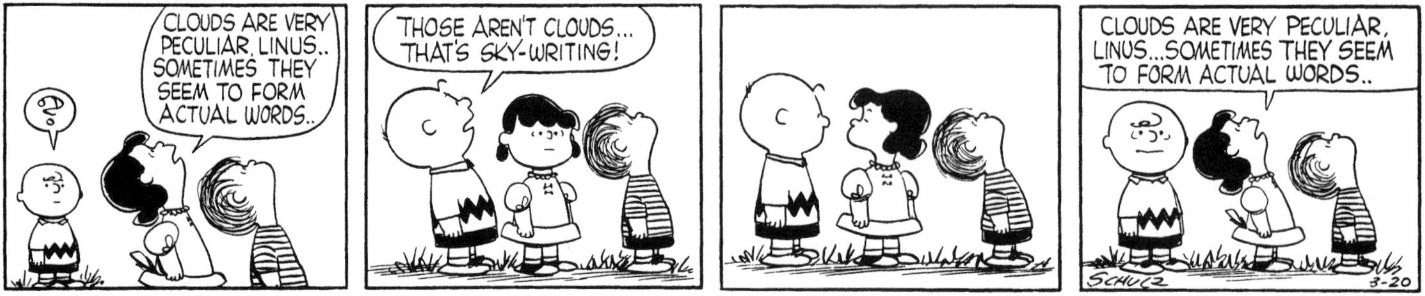
CLOUDS ARE VERY PECULIAR, LINUS.. SOMETIMES THEY SEEM TO FORM ACTUAL WORDS..
THOSE AREN'T CLOUDS... THAT'S SKY-WRITING!
CLOUDS ARE VERY PECULIAR, LINUS...SOMETIMES THEY SEEM TO FORM ACTUAL WORDS..
SCHULZ
3-20

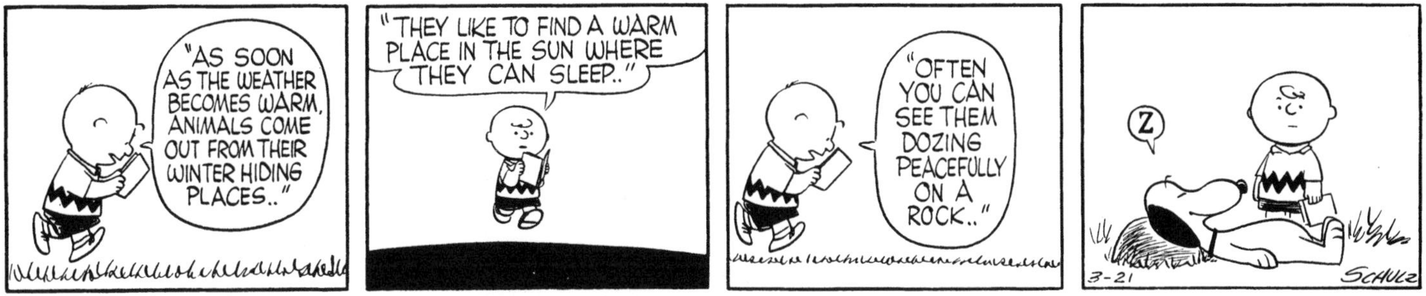
"AS SOON AS THE WEATHER BECOMES WARM, ANIMALS COME OUT FROM THEIR WINTER HIDING PLACES.."
"THEY LIKE TO FIND A WARM PLACE IN THE SUN WHERE THEY CAN SLEEP.."
"OFTEN YOU CAN SEE THEM DOZING PEACEFULLY ON A ROCK.."
Z
3-21
SCHULZ

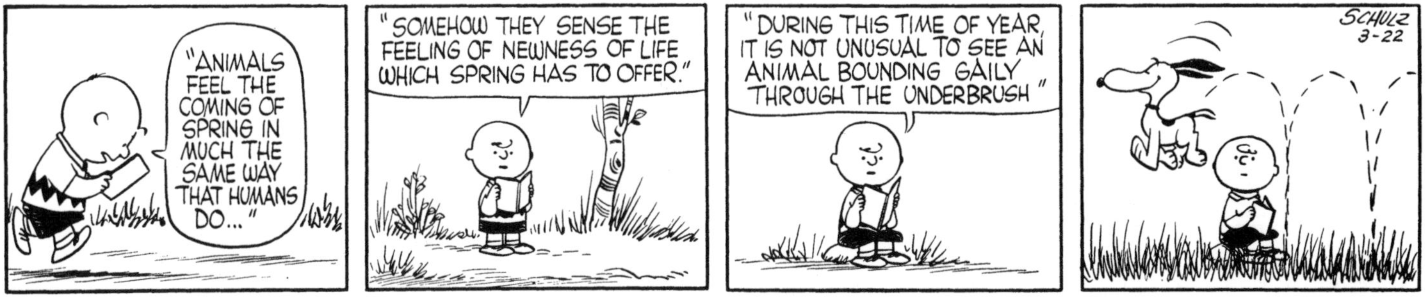
"ANIMALS FEEL THE COMING OF SPRING IN MUCH THE SAME WAY THAT HUMANS DO..."
"SOMEHOW THEY SENSE THE FEELING OF NEWNESS OF LIFE WHICH SPRING HAS TO OFFER."
"DURING THIS TIME OF YEAR, IT IS NOT UNUSUAL TO SEE AN ANIMAL BOUNDING GAILY THROUGH THE UNDERBRUSH"
SCHULZ
3-22

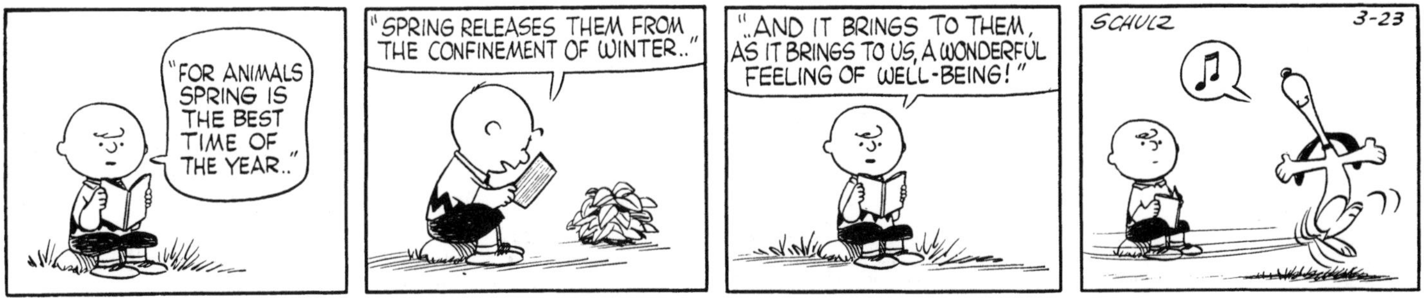
"FOR ANIMALS SPRING IS THE BEST TIME OF THE YEAR.."
"SPRING RELEASES THEM FROM THE CONFINEMENT OF WINTER.."
"..AND IT BRINGS TO THEM, AS IT BRINGS TO US, A WONDERFUL FEELING OF WELL-BEING!"
SCHULZ
3-23

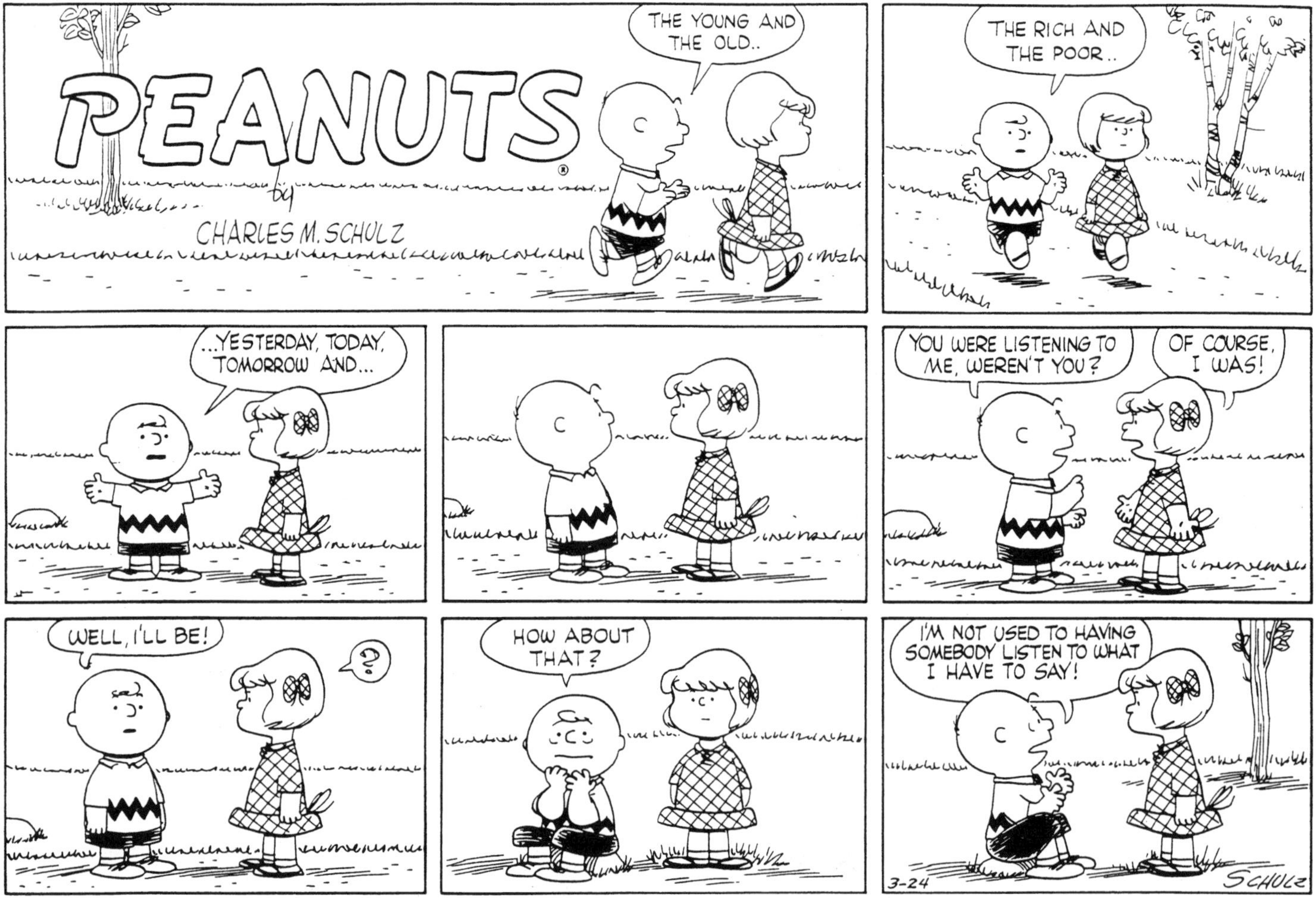
PEANUTS®
by
CHARLES M. SCHULZ
THE YOUNG AND THE OLD..
THE RICH AND THE POOR..
...YESTERDAY, TODAY, TOMORROW AND...
YOU WERE LISTENING TO ME, WEREN'T YOU?
OF COURSE, I WAS!
WELL, I'LL BE!
?
HOW ABOUT THAT?
I'M NOT USED TO HAVING SOMEBODY LISTEN TO WHAT I HAVE TO SAY!
3-24
SCHULZ

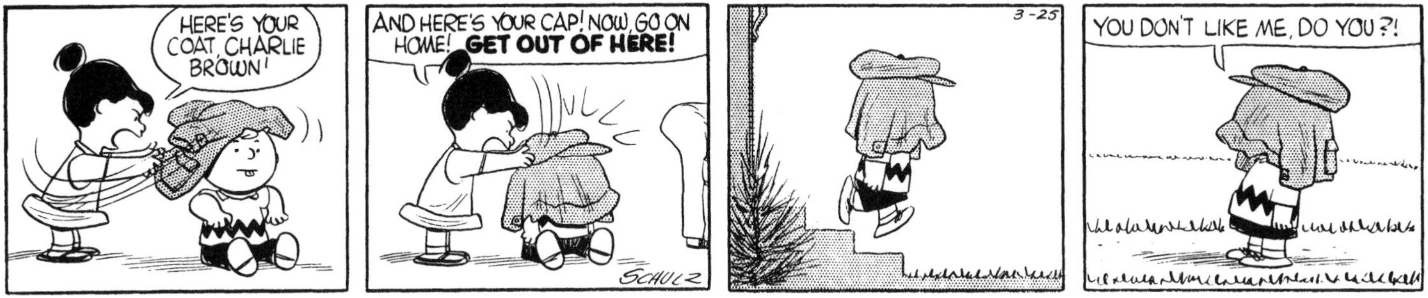
HERE'S YOUR COAT, CHARLIE BROWN!
AND HERE'S YOUR CAP! NOW, GO ON HOME! **GET OUT OF HERE!**
SCHULZ
3-25
YOU DON'T LIKE ME, DO YOU?!

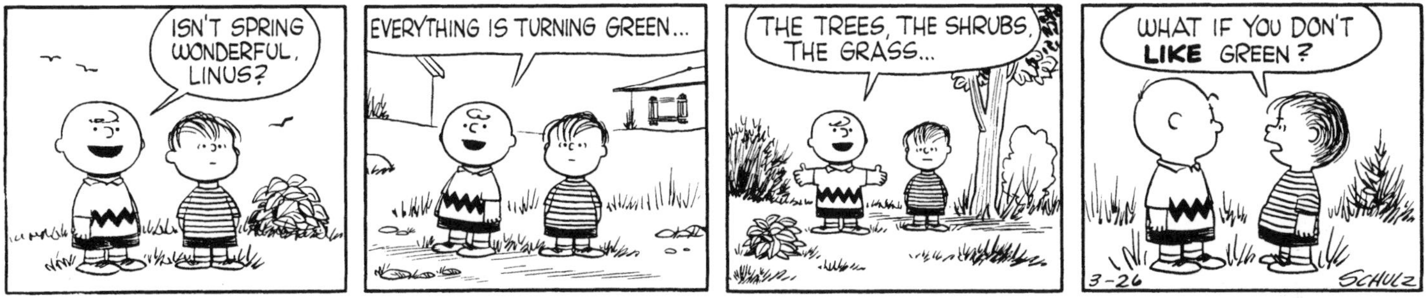
ISN'T SPRING WONDERFUL, LINUS?
EVERYTHING IS TURNING GREEN...
THE TREES, THE SHRUBS, THE GRASS...
WHAT IF YOU DON'T **LIKE** GREEN?
3-26
SCHULZ

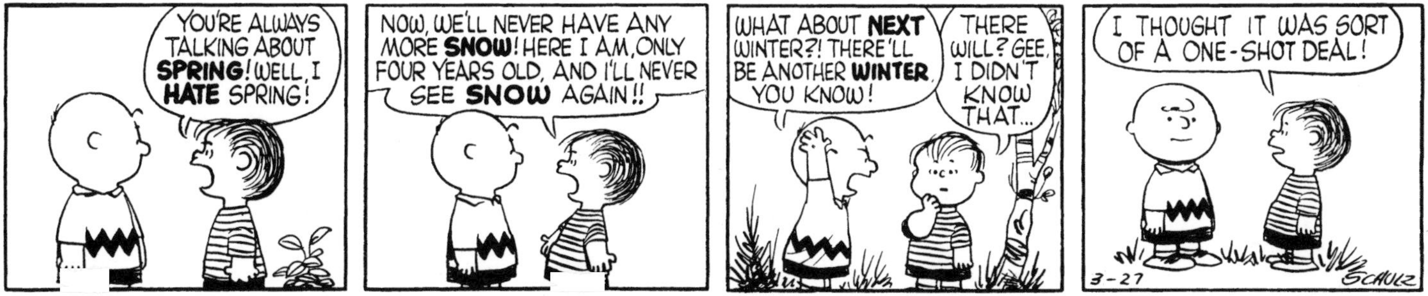
YOU'RE ALWAYS TALKING ABOUT **SPRING**! WELL, I **HATE** SPRING!
NOW, WE'LL NEVER HAVE ANY MORE **SNOW**! HERE I AM, ONLY FOUR YEARS OLD, AND I'LL NEVER SEE **SNOW** AGAIN!!
WHAT ABOUT **NEXT** WINTER?! THERE'LL BE ANOTHER **WINTER**, YOU KNOW!
THERE WILL? GEE, I DIDN'T KNOW THAT...
I THOUGHT IT WAS SORT OF A ONE-SHOT DEAL!
3-27
SCHULZ

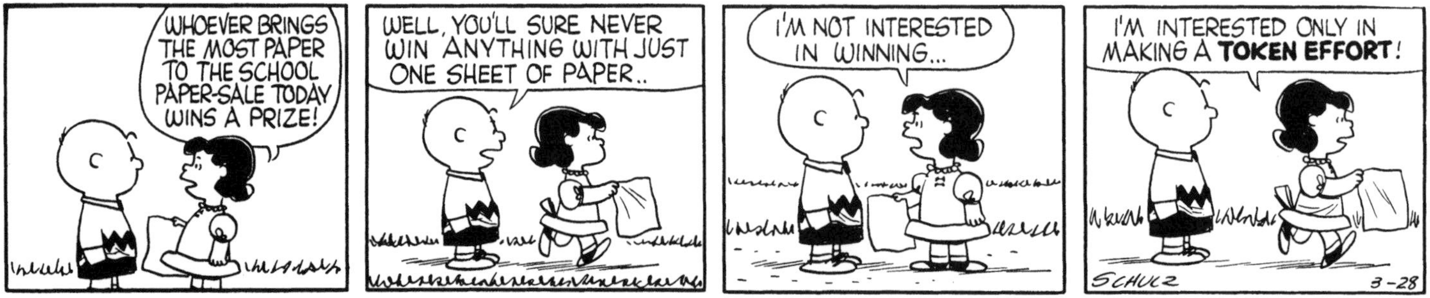
WHOEVER BRINGS THE MOST PAPER TO THE SCHOOL PAPER-SALE TODAY WINS A PRIZE!
WELL, YOU'LL SURE NEVER WIN ANYTHING WITH JUST ONE SHEET OF PAPER..
I'M NOT INTERESTED IN WINNING...
I'M INTERESTED ONLY IN MAKING A **TOKEN EFFORT**!
SCHULZ
3-28

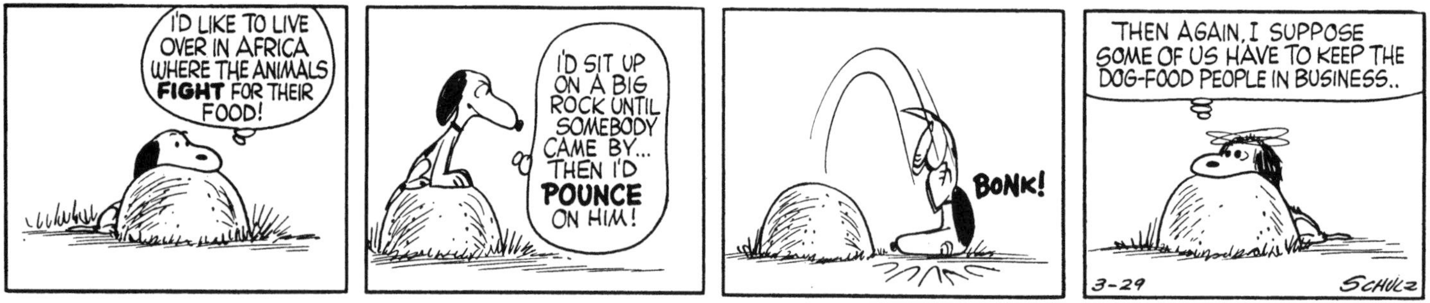
I'D LIKE TO LIVE OVER IN AFRICA WHERE THE ANIMALS **FIGHT** FOR THEIR FOOD!
I'D SIT UP ON A BIG ROCK UNTIL SOMEBODY CAME BY... THEN I'D **POUNCE** ON HIM!
BONK!
THEN AGAIN, I SUPPOSE SOME OF US HAVE TO KEEP THE DOG-FOOD PEOPLE IN BUSINESS..
3-29
SCHULZ

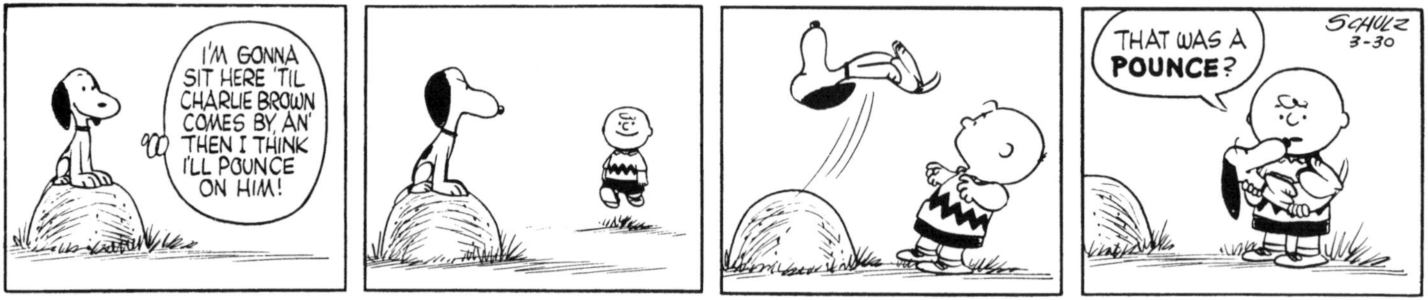
I'M GONNA SIT HERE 'TIL CHARLIE BROWN COMES BY, AN' THEN I THINK I'LL POUNCE ON HIM!
SCHULZ
3-30
THAT WAS A **POUNCE**?

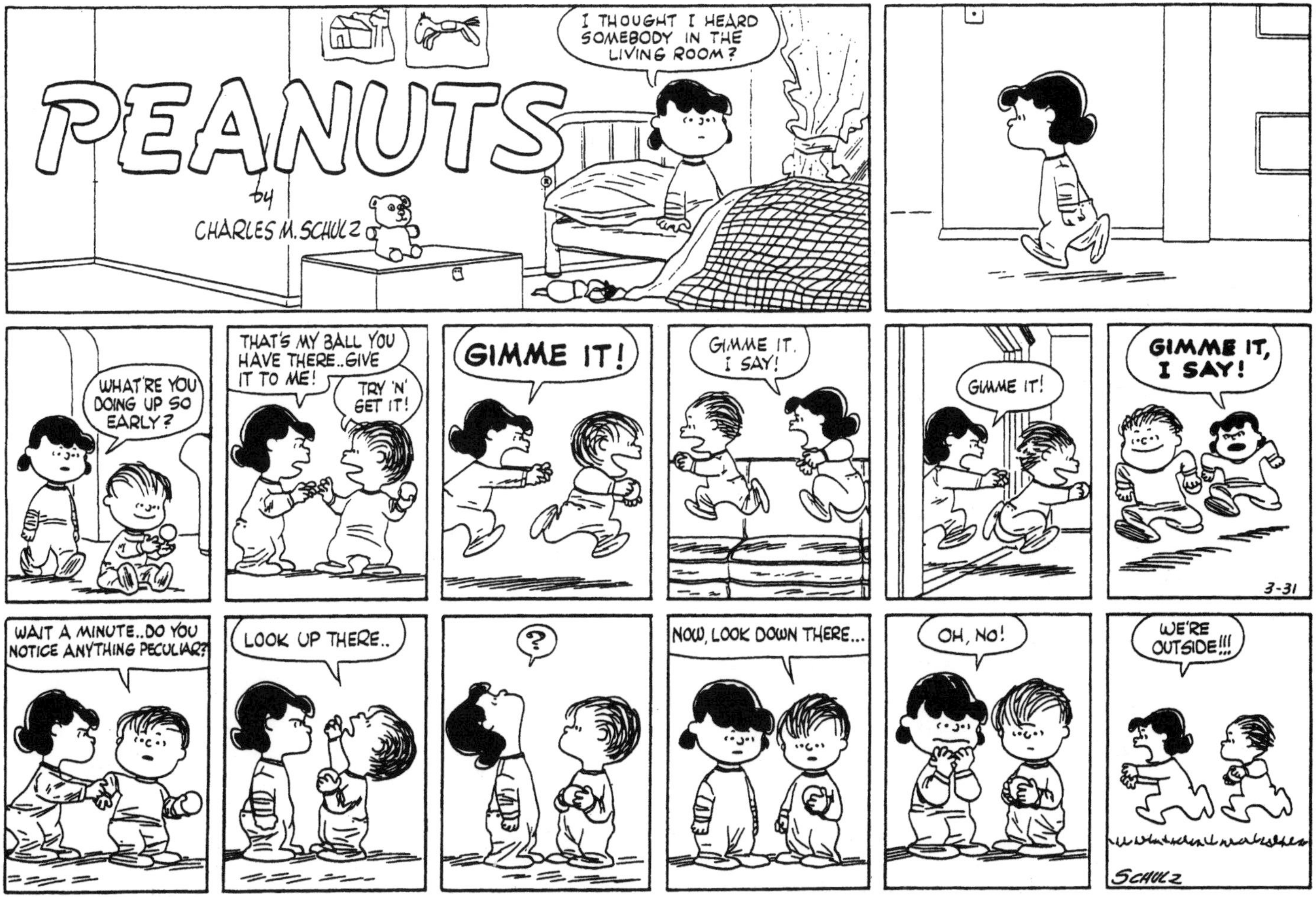
PEANUTS
by CHARLES M. SCHULZ
I THOUGHT I HEARD SOMEBODY IN THE LIVING ROOM?
WHAT'RE YOU DOING UP SO EARLY?
THAT'S MY BALL YOU HAVE THERE..GIVE IT TO ME!
TRY 'N' GET IT!
GIMME IT!
GIMME IT, I SAY!
GIMME IT!
GIMME IT, I SAY!
3-31
WAIT A MINUTE..DO YOU NOTICE ANYTHING PECULIAR?
LOOK UP THERE..
?
NOW, LOOK DOWN THERE...
OH, NO!
WE'RE OUTSIDE!!!
SCHULZ

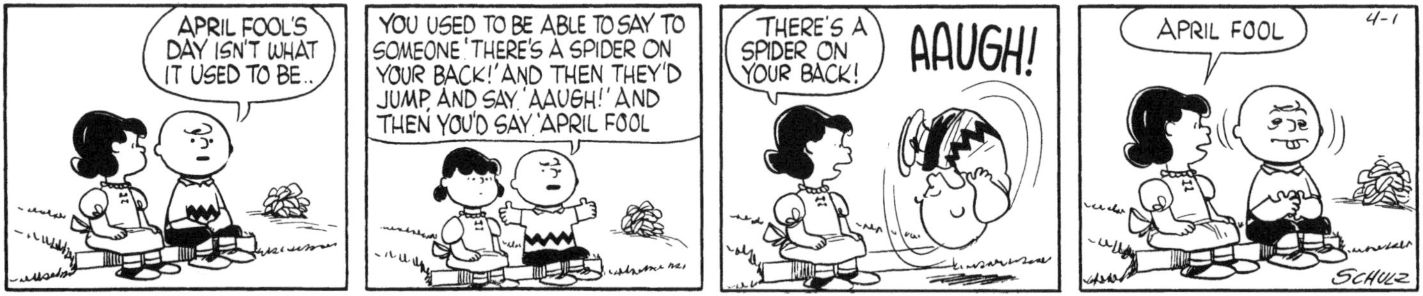
APRIL FOOL'S DAY ISN'T WHAT IT USED TO BE..
YOU USED TO BE ABLE TO SAY TO SOMEONE 'THERE'S A SPIDER ON YOUR BACK!' AND THEN THEY'D JUMP, AND SAY 'AAUGH!' AND THEN YOU'D SAY 'APRIL FOOL
THERE'S A SPIDER ON YOUR BACK!
AAUGH!
APRIL FOOL
4-1
SCHULZ

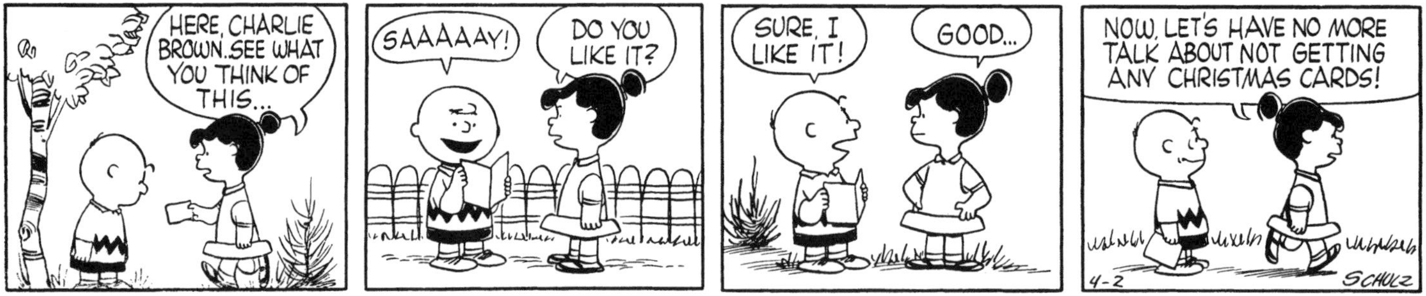
HERE, CHARLIE BROWN..SEE WHAT YOU THINK OF THIS...
SAAAAAY!
DO YOU LIKE IT?
SURE, I LIKE IT!
GOOD...
NOW, LET'S HAVE NO MORE TALK ABOUT NOT GETTING ANY CHRISTMAS CARDS!
4-2
SCHULZ

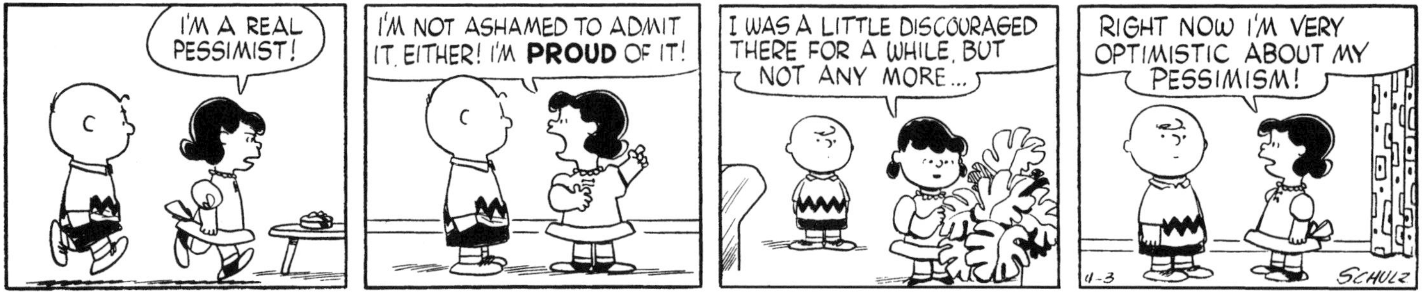
I'M A REAL PESSIMIST!
I'M NOT ASHAMED TO ADMIT IT, EITHER! I'M PROUD OF IT!
I WAS A LITTLE DISCOURAGED THERE FOR A WHILE, BUT NOT ANY MORE...
RIGHT NOW I'M VERY OPTIMISTIC ABOUT MY PESSIMISM!
4-3
SCHULZ

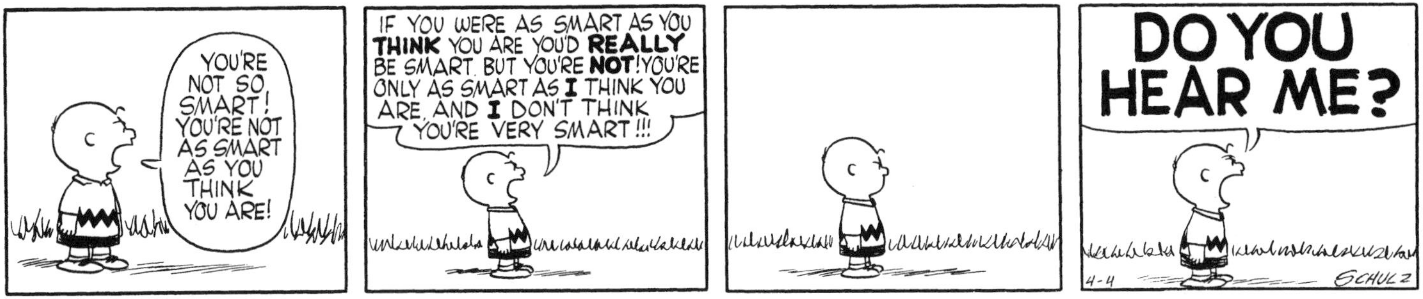
YOU'RE NOT SO SMART! YOU'RE NOT AS SMART AS YOU THINK YOU ARE!
IF YOU WERE AS SMART AS YOU THINK YOU ARE YOU'D REALLY BE SMART. BUT YOU'RE NOT! YOU'RE ONLY AS SMART AS I THINK YOU ARE, AND I DON'T THINK YOU'RE VERY SMART!!!
DO YOU HEAR ME?
4-4
SCHULZ

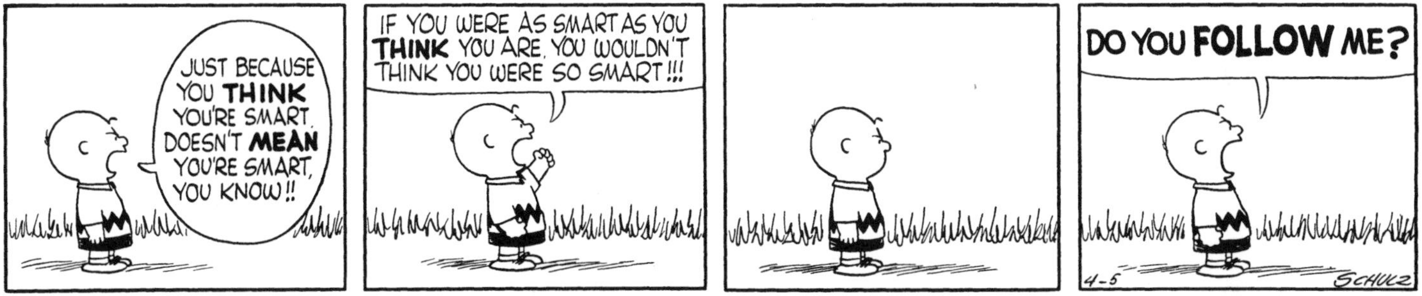
JUST BECAUSE YOU THINK YOU'RE SMART, DOESN'T MEAN YOU'RE SMART, YOU KNOW!!
IF YOU WERE AS SMART AS YOU THINK YOU ARE, YOU WOULDN'T THINK YOU WERE SO SMART!!!
DO YOU FOLLOW ME?
4-5
SCHULZ

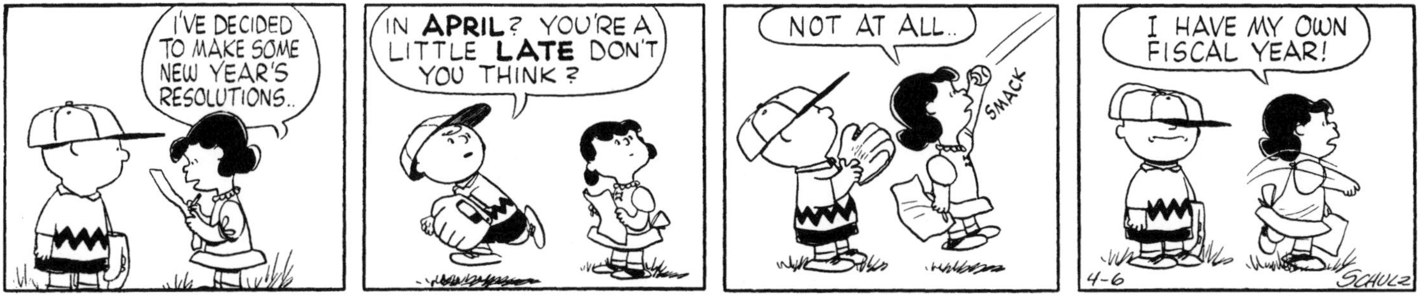
I'VE DECIDED TO MAKE SOME NEW YEAR'S RESOLUTIONS..
IN APRIL? YOU'RE A LITTLE LATE DON'T YOU THINK?
NOT AT ALL..
SMACK
I HAVE MY OWN FISCAL YEAR!
4-6
SCHULZ

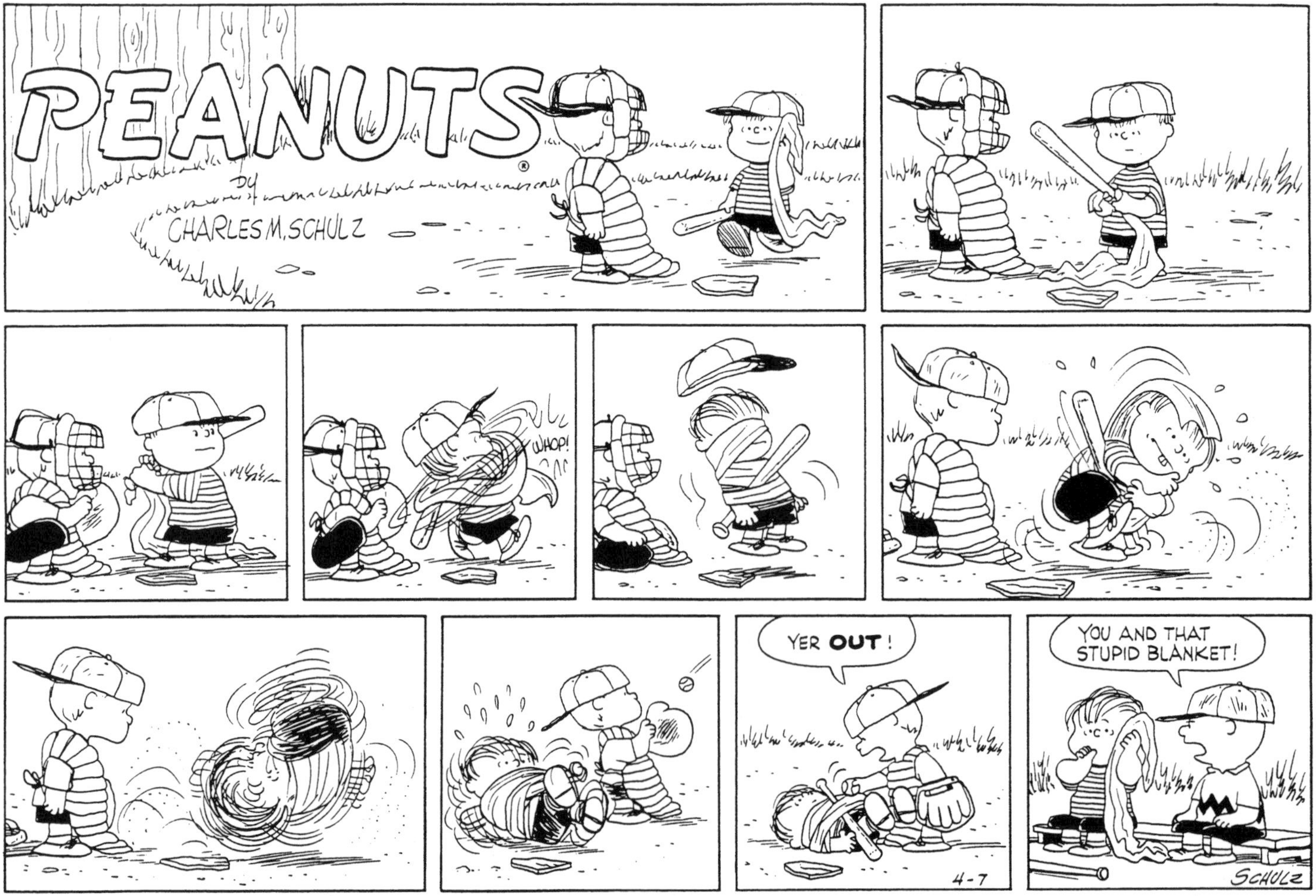
PEANUTS
by
CHARLES M. SCHULZ
WHOP!
YER OUT!
4-7
YOU AND THAT STUPID BLANKET!
SCHULZ

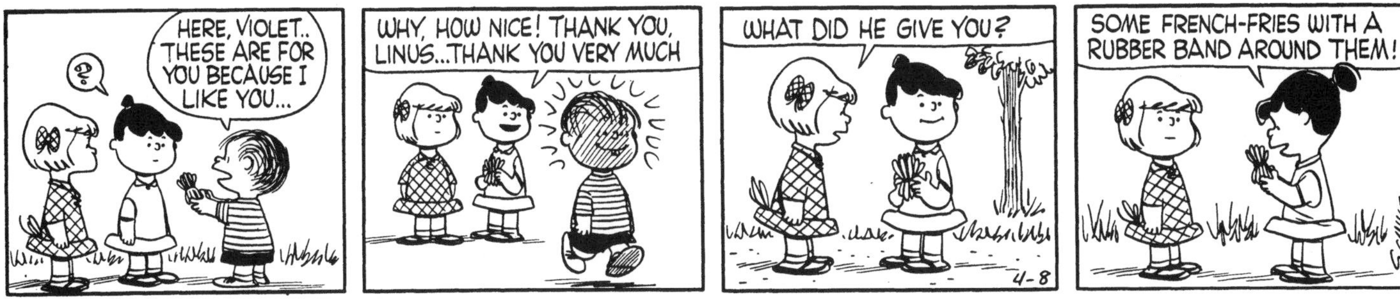
?
HERE, VIOLET.. THESE ARE FOR YOU BECAUSE I LIKE YOU...
WHY, HOW NICE! THANK YOU, LINUS...THANK YOU VERY MUCH
WHAT DID HE GIVE YOU?
4-8
SOME FRENCH-FRIES WITH A RUBBER BAND AROUND THEM!
SCHULZ

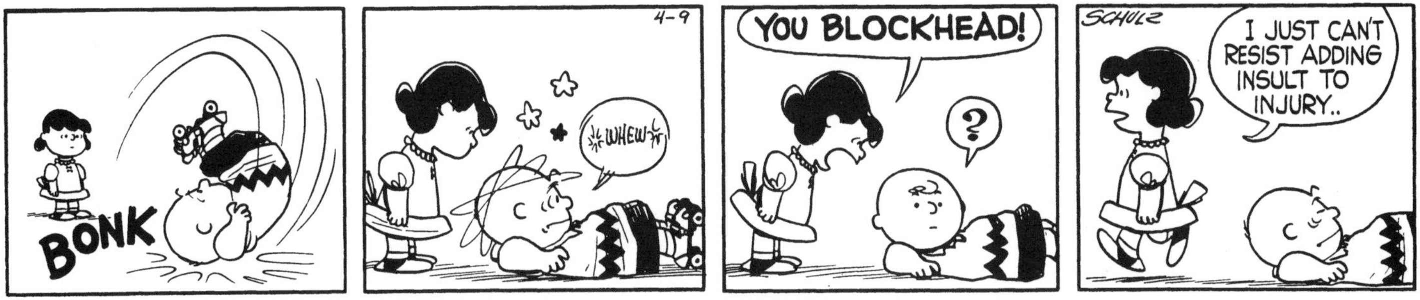
BONK
4-9
WHEW
YOU BLOCKHEAD!
?
SCHULZ
I JUST CAN'T RESIST ADDING INSULT TO INJURY..

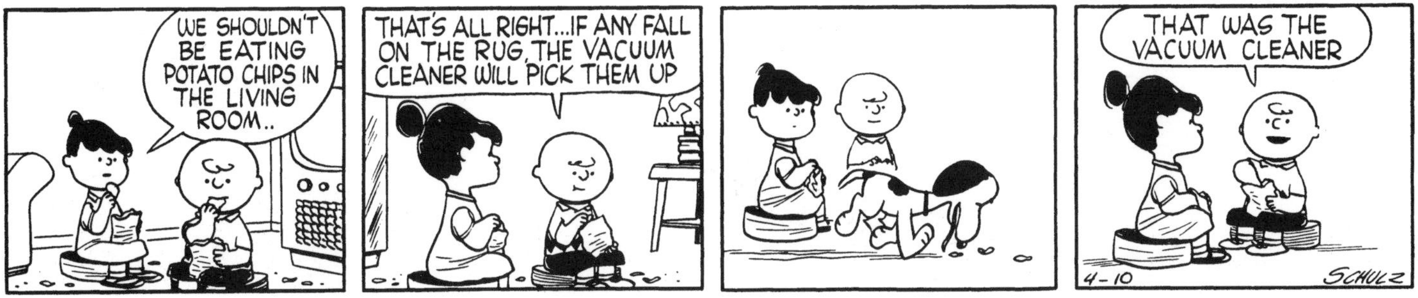
WE SHOULDN'T BE EATING POTATO CHIPS IN THE LIVING ROOM..
THAT'S ALL RIGHT...IF ANY FALL ON THE RUG, THE VACUUM CLEANER WILL PICK THEM UP
THAT WAS THE VACUUM CLEANER
4-10
SCHULZ

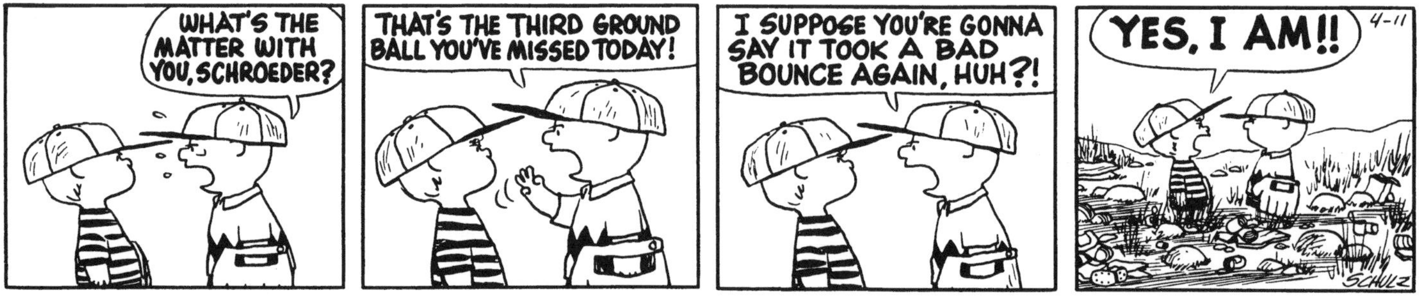
WHAT'S THE MATTER WITH YOU, SCHROEDER?
THAT'S THE THIRD GROUND BALL YOU'VE MISSED TODAY!
I SUPPOSE YOU'RE GONNA SAY IT TOOK A BAD BOUNCE AGAIN, HUH?!
YES, I AM!!
4-11
SCHULZ

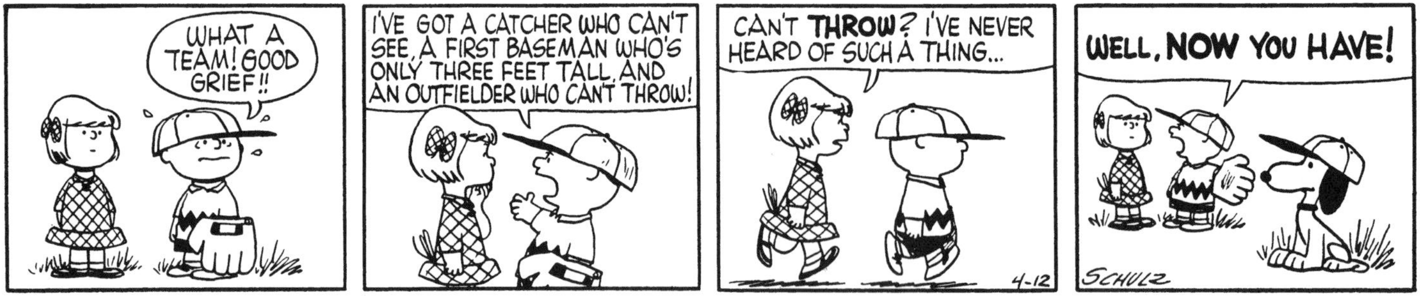
WHAT A TEAM! GOOD GRIEF!!
I'VE GOT A CATCHER WHO CAN'T SEE, A FIRST BASEMAN WHO'S ONLY THREE FEET TALL, AND AN OUTFIELDER WHO CAN'T THROW!
CAN'T THROW? I'VE NEVER HEARD OF SUCH A THING...
4-12
WELL, NOW YOU HAVE!
SCHULZ

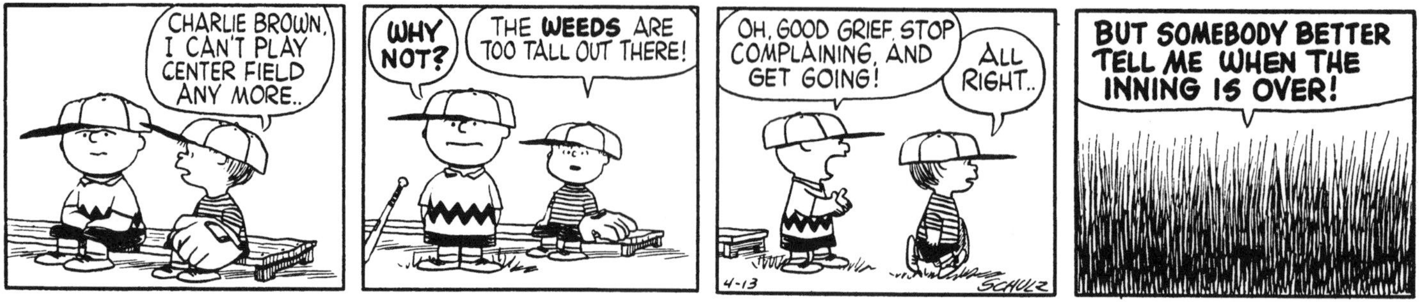
CHARLIE BROWN, I CAN'T PLAY CENTER FIELD ANY MORE..
WHY NOT?
THE WEEDS ARE TOO TALL OUT THERE!
OH, GOOD GRIEF. STOP COMPLAINING, AND GET GOING!
ALL RIGHT..
4-13
SCHULZ
BUT SOMEBODY BETTER TELL ME WHEN THE INNING IS OVER!

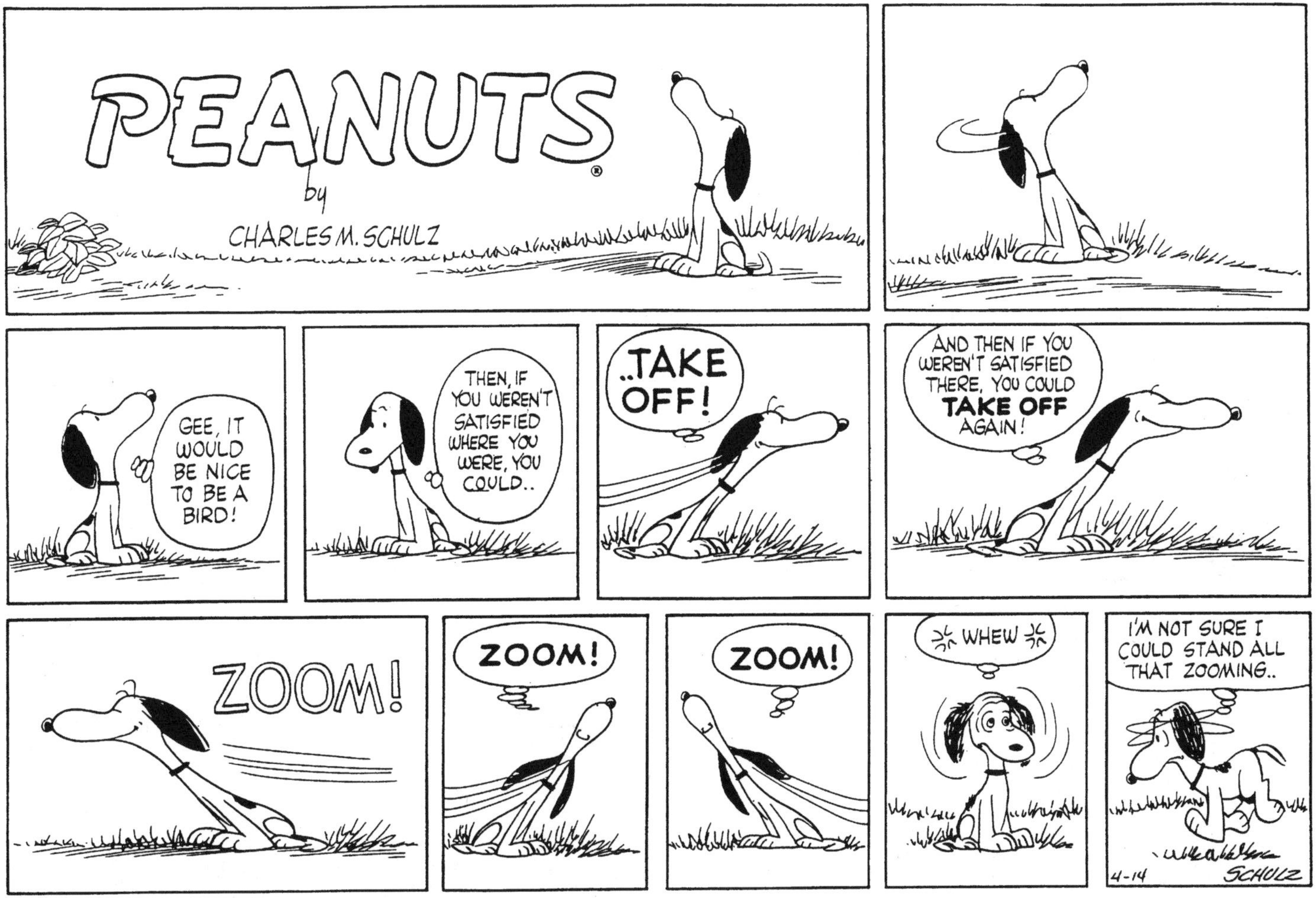
PEANUTS
by
CHARLES M. SCHULZ
GEE, IT WOULD BE NICE TO BE A BIRD!
THEN, IF YOU WEREN'T SATISFIED WHERE YOU WERE, YOU COULD..
..TAKE OFF!
AND THEN IF YOU WEREN'T SATISFIED THERE, YOU COULD **TAKE OFF** AGAIN!
ZOOM!
ZOOM!
ZOOM!
WHEW
I'M NOT SURE I COULD STAND ALL THAT ZOOMING..
4-14
SCHULZ

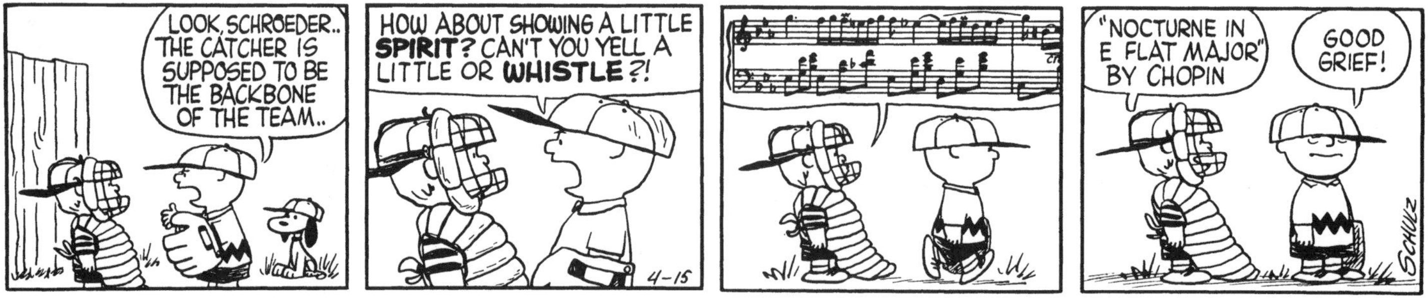
LOOK, SCHROEDER.. THE CATCHER IS SUPPOSED TO BE THE BACKBONE OF THE TEAM..
HOW ABOUT SHOWING A LITTLE SPIRIT? CAN'T YOU YELL A LITTLE OR WHISTLE?!
4-15
"NOCTURNE IN E FLAT MAJOR" BY CHOPIN
GOOD GRIEF!
SCHULZ

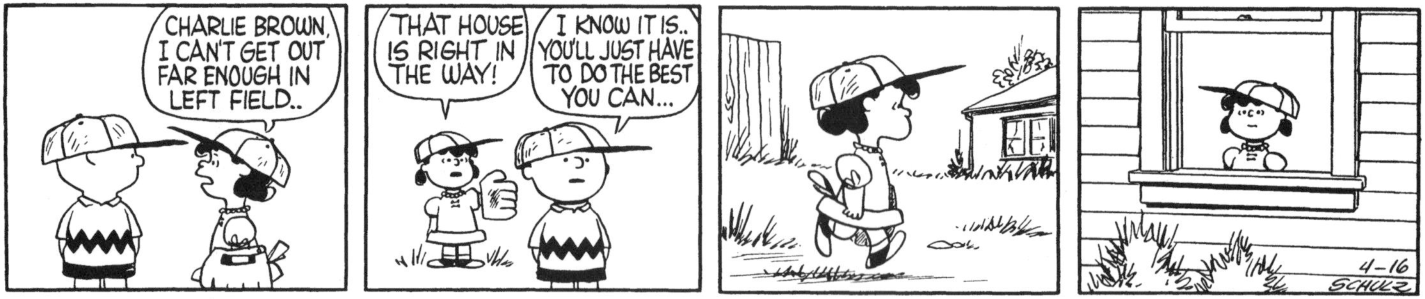
CHARLIE BROWN, I CAN'T GET OUT FAR ENOUGH IN LEFT FIELD..
THAT HOUSE IS RIGHT IN THE WAY!
I KNOW IT IS.. YOU'LL JUST HAVE TO DO THE BEST YOU CAN...
4-16
SCHULZ

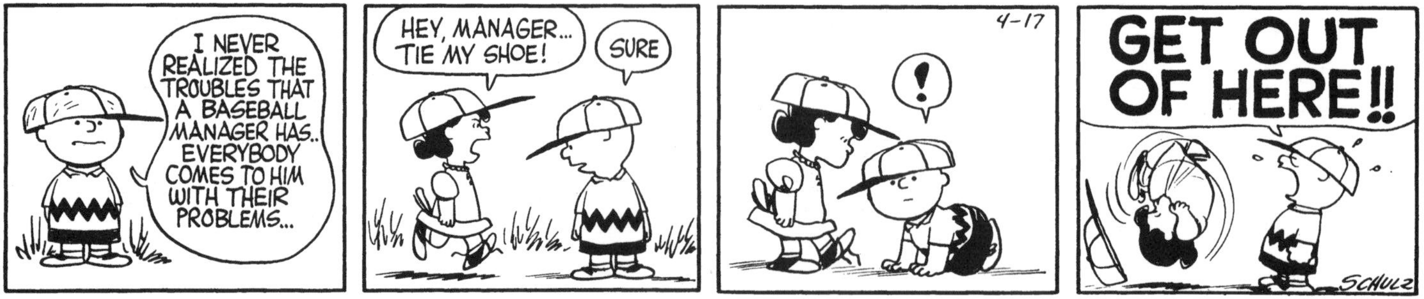
I NEVER REALIZED THE TROUBLES THAT A BASEBALL MANAGER HAS.. EVERYBODY COMES TO HIM WITH THEIR PROBLEMS...
HEY, MANAGER... TIE MY SHOE!
SURE
4-17
!
GET OUT OF HERE!!
SCHULZ

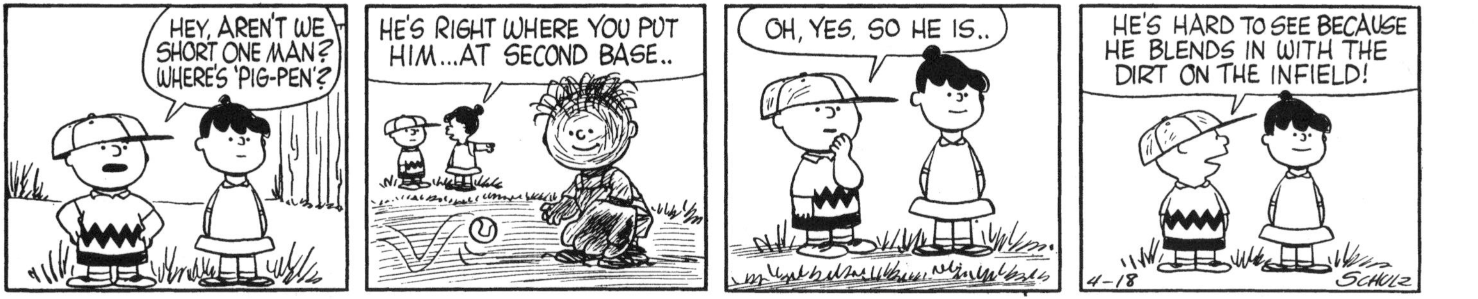
HEY, AREN'T WE SHORT ONE MAN? WHERE'S 'PIG-PEN'?
HE'S RIGHT WHERE YOU PUT HIM...AT SECOND BASE..
OH, YES, SO HE IS..
HE'S HARD TO SEE BECAUSE HE BLENDS IN WITH THE DIRT ON THE INFIELD!
4-18
SCHULZ

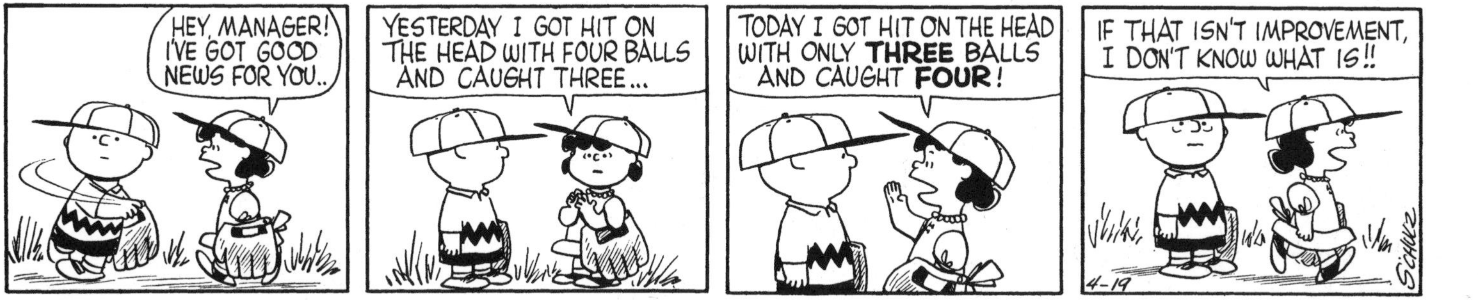
HEY, MANAGER! I'VE GOT GOOD NEWS FOR YOU..
YESTERDAY I GOT HIT ON THE HEAD WITH FOUR BALLS AND CAUGHT THREE...
TODAY I GOT HIT ON THE HEAD WITH ONLY THREE BALLS AND CAUGHT FOUR!
IF THAT ISN'T IMPROVEMENT, I DON'T KNOW WHAT IS!!
4-19
SCHULZ

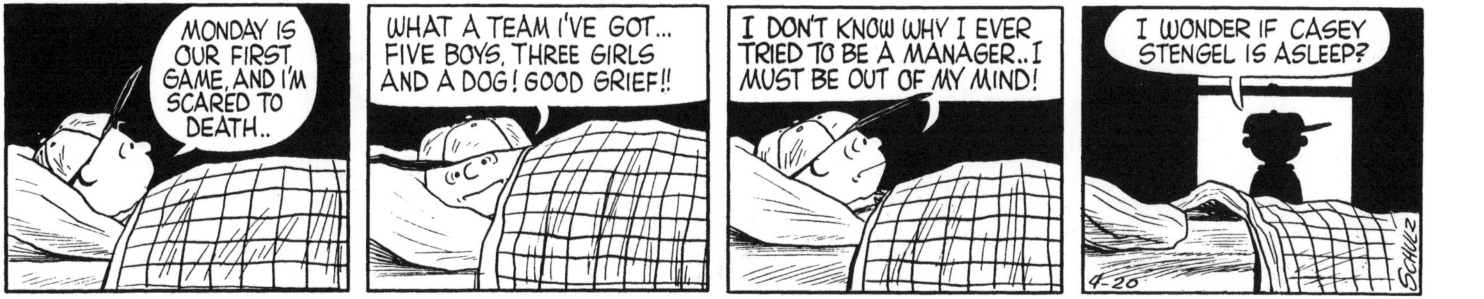
MONDAY IS OUR FIRST GAME, AND I'M SCARED TO DEATH..
WHAT A TEAM I'VE GOT... FIVE BOYS, THREE GIRLS AND A DOG! GOOD GRIEF!!
I DON'T KNOW WHY I EVER TRIED TO BE A MANAGER..I MUST BE OUT OF MY MIND!
I WONDER IF CASEY STENGEL IS ASLEEP?
4-20
SCHULZ

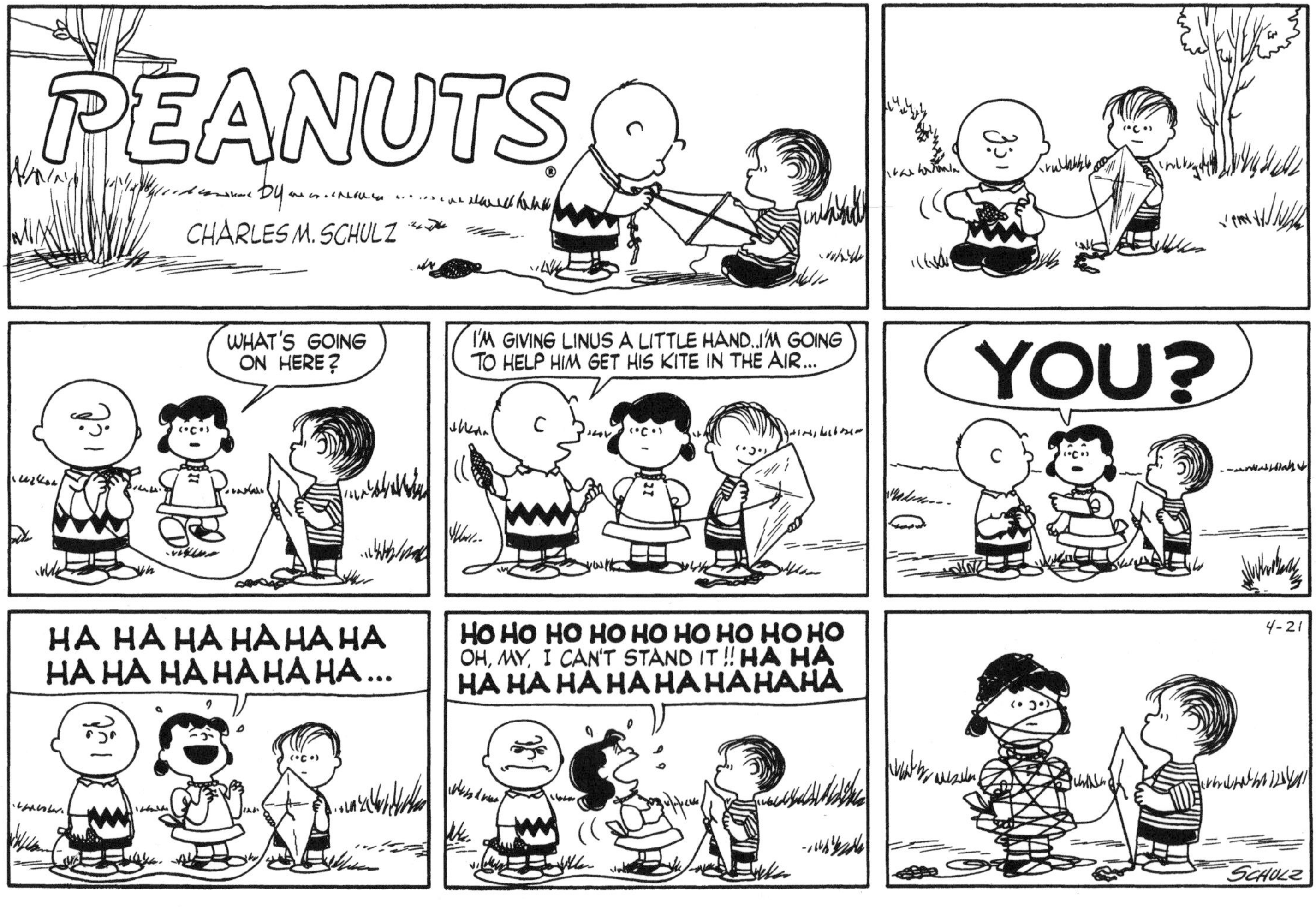
PEANUTS
BY CHARLES M. SCHULZ
WHAT'S GOING ON HERE?
I'M GIVING LINUS A LITTLE HAND..I'M GOING TO HELP HIM GET HIS KITE IN THE AIR...
YOU?
HA HA HA HA HA HA HA HA HA HA HA HA HA HA...
HO HO HO HO HO HO HO HO HO OH, MY, I CAN'T STAND IT!! HA HA HA HA HA HA HA HA HA HA HA
4-21
SCHULZ

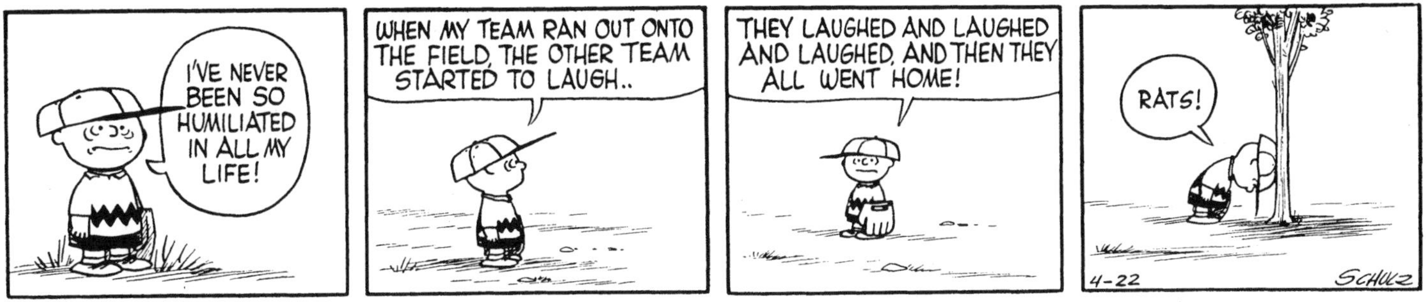
I'VE NEVER BEEN SO HUMILIATED IN ALL MY LIFE!
WHEN MY TEAM RAN OUT ONTO THE FIELD, THE OTHER TEAM STARTED TO LAUGH..
THEY LAUGHED AND LAUGHED AND LAUGHED, AND THEN THEY ALL WENT HOME!
RATS!
4-22
SCHULZ

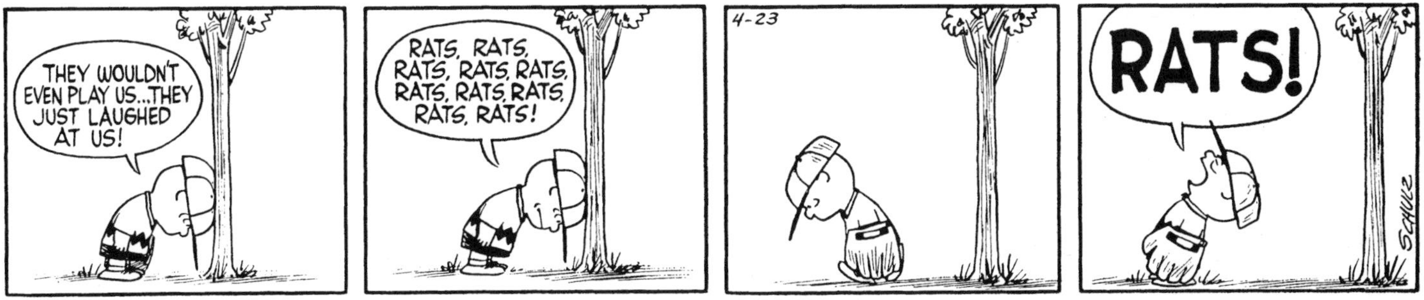
THEY WOULDN'T EVEN PLAY US...THEY JUST LAUGHED AT US!
RATS, RATS, RATS, RATS, RATS, RATS, RATS, RATS, RATS, RATS!
4-23
RATS!
SCHULZ

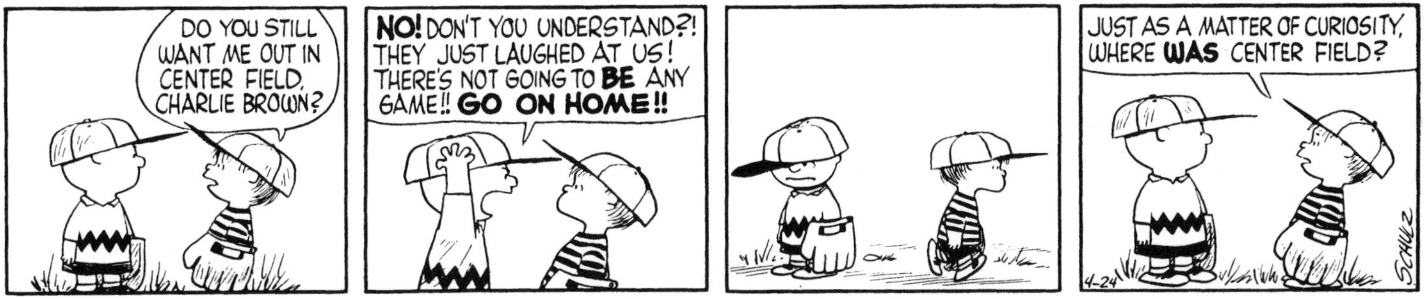
DO YOU STILL WANT ME OUT IN CENTER FIELD, CHARLIE BROWN?
NO! DON'T YOU UNDERSTAND?! THEY JUST LAUGHED AT US! THERE'S NOT GOING TO BE ANY GAME!! GO ON HOME!!
JUST AS A MATTER OF CURIOSITY, WHERE WAS CENTER FIELD?
4-24
SCHULZ

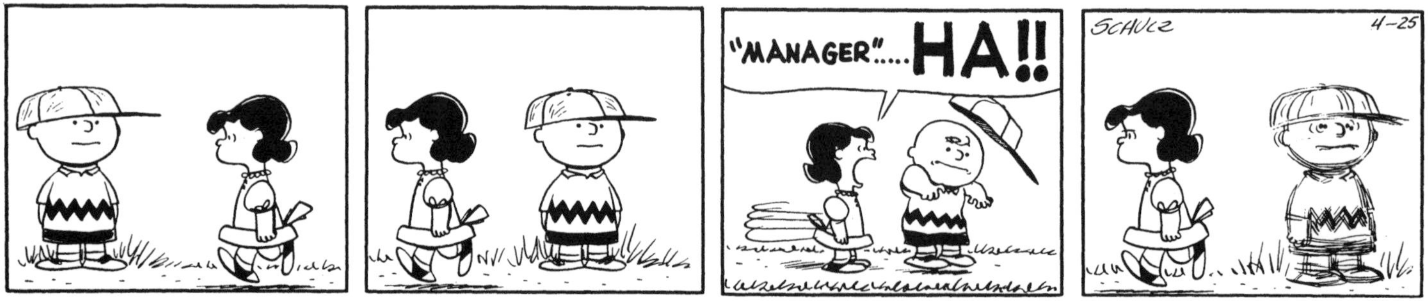
"MANAGER".....HA!!
SCHULZ
4-25

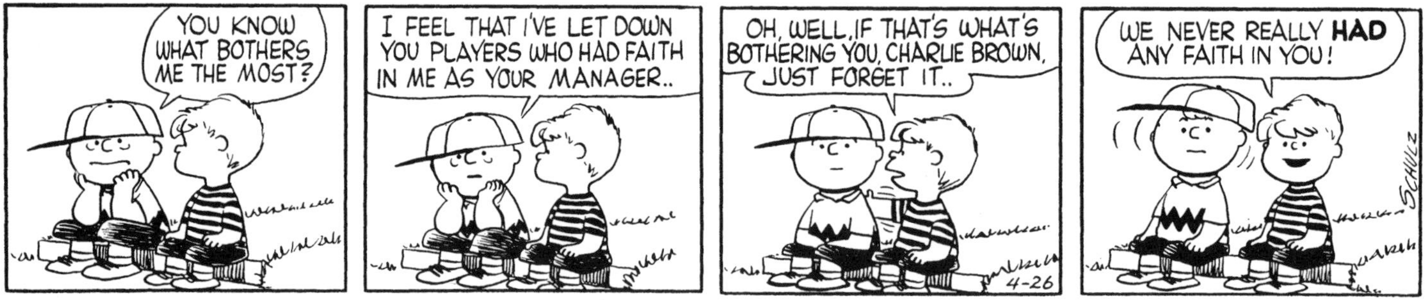
YOU KNOW WHAT BOTHERS ME THE MOST?
I FEEL THAT I'VE LET DOWN YOU PLAYERS WHO HAD FAITH IN ME AS YOUR MANAGER..
OH, WELL, IF THAT'S WHAT'S BOTHERING YOU, CHARLIE BROWN, JUST FORGET IT..
4-26
WE NEVER REALLY **HAD** ANY FAITH IN YOU!
SCHULZ

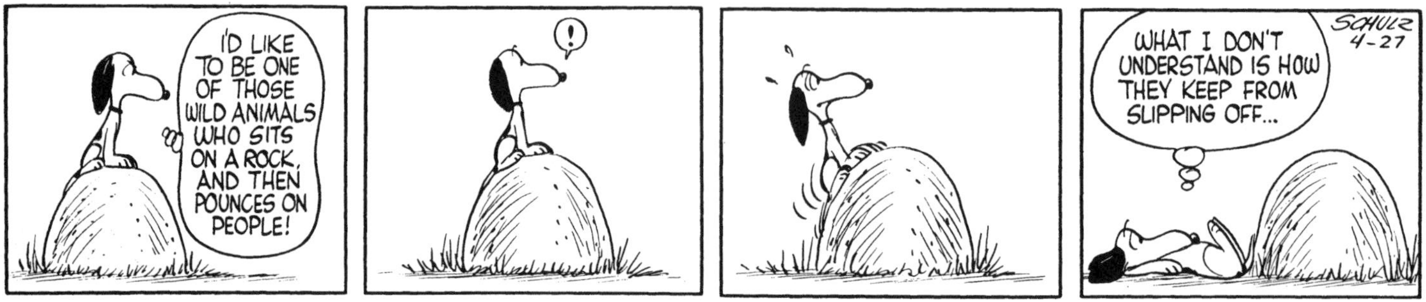
I'D LIKE TO BE ONE OF THOSE WILD ANIMALS WHO SITS ON A ROCK, AND THEN POUNCES ON PEOPLE!
!
SCHULZ
4-27
WHAT I DON'T UNDERSTAND IS HOW THEY KEEP FROM SLIPPING OFF...

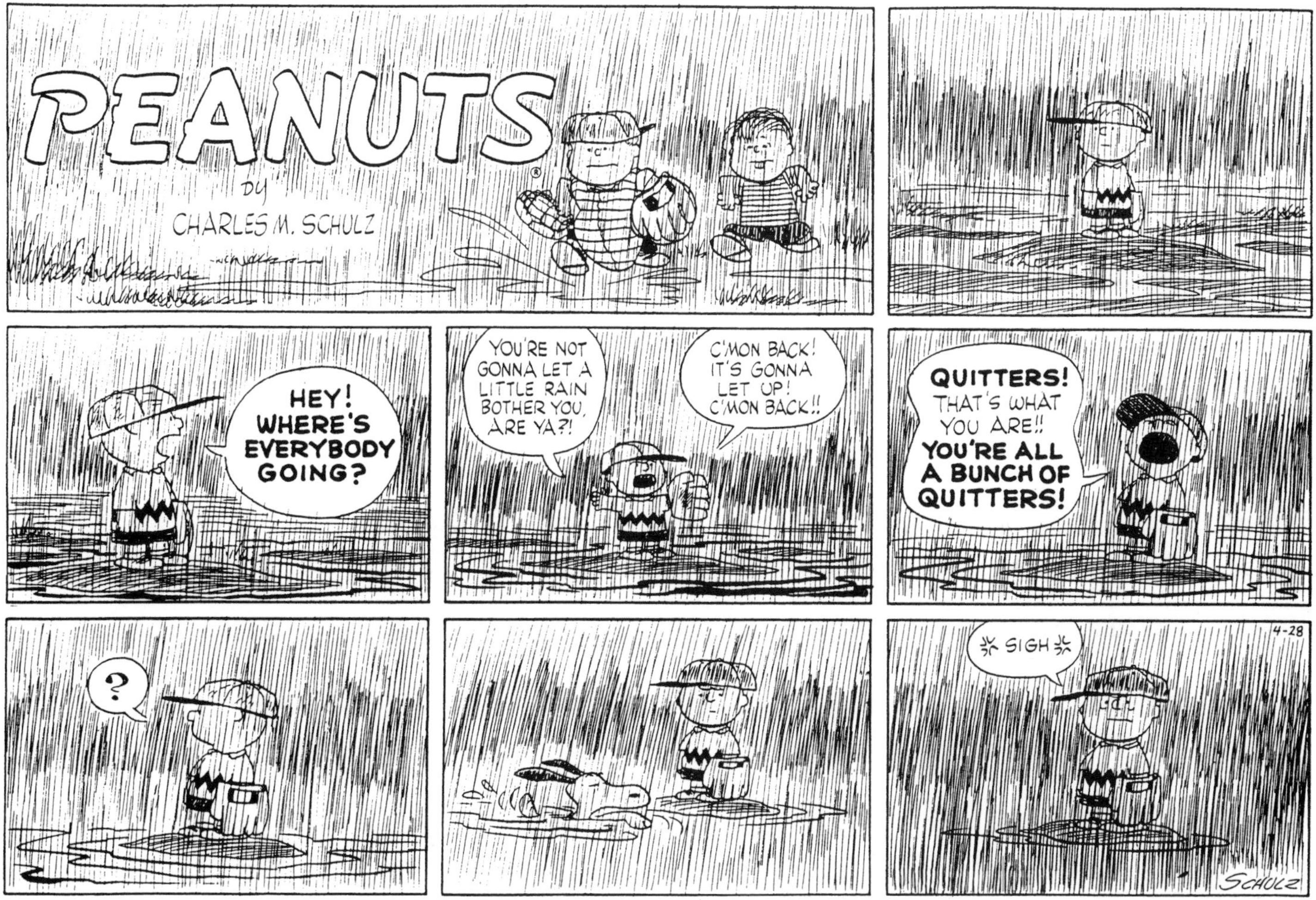
PEANUTS
by
CHARLES M. SCHULZ
HEY! WHERE'S EVERYBODY GOING?
YOU'RE NOT GONNA LET A LITTLE RAIN BOTHER YOU, ARE YA?!
C'MON BACK! IT'S GONNA LET UP! C'MON BACK!!
QUITTERS! THAT'S WHAT YOU ARE!! YOU'RE ALL A BUNCH OF QUITTERS!
?
SIGH
4-28
SCHULZ

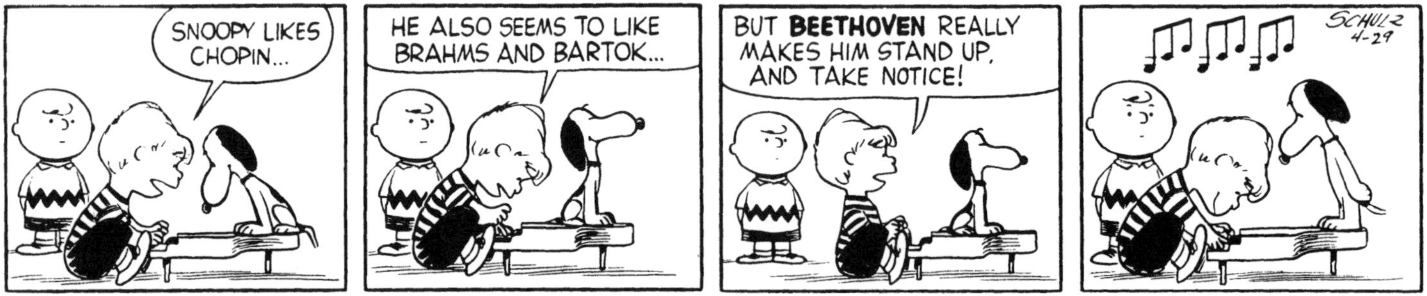
SNOOPY LIKES CHOPIN...
HE ALSO SEEMS TO LIKE BRAHMS AND BARTOK...
BUT **BEETHOVEN** REALLY MAKES HIM STAND UP, AND TAKE NOTICE!
SCHULZ 4-29

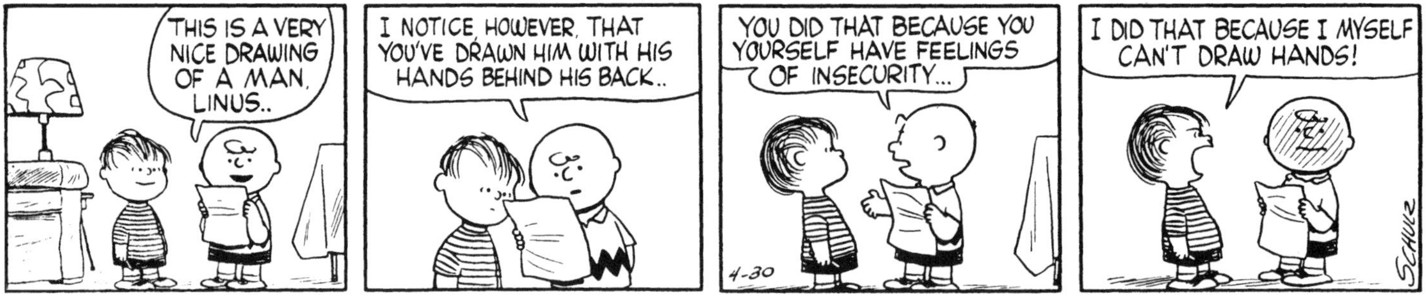
THIS IS A VERY NICE DRAWING OF A MAN, LINUS..
I NOTICE, HOWEVER, THAT YOU'VE DRAWN HIM WITH HIS HANDS BEHIND HIS BACK..
YOU DID THAT BECAUSE YOU YOURSELF HAVE FEELINGS OF INSECURITY...
4-30
I DID THAT BECAUSE I MYSELF CAN'T DRAW HANDS!
SCHULZ

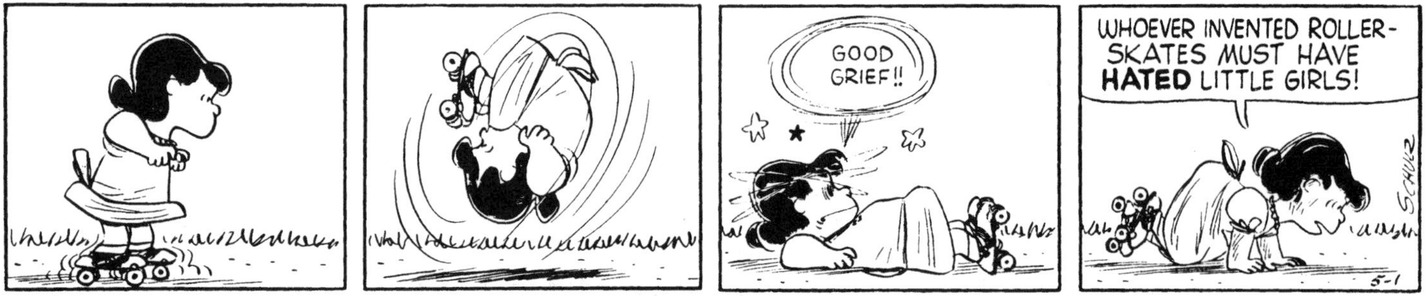
GOOD GRIEF!!
WHOEVER INVENTED ROLLER-SKATES MUST HAVE **HATED** LITTLE GIRLS!
SCHULZ
5-1

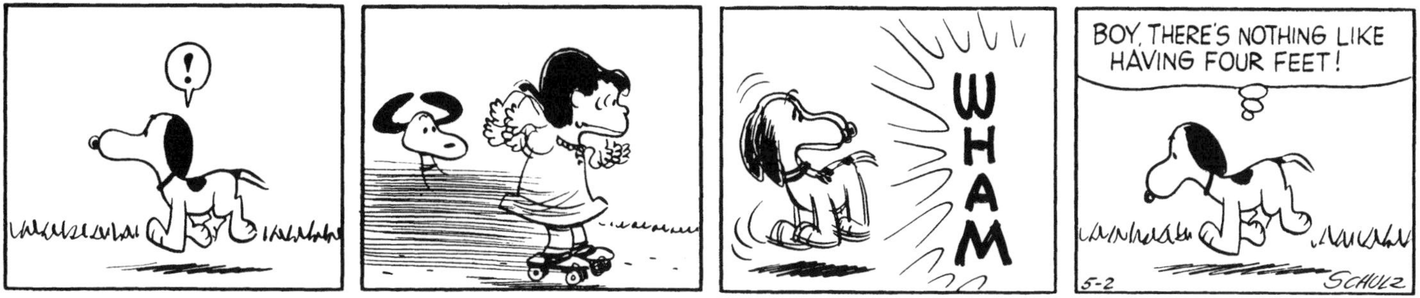
!
WHAM
BOY, THERE'S NOTHING LIKE HAVING FOUR FEET!
5-2
SCHULZ

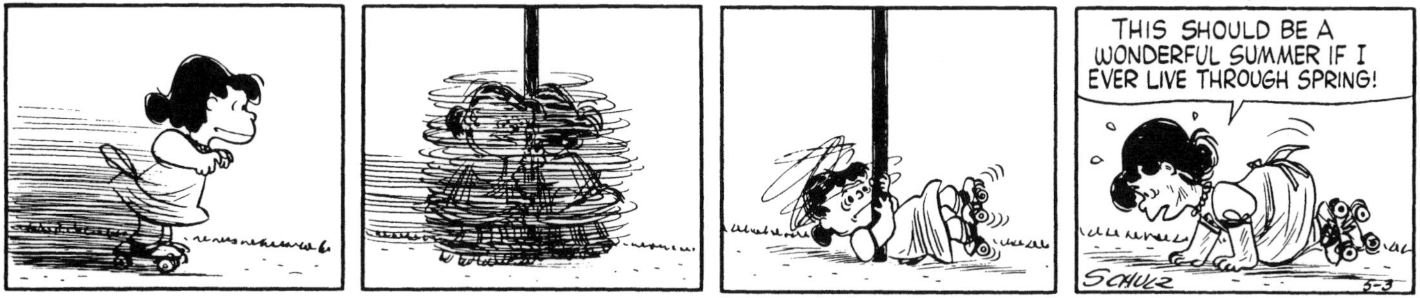
THIS SHOULD BE A WONDERFUL SUMMER IF I EVER LIVE THROUGH SPRING!
SCHULZ
5-3

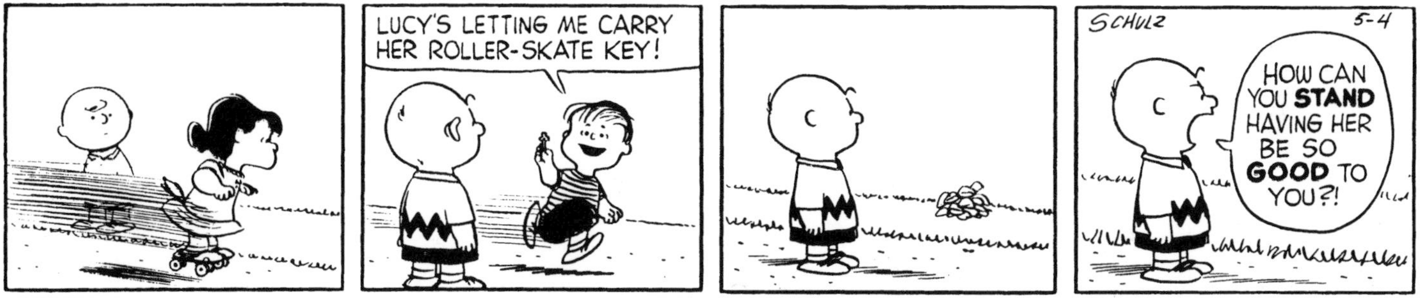
LUCY'S LETTING ME CARRY HER ROLLER-SKATE KEY!
SCHULZ
5-4
HOW CAN YOU **STAND** HAVING HER BE SO **GOOD** TO YOU?!

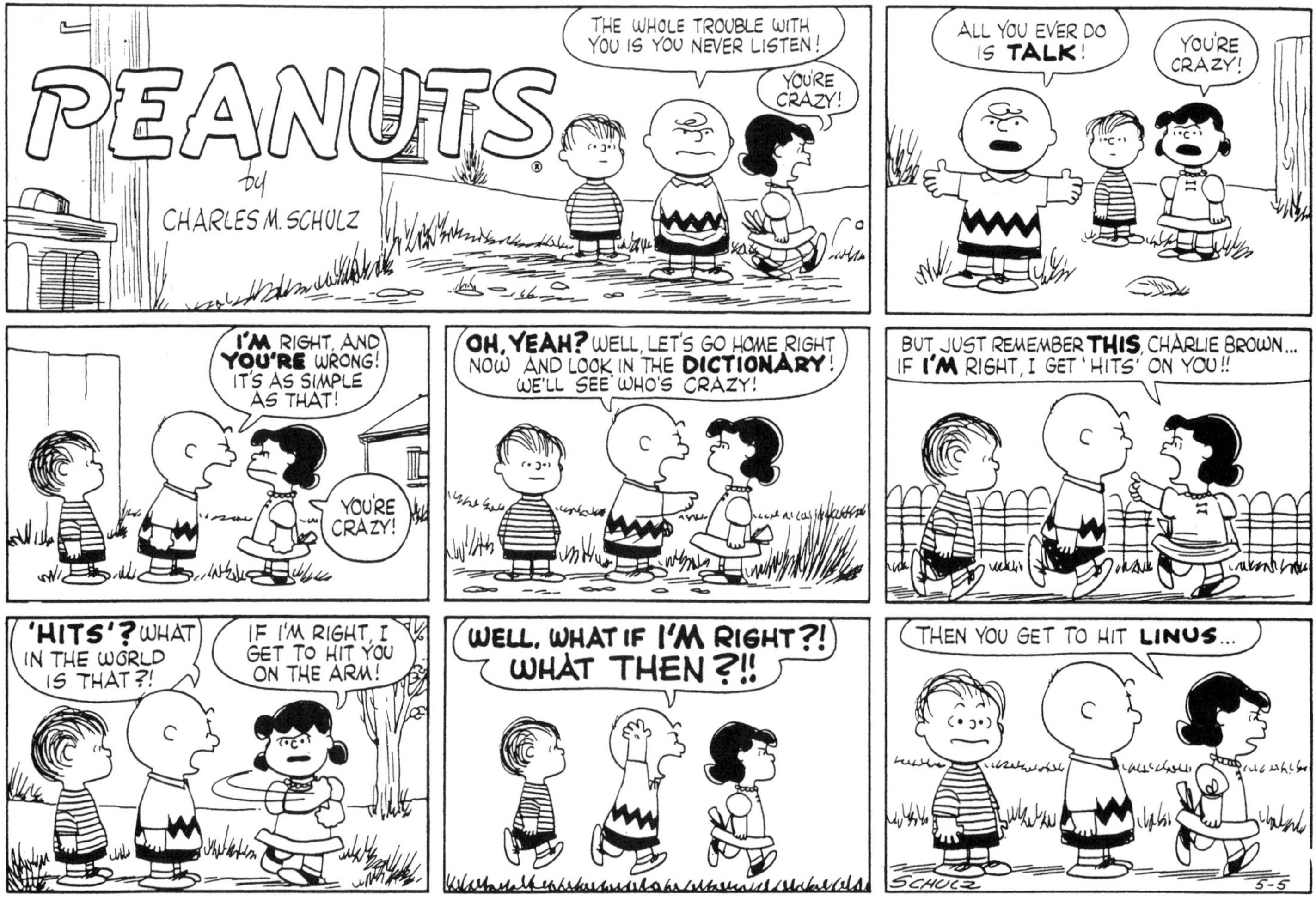
PEANUTS
by CHARLES M. SCHULZ
THE WHOLE TROUBLE WITH YOU IS YOU NEVER LISTEN!
YOU'RE CRAZY!
ALL YOU EVER DO IS TALK!
YOU'RE CRAZY!
I'M RIGHT, AND YOU'RE WRONG! IT'S AS SIMPLE AS THAT!
YOU'RE CRAZY!
OH, YEAH? WELL, LET'S GO HOME RIGHT NOW AND LOOK IN THE DICTIONARY! WE'LL SEE WHO'S CRAZY!
BUT JUST REMEMBER THIS, CHARLIE BROWN... IF I'M RIGHT, I GET 'HITS' ON YOU!!
'HITS'? WHAT IN THE WORLD IS THAT?!
IF I'M RIGHT, I GET TO HIT YOU ON THE ARM!
WELL, WHAT IF I'M RIGHT?! WHAT THEN?!!
THEN YOU GET TO HIT LINUS...
SCHULZ
5-5

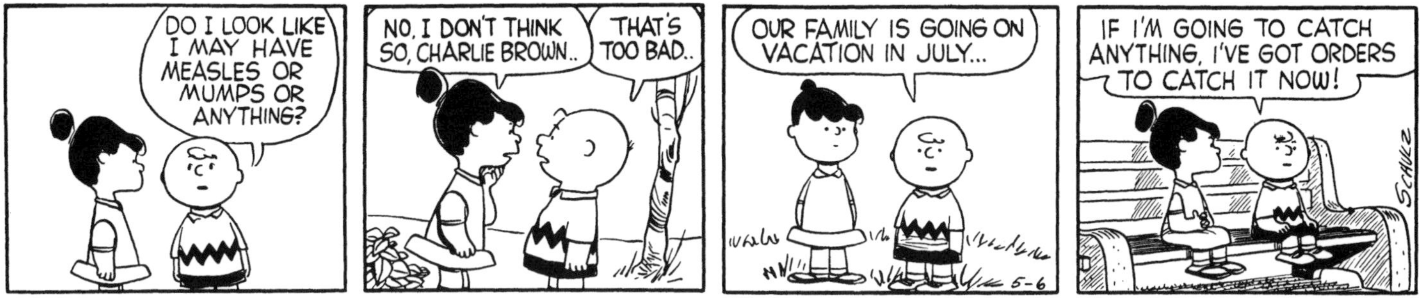
DO I LOOK LIKE I MAY HAVE MEASLES OR MUMPS OR ANYTHING?
NO, I DON'T THINK SO, CHARLIE BROWN..
THAT'S TOO BAD..
OUR FAMILY IS GOING ON VACATION IN JULY...
5-6
IF I'M GOING TO CATCH ANYTHING, I'VE GOT ORDERS TO CATCH IT NOW!
SCHULZ

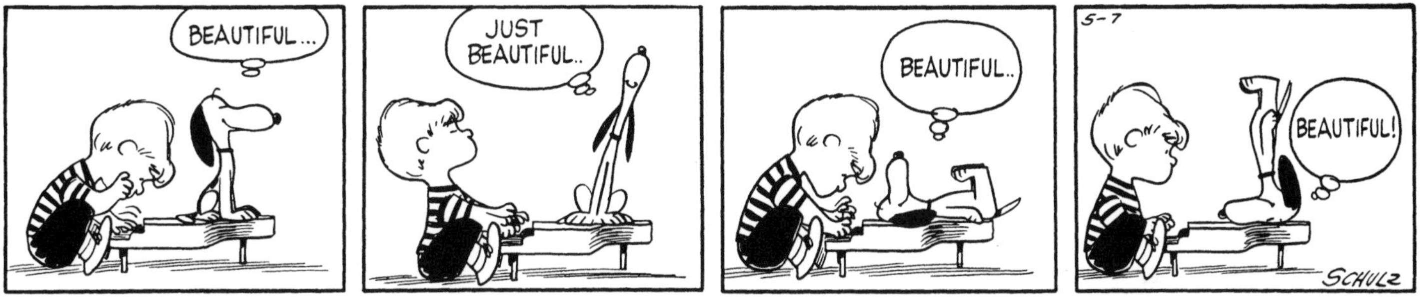
BEAUTIFUL...
JUST BEAUTIFUL..
BEAUTIFUL..
5-7
BEAUTIFUL!
SCHULZ

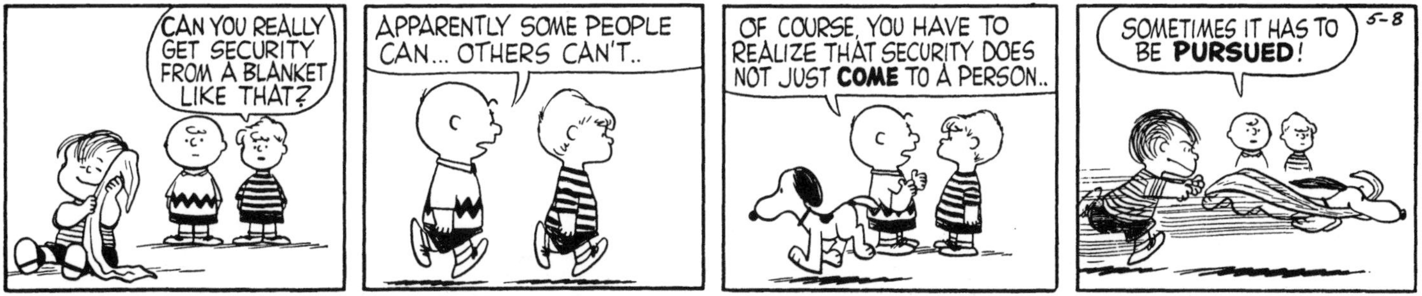
CAN YOU REALLY GET SECURITY FROM A BLANKET LIKE THAT?
APPARENTLY SOME PEOPLE CAN... OTHERS CAN'T..
OF COURSE, YOU HAVE TO REALIZE THAT SECURITY DOES NOT JUST COME TO A PERSON..
5-8
SOMETIMES IT HAS TO BE PURSUED!

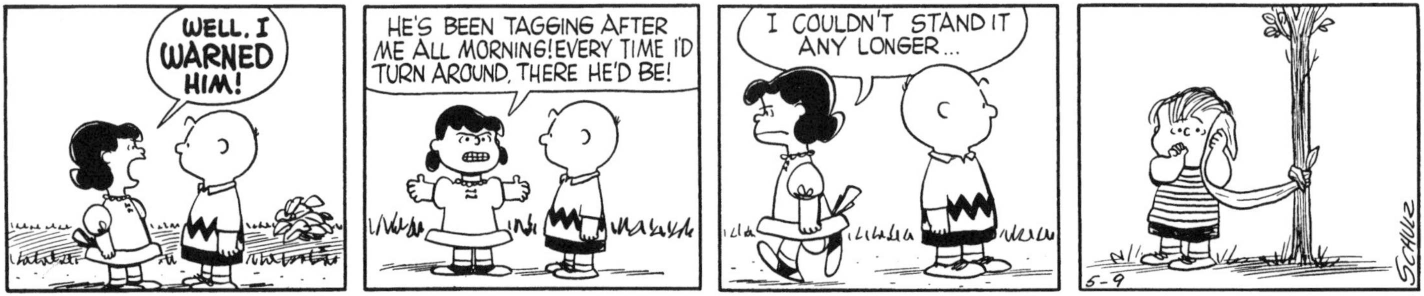
WELL, I WARNED HIM!
HE'S BEEN TAGGING AFTER ME ALL MORNING! EVERY TIME I'D TURN AROUND, THERE HE'D BE!
I COULDN'T STAND IT ANY LONGER...
SCHULZ
5-9

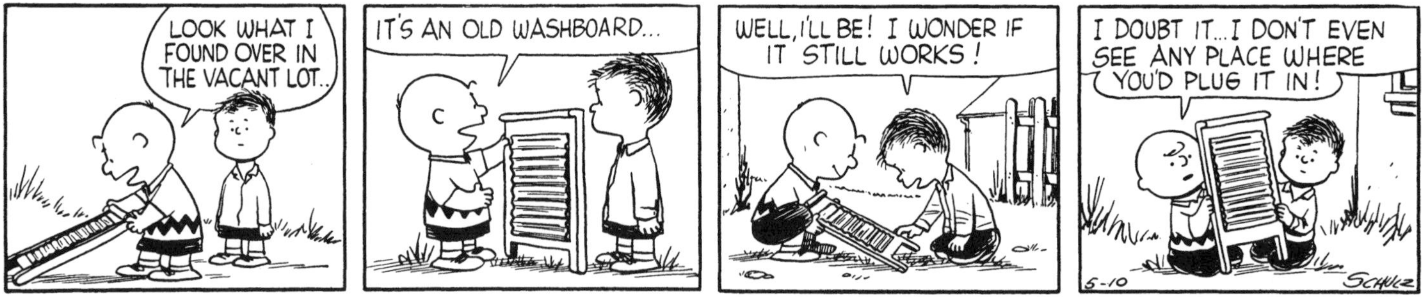
LOOK WHAT I FOUND OVER IN THE VACANT LOT..
IT'S AN OLD WASHBOARD...
WELL, I'LL BE! I WONDER IF IT STILL WORKS!
I DOUBT IT...I DON'T EVEN SEE ANY PLACE WHERE YOU'D PLUG IT IN!
5-10
SCHULZ

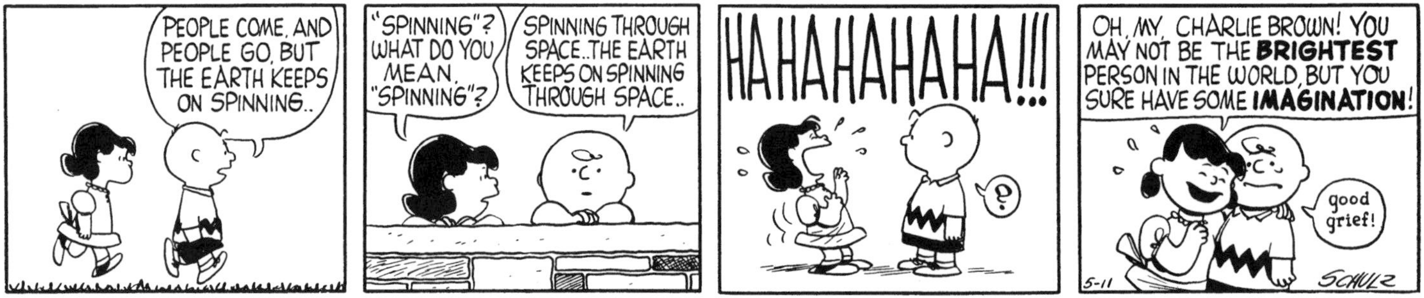
PEOPLE COME, AND PEOPLE GO, BUT THE EARTH KEEPS ON SPINNING..
"SPINNING"? WHAT DO YOU MEAN, "SPINNING"?
SPINNING THROUGH SPACE..THE EARTH KEEPS ON SPINNING THROUGH SPACE..
HAHAHAHAHA!!!..
?
OH, MY, CHARLIE BROWN! YOU MAY NOT BE THE **BRIGHTEST** PERSON IN THE WORLD, BUT YOU SURE HAVE SOME **IMAGINATION**!
good grief!
5-11
SCHULZ

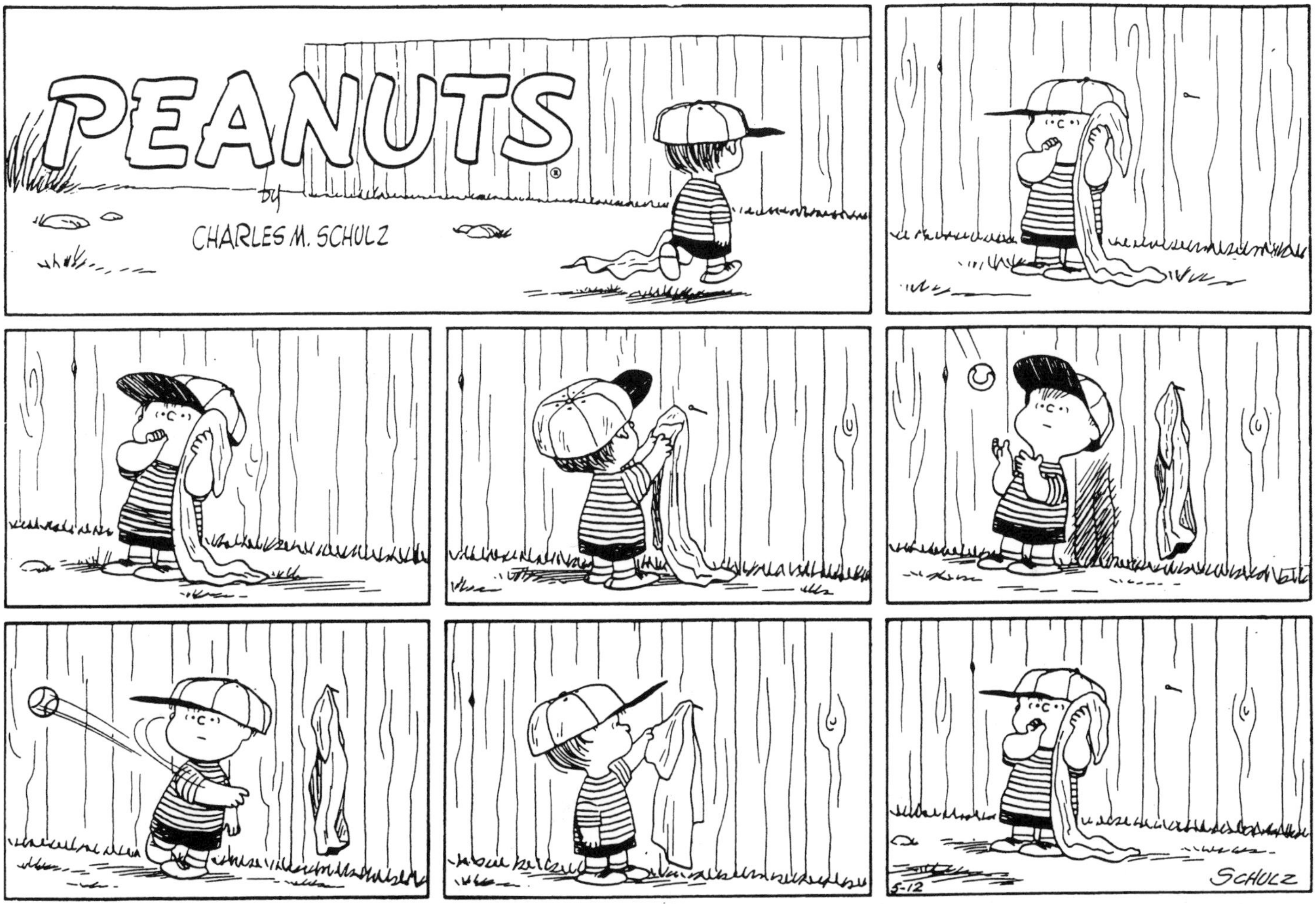
PEANUTS
by
CHARLES M. SCHULZ
SCHULZ
5-12

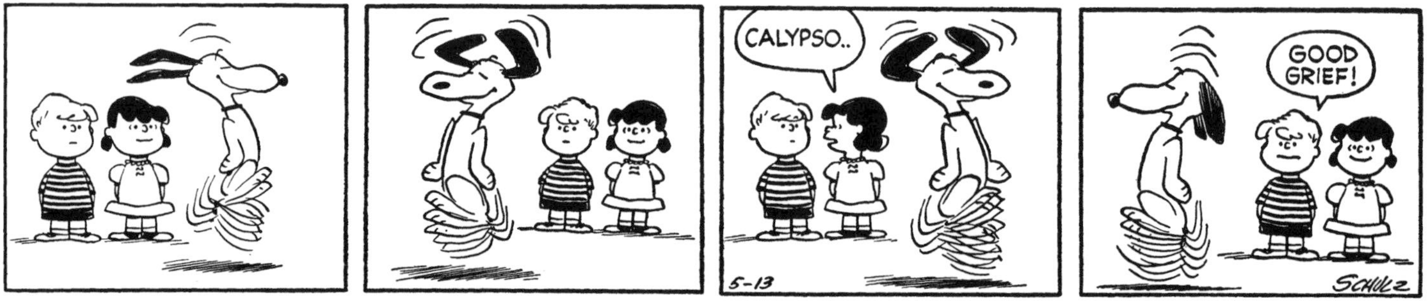
CALYPSO..
5-13
GOOD GRIEF!
SCHULZ

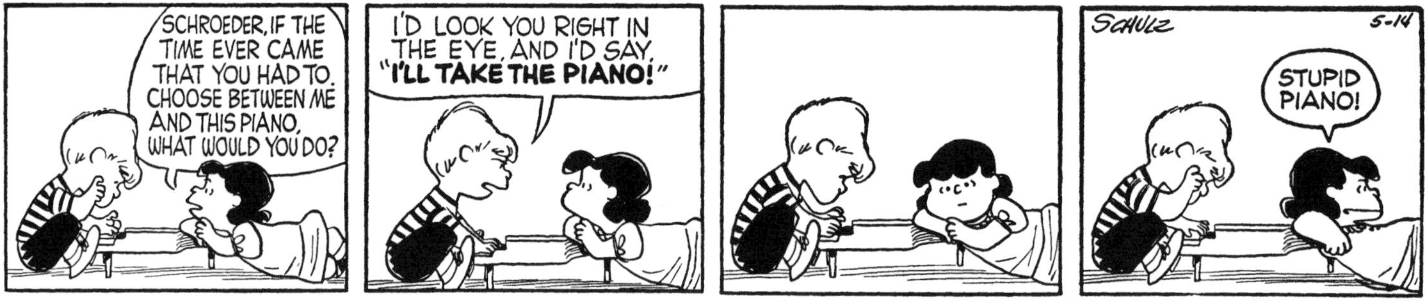
SCHROEDER, IF THE TIME EVER CAME THAT YOU HAD TO CHOOSE BETWEEN ME AND THIS PIANO, WHAT WOULD YOU DO?
I'D LOOK YOU RIGHT IN THE EYE, AND I'D SAY, "I'LL TAKE THE PIANO!"
SCHULZ
5-14
STUPID PIANO!

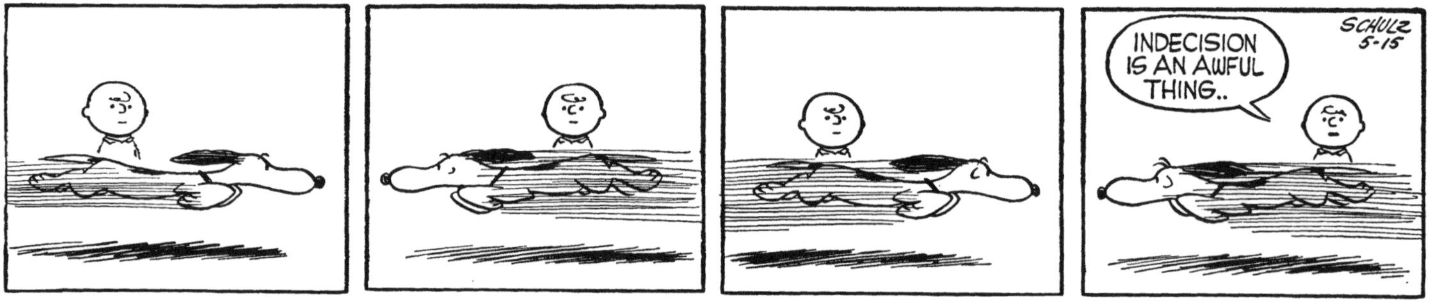
SCHULZ
5-15
INDECISION IS AN AWFUL THING..

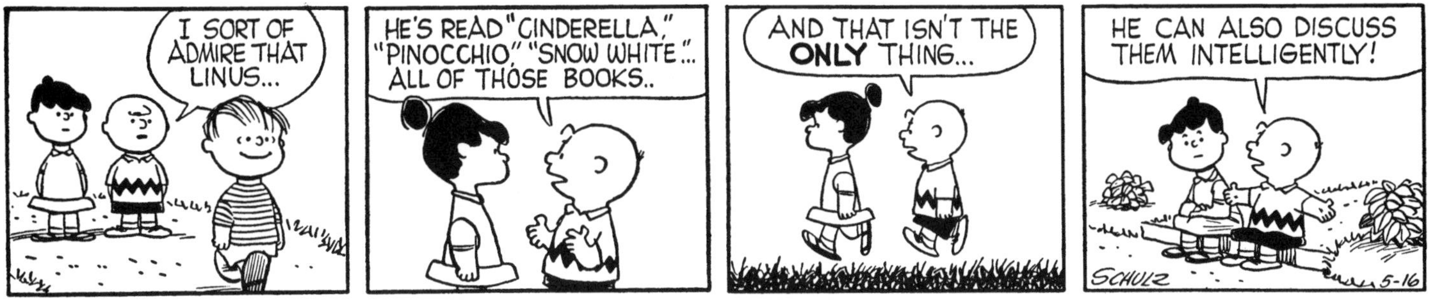
I SORT OF ADMIRE THAT LINUS...
HE'S READ "CINDERELLA," "PINOCCHIO," "SNOW WHITE"... ALL OF THOSE BOOKS..
AND THAT ISN'T THE **ONLY** THING...
HE CAN ALSO DISCUSS THEM INTELLIGENTLY!
SCHULZ
5-16

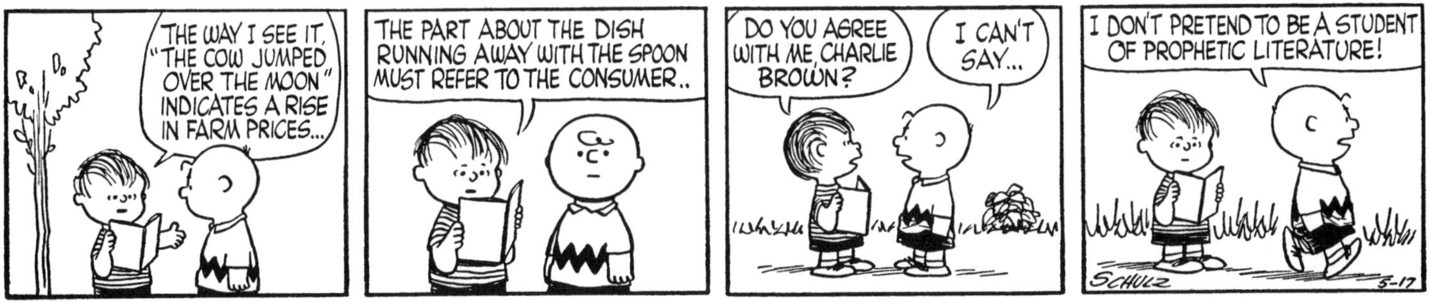
THE WAY I SEE IT, "THE COW JUMPED OVER THE MOON" INDICATES A RISE IN FARM PRICES...
THE PART ABOUT THE DISH RUNNING AWAY WITH THE SPOON MUST REFER TO THE CONSUMER..
DO YOU AGREE WITH ME, CHARLIE BROWN?
I CAN'T SAY...
I DON'T PRETEND TO BE A STUDENT OF PROPHETIC LITERATURE!
SCHULZ
5-17

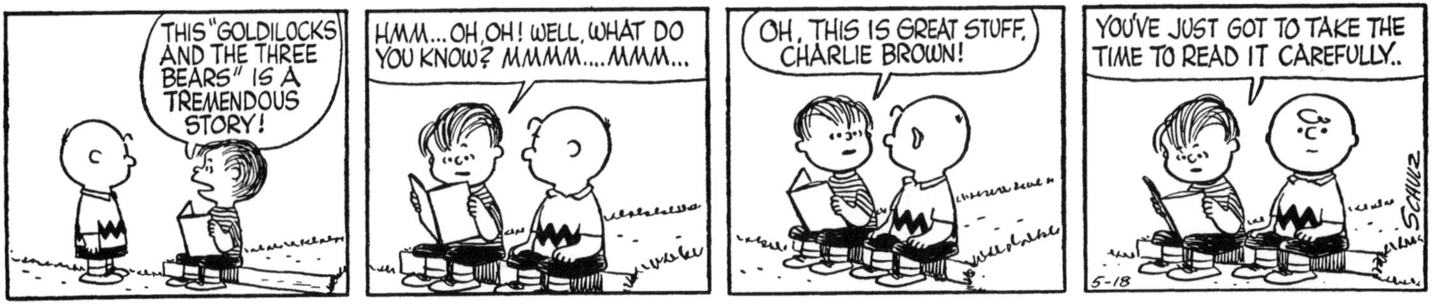
THIS "GOLDILOCKS AND THE THREE BEARS" IS A TREMENDOUS STORY!
HMM... OH, OH! WELL, WHAT DO YOU KNOW? MMMM.... MMM...
OH, THIS IS GREAT STUFF, CHARLIE BROWN!
YOU'VE JUST GOT TO TAKE THE TIME TO READ IT CAREFULLY..
SCHULZ
5-18

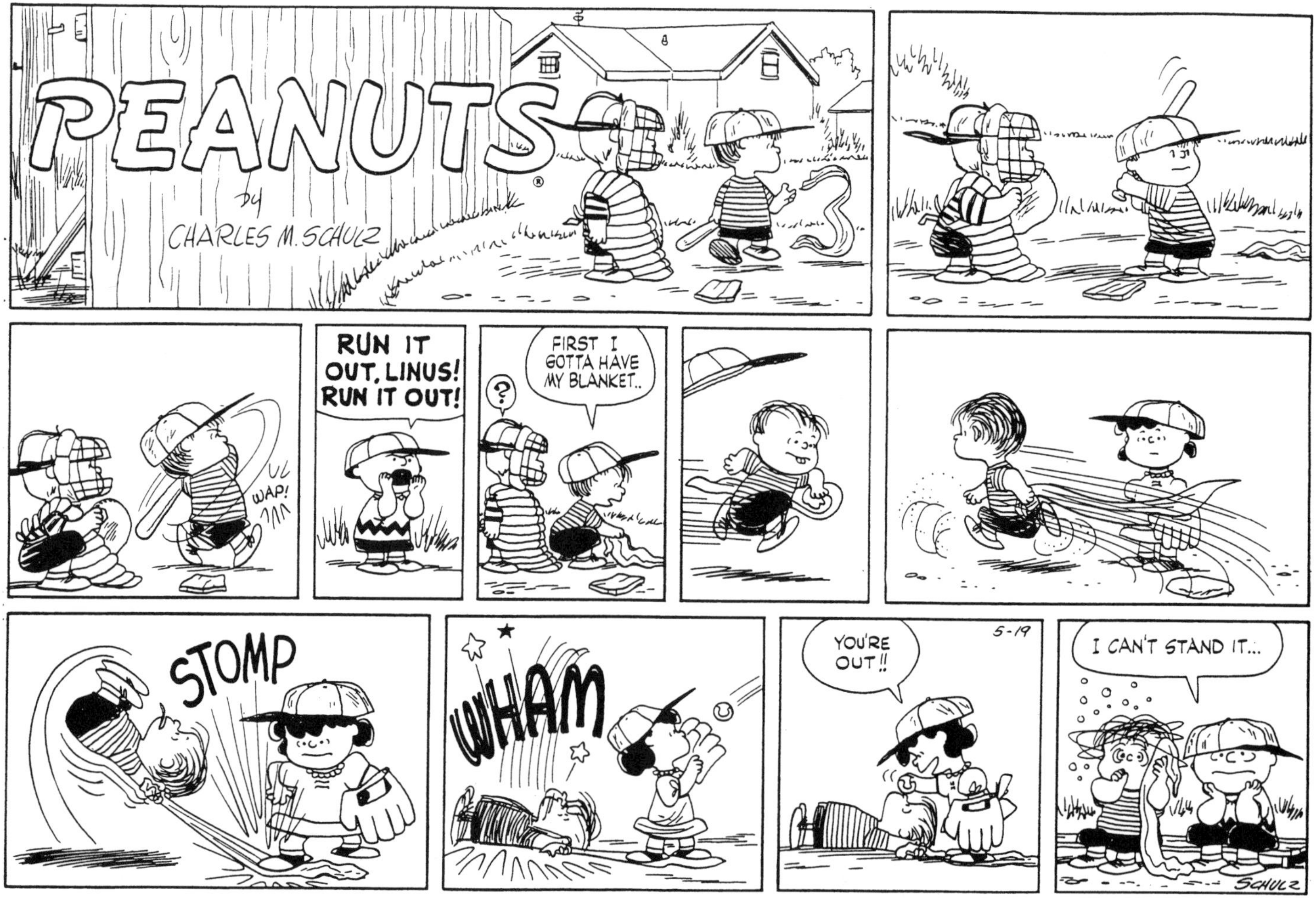
PEANUTS
by
CHARLES M. SCHULZ
WAP!
RUN IT OUT, LINUS! RUN IT OUT!
?
FIRST I GOTTA HAVE MY BLANKET..
STOMP
WHAM
YOU'RE OUT!!
5-19
I CAN'T STAND IT...
SCHULZ

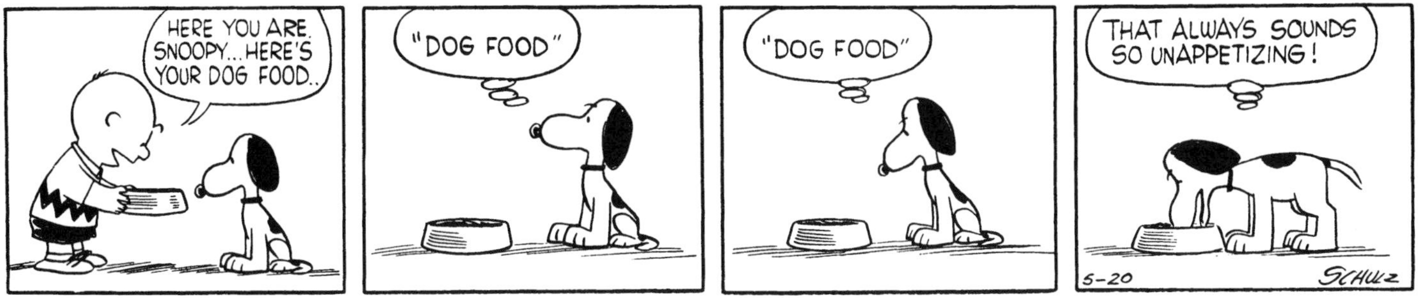
HERE YOU ARE, SNOOPY... HERE'S YOUR DOG FOOD..
"DOG FOOD"
"DOG FOOD"
THAT ALWAYS SOUNDS SO UNAPPETIZING!
5-20
SCHULZ

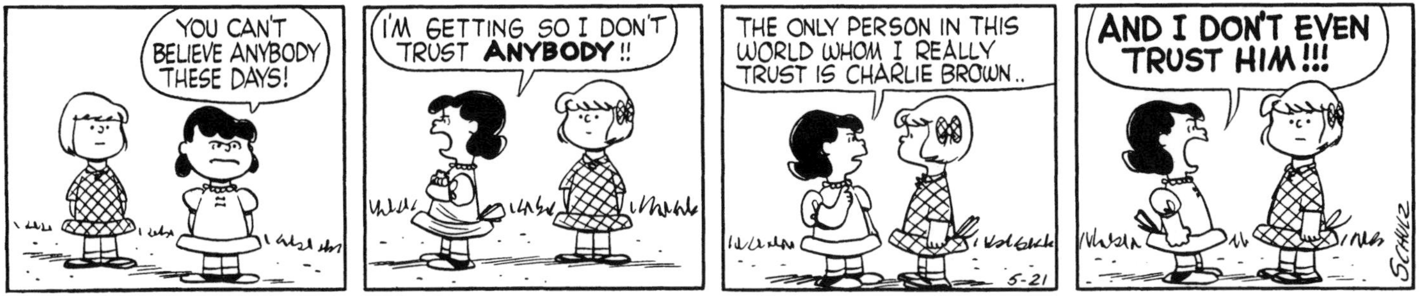
YOU CAN'T BELIEVE ANYBODY THESE DAYS!
I'M GETTING SO I DON'T TRUST ANYBODY!!
THE ONLY PERSON IN THIS WORLD WHOM I REALLY TRUST IS CHARLIE BROWN..
5-21
AND I DON'T EVEN TRUST HIM!!!
SCHULZ

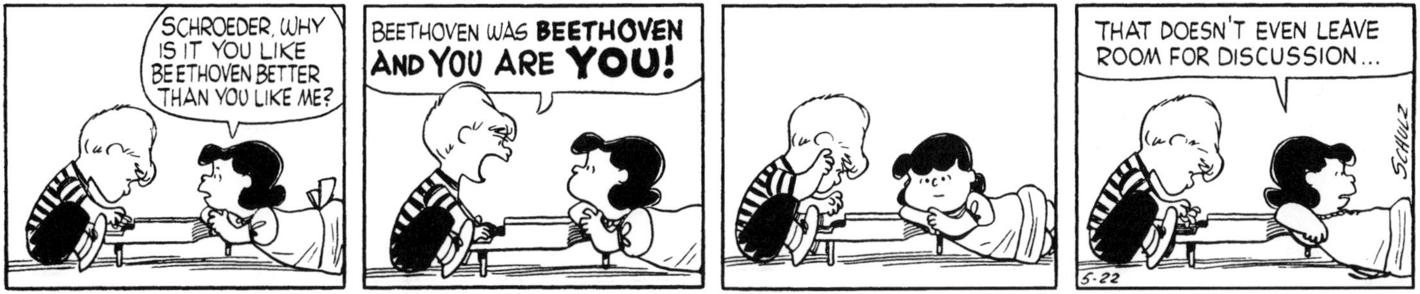
SCHROEDER, WHY IS IT YOU LIKE BEETHOVEN BETTER THAN YOU LIKE ME?
BEETHOVEN WAS BEETHOVEN AND YOU ARE YOU!
THAT DOESN'T EVEN LEAVE ROOM FOR DISCUSSION...
SCHULZ
5-22

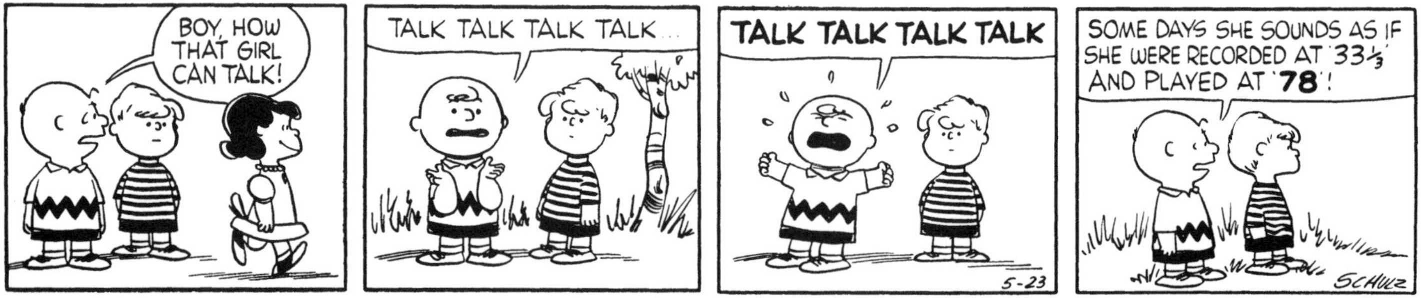
BOY, HOW THAT GIRL CAN TALK!
TALK TALK TALK TALK...
TALK TALK TALK TALK
SOME DAYS SHE SOUNDS AS IF SHE WERE RECORDED AT "33⅓" AND PLAYED AT "78"!
5-23
SCHULZ

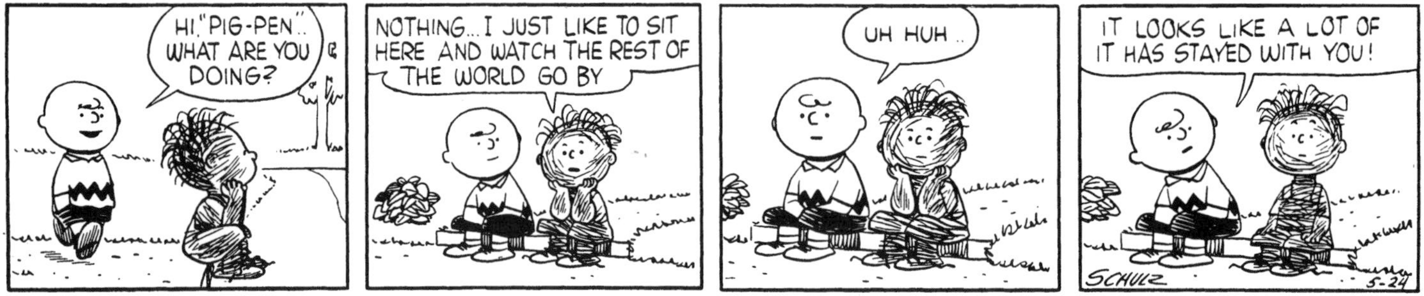
HI, "PIG-PEN"... WHAT ARE YOU DOING?
NOTHING... I JUST LIKE TO SIT HERE AND WATCH THE REST OF THE WORLD GO BY
UH HUH...
IT LOOKS LIKE A LOT OF IT HAS STAYED WITH YOU!
SCHULZ
5-24

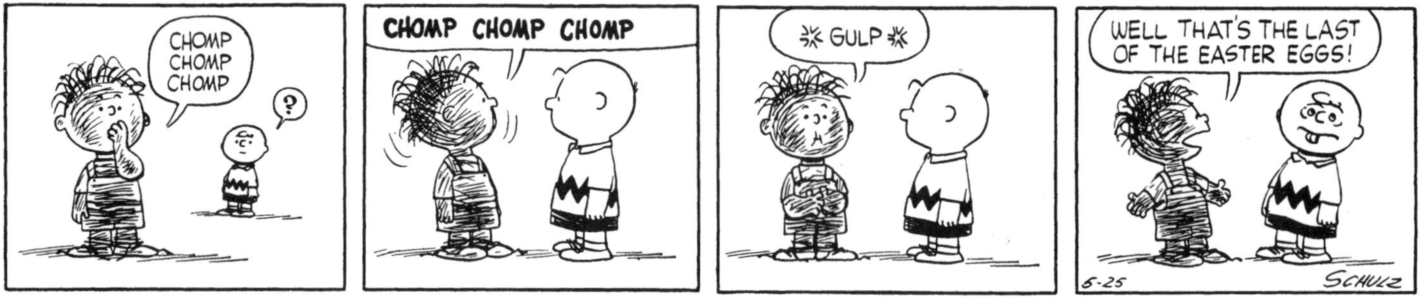
CHOMP CHOMP CHOMP
?
CHOMP CHOMP CHOMP
GULP
WELL THAT'S THE LAST OF THE EASTER EGGS!
5-25
SCHULZ

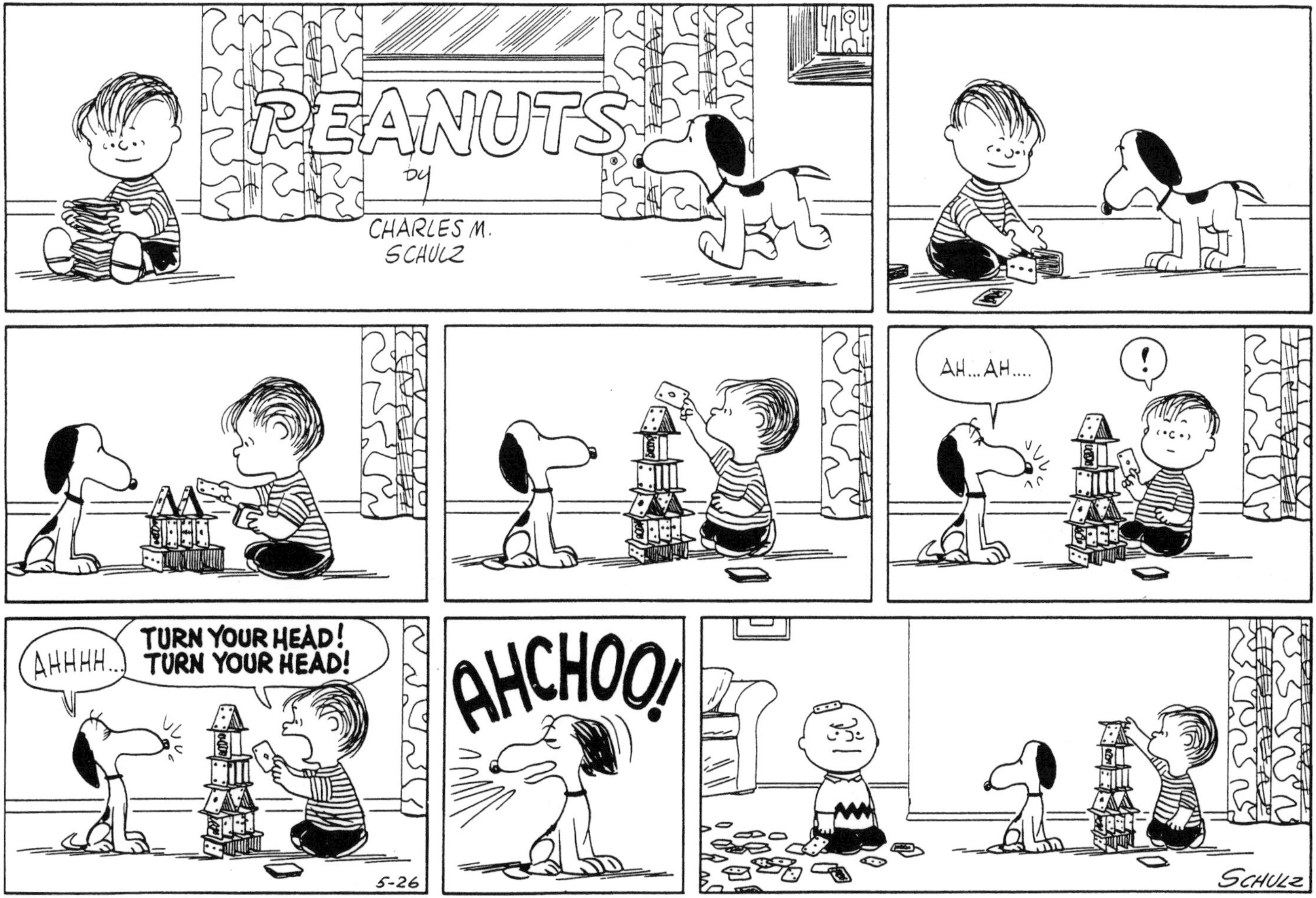
PEANUTS
by
CHARLES M. SCHULZ
AH...AH....
!
AHHHH...
TURN YOUR HEAD! TURN YOUR HEAD!
5-26
AHCHOO!
SCHULZ

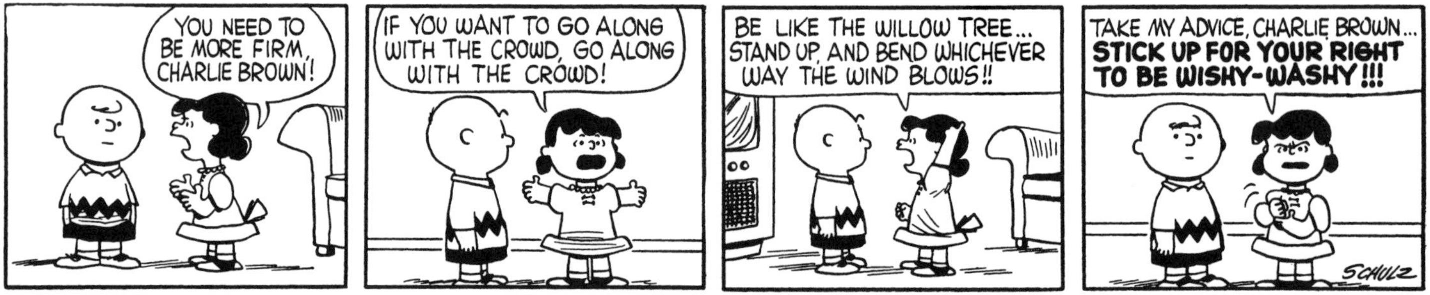
YOU NEED TO BE MORE FIRM, CHARLIE BROWN!
IF YOU WANT TO GO ALONG WITH THE CROWD, GO ALONG WITH THE CROWD!
BE LIKE THE WILLOW TREE... STAND UP, AND BEND WHICHEVER WAY THE WIND BLOWS!!
TAKE MY ADVICE, CHARLIE BROWN... STICK UP FOR YOUR RIGHT TO BE WISHY-WASHY!!!
SCHULZ

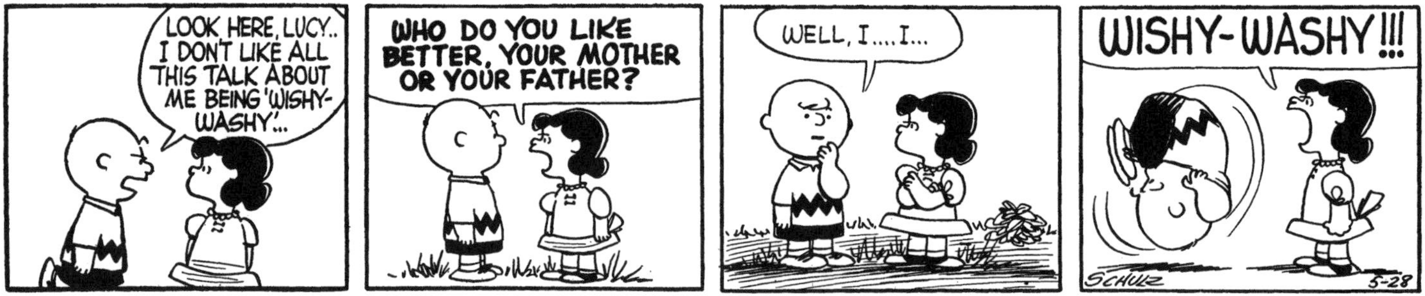
LOOK HERE, LUCY.. I DON'T LIKE ALL THIS TALK ABOUT ME BEING 'WISHY-WASHY'...
WHO DO YOU LIKE BETTER, YOUR MOTHER OR YOUR FATHER?
WELL, I....I...
WISHY-WASHY!!!
SCHULZ
5-28

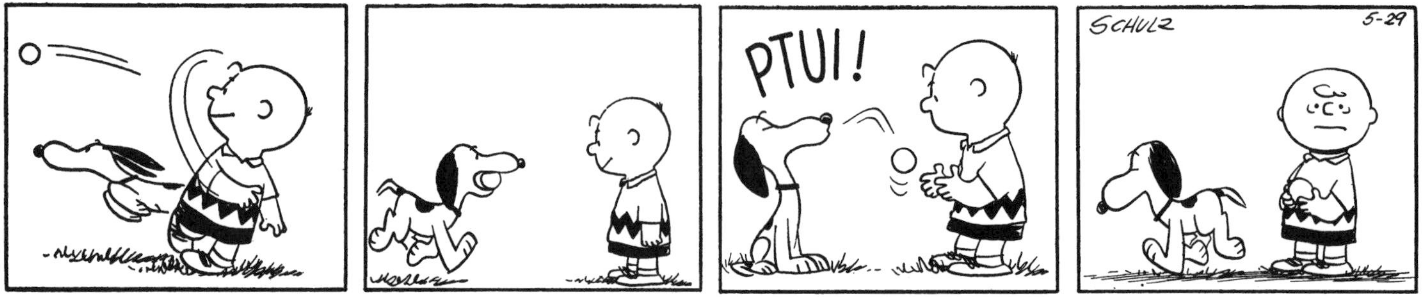
PTUI!
SCHULZ
5-29

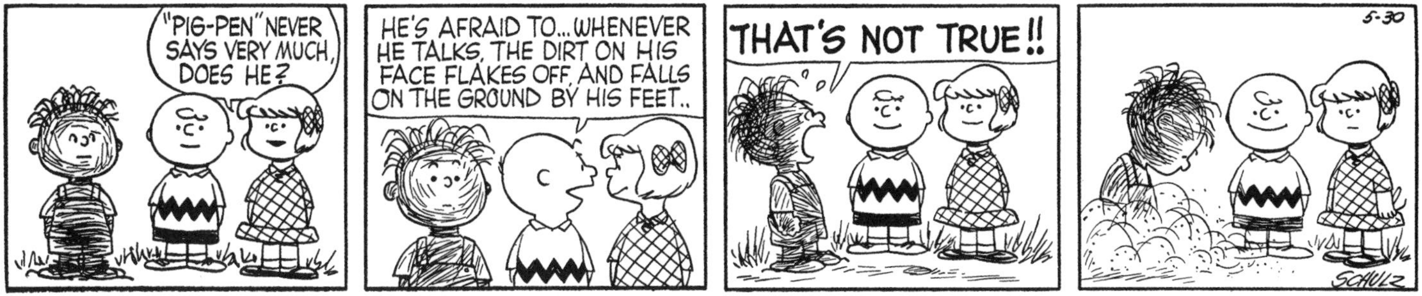
"PIG-PEN" NEVER SAYS VERY MUCH, DOES HE?
HE'S AFRAID TO...WHENEVER HE TALKS, THE DIRT ON HIS FACE FLAKES OFF, AND FALLS ON THE GROUND BY HIS FEET..
THAT'S NOT TRUE!!
5-30
SCHULZ

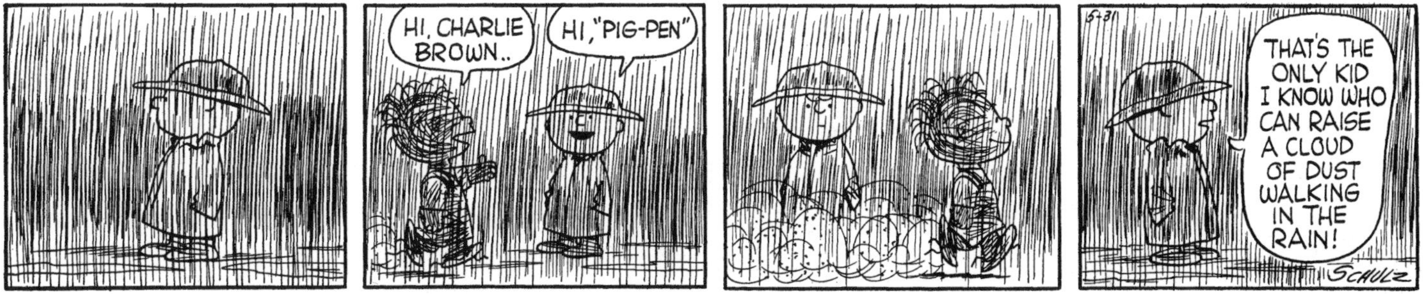
HI, CHARLIE BROWN..
HI, "PIG-PEN"
5-31
THAT'S THE ONLY KID I KNOW WHO CAN RAISE A CLOUD OF DUST WALKING IN THE RAIN!
SCHULZ

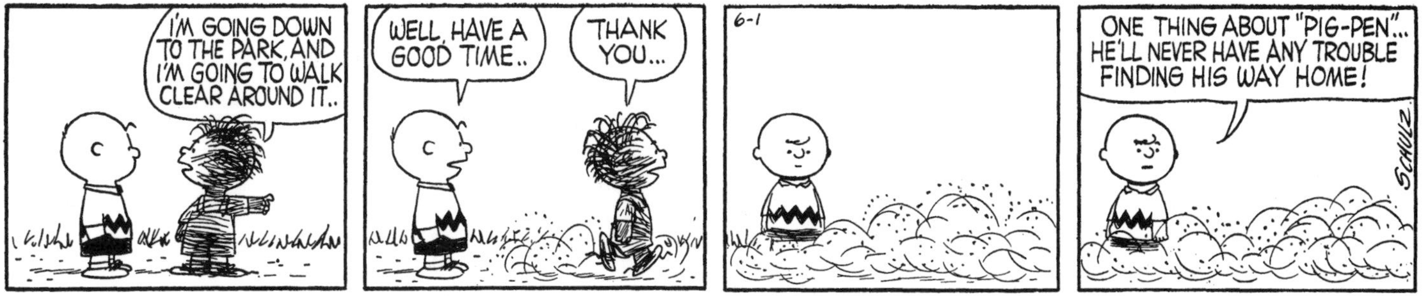
I'M GOING DOWN TO THE PARK, AND I'M GOING TO WALK CLEAR AROUND IT..
WELL, HAVE A GOOD TIME..
THANK YOU...
6-1
ONE THING ABOUT "PIG-PEN"... HE'LL NEVER HAVE ANY TROUBLE FINDING HIS WAY HOME!
SCHULZ

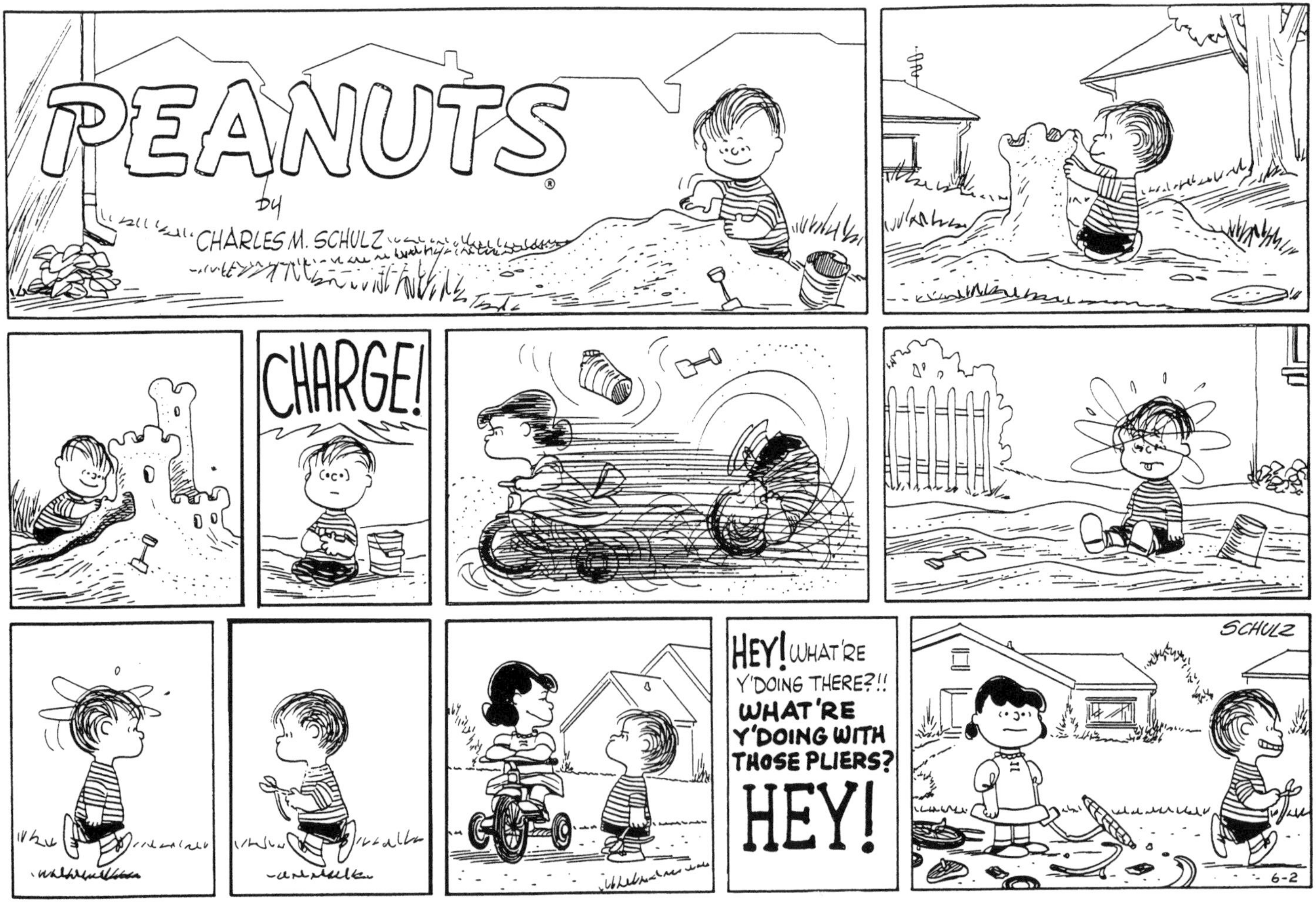
PEANUTS
by
CHARLES M. SCHULZ
CHARGE!
HEY! WHAT'RE Y'DOING THERE?!!
WHAT'RE Y'DOING WITH THOSE PLIERS?
HEY!
SCHULZ
6-2

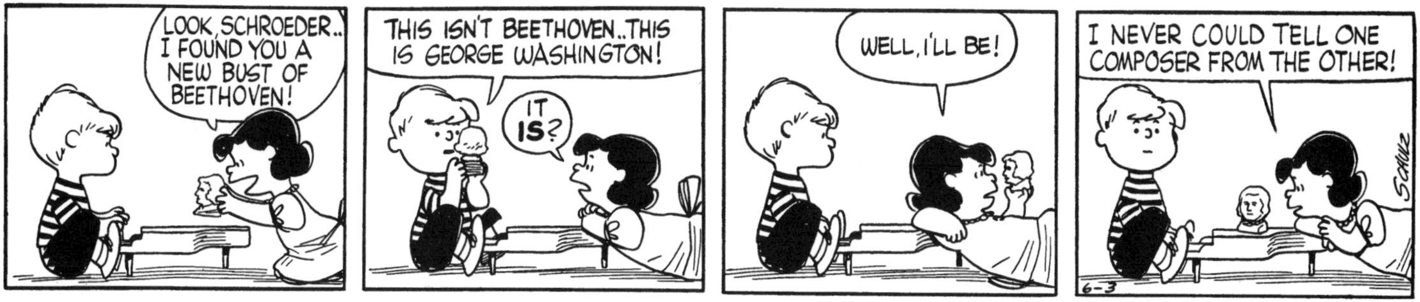
LOOK, SCHROEDER.. I FOUND YOU A NEW BUST OF BEETHOVEN!
THIS ISN'T BEETHOVEN..THIS IS GEORGE WASHINGTON!
IT IS?
WELL, I'LL BE!
I NEVER COULD TELL ONE COMPOSER FROM THE OTHER!
SCHULZ
6-3

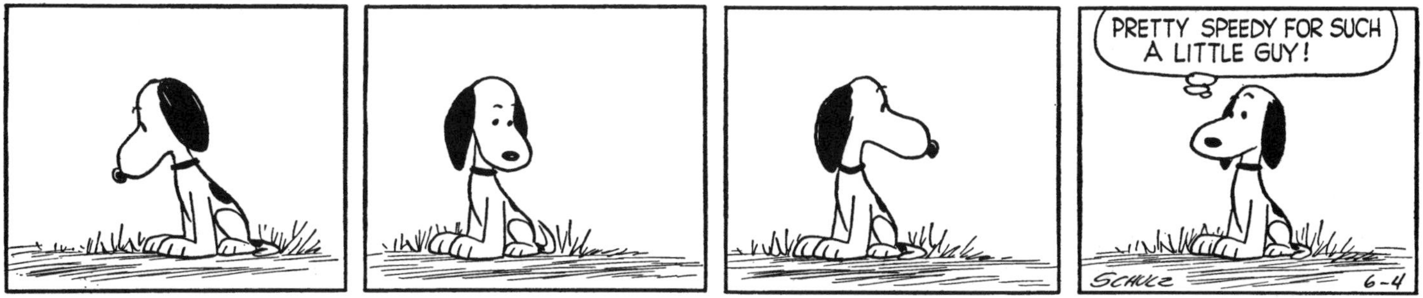
PRETTY SPEEDY FOR SUCH A LITTLE GUY!
SCHULZ
6-4

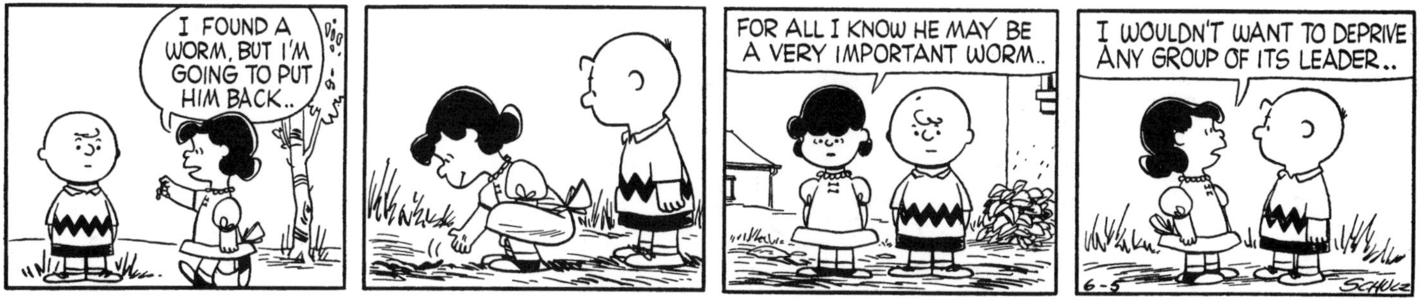
I FOUND A WORM, BUT I'M GOING TO PUT HIM BACK..
FOR ALL I KNOW HE MAY BE A VERY IMPORTANT WORM..
I WOULDN'T WANT TO DEPRIVE ANY GROUP OF ITS LEADER..
6-5
SCHULZ

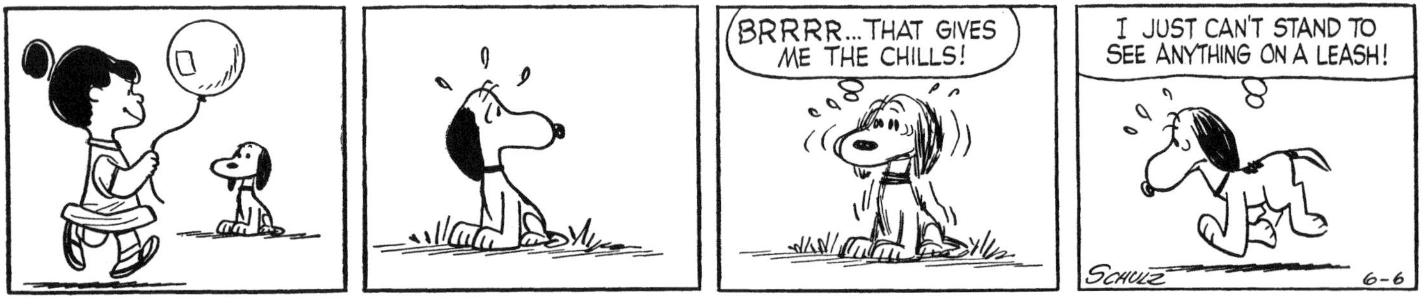
BRRRR...THAT GIVES ME THE CHILLS!
I JUST CAN'T STAND TO SEE ANYTHING ON A LEASH!
SCHULZ
6-6

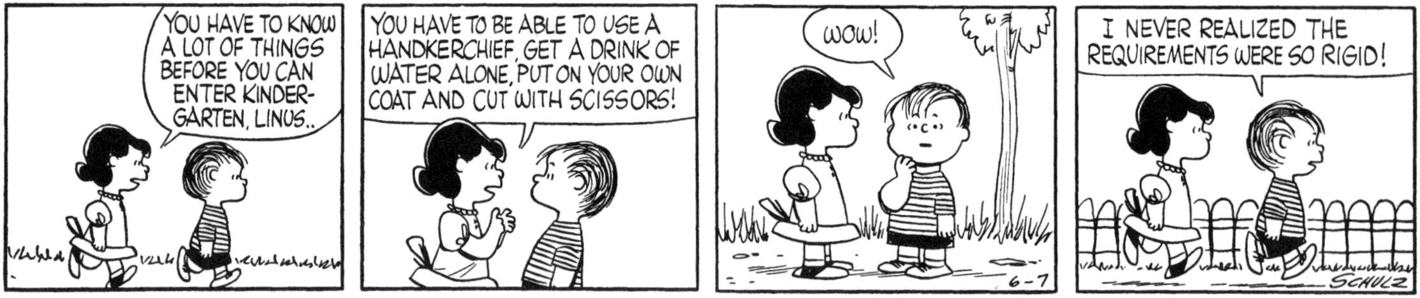
YOU HAVE TO KNOW A LOT OF THINGS BEFORE YOU CAN ENTER KINDER-GARTEN, LINUS..
YOU HAVE TO BE ABLE TO USE A HANDKERCHIEF, GET A DRINK OF WATER ALONE, PUT ON YOUR OWN COAT AND CUT WITH SCISSORS!
WOW!
6-7
I NEVER REALIZED THE REQUIREMENTS WERE SO RIGID!
SCHULZ

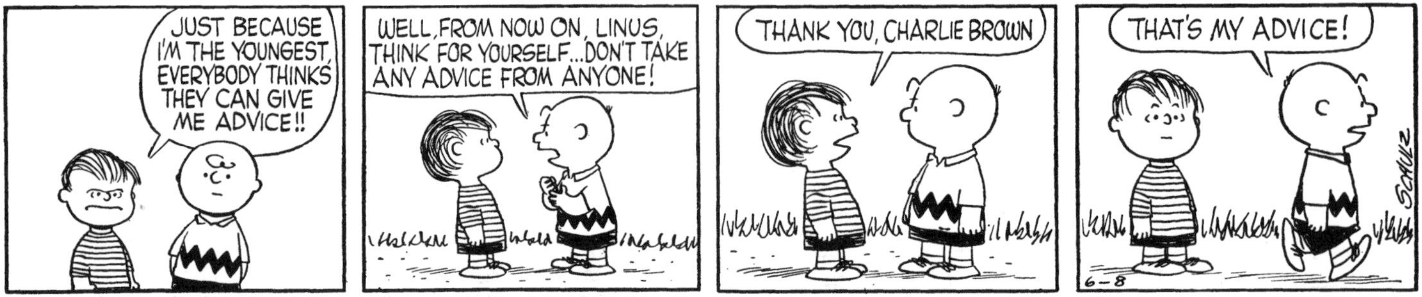
JUST BECAUSE I'M THE YOUNGEST, EVERYBODY THINKS THEY CAN GIVE ME ADVICE!!
WELL, FROM NOW ON, LINUS, THINK FOR YOURSELF...DON'T TAKE ANY ADVICE FROM ANYONE!
THANK YOU, CHARLIE BROWN
THAT'S MY ADVICE!
SCHULZ
6-8

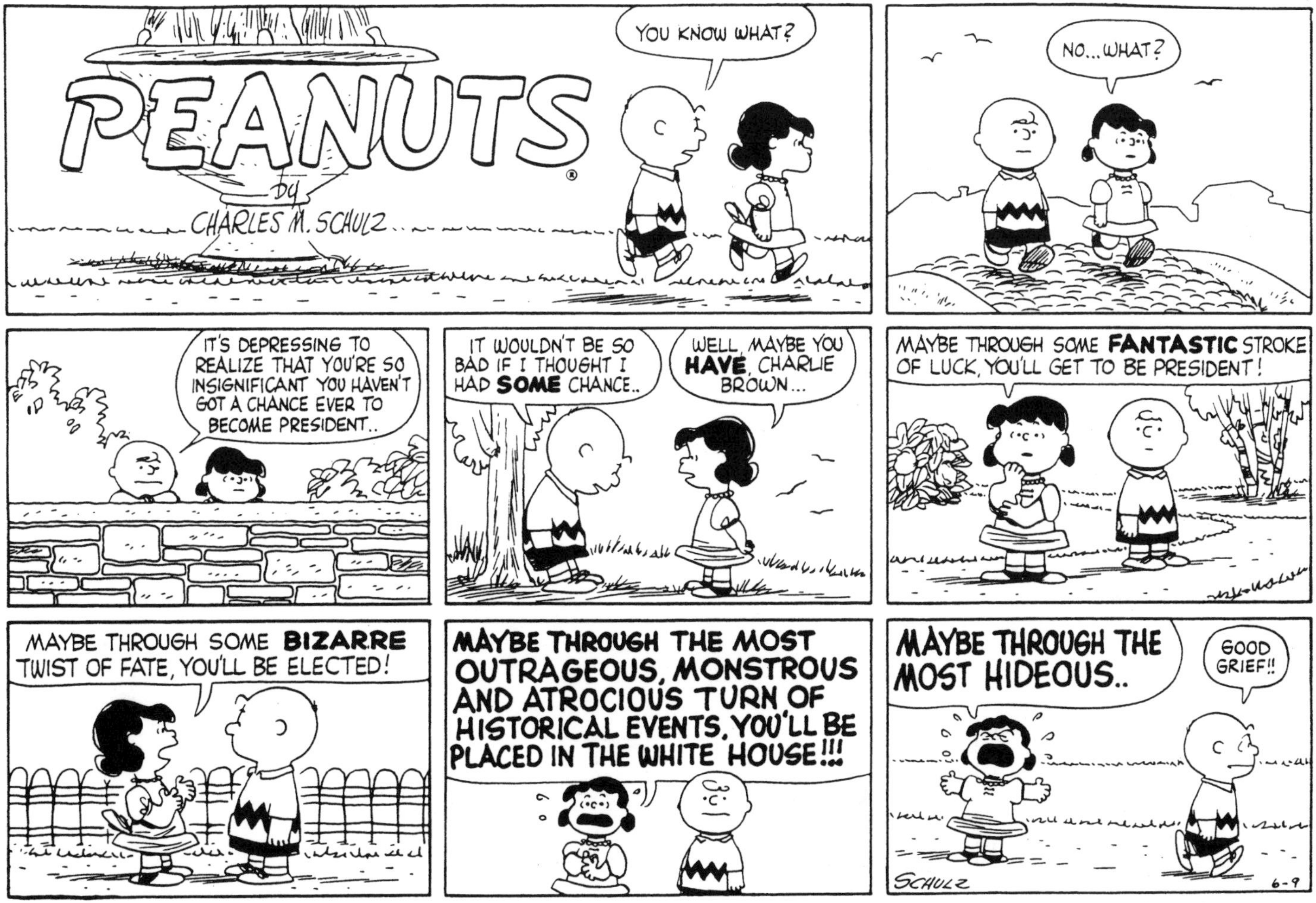
PEANUTS
by CHARLES M. SCHULZ
YOU KNOW WHAT?
NO...WHAT?
IT'S DEPRESSING TO REALIZE THAT YOU'RE SO INSIGNIFICANT YOU HAVEN'T GOT A CHANCE EVER TO BECOME PRESIDENT..
IT WOULDN'T BE SO BAD IF I THOUGHT I HAD **SOME** CHANCE..
WELL, MAYBE YOU **HAVE**, CHARLIE BROWN...
MAYBE THROUGH SOME **FANTASTIC** STROKE OF LUCK, YOU'LL GET TO BE PRESIDENT!
MAYBE THROUGH SOME **BIZARRE** TWIST OF FATE, YOU'LL BE ELECTED!
MAYBE THROUGH THE MOST OUTRAGEOUS, MONSTROUS AND ATROCIOUS TURN OF HISTORICAL EVENTS, YOU'LL BE PLACED IN THE WHITE HOUSE!!!
MAYBE THROUGH THE MOST HIDEOUS..
GOOD GRIEF!!
SCHULZ
6-9

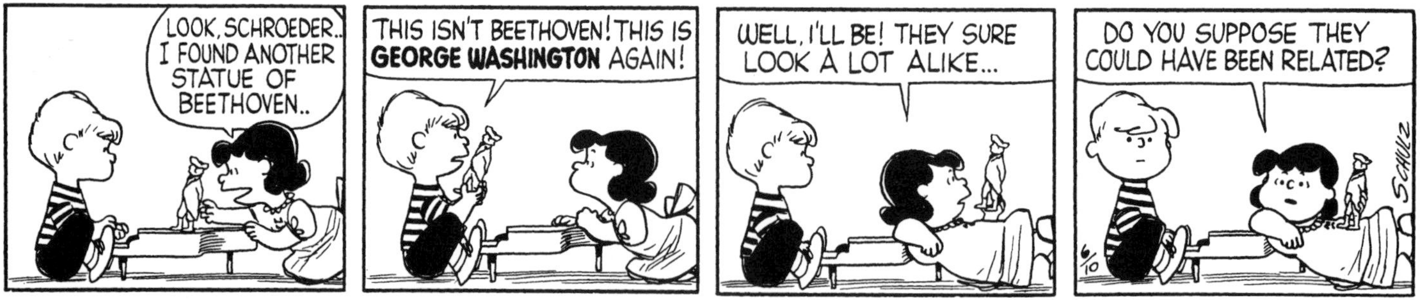
LOOK, SCHROEDER.. I FOUND ANOTHER STATUE OF BEETHOVEN..
THIS ISN'T BEETHOVEN! THIS IS GEORGE WASHINGTON AGAIN!
WELL, I'LL BE! THEY SURE LOOK A LOT ALIKE...
DO YOU SUPPOSE THEY COULD HAVE BEEN RELATED?
SCHULZ
6/10

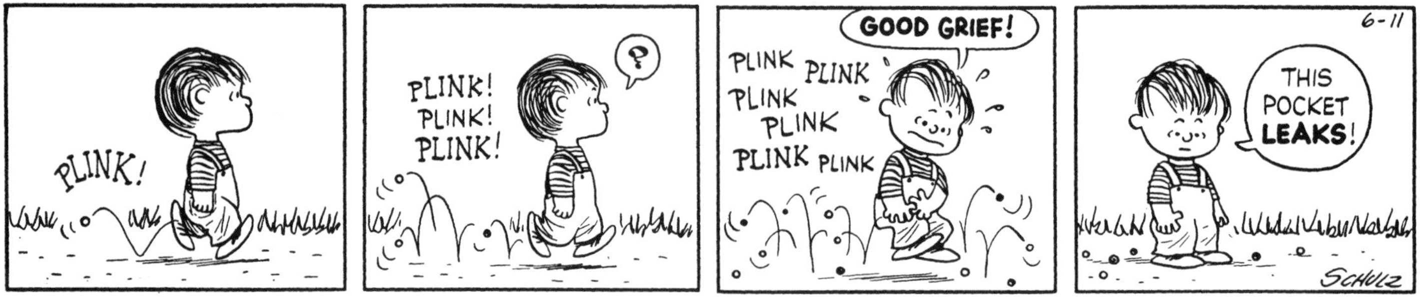
PLINK!
PLINK! PLINK! PLINK!
?
GOOD GRIEF!
PLINK PLINK PLINK PLINK PLINK PLINK
6-11
THIS POCKET LEAKS!
SCHULZ

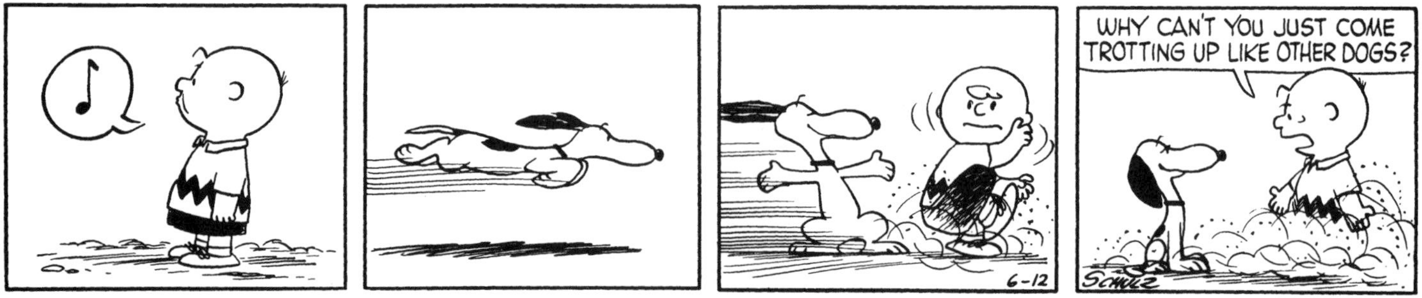
♪
6-12
WHY CAN'T YOU JUST COME TROTTING UP LIKE OTHER DOGS?
SCHULZ

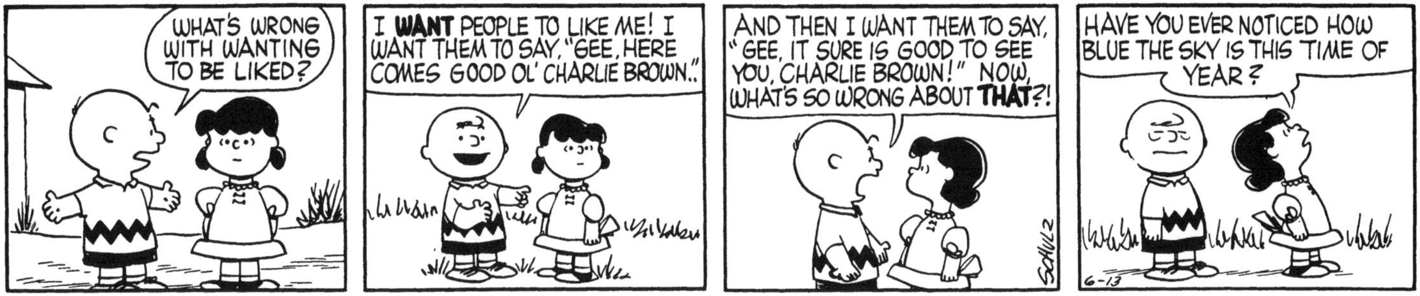
WHAT'S WRONG WITH WANTING TO BE LIKED?
I WANT PEOPLE TO LIKE ME! I WANT THEM TO SAY, "GEE, HERE COMES GOOD OL' CHARLIE BROWN.."
AND THEN I WANT THEM TO SAY, "GEE, IT SURE IS GOOD TO SEE YOU, CHARLIE BROWN!" NOW, WHAT'S SO WRONG ABOUT THAT?!
SCHULZ
HAVE YOU EVER NOTICED HOW BLUE THE SKY IS THIS TIME OF YEAR?
6-13

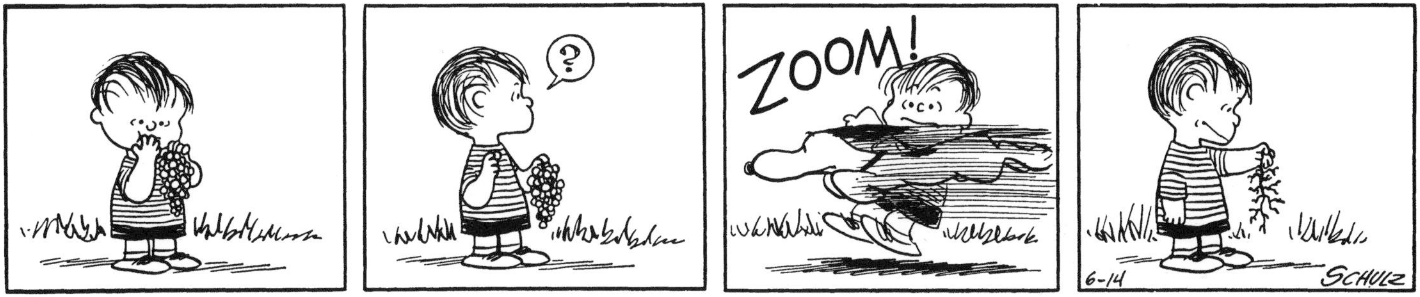
?
ZOOM!
6-14
SCHULZ

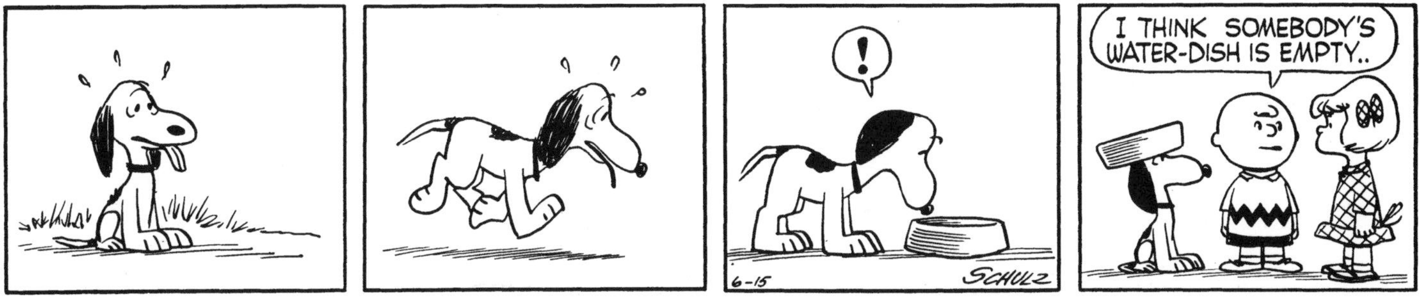
!
6-15
SCHULZ
I THINK SOMEBODY'S WATER-DISH IS EMPTY..

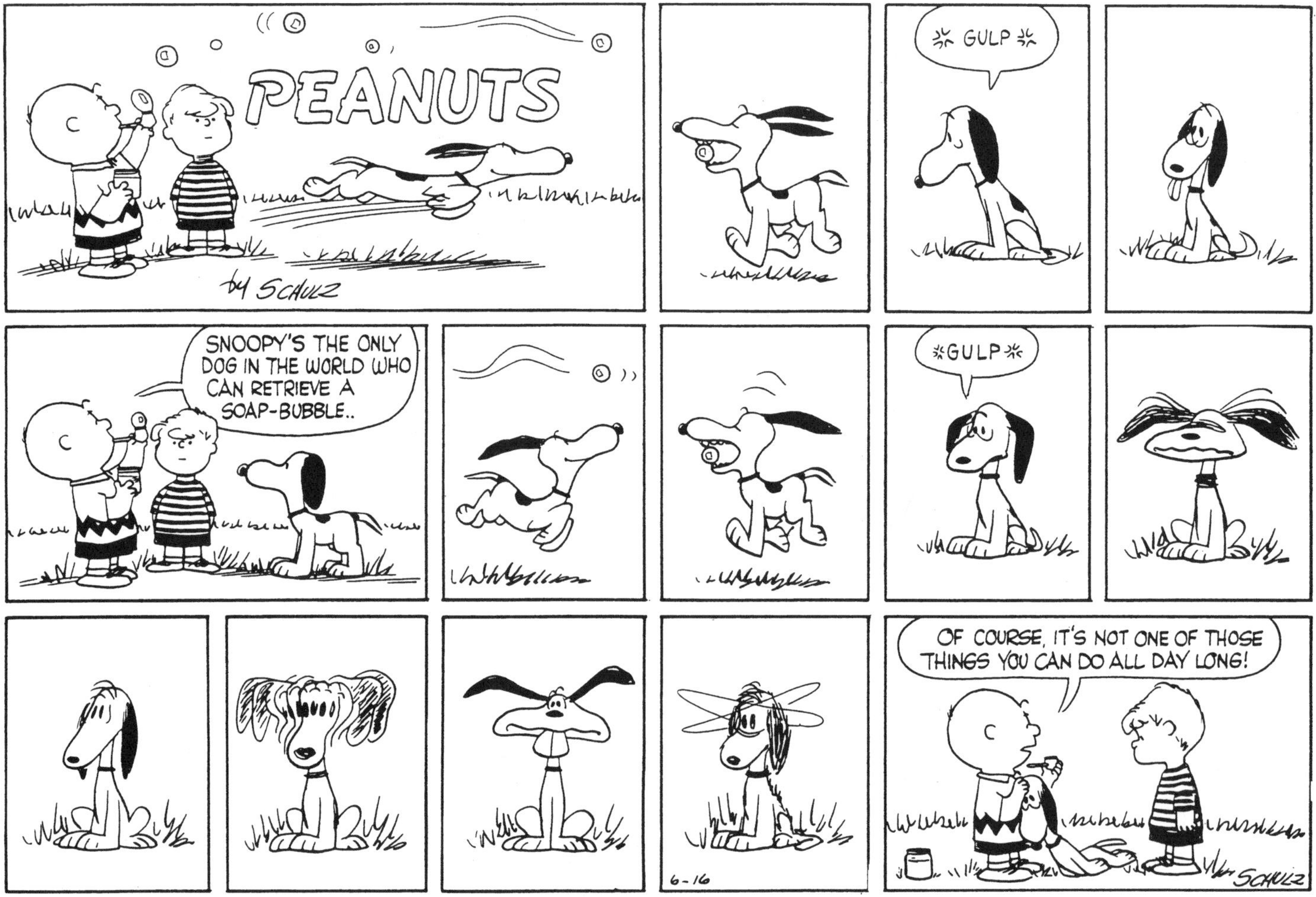
PEANUTS
by SCHULZ
GULP
SNOOPY'S THE ONLY DOG IN THE WORLD WHO CAN RETRIEVE A SOAP-BUBBLE..
GULP
6-16
OF COURSE, IT'S NOT ONE OF THOSE THINGS YOU CAN DO ALL DAY LONG!
SCHULZ

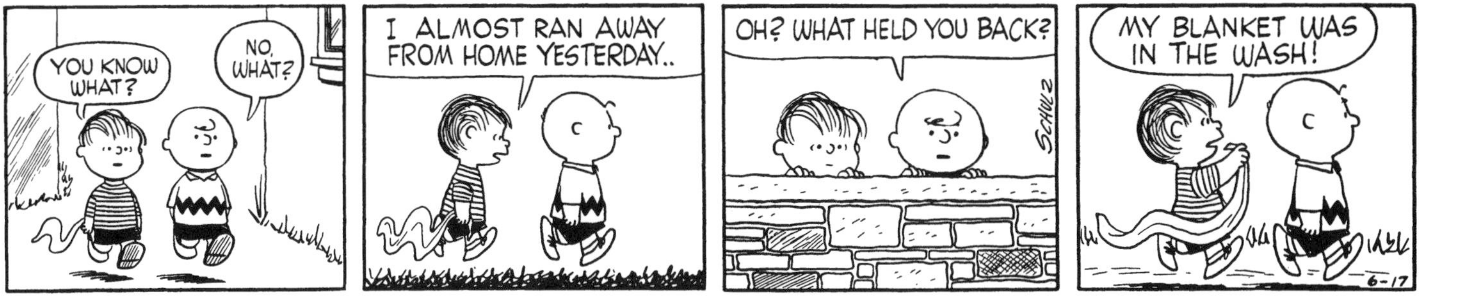
YOU KNOW WHAT?
NO, WHAT?
I ALMOST RAN AWAY FROM HOME YESTERDAY..
OH? WHAT HELD YOU BACK?
SCHULZ
MY BLANKET WAS IN THE WASH!
6-17

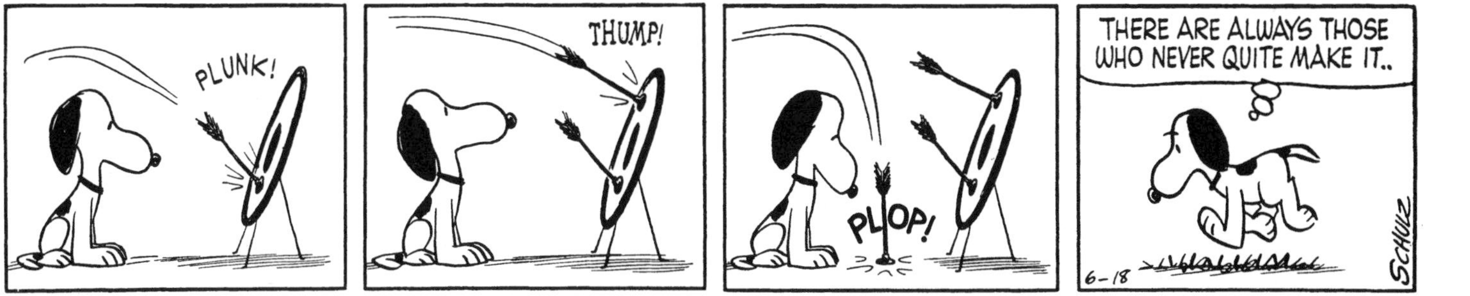
PLUNK!
THUMP!
PLOP!
THERE ARE ALWAYS THOSE WHO NEVER QUITE MAKE IT..
6-18
SCHULZ

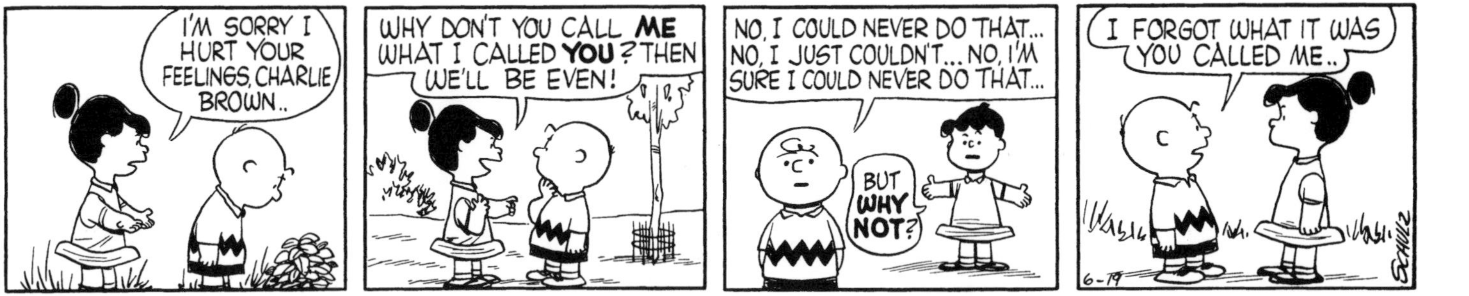
I'M SORRY I HURT YOUR FEELINGS, CHARLIE BROWN..
WHY DON'T YOU CALL ME WHAT I CALLED YOU? THEN WE'LL BE EVEN!
NO, I COULD NEVER DO THAT... NO, I JUST COULDN'T... NO, I'M SURE I COULD NEVER DO THAT...
BUT WHY NOT?
I FORGOT WHAT IT WAS YOU CALLED ME..
6-19
SCHULZ

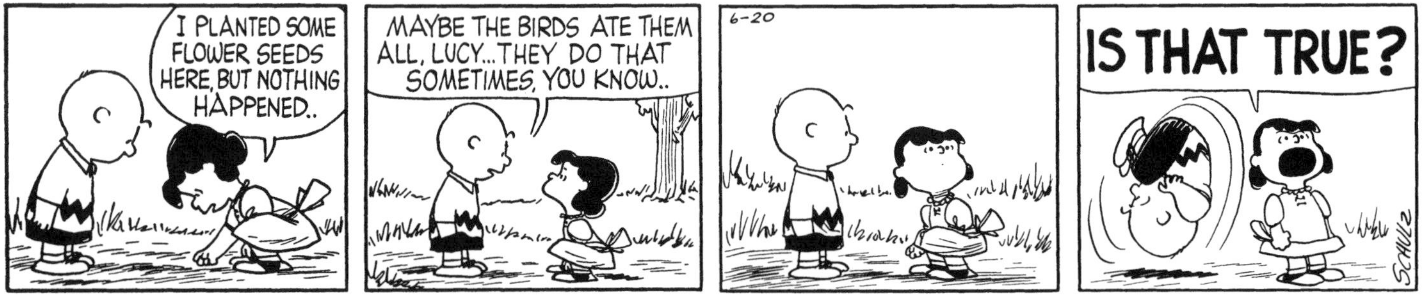
I PLANTED SOME FLOWER SEEDS HERE, BUT NOTHING HAPPENED..
MAYBE THE BIRDS ATE THEM ALL, LUCY...THEY DO THAT SOMETIMES, YOU KNOW..
6-20
IS THAT TRUE?
SCHULZ

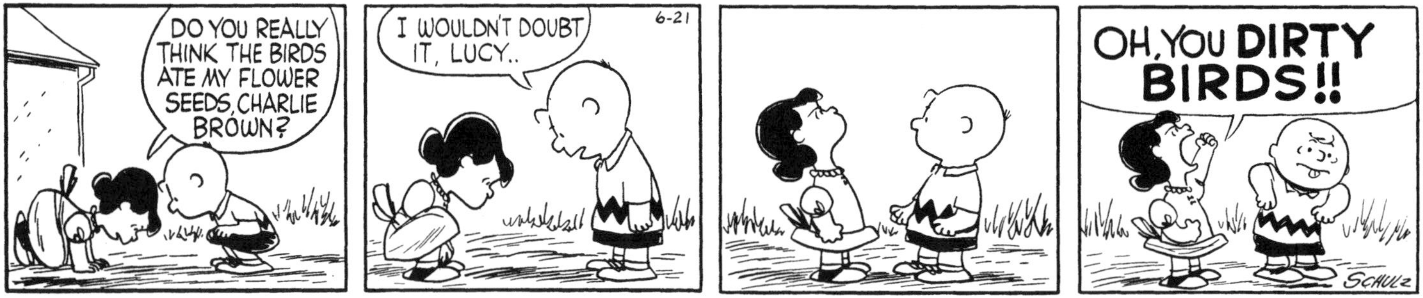
DO YOU REALLY THINK THE BIRDS ATE MY FLOWER SEEDS, CHARLIE BROWN?
I WOULDN'T DOUBT IT, LUCY..
6-21
OH, YOU DIRTY BIRDS!!
SCHULZ

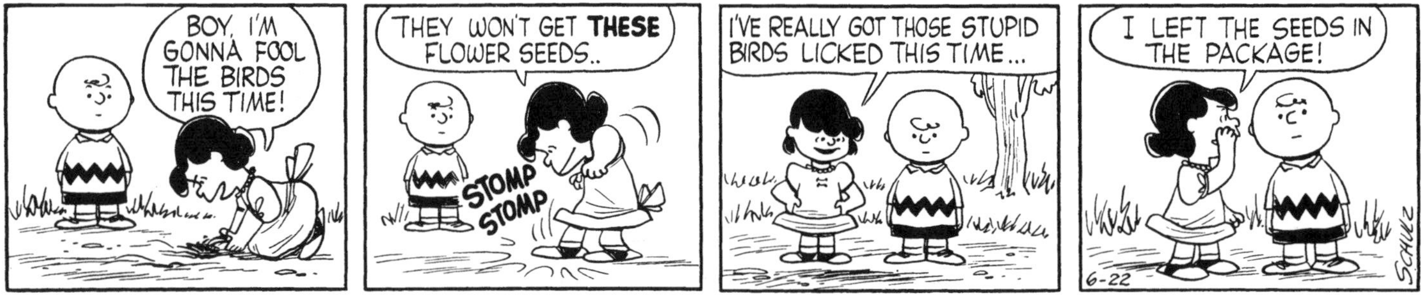
BOY, I'M GONNA FOOL THE BIRDS THIS TIME!
THEY WON'T GET THESE FLOWER SEEDS..
STOMP STOMP
I'VE REALLY GOT THOSE STUPID BIRDS LICKED THIS TIME...
I LEFT THE SEEDS IN THE PACKAGE!
6-22
SCHULZ

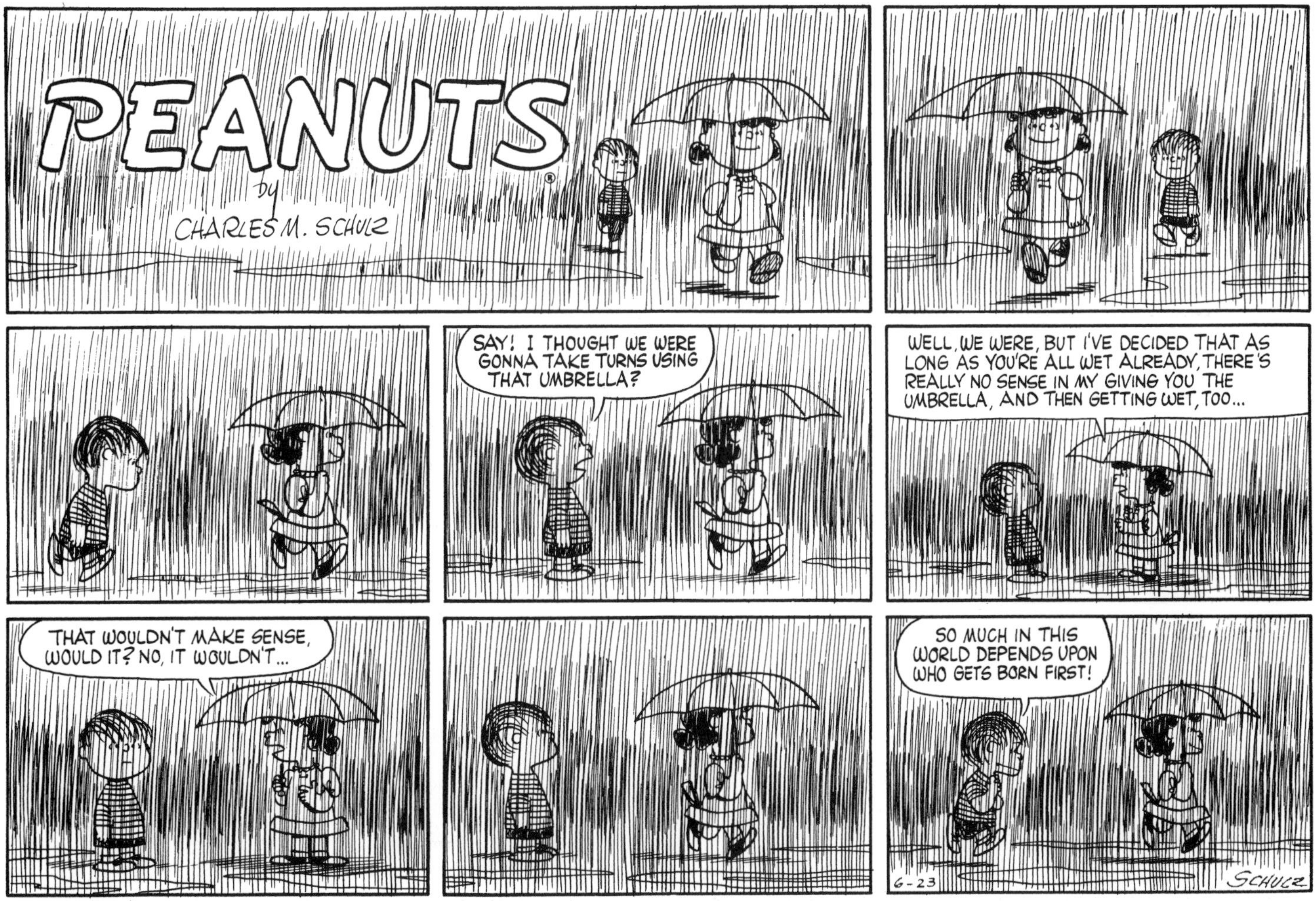
PEANUTS
by CHARLES M. SCHULZ
SAY! I THOUGHT WE WERE GONNA TAKE TURNS USING THAT UMBRELLA?
WELL, WE WERE, BUT I'VE DECIDED THAT AS LONG AS YOU'RE ALL WET ALREADY, THERE'S REALLY NO SENSE IN MY GIVING YOU THE UMBRELLA, AND THEN GETTING WET, TOO...
THAT WOULDN'T MAKE SENSE, WOULD IT? NO, IT WOULDN'T...
SO MUCH IN THIS WORLD DEPENDS UPON WHO GETS BORN FIRST!
6-23
SCHULZ

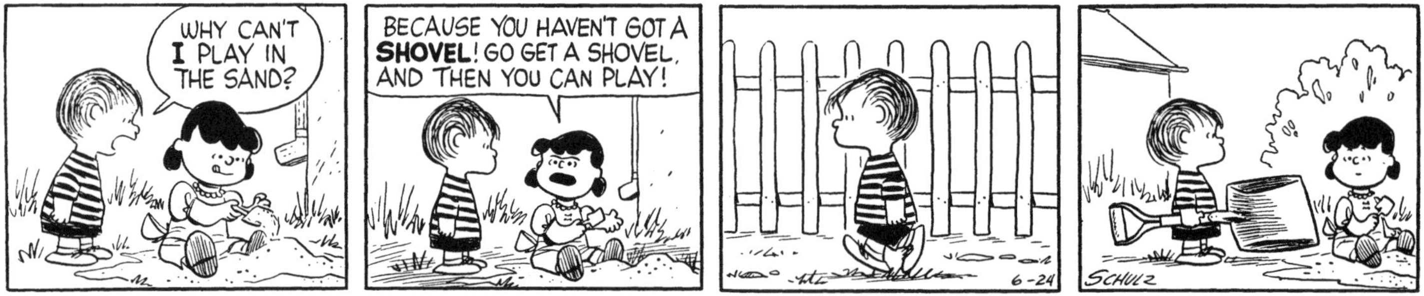
WHY CAN'T **I** PLAY IN THE SAND?
BECAUSE YOU HAVEN'T GOT A **SHOVEL**! GO GET A SHOVEL, AND THEN YOU CAN PLAY!
6-24
SCHULZ

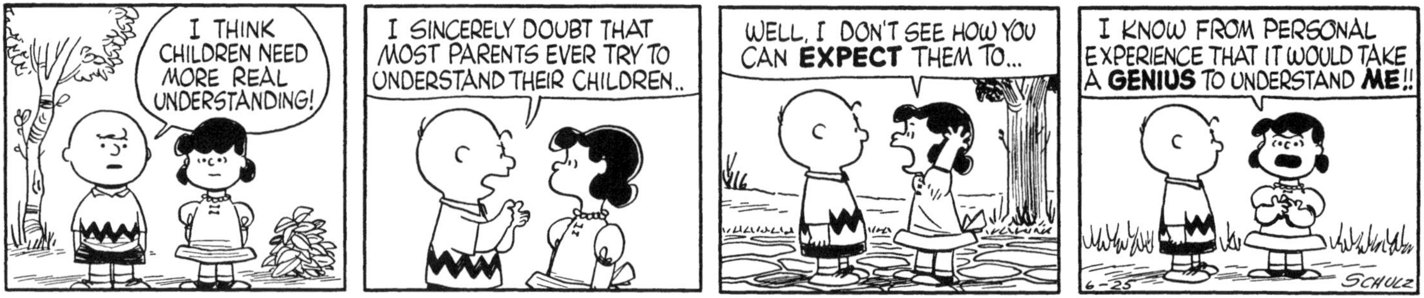
I THINK CHILDREN NEED MORE REAL UNDERSTANDING!
I SINCERELY DOUBT THAT MOST PARENTS EVER TRY TO UNDERSTAND THEIR CHILDREN..
WELL, I DON'T SEE HOW YOU CAN **EXPECT** THEM TO...
I KNOW FROM PERSONAL EXPERIENCE THAT IT WOULD TAKE A **GENIUS** TO UNDERSTAND **ME**!!
6-25
SCHULZ

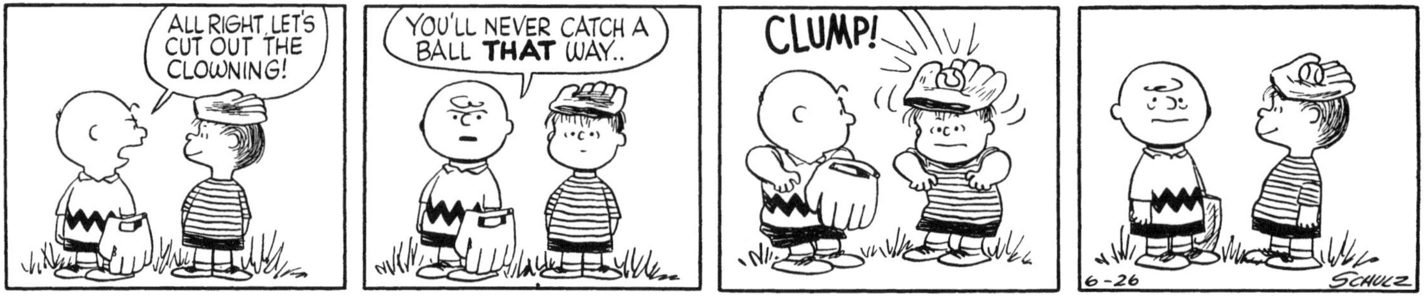
ALL RIGHT, LET'S CUT OUT THE CLOWNING!
YOU'LL NEVER CATCH A BALL **THAT** WAY..
CLUMP!
6-26
SCHULZ

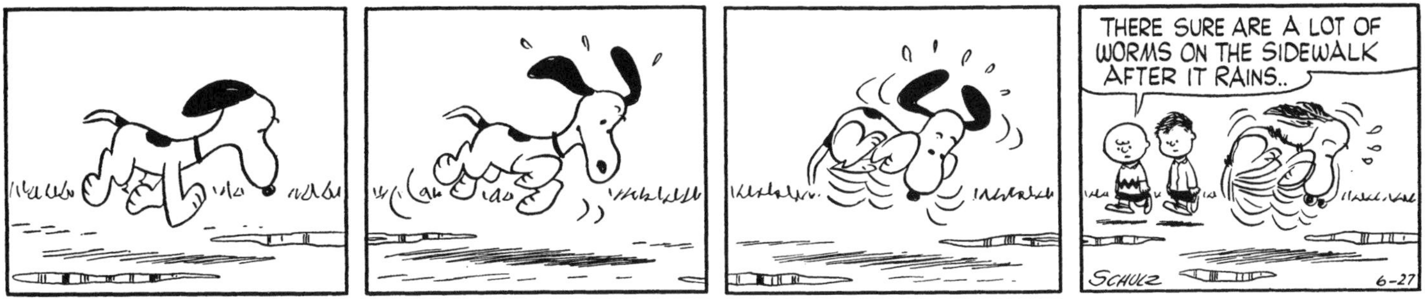
THERE SURE ARE A LOT OF WORMS ON THE SIDEWALK AFTER IT RAINS..
SCHULZ
6-27

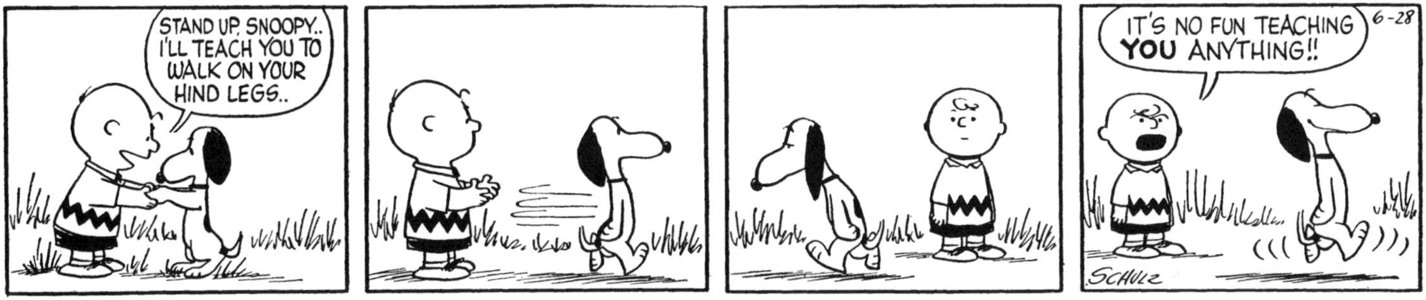
STAND UP, SNOOPY.. I'LL TEACH YOU TO WALK ON YOUR HIND LEGS..
IT'S NO FUN TEACHING **YOU** ANYTHING!!
6-28
SCHULZ

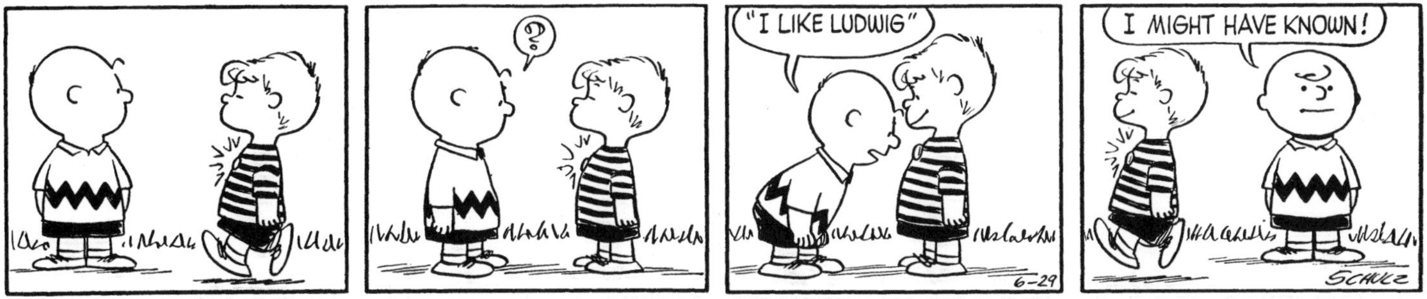
?
"I LIKE LUDWIG"
6-29
I MIGHT HAVE KNOWN!
SCHULZ

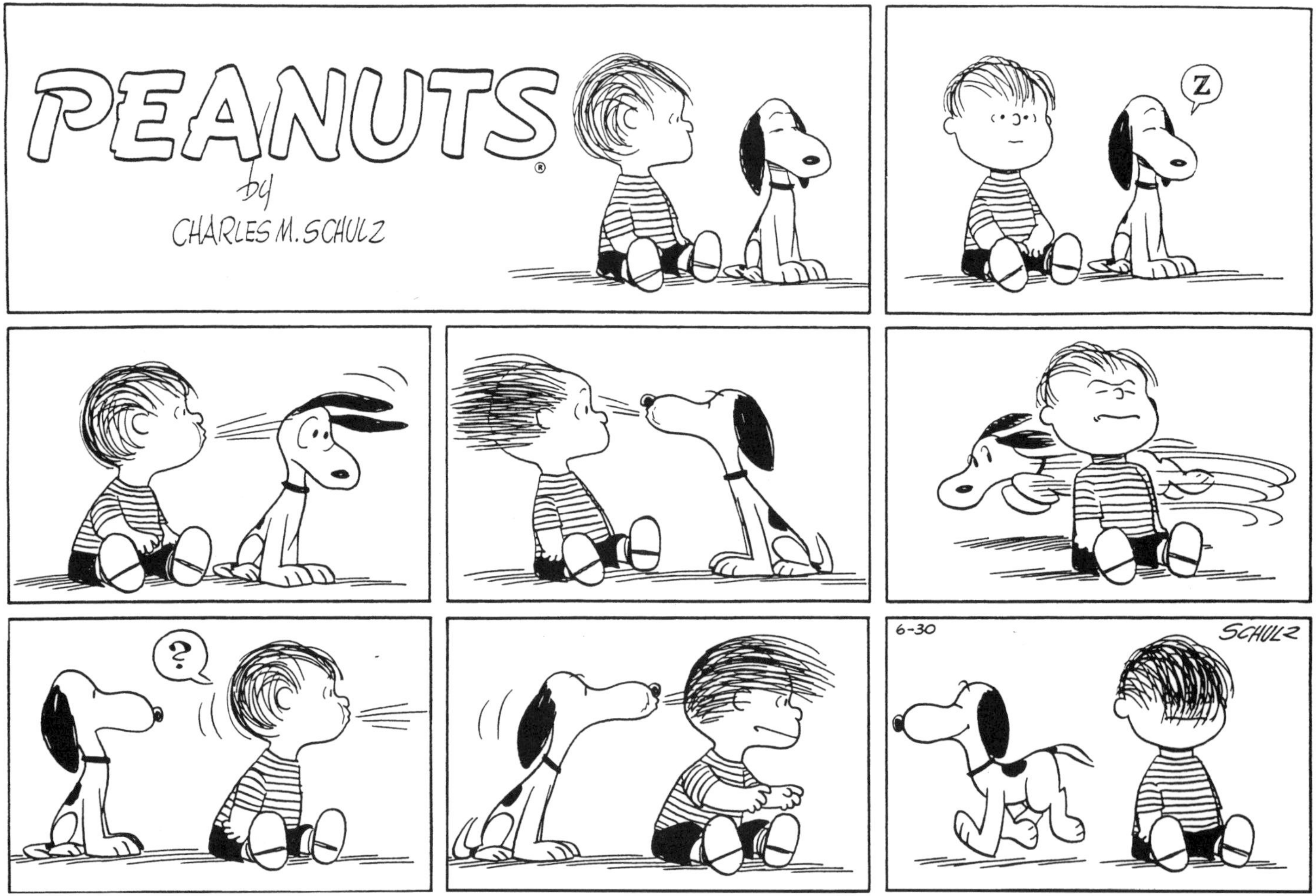
PEANUTS
by CHARLES M. SCHULZ
Z
?
6-30
SCHULZ

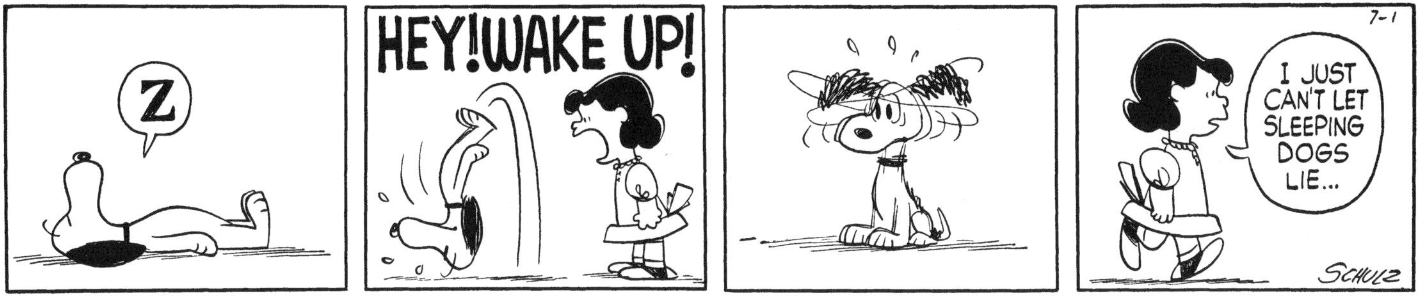
Z
HEY! WAKE UP!
7-1
I JUST CAN'T LET SLEEPING DOGS LIE...
SCHULZ

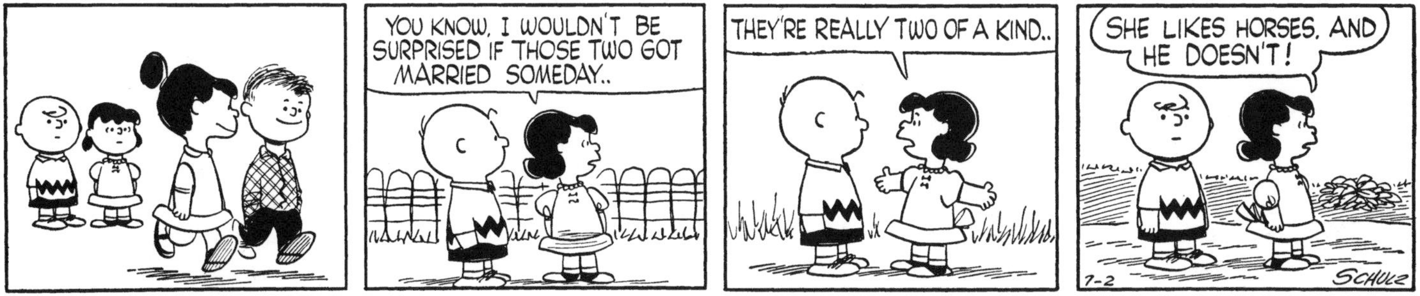
YOU KNOW, I WOULDN'T BE SURPRISED IF THOSE TWO GOT MARRIED SOMEDAY..
THEY'RE REALLY TWO OF A KIND..
SHE LIKES HORSES, AND HE DOESN'T!
7-2
SCHULZ

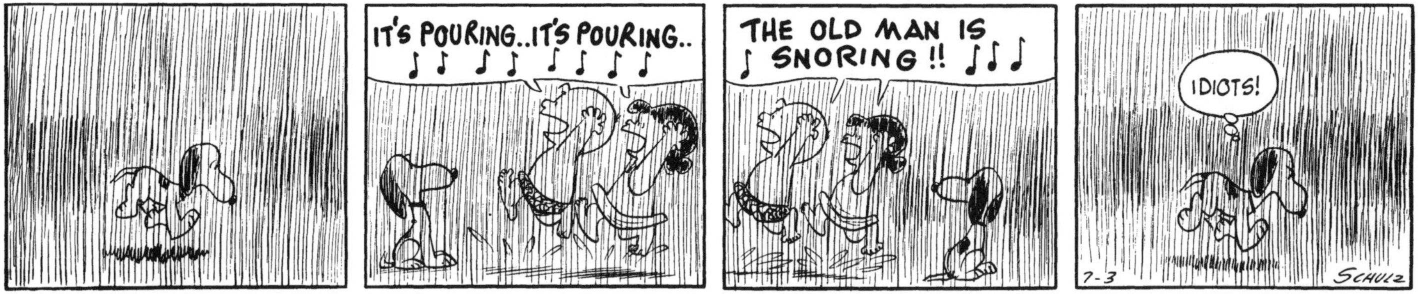
IT'S POURING..IT'S POURING..
THE OLD MAN IS SNORING!!
IDIOTS!
7-3
SCHULZ

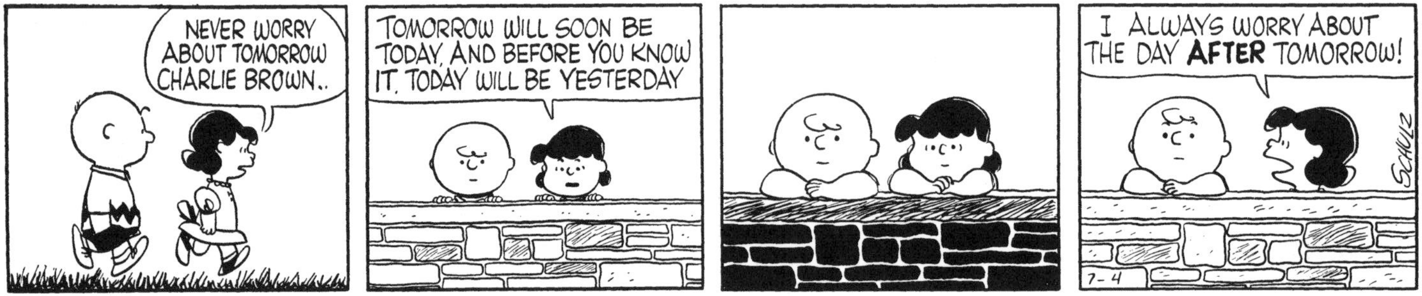
NEVER WORRY ABOUT TOMORROW CHARLIE BROWN..
TOMORROW WILL SOON BE TODAY, AND BEFORE YOU KNOW IT, TODAY WILL BE YESTERDAY
I ALWAYS WORRY ABOUT THE DAY **AFTER** TOMORROW!
7-4

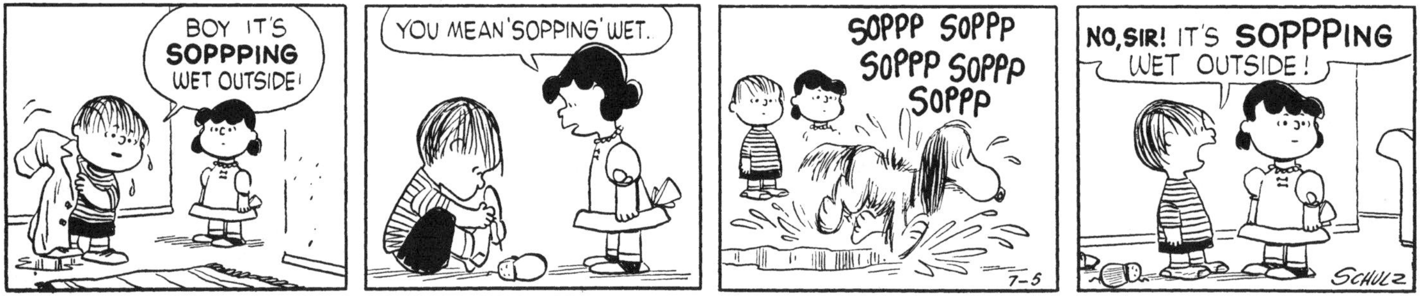
BOY IT'S **SOPPPING** WET OUTSIDE!
YOU MEAN 'SOPPING' WET.
SOPPP SOPPP SOPPP SOPPP SOPPP
7-5
NO, SIR! IT'S **SOPPPING** WET OUTSIDE!

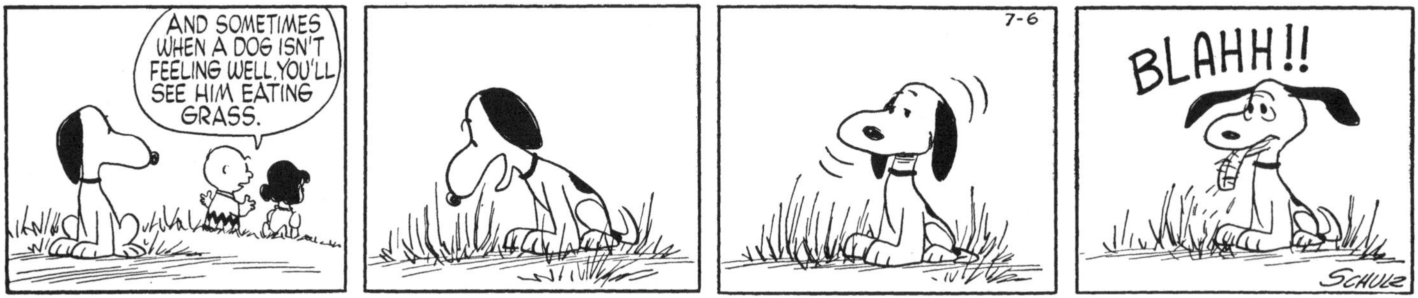
AND SOMETIMES WHEN A DOG ISN'T FEELING WELL, YOU'LL SEE HIM EATING GRASS.
7-6
BLAHH!!

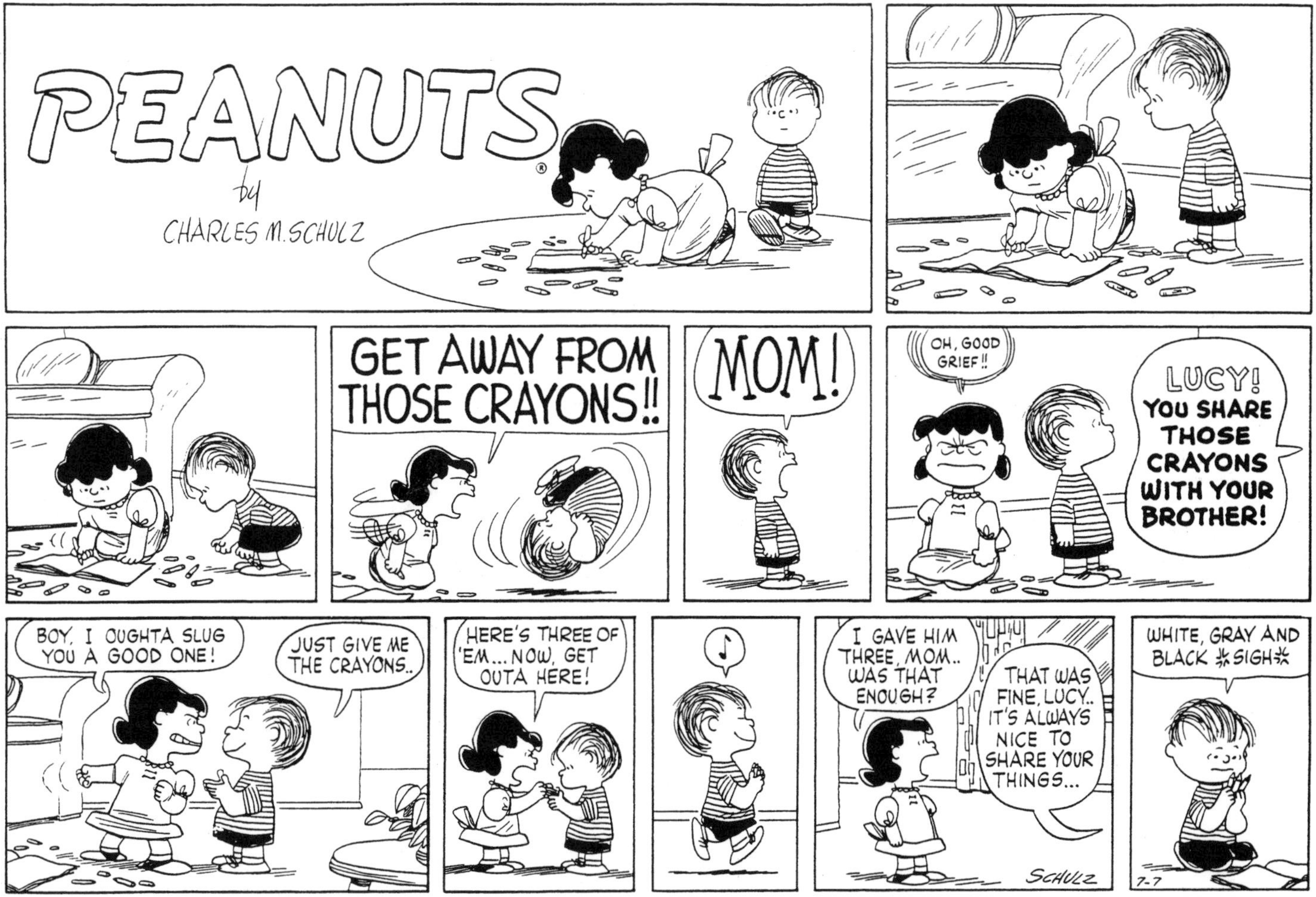
PEANUTS
by
CHARLES M. SCHULZ
GET AWAY FROM THOSE CRAYONS!!
MOM!
OH, GOOD GRIEF!!
LUCY! YOU SHARE THOSE CRAYONS WITH YOUR BROTHER!
BOY, I OUGHTA SLUG YOU A GOOD ONE!
JUST GIVE ME THE CRAYONS..
HERE'S THREE OF 'EM... NOW, GET OUTA HERE!
♪
I GAVE HIM THREE, MOM.. WAS THAT ENOUGH?
THAT WAS FINE, LUCY.. IT'S ALWAYS NICE TO SHARE YOUR THINGS...
SCHULZ
WHITE, GRAY AND BLACK *SIGH*
7-7

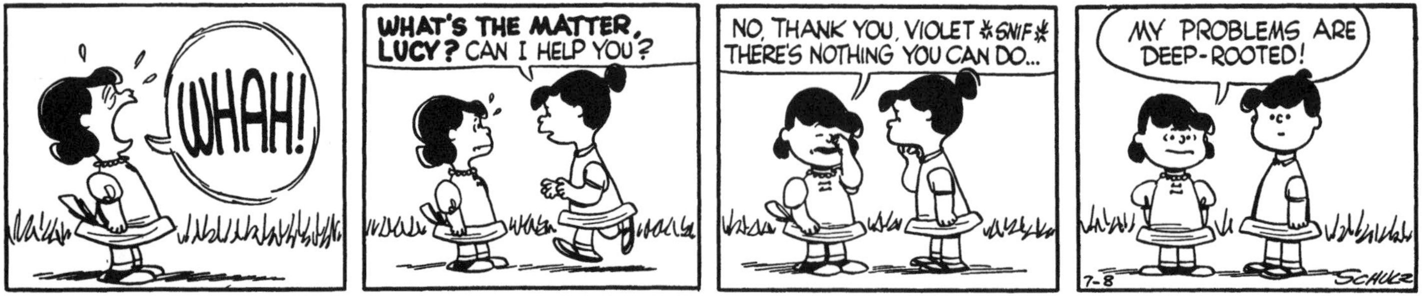
WHAH!
WHAT'S THE MATTER, LUCY? CAN I HELP YOU?
NO, THANK YOU, VIOLET *SNIF* THERE'S NOTHING YOU CAN DO...
MY PROBLEMS ARE DEEP-ROOTED!
7-8
SCHULZ

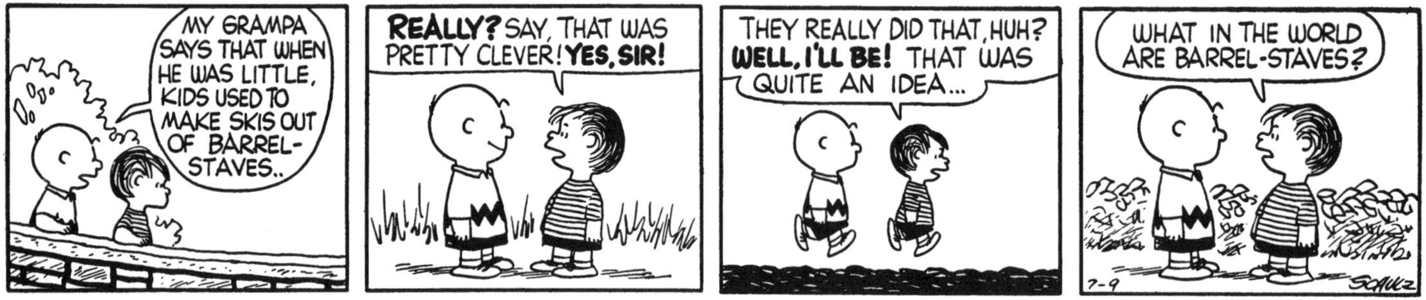
MY GRAMPA SAYS THAT WHEN HE WAS LITTLE, KIDS USED TO MAKE SKIS OUT OF BARREL-STAVES..
REALLY? SAY, THAT WAS PRETTY CLEVER! YES, SIR!
THEY REALLY DID THAT, HUH? WELL, I'LL BE! THAT WAS QUITE AN IDEA...
WHAT IN THE WORLD ARE BARREL-STAVES?
7-9
SCHULZ

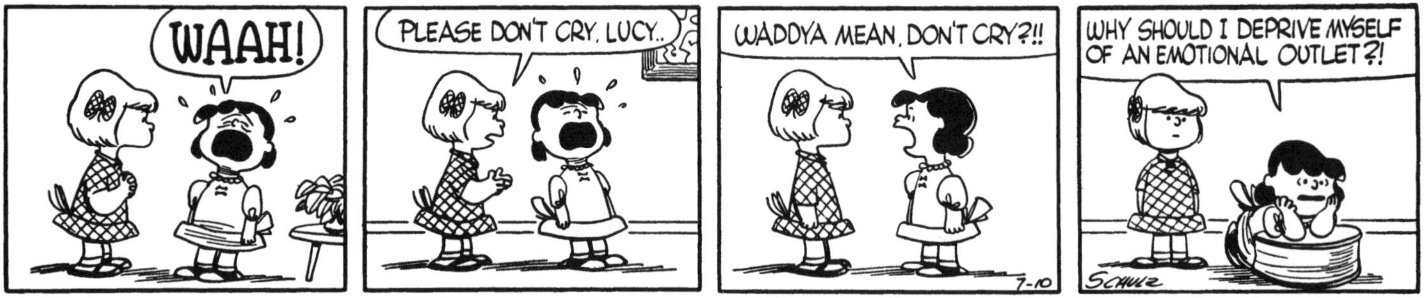
WAAH!
PLEASE DON'T CRY, LUCY..
WADDYA MEAN, DON'T CRY?!!
WHY SHOULD I DEPRIVE MYSELF OF AN EMOTIONAL OUTLET?!
7-10
SCHULZ

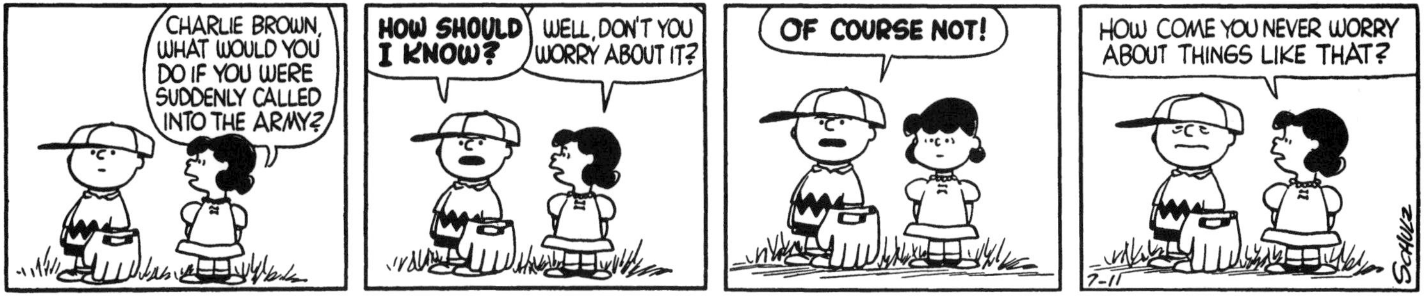
CHARLIE BROWN, WHAT WOULD YOU DO IF YOU WERE SUDDENLY CALLED INTO THE ARMY?
HOW SHOULD I KNOW?
WELL, DON'T YOU WORRY ABOUT IT?
OF COURSE NOT!
HOW COME YOU NEVER WORRY ABOUT THINGS LIKE THAT?
7-11
SCHULZ

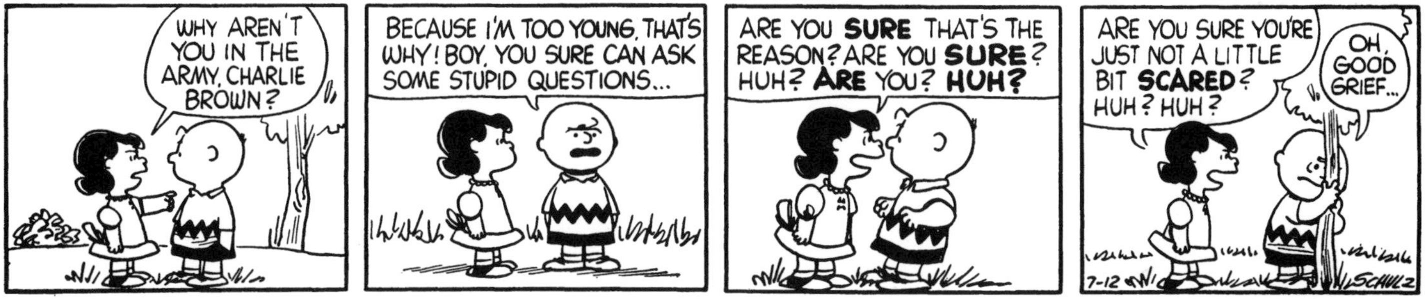
WHY AREN'T YOU IN THE ARMY, CHARLIE BROWN?
BECAUSE I'M TOO YOUNG, THAT'S WHY! BOY, YOU SURE CAN ASK SOME STUPID QUESTIONS...
ARE YOU SURE THAT'S THE REASON? ARE YOU SURE? HUH? ARE YOU? HUH?
ARE YOU SURE YOU'RE JUST NOT A LITTLE BIT SCARED? HUH? HUH?
OH, GOOD GRIEF...
7-12
SCHULZ

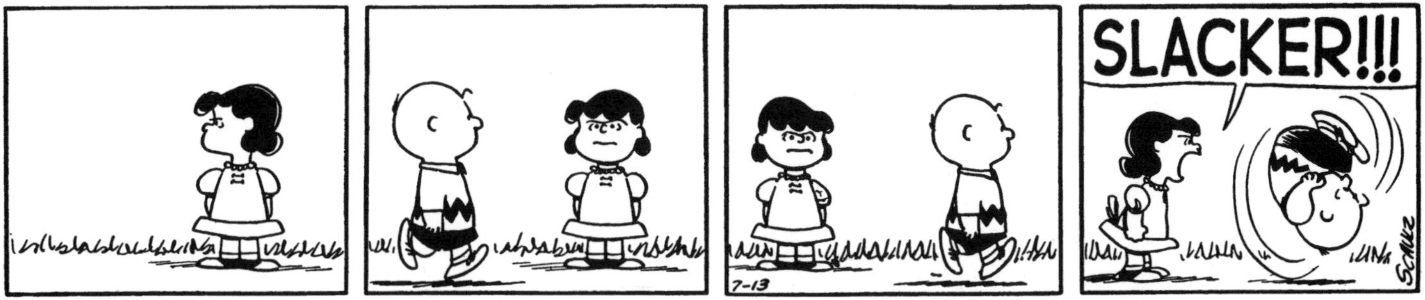
7-13
SLACKER!!!
SCHULZ

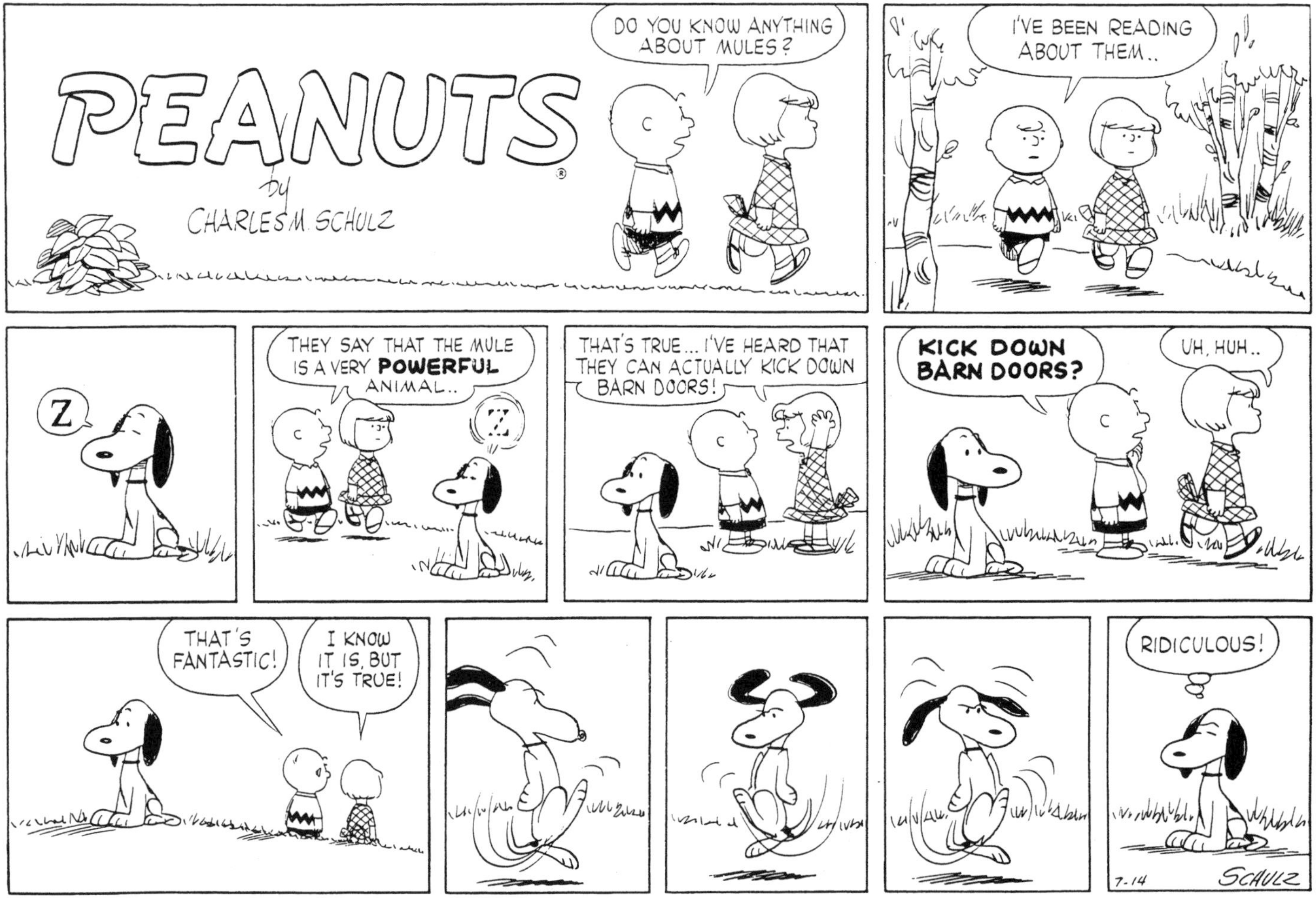
PEANUTS
by CHARLES M. SCHULZ
DO YOU KNOW ANYTHING ABOUT MULES?
I'VE BEEN READING ABOUT THEM..
Z
THEY SAY THAT THE MULE IS A VERY POWERFUL ANIMAL..
Z
THAT'S TRUE... I'VE HEARD THAT THEY CAN ACTUALLY KICK DOWN BARN DOORS!
KICK DOWN BARN DOORS?
UH, HUH..
THAT'S FANTASTIC!
I KNOW IT IS, BUT IT'S TRUE!
RIDICULOUS!
7-14
SCHULZ

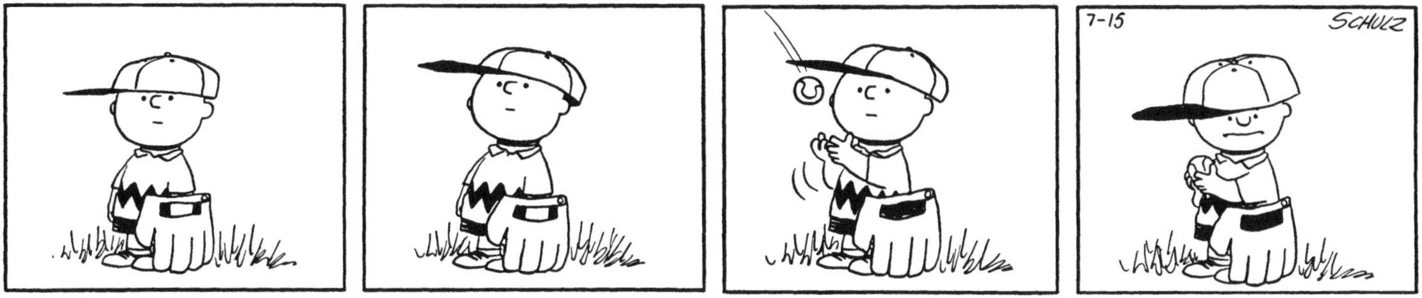
7-15
SCHULZ

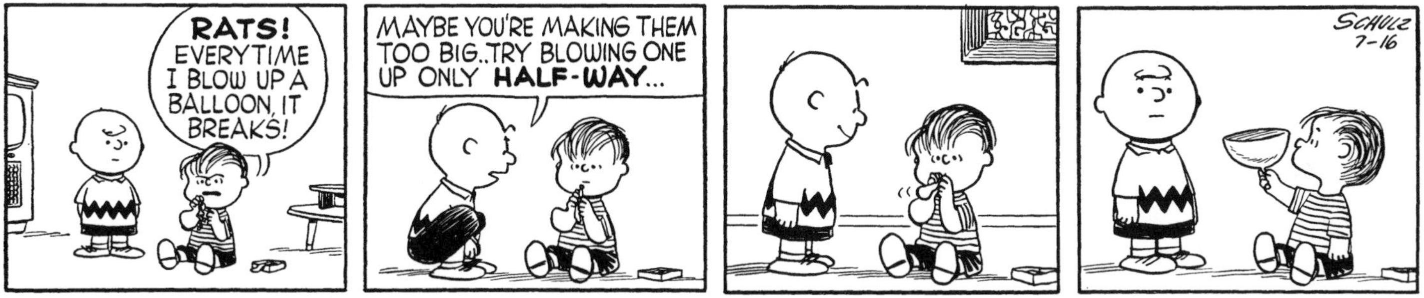
RATS! EVERYTIME I BLOW UP A BALLOON, IT BREAKS!
MAYBE YOU'RE MAKING THEM TOO BIG..TRY BLOWING ONE UP ONLY HALF-WAY...
SCHULZ
7-16

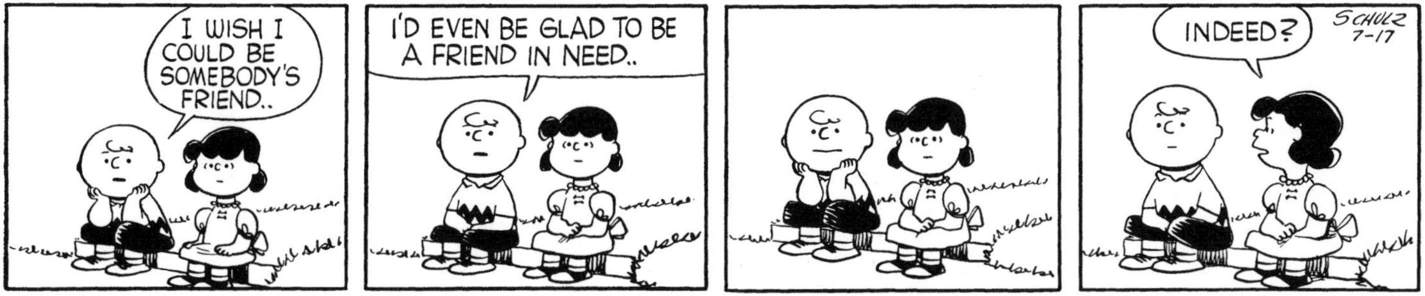
I WISH I COULD BE SOMEBODY'S FRIEND..
I'D EVEN BE GLAD TO BE A FRIEND IN NEED..
INDEED?
SCHULZ
7-17

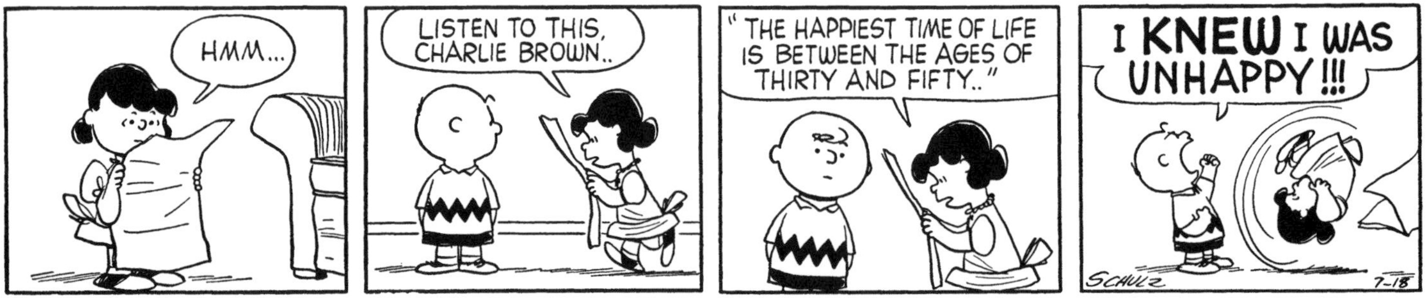
HMM...
LISTEN TO THIS, CHARLIE BROWN..
"THE HAPPIEST TIME OF LIFE IS BETWEEN THE AGES OF THIRTY AND FIFTY.."
I KNEW I WAS UNHAPPY!!!
SCHULZ
7-18

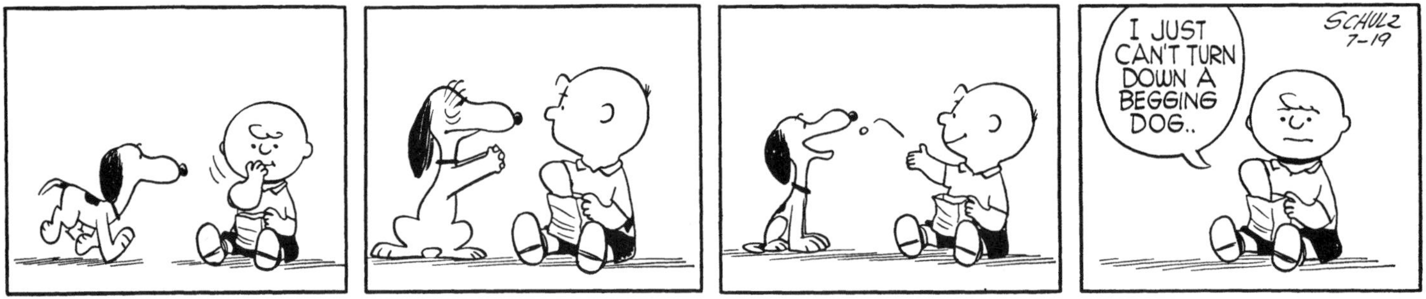
I JUST CAN'T TURN DOWN A BEGGING DOG..
SCHULZ
7-19

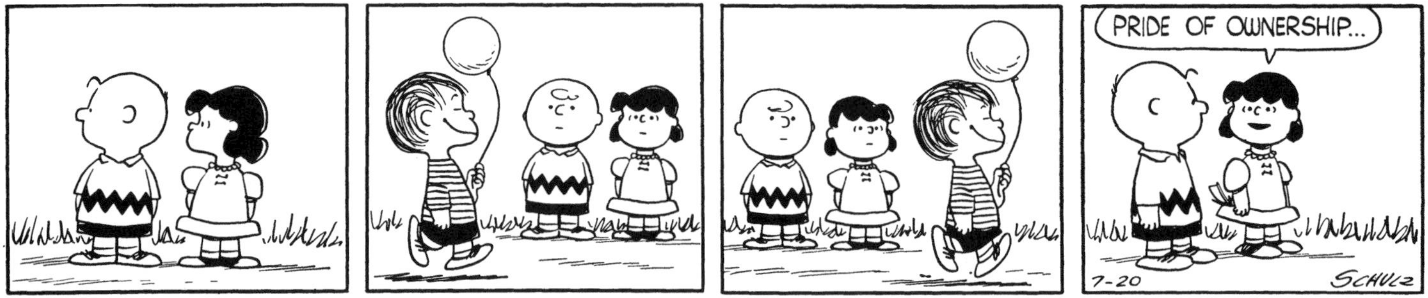
PRIDE OF OWNERSHIP...
7-20
SCHULZ

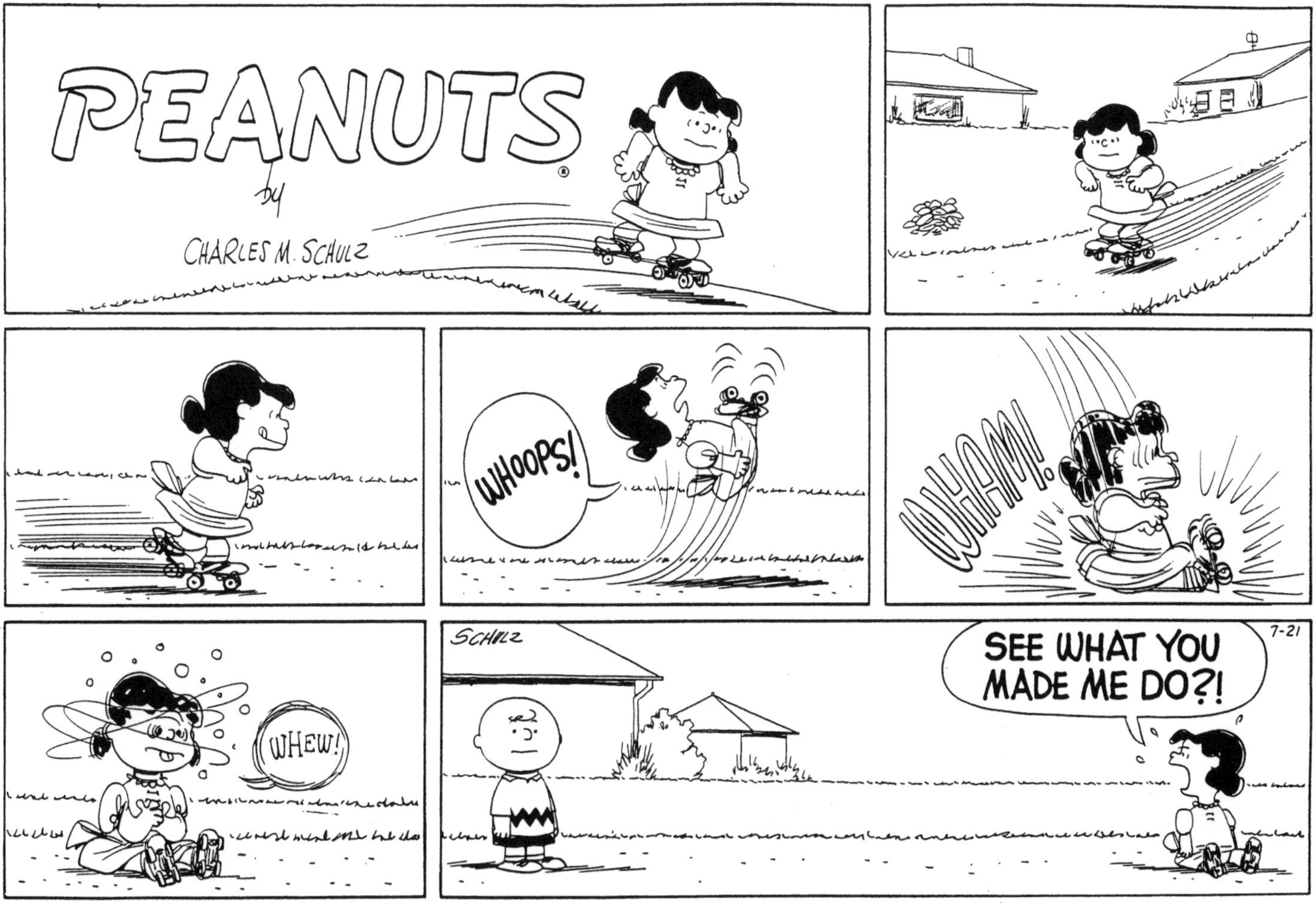
PEANUTS
by
CHARLES M. SCHULZ
WHOOPS!
WHAM!
WHEW!
SCHULZ
7-21
SEE WHAT YOU MADE ME DO?!

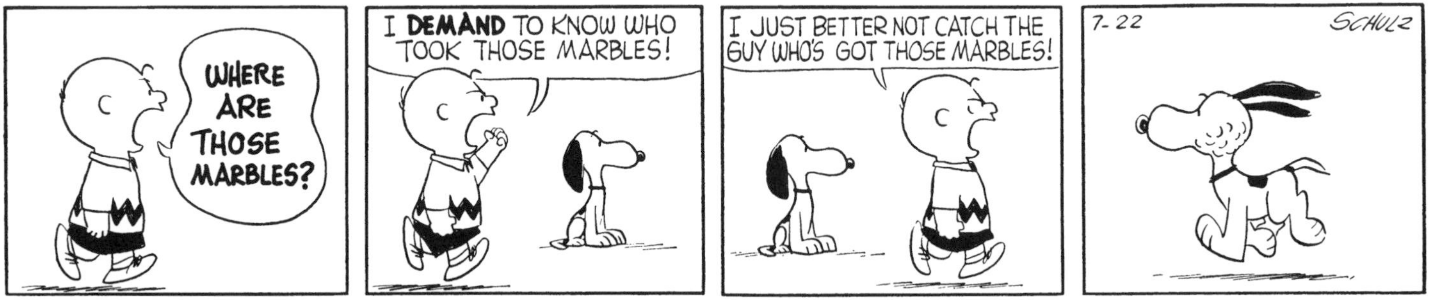
WHERE ARE THOSE MARBLES?
I DEMAND TO KNOW WHO TOOK THOSE MARBLES!
I JUST BETTER NOT CATCH THE GUY WHO'S GOT THOSE MARBLES!
7-22
SCHULZ

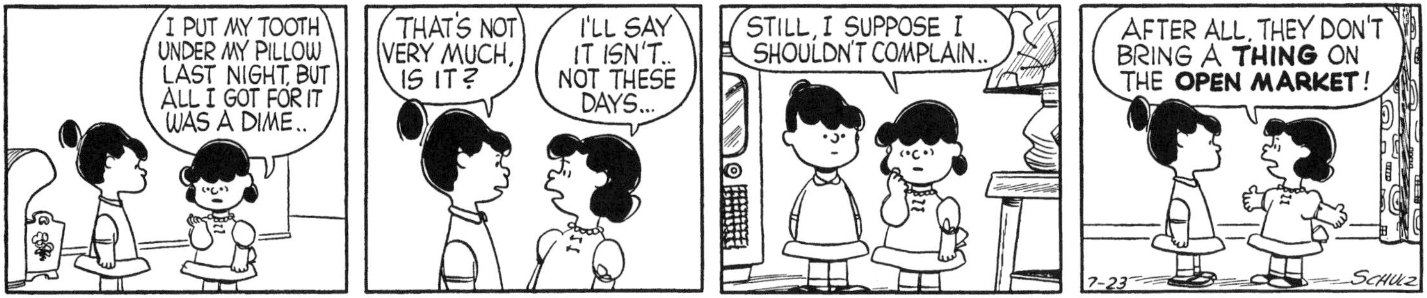
I PUT MY TOOTH UNDER MY PILLOW LAST NIGHT, BUT ALL I GOT FOR IT WAS A DIME..
THAT'S NOT VERY MUCH, IS IT?
I'LL SAY IT ISN'T.. NOT THESE DAYS...
STILL, I SUPPOSE I SHOULDN'T COMPLAIN..
AFTER ALL, THEY DON'T BRING A THING ON THE OPEN MARKET!
7-23
SCHULZ

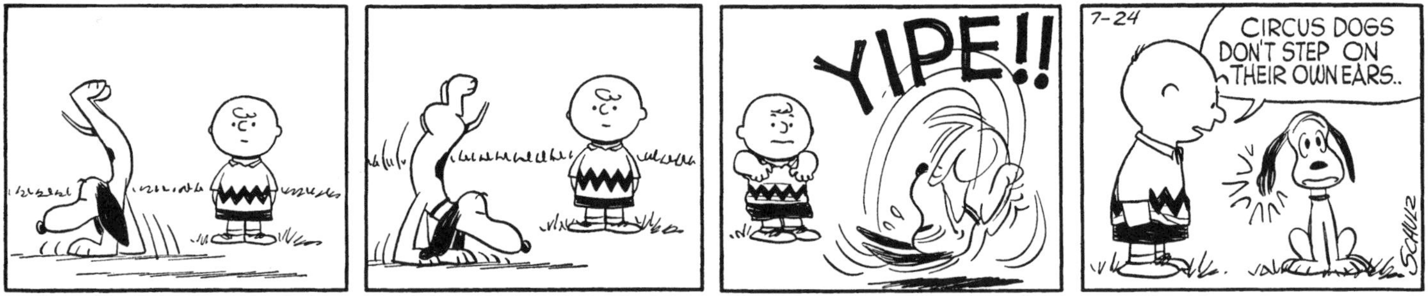
YIPE!!
7-24
CIRCUS DOGS DON'T STEP ON THEIR OWN EARS..
SCHULZ

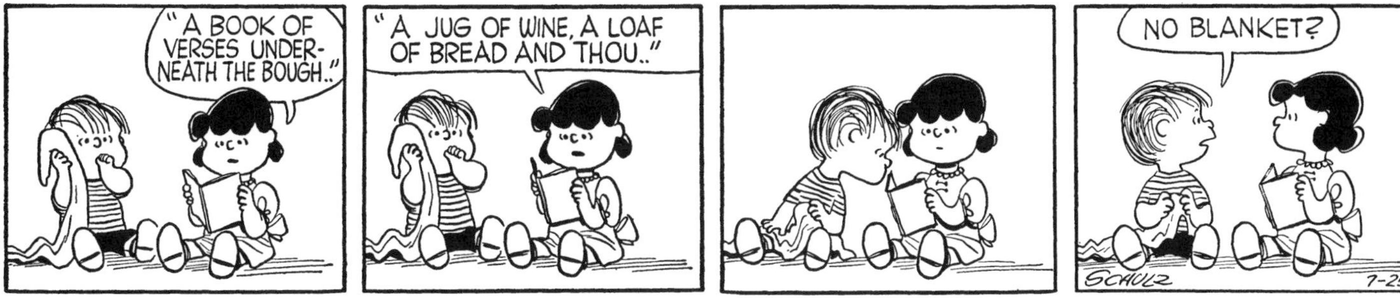
"A BOOK OF VERSES UNDERNEATH THE BOUGH.."
"A JUG OF WINE, A LOAF OF BREAD AND THOU.."
NO BLANKET?
SCHULZ
7-25

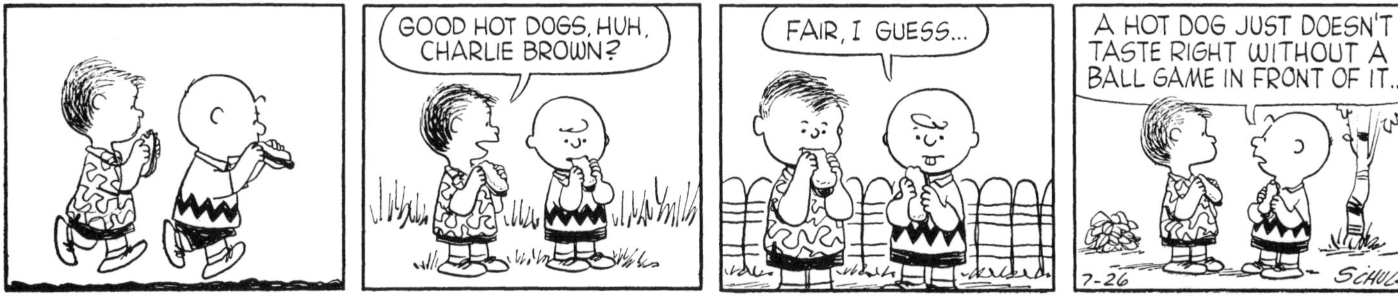
GOOD HOT DOGS, HUH, CHARLIE BROWN?
FAIR, I GUESS...
A HOT DOG JUST DOESN'T TASTE RIGHT WITHOUT A BALL GAME IN FRONT OF IT..
7-26
SCHULZ

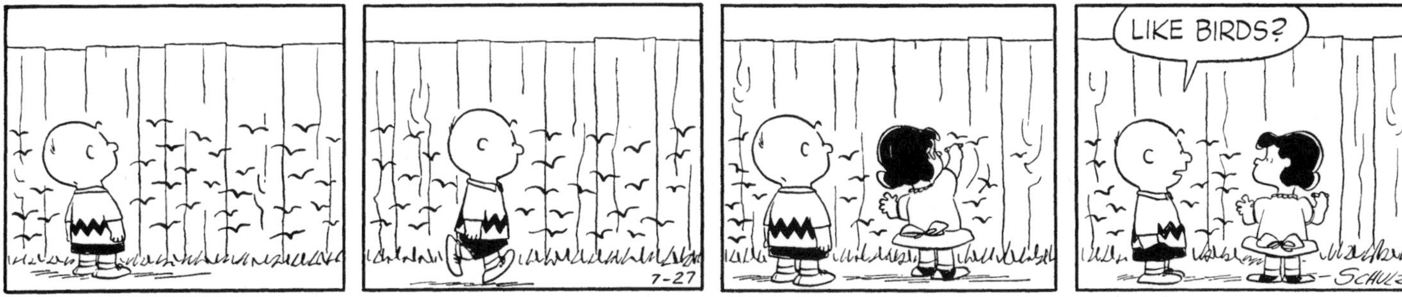
7-27
LIKE BIRDS?
SCHULZ

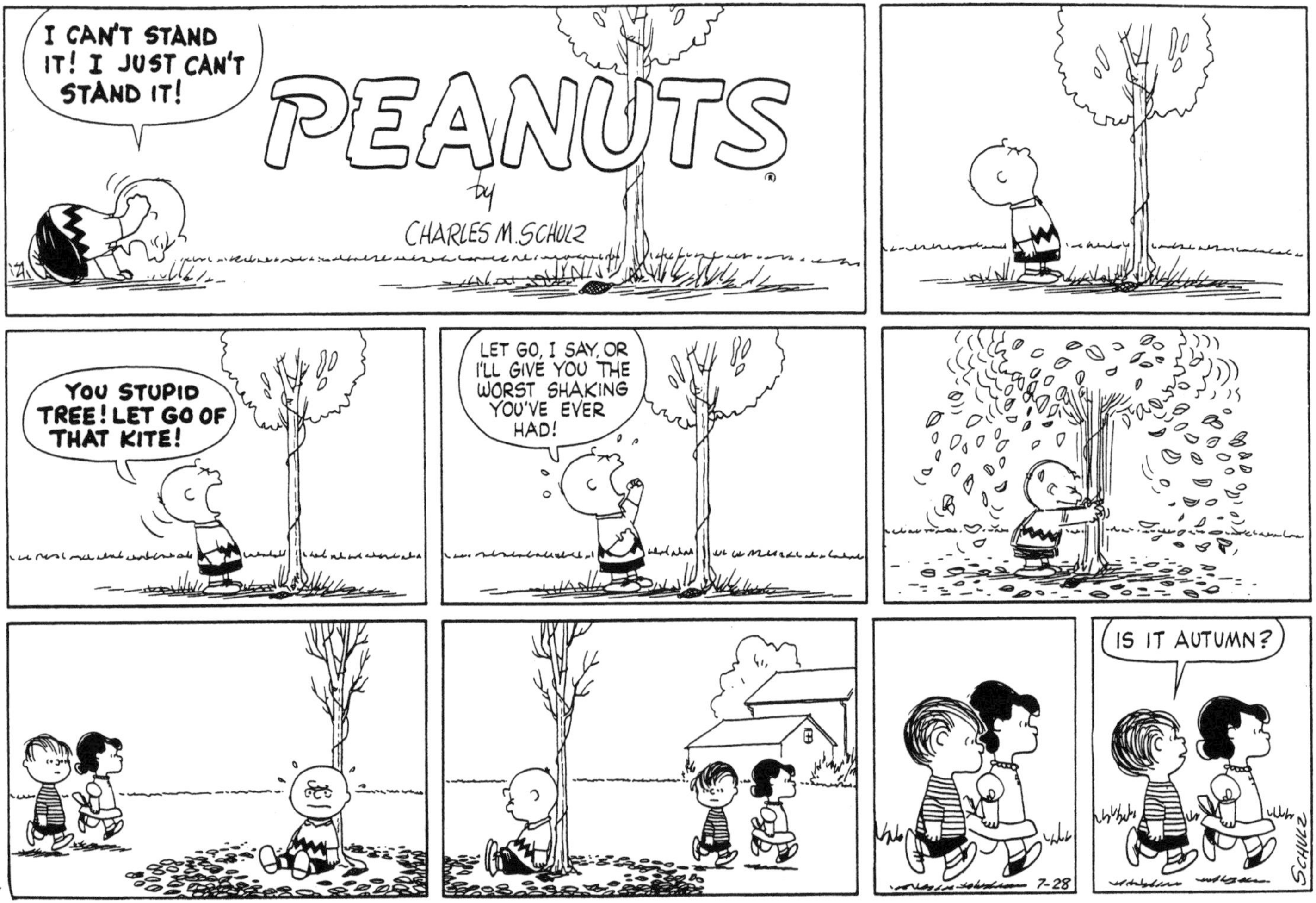
I CAN'T STAND IT! I JUST CAN'T STAND IT!
PEANUTS
by CHARLES M. SCHULZ
YOU STUPID TREE! LET GO OF THAT KITE!
LET GO, I SAY, OR I'LL GIVE YOU THE WORST SHAKING YOU'VE EVER HAD!
7-28
IS IT AUTUMN?
SCHULZ

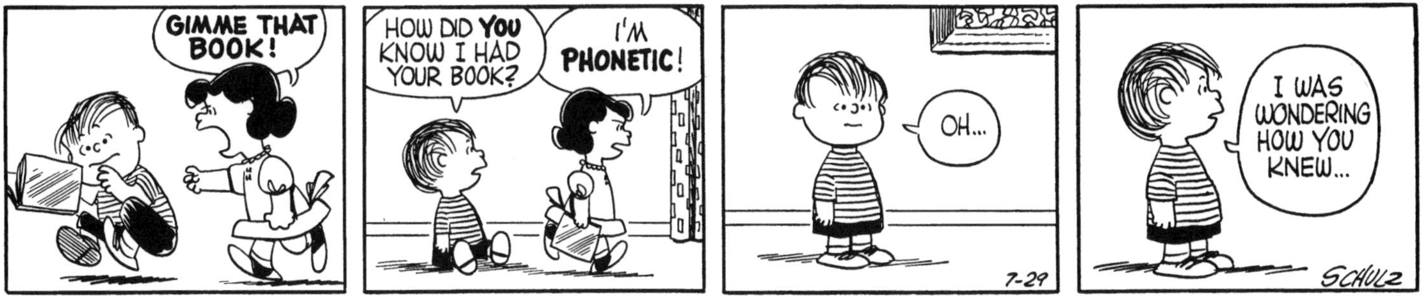
GIMME THAT BOOK!
HOW DID **YOU** KNOW I HAD YOUR BOOK?
I'M **PHONETIC**!
OH...
I WAS WONDERING HOW YOU KNEW...
7-29
SCHULZ

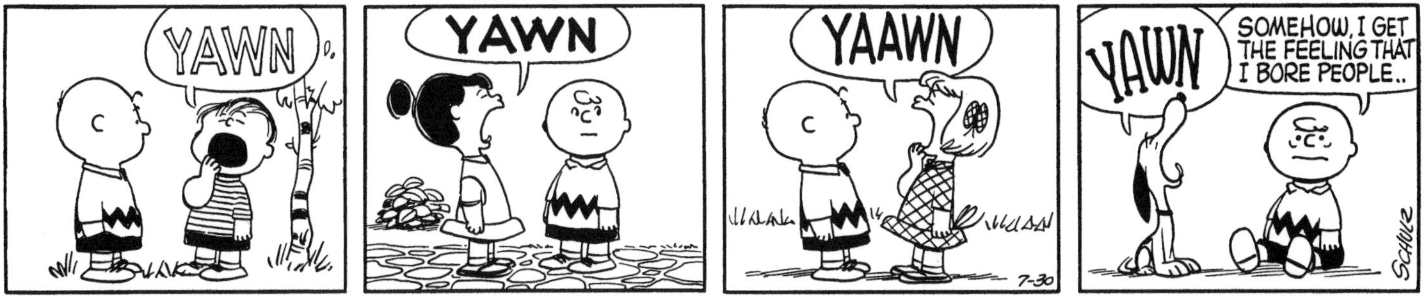
YAWN
YAWN
YAAWN
YAWN
SOMEHOW, I GET THE FEELING THAT I BORE PEOPLE..
7-30
SCHULZ

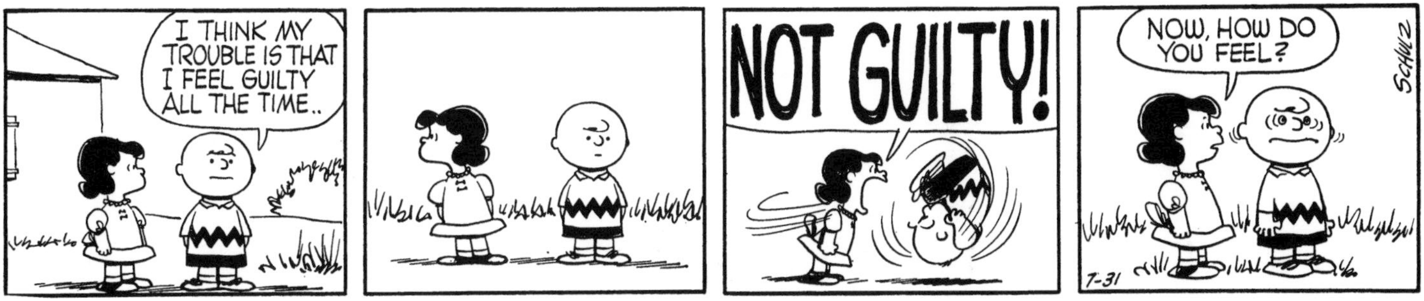
I THINK MY TROUBLE IS THAT I FEEL GUILTY ALL THE TIME..
NOT GUILTY!
NOW, HOW DO YOU FEEL?
7-31
SCHULZ

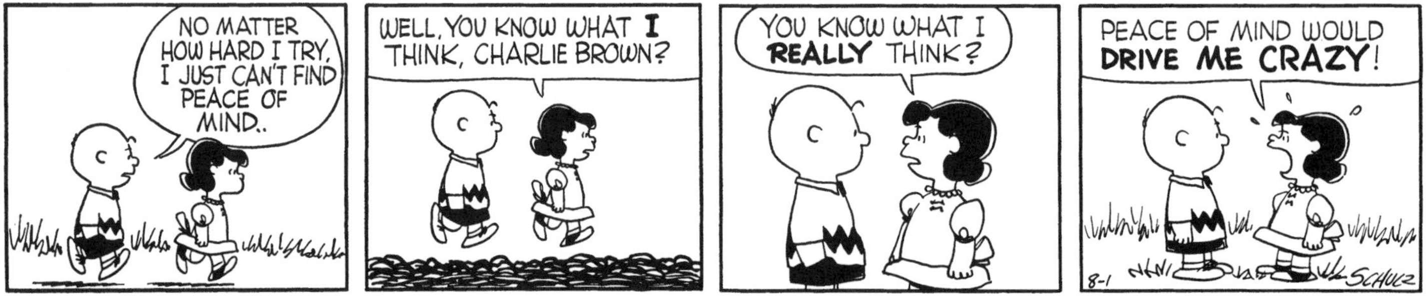
NO MATTER HOW HARD I TRY, I JUST CAN'T FIND PEACE OF MIND..
WELL, YOU KNOW WHAT I THINK, CHARLIE BROWN?
YOU KNOW WHAT I REALLY THINK?
PEACE OF MIND WOULD DRIVE ME CRAZY!
8-1
SCHULZ

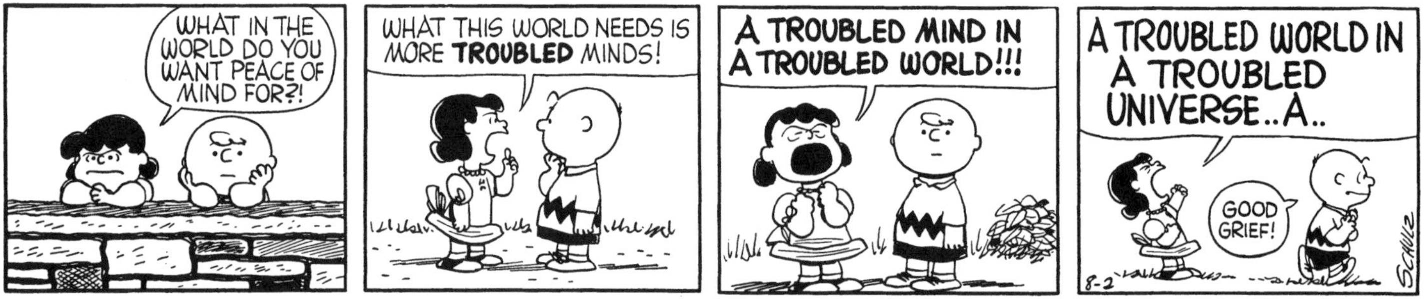
WHAT IN THE WORLD DO YOU WANT PEACE OF MIND FOR?!
WHAT THIS WORLD NEEDS IS MORE TROUBLED MINDS!
A TROUBLED MIND IN A TROUBLED WORLD!!!
A TROUBLED WORLD IN A TROUBLED UNIVERSE..A..
GOOD GRIEF!
8-2
SCHULZ

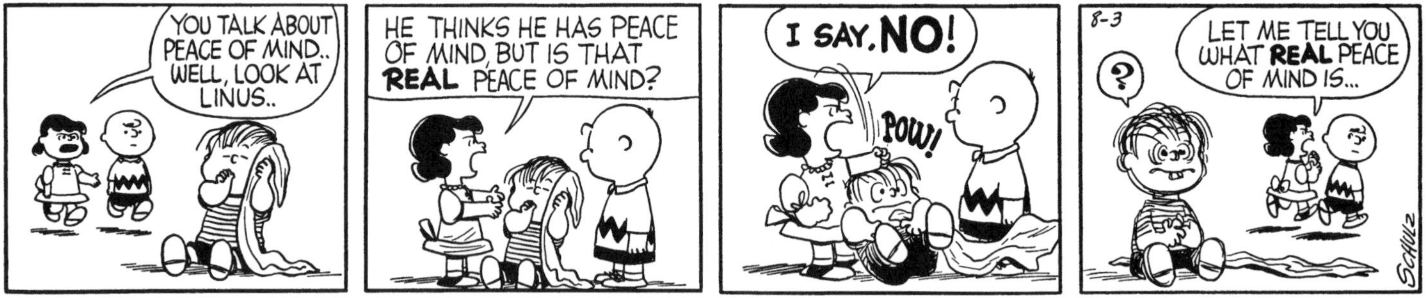
YOU TALK ABOUT PEACE OF MIND.. WELL, LOOK AT LINUS..
HE THINKS HE HAS PEACE OF MIND, BUT IS THAT REAL PEACE OF MIND?
I SAY, NO!
POW!
8-3
?
LET ME TELL YOU WHAT REAL PEACE OF MIND IS...
SCHULZ

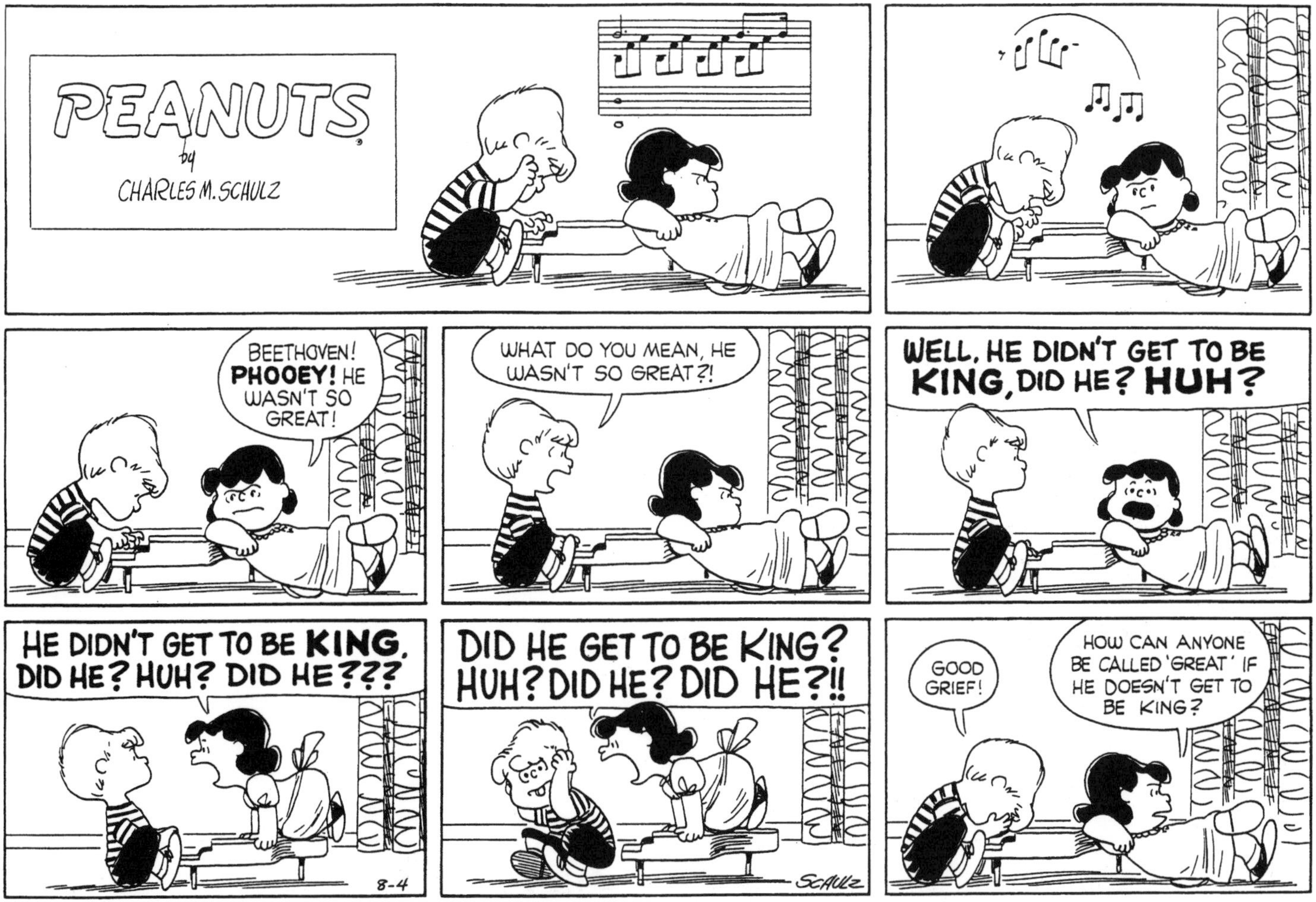
PEANUTS
by
CHARLES M. SCHULZ
BEETHOVEN! PHOOEY! HE WASN'T SO GREAT!
WHAT DO YOU MEAN, HE WASN'T SO GREAT?!
WELL, HE DIDN'T GET TO BE KING, DID HE? HUH?
HE DIDN'T GET TO BE KING, DID HE? HUH? DID HE???
8-4
DID HE GET TO BE KING? HUH? DID HE? DID HE?!!
SCHULZ
GOOD GRIEF!
HOW CAN ANYONE BE CALLED 'GREAT' IF HE DOESN'T GET TO BE KING?

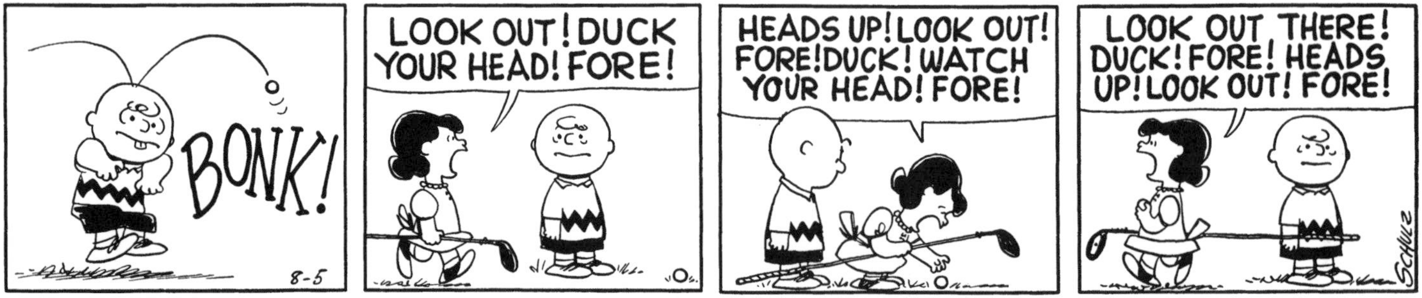
BONK!
8-5
LOOK OUT! DUCK YOUR HEAD! FORE!
HEADS UP! LOOK OUT! FORE! DUCK! WATCH YOUR HEAD! FORE!
LOOK OUT THERE! DUCK! FORE! HEADS UP! LOOK OUT! FORE!
SCHULZ

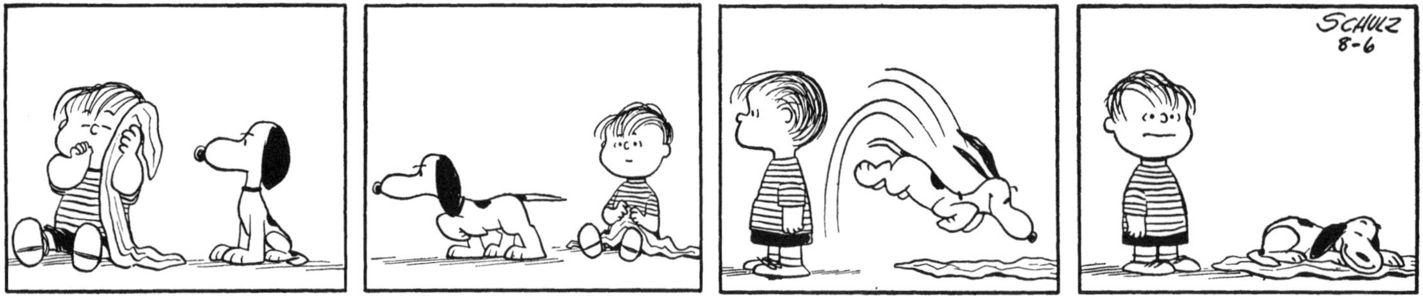
SCHULZ
8-6

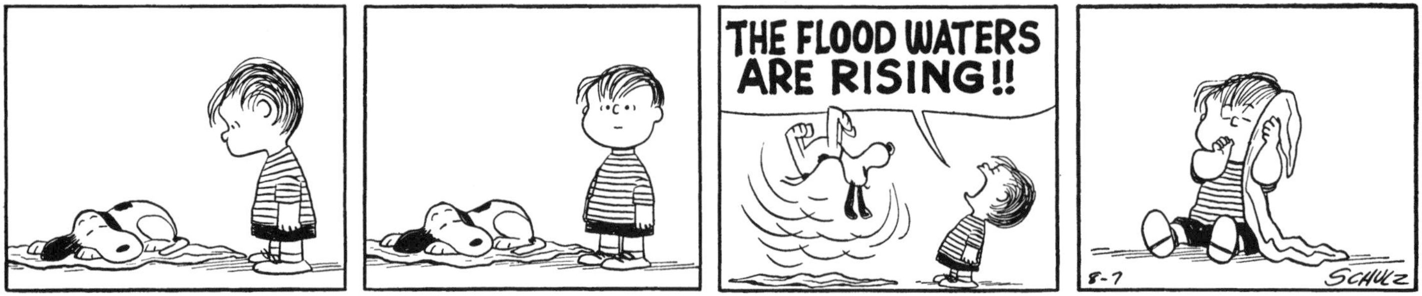
THE FLOOD WATERS ARE RISING!!
8-7
SCHULZ

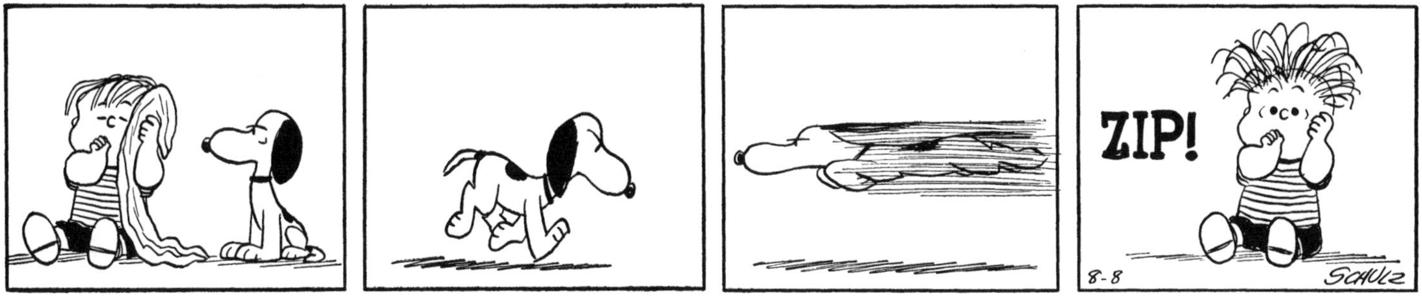
ZIP!
8-8
SCHULZ

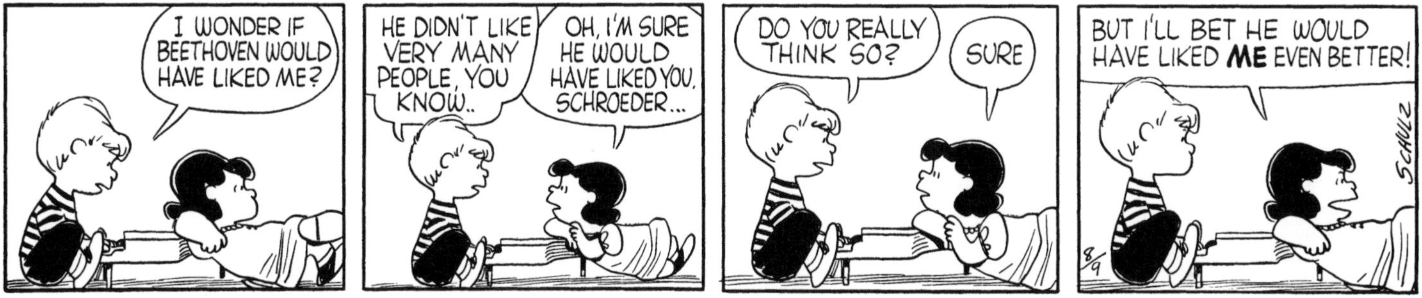
I WONDER IF BEETHOVEN WOULD HAVE LIKED ME?
HE DIDN'T LIKE VERY MANY PEOPLE, YOU KNOW..
OH, I'M SURE HE WOULD HAVE LIKED YOU, SCHROEDER...
DO YOU REALLY THINK SO?
SURE
BUT I'LL BET HE WOULD HAVE LIKED **ME** EVEN BETTER!
SCHULZ
8/9

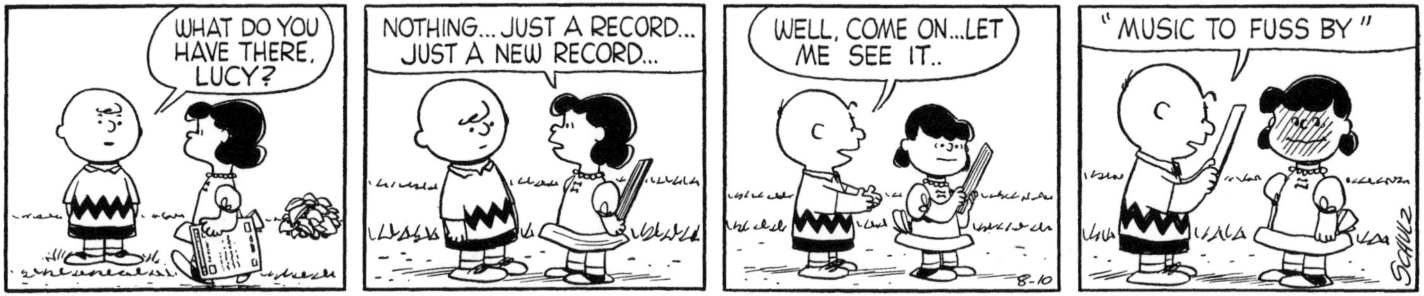
WHAT DO YOU HAVE THERE, LUCY?
NOTHING... JUST A RECORD... JUST A NEW RECORD...
WELL, COME ON...LET ME SEE IT..
8-10
" MUSIC TO FUSS BY "
SCHULZ

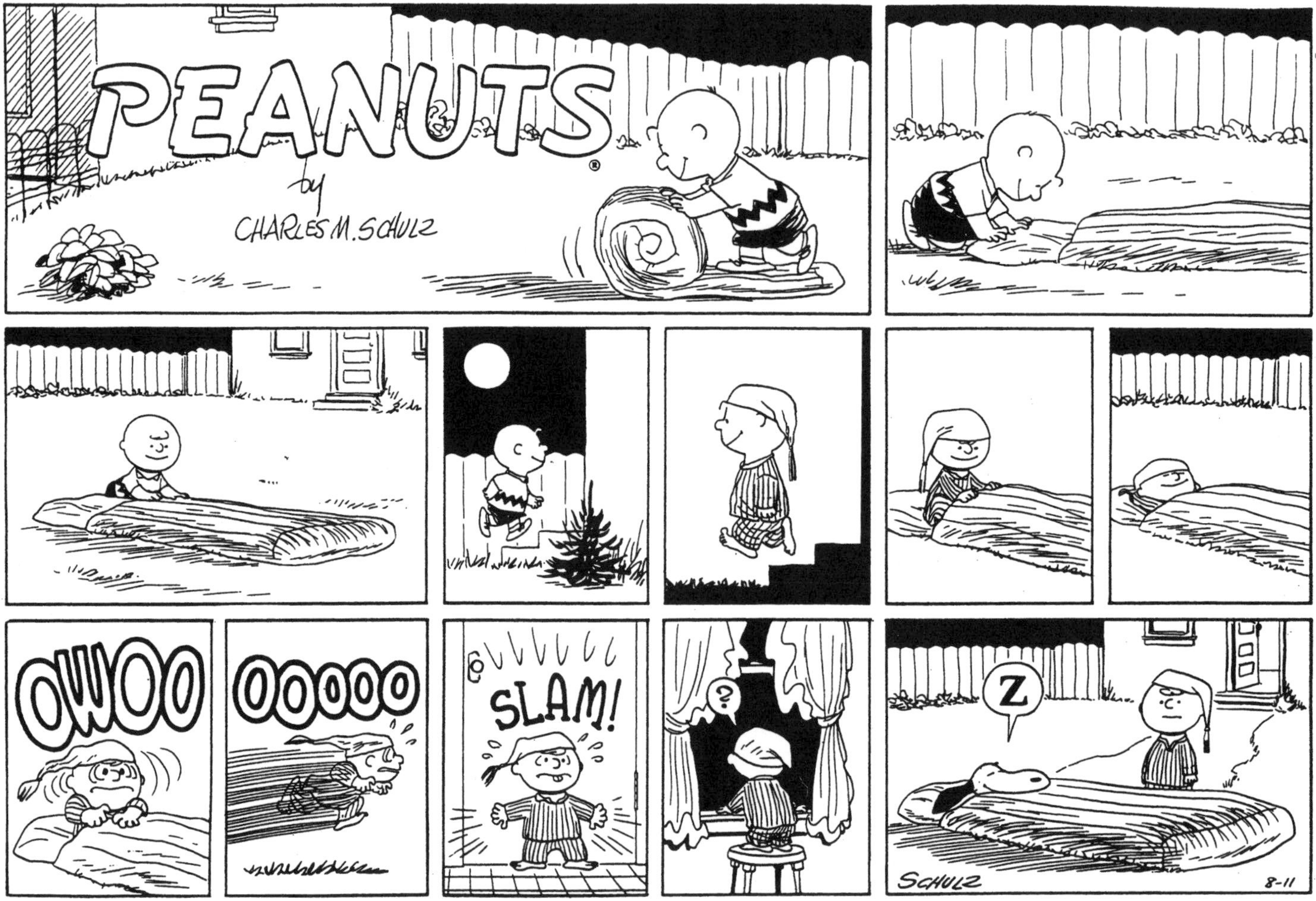
PEANUTS
by CHARLES M. SCHULZ
OWOO
OOOOO
SLAM!
?
Z
SCHULZ
8-11

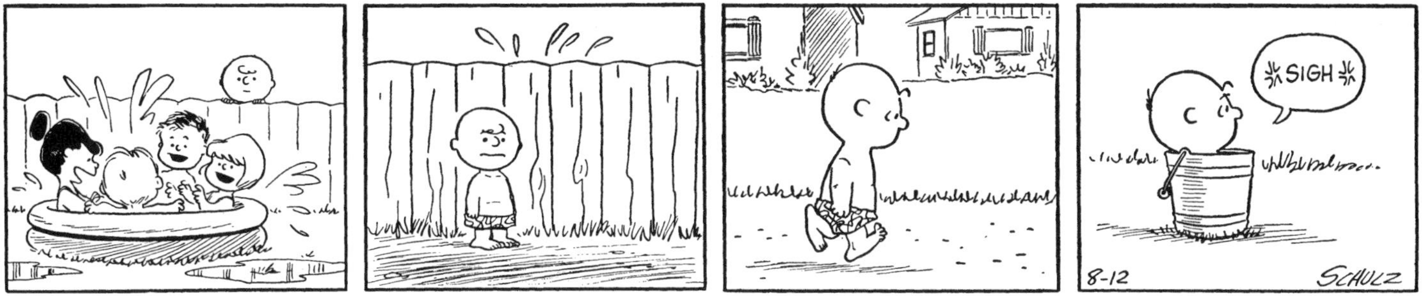
SIGH
8-12
SCHULZ

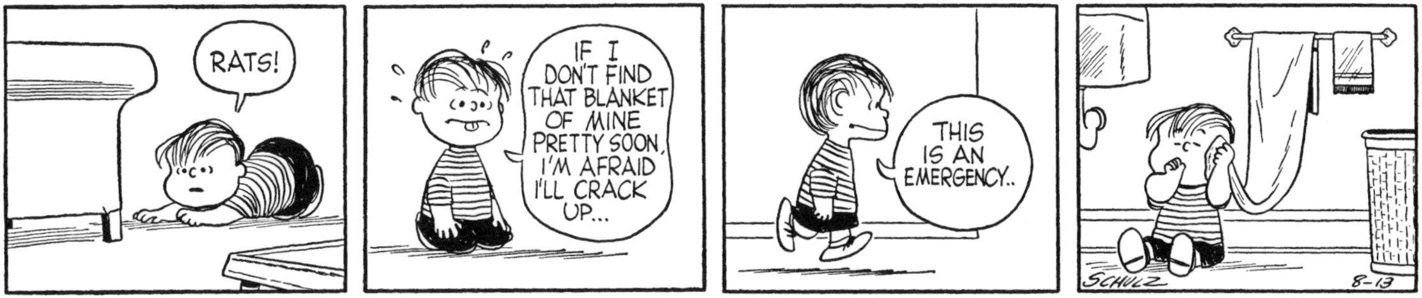
RATS!
IF I DON'T FIND THAT BLANKET OF MINE PRETTY SOON, I'M AFRAID I'LL CRACK UP...
THIS IS AN EMERGENCY..
SCHULZ
8-13

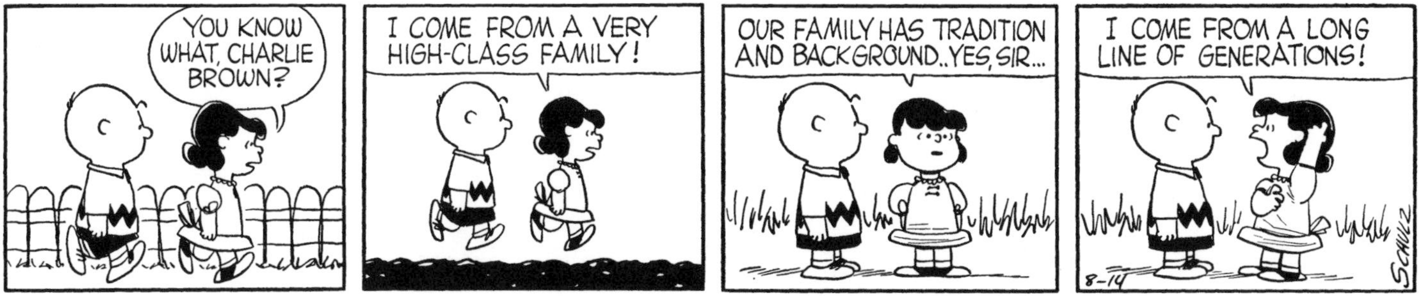
YOU KNOW WHAT, CHARLIE BROWN?
I COME FROM A VERY HIGH-CLASS FAMILY!
OUR FAMILY HAS TRADITION AND BACKGROUND..YES, SIR...
I COME FROM A LONG LINE OF GENERATIONS!
8-14
SCHULZ

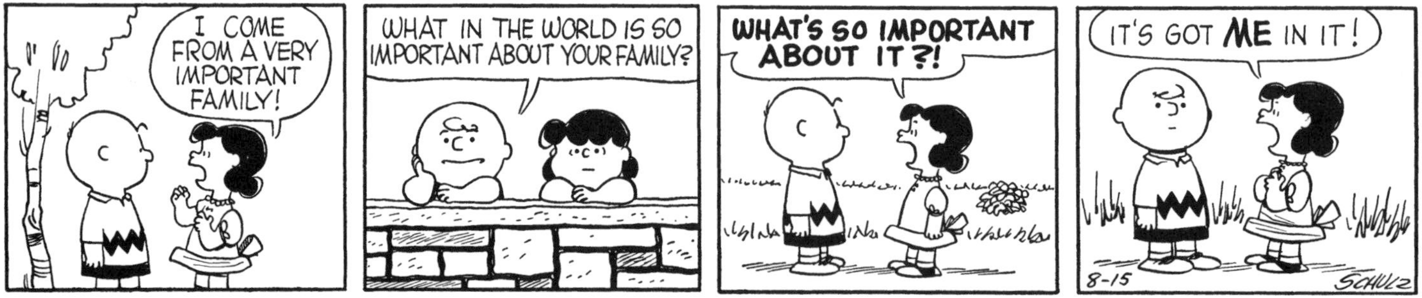
I COME FROM A VERY IMPORTANT FAMILY!
WHAT IN THE WORLD IS SO IMPORTANT ABOUT YOUR FAMILY?
WHAT'S SO IMPORTANT ABOUT IT?!
IT'S GOT ME IN IT!
8-15
SCHULZ

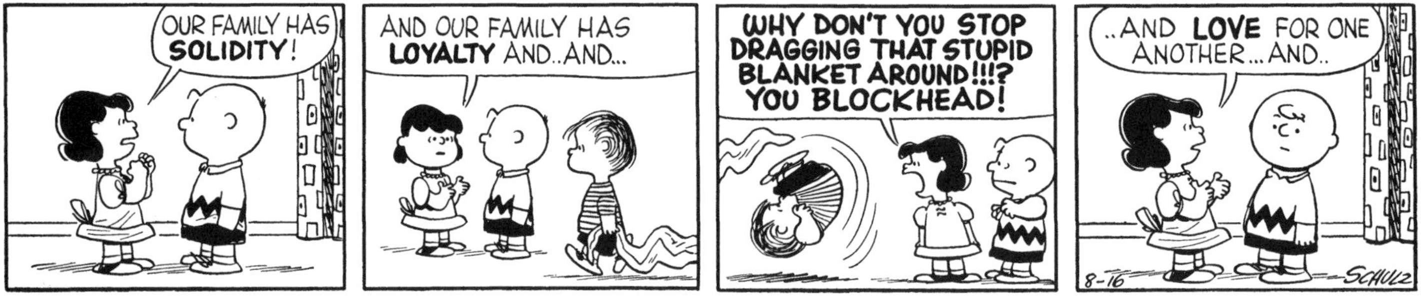
OUR FAMILY HAS SOLIDITY!
AND OUR FAMILY HAS LOYALTY AND..AND...
WHY DON'T YOU STOP DRAGGING THAT STUPID BLANKET AROUND!!!? YOU BLOCKHEAD!
..AND LOVE FOR ONE ANOTHER...AND..
8-16
SCHULZ

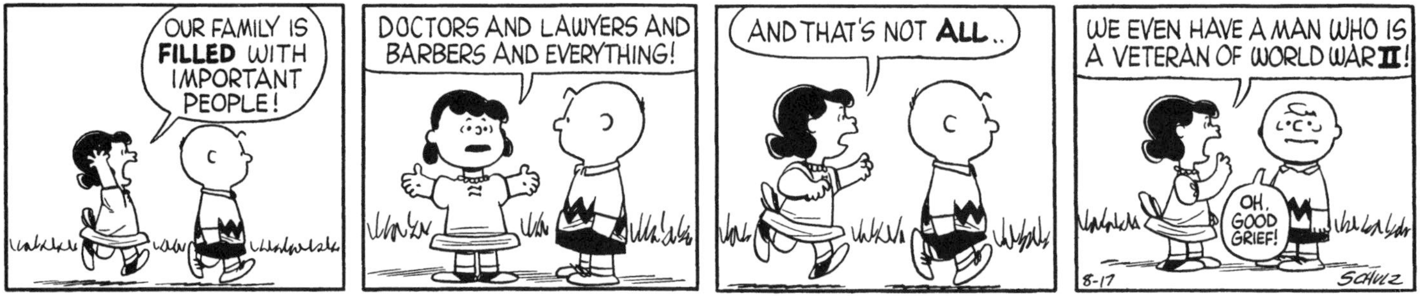
OUR FAMILY IS FILLED WITH IMPORTANT PEOPLE!
DOCTORS AND LAWYERS AND BARBERS AND EVERYTHING!
AND THAT'S NOT ALL..
WE EVEN HAVE A MAN WHO IS A VETERAN OF WORLD WAR II!
OH, GOOD GRIEF!
8-17
SCHULZ

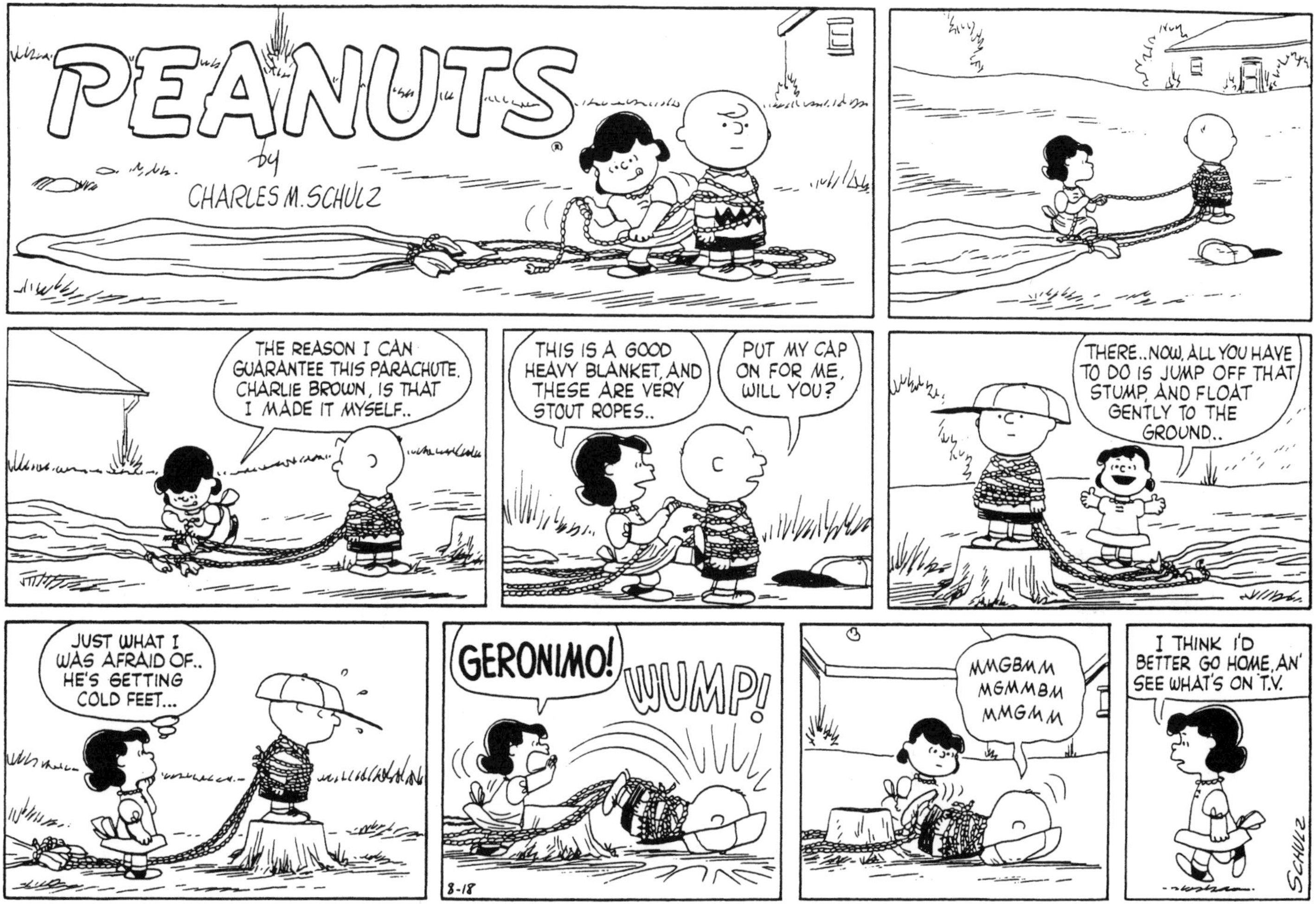
PEANUTS
by CHARLES M. SCHULZ
THE REASON I CAN GUARANTEE THIS PARACHUTE, CHARLIE BROWN, IS THAT I MADE IT MYSELF..
THIS IS A GOOD HEAVY BLANKET, AND THESE ARE VERY STOUT ROPES..
PUT MY CAP ON FOR ME, WILL YOU?
THERE..NOW, ALL YOU HAVE TO DO IS JUMP OFF THAT STUMP, AND FLOAT GENTLY TO THE GROUND..
JUST WHAT I WAS AFRAID OF.. HE'S GETTING COLD FEET...
GERONIMO!
WUMP!
8-18
MMGBMM MGMMBM MMGMM
I THINK I'D BETTER GO HOME, AN' SEE WHAT'S ON T.V.
SCHULZ

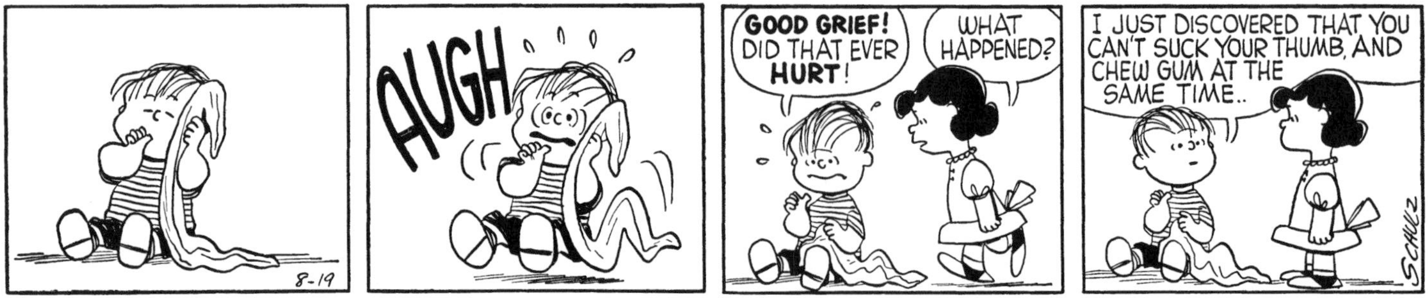
AUGH
GOOD GRIEF! DID THAT EVER HURT!
WHAT HAPPENED?
I JUST DISCOVERED THAT YOU CAN'T SUCK YOUR THUMB, AND CHEW GUM AT THE SAME TIME..
8-19
SCHULZ

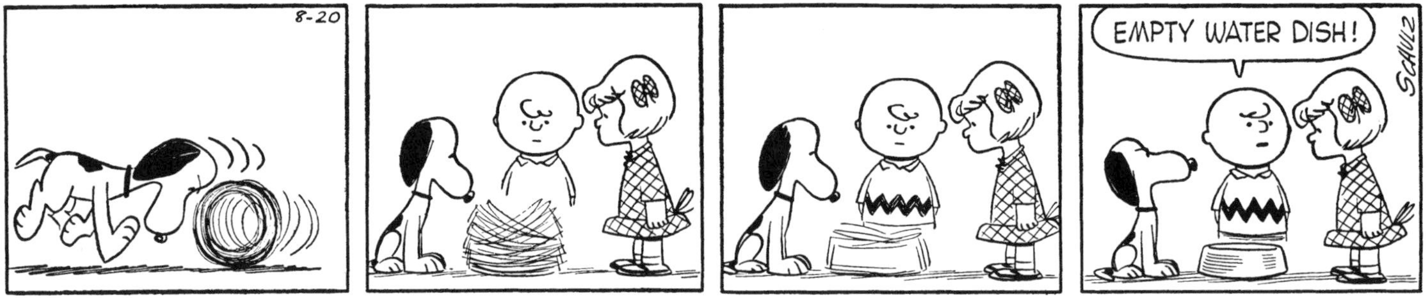
8-20
EMPTY WATER DISH!
SCHULZ

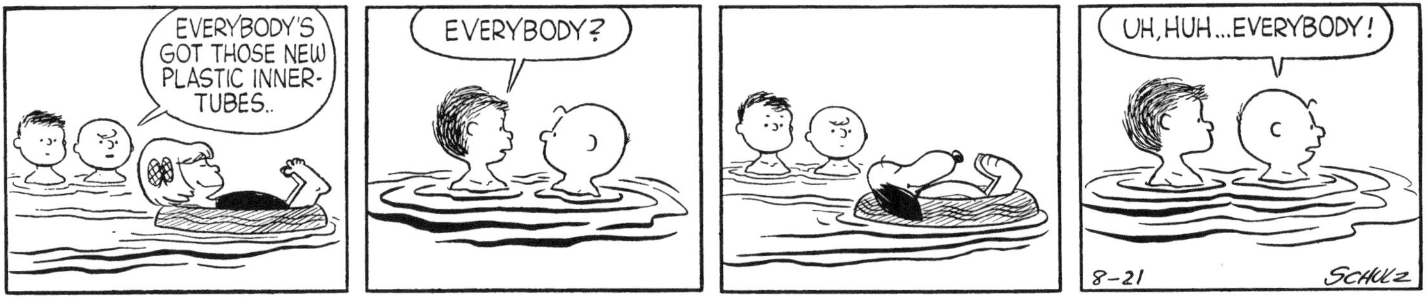
EVERYBODY'S GOT THOSE NEW PLASTIC INNER-TUBES..
EVERYBODY?
UH, HUH...EVERYBODY!
8-21
SCHULZ

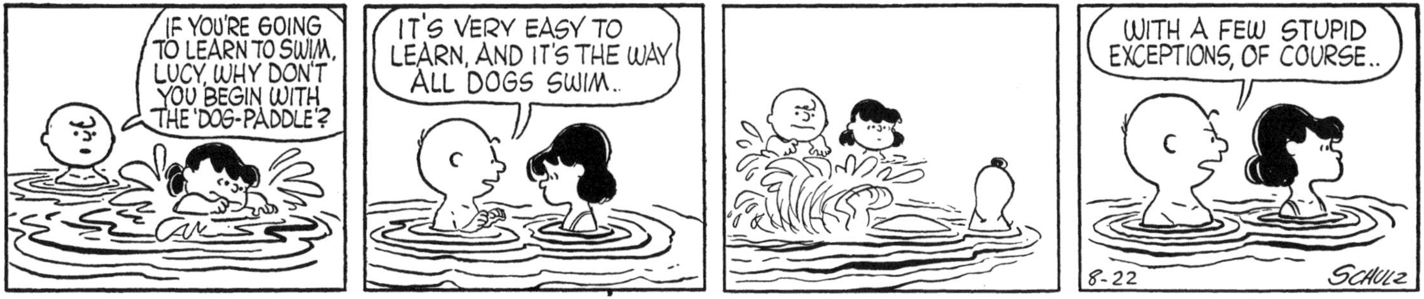
IF YOU'RE GOING TO LEARN TO SWIM, LUCY, WHY DON'T YOU BEGIN WITH THE 'DOG-PADDLE'?
IT'S VERY EASY TO LEARN, AND IT'S THE WAY ALL DOGS SWIM..
WITH A FEW STUPID EXCEPTIONS, OF COURSE..
8-22
SCHULZ

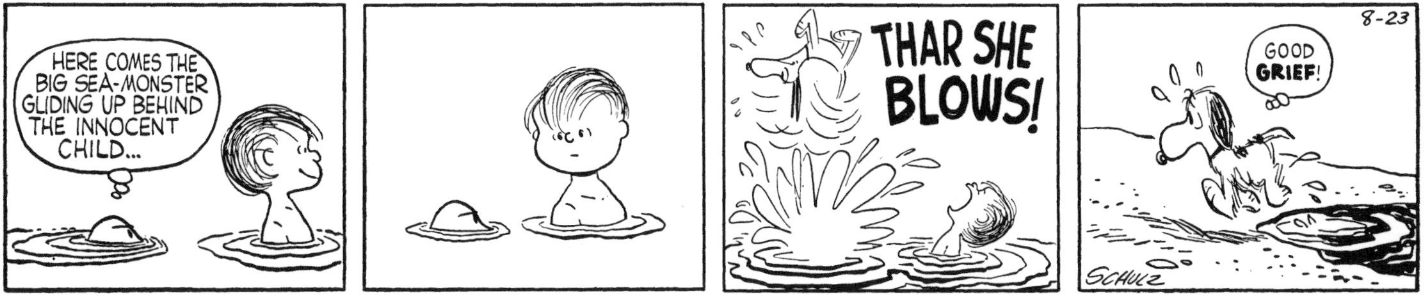
HERE COMES THE BIG SEA-MONSTER GLIDING UP BEHIND THE INNOCENT CHILD...
THAR SHE BLOWS!
8-23
GOOD GRIEF!
SCHULZ

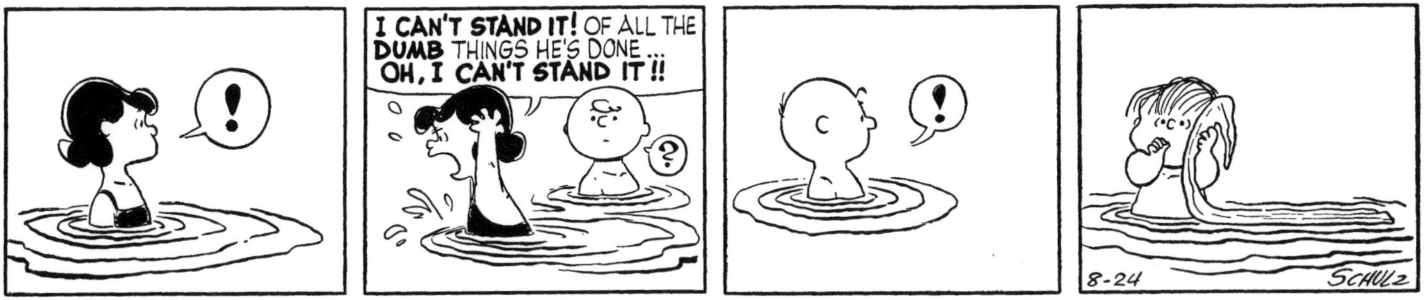
!
I CAN'T STAND IT! OF ALL THE DUMB THINGS HE'S DONE... OH, I CAN'T STAND IT!!
?
!
8-24
SCHULZ

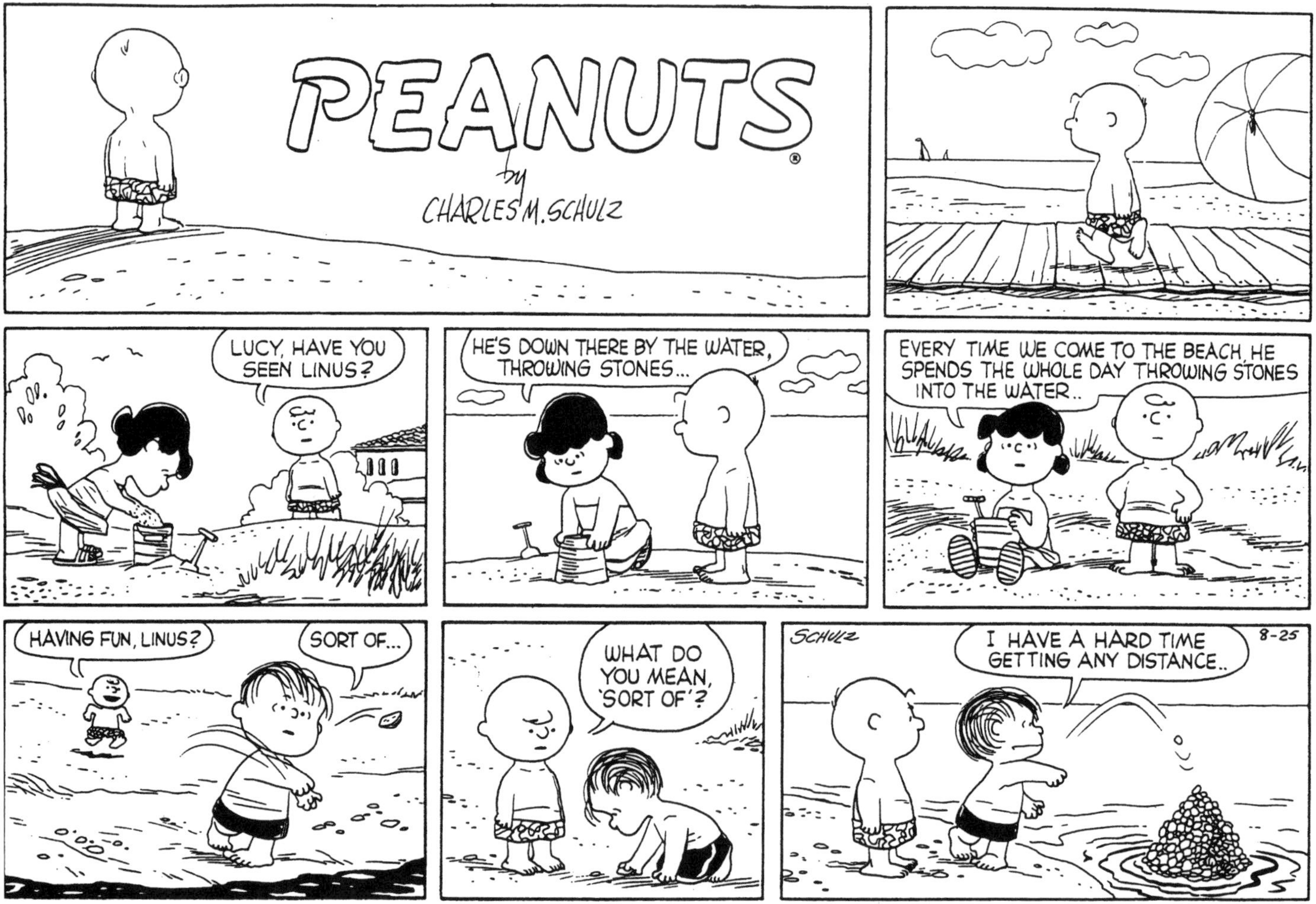
PEANUTS
by CHARLES M. SCHULZ
LUCY, HAVE YOU SEEN LINUS?
HE'S DOWN THERE BY THE WATER, THROWING STONES...
EVERY TIME WE COME TO THE BEACH, HE SPENDS THE WHOLE DAY THROWING STONES INTO THE WATER..
HAVING FUN, LINUS?
SORT OF...
WHAT DO YOU MEAN, 'SORT OF'?
SCHULZ
8-25
I HAVE A HARD TIME GETTING ANY DISTANCE..

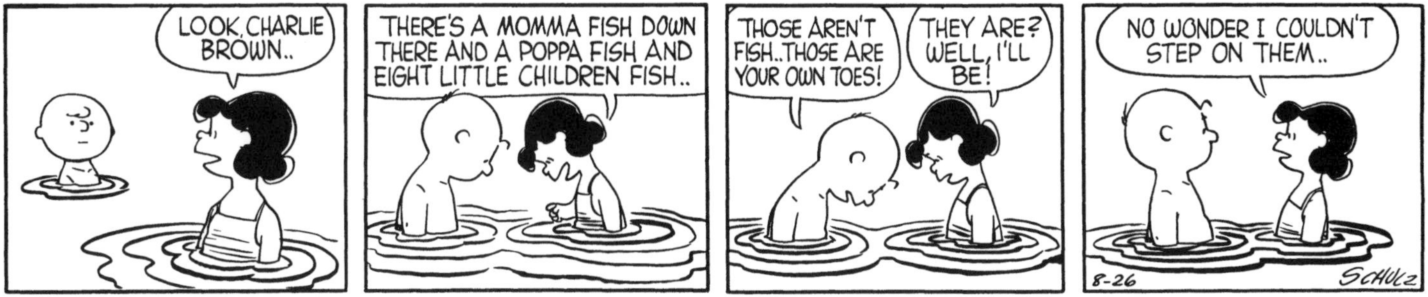
LOOK, CHARLIE BROWN..
THERE'S A MOMMA FISH DOWN THERE AND A POPPA FISH AND EIGHT LITTLE CHILDREN FISH..
THOSE AREN'T FISH..THOSE ARE YOUR OWN TOES!
THEY ARE? WELL, I'LL BE!
NO WONDER I COULDN'T STEP ON THEM..
8-26
SCHULZ

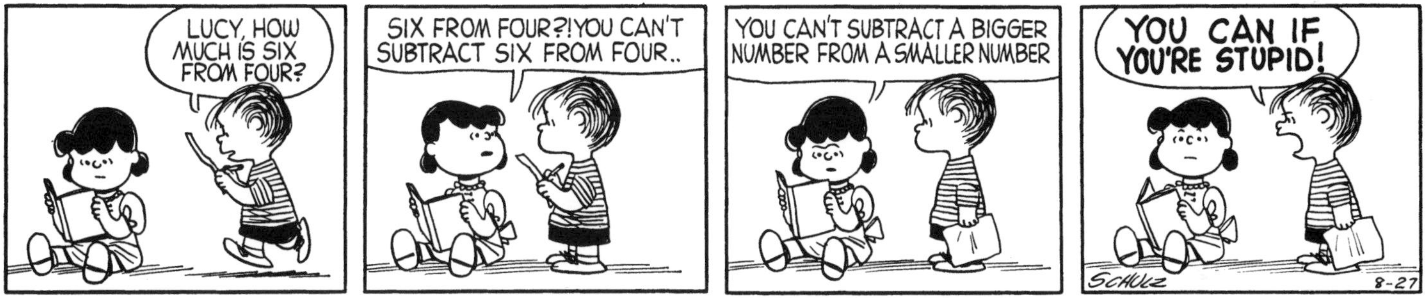
LUCY, HOW MUCH IS SIX FROM FOUR?
SIX FROM FOUR?! YOU CAN'T SUBTRACT SIX FROM FOUR..
YOU CAN'T SUBTRACT A BIGGER NUMBER FROM A SMALLER NUMBER
YOU CAN IF YOU'RE STUPID!
SCHULZ
8-27

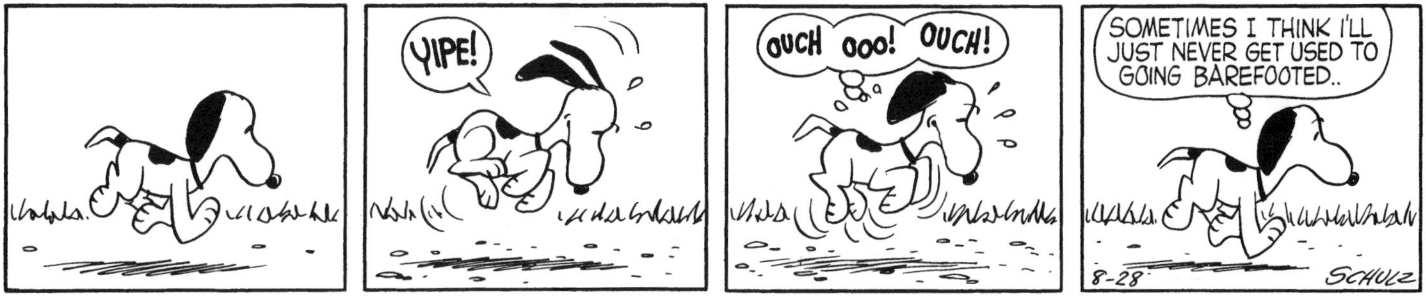
YIPE!
OUCH OOO! OUCH!
SOMETIMES I THINK I'LL JUST NEVER GET USED TO GOING BAREFOOTED..
8-28
SCHULZ

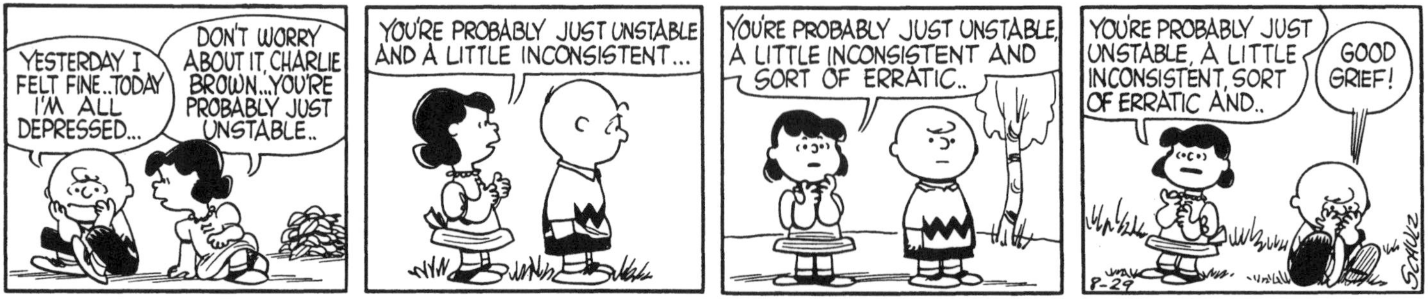
YESTERDAY I FELT FINE..TODAY I'M ALL DEPRESSED...
DON'T WORRY ABOUT IT, CHARLIE BROWN...YOU'RE PROBABLY JUST UNSTABLE..
YOU'RE PROBABLY JUST UNSTABLE AND A LITTLE INCONSISTENT...
YOU'RE PROBABLY JUST UNSTABLE, A LITTLE INCONSISTENT AND SORT OF ERRATIC..
YOU'RE PROBABLY JUST UNSTABLE, A LITTLE INCONSISTENT, SORT OF ERRATIC AND..
GOOD GRIEF!
8-29
SCHULZ

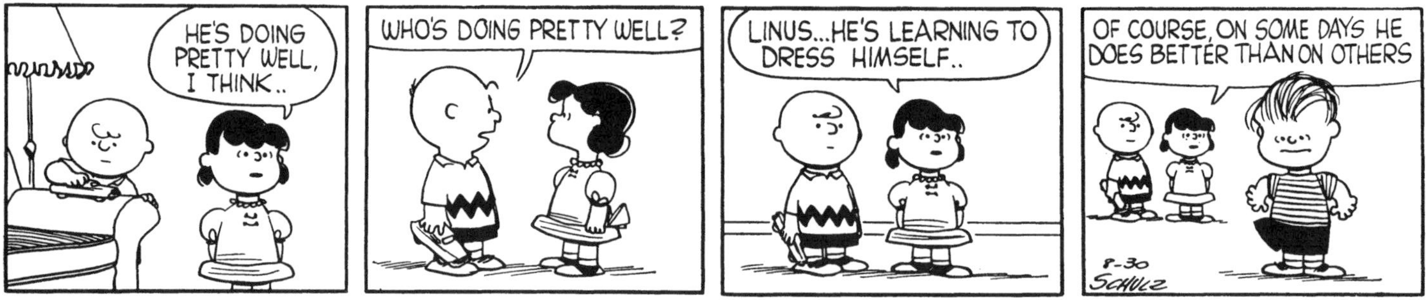
HE'S DOING PRETTY WELL, I THINK..
WHO'S DOING PRETTY WELL?
LINUS...HE'S LEARNING TO DRESS HIMSELF..
OF COURSE, ON SOME DAYS HE DOES BETTER THAN ON OTHERS
8-30
SCHULZ

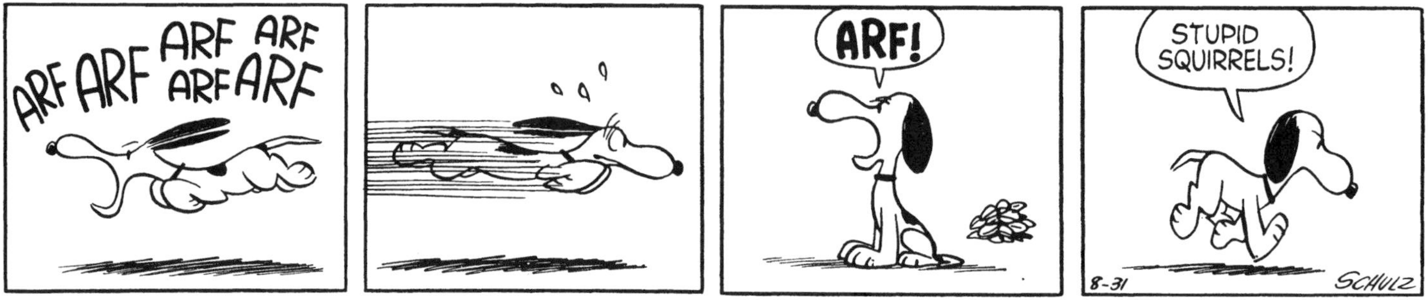
ARF ARF ARF ARF ARF ARF
ARF!
STUPID SQUIRRELS!
8-31
SCHULZ

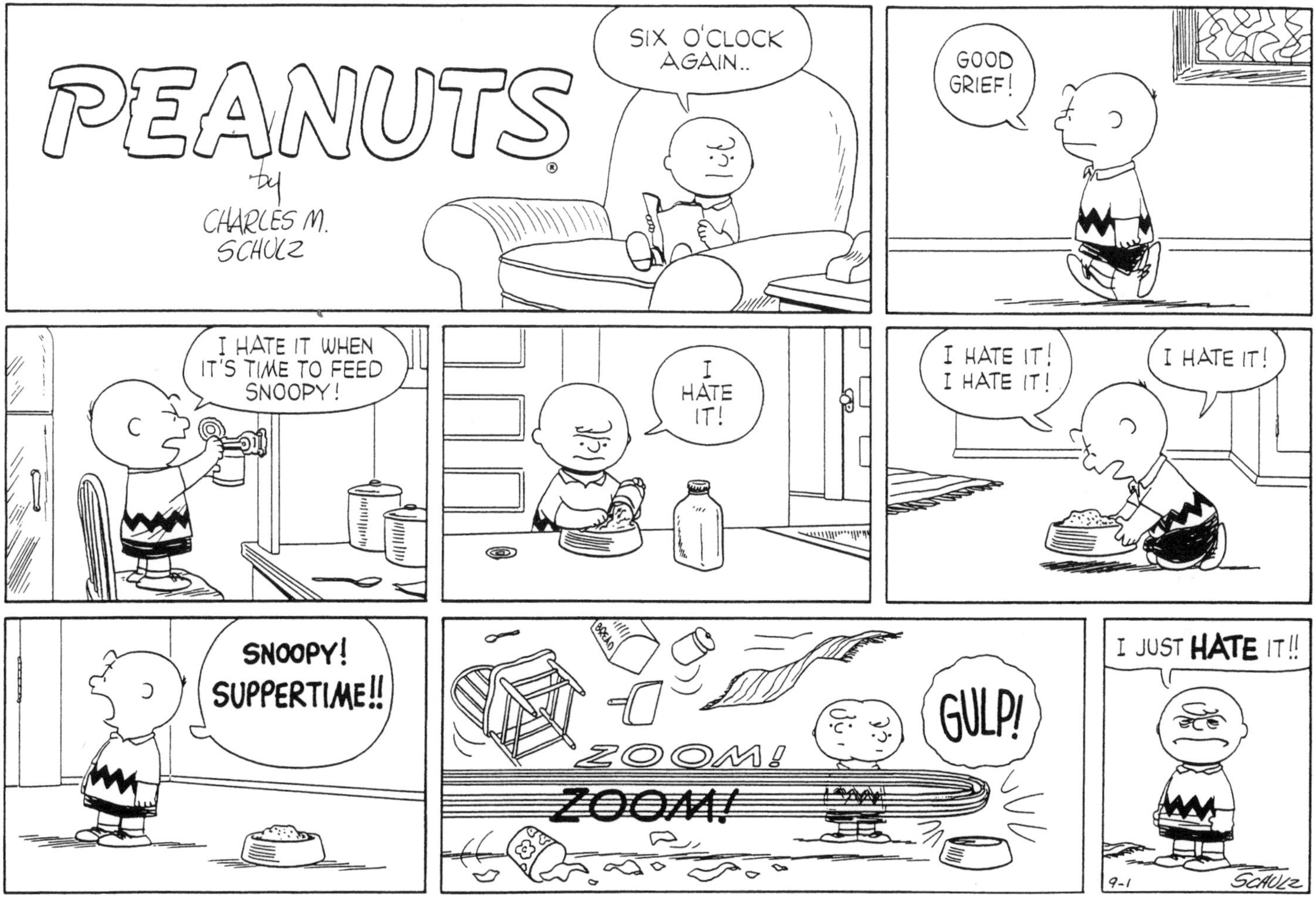
PEANUTS
by CHARLES M. SCHULZ
SIX O'CLOCK AGAIN..
GOOD GRIEF!
I HATE IT WHEN IT'S TIME TO FEED SNOOPY!
I HATE IT!
I HATE IT! I HATE IT!
I HATE IT!
SNOOPY! SUPPERTIME!!
BREAD
ZOOM!
ZOOM!
GULP!
I JUST HATE IT!!
9-1
SCHULZ

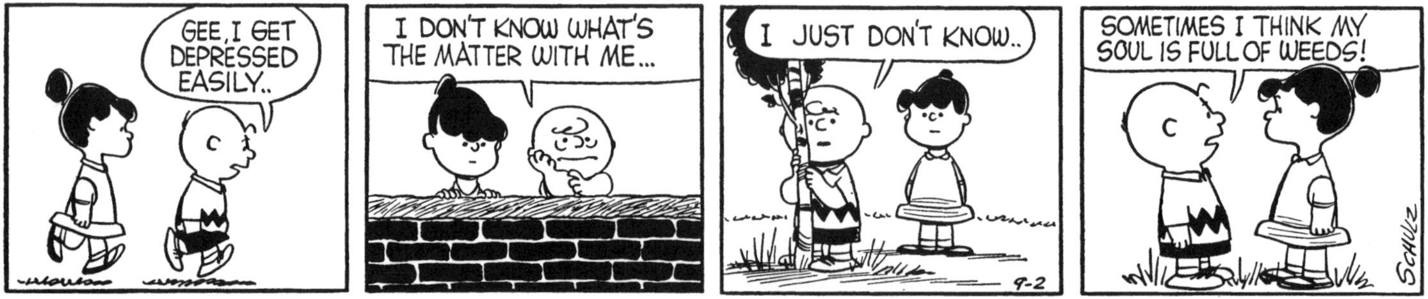
GEE, I GET DEPRESSED EASILY..
I DON'T KNOW WHAT'S THE MATTER WITH ME...
I JUST DON'T KNOW..
SOMETIMES I THINK MY SOUL IS FULL OF WEEDS!
9-2
SCHULZ

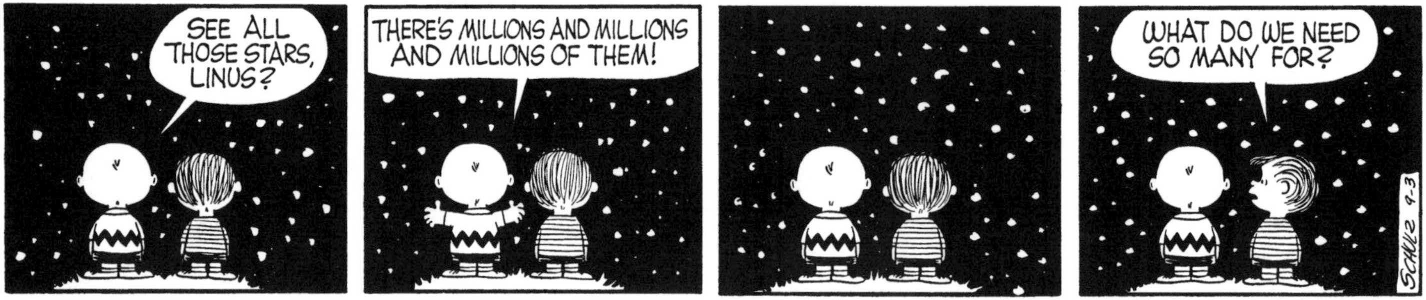
SEE ALL THOSE STARS, LINUS?
THERE'S MILLIONS AND MILLIONS AND MILLIONS OF THEM!
WHAT DO WE NEED SO MANY FOR?
SCHULZ 9-3

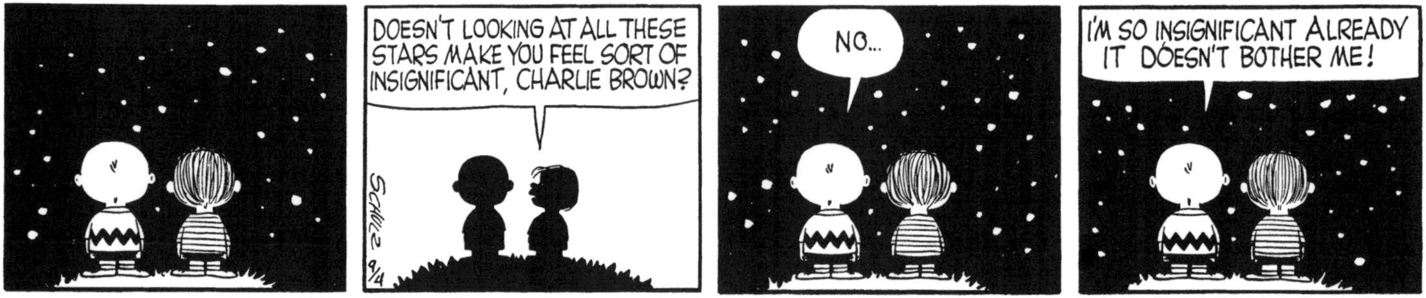
DOESN'T LOOKING AT ALL THESE STARS MAKE YOU FEEL SORT OF INSIGNIFICANT, CHARLIE BROWN?
SCHULZ 9/4
NO...
I'M SO INSIGNIFICANT ALREADY IT DOESN'T BOTHER ME!

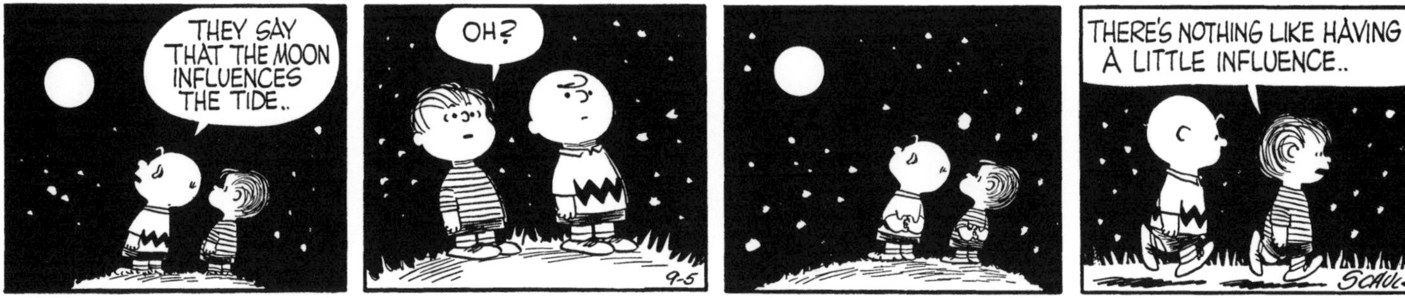
THEY SAY THAT THE MOON INFLUENCES THE TIDE..
OH?
THERE'S NOTHING LIKE HAVING A LITTLE INFLUENCE..

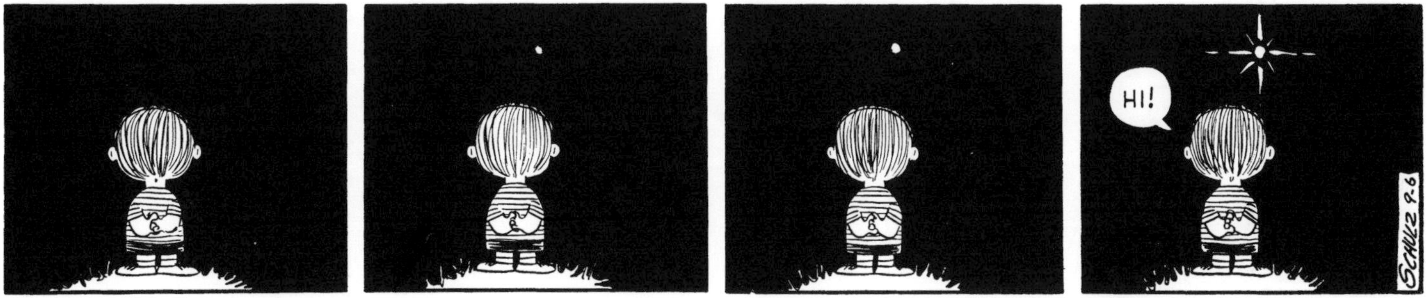
HI!

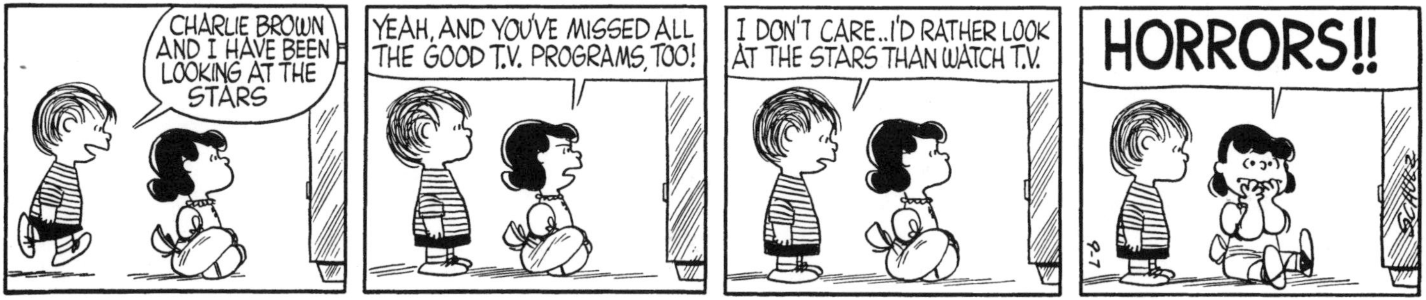
CHARLIE BROWN AND I HAVE BEEN LOOKING AT THE STARS
YEAH, AND YOU'VE MISSED ALL THE GOOD T.V. PROGRAMS, TOO!
I DON'T CARE..I'D RATHER LOOK AT THE STARS THAN WATCH T.V.
HORRORS!!

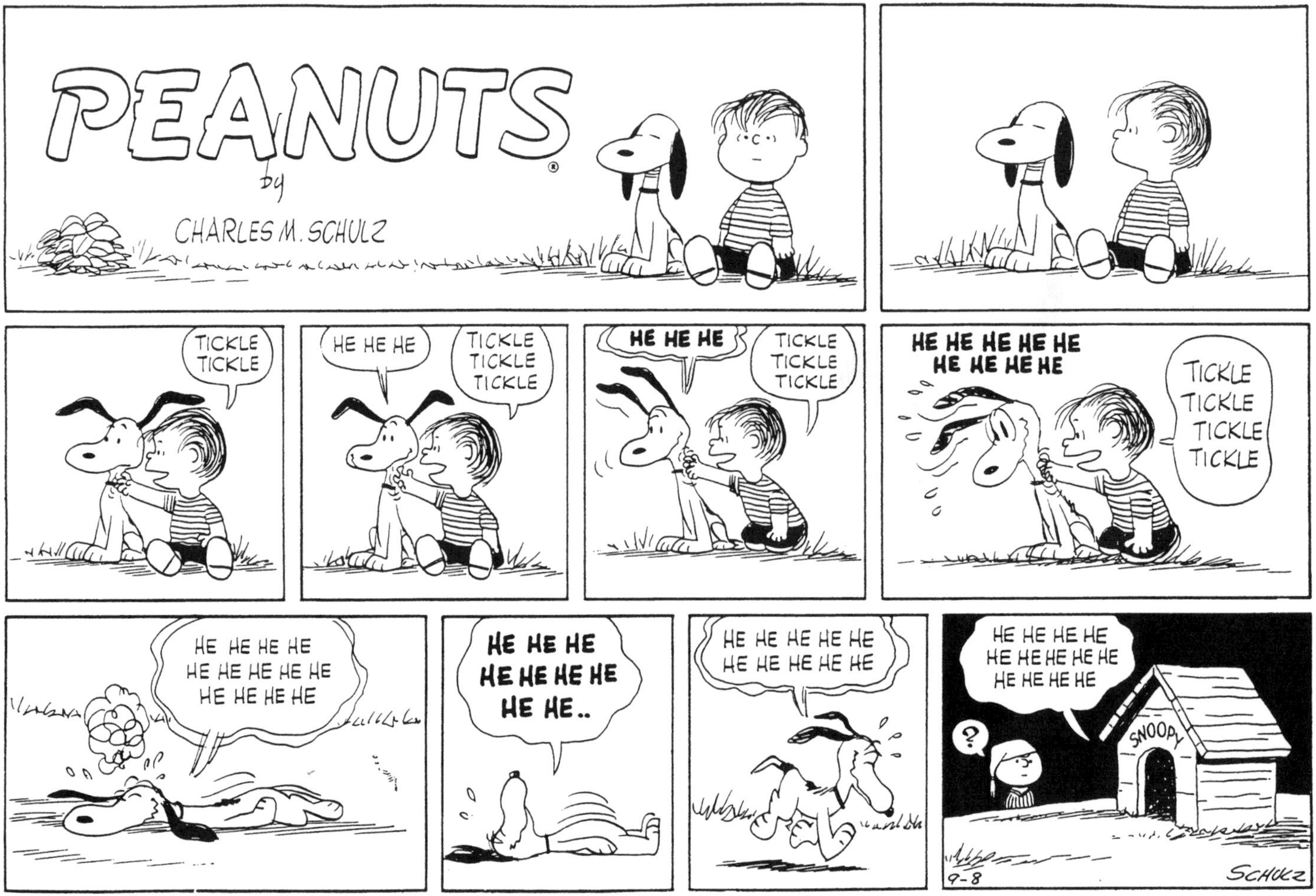
PEANUTS
by
CHARLES M. SCHULZ
TICKLE TICKLE
HE HE HE
TICKLE TICKLE TICKLE
HE HE HE
TICKLE TICKLE TICKLE
HE HE HE HE HE HE HE HE HE
TICKLE TICKLE TICKLE TICKLE
HE HE HE HE HE HE HE HE HE HE HE HE HE
HE HE HE HE HE HE HE HE HE..
HE HE HE HE HE HE HE HE HE HE
HE HE HE HE HE HE HE HE HE HE HE HE HE
?
SNOOPY
9-8
SCHULZ

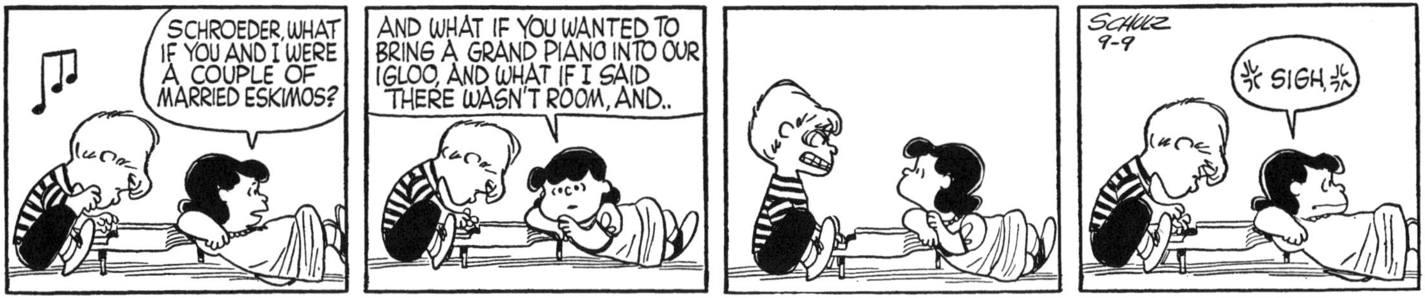
SCHROEDER, WHAT IF YOU AND I WERE A COUPLE OF MARRIED ESKIMOS?
AND WHAT IF YOU WANTED TO BRING A GRAND PIANO INTO OUR IGLOO, AND WHAT IF I SAID THERE WASN'T ROOM, AND..
SCHULZ
9-9
SIGH,

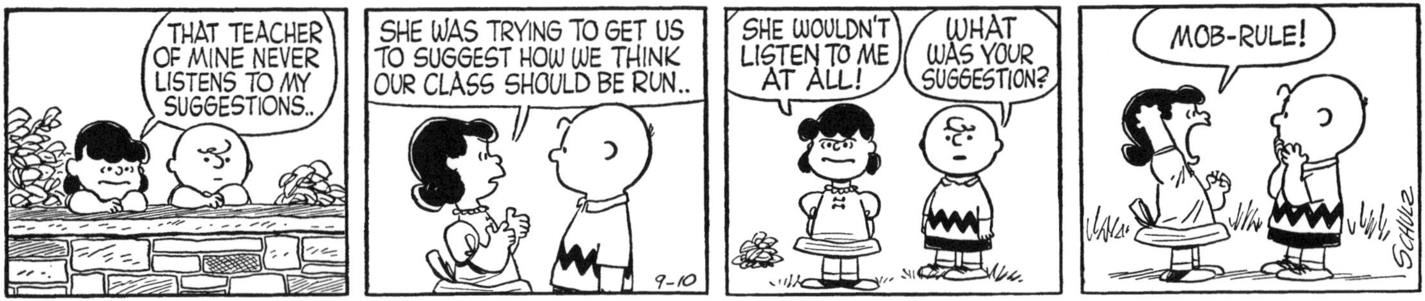
THAT TEACHER OF MINE NEVER LISTENS TO MY SUGGESTIONS..
SHE WAS TRYING TO GET US TO SUGGEST HOW WE THINK OUR CLASS SHOULD BE RUN..
9-10
SHE WOULDN'T LISTEN TO ME AT ALL!
WHAT WAS YOUR SUGGESTION?
MOB-RULE!
SCHULZ

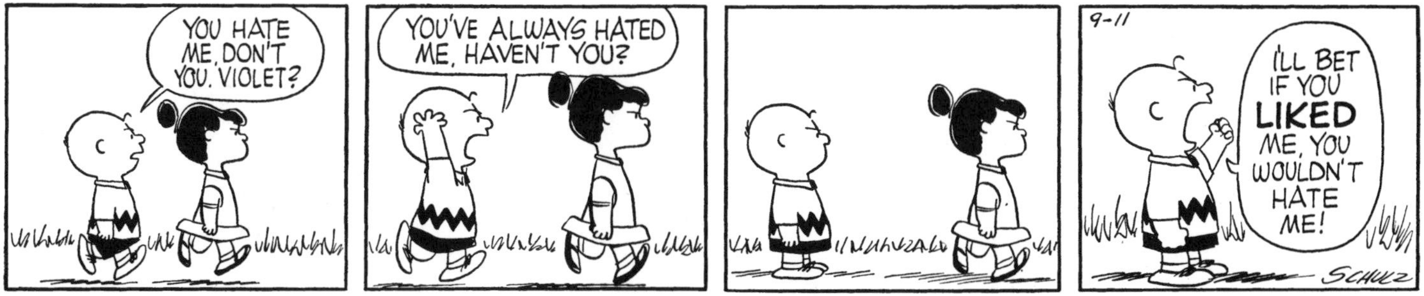
YOU HATE ME, DON'T YOU, VIOLET?
YOU'VE ALWAYS HATED ME, HAVEN'T YOU?
9-11
I'LL BET IF YOU **LIKED** ME, YOU WOULDN'T HATE ME!
SCHULZ

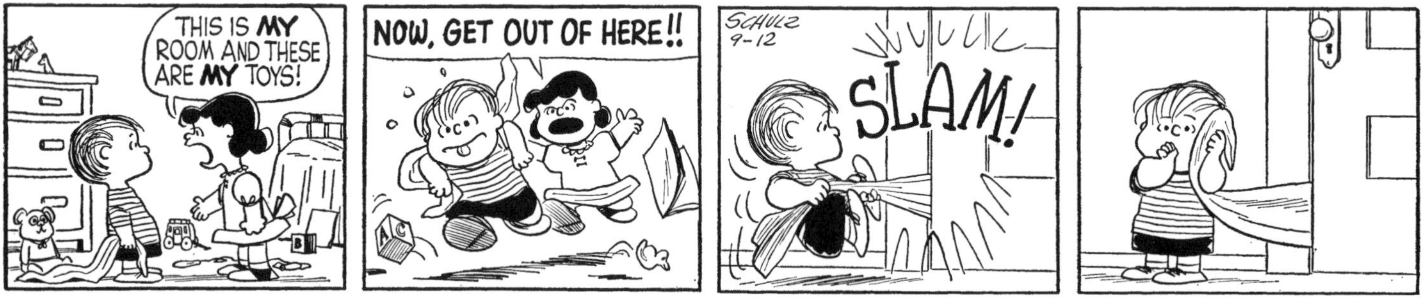
THIS IS MY ROOM AND THESE ARE MY TOYS!
NOW, GET OUT OF HERE!!
SCHULZ 9-12
SLAM!

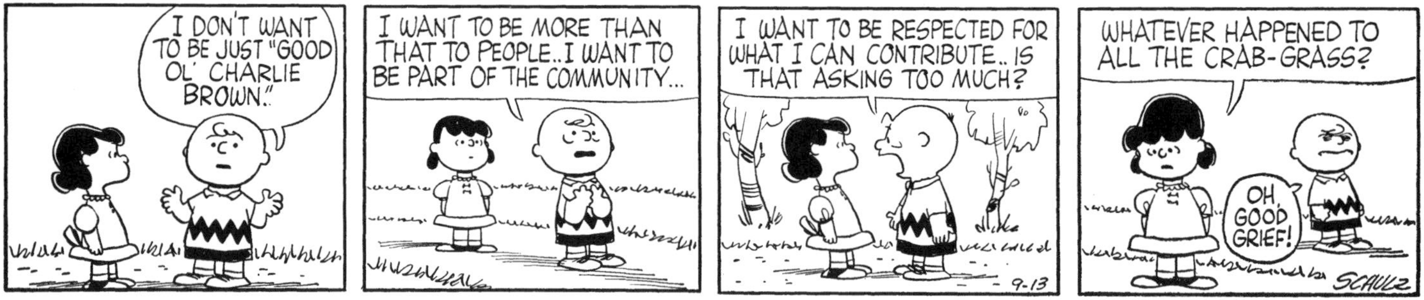
I DON'T WANT TO BE JUST "GOOD OL' CHARLIE BROWN."
I WANT TO BE MORE THAN THAT TO PEOPLE..I WANT TO BE PART OF THE COMMUNITY...
I WANT TO BE RESPECTED FOR WHAT I CAN CONTRIBUTE.. IS THAT ASKING TOO MUCH?
9-13
WHATEVER HAPPENED TO ALL THE CRAB-GRASS?
OH, GOOD GRIEF!
SCHULZ

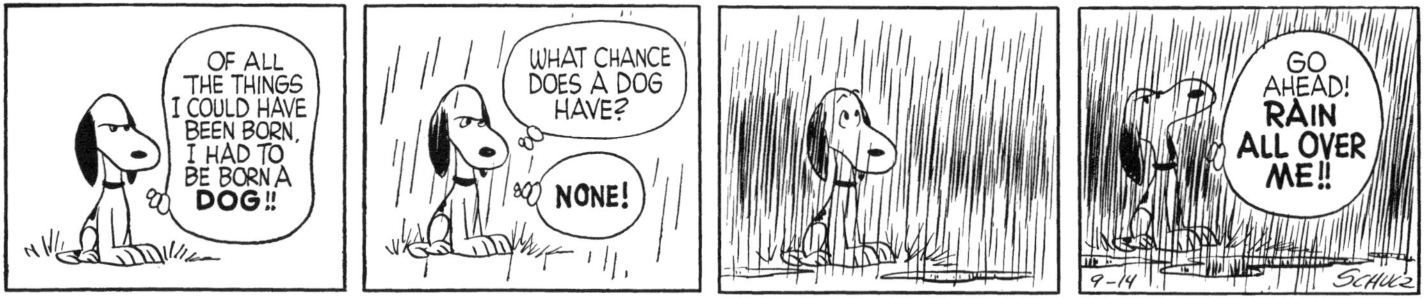
OF ALL THE THINGS I COULD HAVE BEEN BORN, I HAD TO BE BORN A DOG!!
WHAT CHANCE DOES A DOG HAVE?
NONE!
GO AHEAD! RAIN ALL OVER ME!!
9-14
SCHULZ

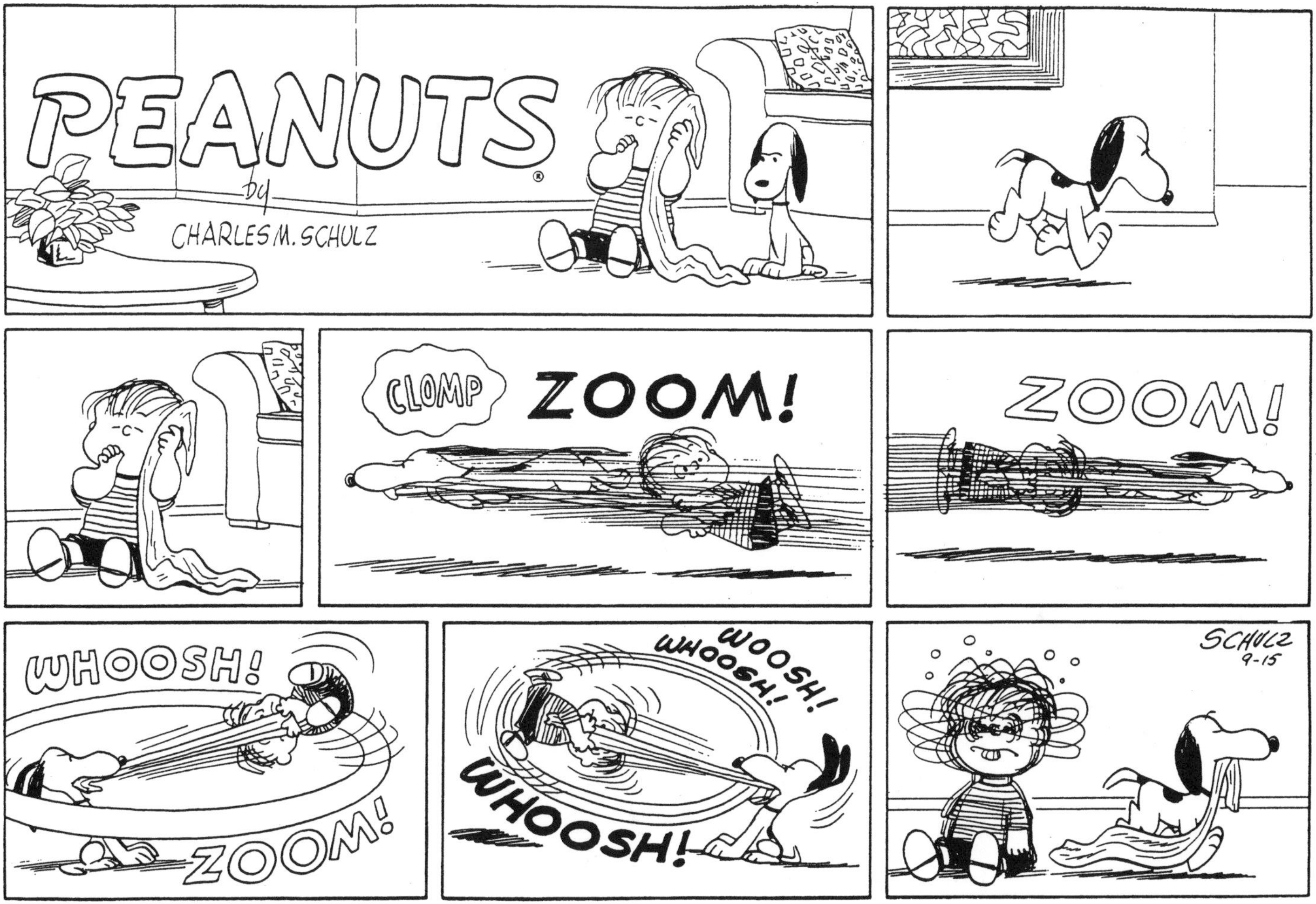
PEANUTS
by
CHARLES M. SCHULZ
CLOMP
ZOOM!
ZOOM!
WHOOSH!
ZOOM!
WOOSH!
WHOOSH!
WHOOSH!
SCHULZ
9-15

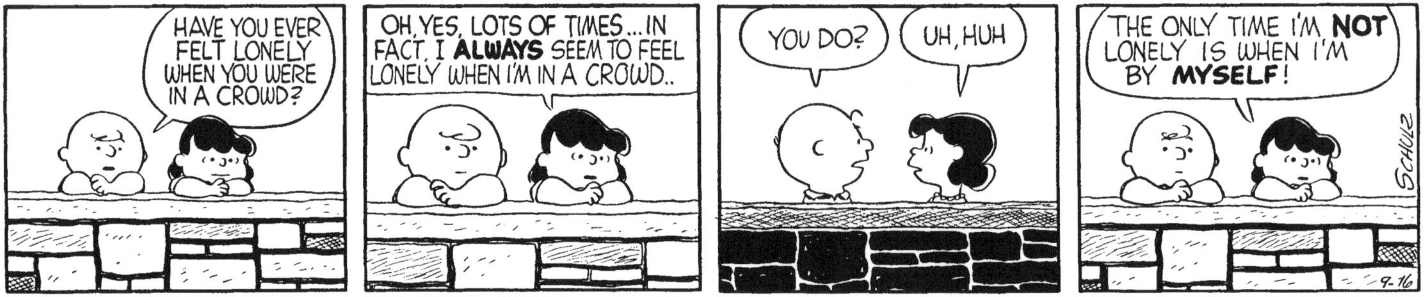
HAVE YOU EVER FELT LONELY WHEN YOU WERE IN A CROWD?
OH, YES, LOTS OF TIMES...IN FACT, I **ALWAYS** SEEM TO FEEL LONELY WHEN I'M IN A CROWD..
YOU DO?
UH, HUH
THE ONLY TIME I'M **NOT** LONELY IS WHEN I'M BY **MYSELF**!
SCHULZ
9-16

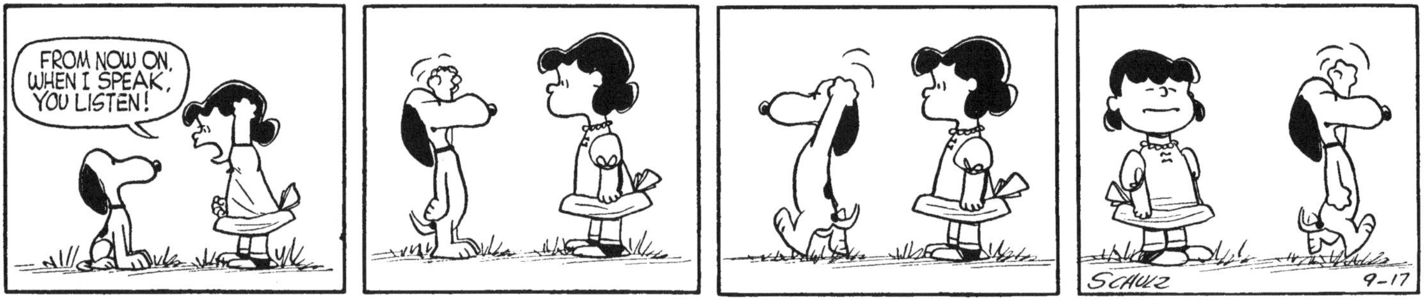
FROM NOW ON, WHEN I SPEAK, YOU LISTEN!
SCHULZ
9-17

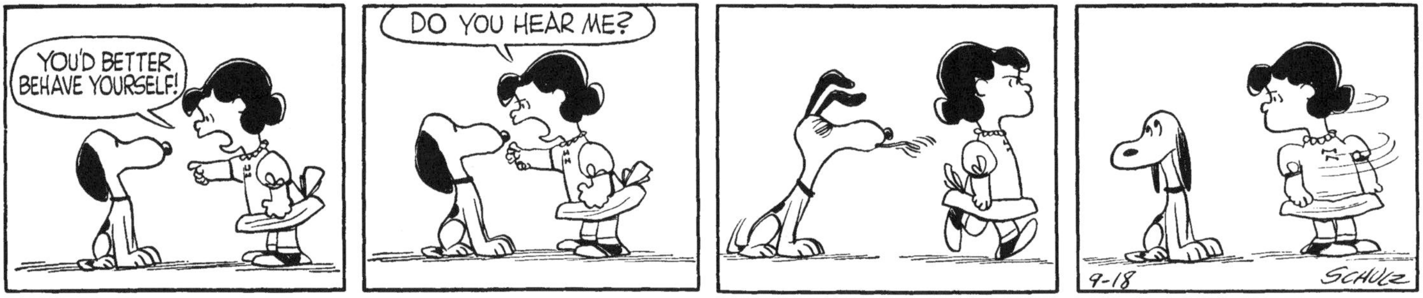
YOU'D BETTER BEHAVE YOURSELF!
DO YOU HEAR ME?
9-18
SCHULZ

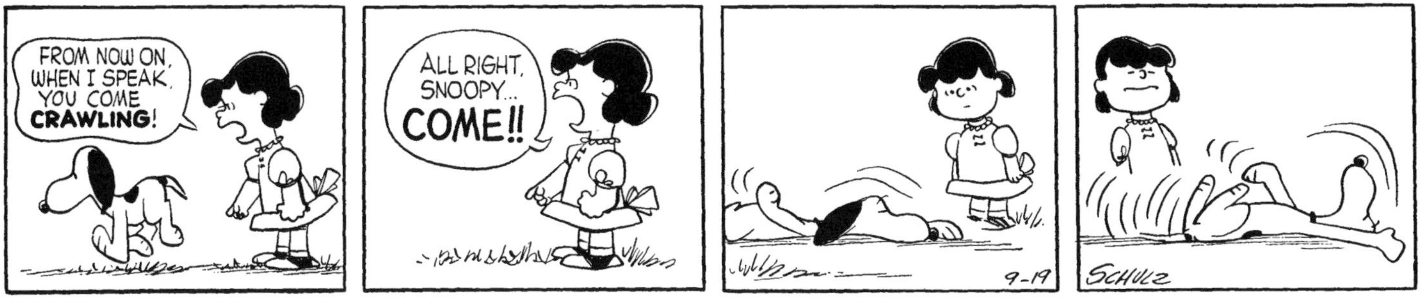
FROM NOW ON, WHEN I SPEAK, YOU COME **CRAWLING**!
ALL RIGHT, SNOOPY... COME!!
9-19
SCHULZ

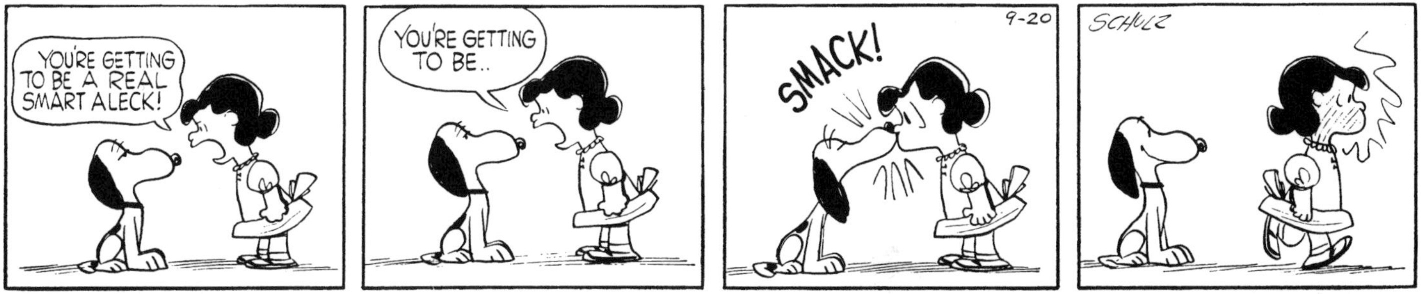
YOU'RE GETTING TO BE A REAL SMART ALECK!
YOU'RE GETTING TO BE..
9-20
SMACK!
SCHULZ

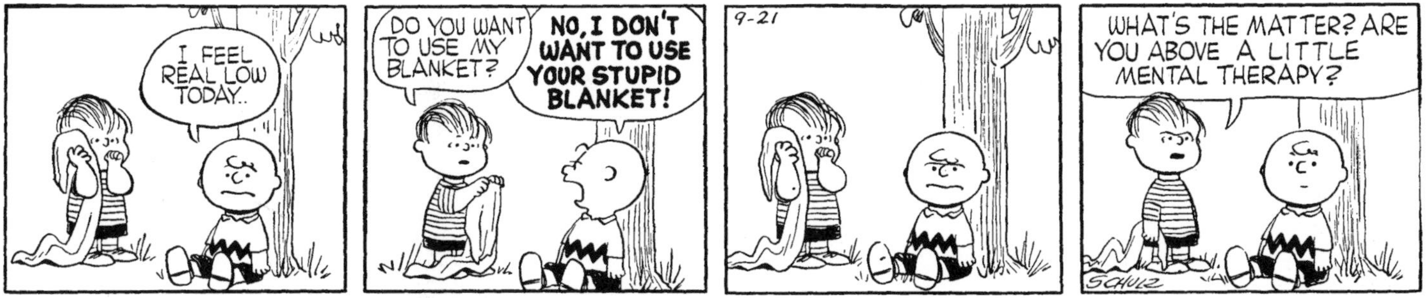
I FEEL REAL LOW TODAY..
DO YOU WANT TO USE MY BLANKET?
NO, I DON'T WANT TO USE YOUR STUPID BLANKET!
9-21
WHAT'S THE MATTER? ARE YOU ABOVE A LITTLE MENTAL THERAPY?
SCHULZ

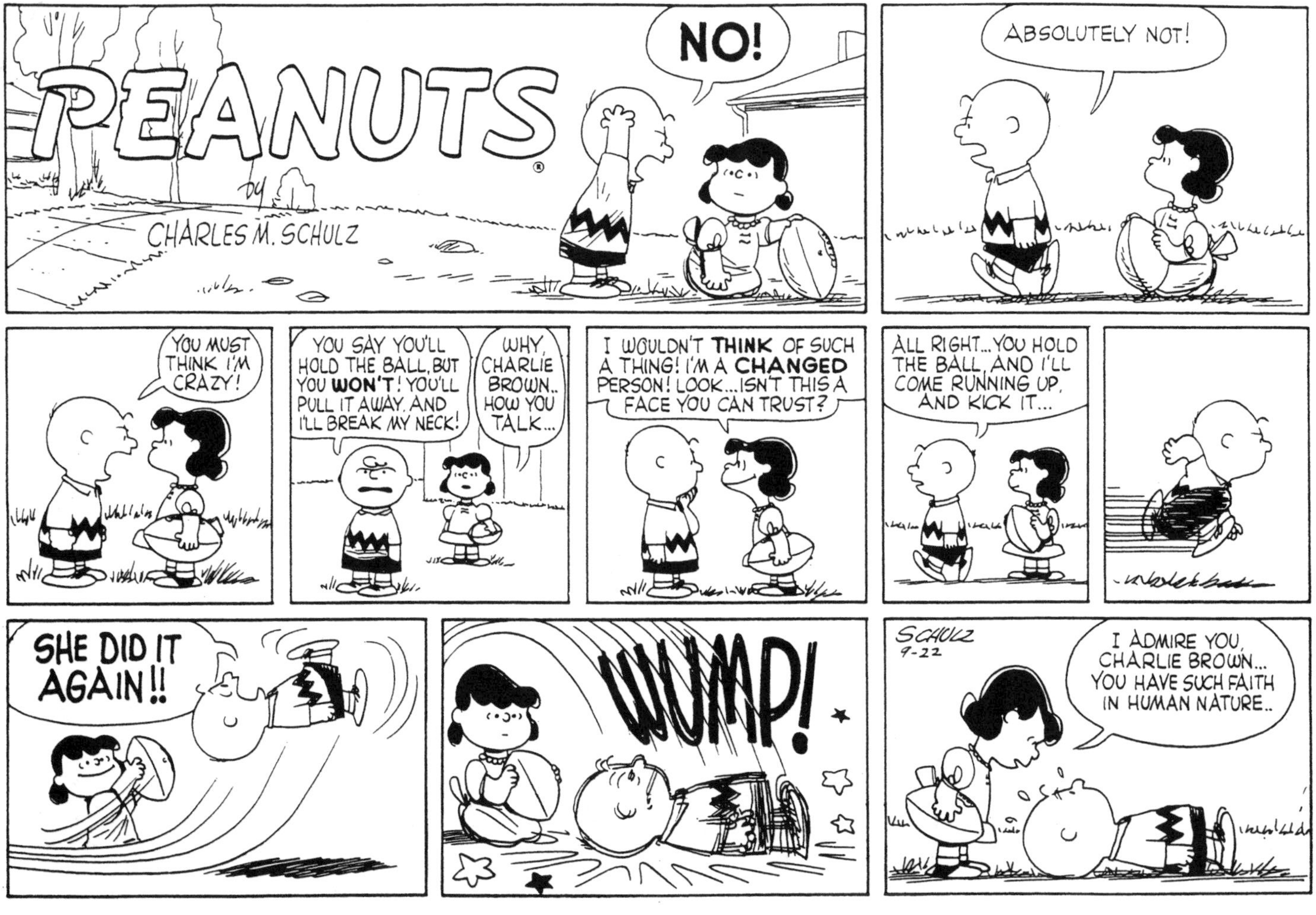
PEANUTS
by
CHARLES M. SCHULZ
NO!
ABSOLUTELY NOT!
YOU MUST THINK I'M CRAZY!
YOU SAY YOU'LL HOLD THE BALL, BUT YOU WON'T! YOU'LL PULL IT AWAY, AND I'LL BREAK MY NECK!
WHY, CHARLIE BROWN.. HOW YOU TALK...
I WOULDN'T THINK OF SUCH A THING! I'M A CHANGED PERSON! LOOK...ISN'T THIS A FACE YOU CAN TRUST?
ALL RIGHT...YOU HOLD THE BALL, AND I'LL COME RUNNING UP, AND KICK IT...
SHE DID IT AGAIN!!
WUMP!
SCHULZ
9-22
I ADMIRE YOU, CHARLIE BROWN... YOU HAVE SUCH FAITH IN HUMAN NATURE..

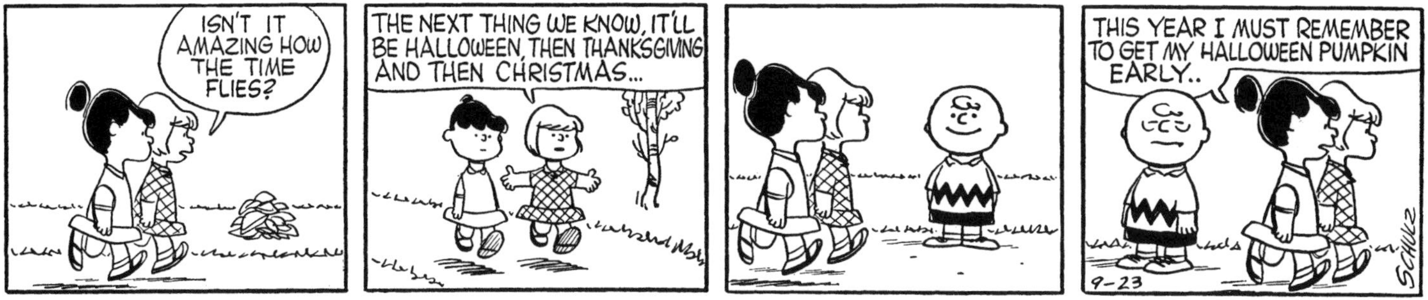
ISN'T IT AMAZING HOW THE TIME FLIES?
THE NEXT THING WE KNOW, IT'LL BE HALLOWEEN, THEN THANKSGIVING AND THEN CHRISTMAS...
THIS YEAR I MUST REMEMBER TO GET MY HALLOWEEN PUMPKIN EARLY..
9-23
SCHULZ

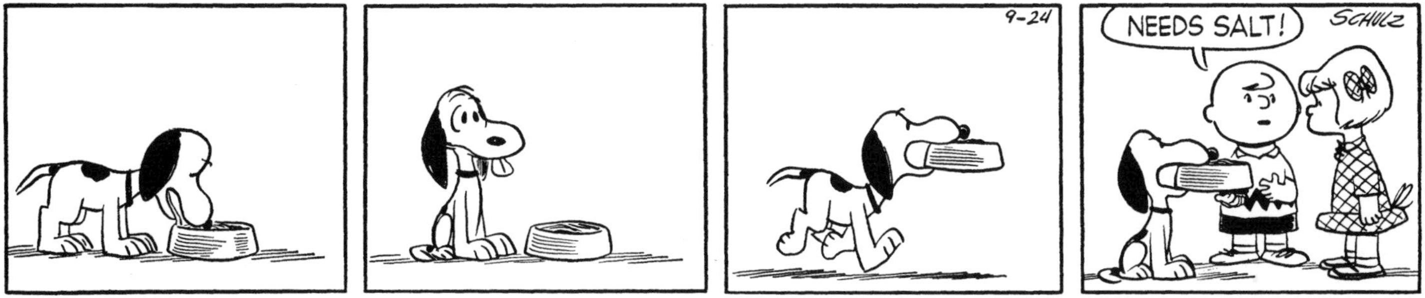
9-24
NEEDS SALT!
SCHULZ

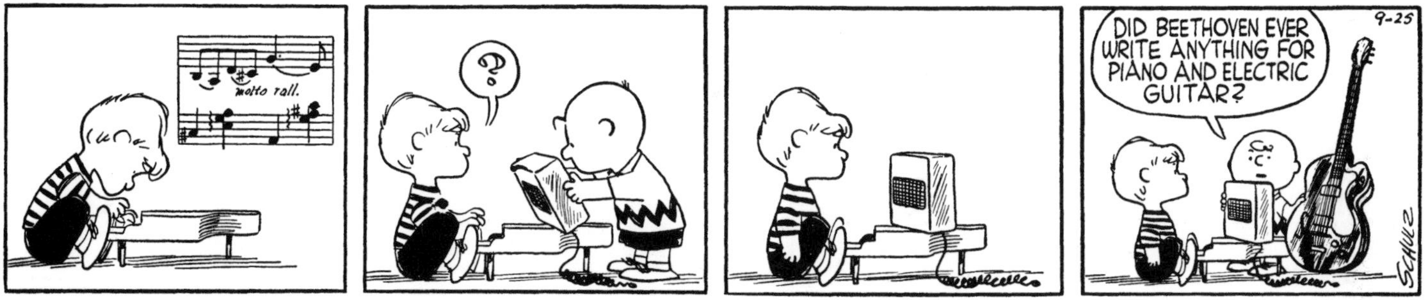
molto rall.
?
9-25
DID BEETHOVEN EVER WRITE ANYTHING FOR PIANO AND ELECTRIC GUITAR?
SCHULZ

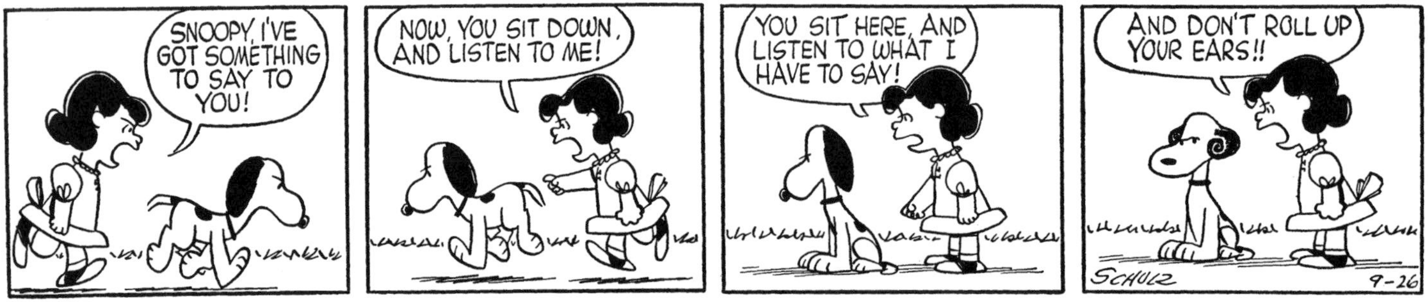
SNOOPY, I'VE GOT SOMETHING TO SAY TO YOU!
NOW, YOU SIT DOWN, AND LISTEN TO ME!
YOU SIT HERE, AND LISTEN TO WHAT I HAVE TO SAY!
AND DON'T ROLL UP YOUR EARS!!
SCHULZ
9-26

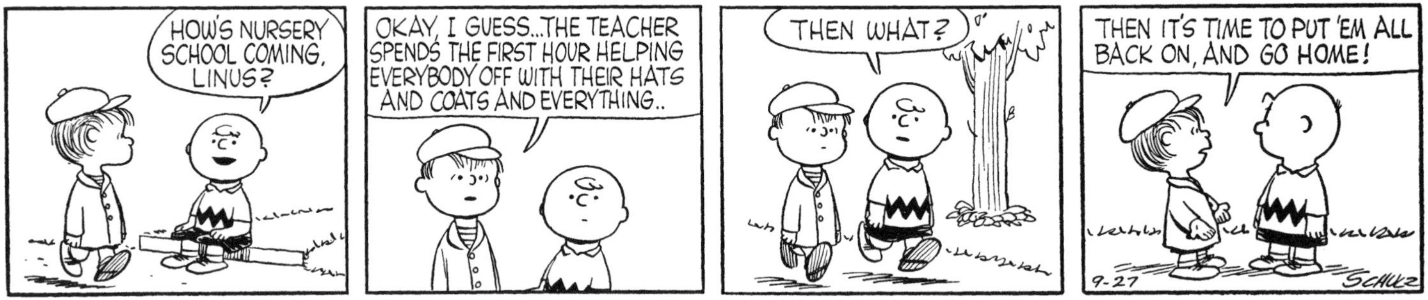
HOW'S NURSERY SCHOOL COMING, LINUS?
OKAY, I GUESS...THE TEACHER SPENDS THE FIRST HOUR HELPING EVERYBODY OFF WITH THEIR HATS AND COATS AND EVERYTHING..
THEN WHAT?
THEN IT'S TIME TO PUT 'EM ALL BACK ON, AND GO HOME!
9-27
SCHULZ

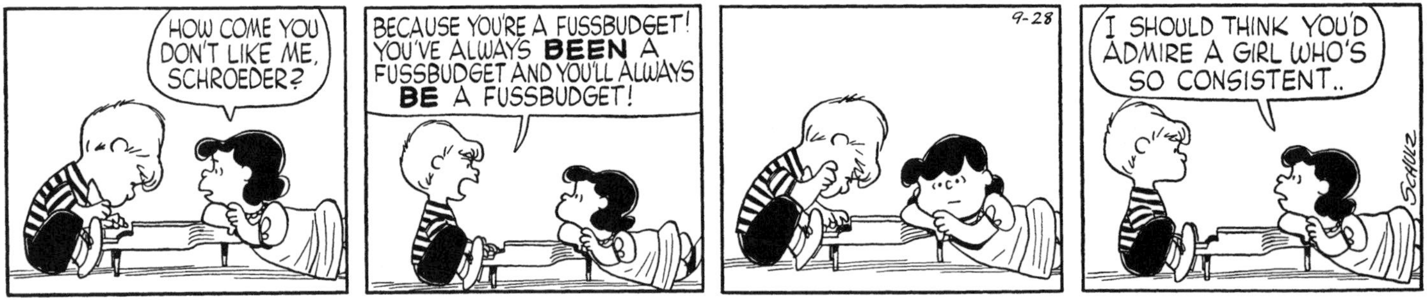
HOW COME YOU DON'T LIKE ME, SCHROEDER?
BECAUSE YOU'RE A FUSSBUDGET! YOU'VE ALWAYS BEEN A FUSSBUDGET AND YOU'LL ALWAYS BE A FUSSBUDGET!
9-28
I SHOULD THINK YOU'D ADMIRE A GIRL WHO'S SO CONSISTENT..
SCHULZ

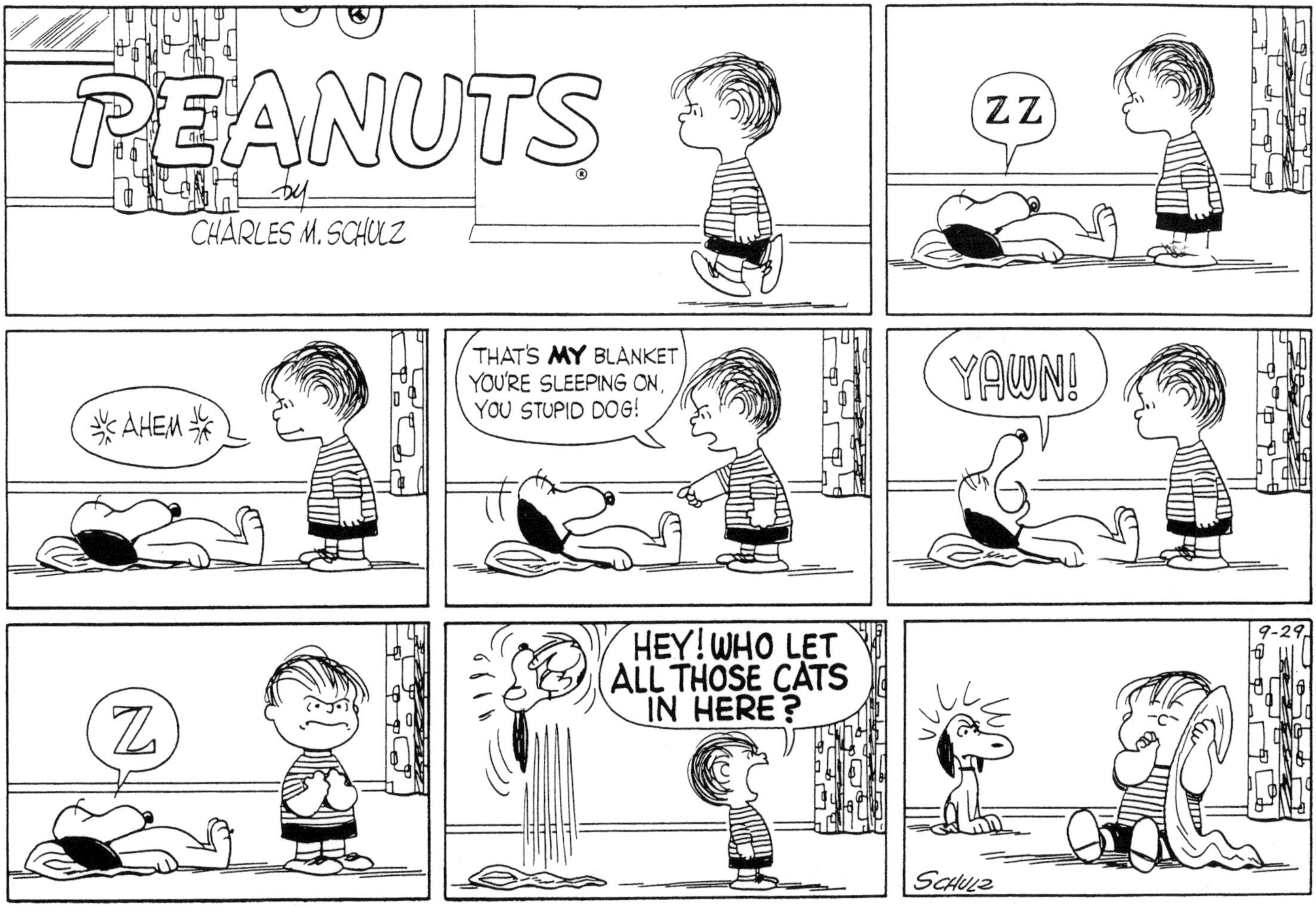
PEANUTS
by CHARLES M. SCHULZ
ZZ
AHEM
THAT'S MY BLANKET YOU'RE SLEEPING ON, YOU STUPID DOG!
YAWN!
Z
HEY! WHO LET ALL THOSE CATS IN HERE?
9-29
SCHULZ

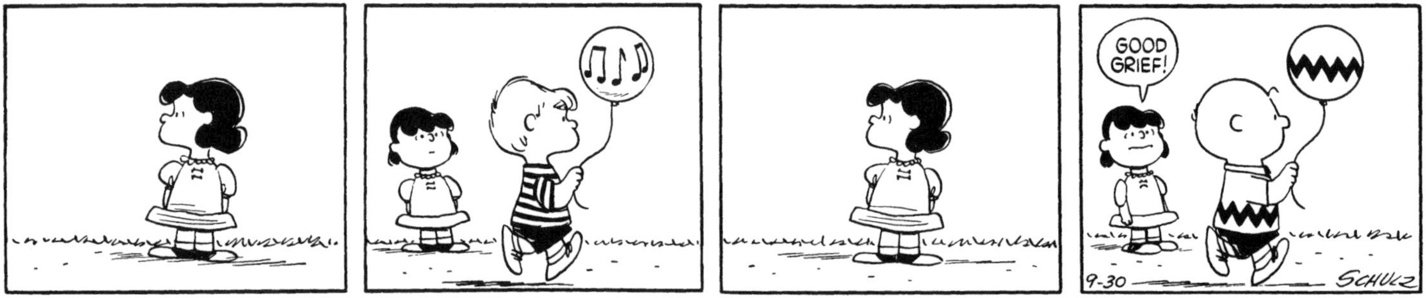
GOOD GRIEF!
9-30
SCHULZ

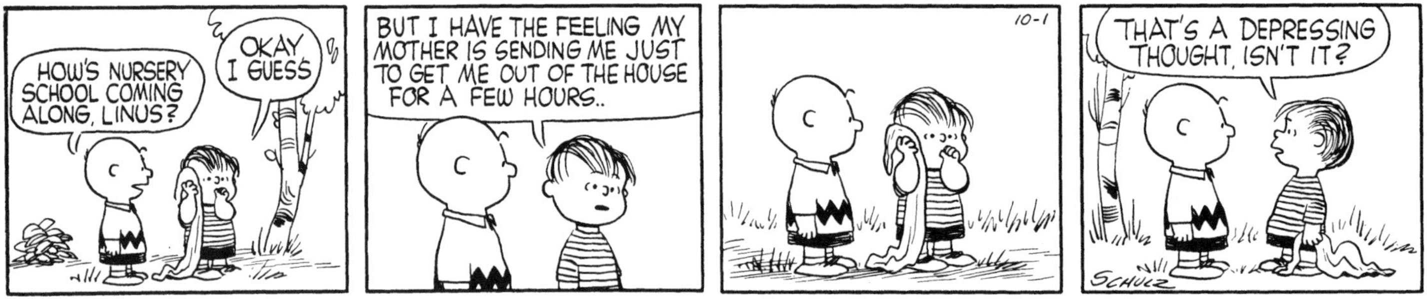
HOW'S NURSERY SCHOOL COMING ALONG, LINUS?
OKAY I GUESS
BUT I HAVE THE FEELING MY MOTHER IS SENDING ME JUST TO GET ME OUT OF THE HOUSE FOR A FEW HOURS..
10-1
THAT'S A DEPRESSING THOUGHT, ISN'T IT?
SCHULZ

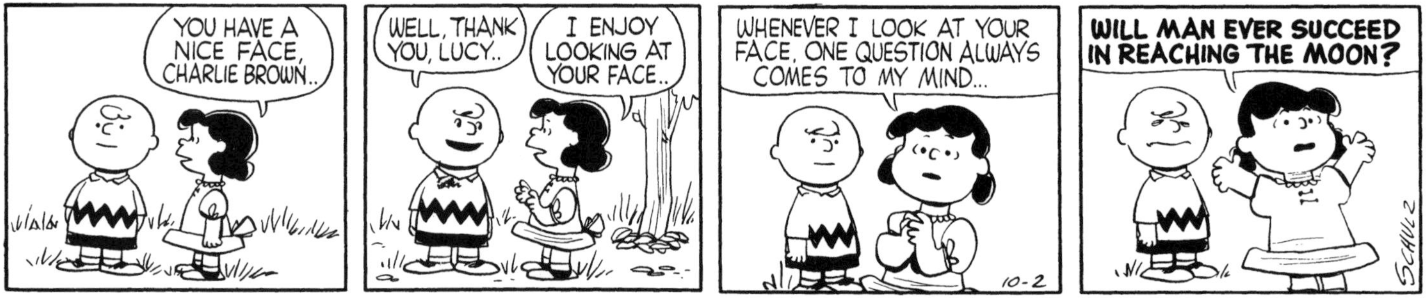
YOU HAVE A NICE FACE, CHARLIE BROWN..
WELL, THANK YOU, LUCY..
I ENJOY LOOKING AT YOUR FACE..
WHENEVER I LOOK AT YOUR FACE, ONE QUESTION ALWAYS COMES TO MY MIND...
10-2
WILL MAN EVER SUCCEED IN REACHING THE MOON?
SCHULZ

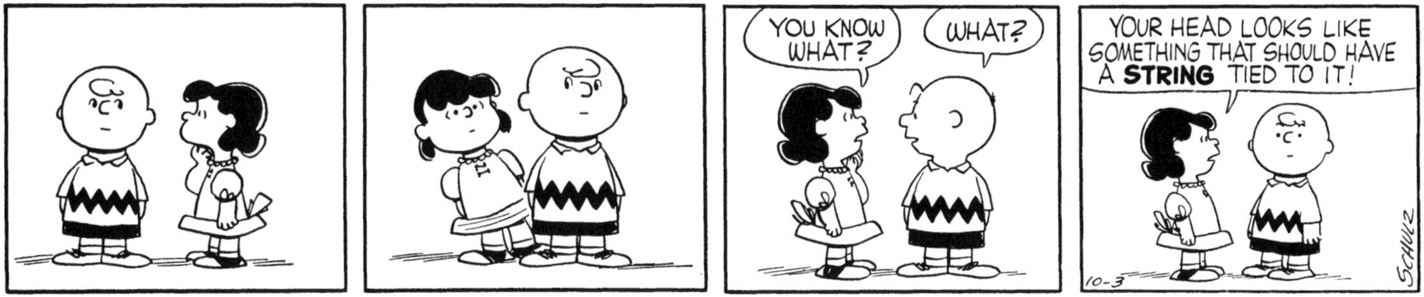
YOU KNOW WHAT?
WHAT?
YOUR HEAD LOOKS LIKE SOMETHING THAT SHOULD HAVE A STRING TIED TO IT!
10-3
SCHULZ

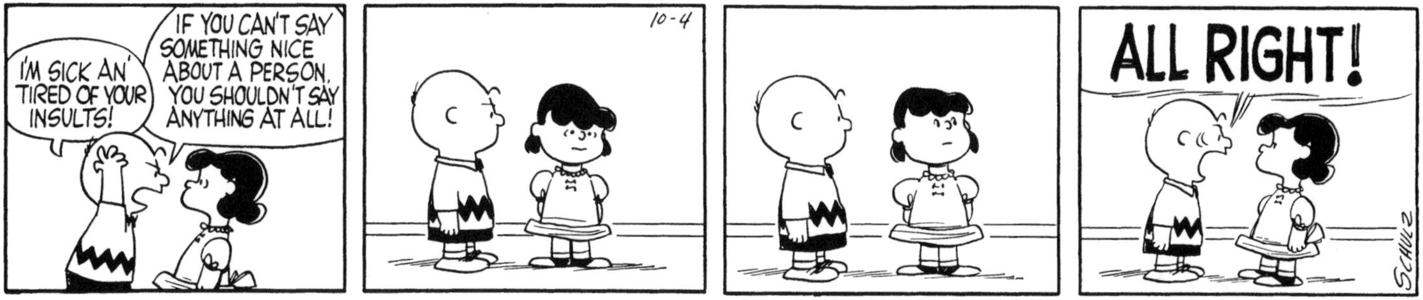
I'M SICK AN' TIRED OF YOUR INSULTS!
IF YOU CAN'T SAY SOMETHING NICE ABOUT A PERSON, YOU SHOULDN'T SAY ANYTHING AT ALL!
10-4
ALL RIGHT!
SCHULZ

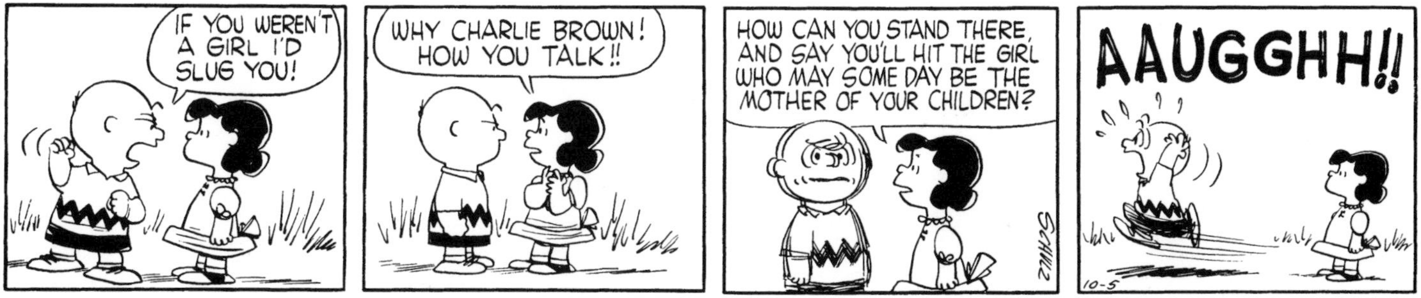
IF YOU WEREN'T A GIRL I'D SLUG YOU!
WHY CHARLIE BROWN! HOW YOU TALK!!
HOW CAN YOU STAND THERE AND SAY YOU'LL HIT THE GIRL WHO MAY SOME DAY BE THE MOTHER OF YOUR CHILDREN?
SCHULZ
AAUGGHH!!
10-5

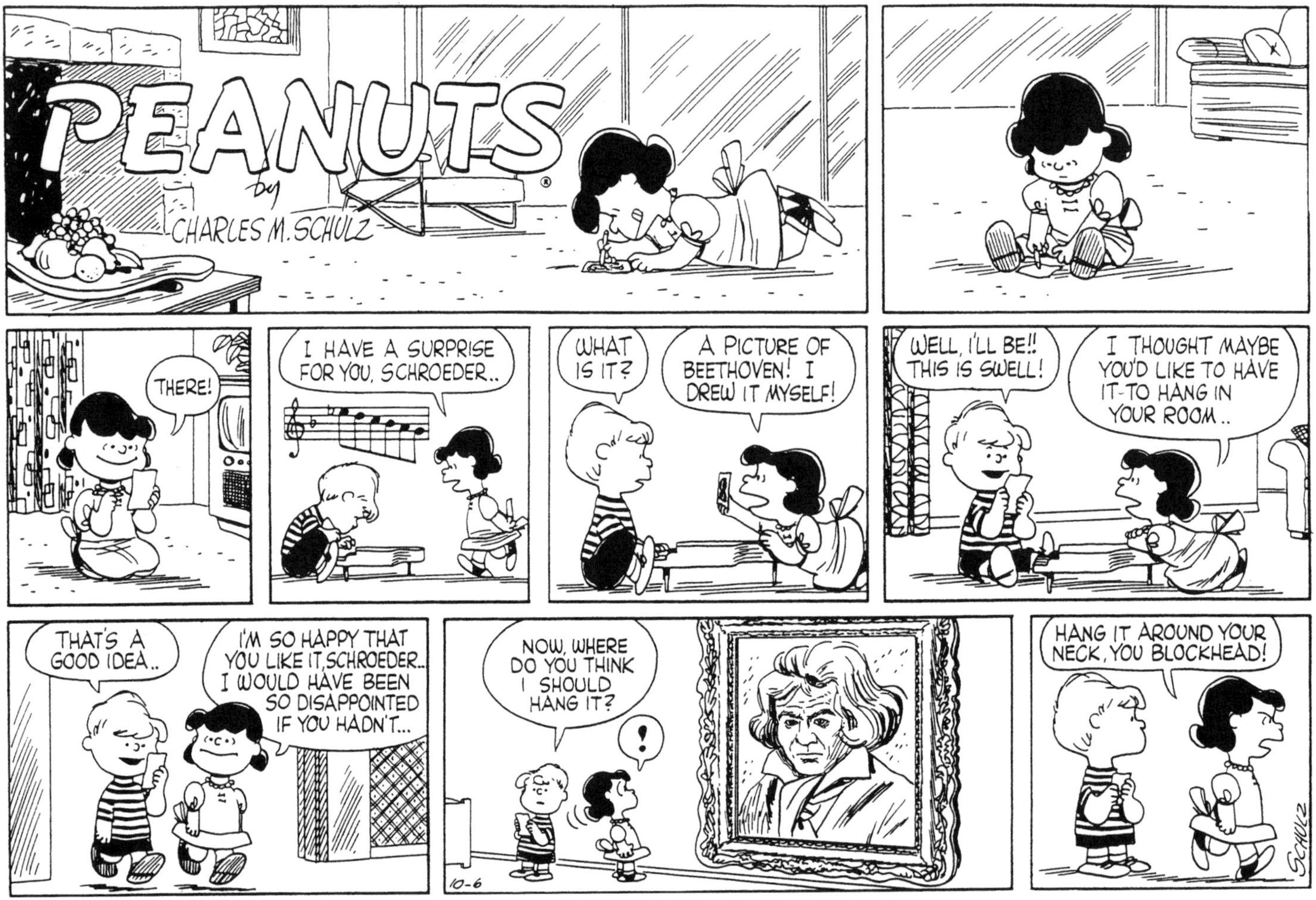
PEANUTS
by
CHARLES M. SCHULZ
THERE!
I HAVE A SURPRISE FOR YOU, SCHROEDER..
WHAT IS IT?
A PICTURE OF BEETHOVEN! I DREW IT MYSELF!
WELL, I'LL BE!! THIS IS SWELL!
I THOUGHT MAYBE YOU'D LIKE TO HAVE IT-TO HANG IN YOUR ROOM..
THAT'S A GOOD IDEA..
I'M SO HAPPY THAT YOU LIKE IT, SCHROEDER.. I WOULD HAVE BEEN SO DISAPPOINTED IF YOU HADN'T...
NOW, WHERE DO YOU THINK I SHOULD HANG IT?
!
10-6
HANG IT AROUND YOUR NECK, YOU BLOCKHEAD!
SCHULZ

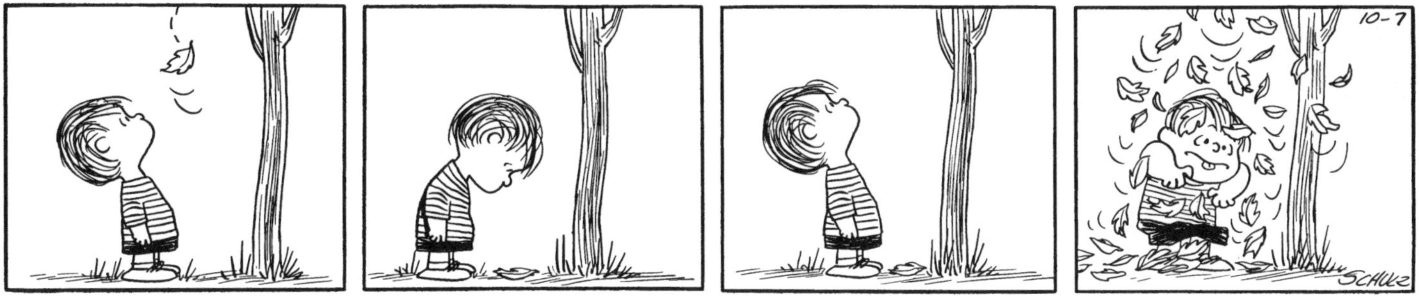
10-7
SCHULZ

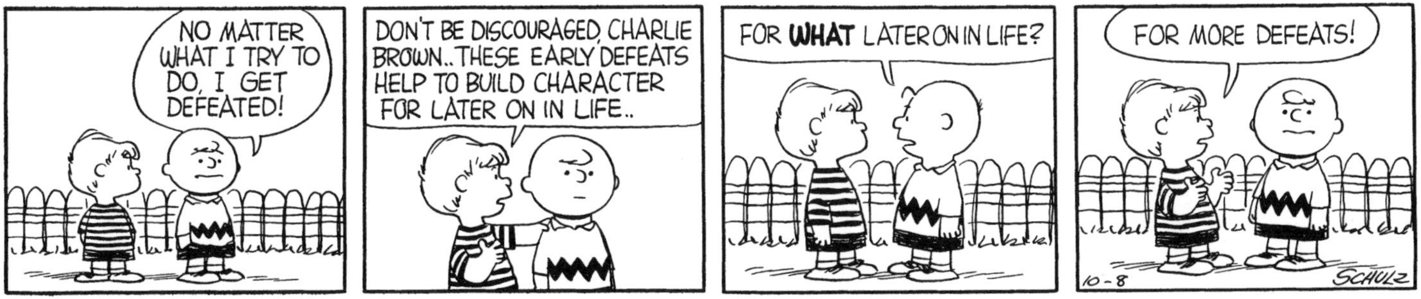
NO MATTER WHAT I TRY TO DO, I GET DEFEATED!
DON'T BE DISCOURAGED, CHARLIE BROWN.. THESE EARLY DEFEATS HELP TO BUILD CHARACTER FOR LATER ON IN LIFE..
FOR WHAT LATER ON IN LIFE?
FOR MORE DEFEATS!
10-8
SCHULZ

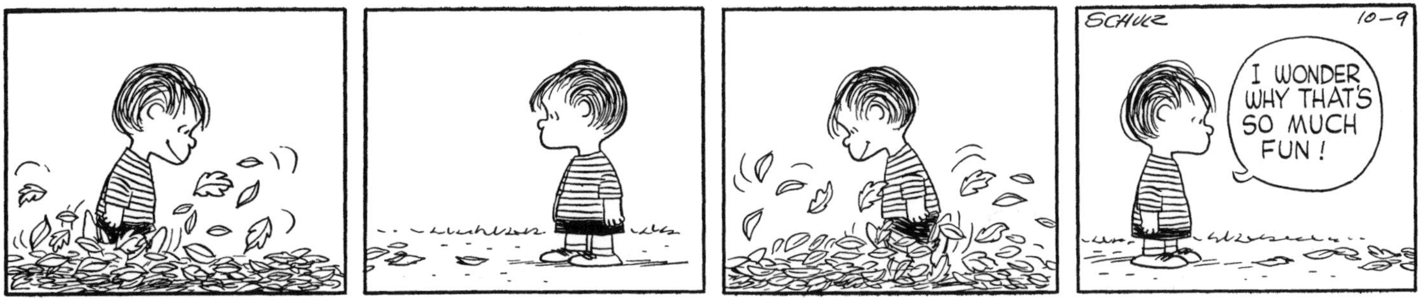
SCHULZ
10-9
I WONDER WHY THAT'S SO MUCH FUN!

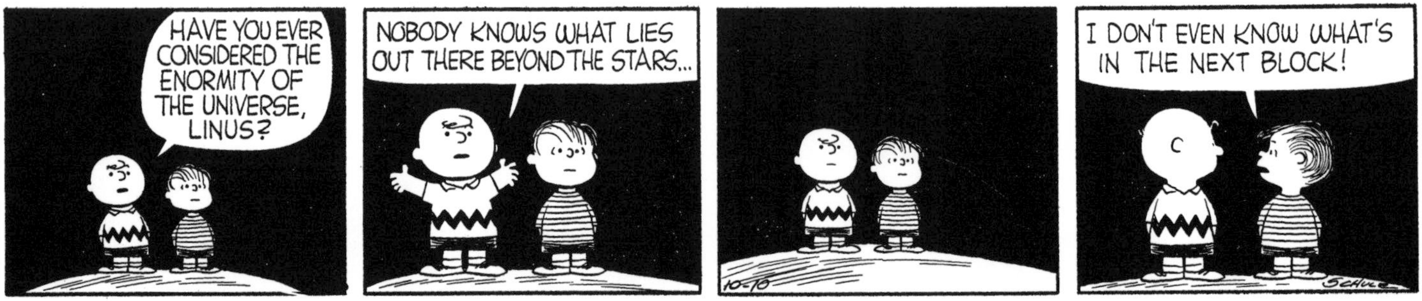
HAVE YOU EVER CONSIDERED THE ENORMITY OF THE UNIVERSE, LINUS?
NOBODY KNOWS WHAT LIES OUT THERE BEYOND THE STARS...
I DON'T EVEN KNOW WHAT'S IN THE NEXT BLOCK!

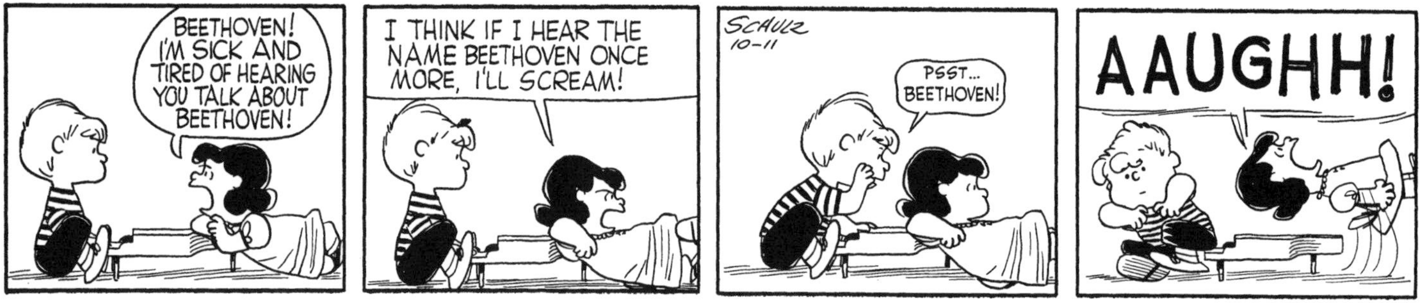
BEETHOVEN! I'M SICK AND TIRED OF HEARING YOU TALK ABOUT BEETHOVEN!
I THINK IF I HEAR THE NAME BEETHOVEN ONCE MORE, I'LL SCREAM!
SCHULZ
10-11
PSST... BEETHOVEN!
AAUGHH!

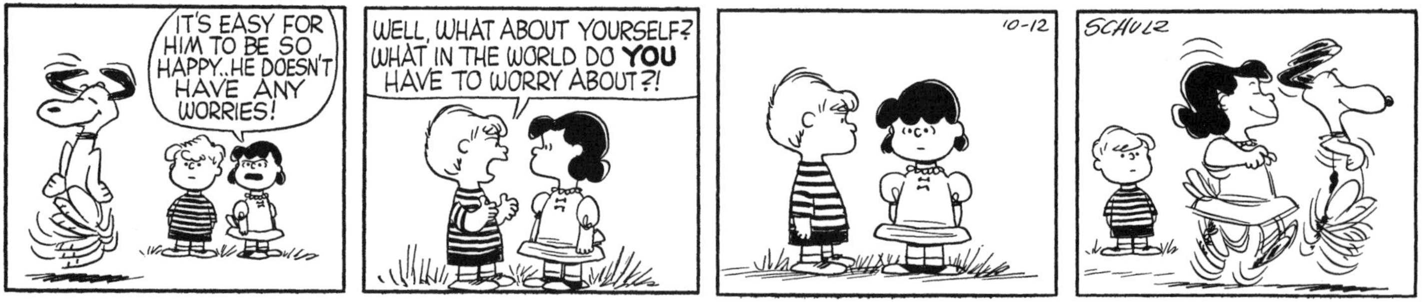
IT'S EASY FOR HIM TO BE SO HAPPY..HE DOESN'T HAVE ANY WORRIES!
WELL, WHAT ABOUT YOURSELF? WHAT IN THE WORLD DO **YOU** HAVE TO WORRY ABOUT?!
10-12
SCHULZ

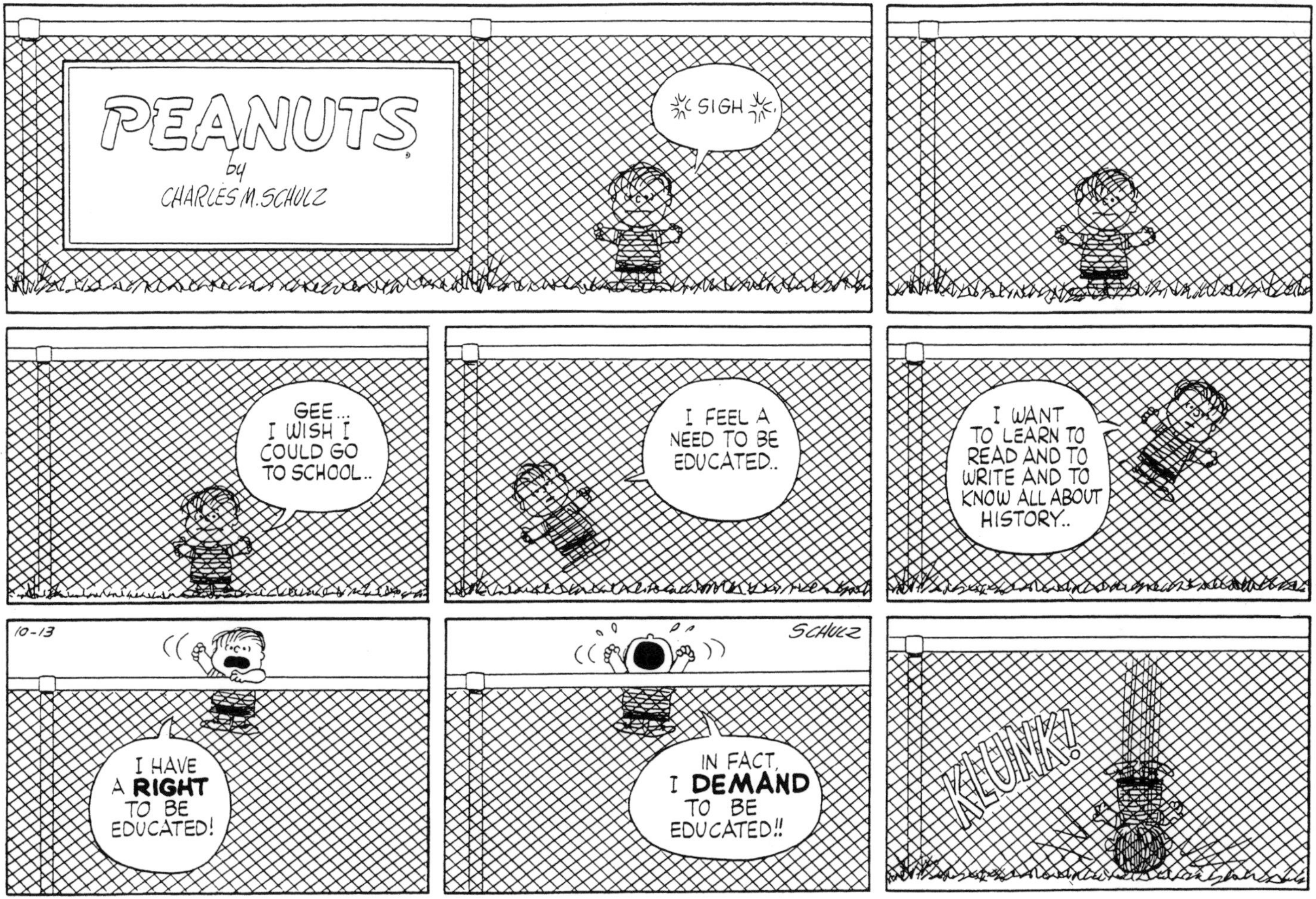

PEANUTS
by
CHARLES M. SCHULZ
SIGH
GEE... I WISH I COULD GO TO SCHOOL..
I FEEL A NEED TO BE EDUCATED..
I WANT TO LEARN TO READ AND TO WRITE AND TO KNOW ALL ABOUT HISTORY..
10-13
I HAVE A **RIGHT** TO BE EDUCATED!
SCHULZ
IN FACT, I **DEMAND** TO BE EDUCATED!!
KLUNK!

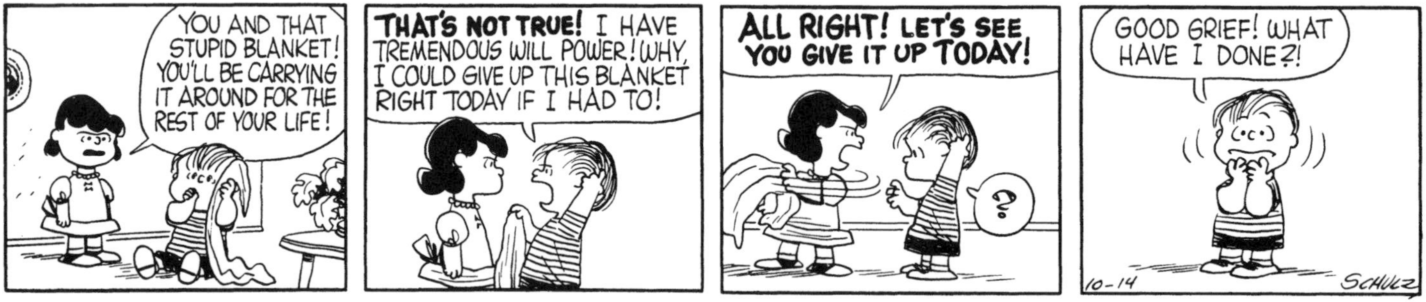
YOU AND THAT STUPID BLANKET! YOU'LL BE CARRYING IT AROUND FOR THE REST OF YOUR LIFE!
THAT'S NOT TRUE! I HAVE TREMENDOUS WILL POWER! WHY, I COULD GIVE UP THIS BLANKET RIGHT TODAY IF I HAD TO!
ALL RIGHT! LET'S SEE YOU GIVE IT UP TODAY!
?
GOOD GRIEF! WHAT HAVE I DONE?!
10-14
SCHULZ

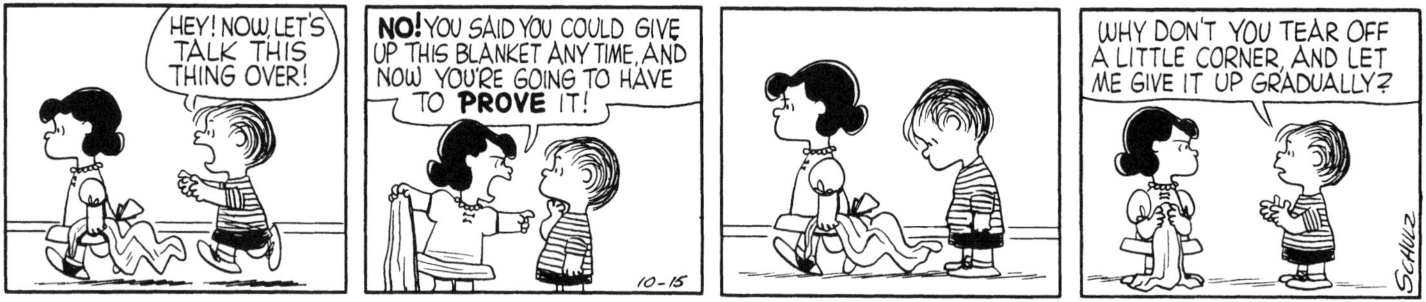
HEY! NOW, LET'S TALK THIS THING OVER!
NO! YOU SAID YOU COULD GIVE UP THIS BLANKET ANY TIME, AND NOW YOU'RE GOING TO HAVE TO PROVE IT!
10-15
WHY DON'T YOU TEAR OFF A LITTLE CORNER, AND LET ME GIVE IT UP GRADUALLY?
SCHULZ

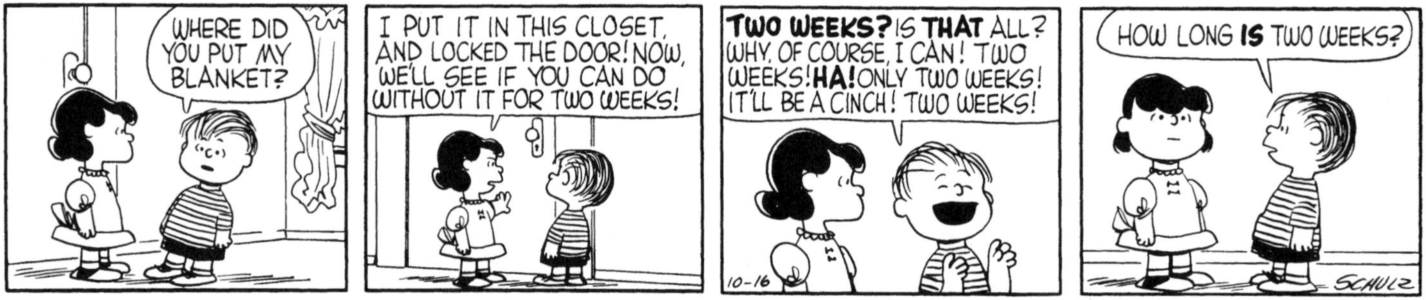
WHERE DID YOU PUT MY BLANKET?
I PUT IT IN THIS CLOSET, AND LOCKED THE DOOR! NOW, WE'LL SEE IF YOU CAN DO WITHOUT IT FOR TWO WEEKS!
TWO WEEKS? IS THAT ALL? WHY, OF COURSE, I CAN! TWO WEEKS! HA! ONLY TWO WEEKS! IT'LL BE A CINCH! TWO WEEKS!
10-16
HOW LONG IS TWO WEEKS?
SCHULZ

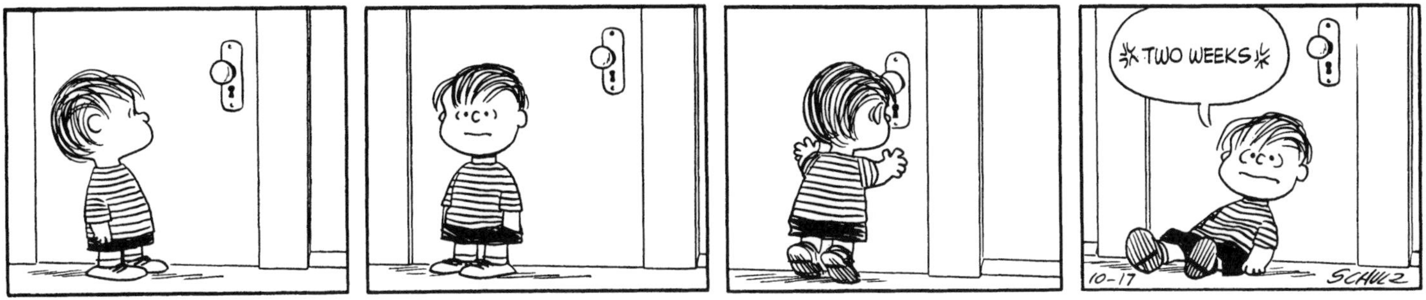
TWO WEEKS
10-17
SCHULZ

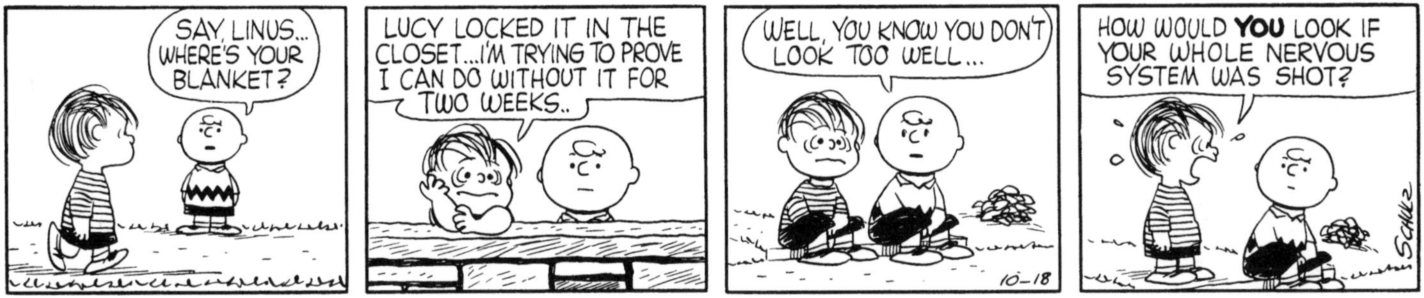
SAY, LINUS... WHERE'S YOUR BLANKET?
LUCY LOCKED IT IN THE CLOSET...I'M TRYING TO PROVE I CAN DO WITHOUT IT FOR TWO WEEKS..
WELL, YOU KNOW YOU DON'T LOOK TOO WELL...
HOW WOULD **YOU** LOOK IF YOUR WHOLE NERVOUS SYSTEM WAS SHOT?
10-18
SCHULZ

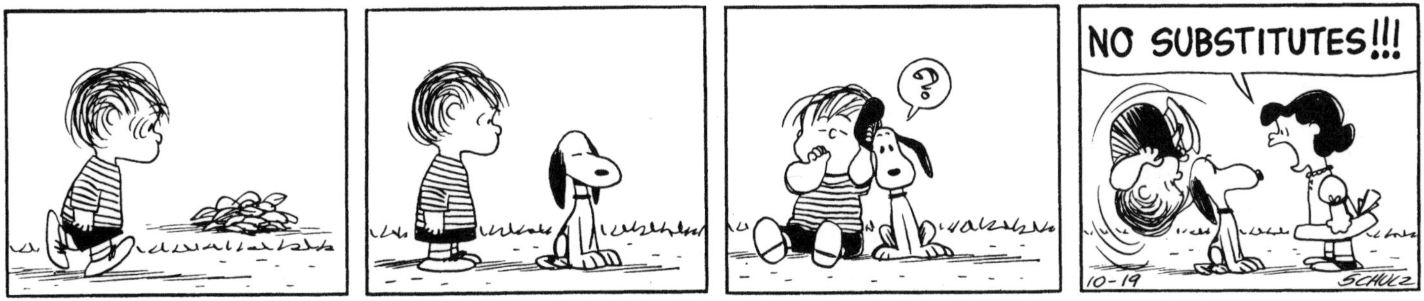
?
NO SUBSTITUTES!!!
10-19
SCHULZ

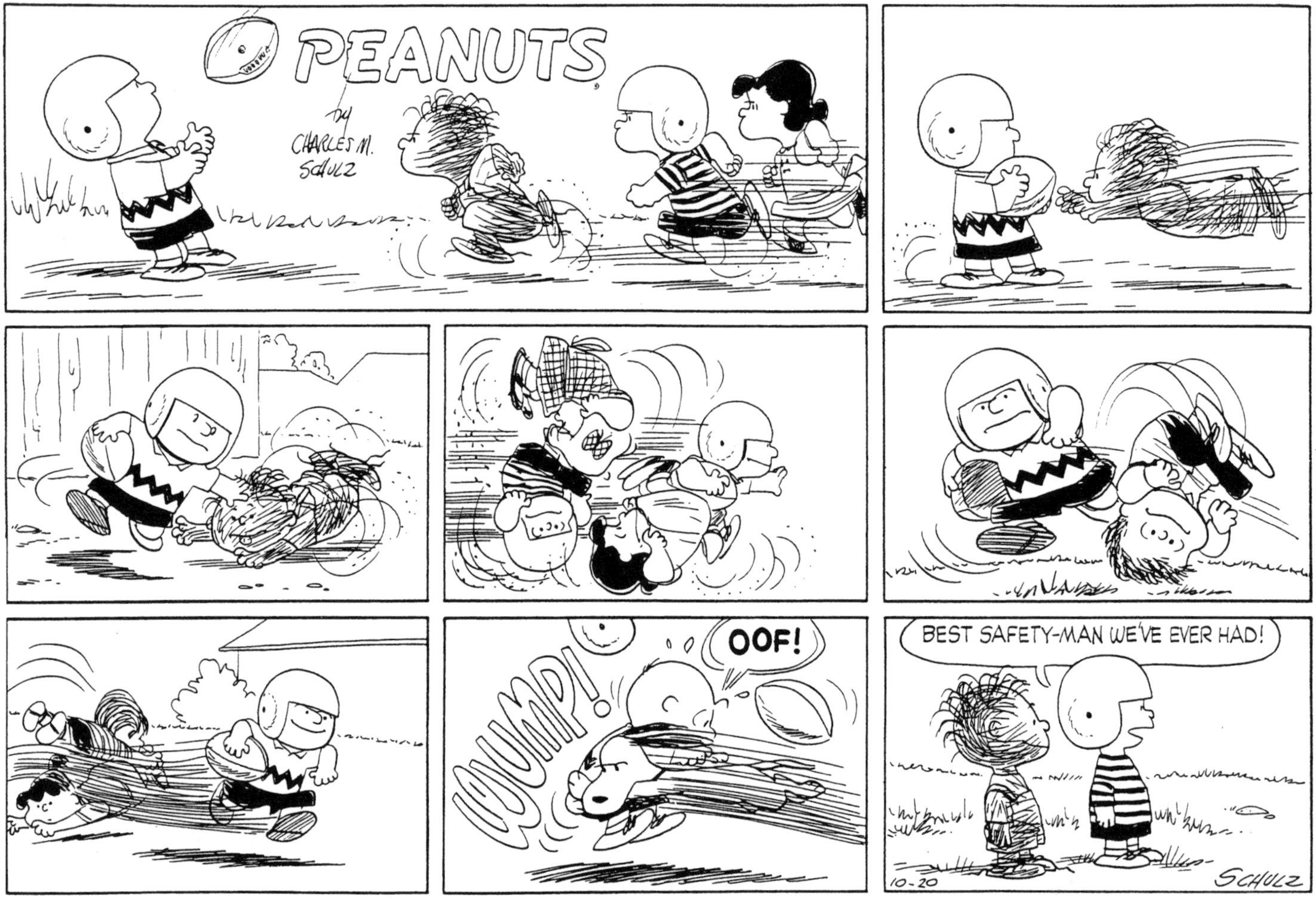
PEANUTS
BY CHARLES M. SCHULZ
OOF!
WUMP!
BEST SAFETY-MAN WE'VE EVER HAD!
10-20
SCHULZ

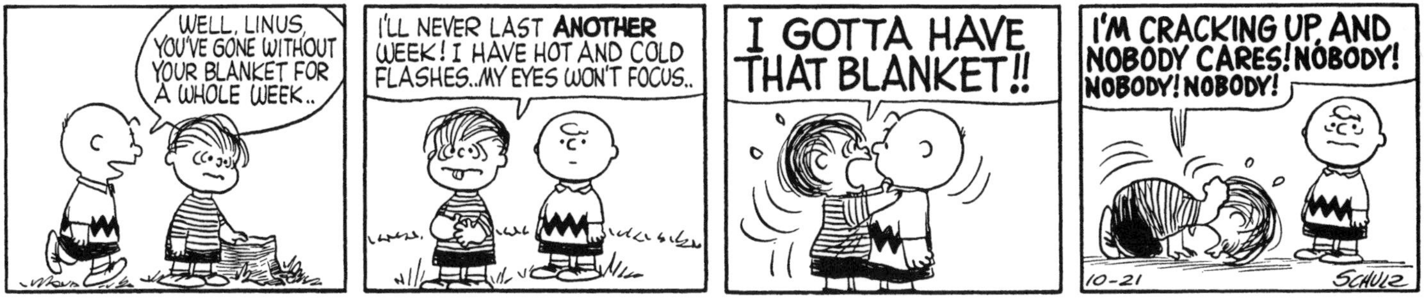
WELL, LINUS, YOU'VE GONE WITHOUT YOUR BLANKET FOR A WHOLE WEEK..
I'LL NEVER LAST **ANOTHER** WEEK! I HAVE HOT AND COLD FLASHES..MY EYES WON'T FOCUS..
I GOTTA HAVE THAT BLANKET!!
I'M CRACKING UP, AND NOBODY CARES! NOBODY! NOBODY! NOBODY!
10-21
SCHULZ

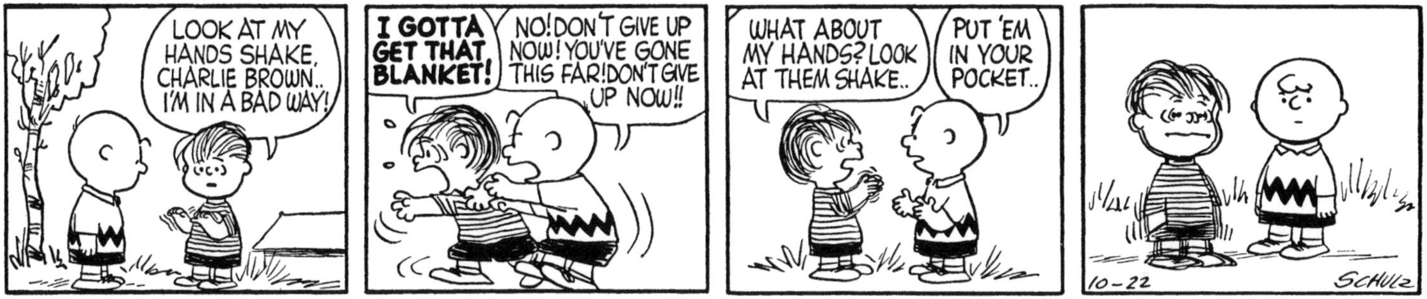
LOOK AT MY HANDS SHAKE, CHARLIE BROWN.. I'M IN A BAD WAY!
I GOTTA GET THAT BLANKET!
NO! DON'T GIVE UP NOW! YOU'VE GONE THIS FAR! DON'T GIVE UP NOW!!
WHAT ABOUT MY HANDS? LOOK AT THEM SHAKE..
PUT 'EM IN YOUR POCKET..
10-22
SCHULZ

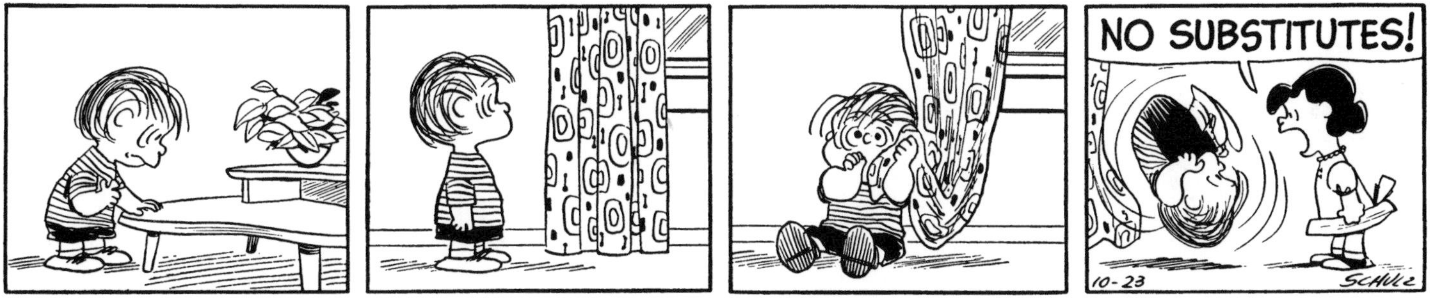
NO SUBSTITUTES!
10-23
SCHULZ

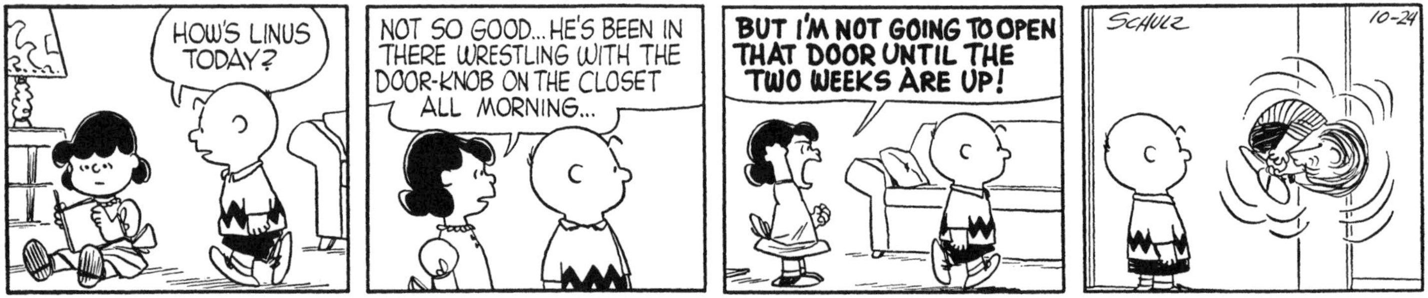
HOW'S LINUS TODAY?
NOT SO GOOD... HE'S BEEN IN THERE WRESTLING WITH THE DOOR-KNOB ON THE CLOSET ALL MORNING...
BUT I'M NOT GOING TO OPEN THAT DOOR UNTIL THE TWO WEEKS ARE UP!
SCHULZ
10-24

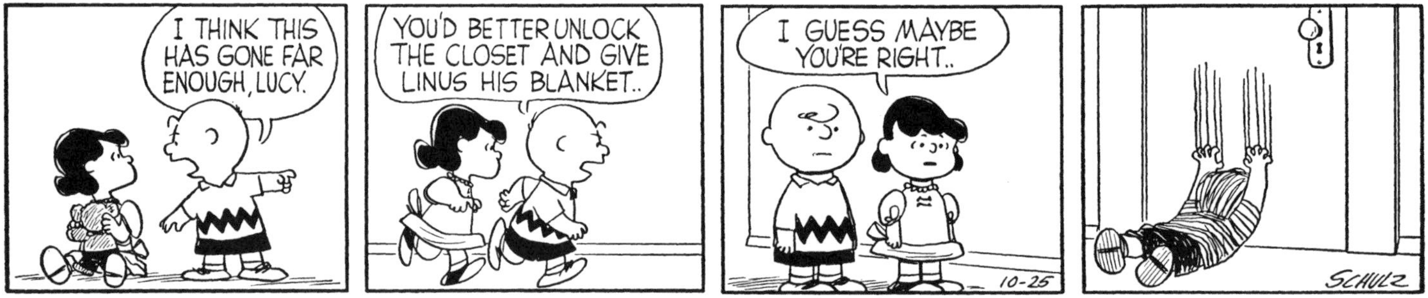
I THINK THIS HAS GONE FAR ENOUGH, LUCY.
YOU'D BETTER UNLOCK THE CLOSET AND GIVE LINUS HIS BLANKET..
I GUESS MAYBE YOU'RE RIGHT..
10-25
SCHULZ

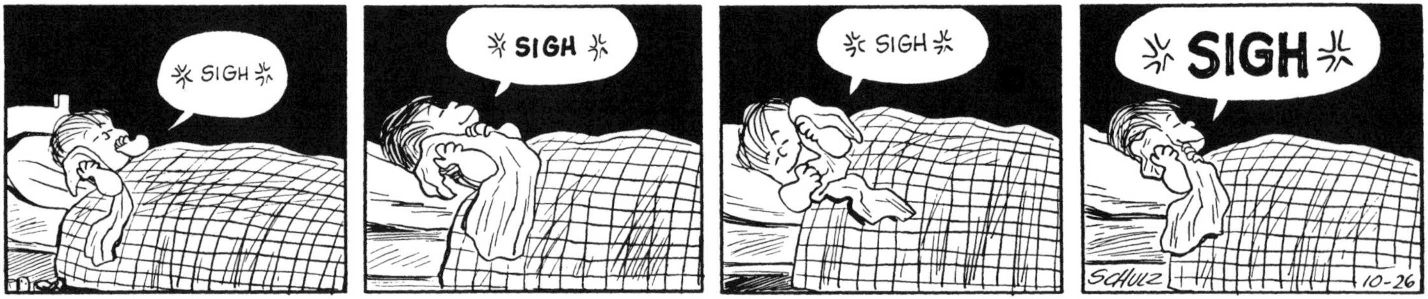
SIGH
SIGH
SIGH
SIGH
SCHULZ
10-26

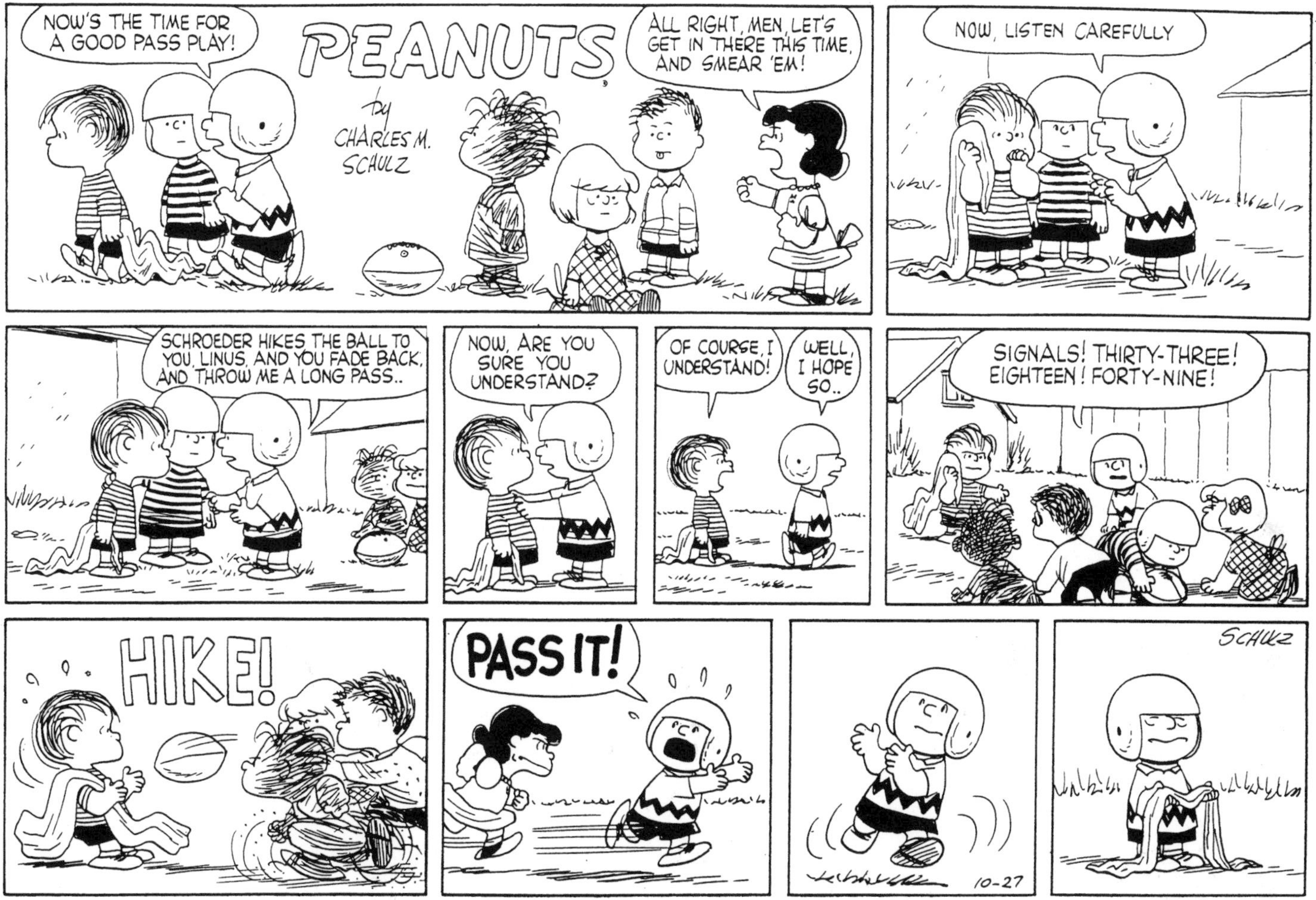
NOW'S THE TIME FOR A GOOD PASS PLAY!
PEANUTS
by CHARLES M. SCHULZ
ALL RIGHT, MEN, LET'S GET IN THERE THIS TIME, AND SMEAR 'EM!
NOW, LISTEN CAREFULLY
SCHROEDER HIKES THE BALL TO YOU, LINUS, AND YOU FADE BACK, AND THROW ME A LONG PASS..
NOW, ARE YOU SURE YOU UNDERSTAND?
OF COURSE, I UNDERSTAND!
WELL, I HOPE SO..
SIGNALS! THIRTY-THREE! EIGHTEEN! FORTY-NINE!
HIKE!
PASS IT!
10-27
SCHULZ

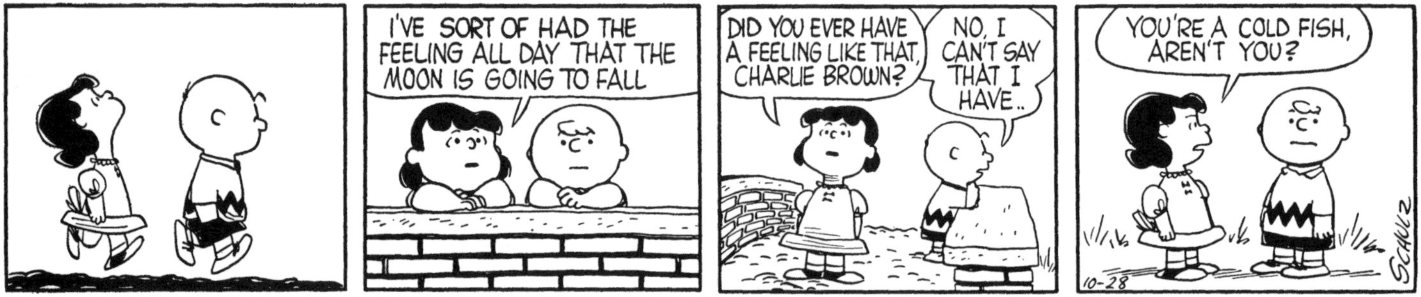
I'VE SORT OF HAD THE FEELING ALL DAY THAT THE MOON IS GOING TO FALL
DID YOU EVER HAVE A FEELING LIKE THAT, CHARLIE BROWN?
NO, I CAN'T SAY THAT I HAVE..
YOU'RE A COLD FISH, AREN'T YOU?
10-28
SCHULZ

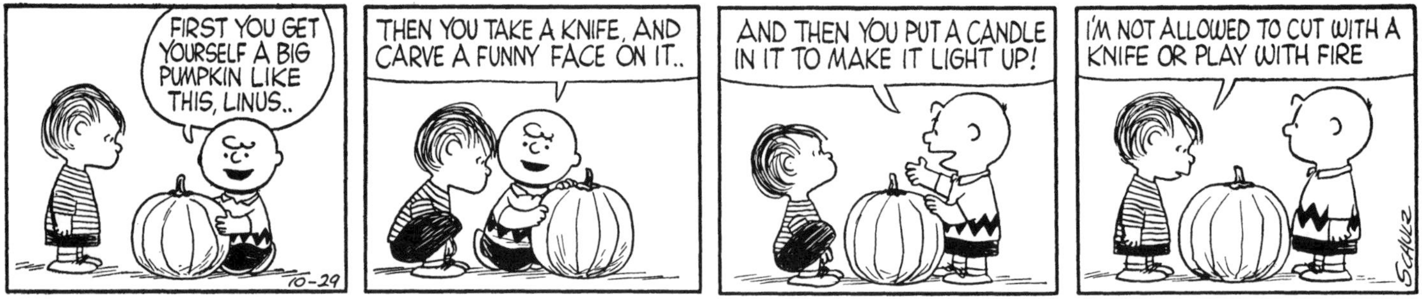
FIRST YOU GET YOURSELF A BIG PUMPKIN LIKE THIS, LINUS..
10-29
THEN YOU TAKE A KNIFE, AND CARVE A FUNNY FACE ON IT..
AND THEN YOU PUT A CANDLE IN IT TO MAKE IT LIGHT UP!
I'M NOT ALLOWED TO CUT WITH A KNIFE OR PLAY WITH FIRE
SCHULZ

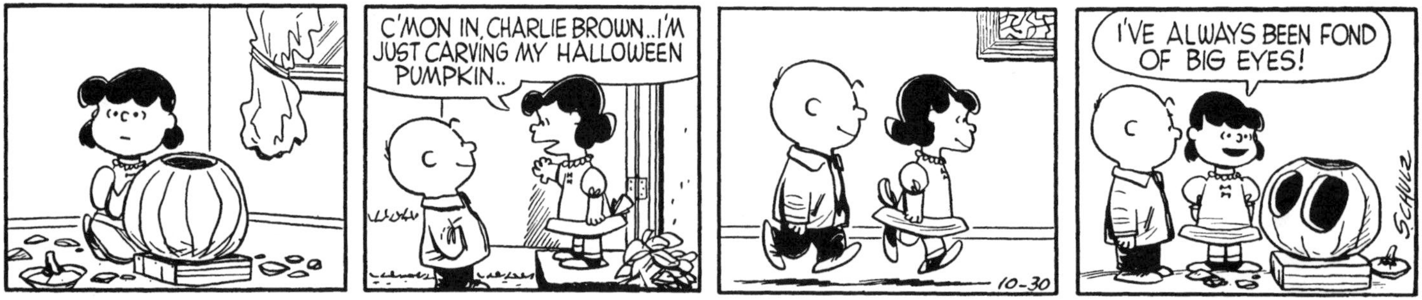
C'MON IN, CHARLIE BROWN..I'M JUST CARVING MY HALLOWEEN PUMPKIN..
10-30
I'VE ALWAYS BEEN FOND OF BIG EYES!
SCHULZ

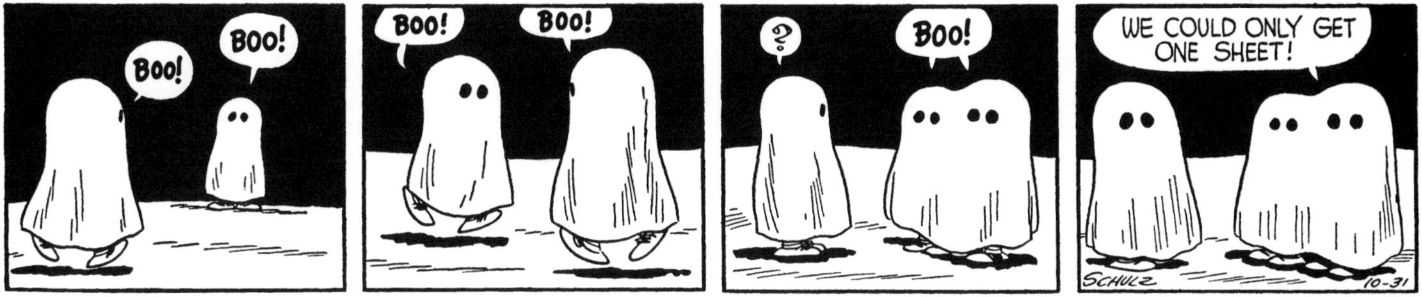
BOO!
BOO!
BOO!
BOO!
?
BOO!
WE COULD ONLY GET ONE SHEET!
SCHULZ
10-31

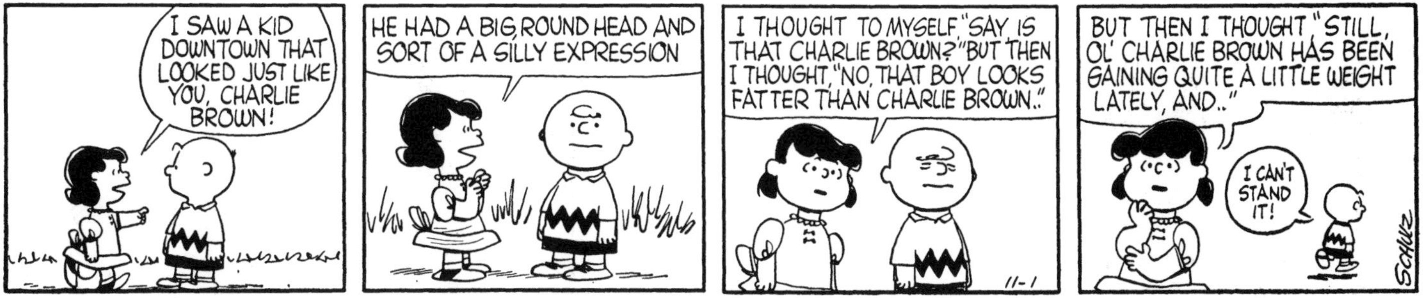
I SAW A KID DOWNTOWN THAT LOOKED JUST LIKE YOU, CHARLIE BROWN!
HE HAD A BIG ROUND HEAD AND SORT OF A SILLY EXPRESSION
I THOUGHT TO MYSELF, "SAY, IS THAT CHARLIE BROWN?" BUT THEN I THOUGHT, "NO, THAT BOY LOOKS FATTER THAN CHARLIE BROWN.."
11-1
BUT THEN I THOUGHT, "STILL, OL' CHARLIE BROWN HAS BEEN GAINING QUITE A LITTLE WEIGHT LATELY, AND.."
I CAN'T STAND IT!
SCHULZ

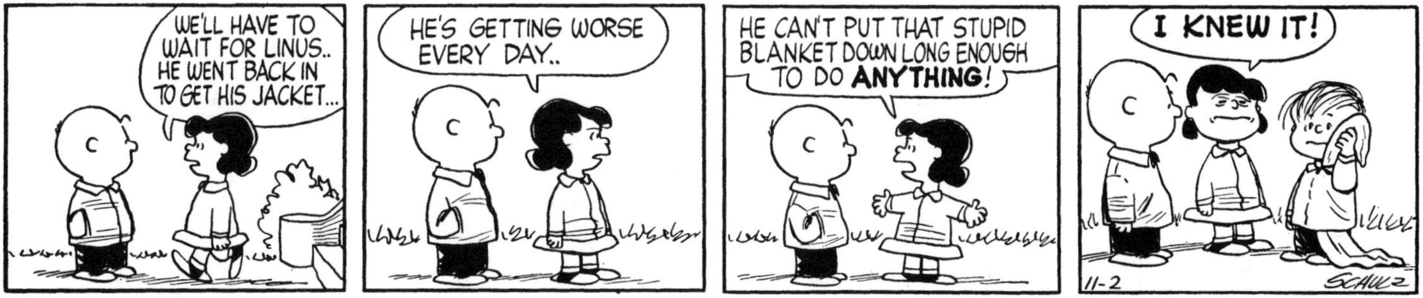
WE'LL HAVE TO WAIT FOR LINUS.. HE WENT BACK IN TO GET HIS JACKET...
HE'S GETTING WORSE EVERY DAY..
HE CAN'T PUT THAT STUPID BLANKET DOWN LONG ENOUGH TO DO ANYTHING!
I KNEW IT!
11-2
SCHULZ

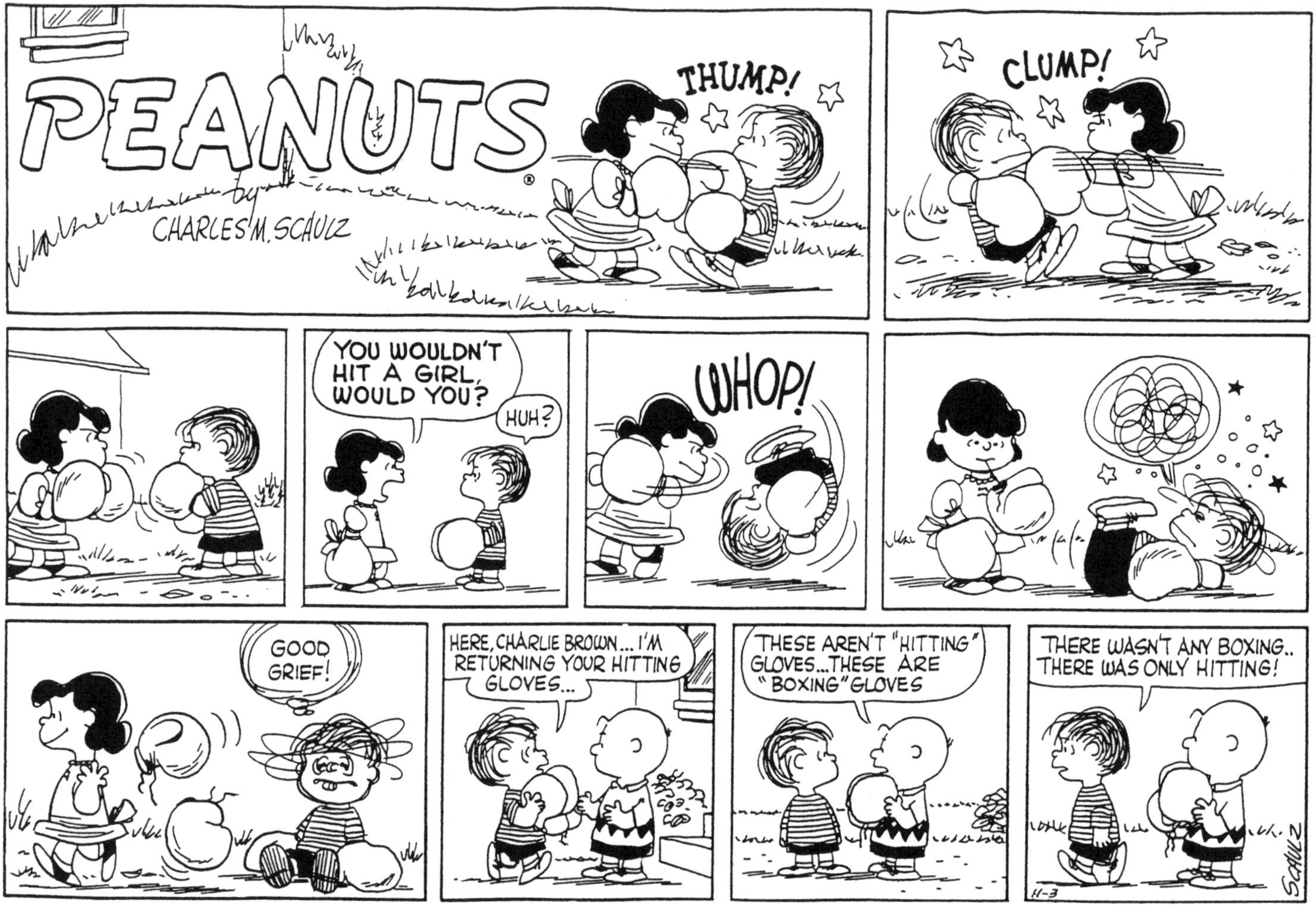
PEANUTS
by CHARLES M. SCHULZ
THUMP!
CLUMP!
YOU WOULDN'T HIT A GIRL, WOULD YOU?
HUH?
WHOP!
GOOD GRIEF!
HERE, CHARLIE BROWN... I'M RETURNING YOUR HITTING GLOVES...
THESE AREN'T "HITTING" GLOVES...THESE ARE "BOXING" GLOVES
THERE WASN'T ANY BOXING.. THERE WAS ONLY HITTING!
11-3
SCHULZ

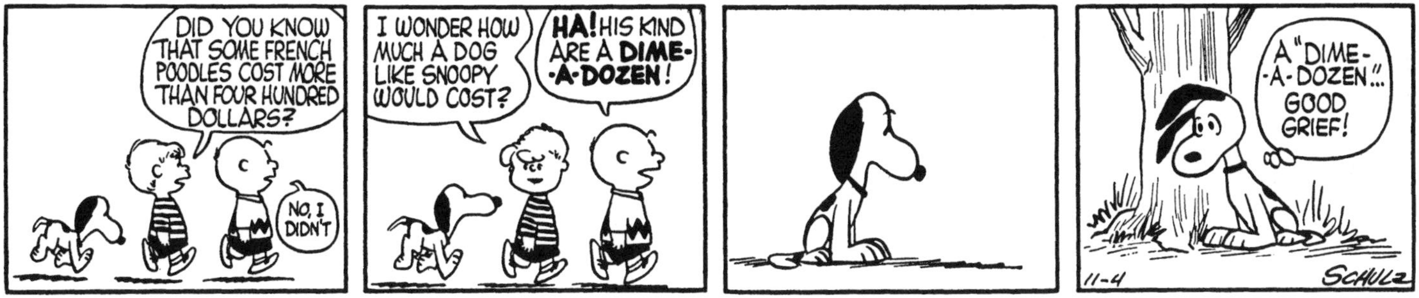
DID YOU KNOW THAT SOME FRENCH POODLES COST MORE THAN FOUR HUNDRED DOLLARS?
NO, I DIDN'T
I WONDER HOW MUCH A DOG LIKE SNOOPY WOULD COST?
HA! HIS KIND ARE A DIME-A-DOZEN!
A "DIME-A-DOZEN"... GOOD GRIEF!
11-4
SCHULZ

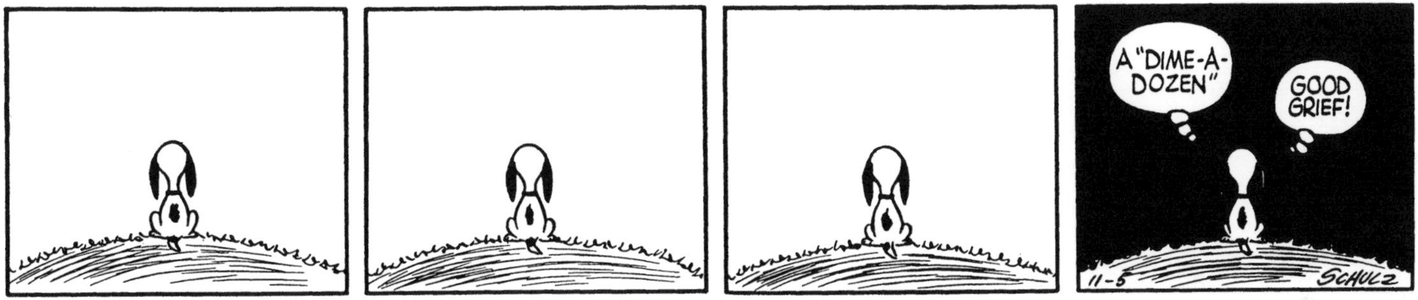
A "DIME-A-DOZEN"
GOOD GRIEF!
11-5
SCHULZ

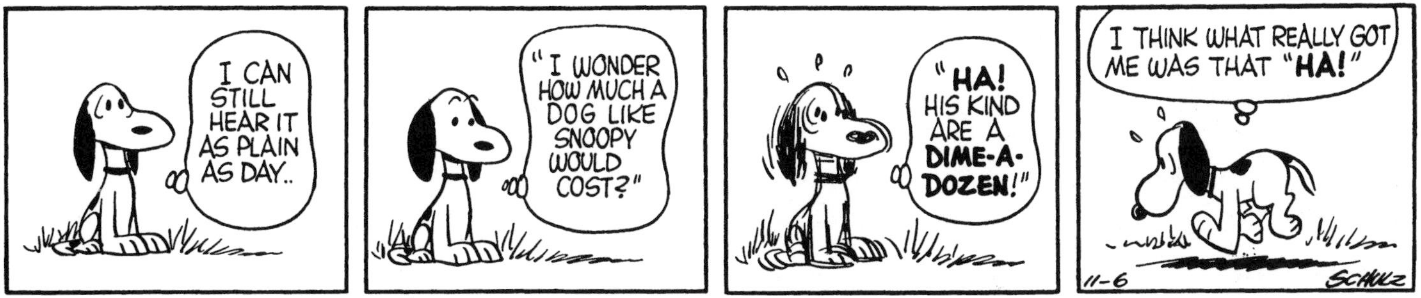
I CAN STILL HEAR IT AS PLAIN AS DAY..
"I WONDER HOW MUCH A DOG LIKE SNOOPY WOULD COST?"
"HA! HIS KIND ARE A DIME-A-DOZEN!"
I THINK WHAT REALLY GOT ME WAS THAT "HA!"
11-6
SCHULZ

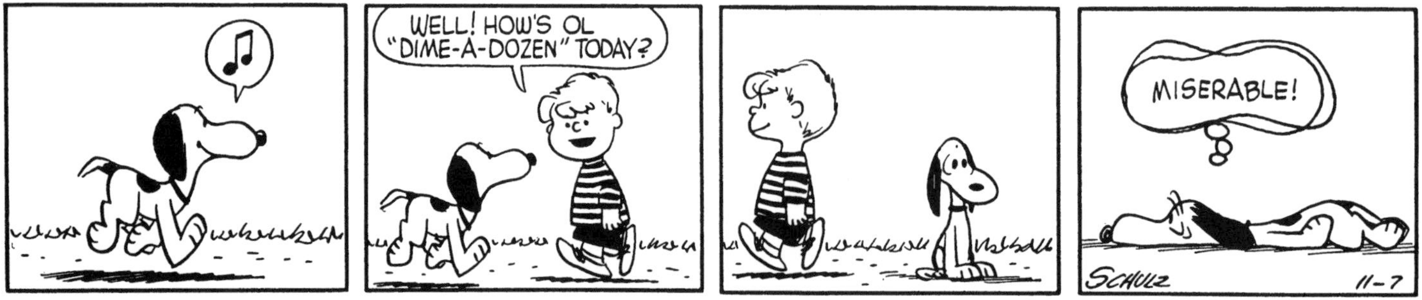
WELL! HOW'S OL "DIME-A-DOZEN" TODAY?
MISERABLE!
SCHULZ
11-7

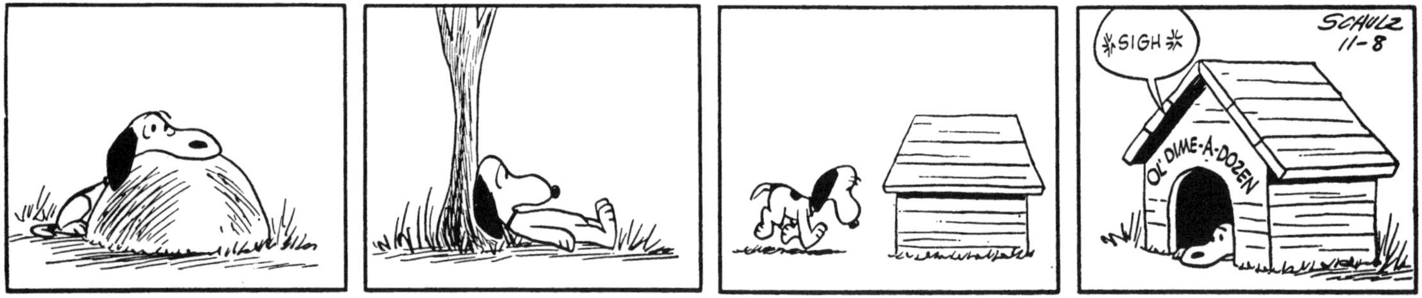
SCHULZ
11-8
SIGH
OL' DIME-A-DOZEN

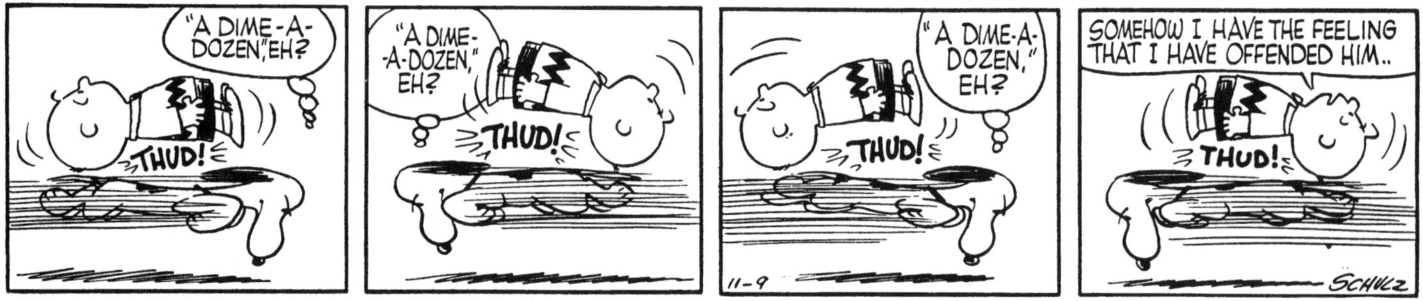
"A DIME-A-DOZEN," EH?
THUD!
"A DIME-A-DOZEN," EH?
THUD!
"A DIME-A-DOZEN," EH?
THUD!
11-9
SOMEHOW I HAVE THE FEELING THAT I HAVE OFFENDED HIM..
THUD!
SCHULZ

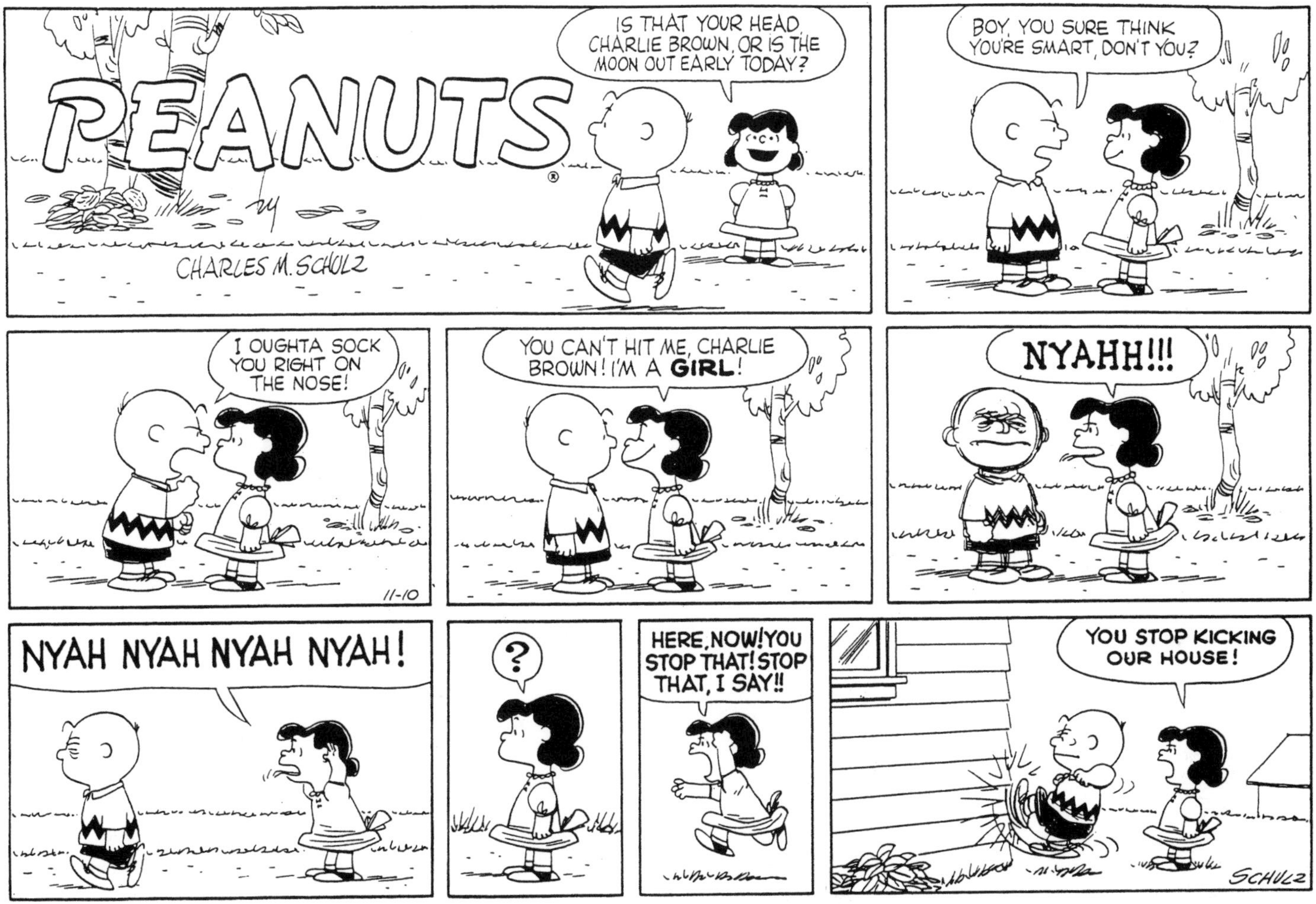
PEANUTS
CHARLES M. SCHULZ
IS THAT YOUR HEAD, CHARLIE BROWN, OR IS THE MOON OUT EARLY TODAY?
BOY, YOU SURE THINK YOU'RE SMART, DON'T YOU?
I OUGHTA SOCK YOU RIGHT ON THE NOSE!
11-10
YOU CAN'T HIT ME, CHARLIE BROWN! I'M A **GIRL**!
NYAHH!!!
NYAH NYAH NYAH NYAH!
?
HERE, NOW! YOU STOP THAT! STOP THAT, I SAY!!
YOU STOP KICKING OUR HOUSE!
SCHULZ

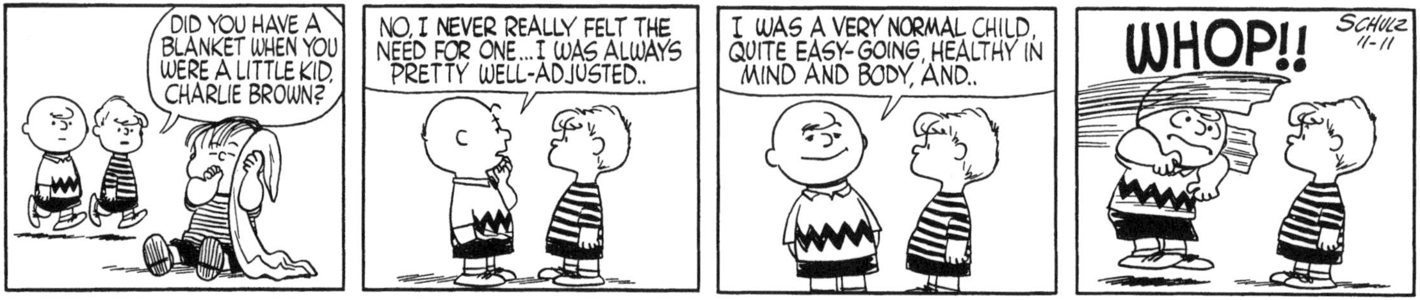
DID YOU HAVE A BLANKET WHEN YOU WERE A LITTLE KID, CHARLIE BROWN?
NO, I NEVER REALLY FELT THE NEED FOR ONE...I WAS ALWAYS PRETTY WELL-ADJUSTED..
I WAS A VERY NORMAL CHILD, QUITE EASY-GOING, HEALTHY IN MIND AND BODY, AND..
WHOP!!
SCHULZ 11-11

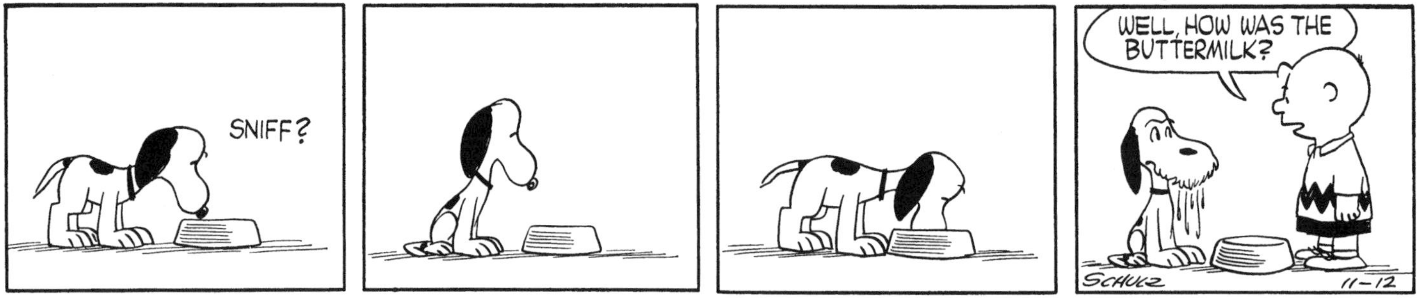
SNIFF?
WELL, HOW WAS THE BUTTERMILK?
SCHULZ
11-12

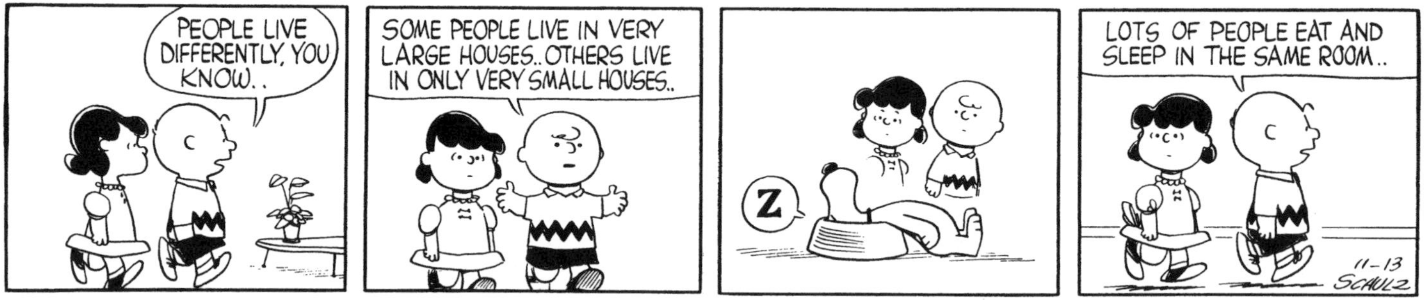
PEOPLE LIVE DIFFERENTLY, YOU KNOW..
SOME PEOPLE LIVE IN VERY LARGE HOUSES..OTHERS LIVE IN ONLY VERY SMALL HOUSES..
Z
LOTS OF PEOPLE EAT AND SLEEP IN THE SAME ROOM..
11-13 SCHULZ

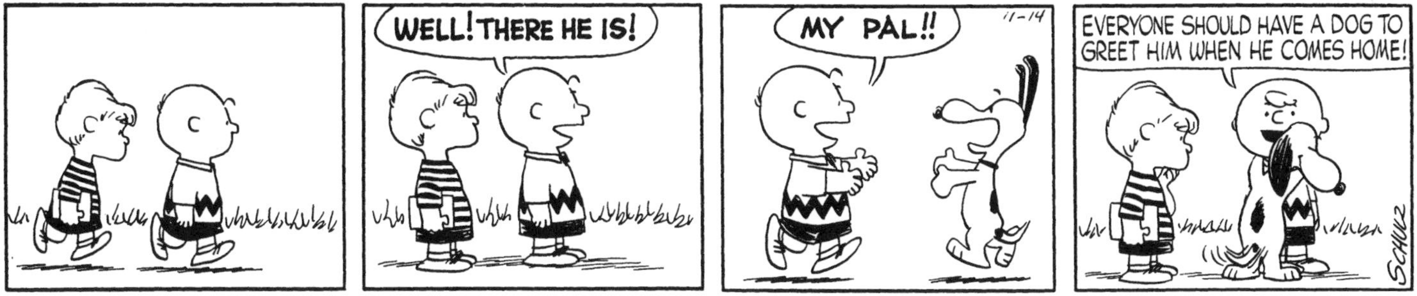
WELL! THERE HE IS!
MY PAL!!
11-14
EVERYONE SHOULD HAVE A DOG TO GREET HIM WHEN HE COMES HOME!
SCHULZ

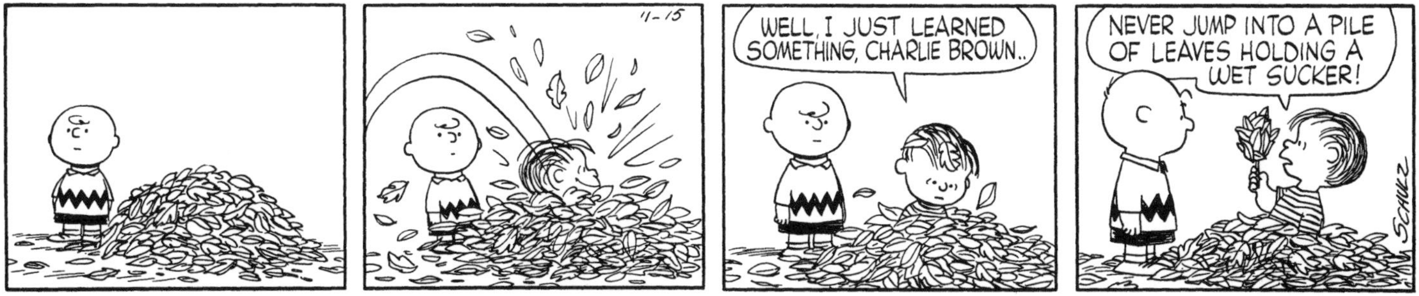
11-15
WELL, I JUST LEARNED SOMETHING, CHARLIE BROWN..
NEVER JUMP INTO A PILE OF LEAVES HOLDING A WET SUCKER!
SCHULZ

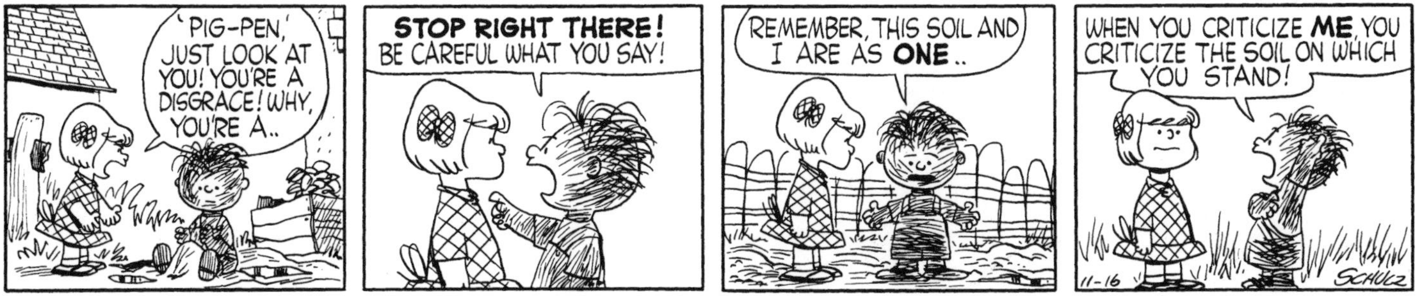
'PIG-PEN,' JUST LOOK AT YOU! YOU'RE A DISGRACE! WHY, YOU'RE A..
STOP RIGHT THERE! BE CAREFUL WHAT YOU SAY!
REMEMBER, THIS SOIL AND I ARE AS ONE..
WHEN YOU CRITICIZE ME, YOU CRITICIZE THE SOIL ON WHICH YOU STAND!
11-16
SCHULZ

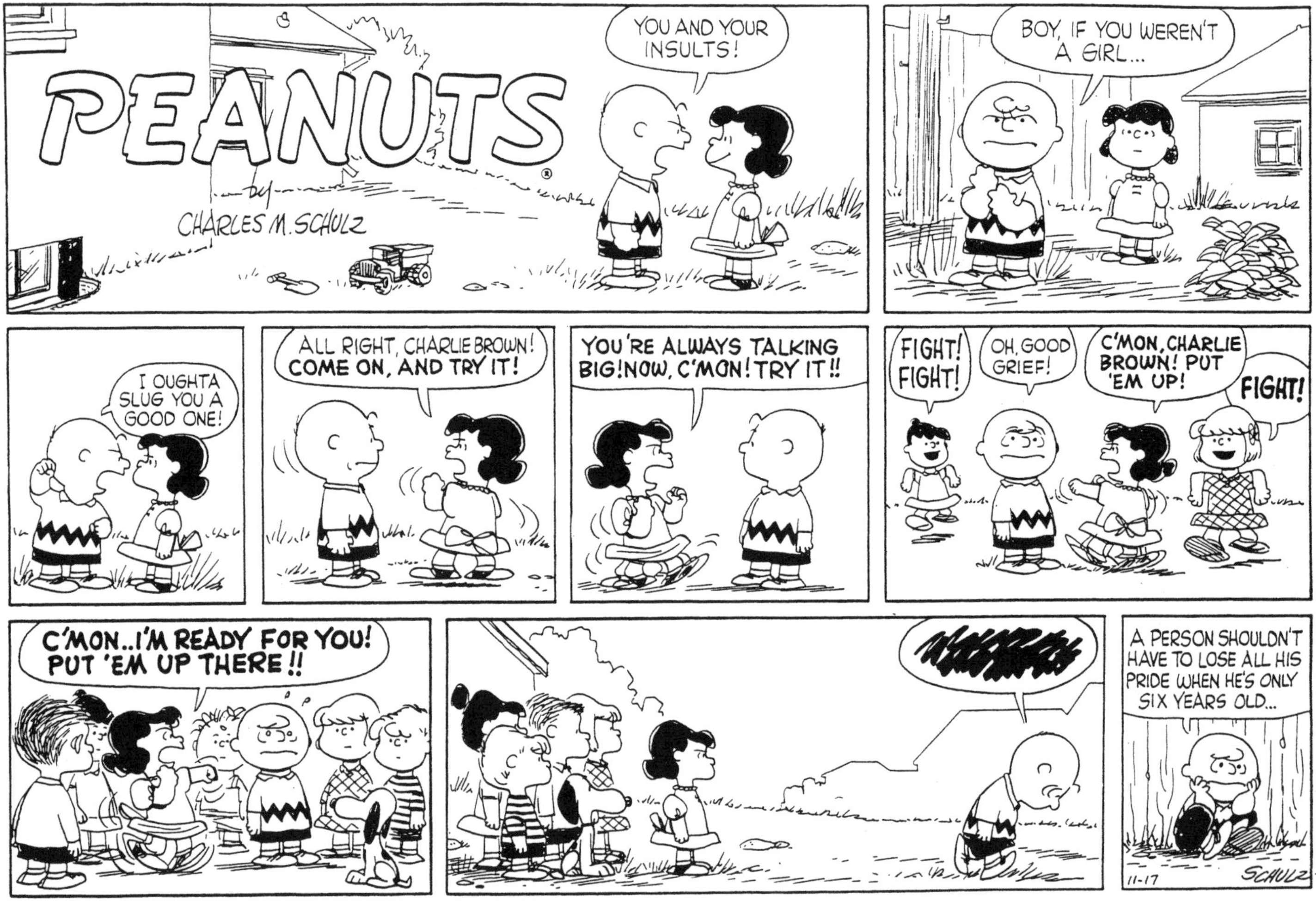
PEANUTS
by CHARLES M. SCHULZ
YOU AND YOUR INSULTS!
BOY, IF YOU WEREN'T A GIRL...
I OUGHTA SLUG YOU A GOOD ONE!
ALL RIGHT, CHARLIE BROWN! COME ON, AND TRY IT!
YOU'RE ALWAYS TALKING BIG! NOW, C'MON! TRY IT!!
FIGHT! FIGHT!
OH, GOOD GRIEF!
C'MON, CHARLIE BROWN! PUT 'EM UP!
FIGHT!
C'MON..I'M READY FOR YOU! PUT 'EM UP THERE!!
A PERSON SHOULDN'T HAVE TO LOSE ALL HIS PRIDE WHEN HE'S ONLY SIX YEARS OLD...
11-17
SCHULZ

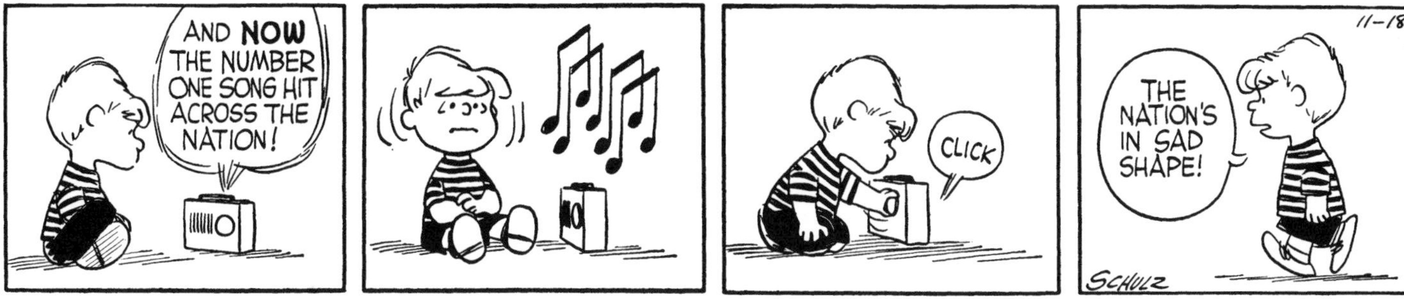
AND **NOW** THE NUMBER ONE SONG HIT ACROSS THE NATION!
CLICK
THE NATION'S IN SAD SHAPE!
11-18
SCHULZ

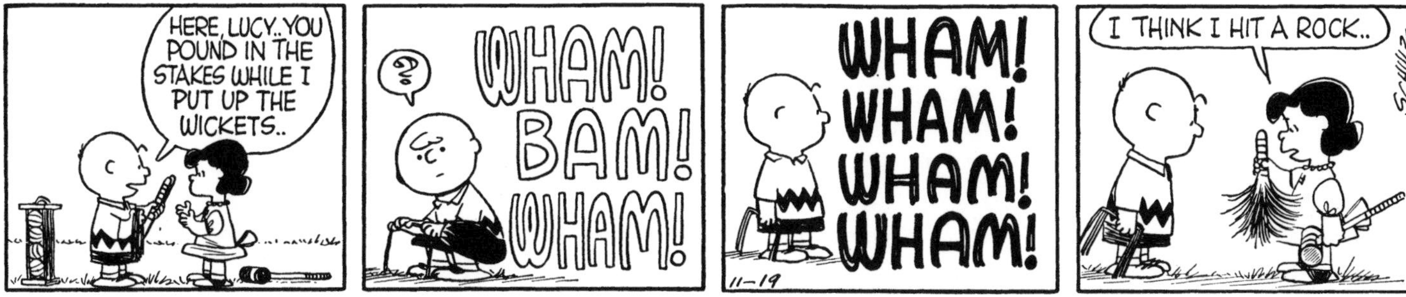
HERE, LUCY.. YOU POUND IN THE STAKES WHILE I PUT UP THE WICKETS..
?
WHAM! BAM! WHAM!
WHAM! WHAM! WHAM! WHAM!
11-19
I THINK I HIT A ROCK..
SCHULZ

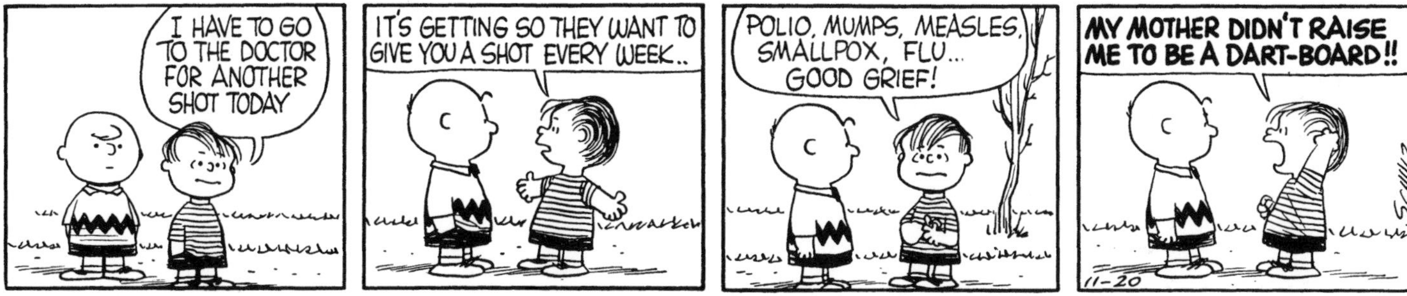
I HAVE TO GO TO THE DOCTOR FOR ANOTHER SHOT TODAY
IT'S GETTING SO THEY WANT TO GIVE YOU A SHOT EVERY WEEK..
POLIO, MUMPS, MEASLES, SMALLPOX, FLU... GOOD GRIEF!
MY MOTHER DIDN'T RAISE ME TO BE A DART-BOARD!!
SCHULZ
11-20

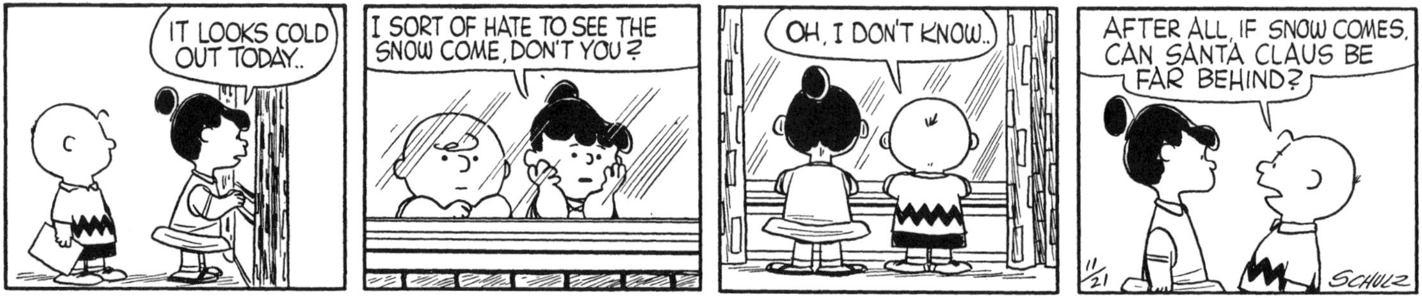
IT LOOKS COLD OUT TODAY..
I SORT OF HATE TO SEE THE SNOW COME, DON'T YOU ?
OH, I DON'T KNOW..
AFTER ALL, IF SNOW COMES, CAN SANTA CLAUS BE FAR BEHIND?
11/21
SCHULZ

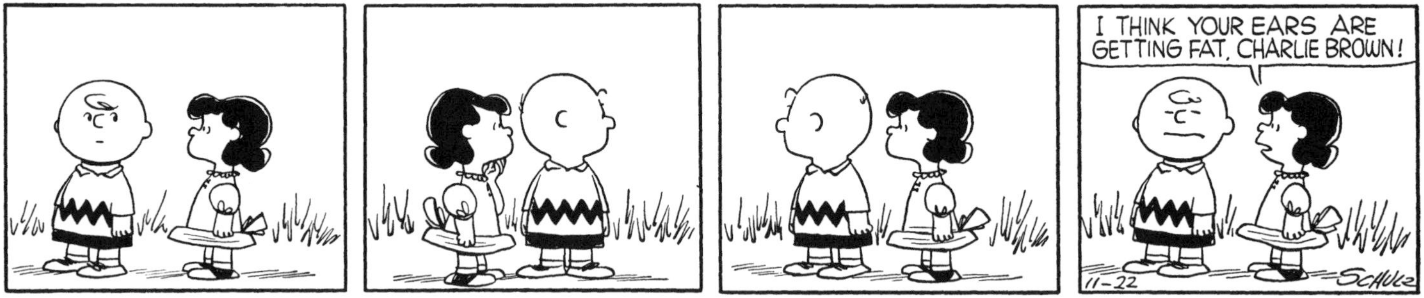
I THINK YOUR EARS ARE GETTING FAT, CHARLIE BROWN!
11-22
SCHULZ

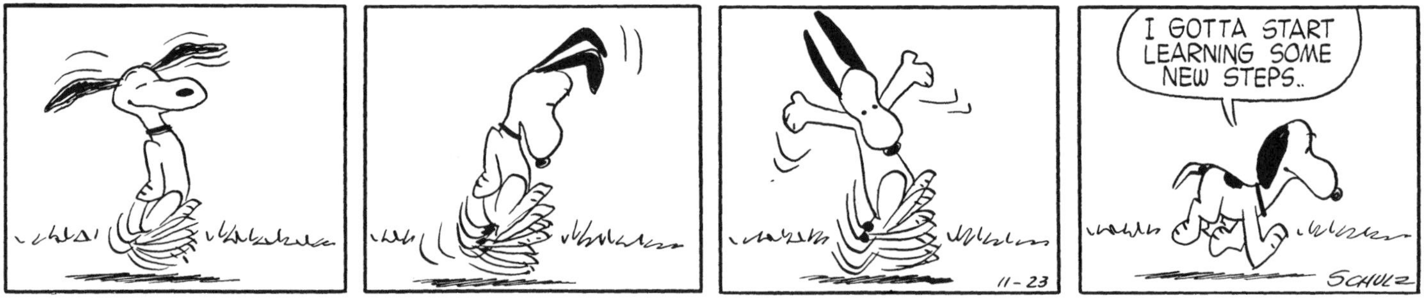
11-23
I GOTTA START LEARNING SOME NEW STEPS..
SCHULZ

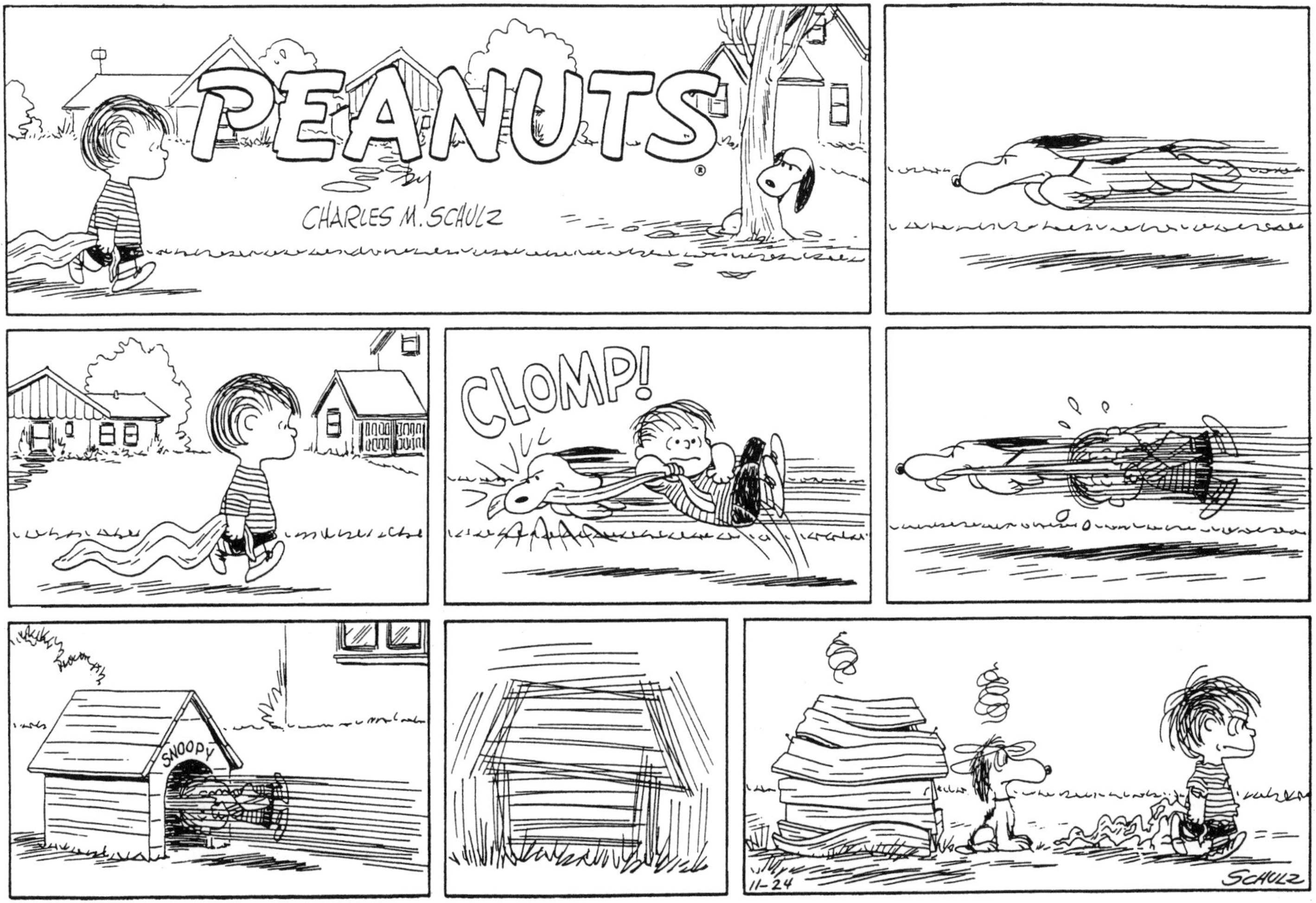
PEANUTS
By
CHARLES M. SCHULZ
CLOMP!
SNOOPY
11-24
SCHULZ

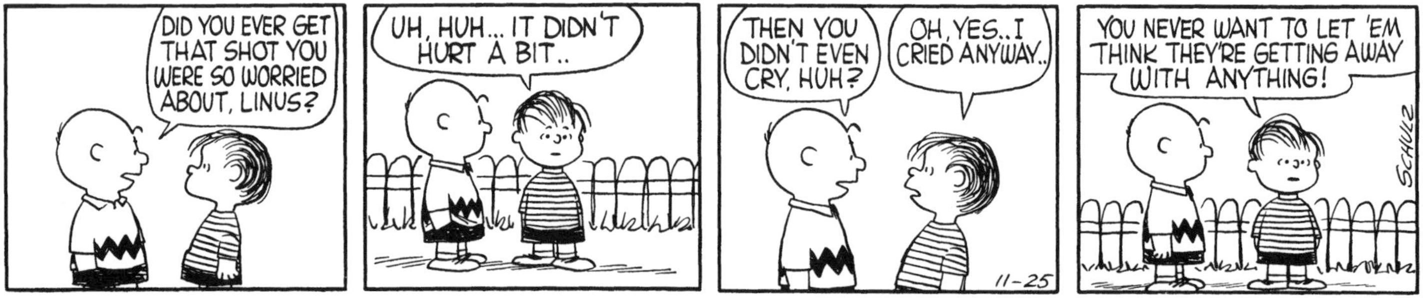
DID YOU EVER GET THAT SHOT YOU WERE SO WORRIED ABOUT, LINUS?
UH, HUH... IT DIDN'T HURT A BIT..
THEN YOU DIDN'T EVEN CRY, HUH?
OH, YES..I CRIED ANYWAY..
11-25
YOU NEVER WANT TO LET 'EM THINK THEY'RE GETTING AWAY WITH ANYTHING!
SCHULZ

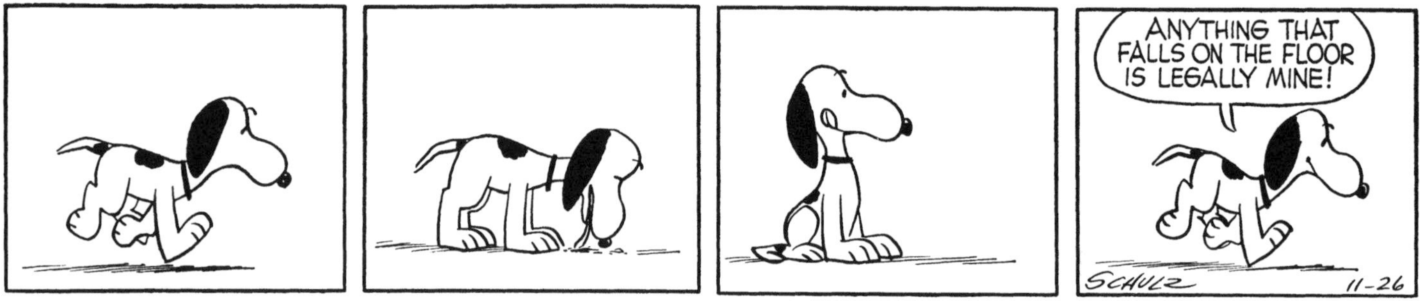
ANYTHING THAT FALLS ON THE FLOOR IS LEGALLY MINE!
SCHULZ
11-26

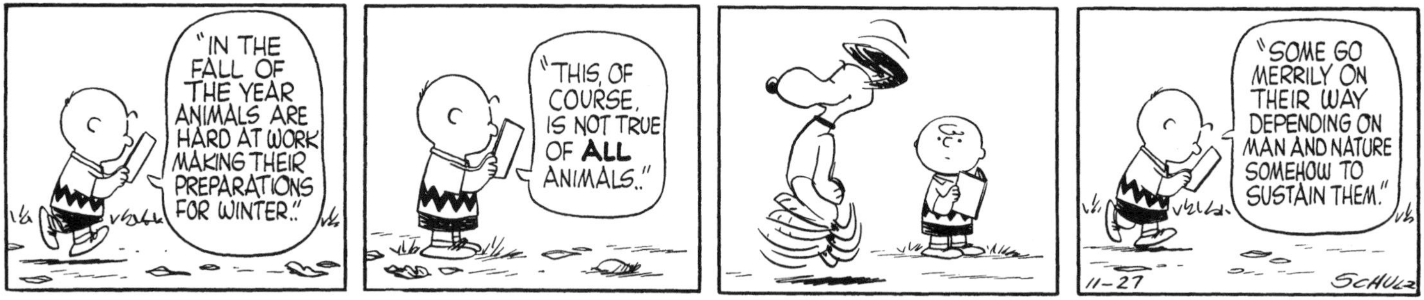
"IN THE FALL OF THE YEAR ANIMALS ARE HARD AT WORK MAKING THEIR PREPARATIONS FOR WINTER."
"THIS, OF COURSE, IS NOT TRUE OF **ALL** ANIMALS."
"SOME GO MERRILY ON THEIR WAY DEPENDING ON MAN AND NATURE SOMEHOW TO SUSTAIN THEM."
11-27
SCHULZ

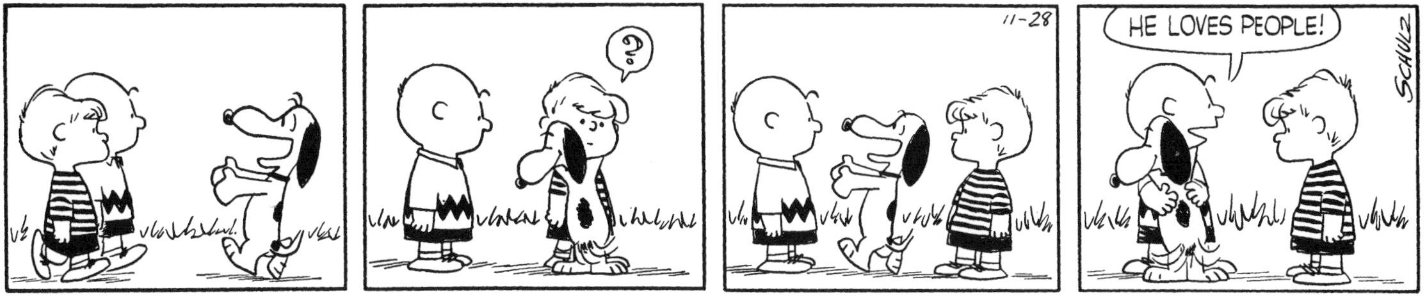
?
11-28
HE LOVES PEOPLE!
SCHULZ

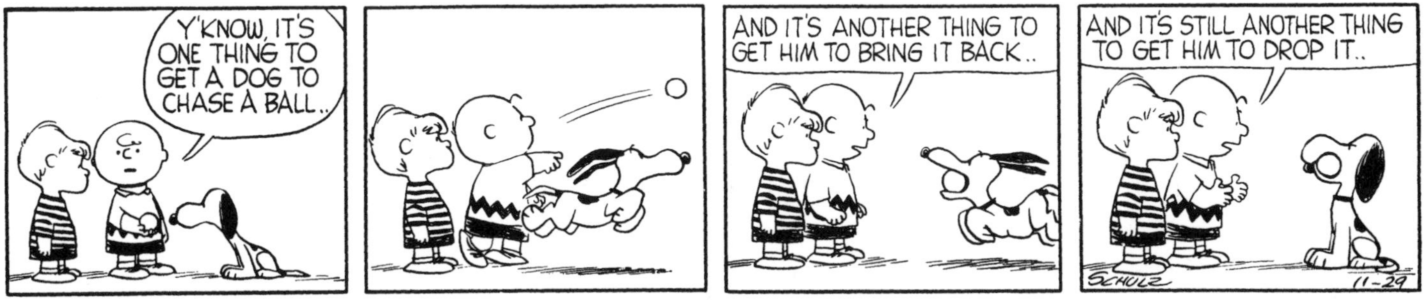
Y'KNOW, IT'S ONE THING TO GET A DOG TO CHASE A BALL..
AND IT'S ANOTHER THING TO GET HIM TO BRING IT BACK..
AND IT'S STILL ANOTHER THING TO GET HIM TO DROP IT..
SCHULZ
11-29

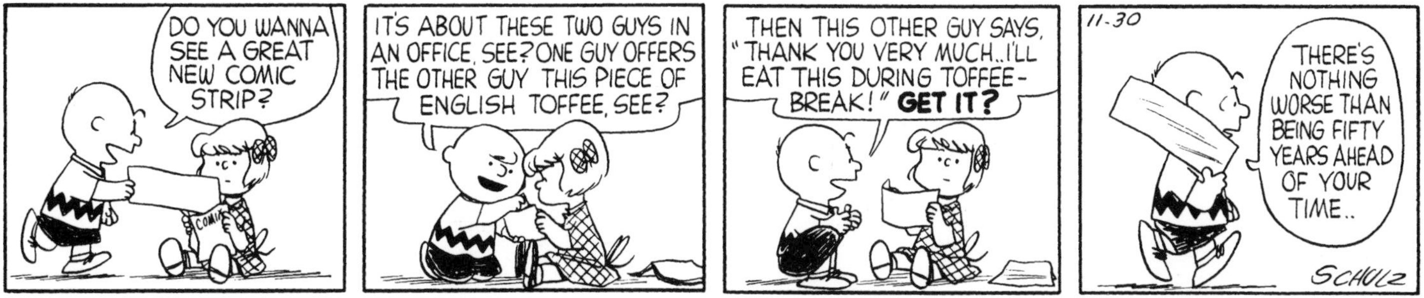
DO YOU WANNA SEE A GREAT NEW COMIC STRIP?
COMIC
IT'S ABOUT THESE TWO GUYS IN AN OFFICE, SEE? ONE GUY OFFERS THE OTHER GUY THIS PIECE OF ENGLISH TOFFEE, SEE?
THEN THIS OTHER GUY SAYS, "THANK YOU VERY MUCH..I'LL EAT THIS DURING TOFFEE-BREAK!" GET IT?
11-30
THERE'S NOTHING WORSE THAN BEING FIFTY YEARS AHEAD OF YOUR TIME..
SCHULZ

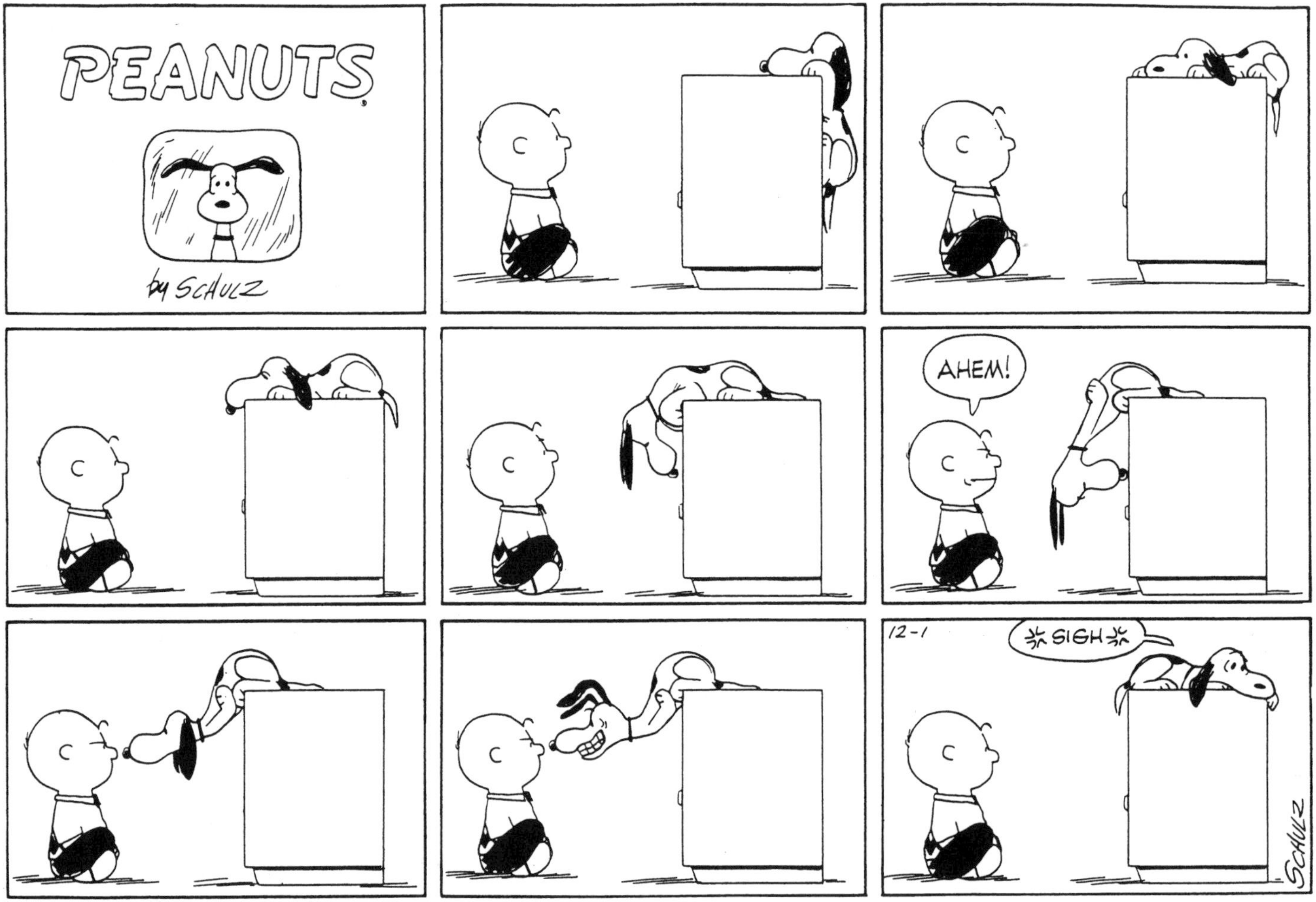
PEANUTS
by SCHULZ
AHEM!
12-1
SIGH
SCHULZ

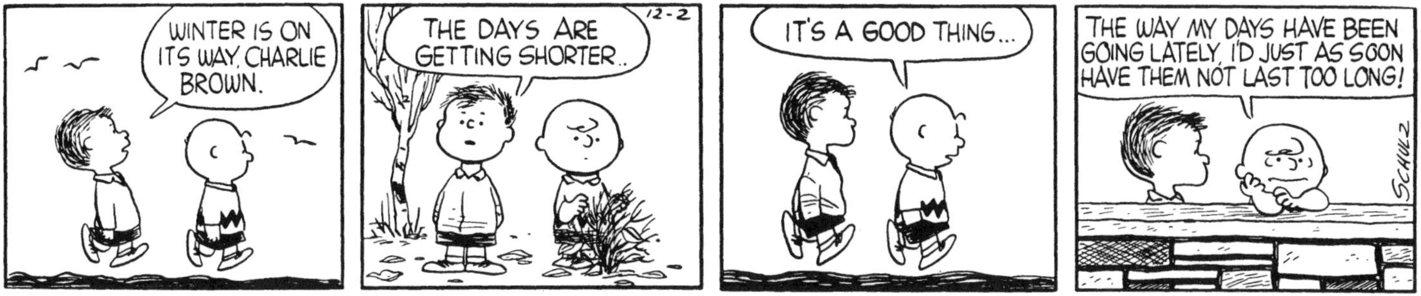
WINTER IS ON ITS WAY, CHARLIE BROWN.
THE DAYS ARE GETTING SHORTER..
12-2
IT'S A GOOD THING...
THE WAY MY DAYS HAVE BEEN GOING LATELY, I'D JUST AS SOON HAVE THEM NOT LAST TOO LONG!

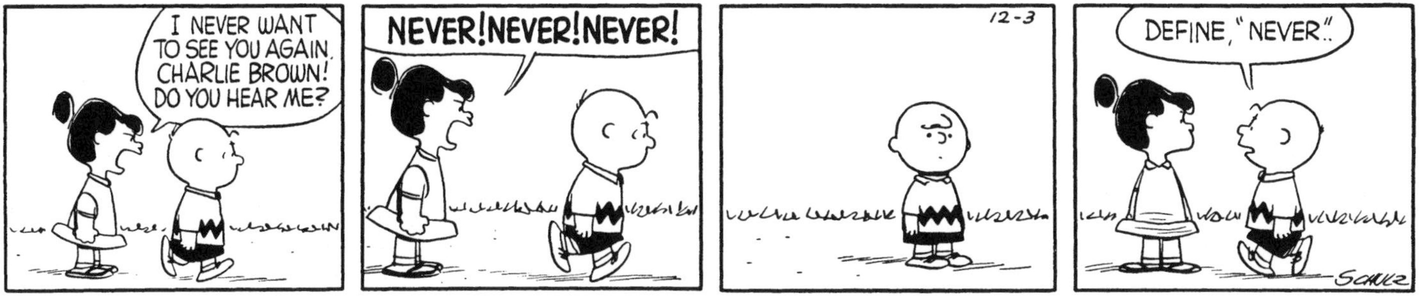
I NEVER WANT TO SEE YOU AGAIN, CHARLIE BROWN! DO YOU HEAR ME?
NEVER! NEVER! NEVER!
12-3
DEFINE, "NEVER"..

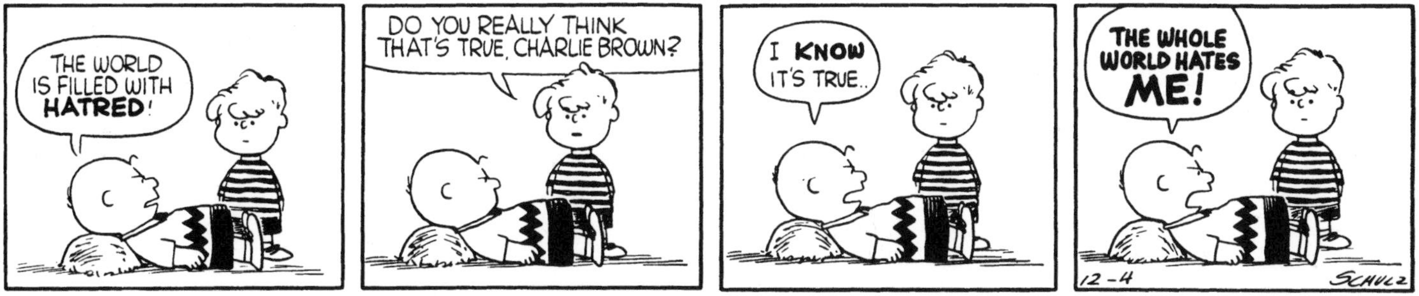
THE WORLD IS FILLED WITH **HATRED**!
DO YOU REALLY THINK THAT'S TRUE, CHARLIE BROWN?
I **KNOW** IT'S TRUE..
THE WHOLE WORLD HATES ME!
12-4

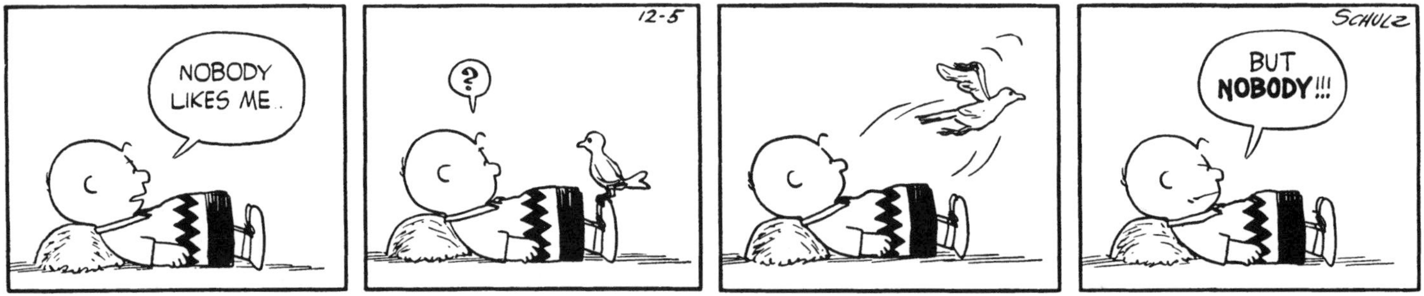
NOBODY LIKES ME..
?
12-5
SCHULZ
BUT **NOBODY**!!!

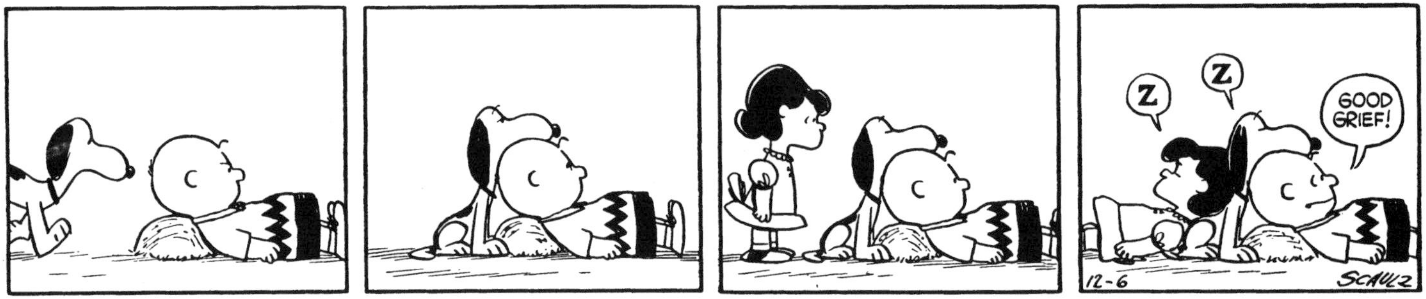
Z
Z
GOOD GRIEF!
12-6
SCHULZ

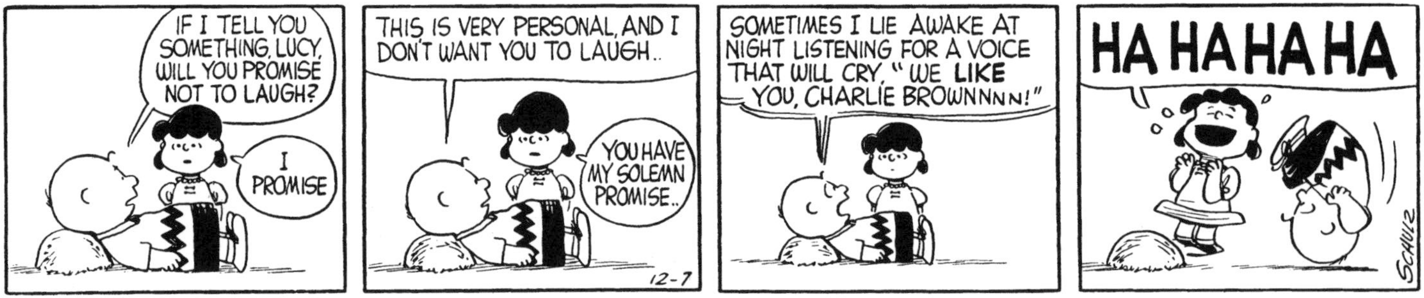
IF I TELL YOU SOMETHING, LUCY, WILL YOU PROMISE NOT TO LAUGH?
I PROMISE
THIS IS VERY PERSONAL, AND I DON'T WANT YOU TO LAUGH..
YOU HAVE MY SOLEMN PROMISE..
12-7
SOMETIMES I LIE AWAKE AT NIGHT LISTENING FOR A VOICE THAT WILL CRY, "WE **LIKE** YOU, CHARLIE BROWNNNNN!"
HA HA HA HA HA
SCHULZ

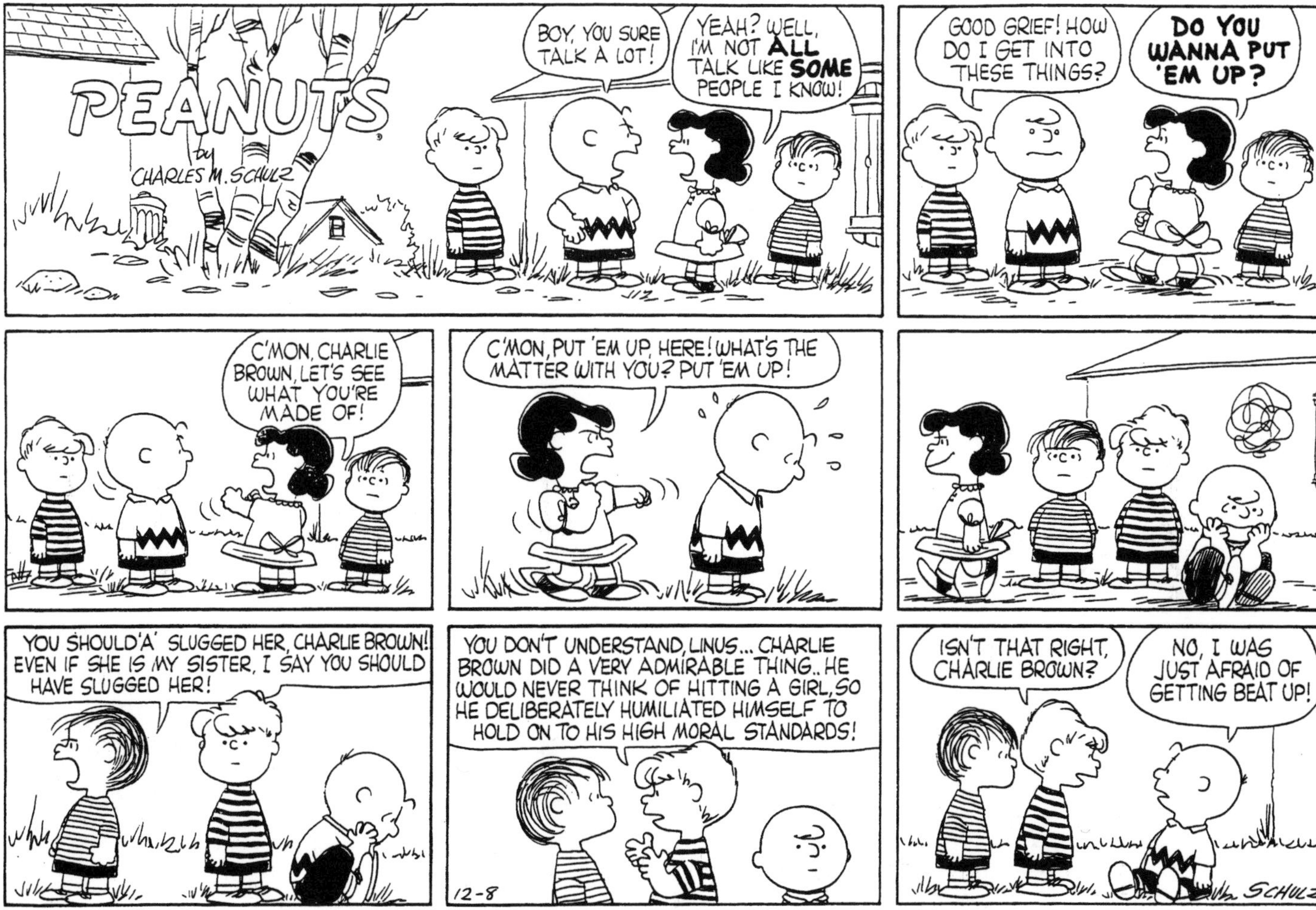
PEANUTS
by CHARLES M. SCHULZ
BOY, YOU SURE TALK A LOT!
YEAH? WELL, I'M NOT ALL TALK LIKE SOME PEOPLE I KNOW!
GOOD GRIEF! HOW DO I GET INTO THESE THINGS?
DO YOU WANNA PUT 'EM UP?
C'MON, CHARLIE BROWN, LET'S SEE WHAT YOU'RE MADE OF!
C'MON, PUT 'EM UP, HERE! WHAT'S THE MATTER WITH YOU? PUT 'EM UP!
YOU SHOULD'A' SLUGGED HER, CHARLIE BROWN! EVEN IF SHE IS MY SISTER, I SAY YOU SHOULD HAVE SLUGGED HER!
YOU DON'T UNDERSTAND, LINUS... CHARLIE BROWN DID A VERY ADMIRABLE THING.. HE WOULD NEVER THINK OF HITTING A GIRL, SO HE DELIBERATELY HUMILIATED HIMSELF TO HOLD ON TO HIS HIGH MORAL STANDARDS!
12-8
ISN'T THAT RIGHT, CHARLIE BROWN?
NO, I WAS JUST AFRAID OF GETTING BEAT UP!
SCHULZ

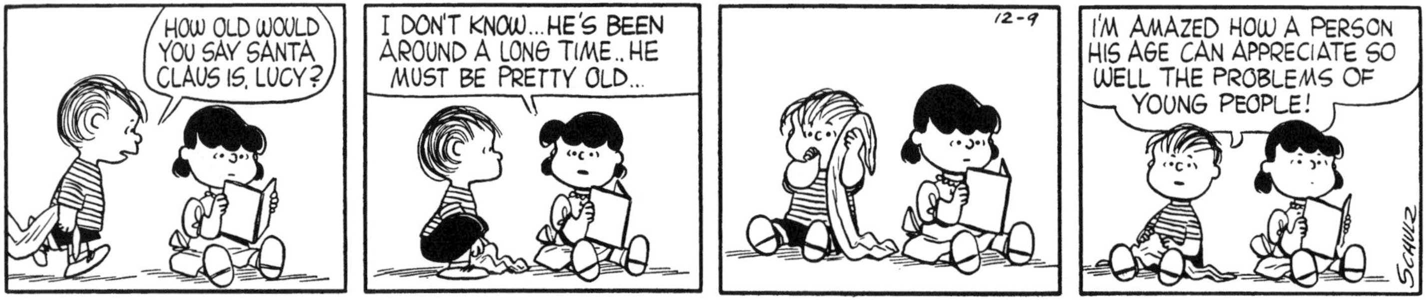
HOW OLD WOULD YOU SAY SANTA CLAUS IS, LUCY?
I DON'T KNOW... HE'S BEEN AROUND A LONG TIME.. HE MUST BE PRETTY OLD...
12-9
I'M AMAZED HOW A PERSON HIS AGE CAN APPRECIATE SO WELL THE PROBLEMS OF YOUNG PEOPLE!
SCHULZ

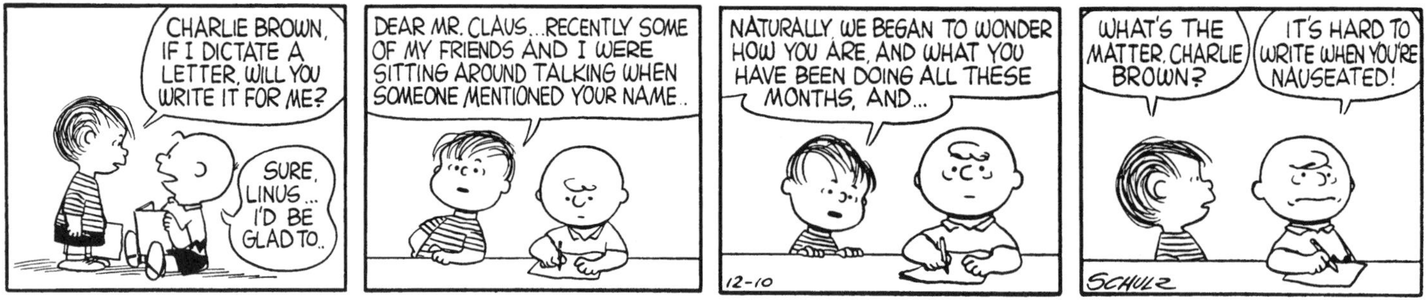
CHARLIE BROWN, IF I DICTATE A LETTER, WILL YOU WRITE IT FOR ME?
SURE, LINUS... I'D BE GLAD TO..
DEAR MR. CLAUS... RECENTLY SOME OF MY FRIENDS AND I WERE SITTING AROUND TALKING WHEN SOMEONE MENTIONED YOUR NAME..
NATURALLY, WE BEGAN TO WONDER HOW YOU ARE, AND WHAT YOU HAVE BEEN DOING ALL THESE MONTHS, AND...
12-10
WHAT'S THE MATTER, CHARLIE BROWN?
IT'S HARD TO WRITE WHEN YOU'RE NAUSEATED!
SCHULZ

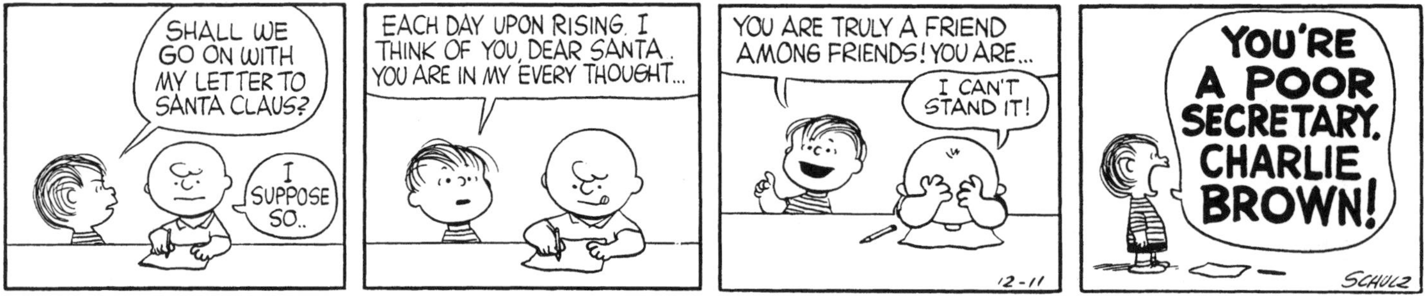
SHALL WE GO ON WITH MY LETTER TO SANTA CLAUS?
I SUPPOSE SO..
EACH DAY UPON RISING, I THINK OF YOU, DEAR SANTA. YOU ARE IN MY EVERY THOUGHT...
YOU ARE TRULY A FRIEND AMONG FRIENDS! YOU ARE...
I CAN'T STAND IT!
12-11
YOU'RE A POOR SECRETARY, CHARLIE BROWN!
SCHULZ

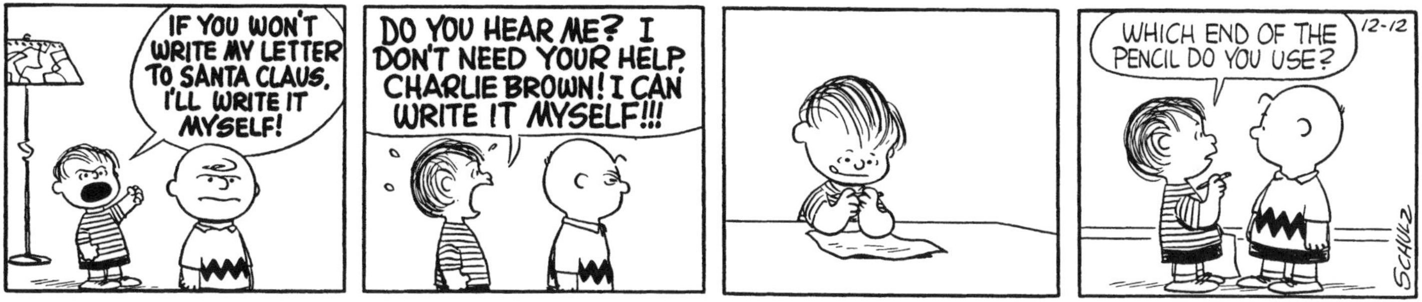
IF YOU WON'T WRITE MY LETTER TO SANTA CLAUS, I'LL WRITE IT MYSELF!
DO YOU HEAR ME? I DON'T NEED YOUR HELP, CHARLIE BROWN! I CAN WRITE IT MYSELF!!!
12-12
WHICH END OF THE PENCIL DO YOU USE?
SCHULZ

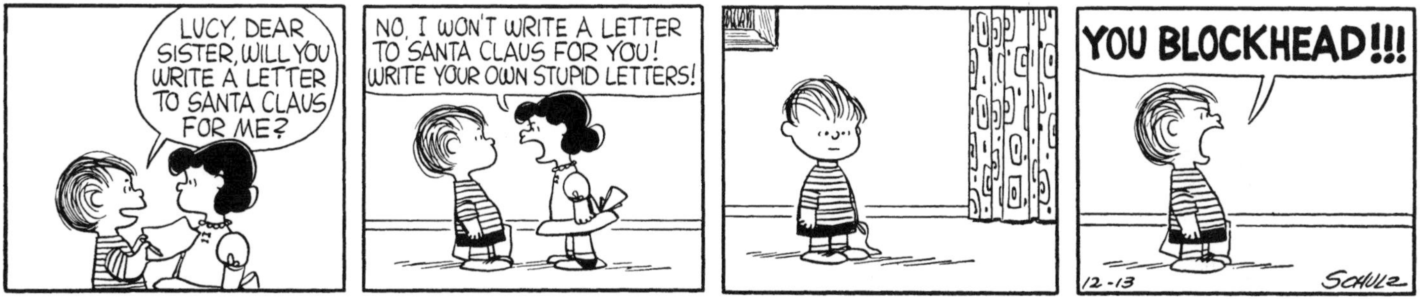
LUCY, DEAR SISTER, WILL YOU WRITE A LETTER TO SANTA CLAUS FOR ME?
NO, I WON'T WRITE A LETTER TO SANTA CLAUS FOR YOU! WRITE YOUR OWN STUPID LETTERS!
YOU BLOCKHEAD!!!
12-13
SCHULZ

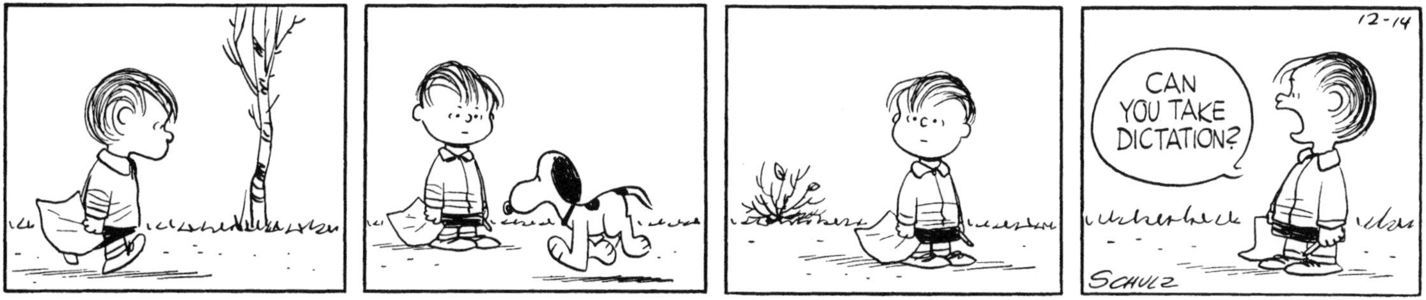
12-14
CAN YOU TAKE DICTATION?
SCHULZ

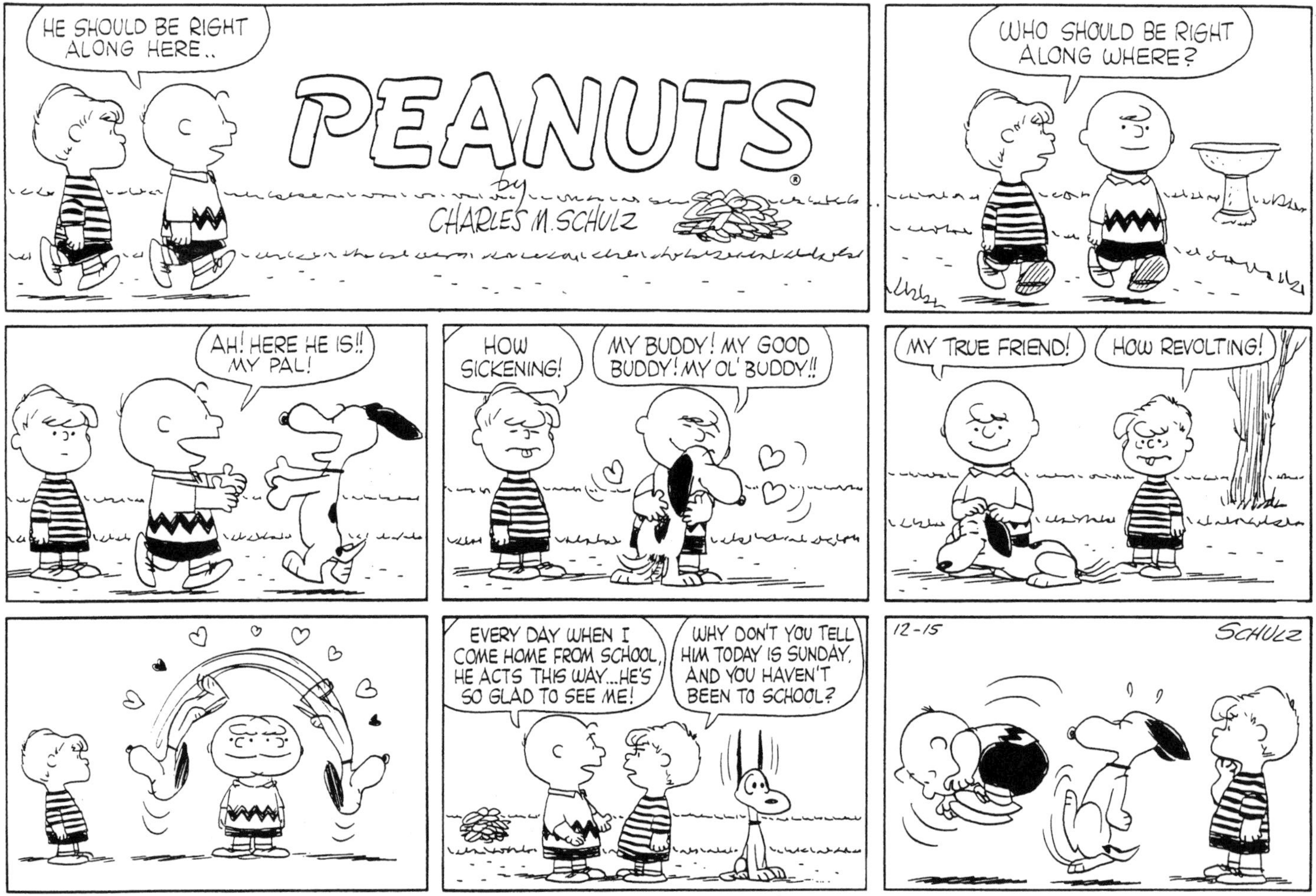
HE SHOULD BE RIGHT ALONG HERE..
PEANUTS
by CHARLES M. SCHULZ
WHO SHOULD BE RIGHT ALONG WHERE?
AH! HERE HE IS!! MY PAL!
HOW SICKENING!
MY BUDDY! MY GOOD BUDDY! MY OL' BUDDY!!
MY TRUE FRIEND!
HOW REVOLTING!
EVERY DAY WHEN I COME HOME FROM SCHOOL, HE ACTS THIS WAY...HE'S SO GLAD TO SEE ME!
WHY DON'T YOU TELL HIM TODAY IS SUNDAY, AND YOU HAVEN'T BEEN TO SCHOOL?
12-15
SCHULZ

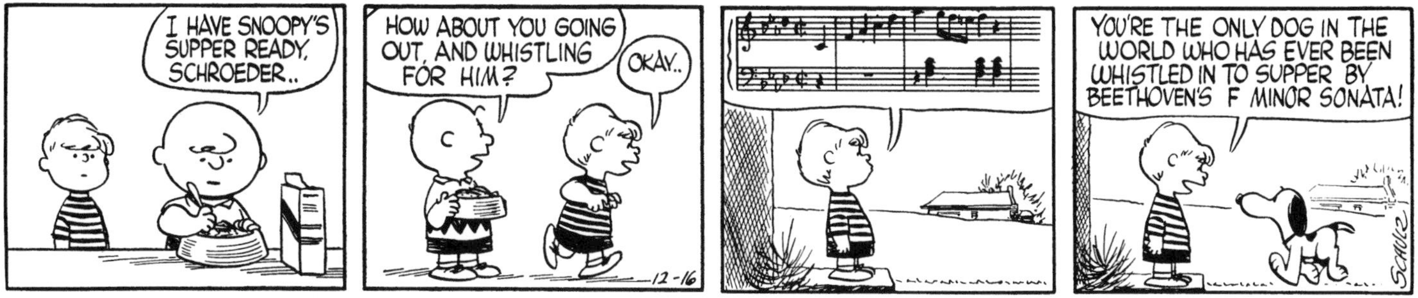
I HAVE SNOOPY'S SUPPER READY, SCHROEDER..
HOW ABOUT YOU GOING OUT, AND WHISTLING FOR HIM?
OKAY..
12-16
YOU'RE THE ONLY DOG IN THE WORLD WHO HAS EVER BEEN WHISTLED IN TO SUPPER BY BEETHOVEN'S F MINOR SONATA!
SCHULZ

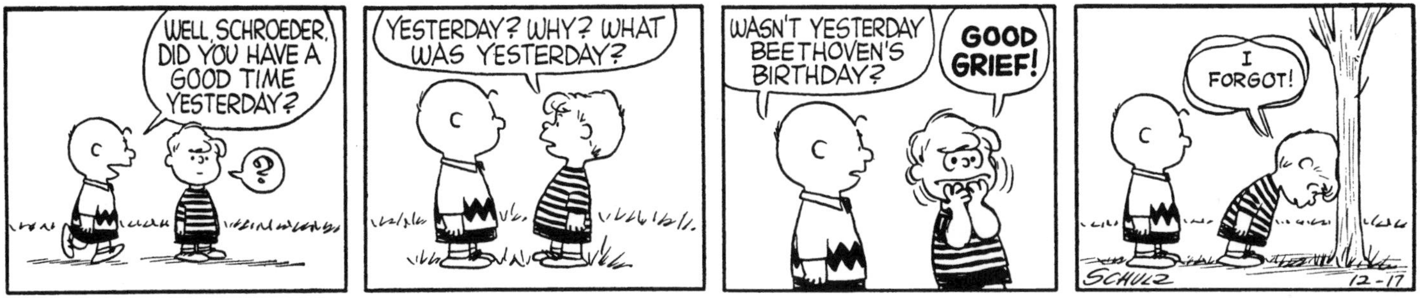
WELL, SCHROEDER, DID YOU HAVE A GOOD TIME YESTERDAY?
?
YESTERDAY? WHY? WHAT WAS YESTERDAY?
WASN'T YESTERDAY BEETHOVEN'S BIRTHDAY?
GOOD GRIEF!
I FORGOT!
SCHULZ
12-17

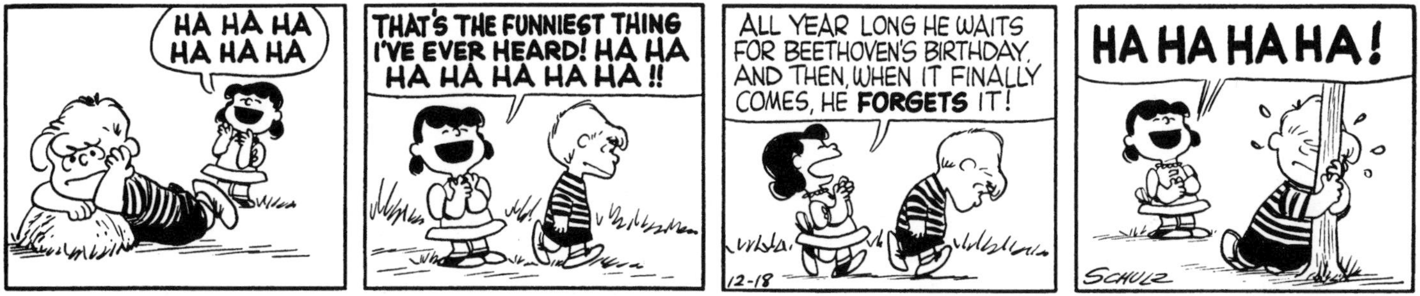
HA HA HA HA HA HA
THAT'S THE FUNNIEST THING I'VE EVER HEARD! HA HA HA HA HA HA HA !!
ALL YEAR LONG HE WAITS FOR BEETHOVEN'S BIRTHDAY, AND THEN, WHEN IT FINALLY COMES, HE FORGETS IT!
12-18
HA HA HA HA HA!
SCHULZ

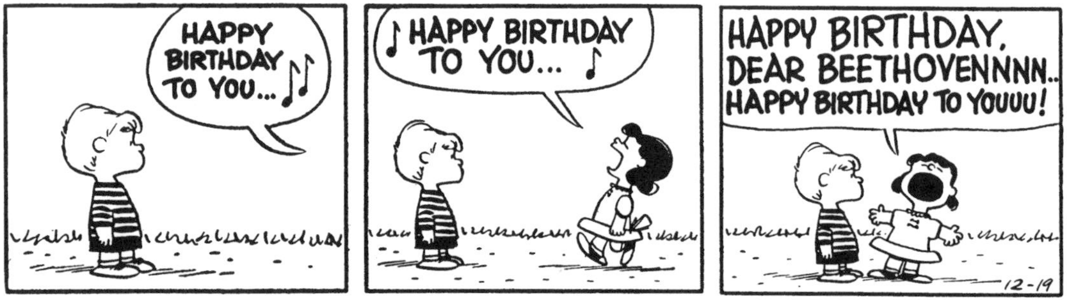
HAPPY BIRTHDAY TO YOU...
HAPPY BIRTHDAY TO YOU...
HAPPY BIRTHDAY, DEAR BEETHOVENNNN.. HAPPY BIRTHDAY TO YOUUU!
12-19
HA HA HA HA HA HA
SCHULZ

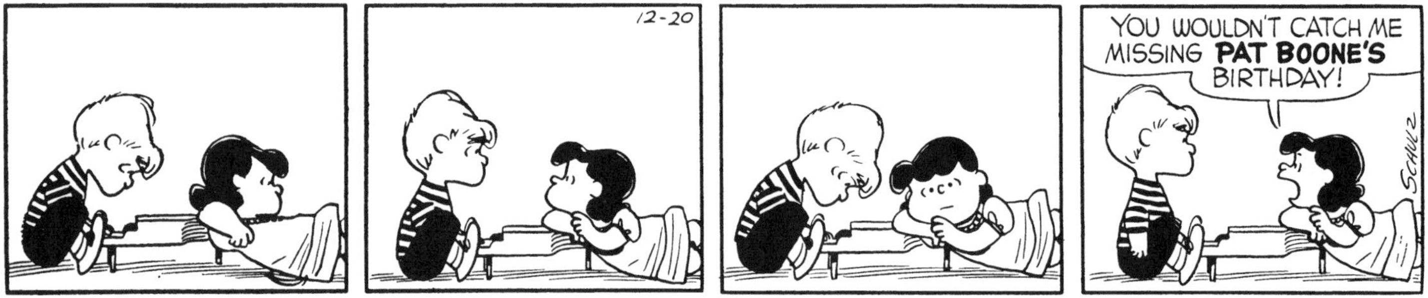
12-20
YOU WOULDN'T CATCH ME MISSING **PAT BOONE'S** BIRTHDAY!
SCHULZ

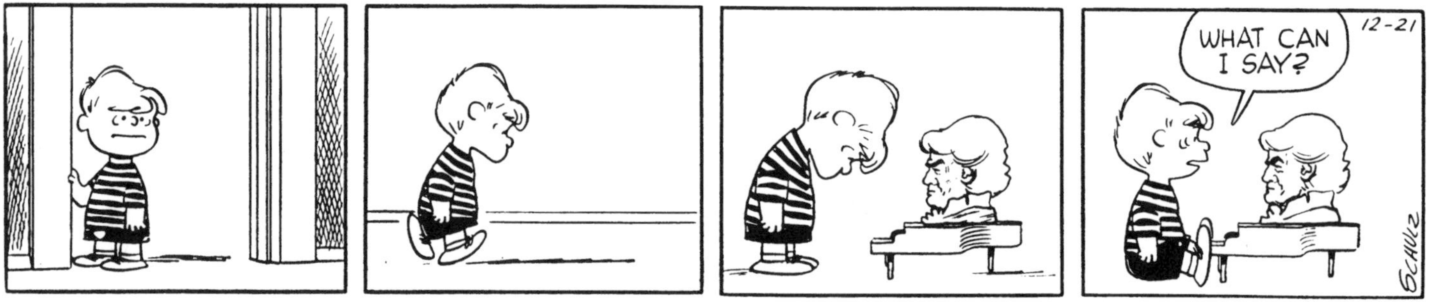
12-21
WHAT CAN I SAY?
SCHULZ

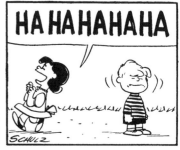

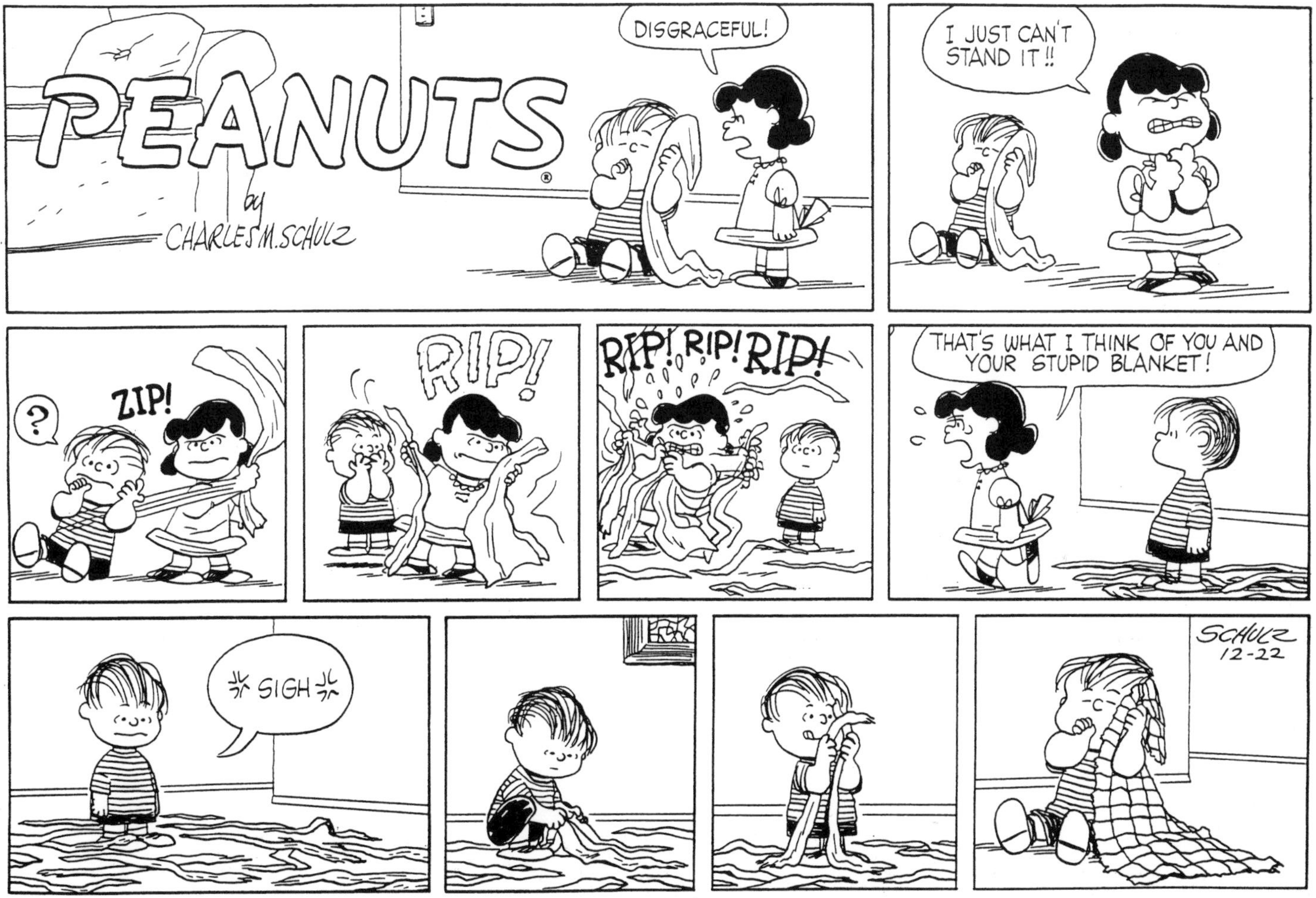
PEANUTS
by
CHARLES M. SCHULZ
DISGRACEFUL!
I JUST CAN'T STAND IT!!
?
ZIP!
RIP!
RIP! RIP! RIP!
THAT'S WHAT I THINK OF YOU AND YOUR STUPID BLANKET!
SIGH
SCHULZ
12-22

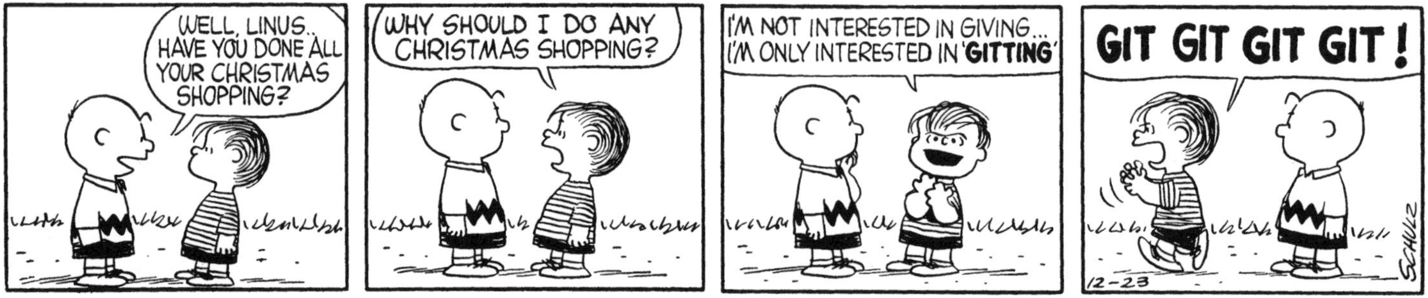
WELL, LINUS.. HAVE YOU DONE ALL YOUR CHRISTMAS SHOPPING?
WHY SHOULD I DO ANY CHRISTMAS SHOPPING?
I'M NOT INTERESTED IN GIVING... I'M ONLY INTERESTED IN 'GITTING'
GIT GIT GIT GIT!
SCHULZ
12-23

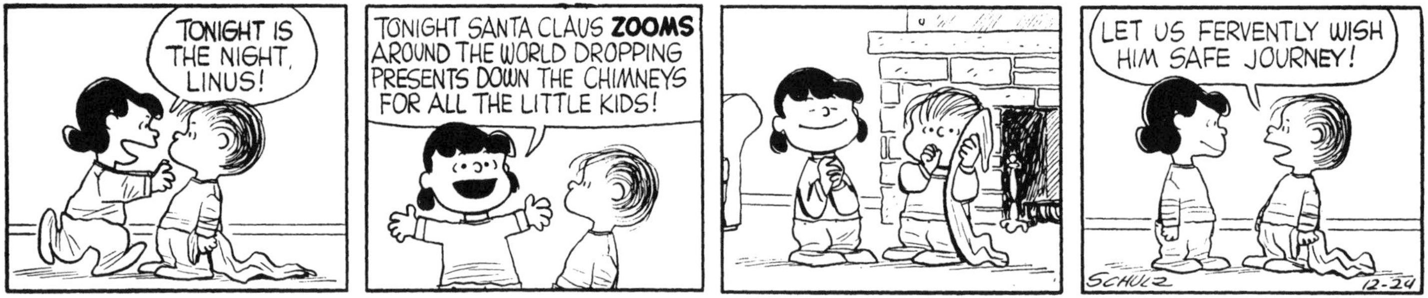
TONIGHT IS THE NIGHT, LINUS!
TONIGHT SANTA CLAUS ZOOMS AROUND THE WORLD DROPPING PRESENTS DOWN THE CHIMNEYS FOR ALL THE LITTLE KIDS!
LET US FERVENTLY WISH HIM SAFE JOURNEY!
SCHULZ
12-24

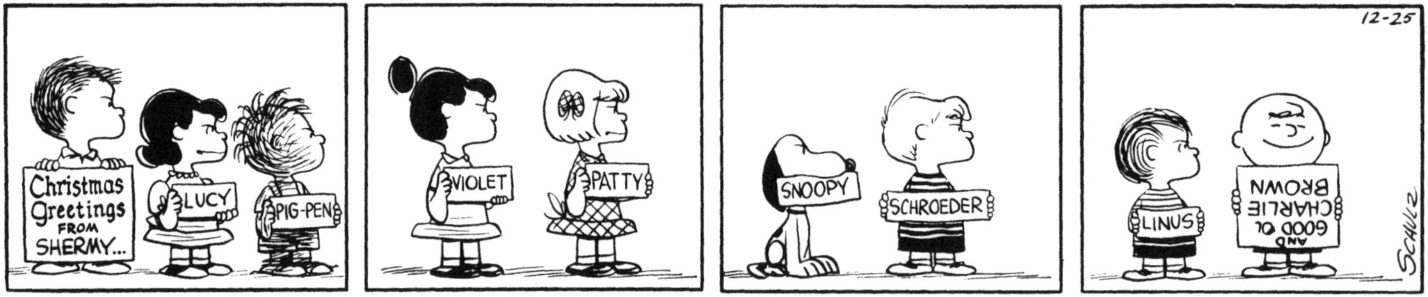
Christmas Greetings FROM SHERMY...
LUCY
PIG-PEN
VIOLET
PATTY
SNOOPY
SCHROEDER
LINUS
AND GOOD OL' CHARLIE BROWN
12-25
SCHULZ

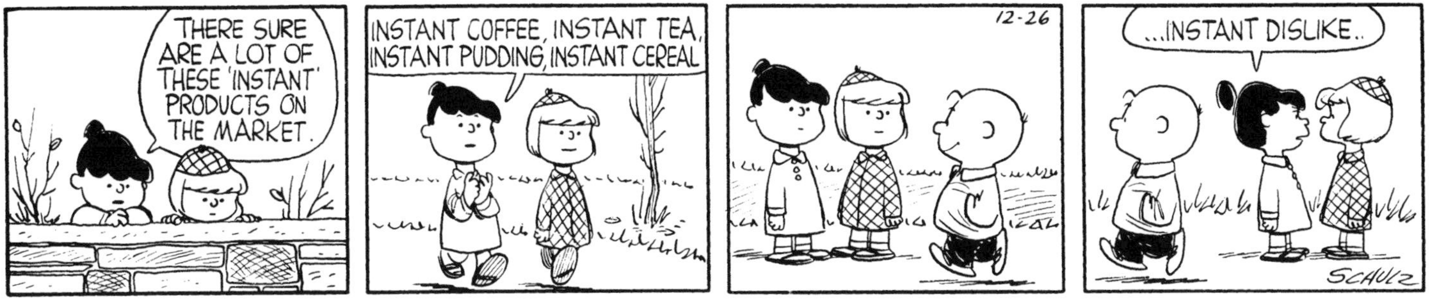
THERE SURE ARE A LOT OF THESE 'INSTANT' PRODUCTS ON THE MARKET.
INSTANT COFFEE, INSTANT TEA, INSTANT PUDDING, INSTANT CEREAL
12-26
...INSTANT DISLIKE..
SCHULZ

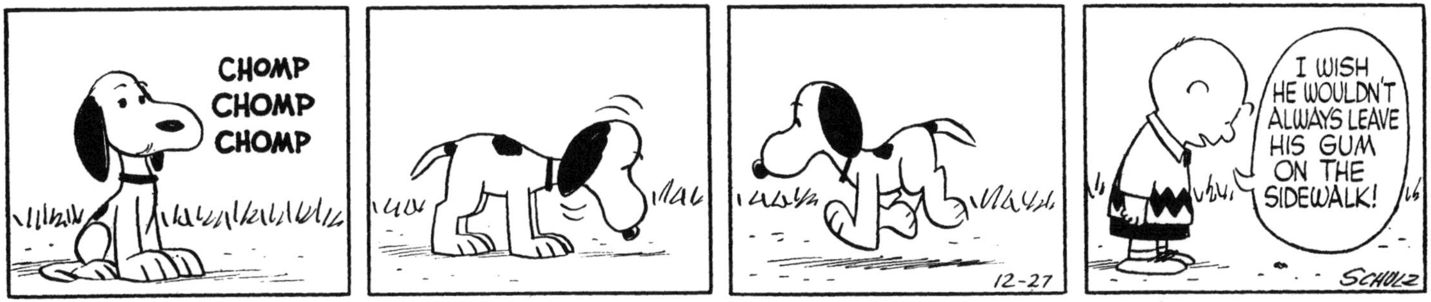
CHOMP
CHOMP
CHOMP
12-27
I WISH HE WOULDN'T ALWAYS LEAVE HIS GUM ON THE SIDEWALK!
SCHULZ

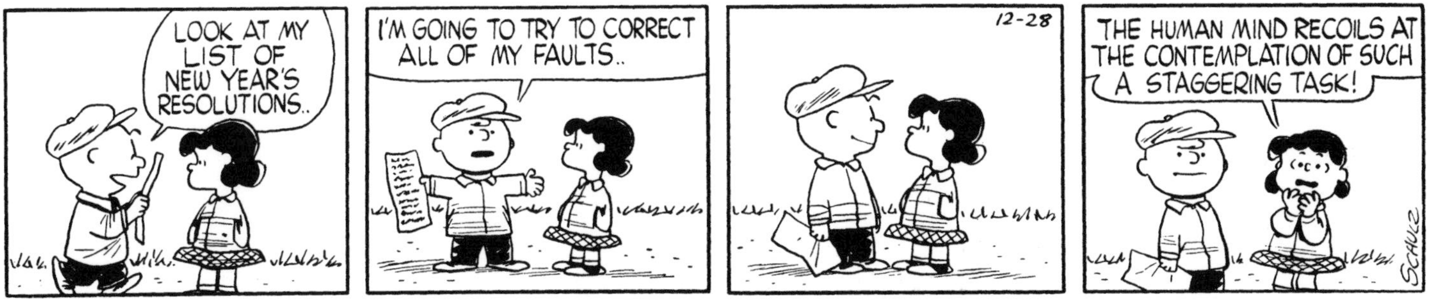
LOOK AT MY LIST OF NEW YEAR'S RESOLUTIONS..
I'M GOING TO TRY TO CORRECT ALL OF MY FAULTS..
12-28
THE HUMAN MIND RECOILS AT THE CONTEMPLATION OF SUCH A STAGGERING TASK!
SCHULZ

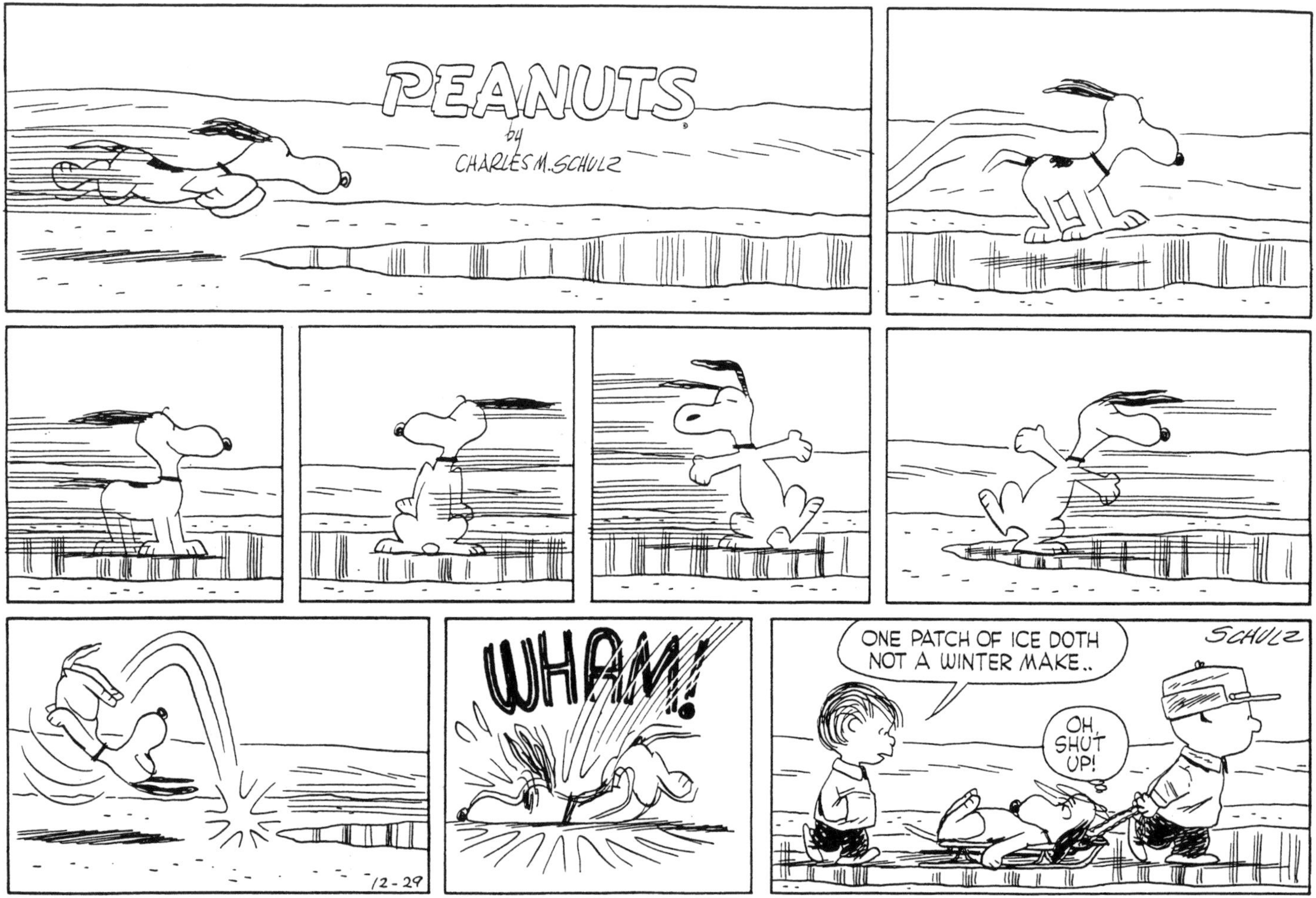
PEANUTS
by
CHARLES M. SCHULZ
12-29
WHAM!
SCHULZ
ONE PATCH OF ICE DOTH NOT A WINTER MAKE..
OH, SHUT UP!

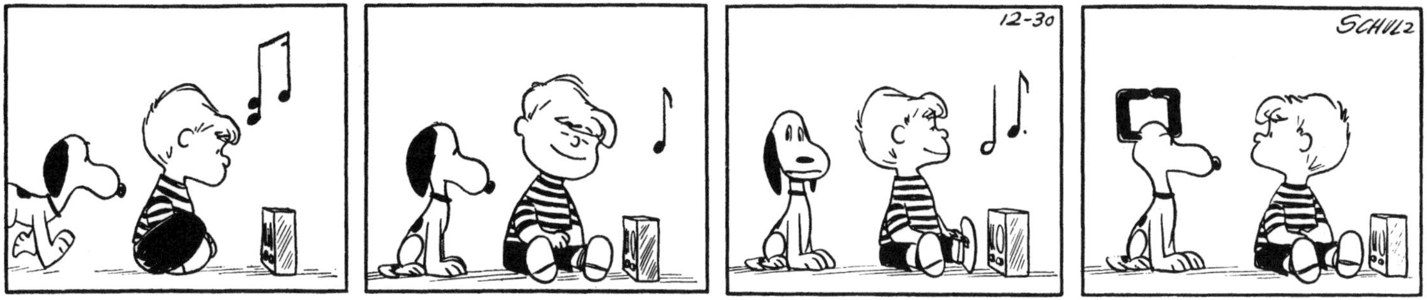
12-30
SCHULZ

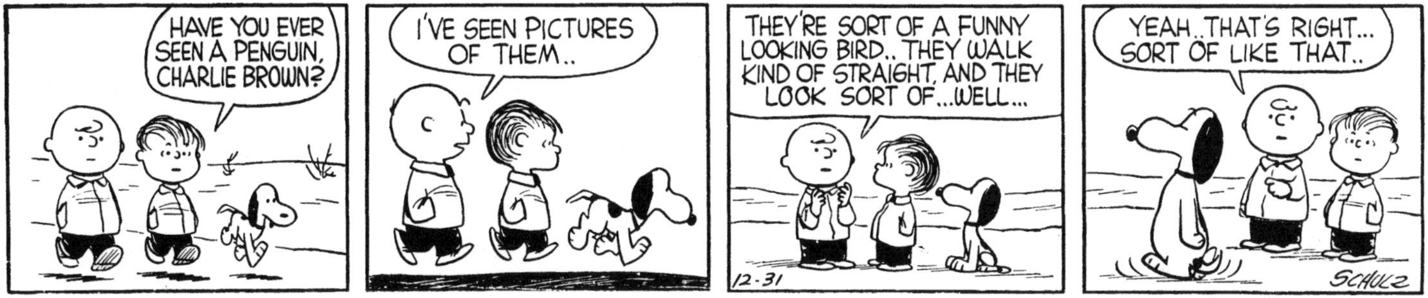
HAVE YOU EVER SEEN A PENGUIN, CHARLIE BROWN?
I'VE SEEN PICTURES OF THEM..
THEY'RE SORT OF A FUNNY LOOKING BIRD.. THEY WALK KIND OF STRAIGHT, AND THEY LOOK SORT OF...WELL...
12-31
YEAH..THAT'S RIGHT... SORT OF LIKE THAT..
SCHULZ

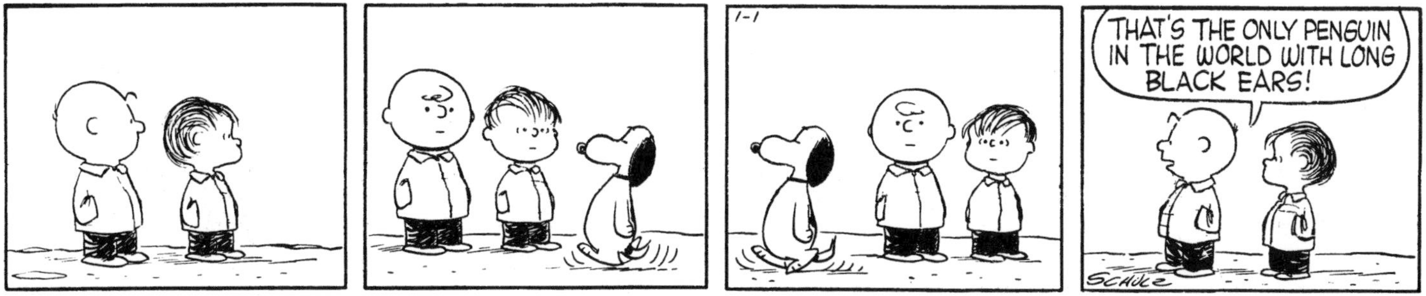
1-1
THAT'S THE ONLY PENGUIN IN THE WORLD WITH LONG BLACK EARS!
SCHULZ

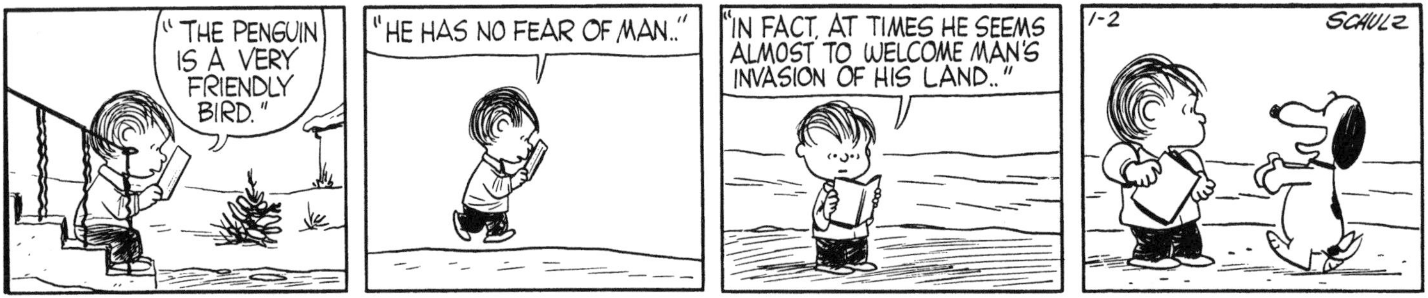
"THE PENGUIN IS A VERY FRIENDLY BIRD."
"HE HAS NO FEAR OF MAN.."
"IN FACT, AT TIMES HE SEEMS ALMOST TO WELCOME MAN'S INVASION OF HIS LAND.."
1-2
SCHULZ

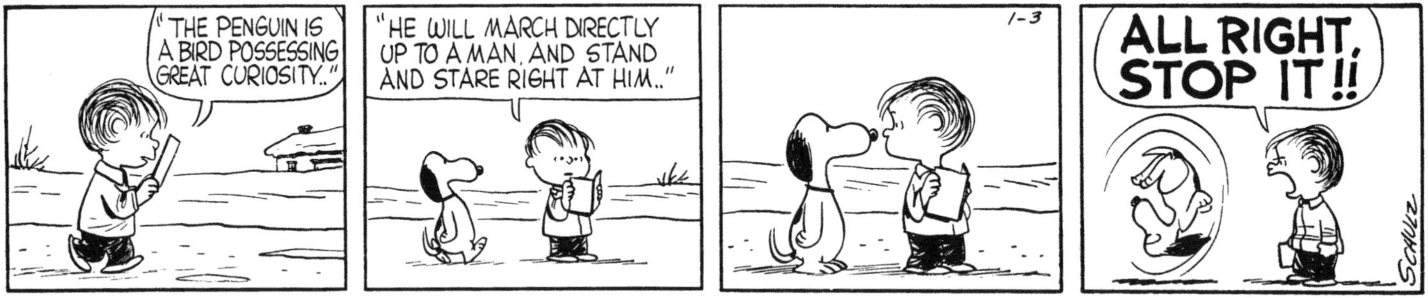
"THE PENGUIN IS A BIRD POSSESSING GREAT CURIOSITY.."
"HE WILL MARCH DIRECTLY UP TO A MAN, AND STAND AND STARE RIGHT AT HIM.."
1-3
ALL RIGHT, STOP IT !!
SCHULZ

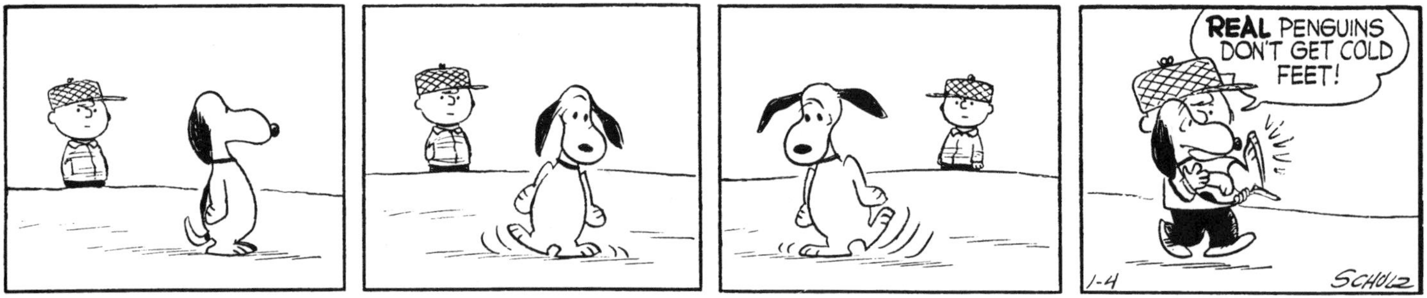
REAL PENGUINS DON'T GET COLD FEET!
1-4
SCHULZ

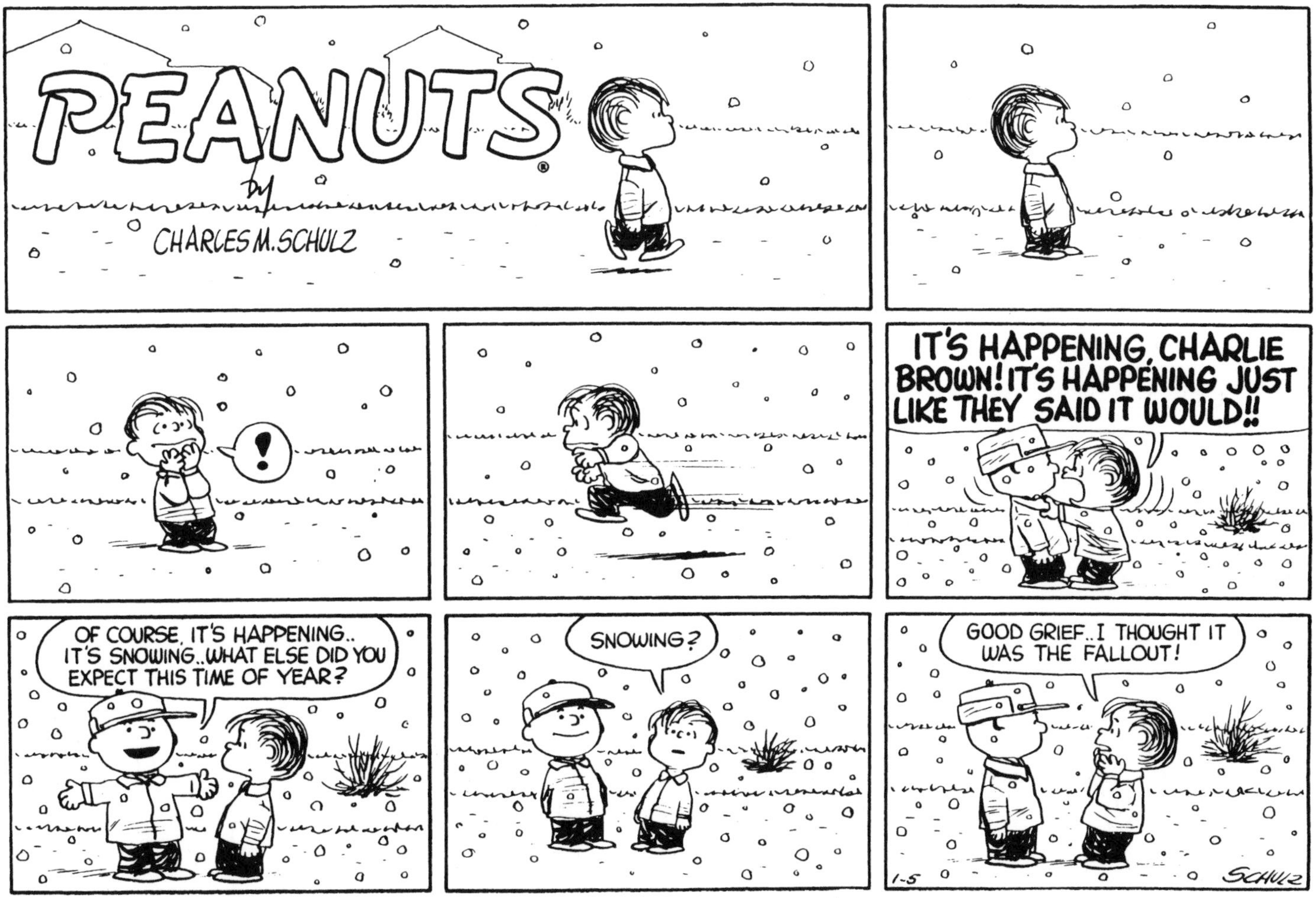
PEANUTS
by CHARLES M. SCHULZ
!
IT'S HAPPENING, CHARLIE BROWN! IT'S HAPPENING JUST LIKE THEY SAID IT WOULD!!
OF COURSE, IT'S HAPPENING.. IT'S SNOWING..WHAT ELSE DID YOU EXPECT THIS TIME OF YEAR?
SNOWING?
GOOD GRIEF..I THOUGHT IT WAS THE FALLOUT!
1-5
SCHULZ

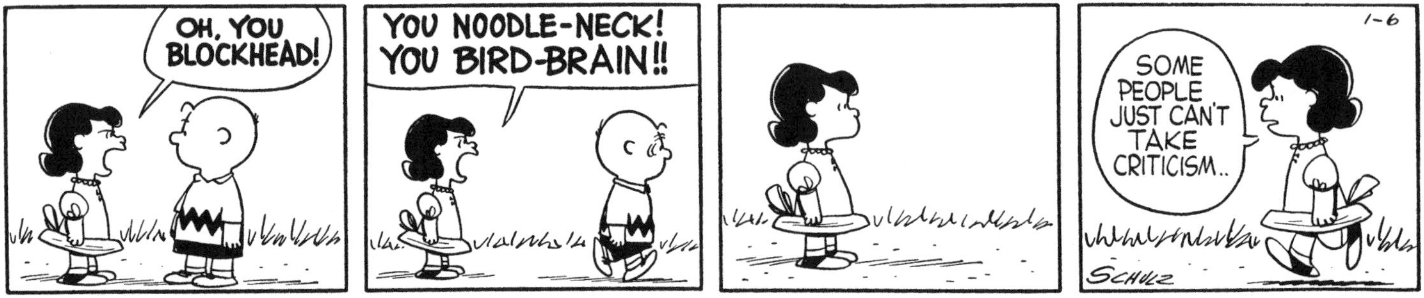
OH, YOU BLOCKHEAD!
YOU NOODLE-NECK! YOU BIRD-BRAIN!!
SOME PEOPLE JUST CAN'T TAKE CRITICISM..

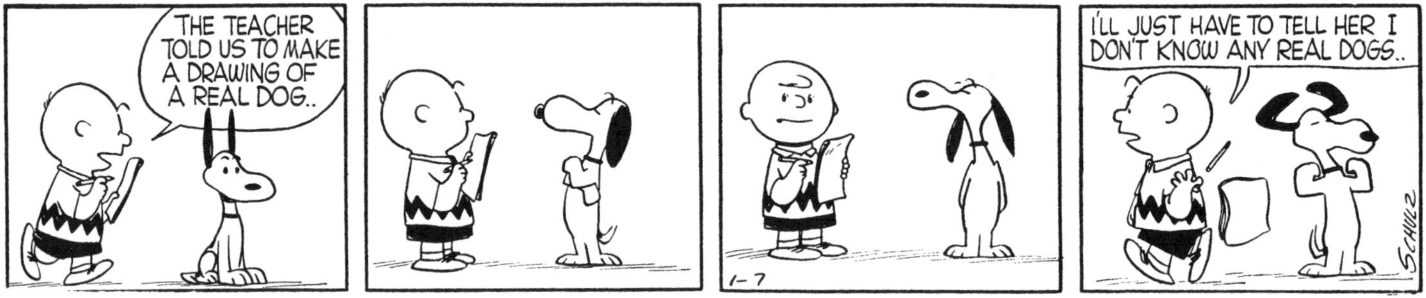
THE TEACHER TOLD US TO MAKE A DRAWING OF A REAL DOG..
I'LL JUST HAVE TO TELL HER I DON'T KNOW ANY REAL DOGS..

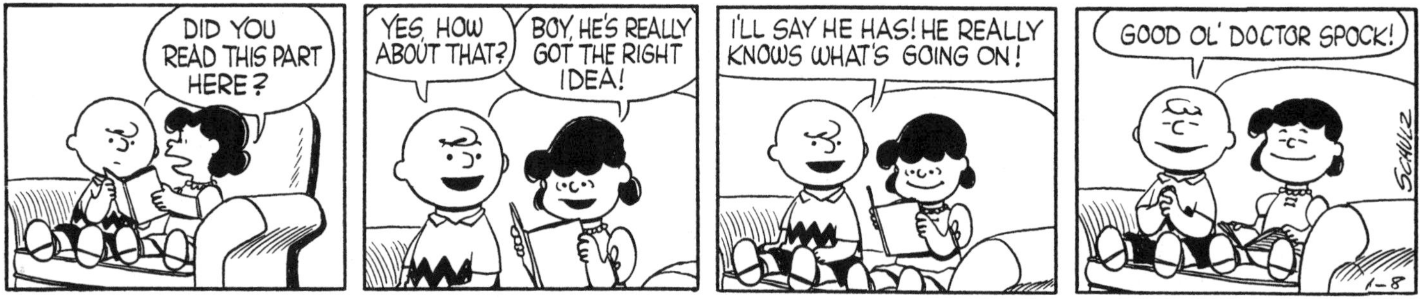
DID YOU READ THIS PART HERE?
YES, HOW ABOUT THAT?
BOY, HE'S REALLY GOT THE RIGHT IDEA!
I'LL SAY HE HAS! HE REALLY KNOWS WHAT'S GOING ON!
GOOD OL' DOCTOR SPOCK!

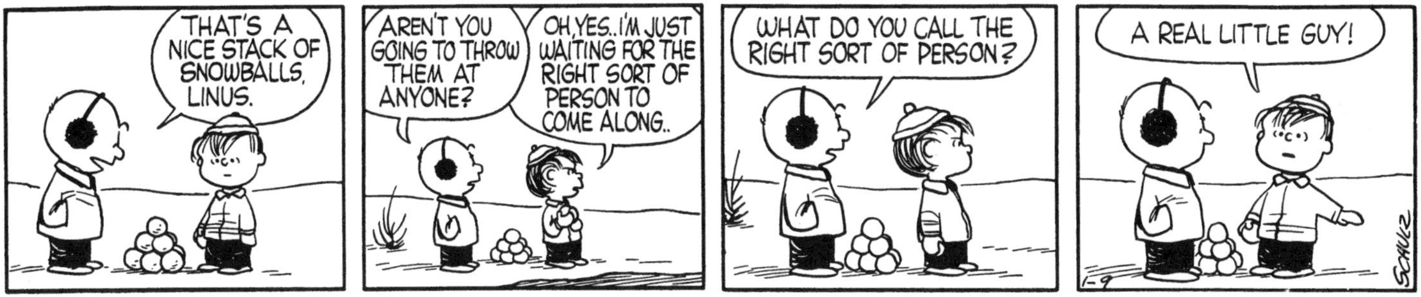
THAT'S A NICE STACK OF SNOWBALLS, LINUS.
AREN'T YOU GOING TO THROW THEM AT ANYONE?
OH, YES.. I'M JUST WAITING FOR THE RIGHT SORT OF PERSON TO COME ALONG..
WHAT DO YOU CALL THE RIGHT SORT OF PERSON?
A REAL LITTLE GUY!
1-9
SCHULZ

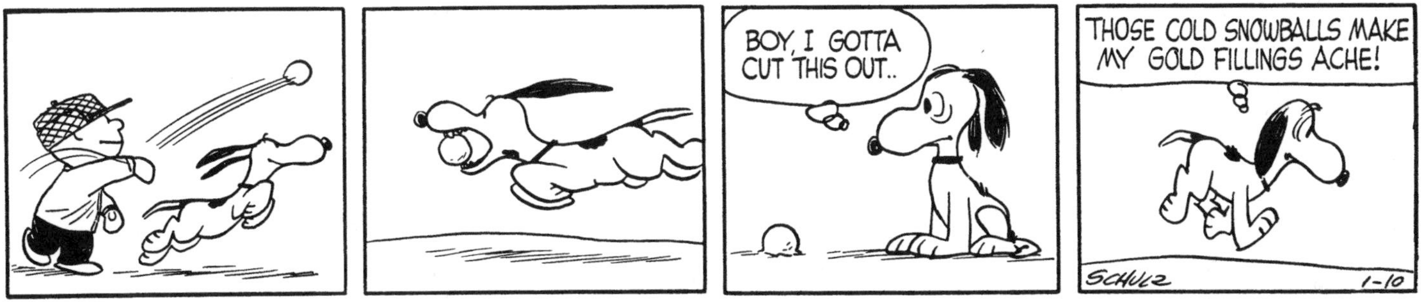
BOY, I GOTTA CUT THIS OUT..
THOSE COLD SNOWBALLS MAKE MY GOLD FILLINGS ACHE!
SCHULZ
1-10

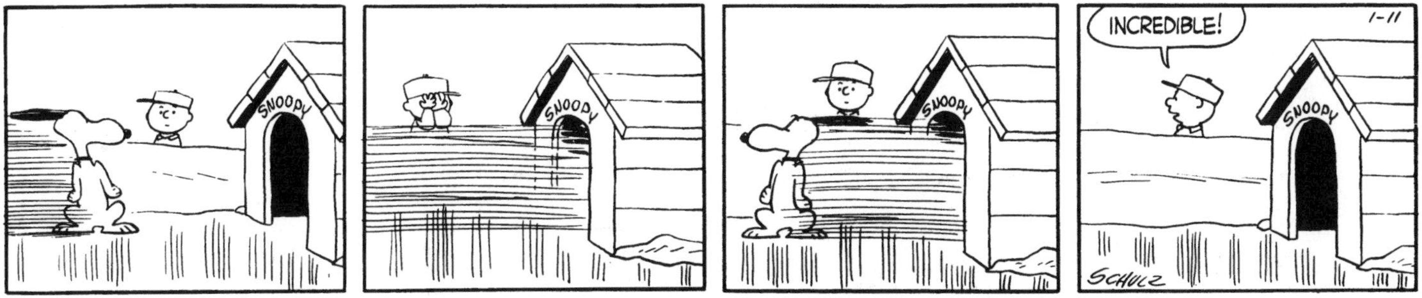
SNOOPY
SNOOPY
SNOOPY
INCREDIBLE!
1-11
SNOOPY
SCHULZ

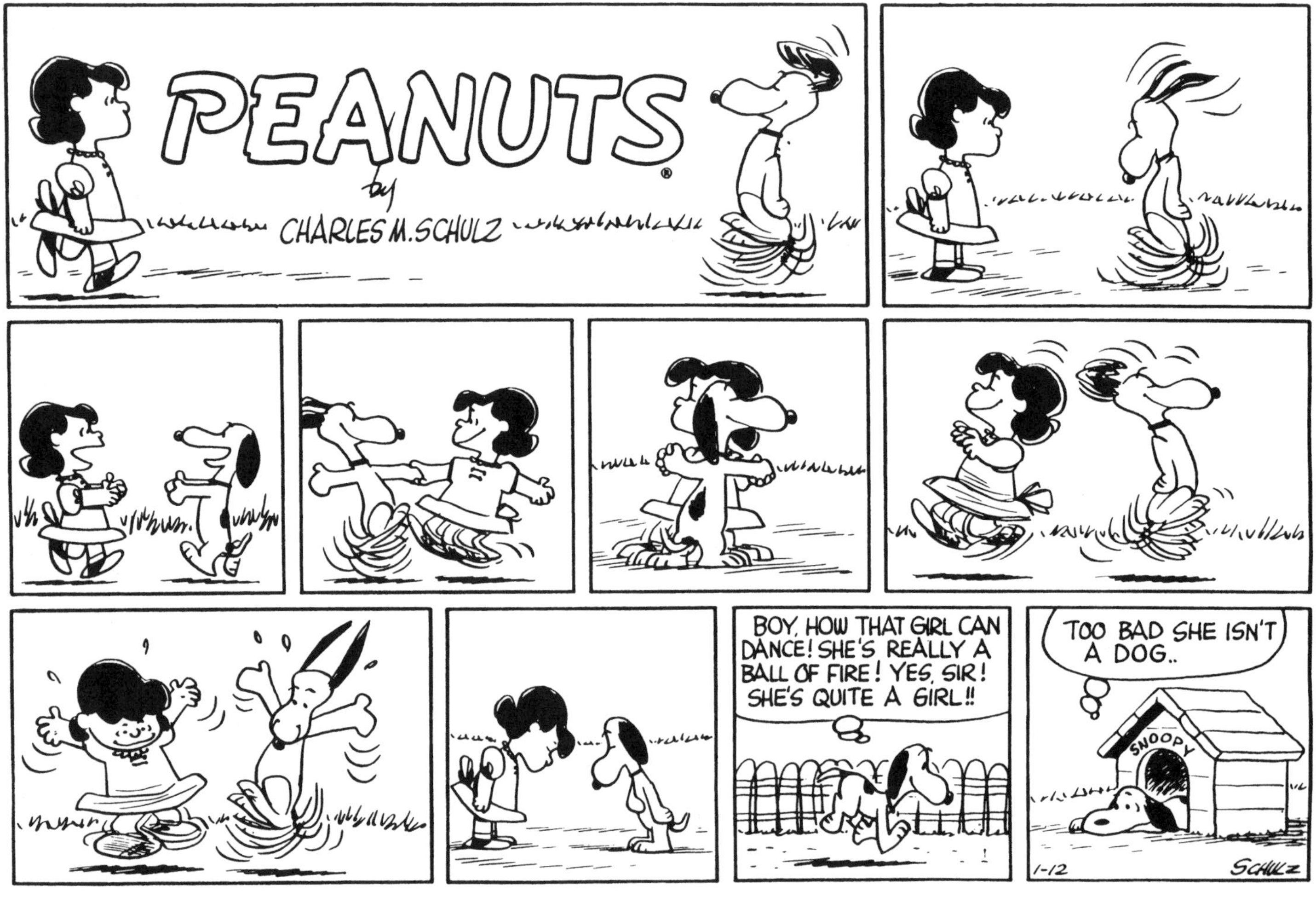
PEANUTS
by
CHARLES M. SCHULZ
BOY, HOW THAT GIRL CAN DANCE! SHE'S REALLY A BALL OF FIRE! YES, SIR! SHE'S QUITE A GIRL!!
TOO BAD SHE ISN'T A DOG..
SNOOPY
1-12
SCHULZ

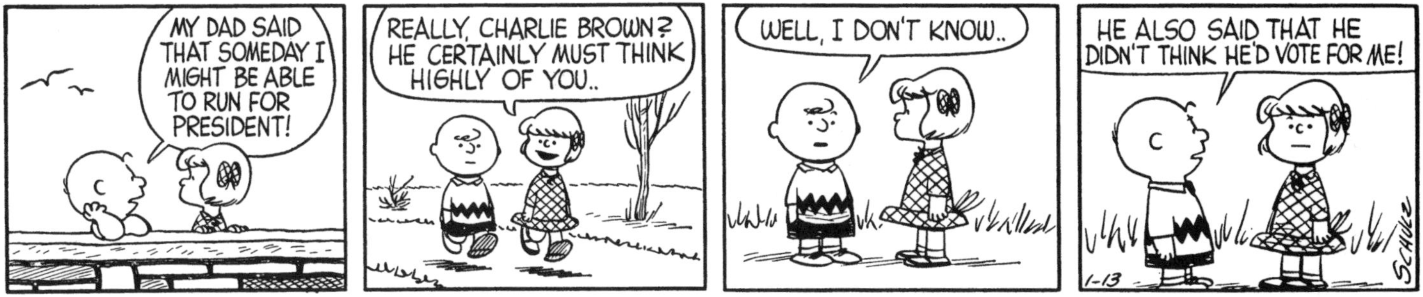
MY DAD SAID THAT SOMEDAY I MIGHT BE ABLE TO RUN FOR PRESIDENT!
REALLY, CHARLIE BROWN? HE CERTAINLY MUST THINK HIGHLY OF YOU..
WELL, I DON'T KNOW..
HE ALSO SAID THAT HE DIDN'T THINK HE'D VOTE FOR ME!
1-13
SCHULZ

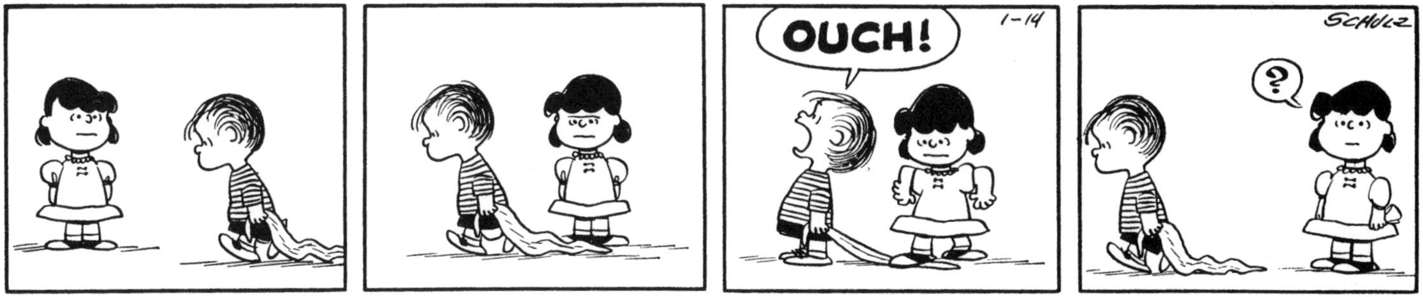
OUCH!
1-14
SCHULZ
?

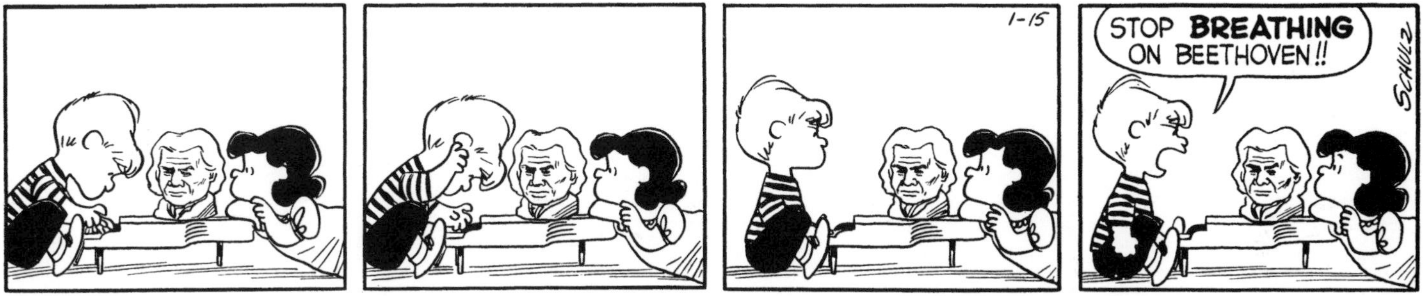
1-15
STOP **BREATHING** ON BEETHOVEN!!
SCHULZ

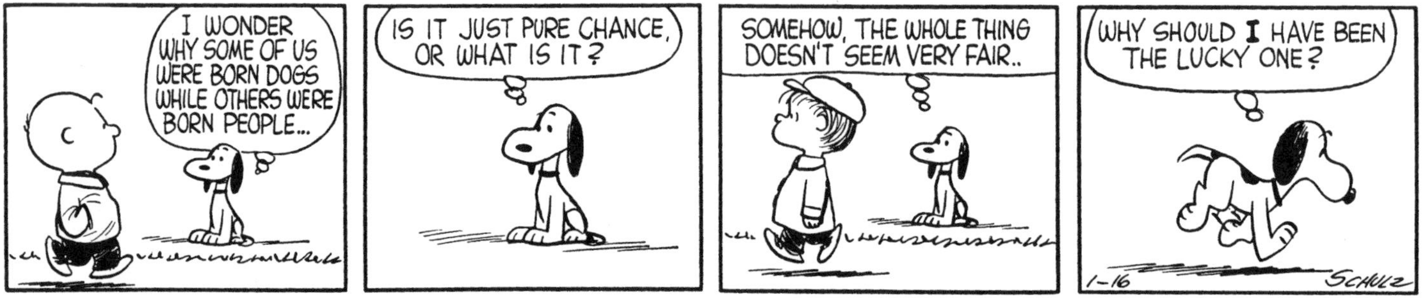
I WONDER WHY SOME OF US WERE BORN DOGS WHILE OTHERS WERE BORN PEOPLE...
IS IT JUST PURE CHANCE, OR WHAT IS IT?
SOMEHOW, THE WHOLE THING DOESN'T SEEM VERY FAIR..
WHY SHOULD I HAVE BEEN THE LUCKY ONE?
1-16
SCHULZ

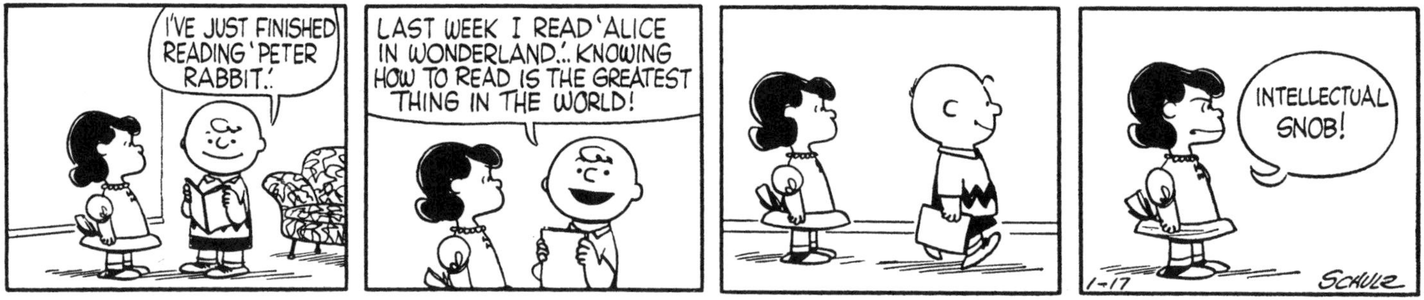
I'VE JUST FINISHED READING 'PETER RABBIT.'
LAST WEEK I READ 'ALICE IN WONDERLAND.'.. KNOWING HOW TO READ IS THE GREATEST THING IN THE WORLD!
INTELLECTUAL SNOB!
1-17
SCHULZ

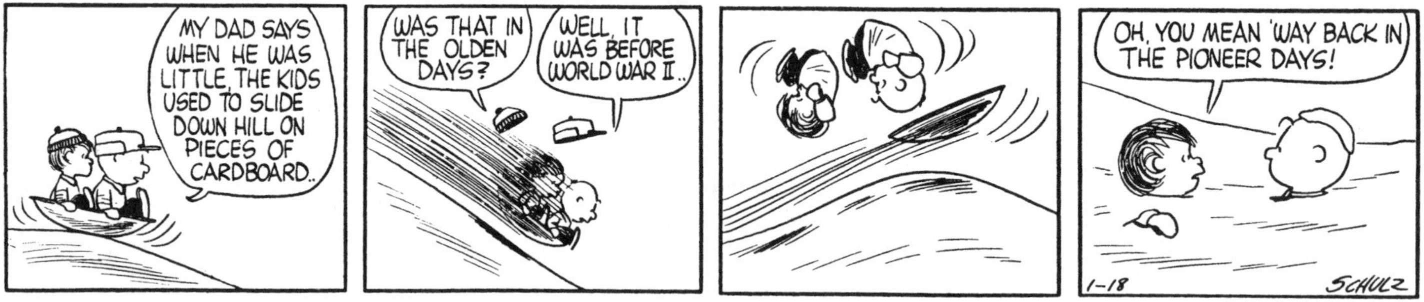
MY DAD SAYS WHEN HE WAS LITTLE, THE KIDS USED TO SLIDE DOWN HILL ON PIECES OF CARDBOARD..
WAS THAT IN THE OLDEN DAYS?
WELL, IT WAS BEFORE WORLD WAR II..
OH, YOU MEAN 'WAY BACK IN THE PIONEER DAYS!
1-18
SCHULZ

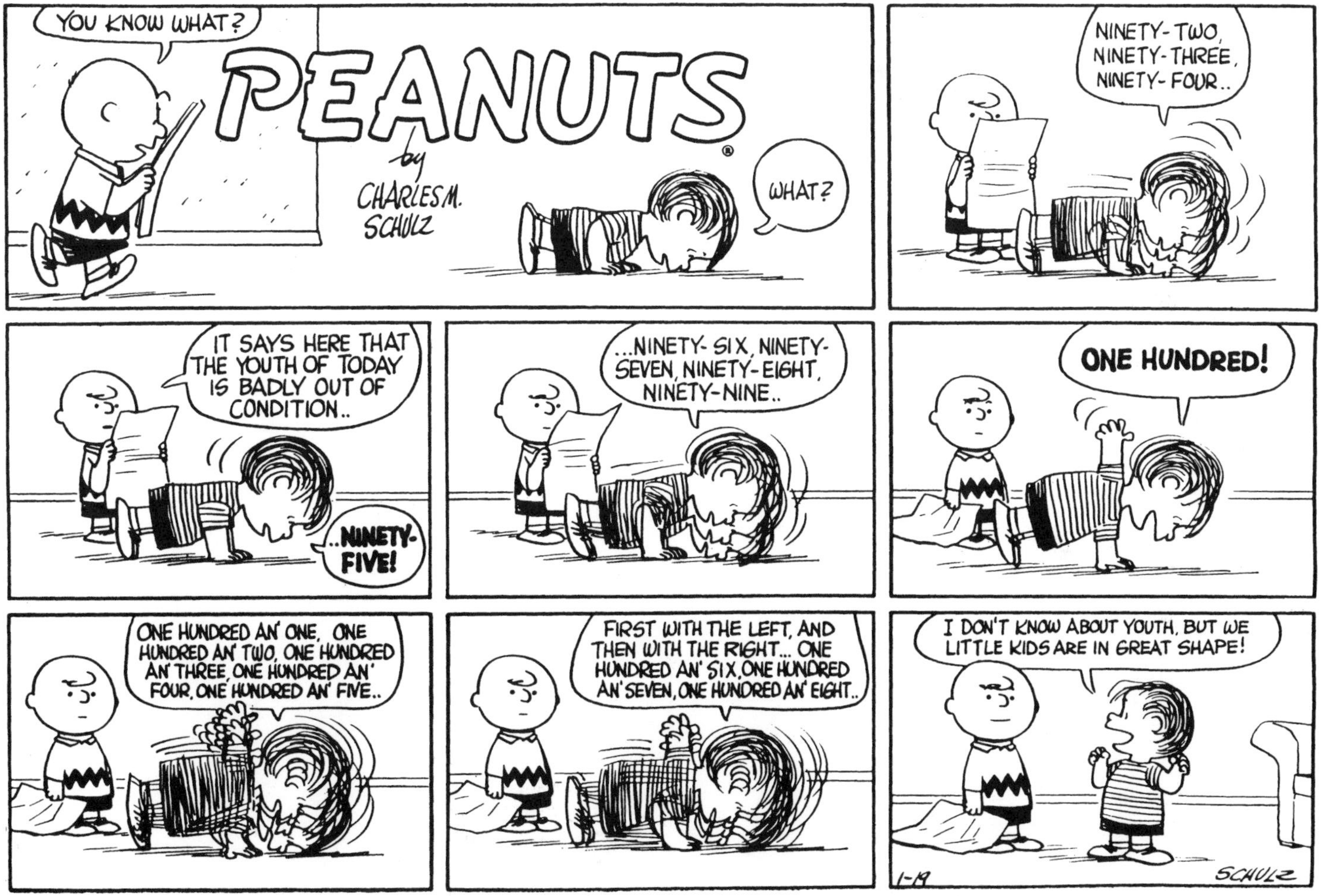
YOU KNOW WHAT?
PEANUTS
by CHARLES M. SCHULZ
WHAT?
NINETY-TWO, NINETY-THREE, NINETY-FOUR..
IT SAYS HERE THAT THE YOUTH OF TODAY IS BADLY OUT OF CONDITION..
..NINETY-FIVE!
...NINETY-SIX, NINETY-SEVEN, NINETY-EIGHT, NINETY-NINE..
ONE HUNDRED!
ONE HUNDRED AN' ONE, ONE HUNDRED AN' TWO, ONE HUNDRED AN' THREE, ONE HUNDRED AN' FOUR, ONE HUNDRED AN' FIVE..
FIRST WITH THE LEFT, AND THEN WITH THE RIGHT... ONE HUNDRED AN' SIX, ONE HUNDRED AN' SEVEN, ONE HUNDRED AN' EIGHT..
I DON'T KNOW ABOUT YOUTH, BUT WE LITTLE KIDS ARE IN GREAT SHAPE!
1-19
SCHULZ

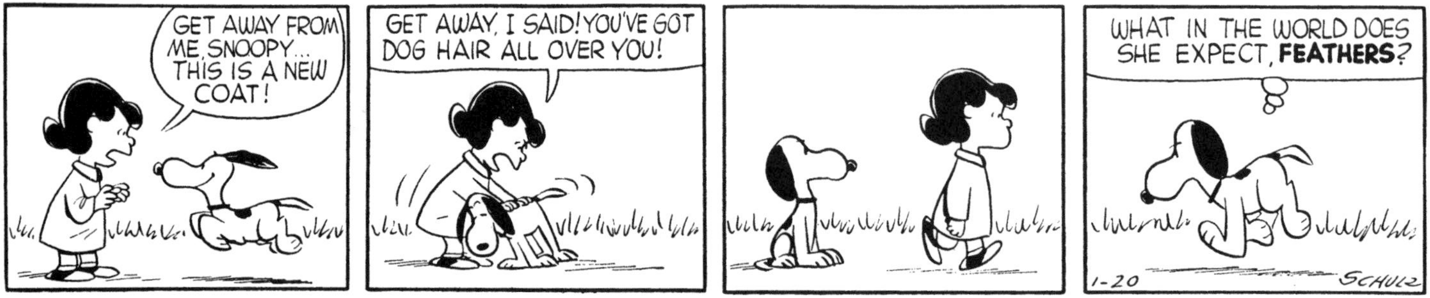
GET AWAY FROM ME, SNOOPY... THIS IS A NEW COAT!
GET AWAY, I SAID! YOU'VE GOT DOG HAIR ALL OVER YOU!
WHAT IN THE WORLD DOES SHE EXPECT, **FEATHERS**?
1-20
SCHULZ

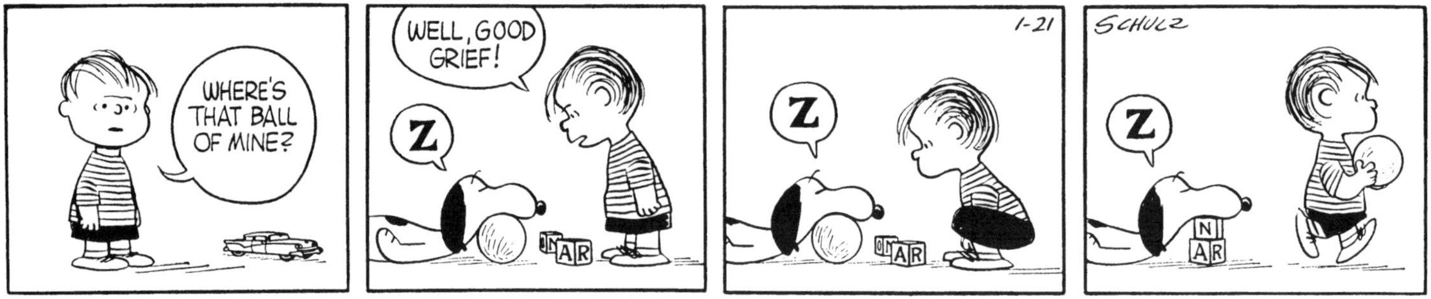
WHERE'S THAT BALL OF MINE?
WELL, GOOD GRIEF!
Z
1-21
Z
SCHULZ
Z

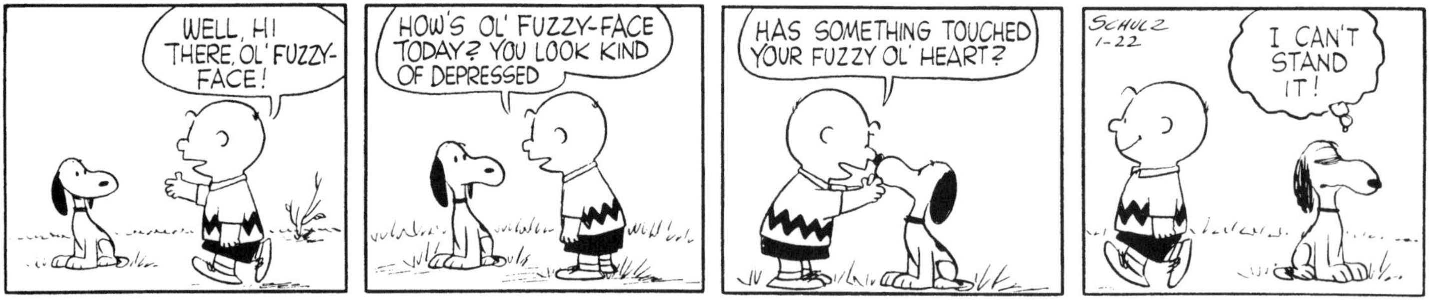
WELL, HI THERE, OL' FUZZY-FACE!
HOW'S OL' FUZZY-FACE TODAY? YOU LOOK KIND OF DEPRESSED
HAS SOMETHING TOUCHED YOUR FUZZY OL' HEART?
SCHULZ
1-22
I CAN'T STAND IT!

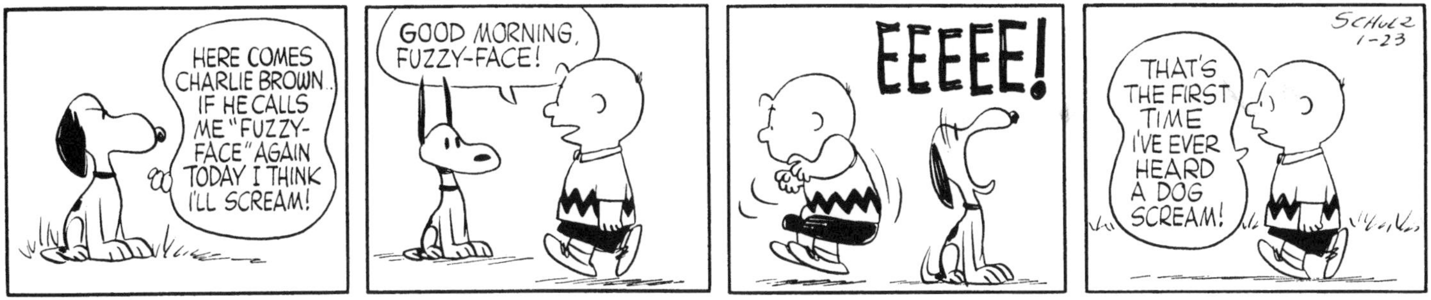
HERE COMES CHARLIE BROWN.. IF HE CALLS ME "FUZZY-FACE" AGAIN TODAY I THINK I'LL SCREAM!
GOOD MORNING, FUZZY-FACE!
EEEEE!
SCHULZ 1-23
THAT'S THE FIRST TIME I'VE EVER HEARD A DOG SCREAM!

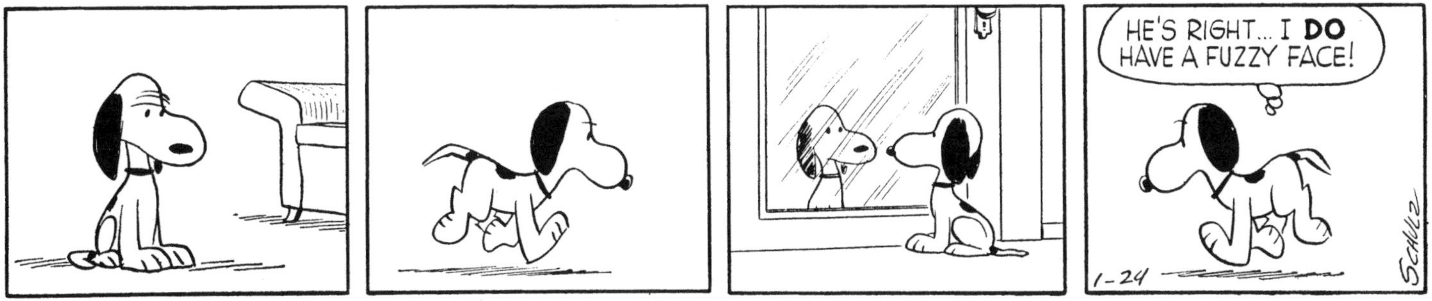
HE'S RIGHT... I **DO** HAVE A FUZZY FACE!
1-24
SCHULZ

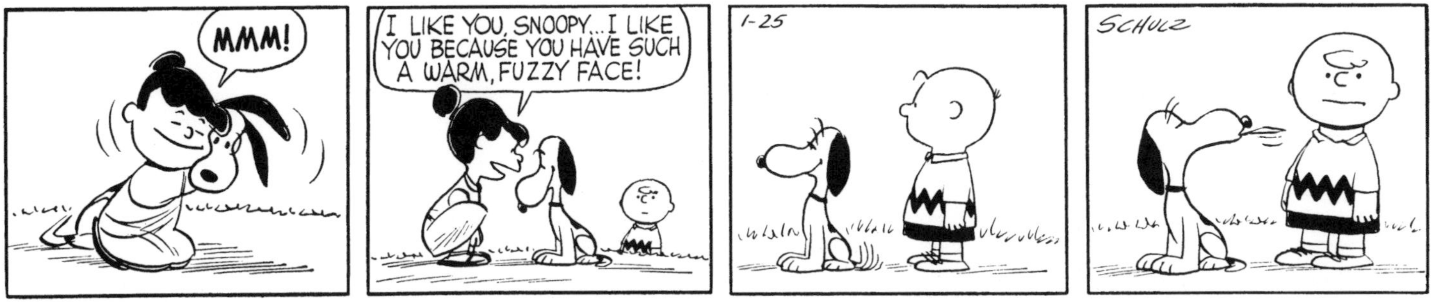
MMM!
I LIKE YOU, SNOOPY... I LIKE YOU BECAUSE YOU HAVE SUCH A WARM, FUZZY FACE!
1-25
SCHULZ

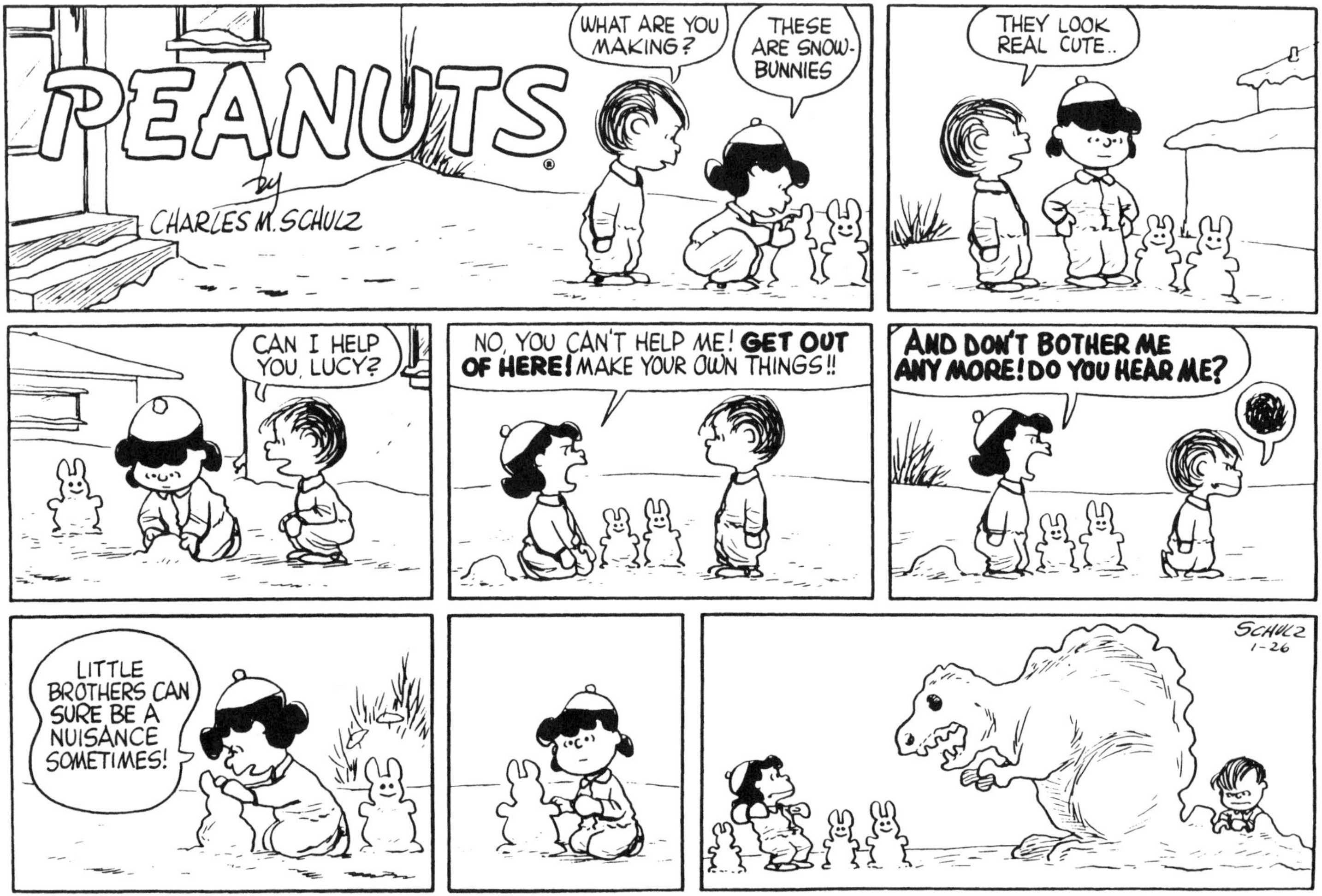
PEANUTS
by CHARLES M. SCHULZ
WHAT ARE YOU MAKING?
THESE ARE SNOW-BUNNIES
THEY LOOK REAL CUTE..
CAN I HELP YOU, LUCY?
NO, YOU CAN'T HELP ME! GET OUT OF HERE! MAKE YOUR OWN THINGS!!
AND DON'T BOTHER ME ANY MORE! DO YOU HEAR ME?
LITTLE BROTHERS CAN SURE BE A NUISANCE SOMETIMES!
SCHULZ 1-26

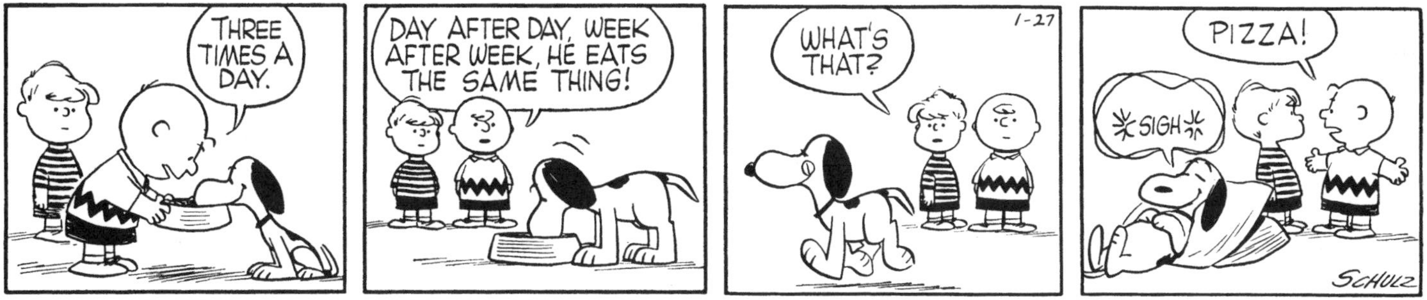
THREE TIMES A DAY.
DAY AFTER DAY, WEEK AFTER WEEK, HE EATS THE SAME THING!
1-27
WHAT'S THAT?
PIZZA!
SIGH
SCHULZ

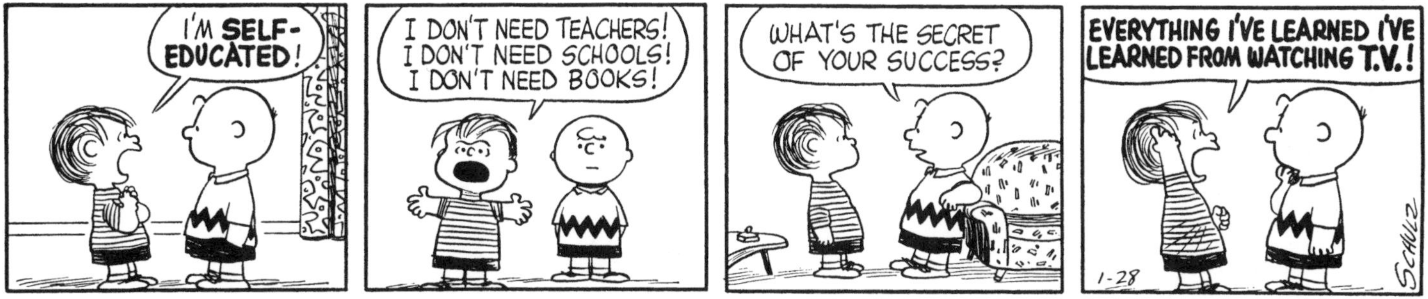
I'M **SELF-EDUCATED**!
I DON'T NEED TEACHERS! I DON'T NEED SCHOOLS! I DON'T NEED BOOKS!
WHAT'S THE SECRET OF YOUR SUCCESS?
EVERYTHING I'VE LEARNED I'VE LEARNED FROM WATCHING T.V.!
1-28
SCHULZ

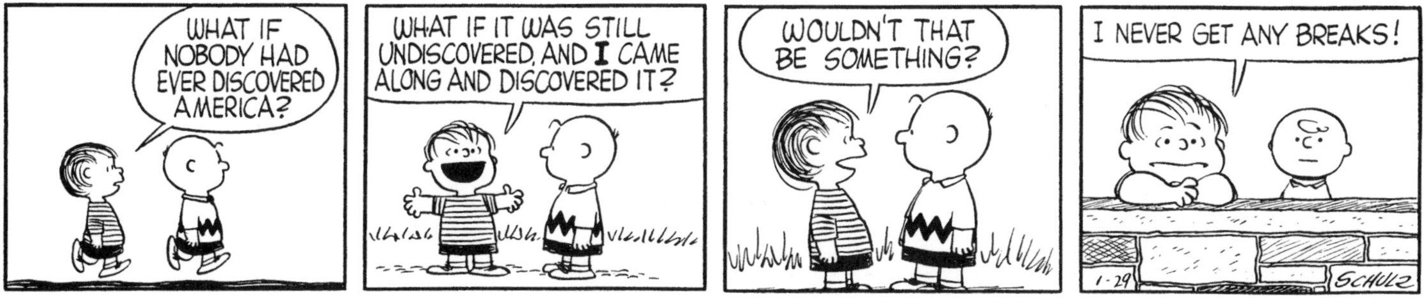
WHAT IF NOBODY HAD EVER DISCOVERED AMERICA?
WHAT IF IT WAS STILL UNDISCOVERED, AND **I** CAME ALONG AND DISCOVERED IT?
WOULDN'T THAT BE SOMETHING?
I NEVER GET ANY BREAKS!
1-29
SCHULZ

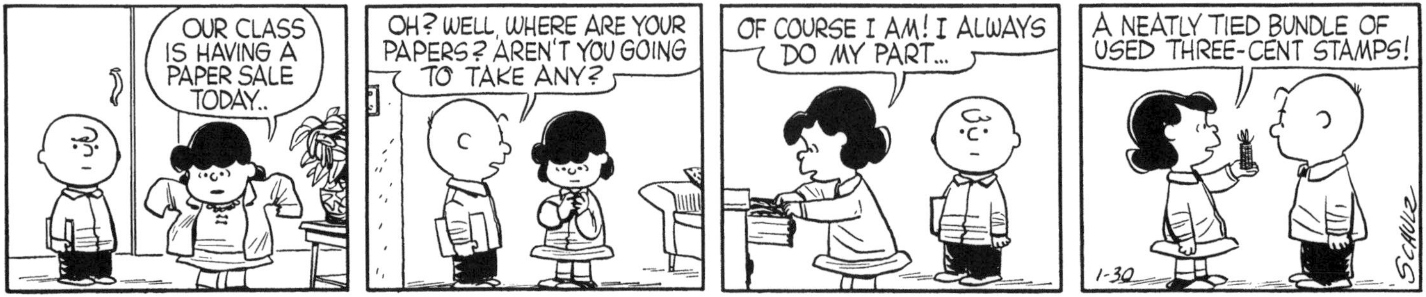
OUR CLASS IS HAVING A PAPER SALE TODAY..
OH? WELL, WHERE ARE YOUR PAPERS? AREN'T YOU GOING TO TAKE ANY?
OF COURSE I AM! I ALWAYS DO MY PART...
A NEATLY TIED BUNDLE OF USED THREE-CENT STAMPS!
1-30

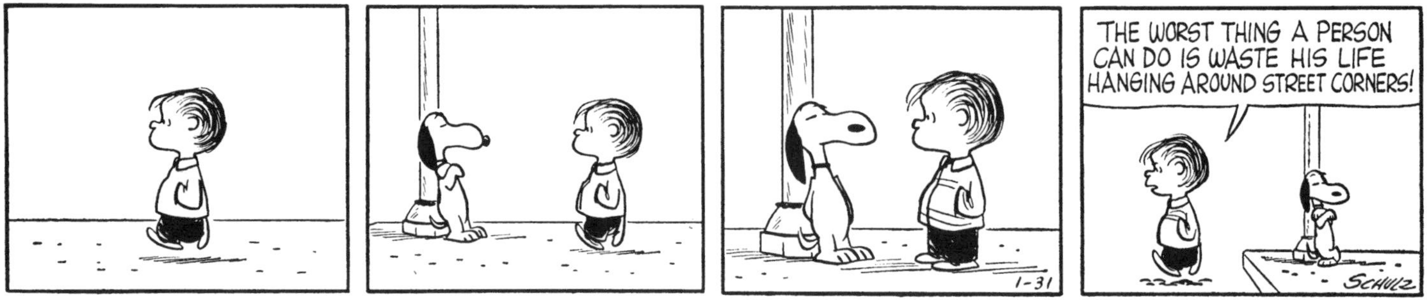
1-31
THE WORST THING A PERSON CAN DO IS WASTE HIS LIFE HANGING AROUND STREET CORNERS!

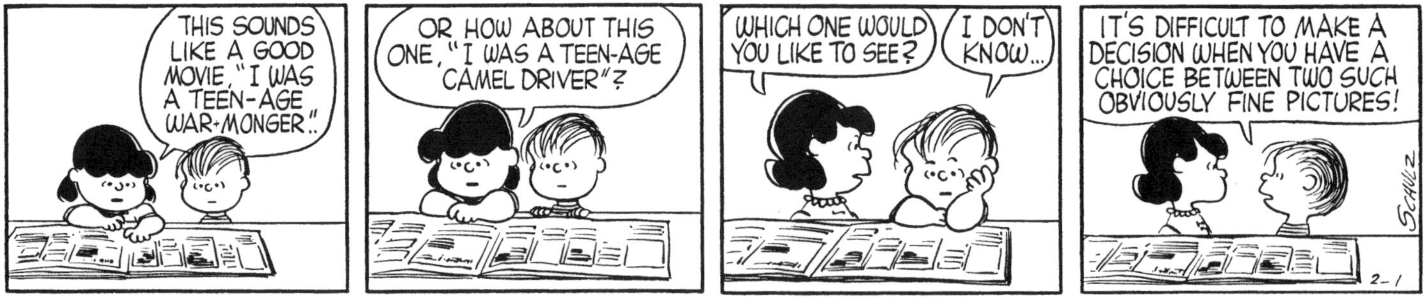
THIS SOUNDS LIKE A GOOD MOVIE, "I WAS A TEEN-AGE WAR-MONGER"..
OR HOW ABOUT THIS ONE, "I WAS A TEEN-AGE CAMEL DRIVER"?
WHICH ONE WOULD YOU LIKE TO SEE?
I DON'T KNOW...
IT'S DIFFICULT TO MAKE A DECISION WHEN YOU HAVE A CHOICE BETWEEN TWO SUCH OBVIOUSLY FINE PICTURES!
2-1

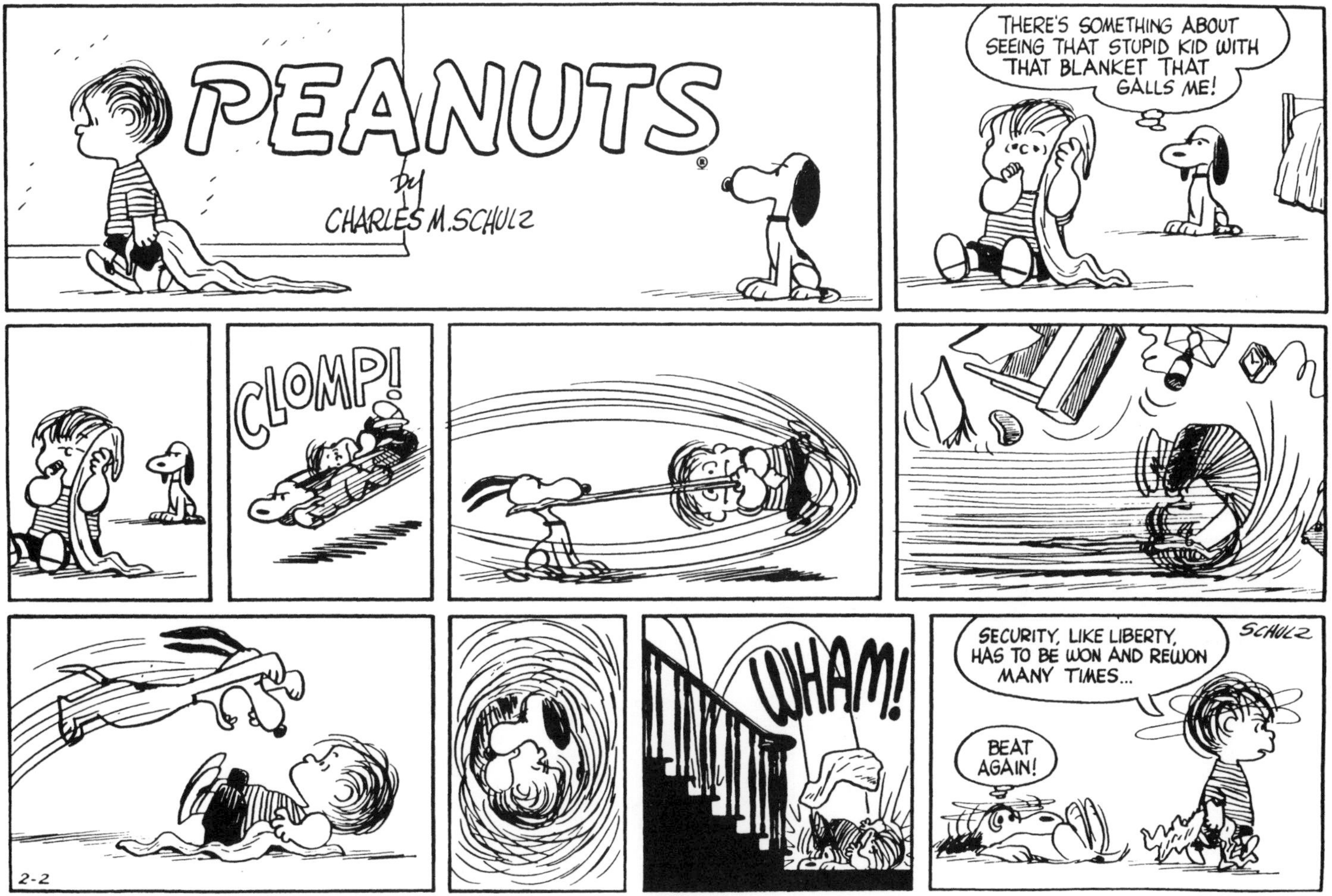
PEANUTS
by
CHARLES M. SCHULZ
THERE'S SOMETHING ABOUT SEEING THAT STUPID KID WITH THAT BLANKET THAT GALLS ME!
CLOMP!
WHAM!
SECURITY, LIKE LIBERTY, HAS TO BE WON AND REWON MANY TIMES...
BEAT AGAIN!
SCHULZ
2-2

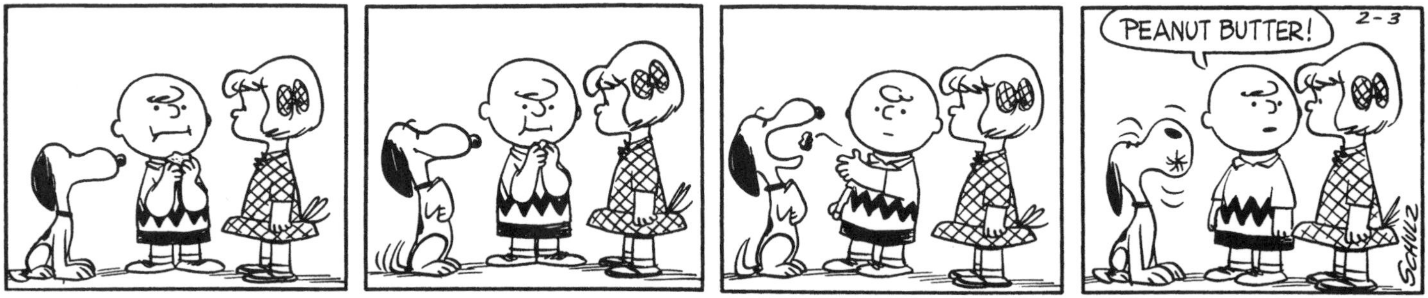
PEANUT BUTTER!

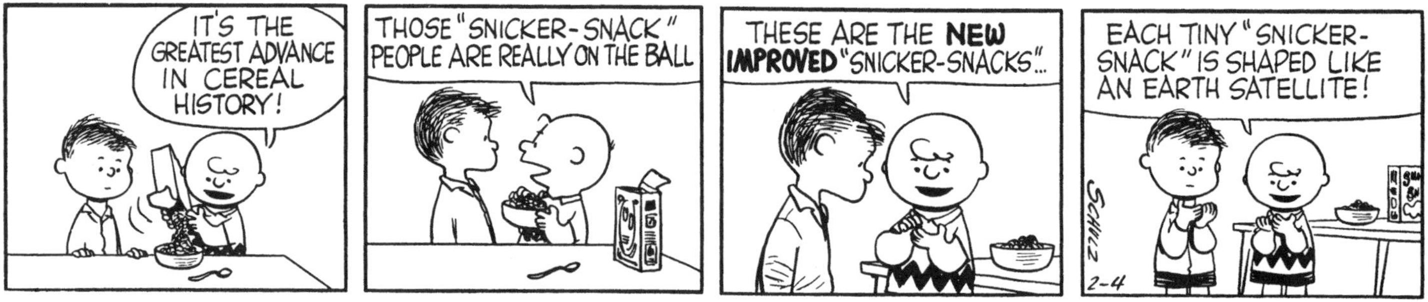
IT'S THE GREATEST ADVANCE IN CEREAL HISTORY!
THOSE "SNICKER-SNACK" PEOPLE ARE REALLY ON THE BALL
THESE ARE THE NEW IMPROVED "SNICKER-SNACKS"...
EACH TINY "SNICKER-SNACK" IS SHAPED LIKE AN EARTH SATELLITE!

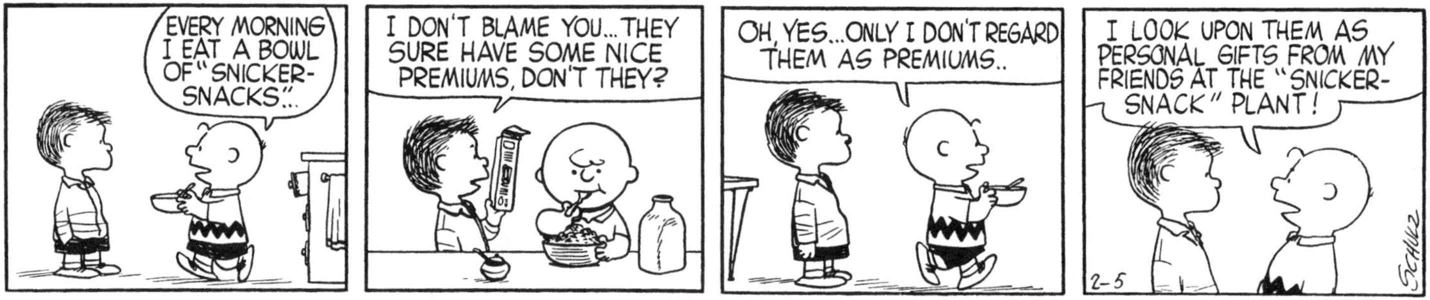
EVERY MORNING I EAT A BOWL OF "SNICKER-SNACKS"...
I DON'T BLAME YOU... THEY SURE HAVE SOME NICE PREMIUMS, DON'T THEY?
OH, YES... ONLY I DON'T REGARD THEM AS PREMIUMS..
I LOOK UPON THEM AS PERSONAL GIFTS FROM MY FRIENDS AT THE "SNICKER-SNACK" PLANT!

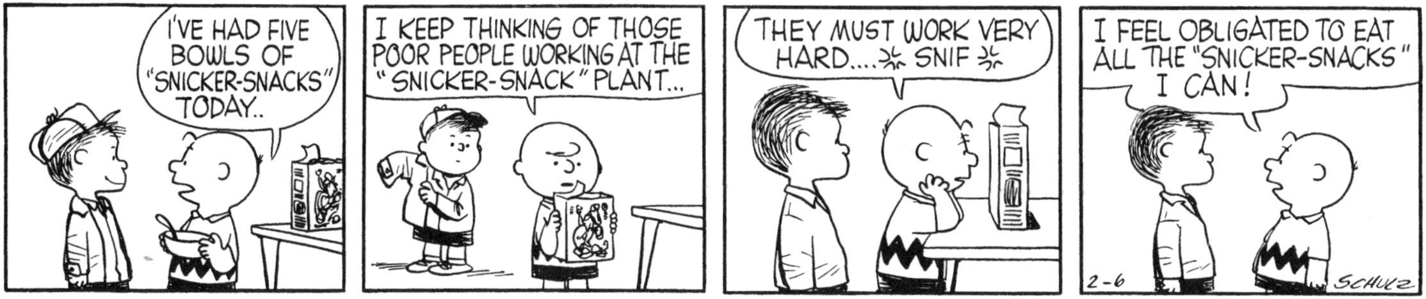
I'VE HAD FIVE BOWLS OF "SNICKER-SNACKS" TODAY..
I KEEP THINKING OF THOSE POOR PEOPLE WORKING AT THE "SNICKER-SNACK" PLANT...
THEY MUST WORK VERY HARD.... SNIF
I FEEL OBLIGATED TO EAT ALL THE "SNICKER-SNACKS" I CAN!
2-6
SCHULZ

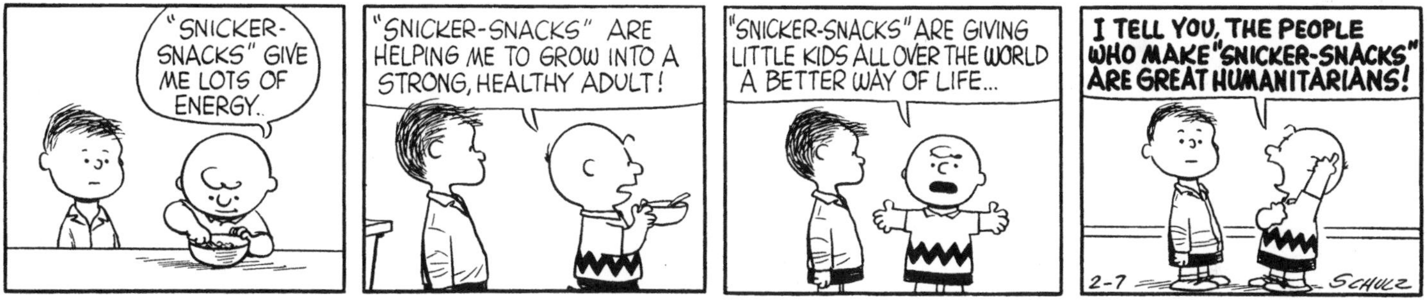
"SNICKER-SNACKS" GIVE ME LOTS OF ENERGY..
"SNICKER-SNACKS" ARE HELPING ME TO GROW INTO A STRONG, HEALTHY ADULT!
"SNICKER-SNACKS" ARE GIVING LITTLE KIDS ALL OVER THE WORLD A BETTER WAY OF LIFE...
I TELL YOU, THE PEOPLE WHO MAKE "SNICKER-SNACKS" ARE GREAT HUMANITARIANS!
2-7
SCHULZ

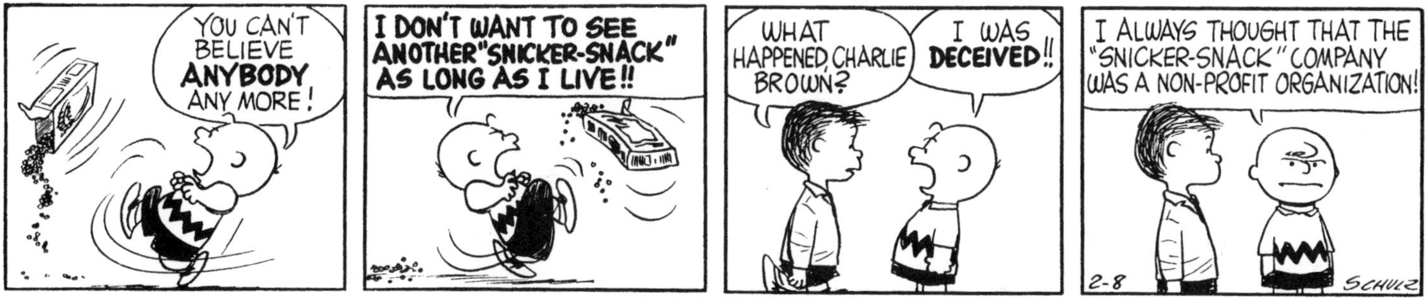
YOU CAN'T BELIEVE ANYBODY ANY MORE!
I DON'T WANT TO SEE ANOTHER "SNICKER-SNACK" AS LONG AS I LIVE!!
WHAT HAPPENED, CHARLIE BROWN?
I WAS DECEIVED!!
I ALWAYS THOUGHT THAT THE "SNICKER-SNACK" COMPANY WAS A NON-PROFIT ORGANIZATION!
2-8
SCHULZ

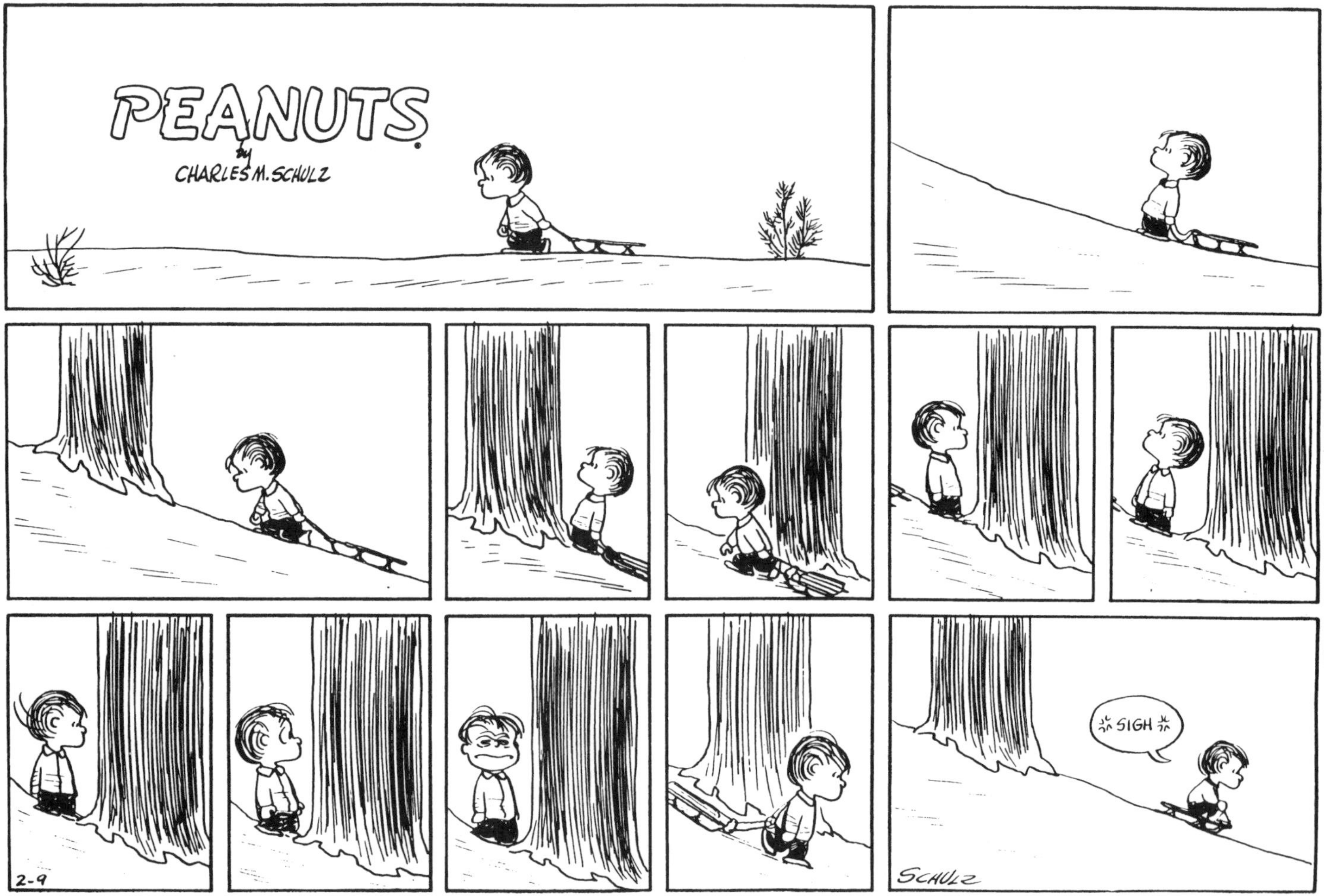
PEANUTS
by
CHARLES M. SCHULZ
2-9
SIGH
SCHULZ

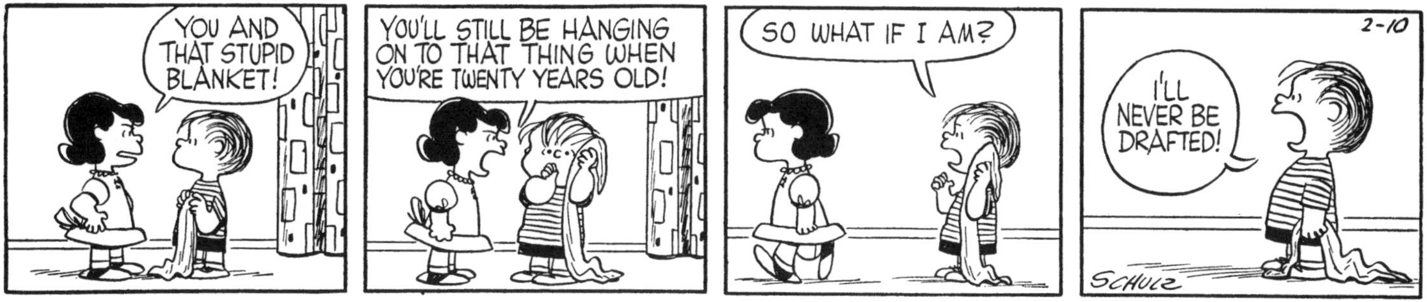
YOU AND THAT STUPID BLANKET!
YOU'LL STILL BE HANGING ON TO THAT THING WHEN YOU'RE TWENTY YEARS OLD!
SO WHAT IF I AM?
I'LL NEVER BE DRAFTED!
2-10
SCHULZ

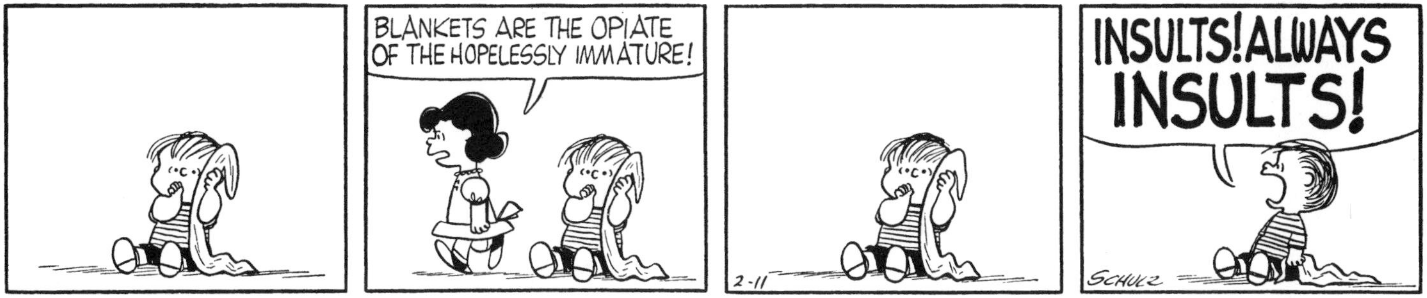
BLANKETS ARE THE OPIATE OF THE HOPELESSLY IMMATURE!
2-11
INSULTS! ALWAYS INSULTS!
SCHULZ

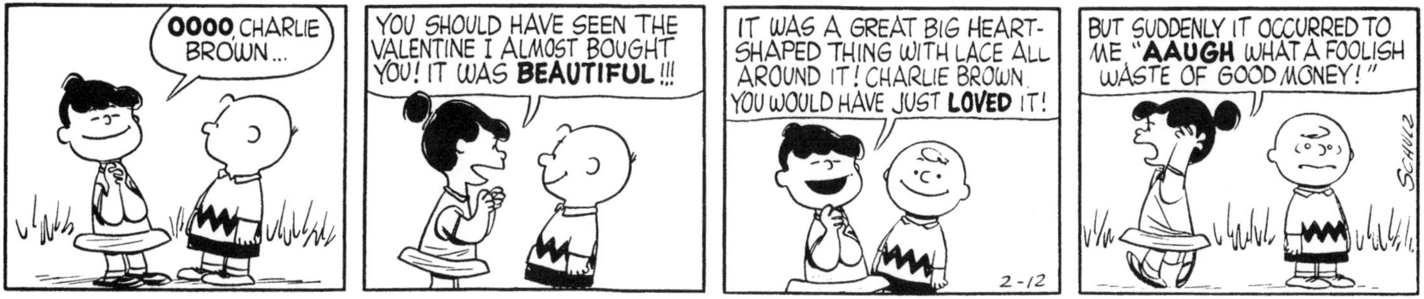
OOOO CHARLIE BROWN...
YOU SHOULD HAVE SEEN THE VALENTINE I ALMOST BOUGHT YOU! IT WAS BEAUTIFUL!!!
IT WAS A GREAT BIG HEART-SHAPED THING WITH LACE ALL AROUND IT! CHARLIE BROWN, YOU WOULD HAVE JUST LOVED IT!
2-12
BUT SUDDENLY IT OCCURRED TO ME, "AAUGH WHAT A FOOLISH WASTE OF GOOD MONEY!"
SCHULZ

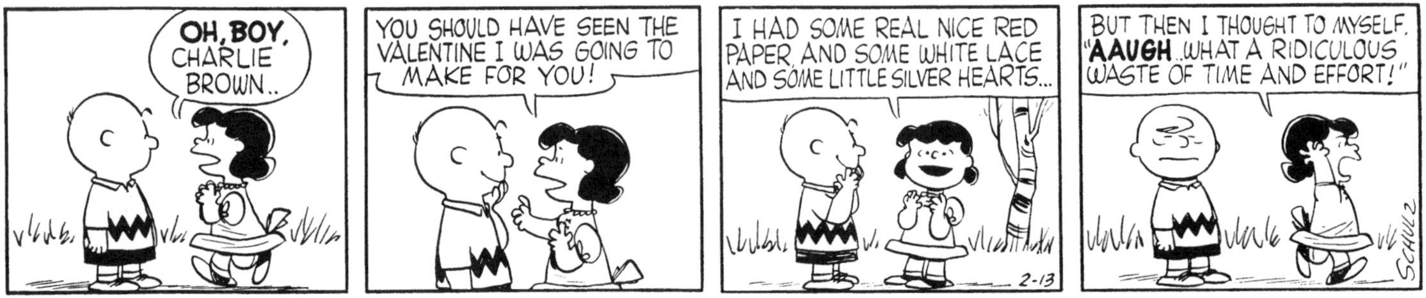
OH, BOY, CHARLIE BROWN..
YOU SHOULD HAVE SEEN THE VALENTINE I WAS GOING TO MAKE FOR YOU!
I HAD SOME REAL NICE RED PAPER, AND SOME WHITE LACE AND SOME LITTLE SILVER HEARTS...
2-13
BUT THEN I THOUGHT TO MYSELF, "AAUGH..WHAT A RIDICULOUS WASTE OF TIME AND EFFORT!"
SCHULZ

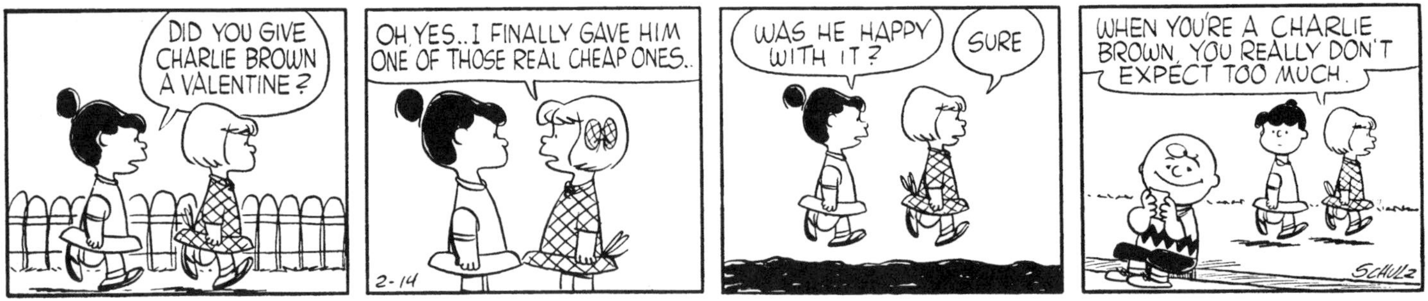
DID YOU GIVE CHARLIE BROWN A VALENTINE?
OH, YES..I FINALLY GAVE HIM ONE OF THOSE REAL CHEAP ONES..
2-14
WAS HE HAPPY WITH IT?
SURE
WHEN YOU'RE A CHARLIE BROWN, YOU REALLY DON'T EXPECT TOO MUCH.
SCHULZ

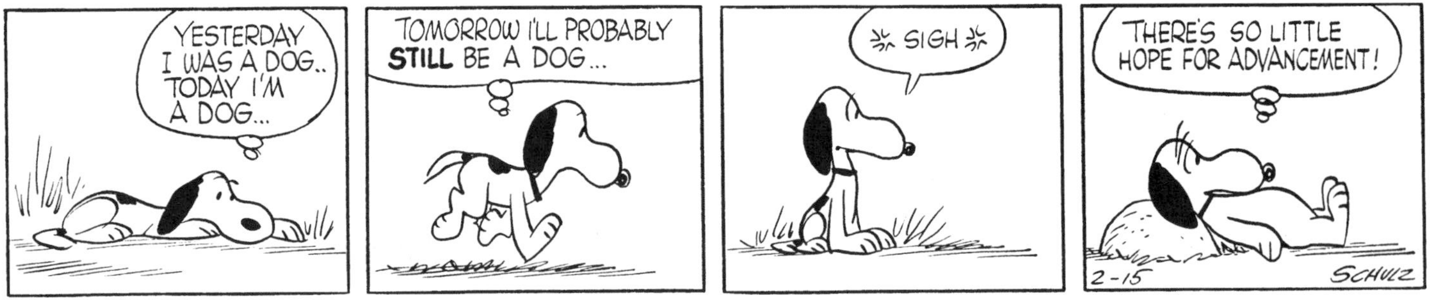
YESTERDAY I WAS A DOG.. TODAY I'M A DOG...
TOMORROW I'LL PROBABLY STILL BE A DOG...
SIGH
THERE'S SO LITTLE HOPE FOR ADVANCEMENT!
2-15
SCHULZ

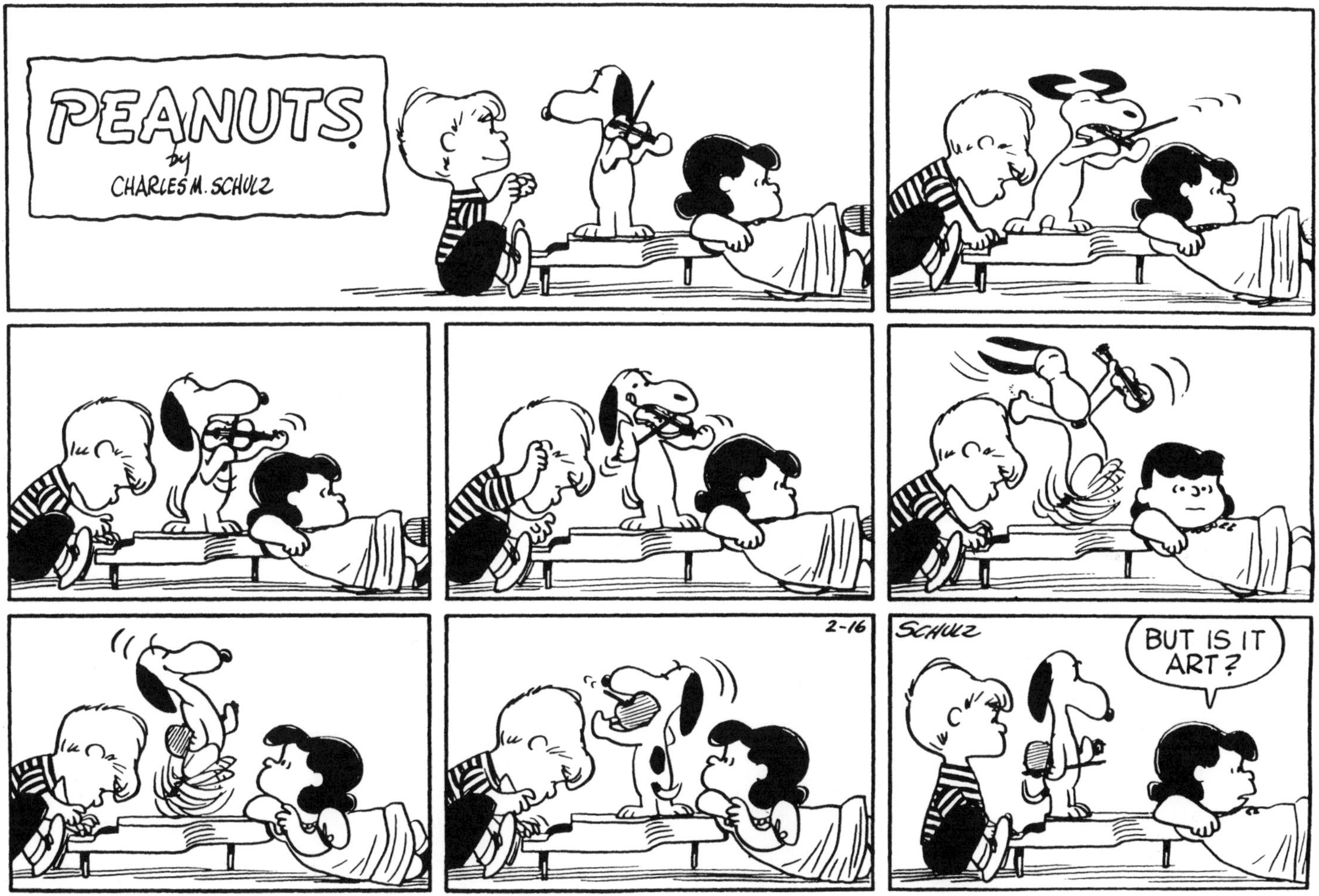
PEANUTS
by
CHARLES M. SCHULZ
2-16
SCHULZ
BUT IS IT ART?

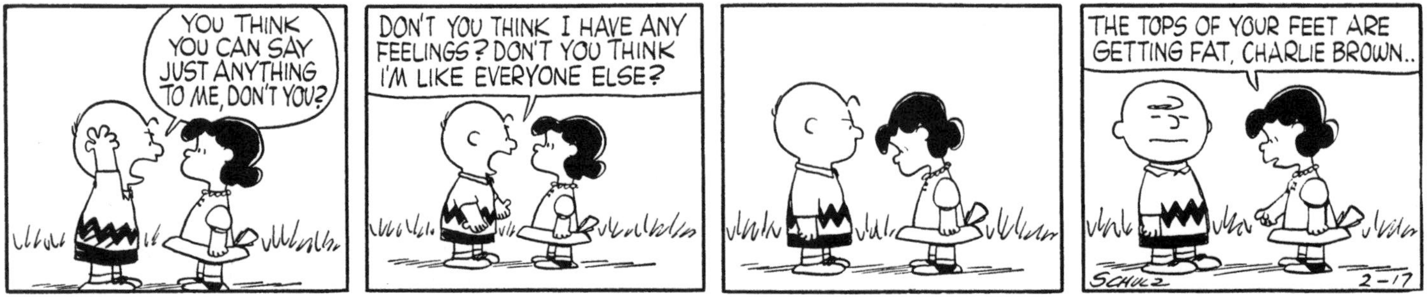
YOU THINK YOU CAN SAY JUST ANYTHING TO ME, DON'T YOU?
DON'T YOU THINK I HAVE ANY FEELINGS? DON'T YOU THINK I'M LIKE EVERYONE ELSE?
THE TOPS OF YOUR FEET ARE GETTING FAT, CHARLIE BROWN..
SCHULZ
2-17

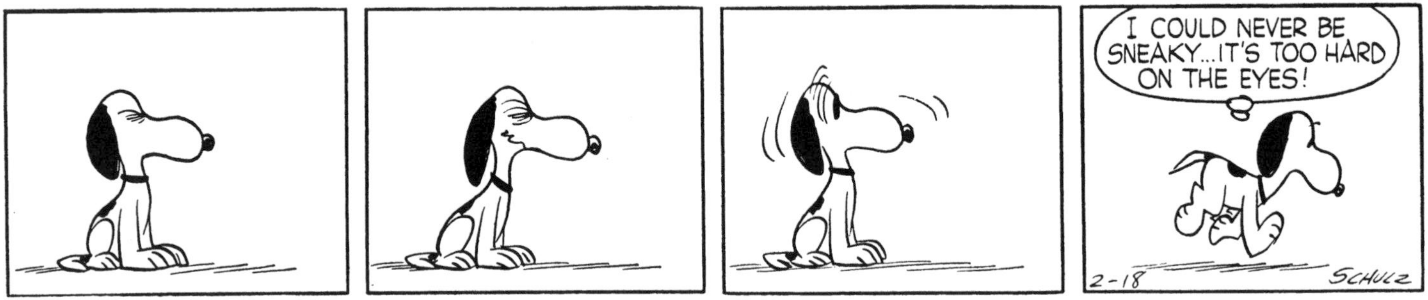
I COULD NEVER BE SNEAKY...IT'S TOO HARD ON THE EYES!
2-18
SCHULZ

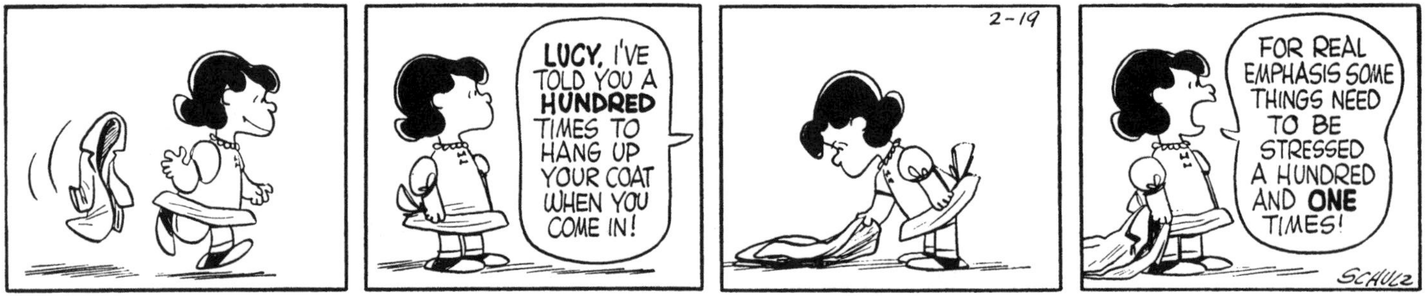
LUCY, I'VE TOLD YOU A HUNDRED TIMES TO HANG UP YOUR COAT WHEN YOU COME IN!
2-19
FOR REAL EMPHASIS SOME THINGS NEED TO BE STRESSED A HUNDRED AND ONE TIMES!
SCHULZ

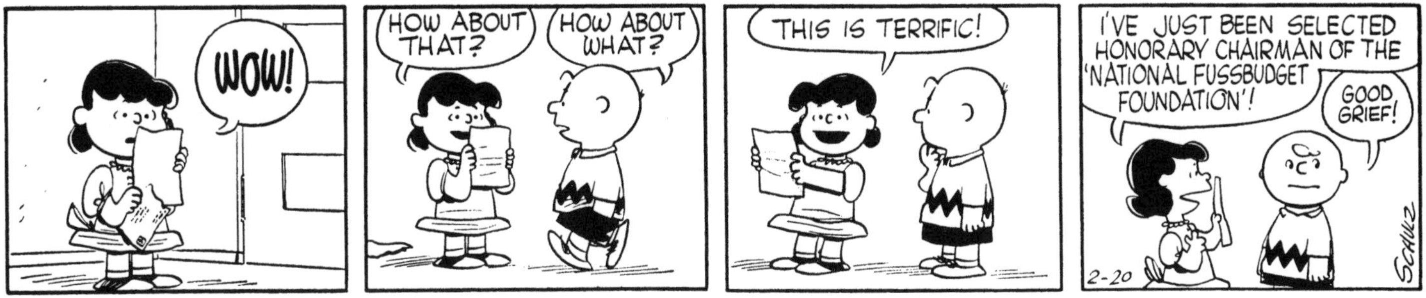

WOW!
HOW ABOUT THAT?
HOW ABOUT WHAT?
THIS IS TERRIFIC!
I'VE JUST BEEN SELECTED HONORARY CHAIRMAN OF THE 'NATIONAL FUSSBUDGET FOUNDATION'!
GOOD GRIEF!
2-20
SCHULZ

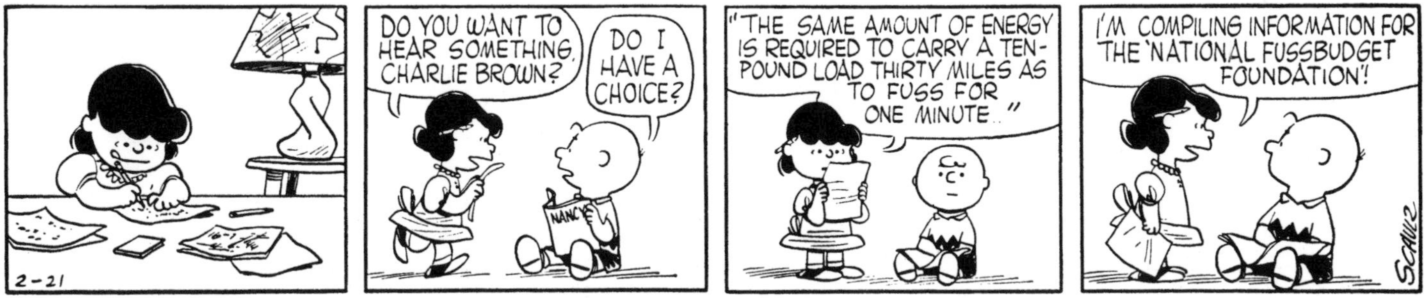

2-21
DO YOU WANT TO HEAR SOMETHING, CHARLIE BROWN?
DO I HAVE A CHOICE?
NANCY
"THE SAME AMOUNT OF ENERGY IS REQUIRED TO CARRY A TEN-POUND LOAD THIRTY MILES AS TO FUSS FOR ONE MINUTE..."
I'M COMPILING INFORMATION FOR THE 'NATIONAL FUSSBUDGET FOUNDATION'!
SCHULZ

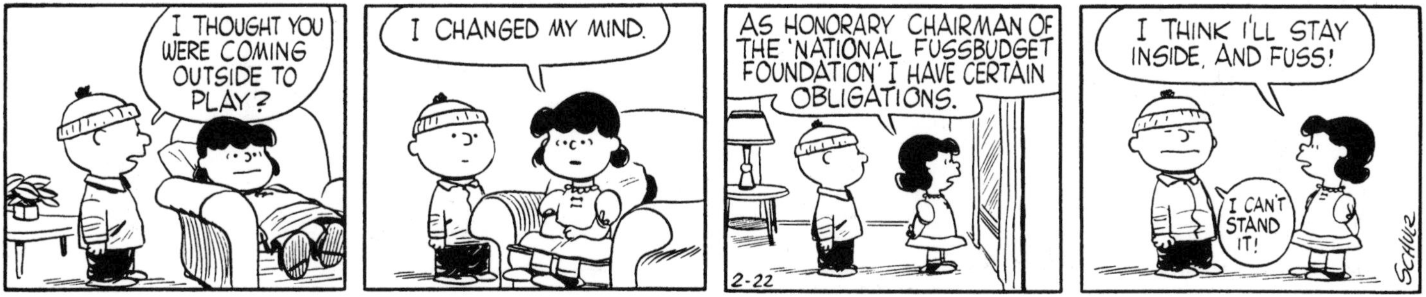

I THOUGHT YOU WERE COMING OUTSIDE TO PLAY?
I CHANGED MY MIND.
AS HONORARY CHAIRMAN OF THE 'NATIONAL FUSSBUDGET FOUNDATION' I HAVE CERTAIN OBLIGATIONS.
2-22
I THINK I'LL STAY INSIDE, AND FUSS!
I CAN'T STAND IT!
SCHULZ

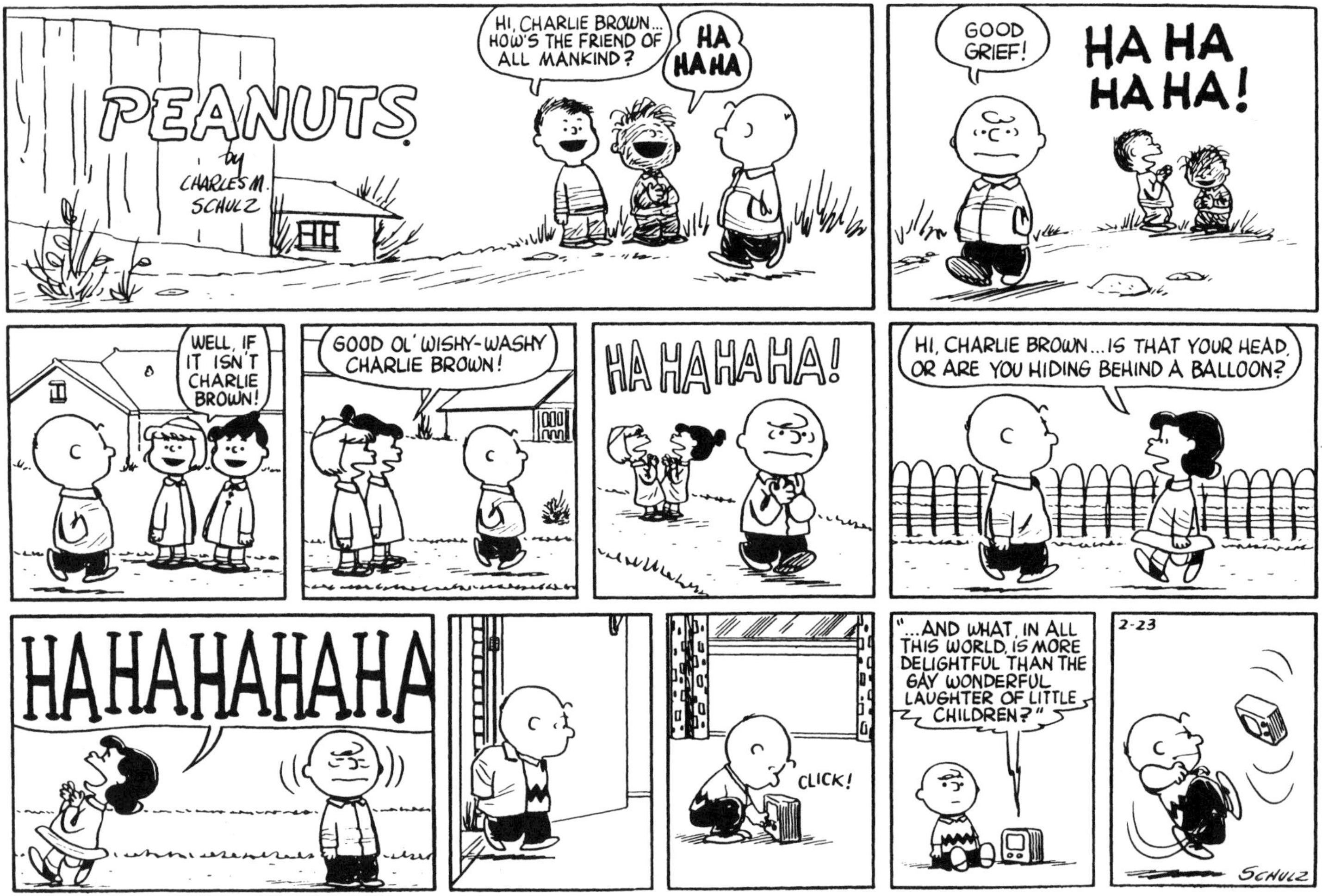
PEANUTS
by CHARLES M. SCHULZ
HI, CHARLIE BROWN... HOW'S THE FRIEND OF ALL MANKIND?
HA HA HA
GOOD GRIEF!
HA HA HA HA!
WELL, IF IT ISN'T CHARLIE BROWN!
GOOD OL' WISHY-WASHY CHARLIE BROWN!
HA HA HA HA HA!
HI, CHARLIE BROWN... IS THAT YOUR HEAD, OR ARE YOU HIDING BEHIND A BALLOON?
HAHAHAHAHAHA
CLICK!
"...AND WHAT, IN ALL THIS WORLD, IS MORE DELIGHTFUL THAN THE GAY WONDERFUL LAUGHTER OF LITTLE CHILDREN?"
2-23
SCHULZ

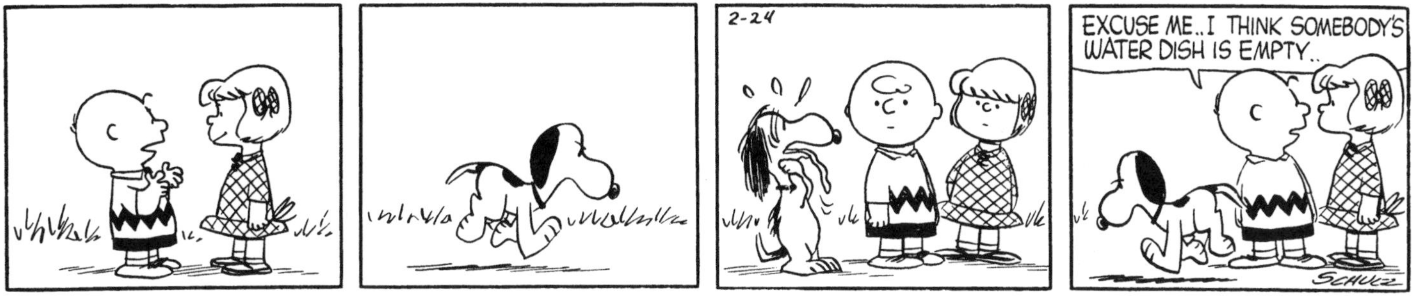
2-24
EXCUSE ME.. I THINK SOMEBODY'S WATER DISH IS EMPTY..
SCHULZ

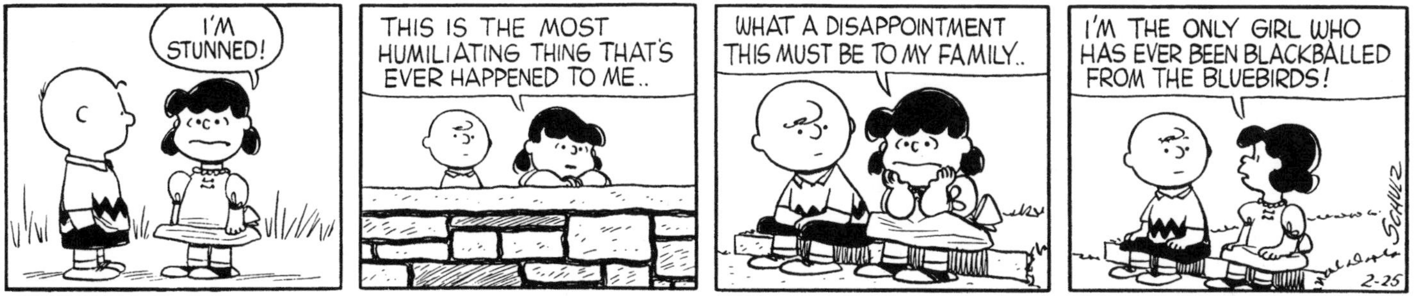
I'M STUNNED!
THIS IS THE MOST HUMILIATING THING THAT'S EVER HAPPENED TO ME..
WHAT A DISAPPOINTMENT THIS MUST BE TO MY FAMILY..
I'M THE ONLY GIRL WHO HAS EVER BEEN BLACKBALLED FROM THE BLUEBIRDS!
SCHULZ
2-25

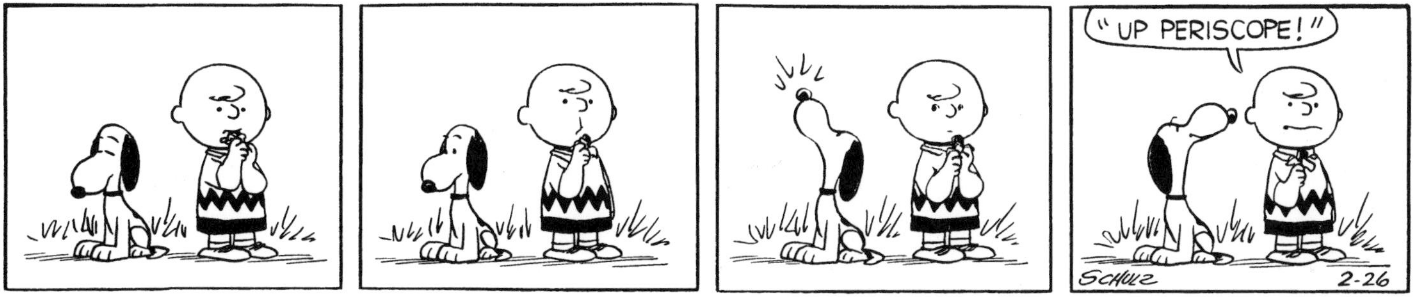
"UP PERISCOPE!"
SCHULZ
2-26

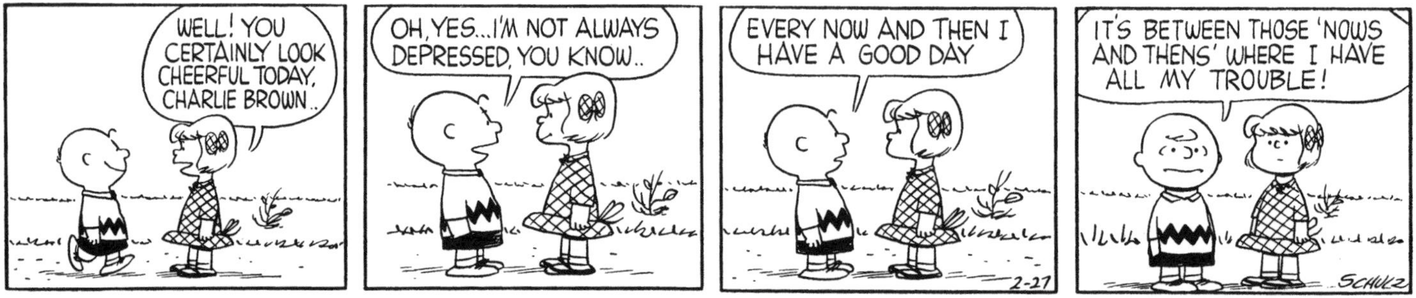
WELL! YOU CERTAINLY LOOK CHEERFUL TODAY, CHARLIE BROWN..
OH, YES...I'M NOT ALWAYS DEPRESSED, YOU KNOW..
EVERY NOW AND THEN I HAVE A GOOD DAY
2-27
IT'S BETWEEN THOSE 'NOWS AND THENS' WHERE I HAVE ALL MY TROUBLE!
SCHULZ

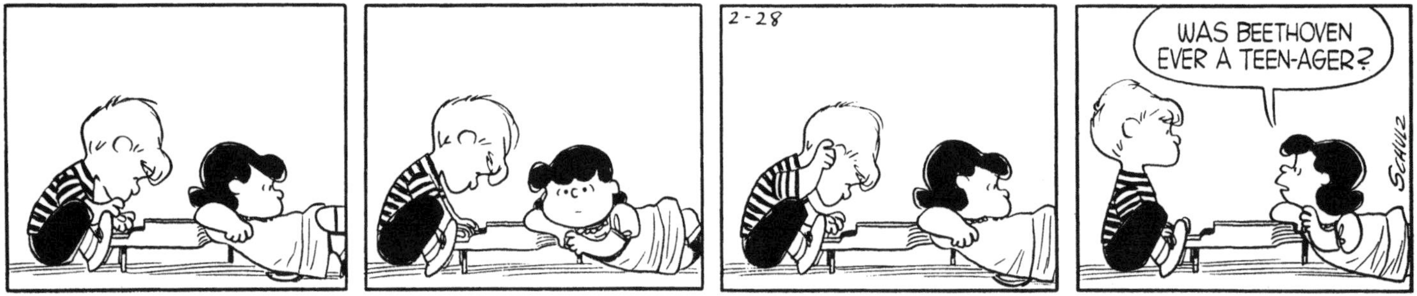
2-28
WAS BEETHOVEN EVER A TEEN-AGER?
SCHULZ

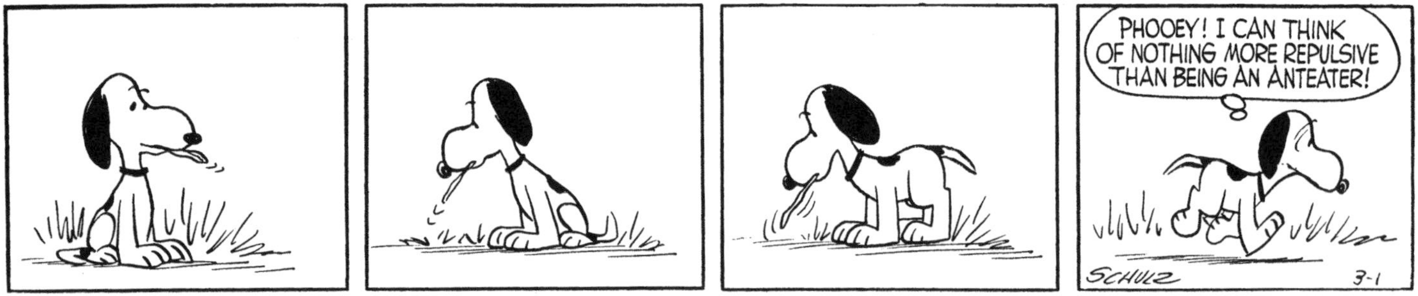
PHOOEY! I CAN THINK OF NOTHING MORE REPULSIVE THAN BEING AN ANTEATER!
SCHULZ
3-1

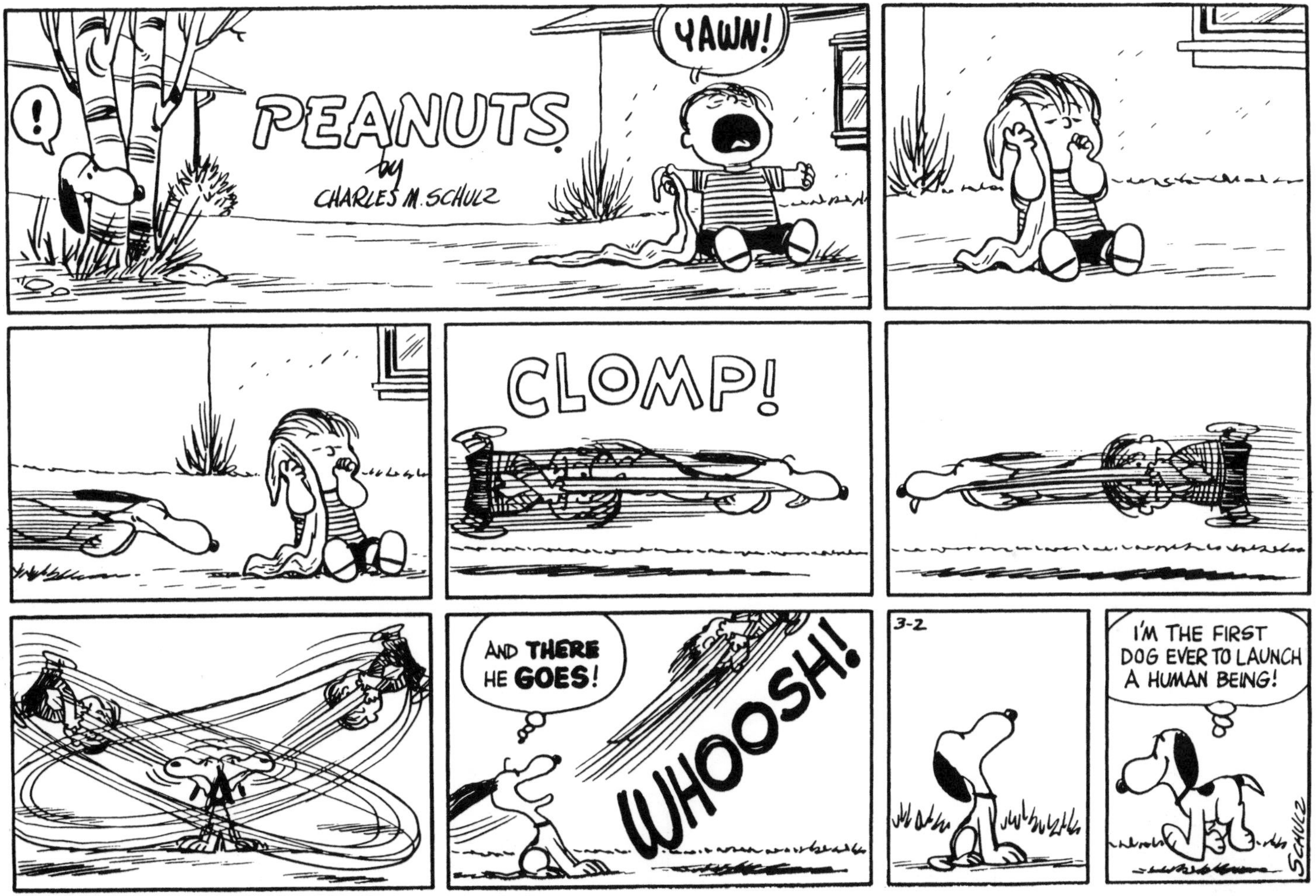
!
YAWN!
PEANUTS
by
CHARLES M. SCHULZ
CLOMP!
AND THERE HE GOES!
WHOOSH!
3-2
I'M THE FIRST DOG EVER TO LAUNCH A HUMAN BEING!
SCHULZ

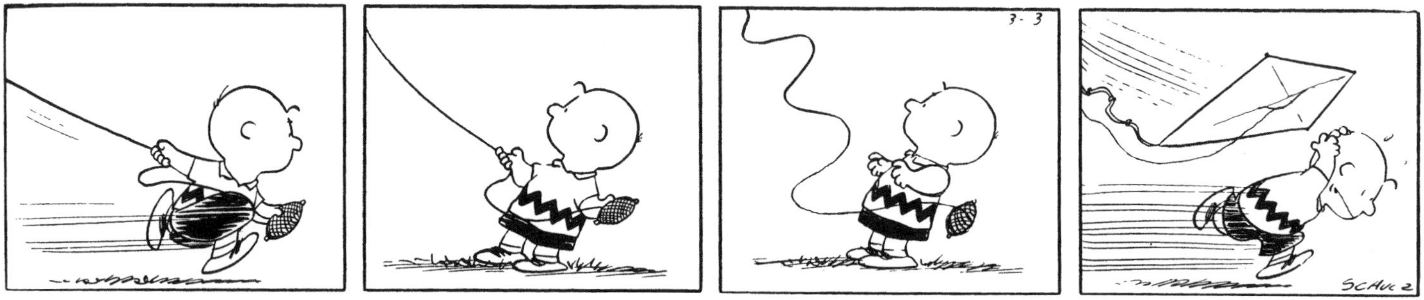
3-3
SCHULZ

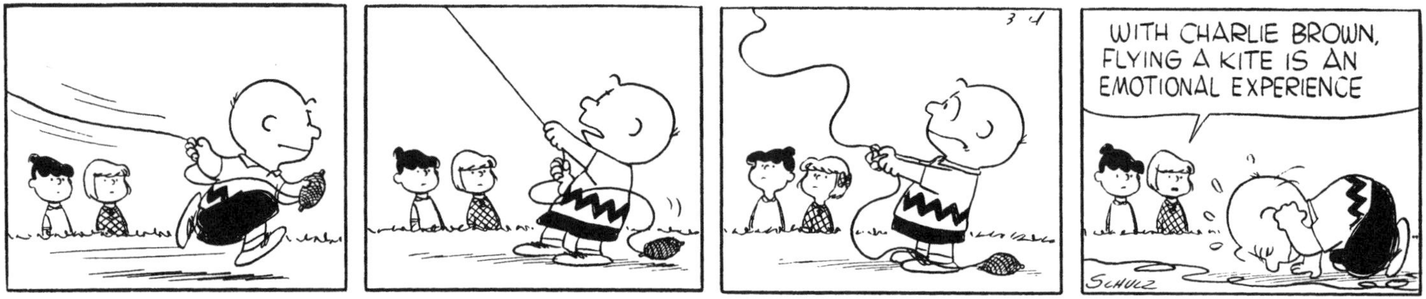
3-4
WITH CHARLIE BROWN, FLYING A KITE IS AN EMOTIONAL EXPERIENCE
SCHULZ

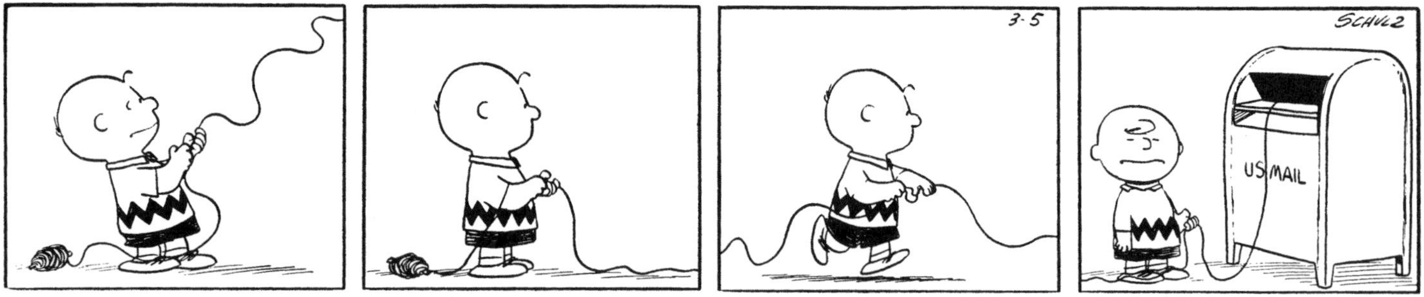
3-5
SCHULZ
US MAIL

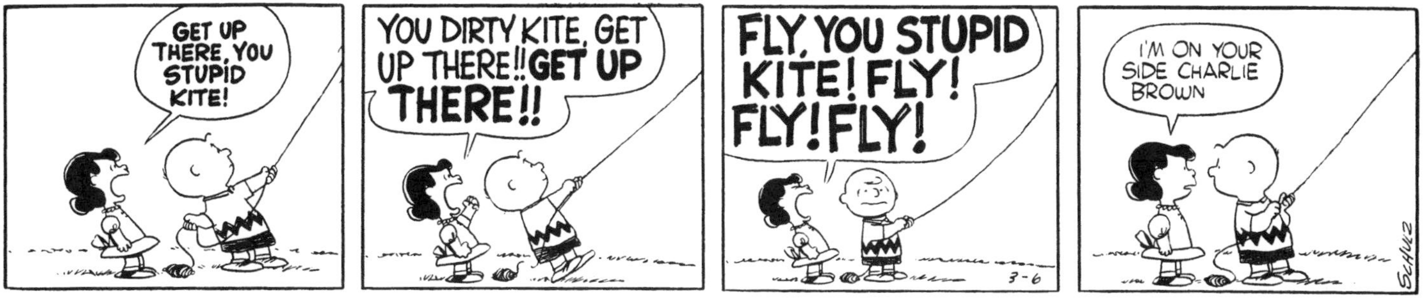
GET UP THERE, YOU STUPID KITE!
YOU DIRTY KITE, GET UP THERE!! GET UP THERE!!
FLY, YOU STUPID KITE! FLY! FLY! FLY!
3-6
I'M ON YOUR SIDE CHARLIE BROWN
SCHULZ

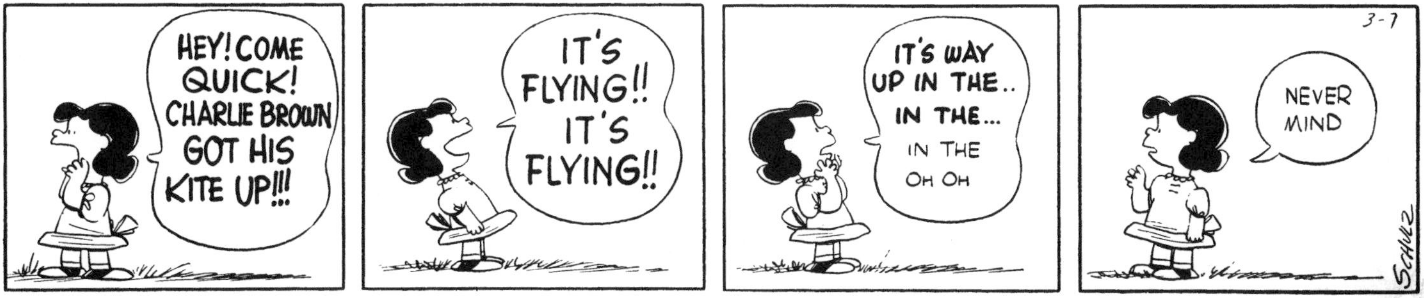
HEY! COME QUICK! CHARLIE BROWN GOT HIS KITE UP!!!
IT'S FLYING!! IT'S FLYING!!
IT'S WAY UP IN THE.. IN THE... IN THE OH OH
3-7
NEVER MIND
SCHULZ

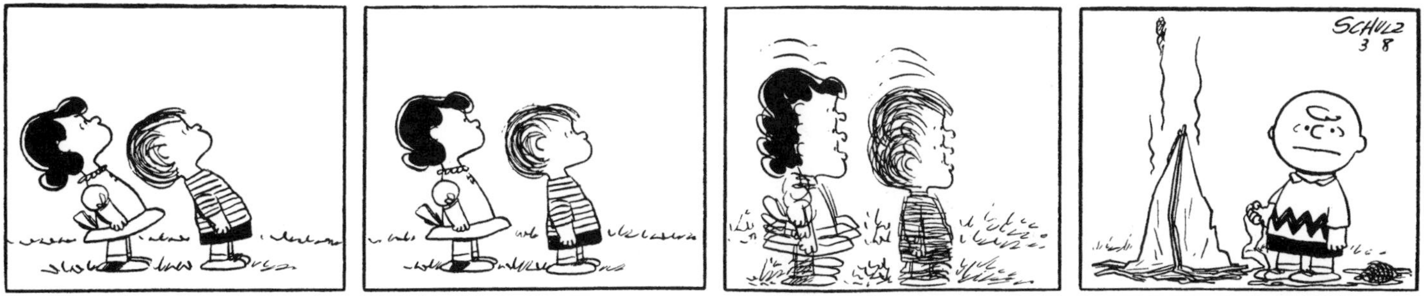
SCHULZ
3 8

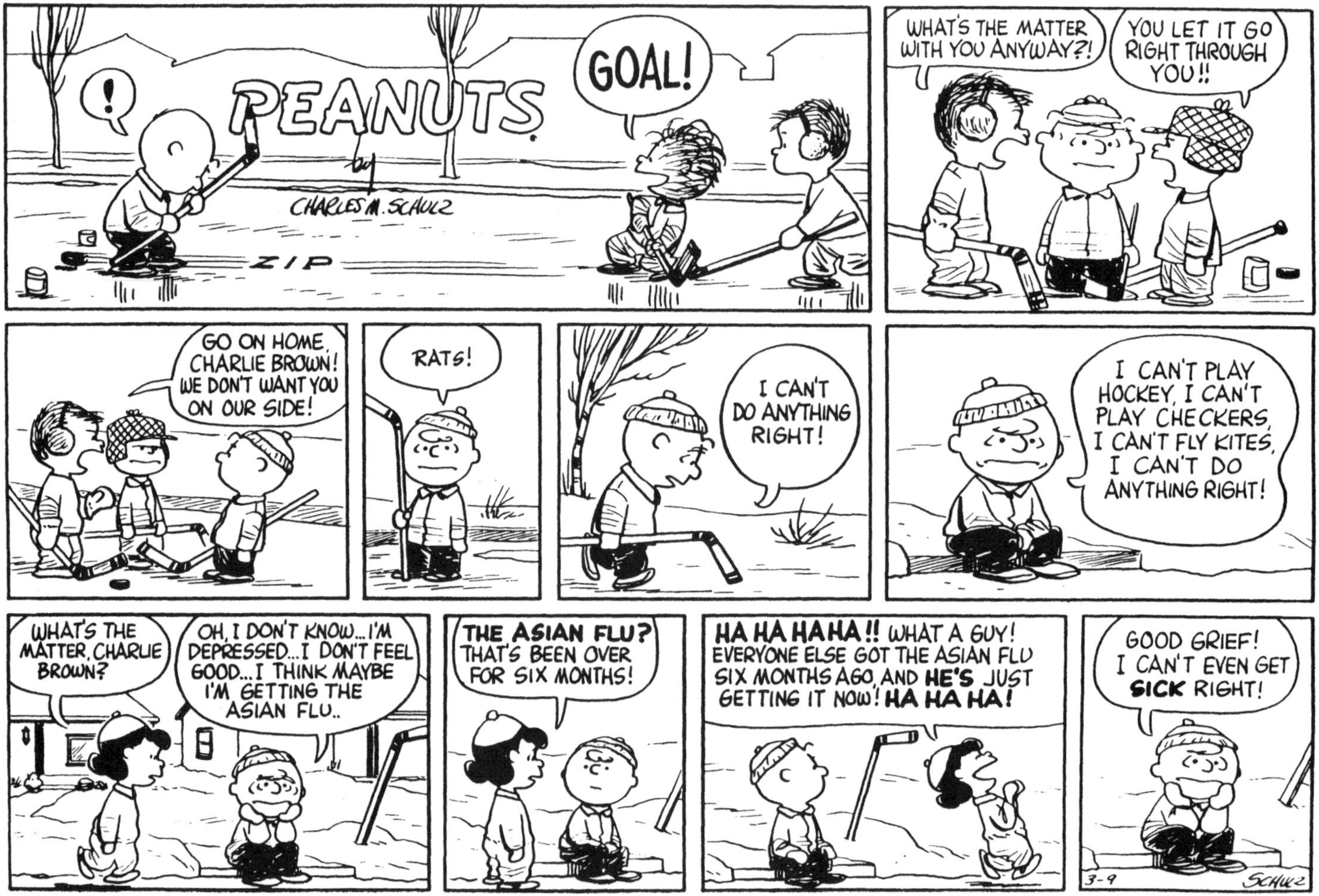
!
PEANUTS
by
CHARLES M. SCHULZ
ZIP
GOAL!
WHAT'S THE MATTER WITH YOU ANYWAY?!
YOU LET IT GO RIGHT THROUGH YOU!!
GO ON HOME, CHARLIE BROWN! WE DON'T WANT YOU ON OUR SIDE!
RATS!
I CAN'T DO ANYTHING RIGHT!
I CAN'T PLAY HOCKEY, I CAN'T PLAY CHECKERS, I CAN'T FLY KITES, I CAN'T DO ANYTHING RIGHT!
WHAT'S THE MATTER, CHARLIE BROWN?
OH, I DON'T KNOW...I'M DEPRESSED...I DON'T FEEL GOOD...I THINK MAYBE I'M GETTING THE ASIAN FLU..
THE ASIAN FLU? THAT'S BEEN OVER FOR SIX MONTHS!
HA HA HA HA!! WHAT A GUY! EVERYONE ELSE GOT THE ASIAN FLU SIX MONTHS AGO, AND HE'S JUST GETTING IT NOW! HA HA HA!
GOOD GRIEF! I CAN'T EVEN GET SICK RIGHT!
3-9
SCHULZ

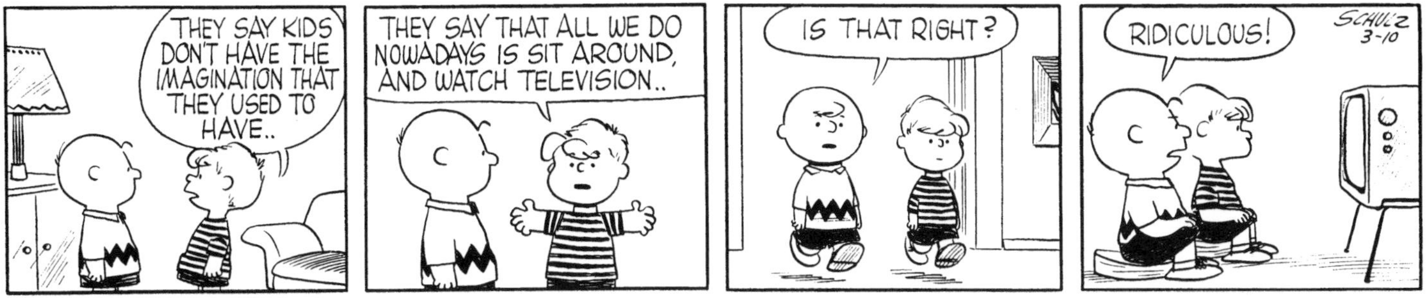
THEY SAY KIDS DON'T HAVE THE IMAGINATION THAT THEY USED TO HAVE..
THEY SAY THAT ALL WE DO NOWADAYS IS SIT AROUND, AND WATCH TELEVISION..
IS THAT RIGHT?
RIDICULOUS!
SCHULZ 3-10

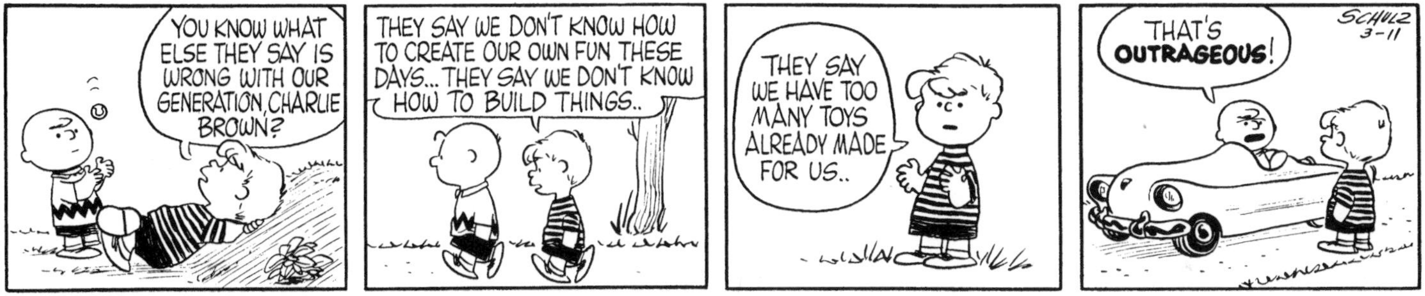
YOU KNOW WHAT ELSE THEY SAY IS WRONG WITH OUR GENERATION, CHARLIE BROWN?
THEY SAY WE DON'T KNOW HOW TO CREATE OUR OWN FUN THESE DAYS... THEY SAY WE DON'T KNOW HOW TO BUILD THINGS..
THEY SAY WE HAVE TOO MANY TOYS ALREADY MADE FOR US..
THAT'S **OUTRAGEOUS**!
SCHULZ 3-11

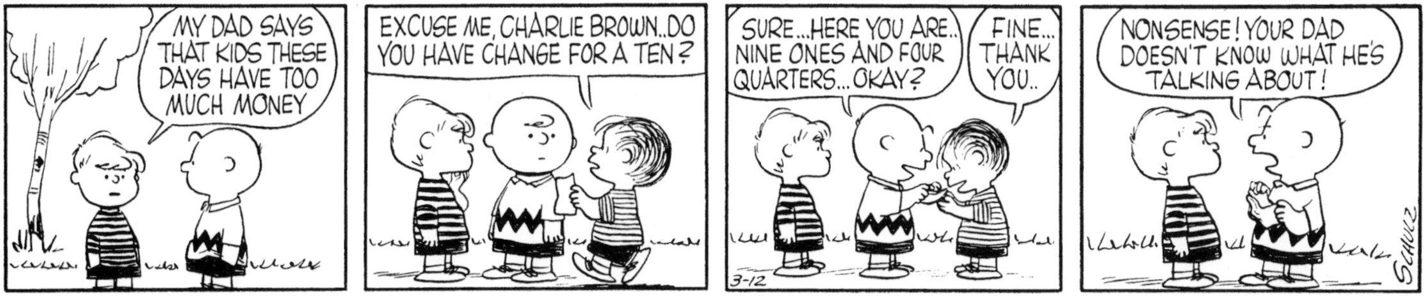
MY DAD SAYS THAT KIDS THESE DAYS HAVE TOO MUCH MONEY
EXCUSE ME, CHARLIE BROWN..DO YOU HAVE CHANGE FOR A TEN?
SURE...HERE YOU ARE.. NINE ONES AND FOUR QUARTERS...OKAY?
FINE... THANK YOU..
3-12
NONSENSE! YOUR DAD DOESN'T KNOW WHAT HE'S TALKING ABOUT!
SCHULZ

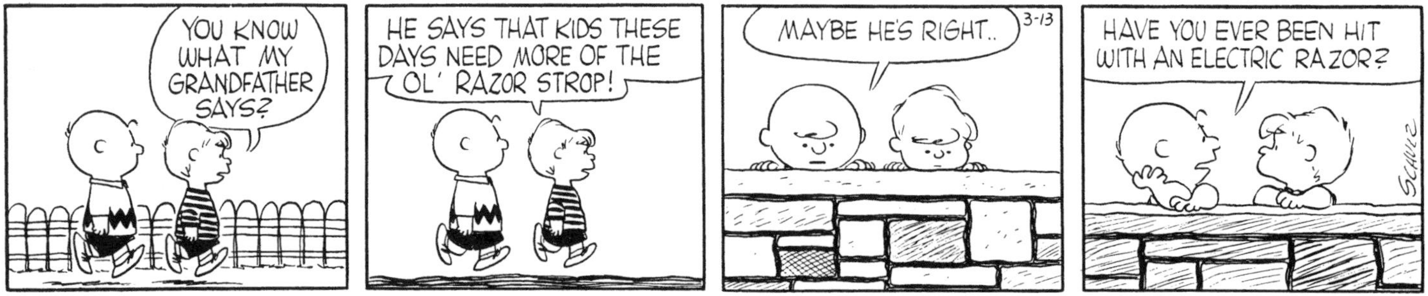

YOU KNOW WHAT MY GRANDFATHER SAYS?
HE SAYS THAT KIDS THESE DAYS NEED MORE OF THE OL' RAZOR STROP!
MAYBE HE'S RIGHT..
3-13
HAVE YOU EVER BEEN HIT WITH AN ELECTRIC RAZOR?
SCHULZ

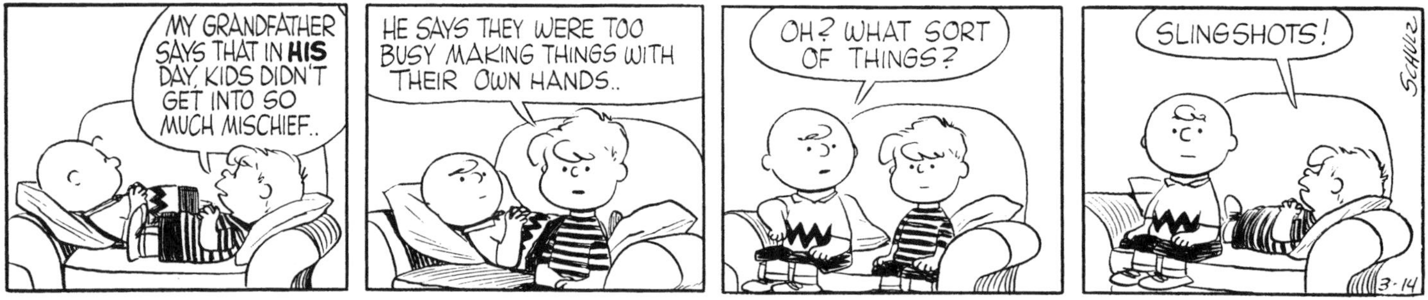

MY GRANDFATHER SAYS THAT IN **HIS** DAY, KIDS DIDN'T GET INTO SO MUCH MISCHIEF..
HE SAYS THEY WERE TOO BUSY MAKING THINGS WITH THEIR OWN HANDS..
OH? WHAT SORT OF THINGS?
SLINGSHOTS!
SCHULZ
3-14

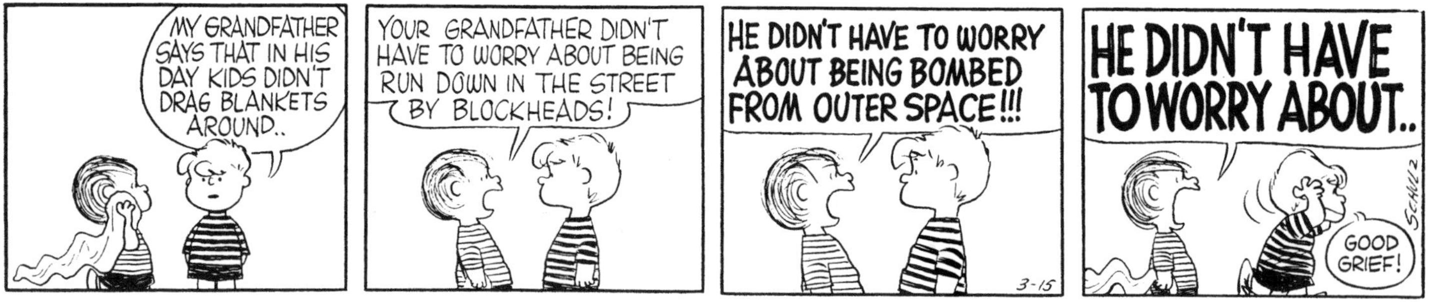

MY GRANDFATHER SAYS THAT IN HIS DAY KIDS DIDN'T DRAG BLANKETS AROUND..
YOUR GRANDFATHER DIDN'T HAVE TO WORRY ABOUT BEING RUN DOWN IN THE STREET BY BLOCKHEADS!
HE DIDN'T HAVE TO WORRY ABOUT BEING BOMBED FROM OUTER SPACE!!!
3-15
HE DIDN'T HAVE TO WORRY ABOUT..
SCHULZ
GOOD GRIEF!

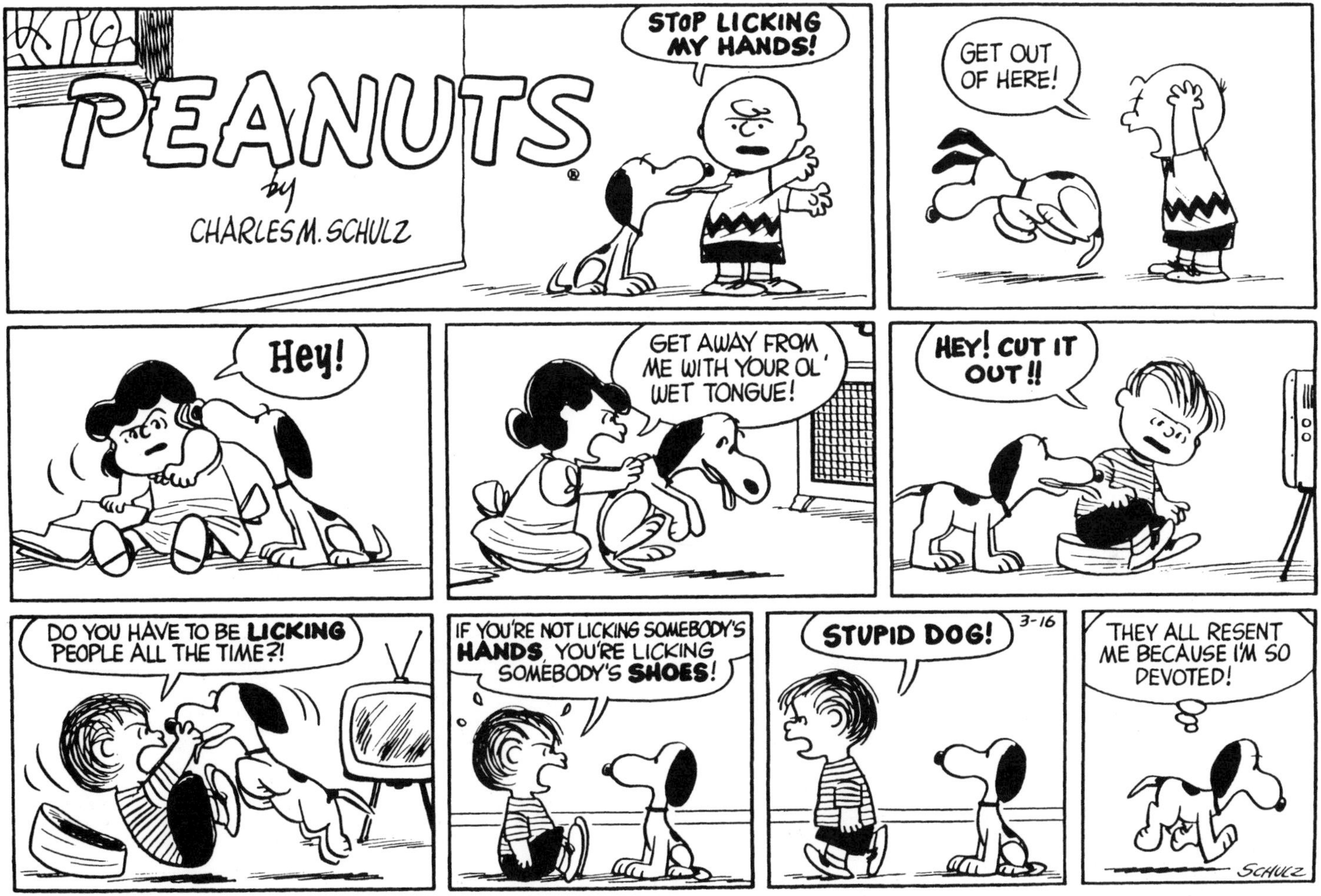
PEANUTS
by
CHARLES M. SCHULZ
STOP LICKING MY HANDS!
GET OUT OF HERE!
Hey!
GET AWAY FROM ME WITH YOUR OL' WET TONGUE!
HEY! CUT IT OUT!!
DO YOU HAVE TO BE LICKING PEOPLE ALL THE TIME?!
IF YOU'RE NOT LICKING SOMEBODY'S HANDS, YOU'RE LICKING SOMEBODY'S SHOES!
STUPID DOG!
3-16
THEY ALL RESENT ME BECAUSE I'M SO DEVOTED!
SCHULZ

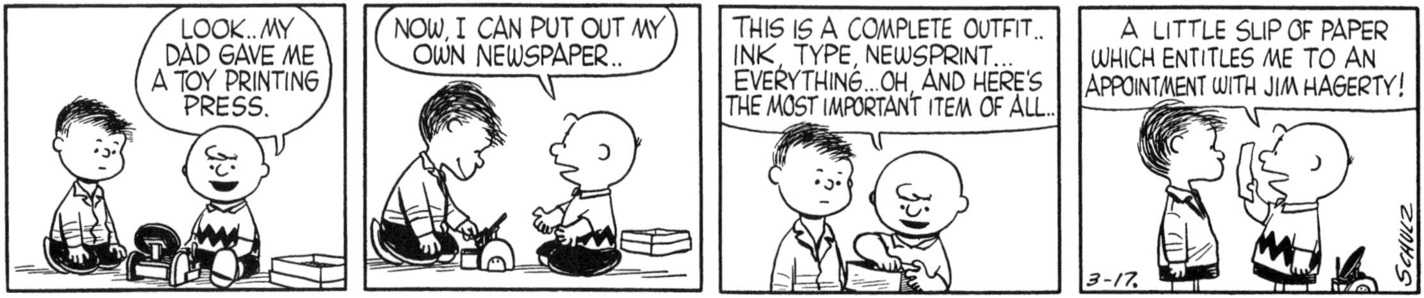
LOOK.. MY DAD GAVE ME A TOY PRINTING PRESS.
NOW, I CAN PUT OUT MY OWN NEWSPAPER..
THIS IS A COMPLETE OUTFIT.. INK, TYPE, NEWSPRINT... EVERYTHING...OH, AND HERE'S THE MOST IMPORTANT ITEM OF ALL..
A LITTLE SLIP OF PAPER WHICH ENTITLES ME TO AN APPOINTMENT WITH JIM HAGERTY!
3-17.
SCHULZ

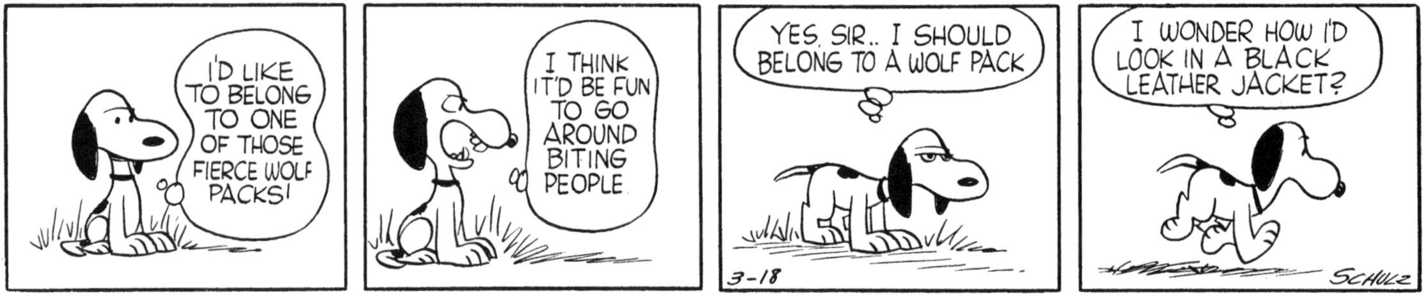
I'D LIKE TO BELONG TO ONE OF THOSE FIERCE WOLF PACKS!
I THINK IT'D BE FUN TO GO AROUND BITING PEOPLE
YES, SIR.. I SHOULD BELONG TO A WOLF PACK
3-18
I WONDER HOW I'D LOOK IN A BLACK LEATHER JACKET?
SCHULZ

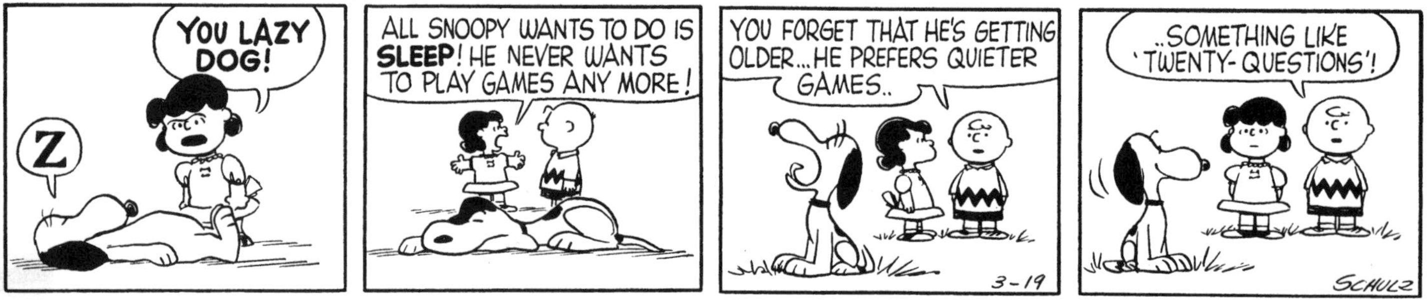
Z
YOU LAZY DOG!
ALL SNOOPY WANTS TO DO IS SLEEP! HE NEVER WANTS TO PLAY GAMES ANY MORE!
YOU FORGET THAT HE'S GETTING OLDER...HE PREFERS QUIETER GAMES..
3-19
..SOMETHING LIKE 'TWENTY-QUESTIONS'!
SCHULZ

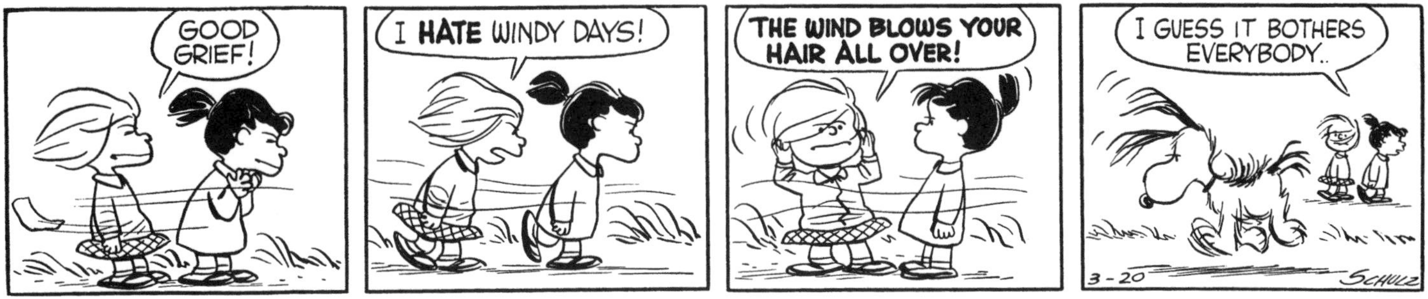
GOOD GRIEF!
I HATE WINDY DAYS!
THE WIND BLOWS YOUR HAIR ALL OVER!
I GUESS IT BOTHERS EVERYBODY..
3-20
SCHULZ

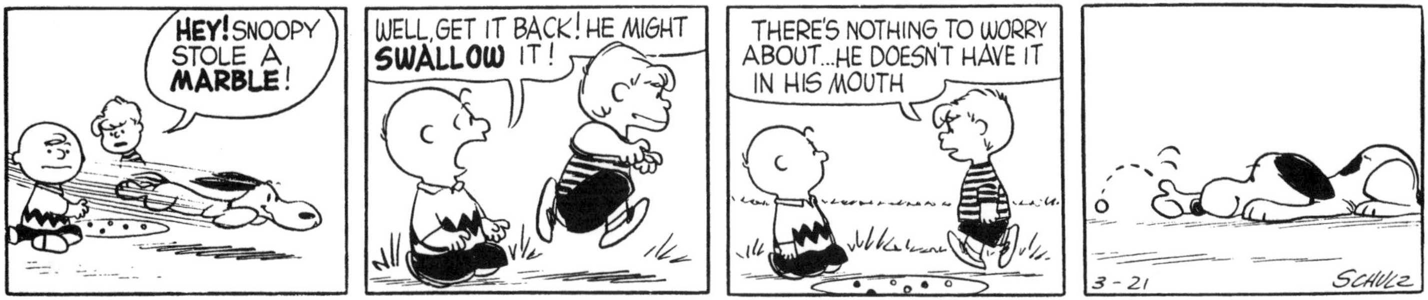
HEY! SNOOPY STOLE A MARBLE!
WELL, GET IT BACK! HE MIGHT SWALLOW IT!
THERE'S NOTHING TO WORRY ABOUT...HE DOESN'T HAVE IT IN HIS MOUTH
3-21
SCHULZ

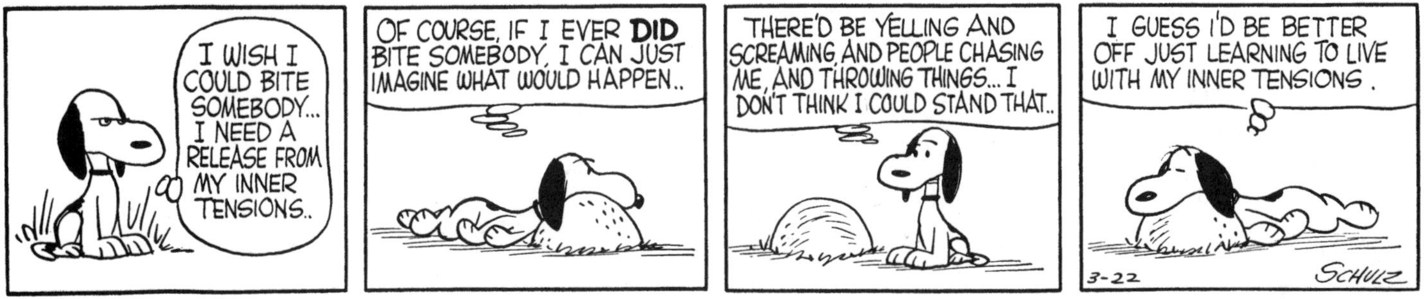
I WISH I COULD BITE SOMEBODY... I NEED A RELEASE FROM MY INNER TENSIONS..
OF COURSE, IF I EVER DID BITE SOMEBODY, I CAN JUST IMAGINE WHAT WOULD HAPPEN..
THERE'D BE YELLING AND SCREAMING, AND PEOPLE CHASING ME, AND THROWING THINGS... I DON'T THINK I COULD STAND THAT..
I GUESS I'D BE BETTER OFF JUST LEARNING TO LIVE WITH MY INNER TENSIONS.
3-22
SCHULZ

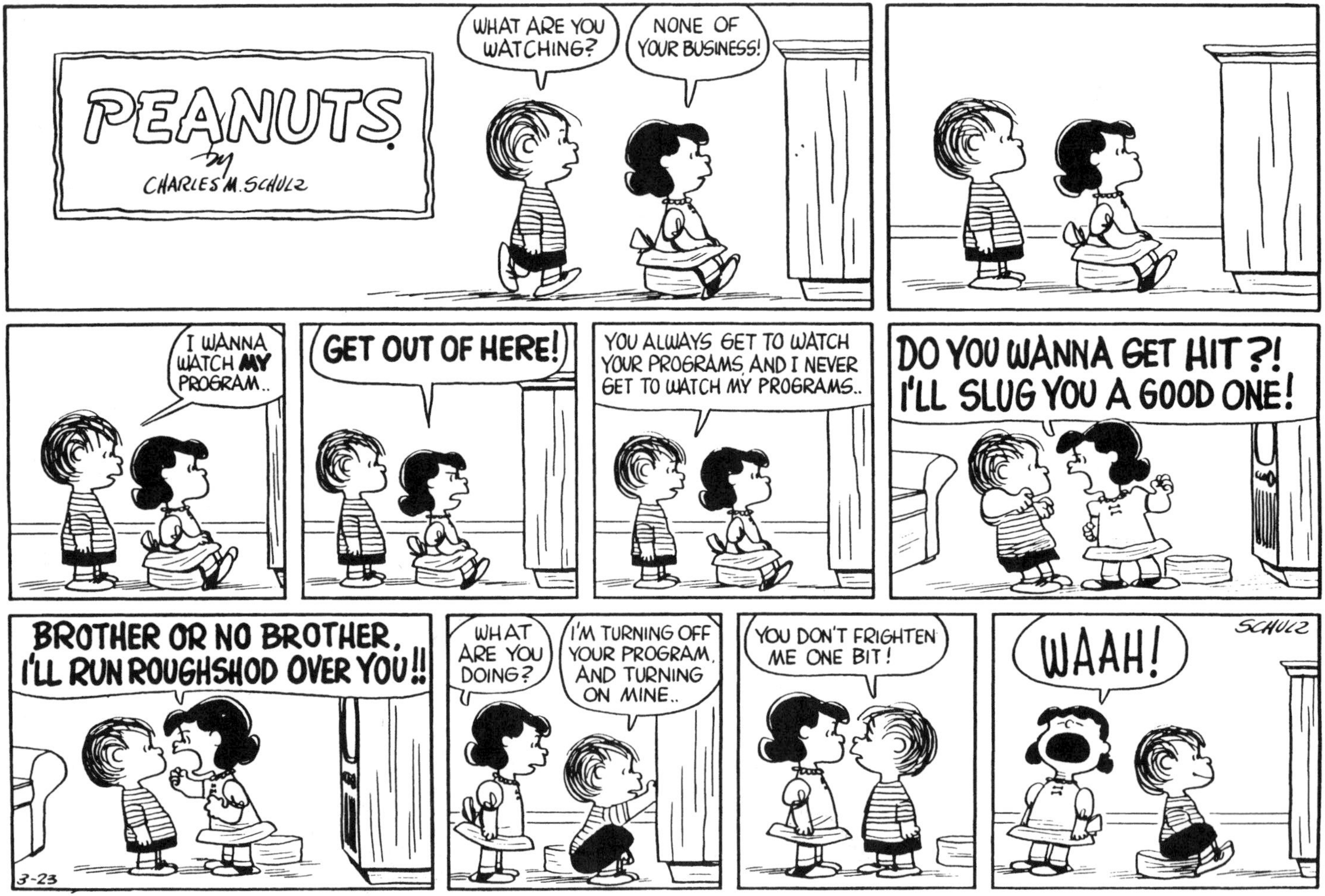
PEANUTS
by CHARLES M. SCHULZ
WHAT ARE YOU WATCHING?
NONE OF YOUR BUSINESS!
I WANNA WATCH **MY** PROGRAM..
GET OUT OF HERE!
YOU ALWAYS GET TO WATCH YOUR PROGRAMS, AND I NEVER GET TO WATCH MY PROGRAMS..
DO YOU WANNA GET HIT?! I'LL SLUG YOU A GOOD ONE!
BROTHER OR NO BROTHER, I'LL RUN ROUGHSHOD OVER YOU!!
3-23
WHAT ARE YOU DOING?
I'M TURNING OFF YOUR PROGRAM, AND TURNING ON MINE..
YOU DON'T FRIGHTEN ME ONE BIT!
WAAH!
SCHULZ

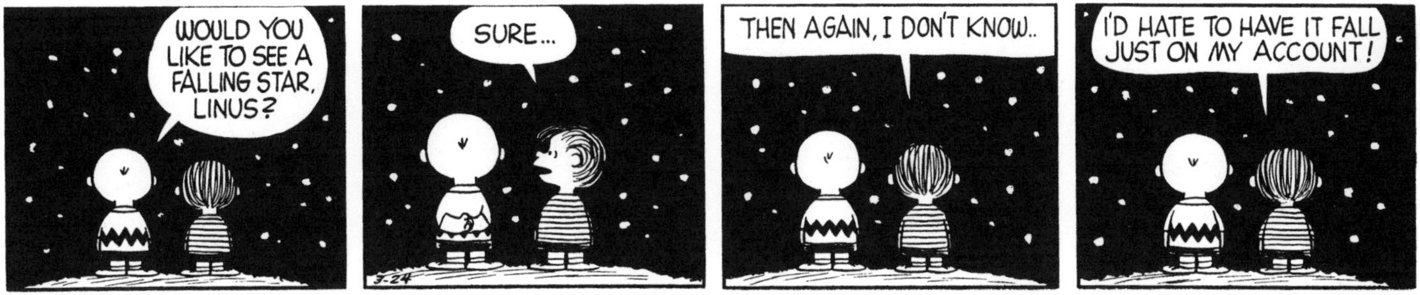
WOULD YOU LIKE TO SEE A FALLING STAR, LINUS?
SURE...
THEN AGAIN, I DON'T KNOW..
I'D HATE TO HAVE IT FALL JUST ON MY ACCOUNT!

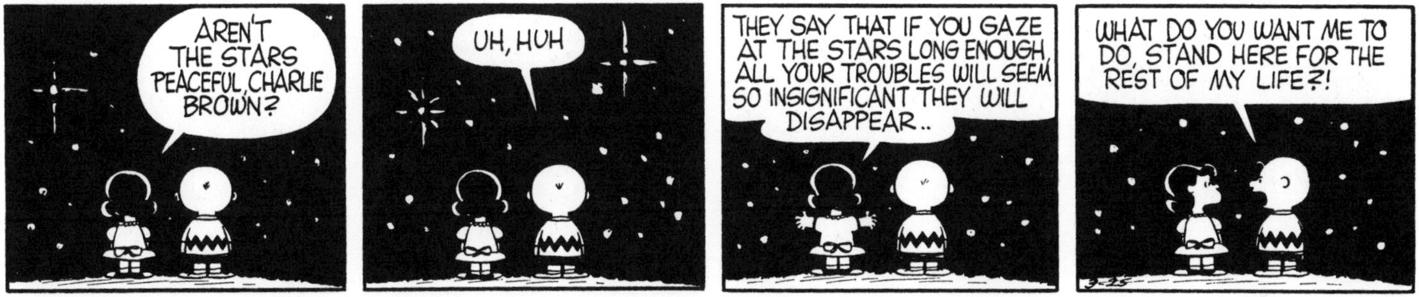
AREN'T THE STARS PEACEFUL, CHARLIE BROWN?
UH, HUH
THEY SAY THAT IF YOU GAZE AT THE STARS LONG ENOUGH ALL YOUR TROUBLES WILL SEEM SO INSIGNIFICANT THEY WILL DISAPPEAR..
WHAT DO YOU WANT ME TO DO, STAND HERE FOR THE REST OF MY LIFE?!

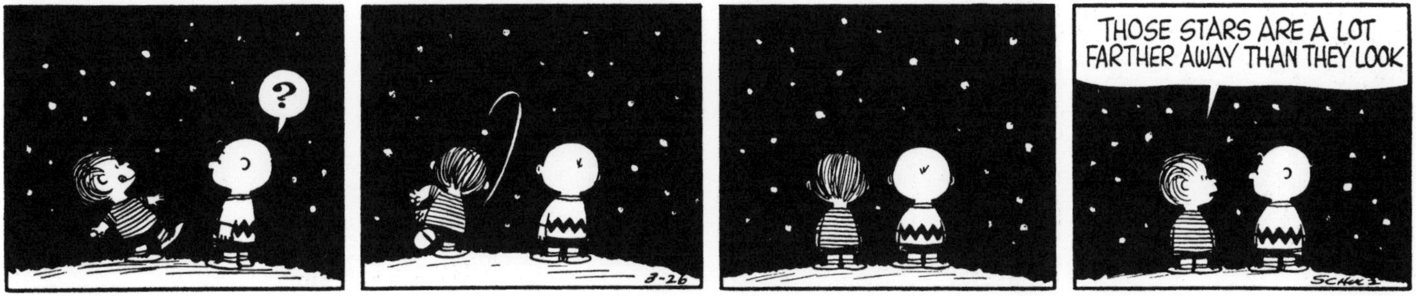
?
THOSE STARS ARE A LOT FARTHER AWAY THAN THEY LOOK

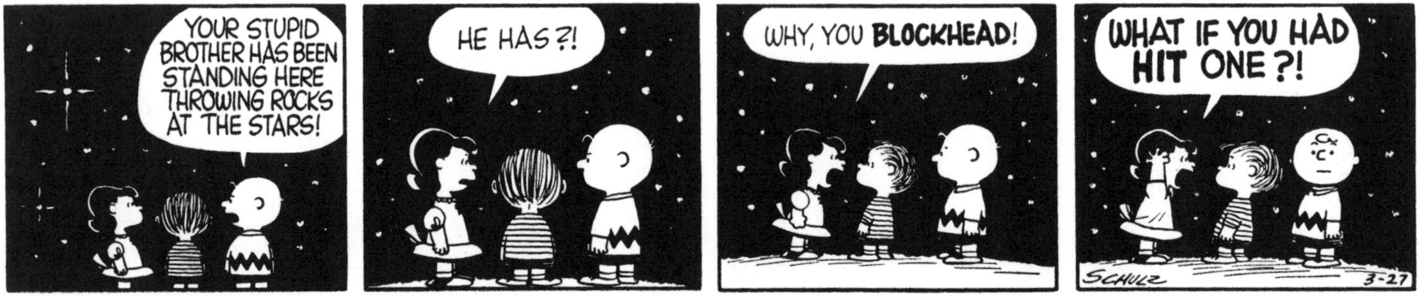
YOUR STUPID BROTHER HAS BEEN STANDING HERE THROWING ROCKS AT THE STARS!
HE HAS?!
WHY, YOU BLOCKHEAD!
WHAT IF YOU HAD HIT ONE?!
SCHULZ
3-27

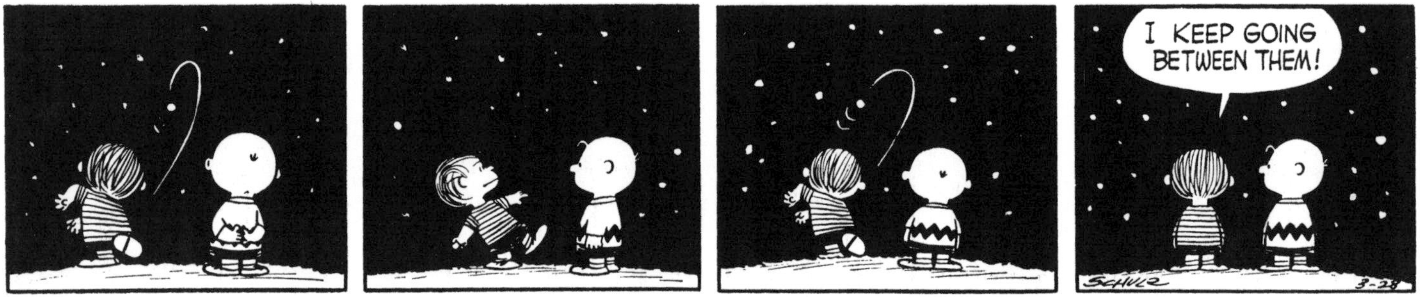
I KEEP GOING BETWEEN THEM!
SCHULZ
3-28

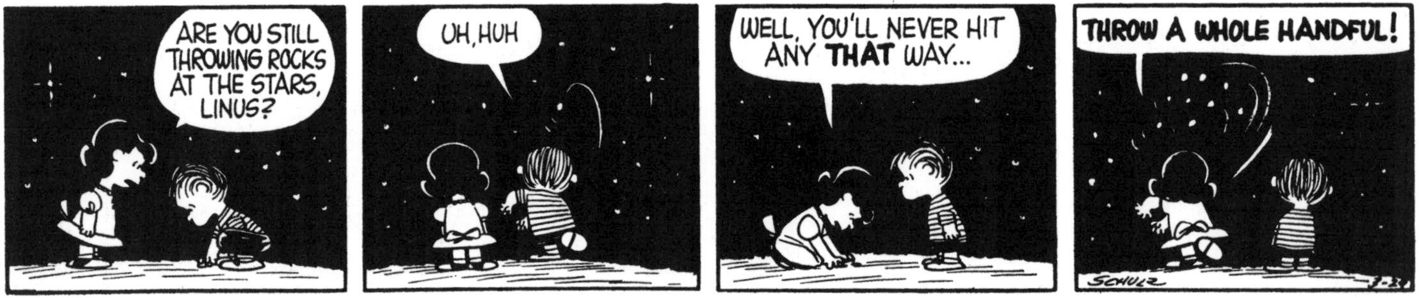
ARE YOU STILL THROWING ROCKS AT THE STARS, LINUS?
UH, HUH
WELL, YOU'LL NEVER HIT ANY THAT WAY...
THROW A WHOLE HANDFUL!
SCHULZ

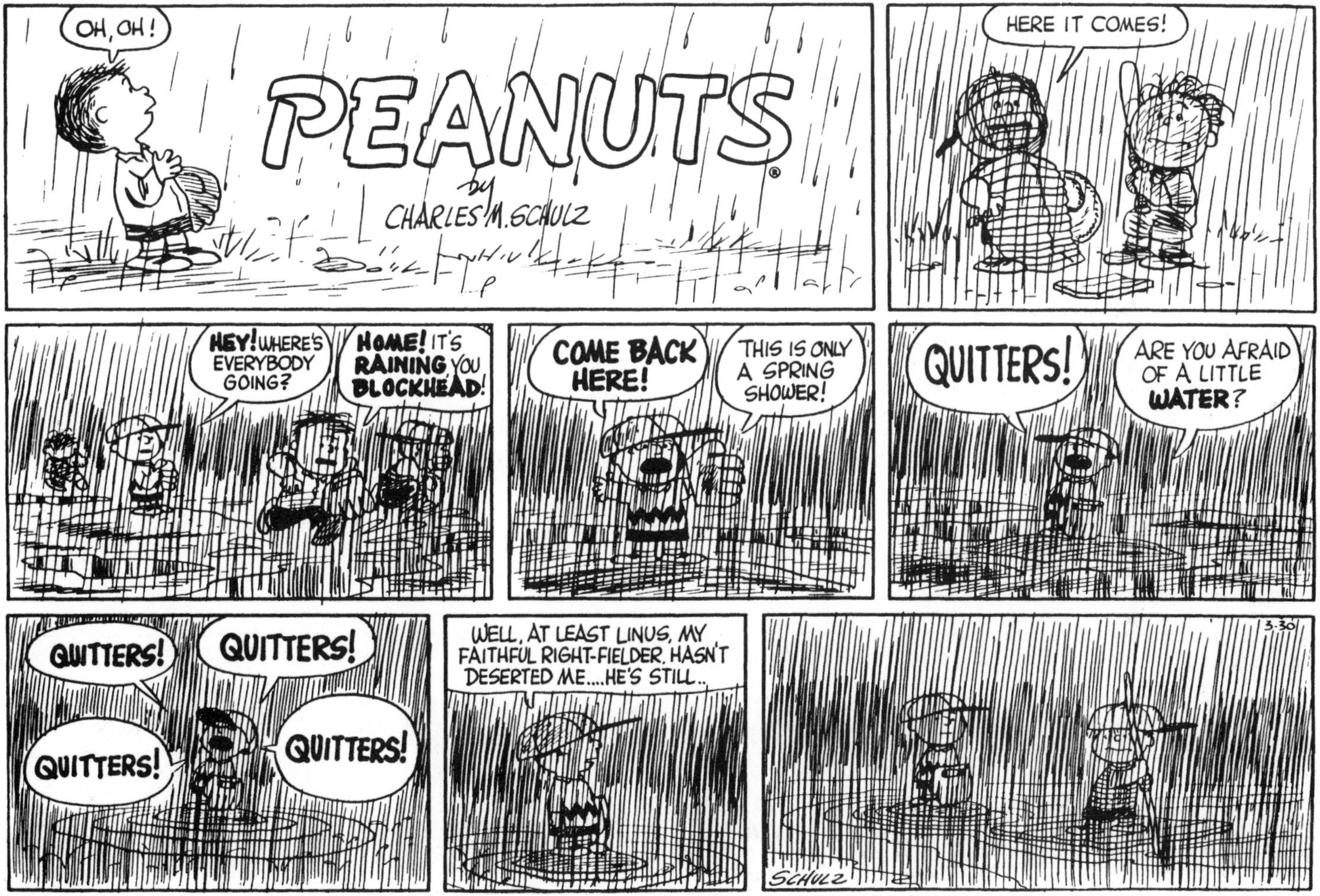
OH, OH!
PEANUTS
by CHARLES M. SCHULZ
HERE IT COMES!
HEY! WHERE'S EVERYBODY GOING?
HOME! IT'S RAINING YOU BLOCKHEAD!
COME BACK HERE!
THIS IS ONLY A SPRING SHOWER!
QUITTERS!
ARE YOU AFRAID OF A LITTLE WATER?
QUITTERS!
QUITTERS!
QUITTERS!
QUITTERS!
WELL, AT LEAST LINUS, MY FAITHFUL RIGHT-FIELDER, HASN'T DESERTED ME....HE'S STILL..
3-30
SCHULZ

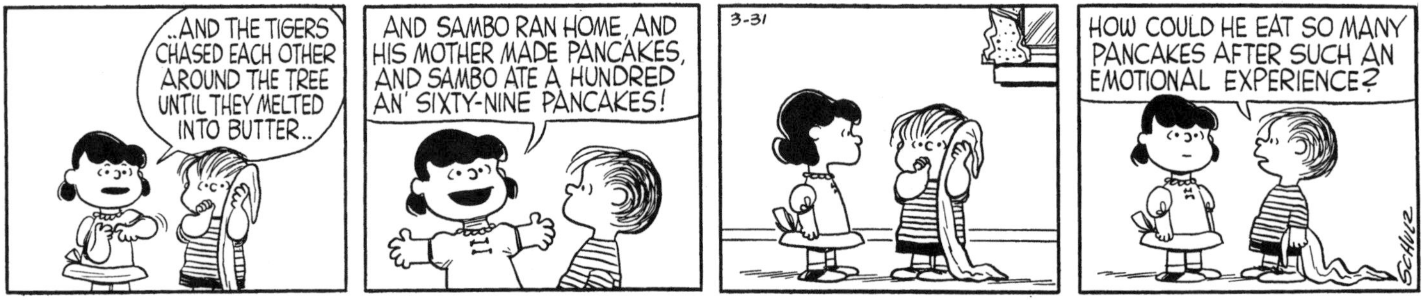
..AND THE TIGERS CHASED EACH OTHER AROUND THE TREE UNTIL THEY MELTED INTO BUTTER..
AND SAMBO RAN HOME, AND HIS MOTHER MADE PANCAKES, AND SAMBO ATE A HUNDRED AN' SIXTY-NINE PANCAKES!
3-31
HOW COULD HE EAT SO MANY PANCAKES AFTER SUCH AN EMOTIONAL EXPERIENCE?
SCHULZ

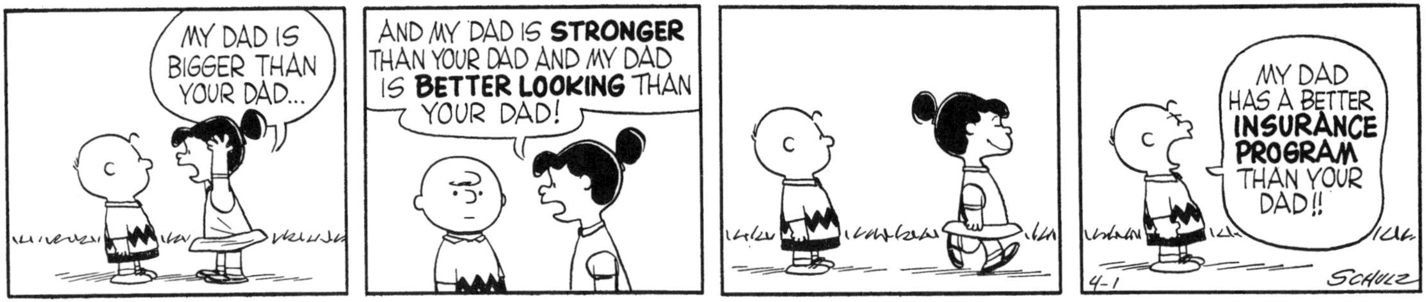
MY DAD IS BIGGER THAN YOUR DAD...
AND MY DAD IS **STRONGER** THAN YOUR DAD AND MY DAD IS **BETTER LOOKING** THAN YOUR DAD!
MY DAD HAS A BETTER **INSURANCE PROGRAM** THAN YOUR DAD!!
4-1
SCHULZ

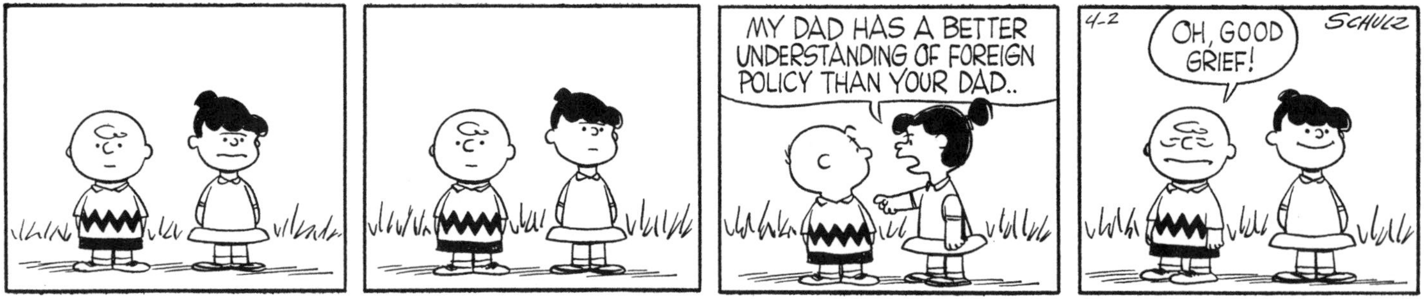
MY DAD HAS A BETTER UNDERSTANDING OF FOREIGN POLICY THAN YOUR DAD..
4-2
SCHULZ
OH, GOOD GRIEF!

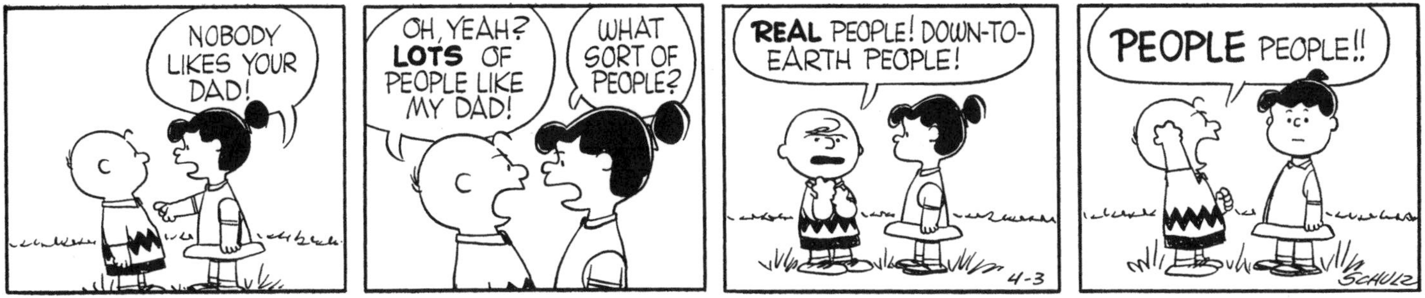
NOBODY LIKES YOUR DAD!
OH, YEAH? LOTS OF PEOPLE LIKE MY DAD!
WHAT SORT OF PEOPLE?
REAL PEOPLE! DOWN-TO-EARTH PEOPLE!
4-3
PEOPLE PEOPLE!!
SCHULZ

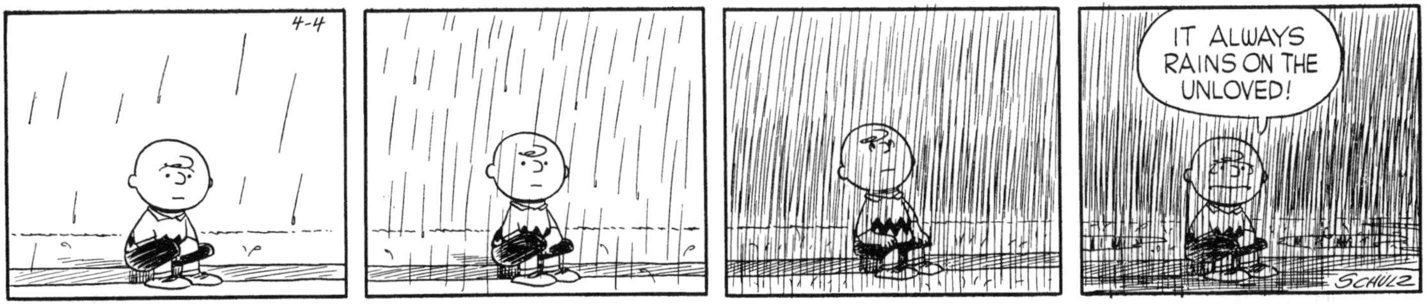
4-4
IT ALWAYS RAINS ON THE UNLOVED!
SCHULZ

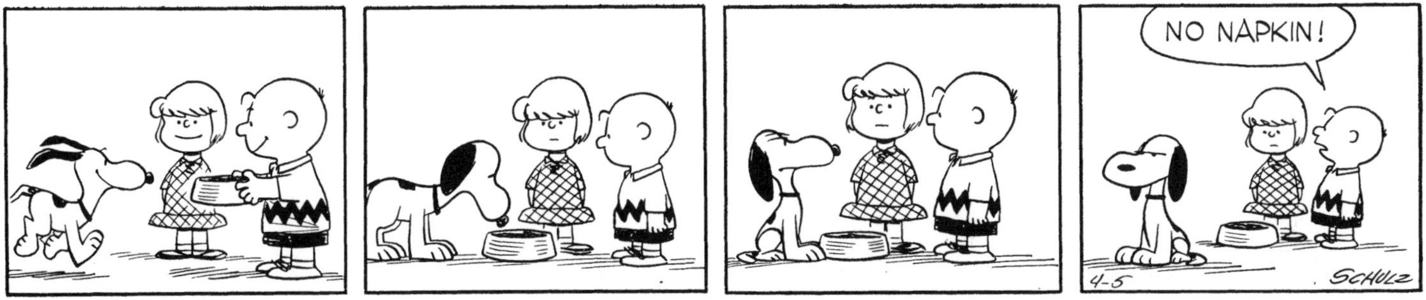
NO NAPKIN!
4-5
SCHULZ

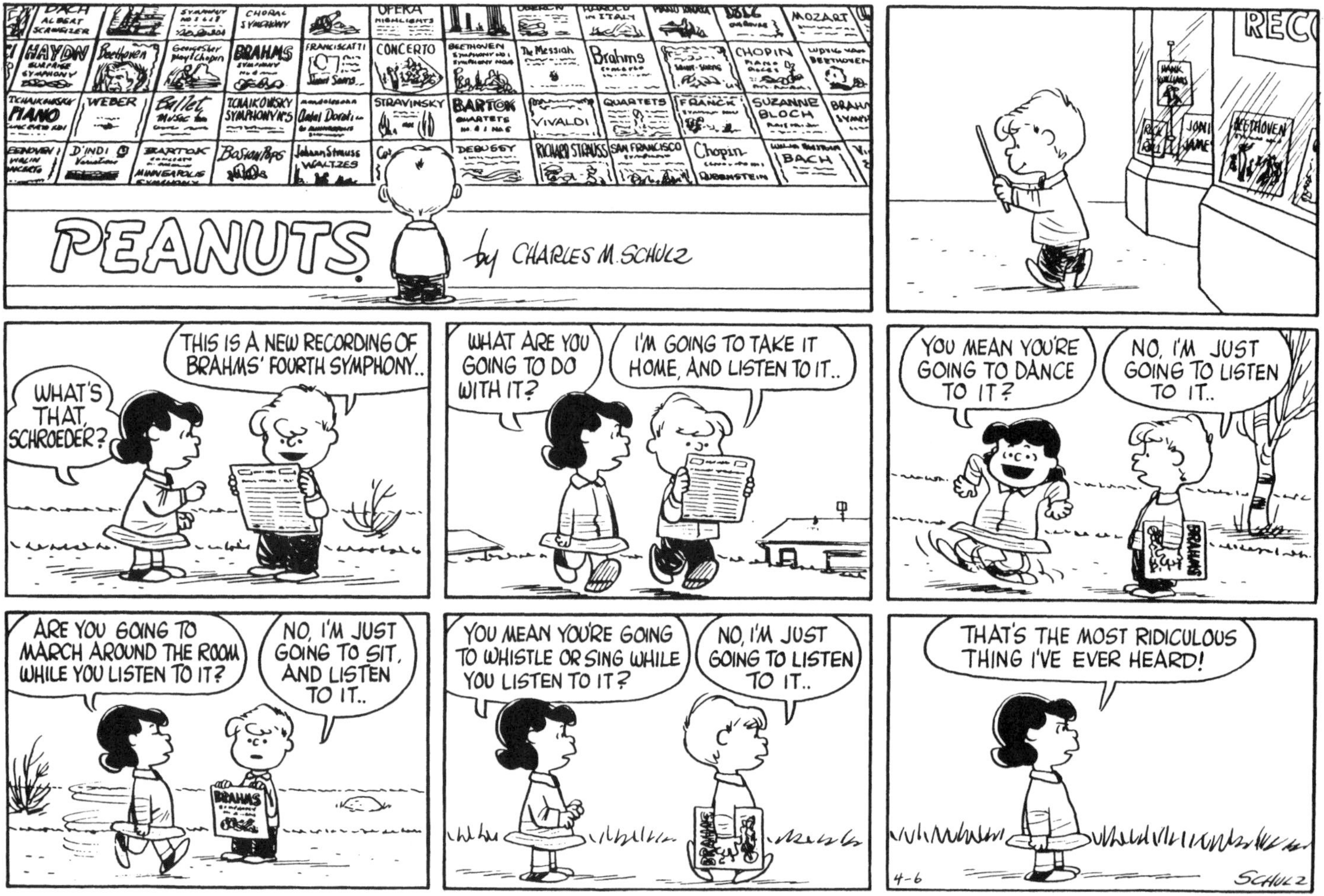
PEANUTS
by CHARLES M. SCHULZ
WHAT'S THAT, SCHROEDER?
THIS IS A NEW RECORDING OF BRAHMS' FOURTH SYMPHONY..
WHAT ARE YOU GOING TO DO WITH IT?
I'M GOING TO TAKE IT HOME, AND LISTEN TO IT..
YOU MEAN YOU'RE GOING TO DANCE TO IT?
NO, I'M JUST GOING TO LISTEN TO IT..
ARE YOU GOING TO MARCH AROUND THE ROOM WHILE YOU LISTEN TO IT?
NO, I'M JUST GOING TO SIT, AND LISTEN TO IT..
YOU MEAN YOU'RE GOING TO WHISTLE OR SING WHILE YOU LISTEN TO IT?
NO, I'M JUST GOING TO LISTEN TO IT..
THAT'S THE MOST RIDICULOUS THING I'VE EVER HEARD!
4-6
SCHULZ

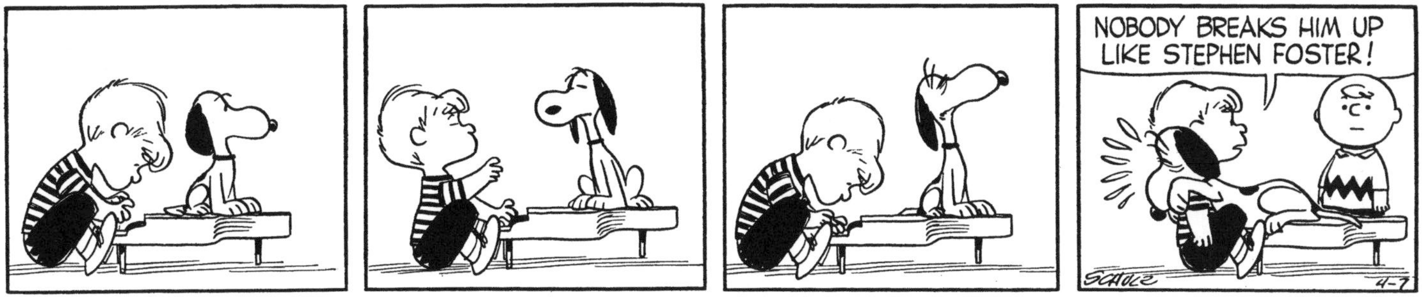
NOBODY BREAKS HIM UP LIKE STEPHEN FOSTER!
SCHULZ
4-7

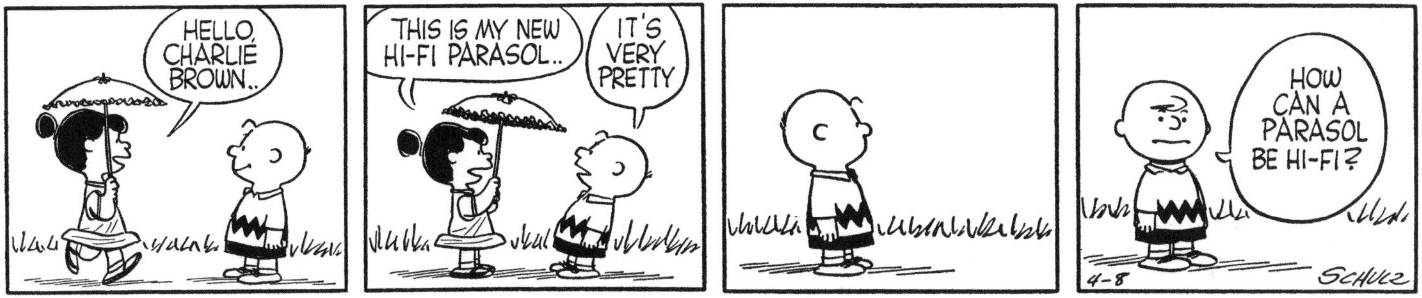
HELLO, CHARLIE BROWN..
THIS IS MY NEW HI-FI PARASOL..
IT'S VERY PRETTY
HOW CAN A PARASOL BE HI-FI?
4-8
SCHULZ

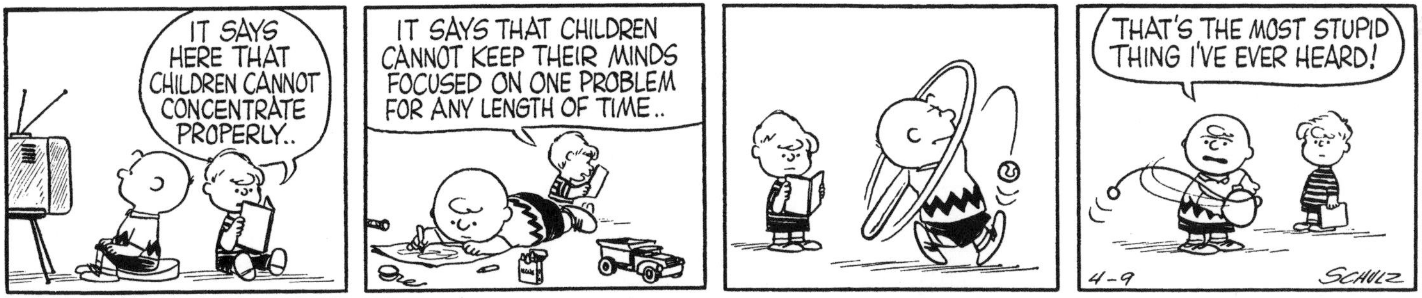
IT SAYS HERE THAT CHILDREN CANNOT CONCENTRATE PROPERLY..
IT SAYS THAT CHILDREN CANNOT KEEP THEIR MINDS FOCUSED ON ONE PROBLEM FOR ANY LENGTH OF TIME..
THAT'S THE MOST STUPID THING I'VE EVER HEARD!
4-9
SCHULZ

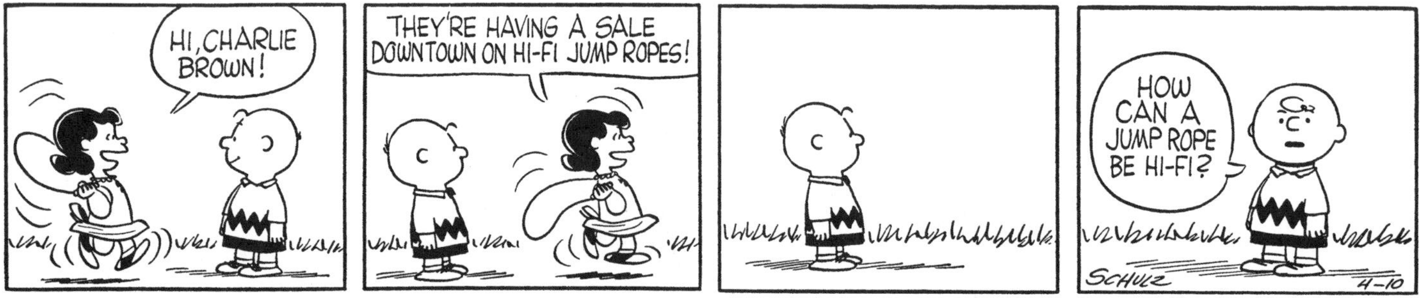
HI, CHARLIE BROWN!
THEY'RE HAVING A SALE DOWNTOWN ON HI-FI JUMP ROPES!
HOW CAN A JUMP ROPE BE HI-FI?
SCHULZ
4-10

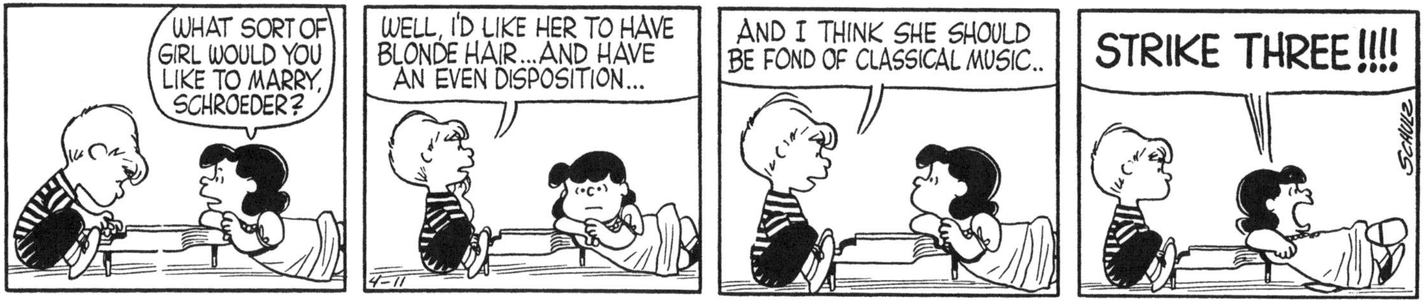
WHAT SORT OF GIRL WOULD YOU LIKE TO MARRY, SCHROEDER?
WELL, I'D LIKE HER TO HAVE BLONDE HAIR...AND HAVE AN EVEN DISPOSITION...
4-11
AND I THINK SHE SHOULD BE FOND OF CLASSICAL MUSIC..
STRIKE THREE!!!!
SCHULZ

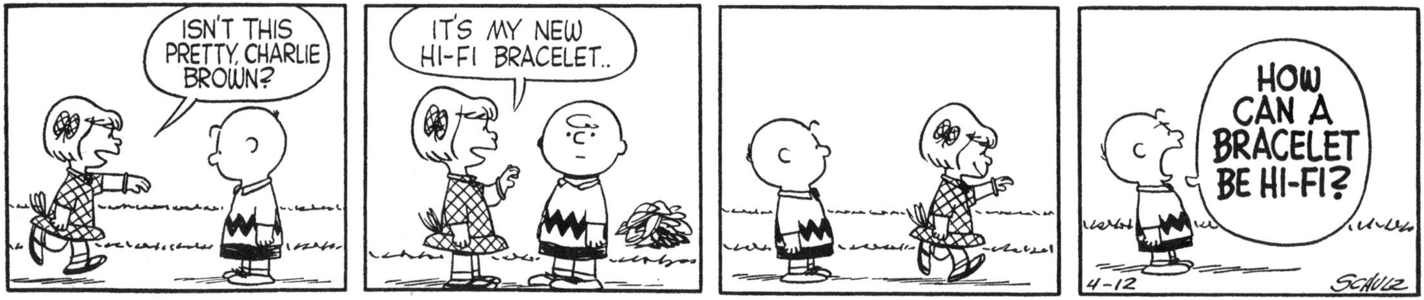
ISN'T THIS PRETTY, CHARLIE BROWN?
IT'S MY NEW HI-FI BRACELET..
HOW CAN A BRACELET BE HI-FI?
4-12
SCHULZ

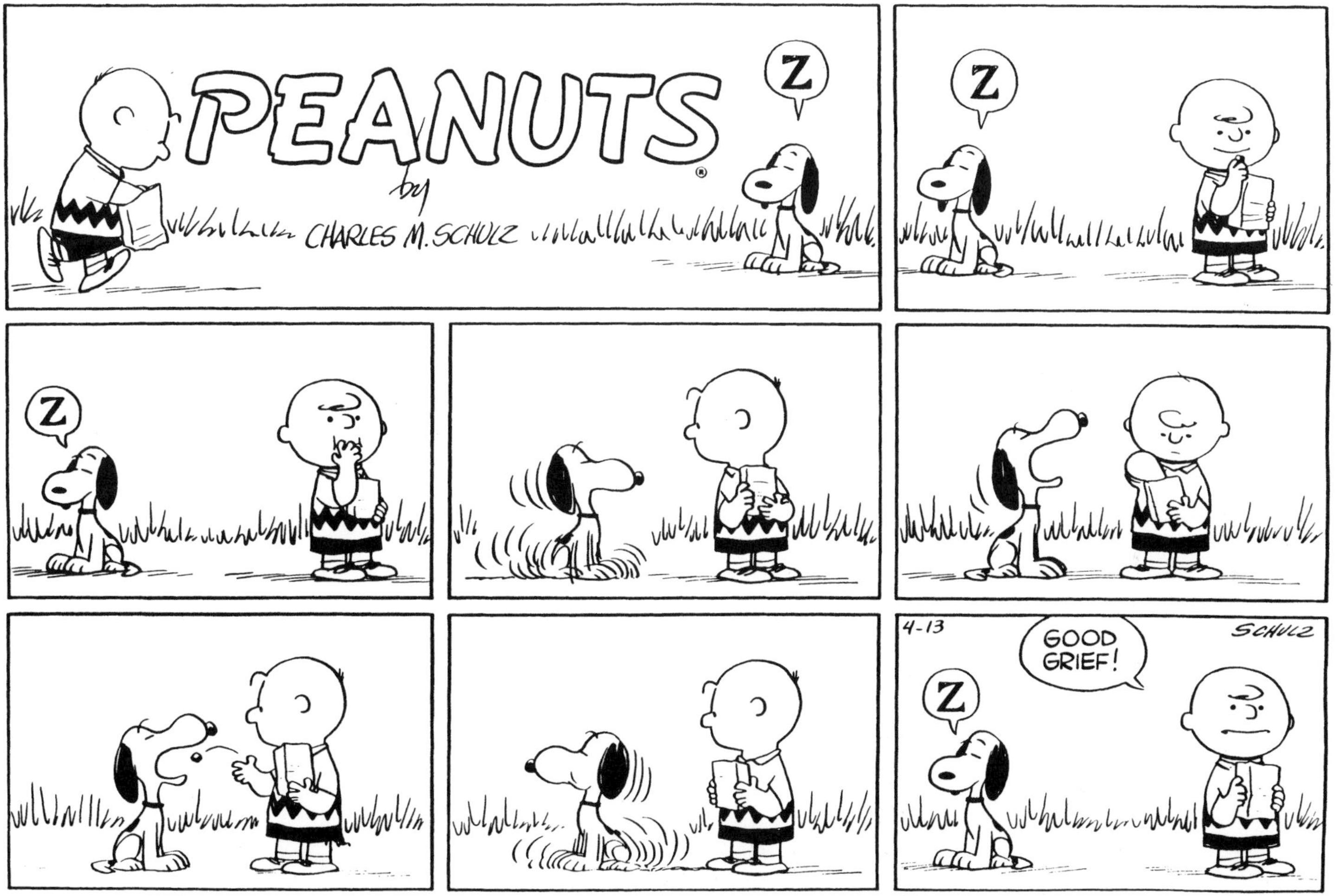
PEANUTS
by CHARLES M. SCHULZ
Z
Z
Z
4-13
SCHULZ
GOOD GRIEF!
Z

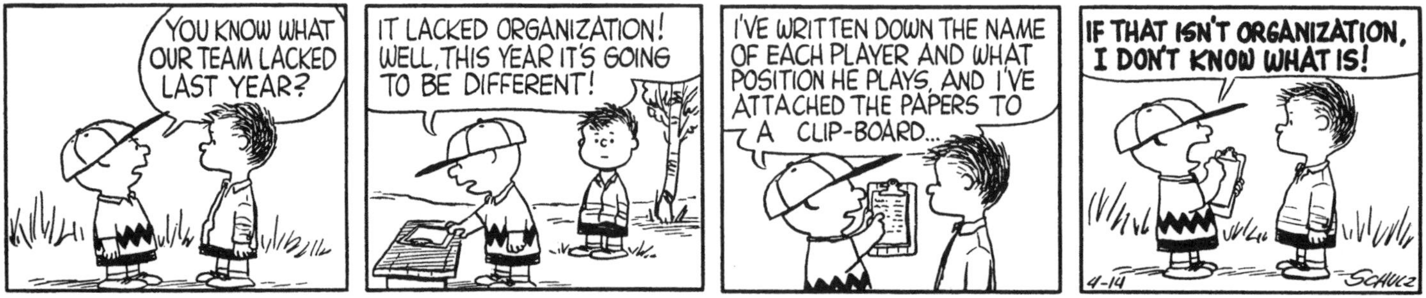
YOU KNOW WHAT OUR TEAM LACKED LAST YEAR?
IT LACKED ORGANIZATION! WELL, THIS YEAR IT'S GOING TO BE DIFFERENT!
I'VE WRITTEN DOWN THE NAME OF EACH PLAYER AND WHAT POSITION HE PLAYS, AND I'VE ATTACHED THE PAPERS TO A CLIP-BOARD...
IF THAT ISN'T ORGANIZATION, I DON'T KNOW WHAT IS!
4-14
SCHULZ

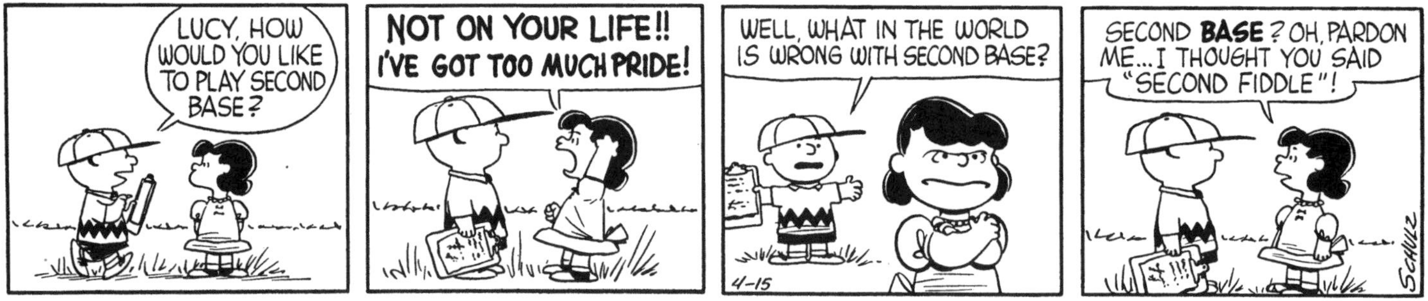
LUCY, HOW WOULD YOU LIKE TO PLAY SECOND BASE?
NOT ON YOUR LIFE!! I'VE GOT TOO MUCH PRIDE!
WELL, WHAT IN THE WORLD IS WRONG WITH SECOND BASE?
4-15
SECOND BASE? OH, PARDON ME...I THOUGHT YOU SAID "SECOND FIDDLE"!
SCHULZ

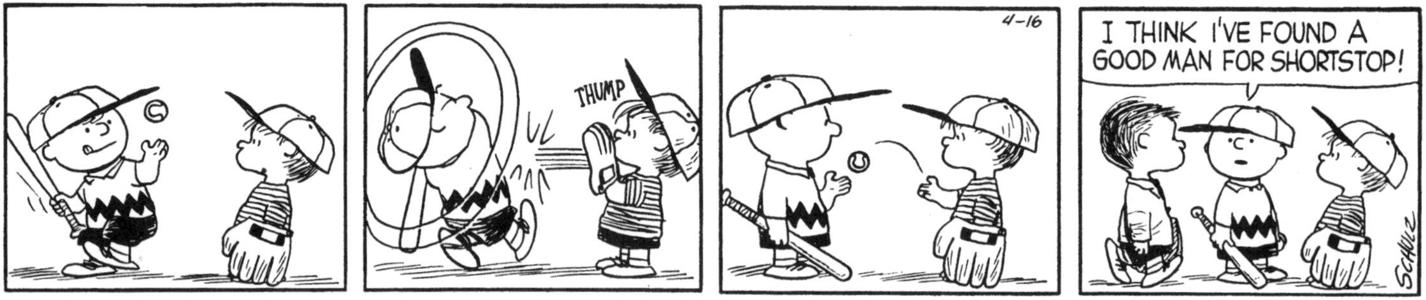
THUMP
4-16
I THINK I'VE FOUND A GOOD MAN FOR SHORTSTOP!
SCHULZ

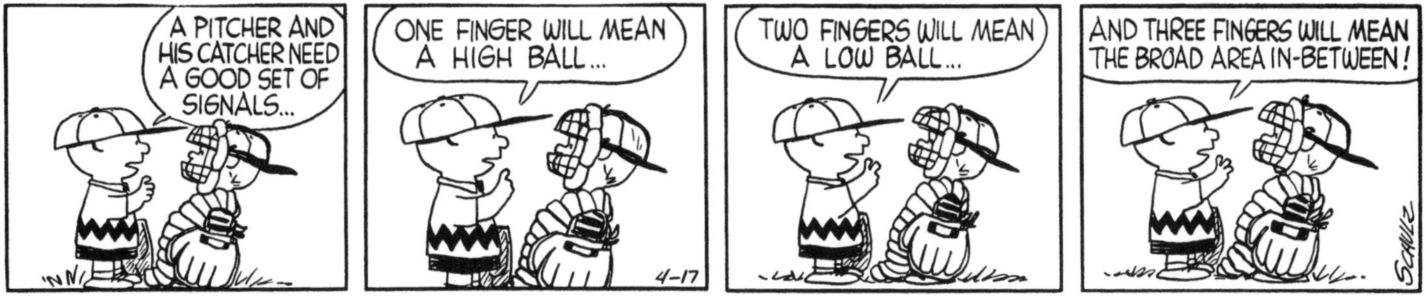
A PITCHER AND HIS CATCHER NEED A GOOD SET OF SIGNALS...
ONE FINGER WILL MEAN A HIGH BALL...
4-17
TWO FINGERS WILL MEAN A LOW BALL...
AND THREE FINGERS WILL MEAN THE BROAD AREA IN-BETWEEN!
SCHULZ

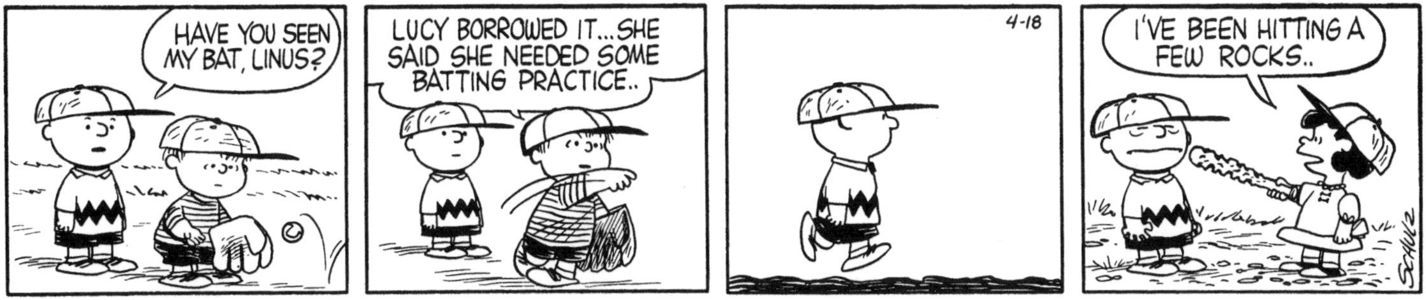
HAVE YOU SEEN MY BAT, LINUS?
LUCY BORROWED IT...SHE SAID SHE NEEDED SOME BATTING PRACTICE..
4-18
I'VE BEEN HITTING A FEW ROCKS..
SCHULZ

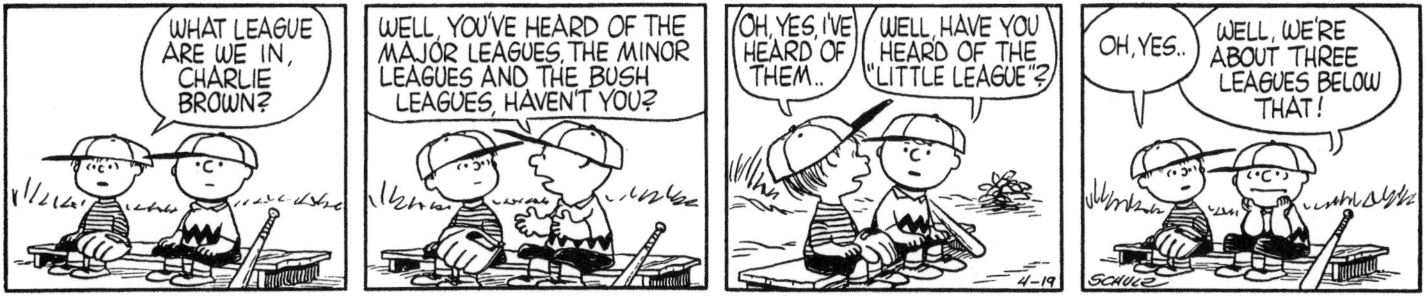
WHAT LEAGUE ARE WE IN, CHARLIE BROWN?
WELL, YOU'VE HEARD OF THE MAJOR LEAGUES, THE MINOR LEAGUES AND THE BUSH LEAGUES, HAVEN'T YOU?
OH, YES, I'VE HEARD OF THEM..
WELL, HAVE YOU HEARD OF THE "LITTLE LEAGUE"?
4-19
OH, YES..
WELL, WE'RE ABOUT THREE LEAGUES BELOW THAT!
SCHULZ

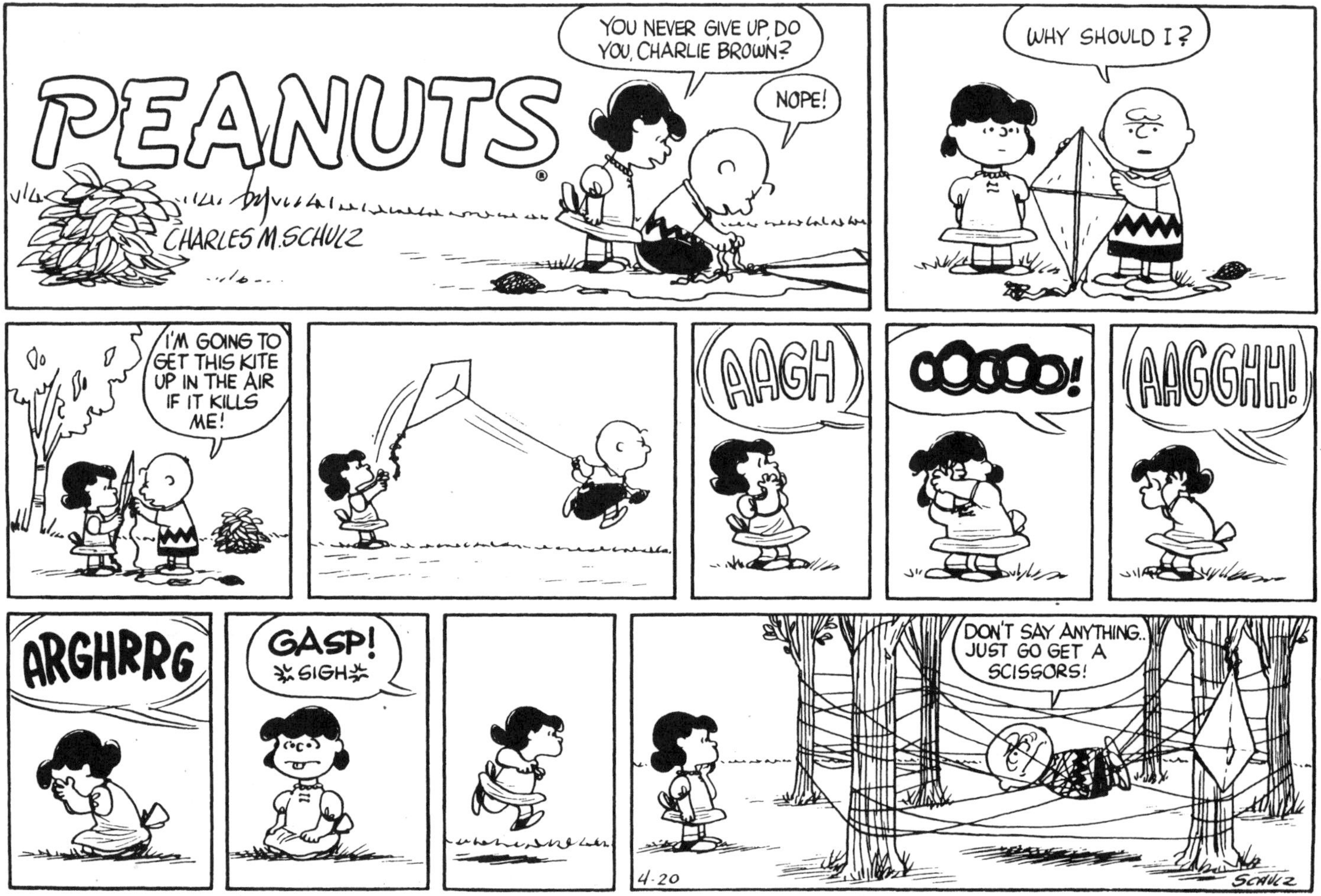
PEANUTS
by Charles M. Schulz
YOU NEVER GIVE UP, DO YOU, CHARLIE BROWN?
NOPE!
WHY SHOULD I?
I'M GOING TO GET THIS KITE UP IN THE AIR IF IT KILLS ME!
AAGH
OOOOOO!
AAGGHH!
ARGHRRG
GASP!
SIGH
DON'T SAY ANYTHING.. JUST GO GET A SCISSORS!
4-20
SCHULZ

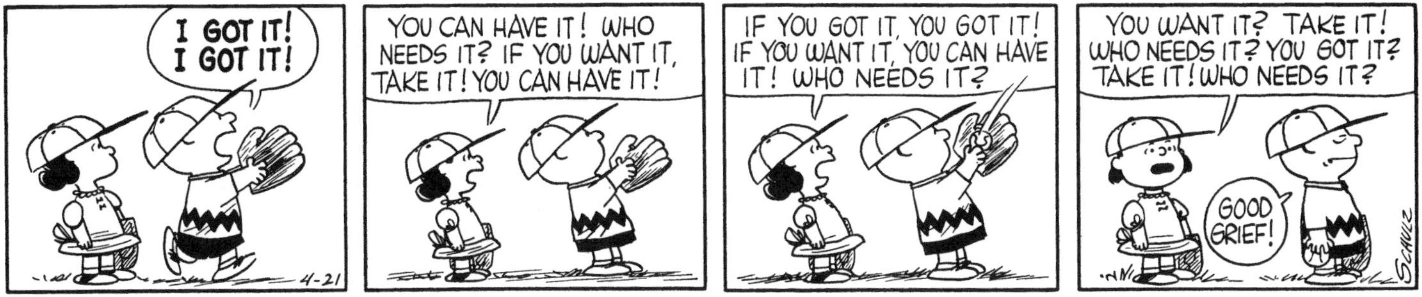
I GOT IT! I GOT IT!
4-21
YOU CAN HAVE IT! WHO NEEDS IT? IF YOU WANT IT, TAKE IT! YOU CAN HAVE IT!
IF YOU GOT IT, YOU GOT IT! IF YOU WANT IT, YOU CAN HAVE IT! WHO NEEDS IT?
YOU WANT IT? TAKE IT! WHO NEEDS IT? YOU GOT IT? TAKE IT! WHO NEEDS IT?
GOOD GRIEF!
SCHULZ

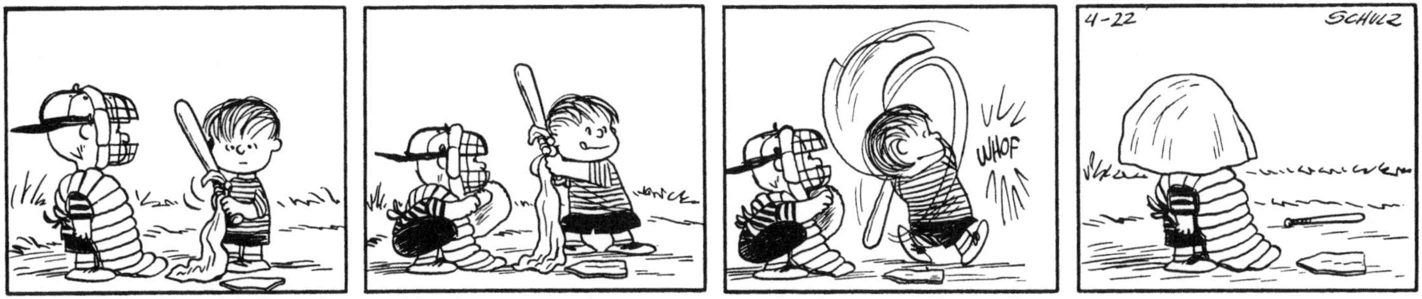
WHOF
4-22
SCHULZ

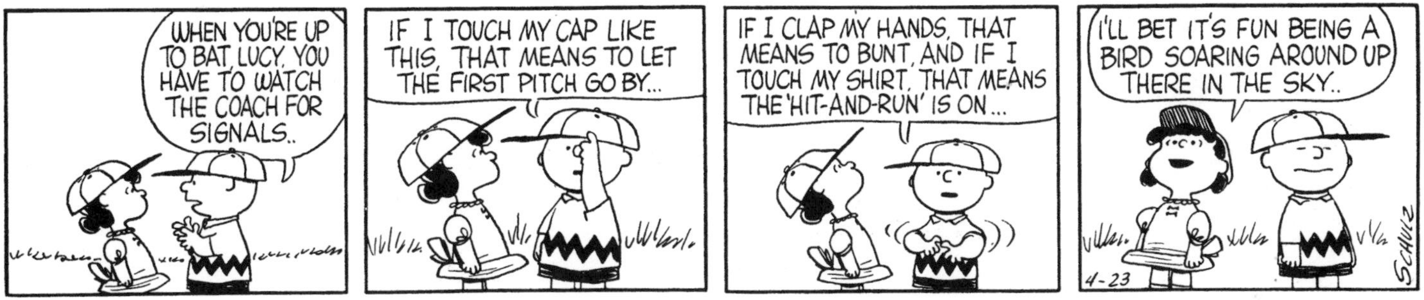
WHEN YOU'RE UP TO BAT, LUCY, YOU HAVE TO WATCH THE COACH FOR SIGNALS..
IF I TOUCH MY CAP LIKE THIS, THAT MEANS TO LET THE FIRST PITCH GO BY...
IF I CLAP MY HANDS, THAT MEANS TO BUNT, AND IF I TOUCH MY SHIRT, THAT MEANS THE 'HIT-AND-RUN' IS ON...
I'LL BET IT'S FUN BEING A BIRD SOARING AROUND UP THERE IN THE SKY..
SCHULZ
4-23

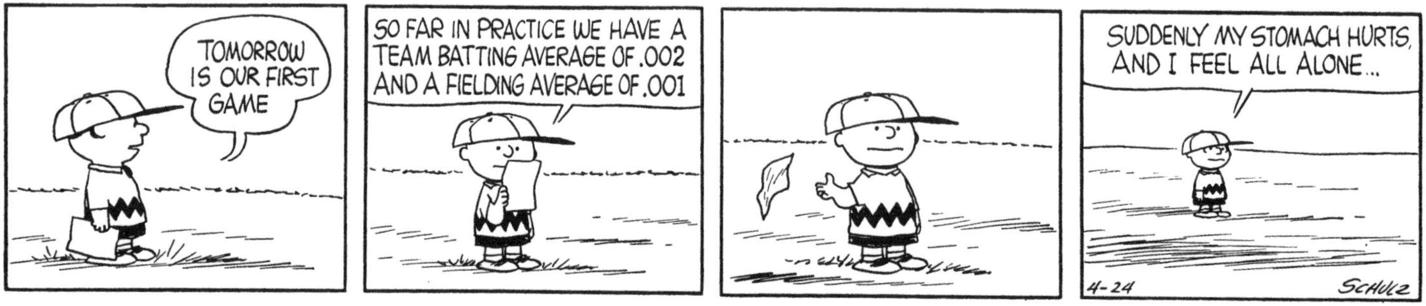
TOMORROW IS OUR FIRST GAME
SO FAR IN PRACTICE WE HAVE A TEAM BATTING AVERAGE OF .002 AND A FIELDING AVERAGE OF .001
SUDDENLY MY STOMACH HURTS, AND I FEEL ALL ALONE...
4-24
SCHULZ

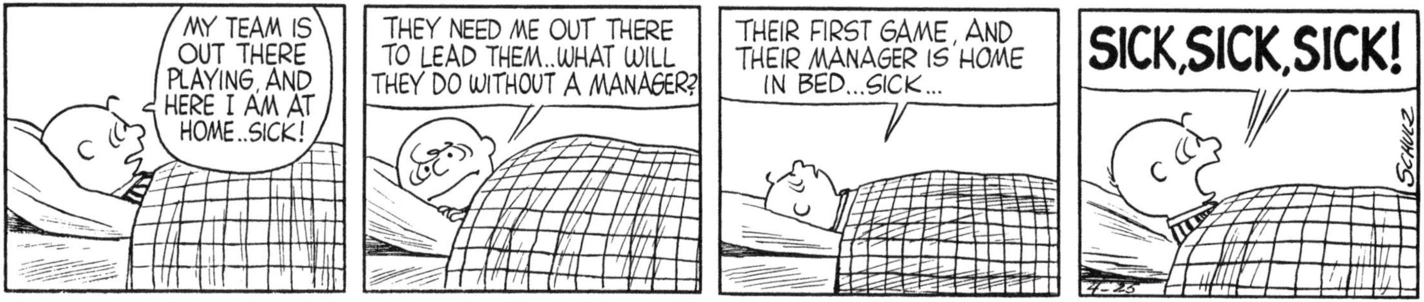
MY TEAM IS OUT THERE PLAYING, AND HERE I AM AT HOME..SICK!
THEY NEED ME OUT THERE TO LEAD THEM..WHAT WILL THEY DO WITHOUT A MANAGER?
THEIR FIRST GAME, AND THEIR MANAGER IS HOME IN BED...SICK...
SICK, SICK, SICK!
SCHULZ
4-25

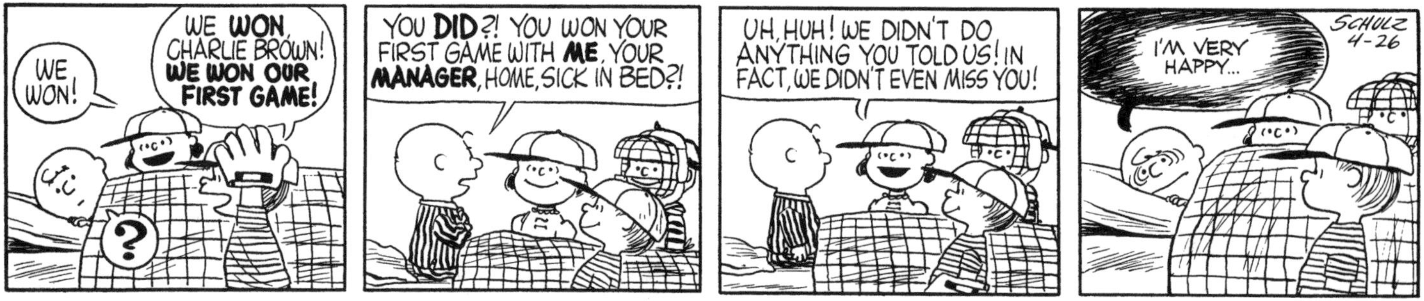
WE WON!
WE **WON**, CHARLIE BROWN! **WE WON OUR FIRST GAME!**
?
YOU **DID**?! YOU WON YOUR FIRST GAME WITH **ME**, YOUR **MANAGER**, HOME, SICK IN BED?!
UH, HUH! WE DIDN'T DO ANYTHING YOU TOLD US! IN FACT, WE DIDN'T EVEN MISS YOU!
SCHULZ 4-26
I'M VERY HAPPY...

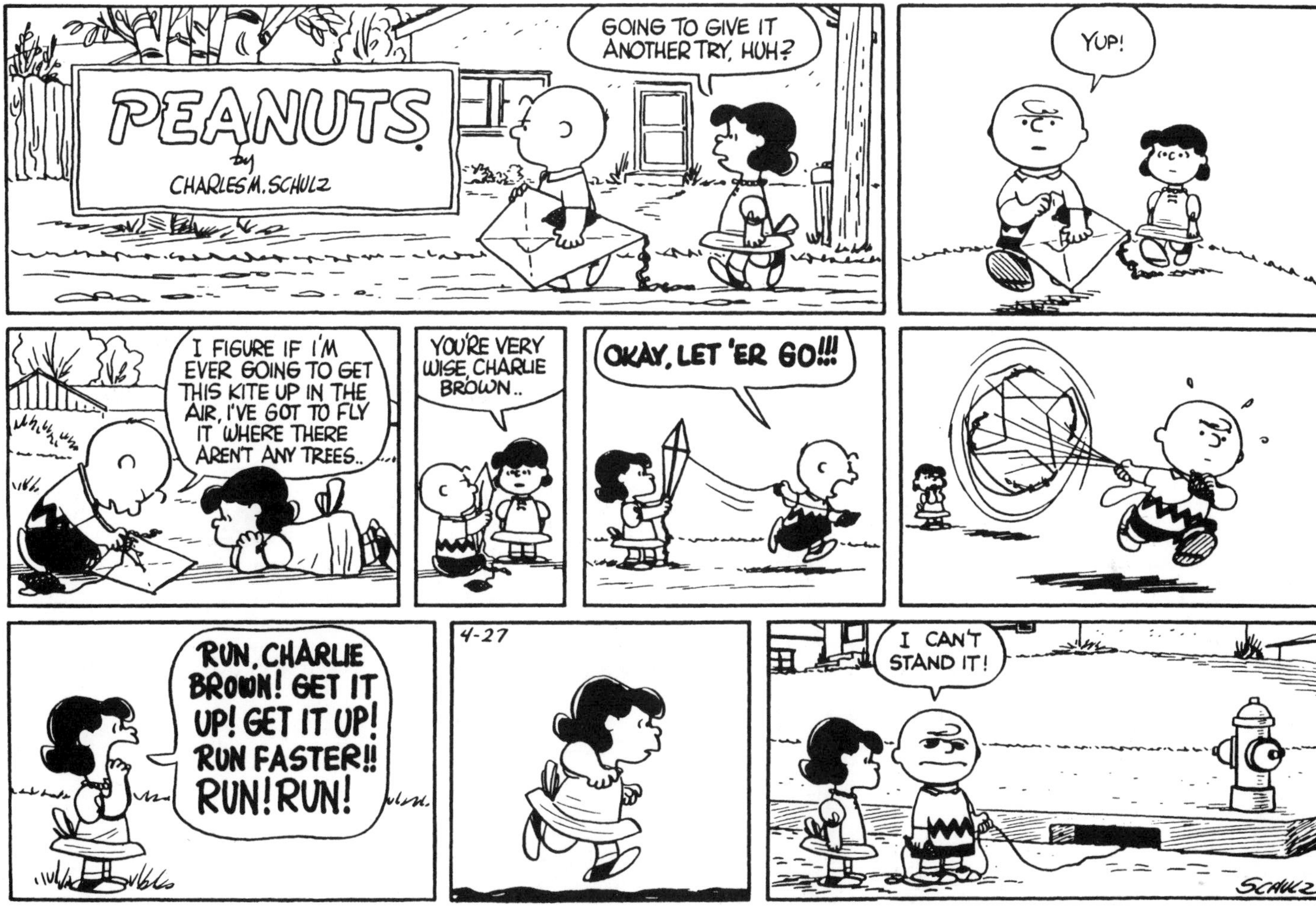
PEANUTS
by
CHARLES M. SCHULZ
GOING TO GIVE IT ANOTHER TRY, HUH?
YUP!
I FIGURE IF I'M EVER GOING TO GET THIS KITE UP IN THE AIR, I'VE GOT TO FLY IT WHERE THERE AREN'T ANY TREES..
YOU'RE VERY WISE, CHARLIE BROWN..
OKAY, LET 'ER GO!!!
RUN, CHARLIE BROWN! GET IT UP! GET IT UP! RUN FASTER!! RUN! RUN!
4-27
I CAN'T STAND IT!
SCHULZ

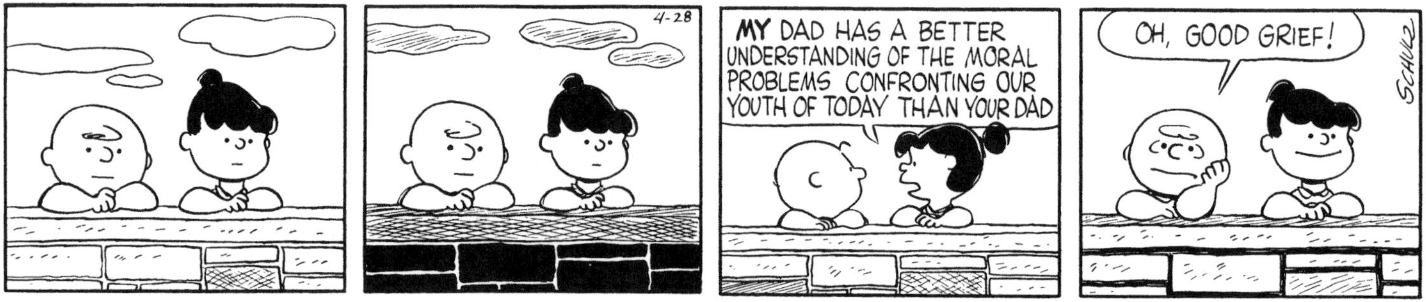
4-28
MY DAD HAS A BETTER UNDERSTANDING OF THE MORAL PROBLEMS CONFRONTING OUR YOUTH OF TODAY THAN YOUR DAD
OH, GOOD GRIEF!
SCHULZ

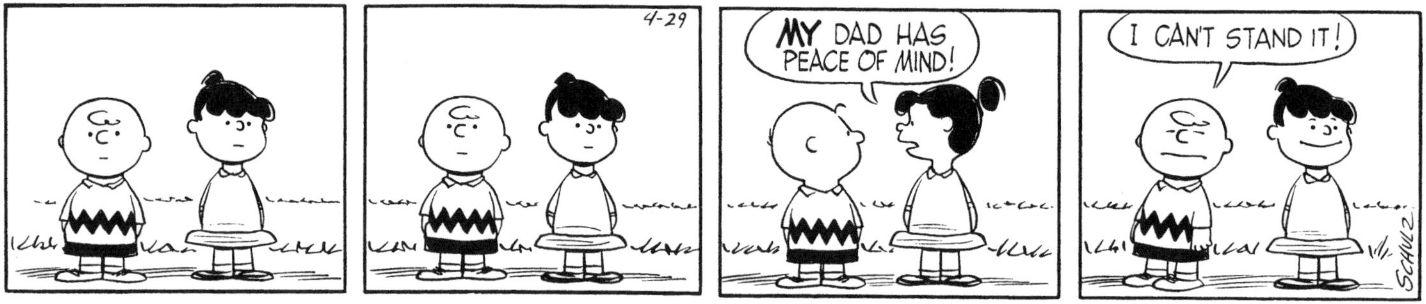
4-29
MY DAD HAS PEACE OF MIND!
I CAN'T STAND IT!
SCHULZ

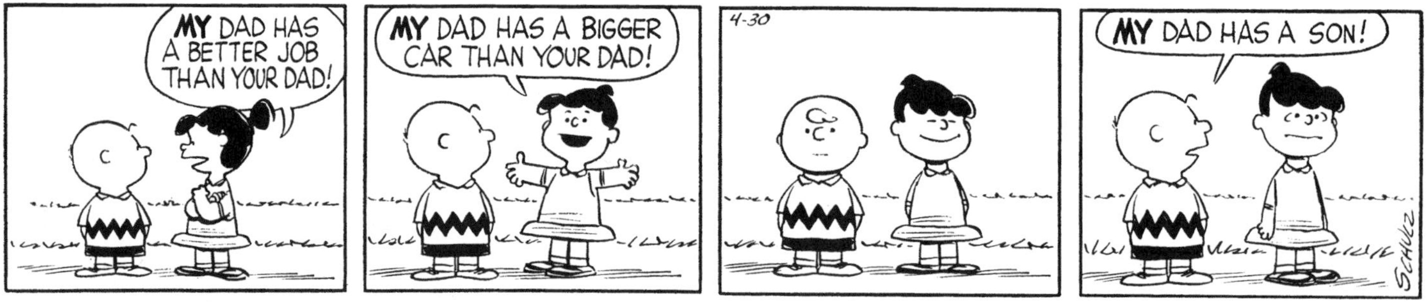
MY DAD HAS A BETTER JOB THAN YOUR DAD!
MY DAD HAS A BIGGER CAR THAN YOUR DAD!
4-30
MY DAD HAS A SON!
SCHULZ

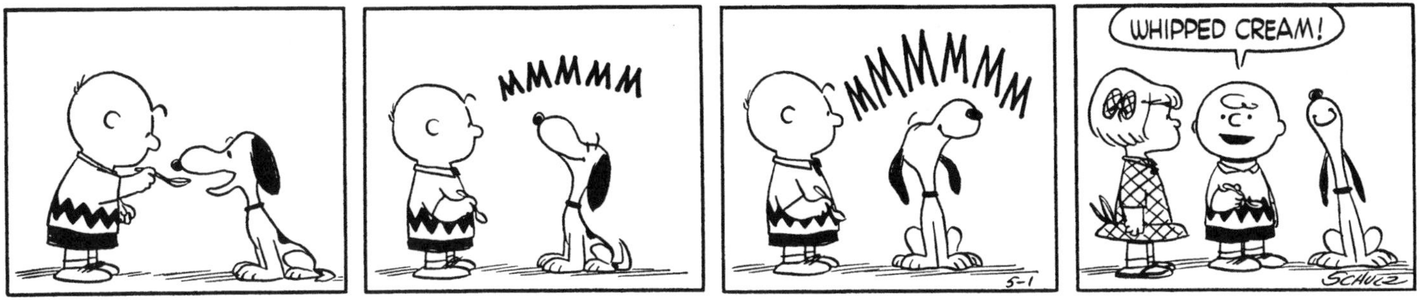
MMMMM
MMMMMM
WHIPPED CREAM!

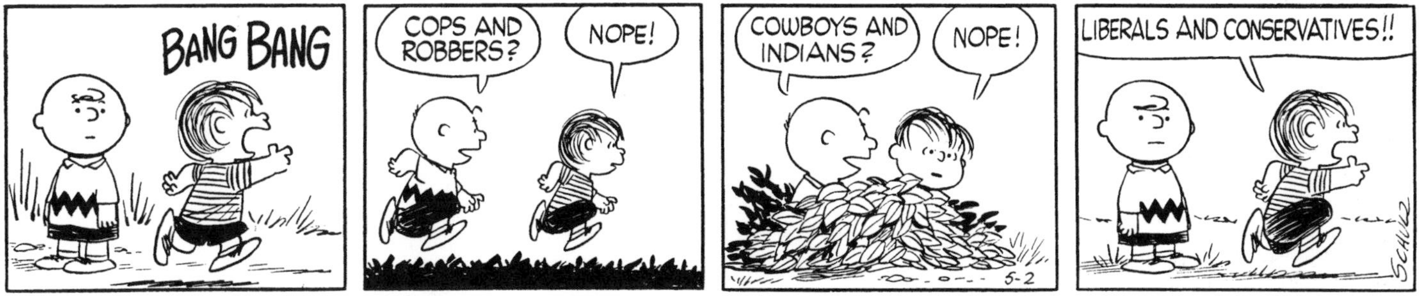
BANG BANG
COPS AND ROBBERS?
NOPE!
COWBOYS AND INDIANS?
NOPE!
LIBERALS AND CONSERVATIVES!!

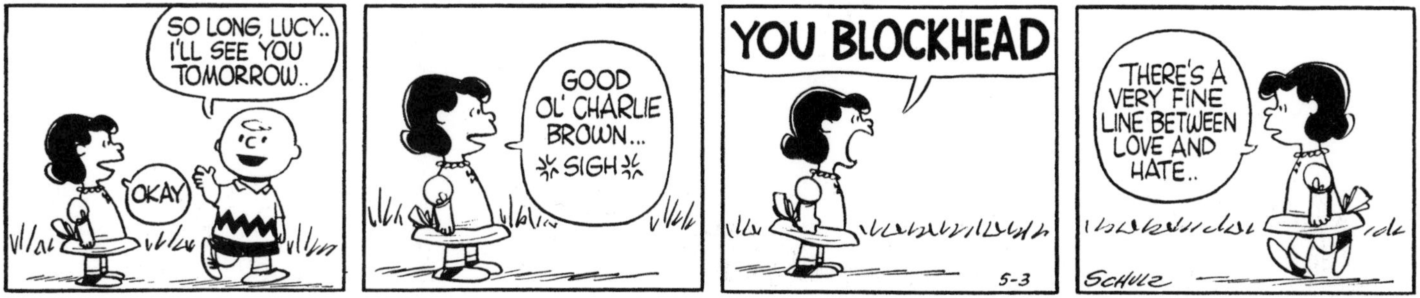
SO LONG, LUCY.. I'LL SEE YOU TOMORROW..
OKAY
GOOD OL' CHARLIE BROWN...
SIGH
YOU BLOCKHEAD
THERE'S A VERY FINE LINE BETWEEN LOVE AND HATE..

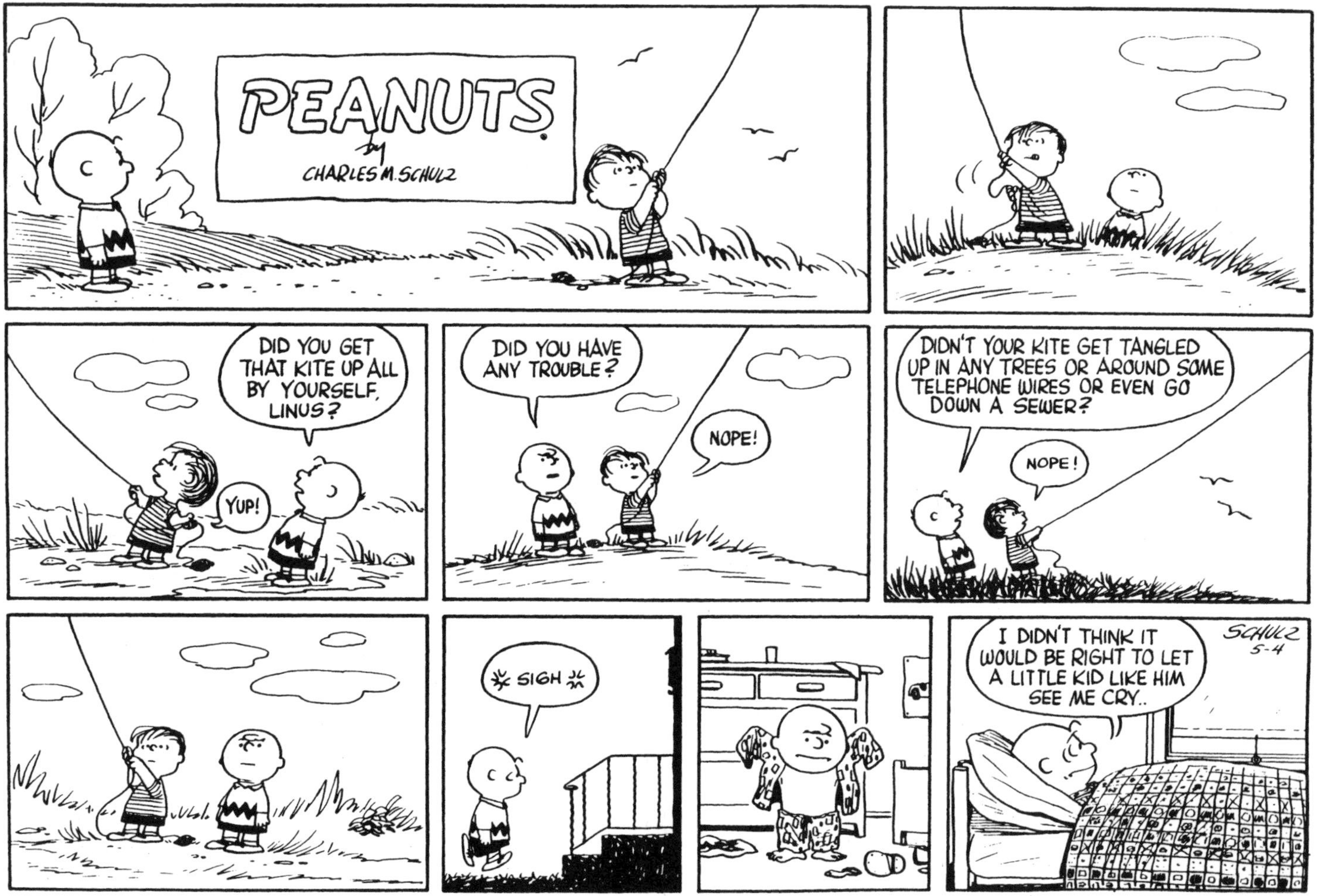
PEANUTS
by
CHARLES M. SCHULZ
DID YOU GET THAT KITE UP ALL BY YOURSELF, LINUS?
YUP!
DID YOU HAVE ANY TROUBLE?
NOPE!
DIDN'T YOUR KITE GET TANGLED UP IN ANY TREES OR AROUND SOME TELEPHONE WIRES OR EVEN GO DOWN A SEWER?
NOPE!
SIGH
I DIDN'T THINK IT WOULD BE RIGHT TO LET A LITTLE KID LIKE HIM SEE ME CRY..
SCHULZ 5-4

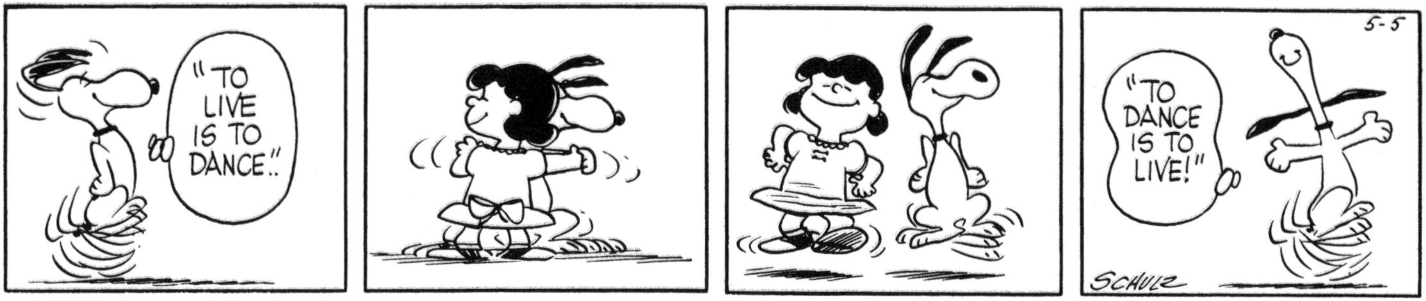
"TO LIVE IS TO DANCE."
"TO DANCE IS TO LIVE!"
5-5
SCHULZ

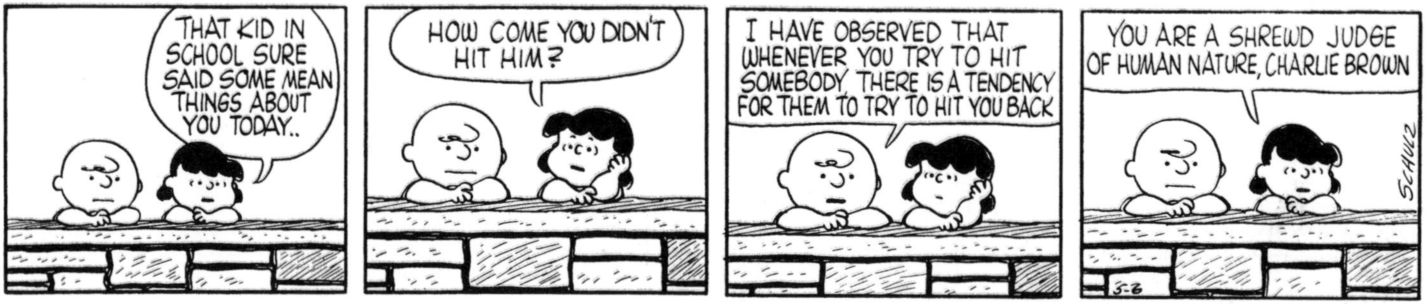
THAT KID IN SCHOOL SURE SAID SOME MEAN THINGS ABOUT YOU TODAY..
HOW COME YOU DIDN'T HIT HIM?
I HAVE OBSERVED THAT WHENEVER YOU TRY TO HIT SOMEBODY, THERE IS A TENDENCY FOR THEM TO TRY TO HIT YOU BACK
YOU ARE A SHREWD JUDGE OF HUMAN NATURE, CHARLIE BROWN
SCHULZ
5-6

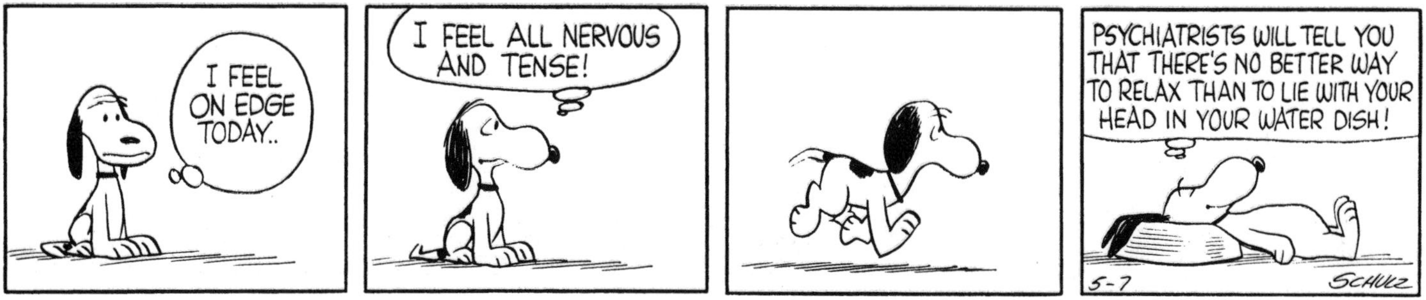
I FEEL ON EDGE TODAY..
I FEEL ALL NERVOUS AND TENSE!
PSYCHIATRISTS WILL TELL YOU THAT THERE'S NO BETTER WAY TO RELAX THAN TO LIE WITH YOUR HEAD IN YOUR WATER DISH!
5-7
SCHULZ

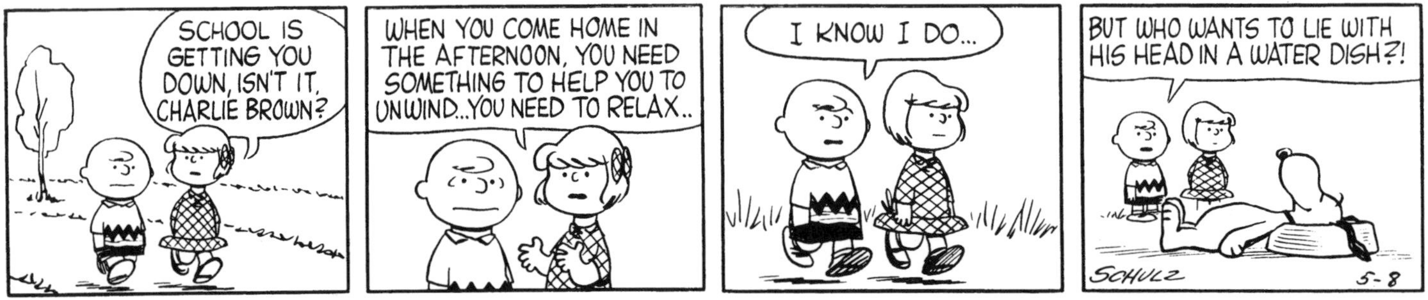
SCHOOL IS GETTING YOU DOWN, ISN'T IT, CHARLIE BROWN?
WHEN YOU COME HOME IN THE AFTERNOON, YOU NEED SOMETHING TO HELP YOU TO UNWIND...YOU NEED TO RELAX..
I KNOW I DO...
BUT WHO WANTS TO LIE WITH HIS HEAD IN A WATER DISH?!
SCHULZ
5-8

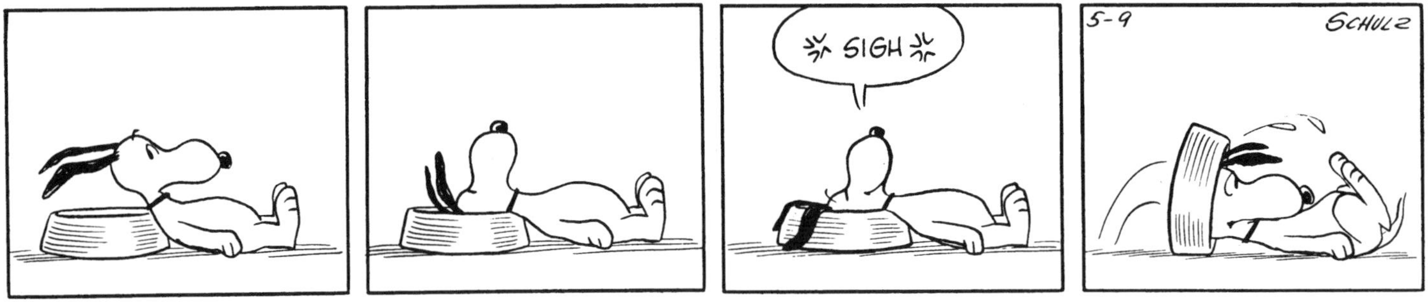
SIGH
5-9
SCHULZ

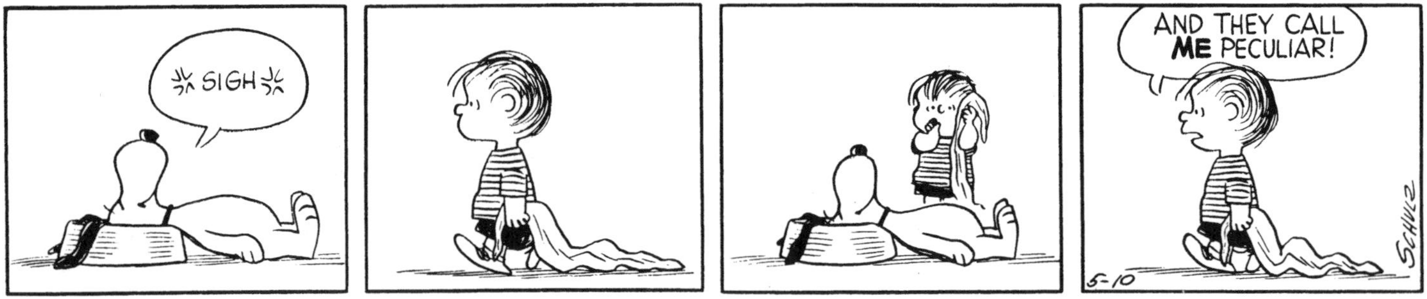
SIGH
AND THEY CALL **ME** PECULIAR!
SCHULZ
5-10

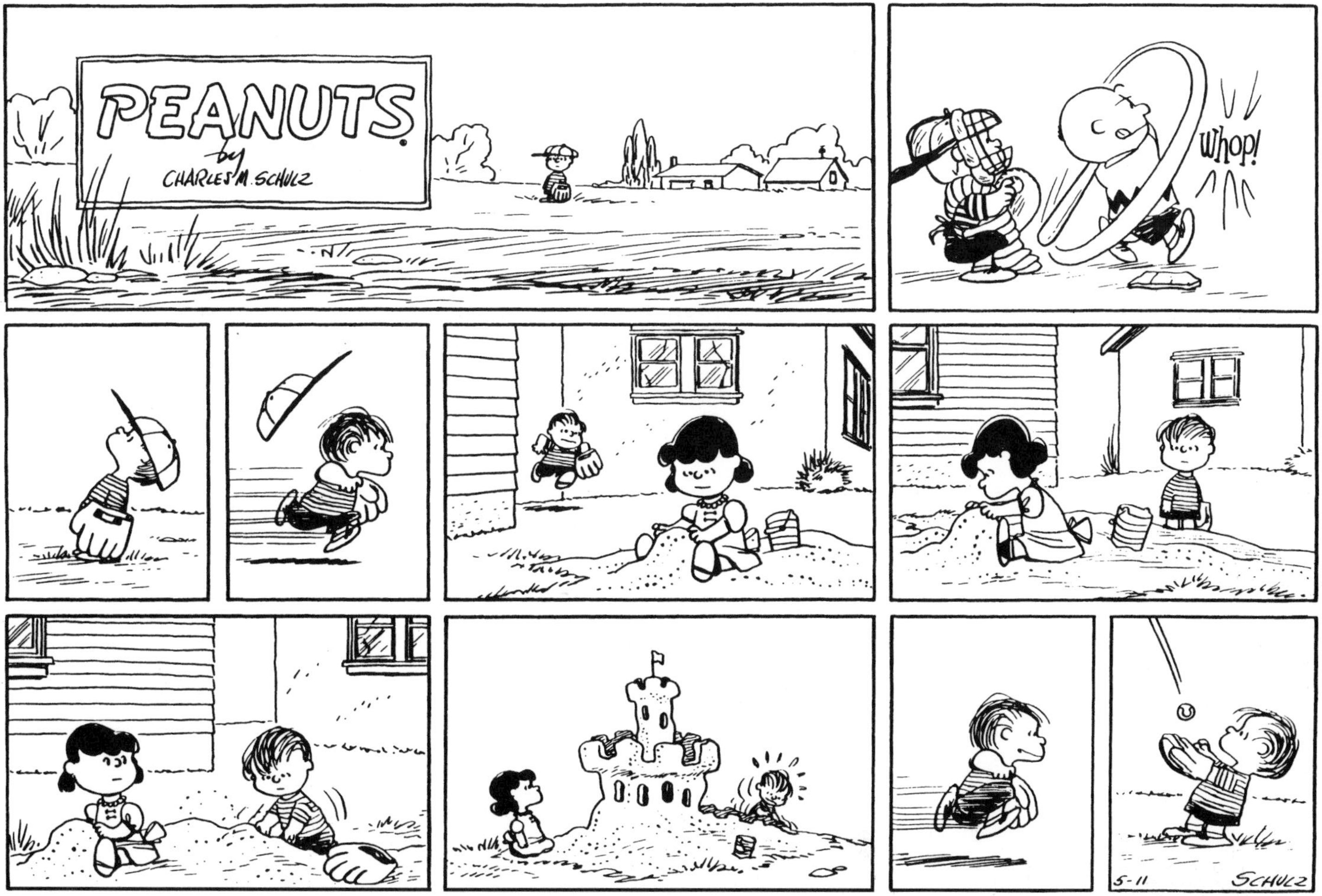
PEANUTS
by
CHARLES M. SCHULZ
Whop!
5-11
SCHULZ

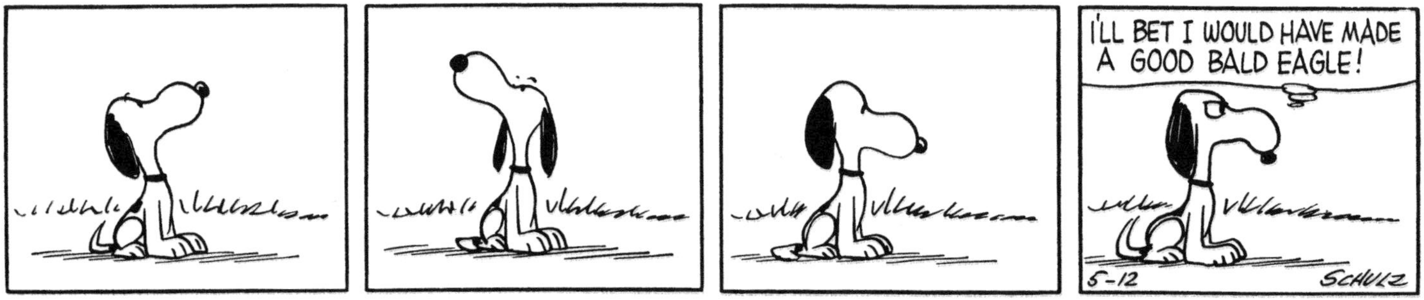
I'LL BET I WOULD HAVE MADE A GOOD BALD EAGLE!
5-12
SCHULZ

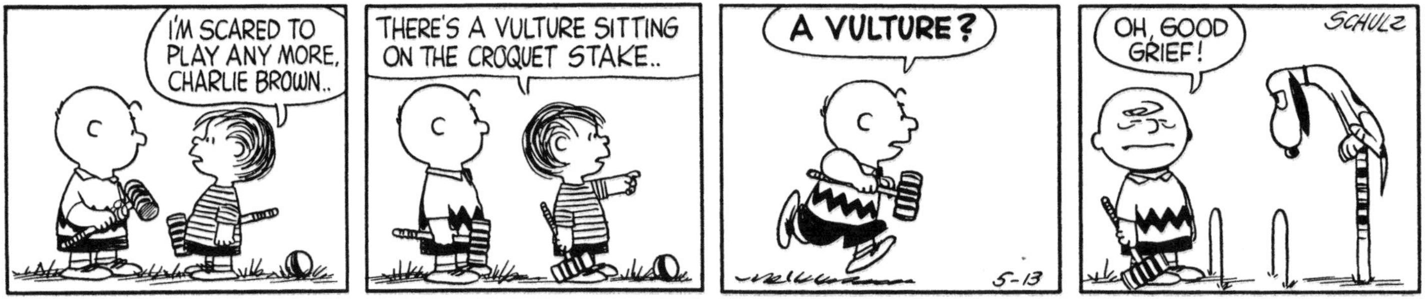
I'M SCARED TO PLAY ANY MORE, CHARLIE BROWN..
THERE'S A VULTURE SITTING ON THE CROQUET STAKE..
A VULTURE?
5-13
SCHULZ
OH, GOOD GRIEF!

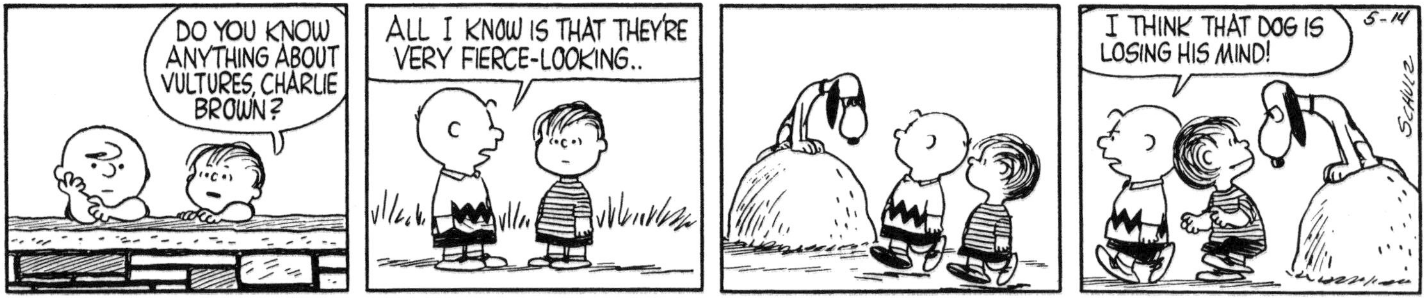
DO YOU KNOW ANYTHING ABOUT VULTURES, CHARLIE BROWN?
ALL I KNOW IS THAT THEY'RE VERY FIERCE-LOOKING..
5-14
SCHULZ
I THINK THAT DOG IS LOSING HIS MIND!

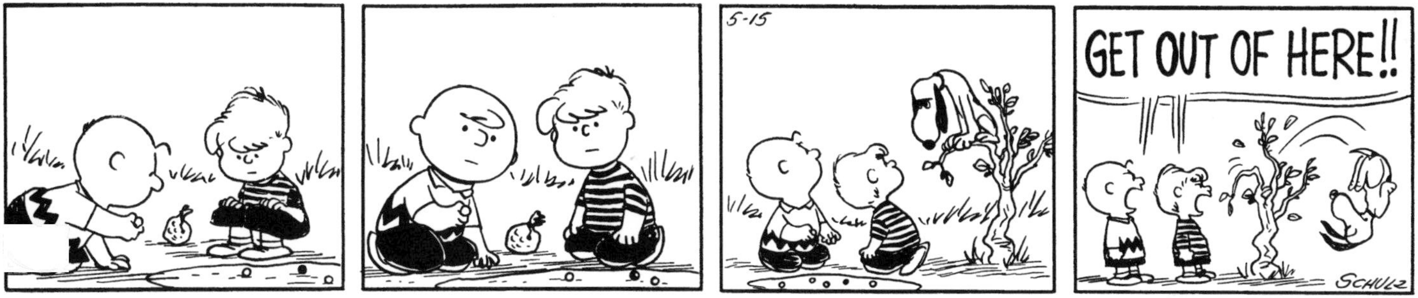
5-15
GET OUT OF HERE!!
SCHULZ

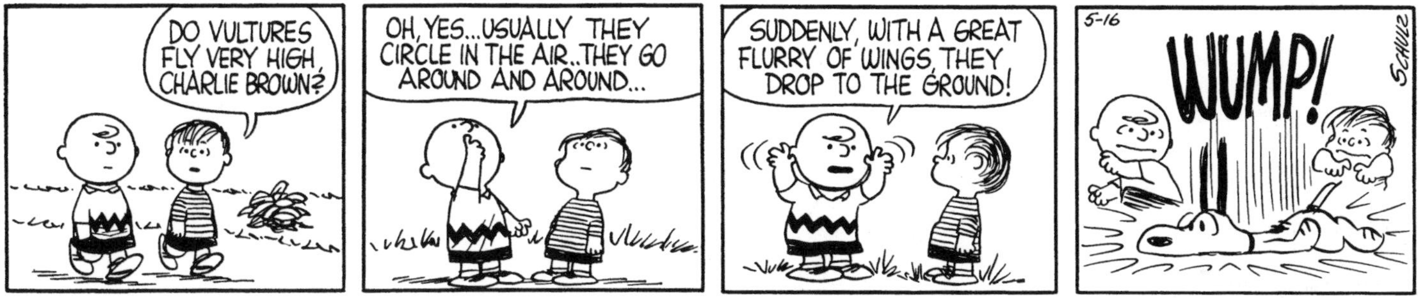
DO VULTURES FLY VERY HIGH, CHARLIE BROWN?
OH, YES...USUALLY THEY CIRCLE IN THE AIR..THEY GO AROUND AND AROUND...
SUDDENLY, WITH A GREAT FLURRY OF WINGS, THEY DROP TO THE GROUND!
5-16
WUMP!
SCHULZ

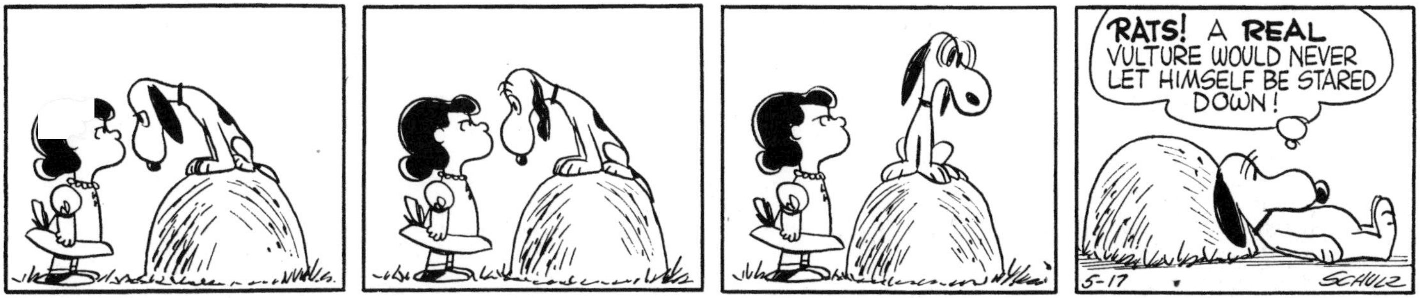
RATS! A REAL VULTURE WOULD NEVER LET HIMSELF BE STARED DOWN!
5-17
SCHULZ

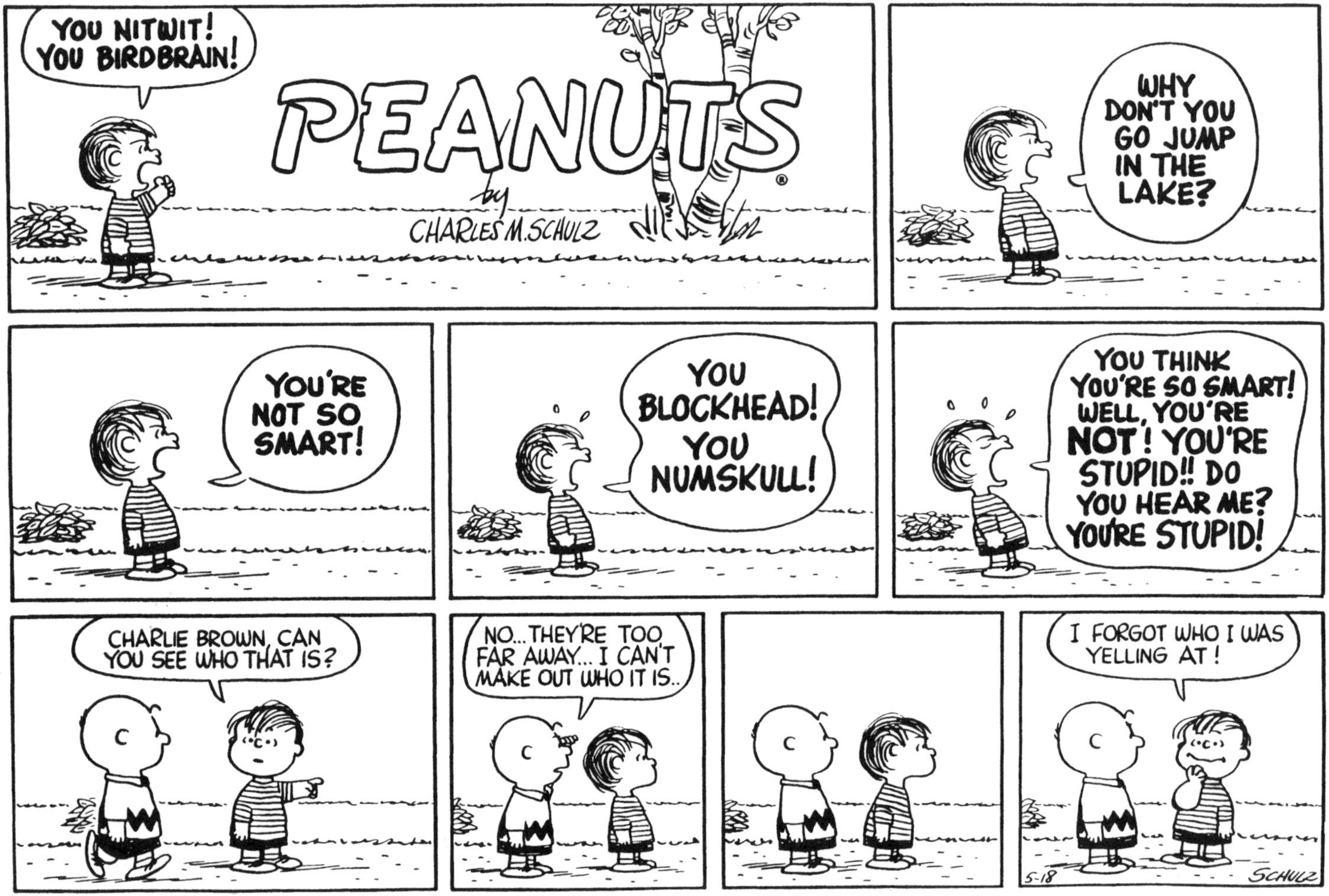
YOU NITWIT! YOU BIRDBRAIN!
PEANUTS
by CHARLES M. SCHULZ
WHY DON'T YOU GO JUMP IN THE LAKE?
YOU'RE NOT SO SMART!
YOU BLOCKHEAD! YOU NUMSKULL!
YOU THINK YOU'RE SO SMART! WELL, YOU'RE NOT! YOU'RE STUPID!! DO YOU HEAR ME? YOU'RE STUPID!
CHARLIE BROWN, CAN YOU SEE WHO THAT IS?
NO... THEY'RE TOO FAR AWAY... I CAN'T MAKE OUT WHO IT IS..
I FORGOT WHO I WAS YELLING AT!
5-18
SCHULZ

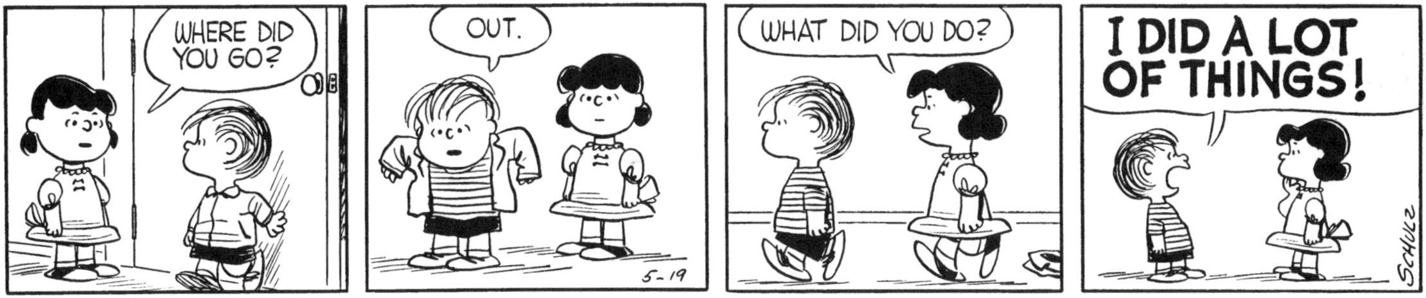
WHERE DID YOU GO?
OUT.
5-19
WHAT DID YOU DO?
I DID A LOT OF THINGS!
SCHULZ

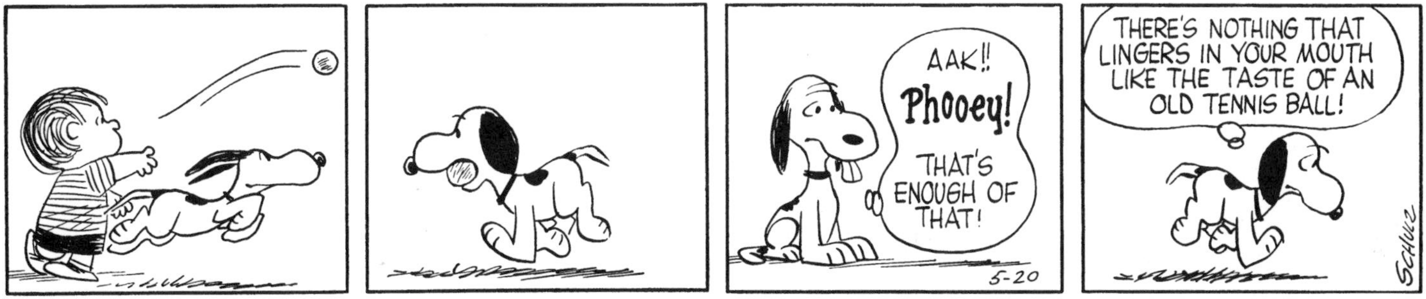
AAK!! Phooey! THAT'S ENOUGH OF THAT!
5-20
THERE'S NOTHING THAT LINGERS IN YOUR MOUTH LIKE THE TASTE OF AN OLD TENNIS BALL!
SCHULZ

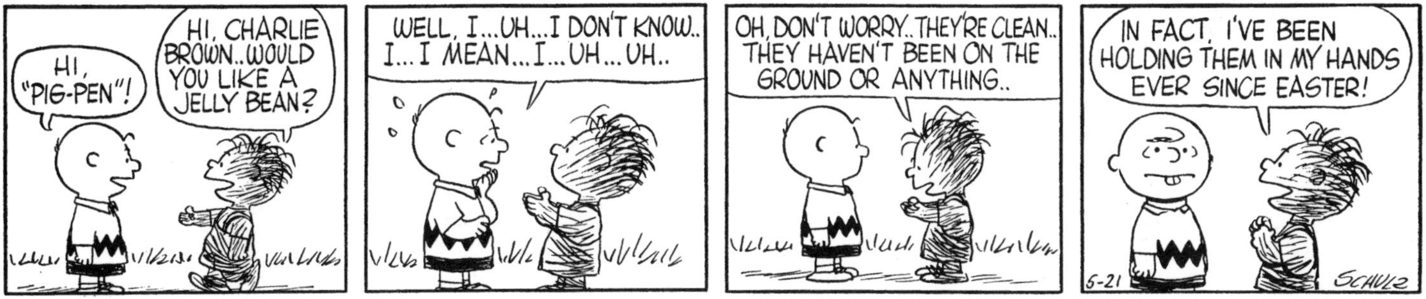
HI, "PIG-PEN"!
HI, CHARLIE BROWN..WOULD YOU LIKE A JELLY BEAN?
WELL, I...UH...I DON'T KNOW.. I... I MEAN... I... UH... UH..
OH, DON'T WORRY..THEY'RE CLEAN.. THEY HAVEN'T BEEN ON THE GROUND OR ANYTHING..
IN FACT, I'VE BEEN HOLDING THEM IN MY HANDS EVER SINCE EASTER!
5-21
SCHULZ

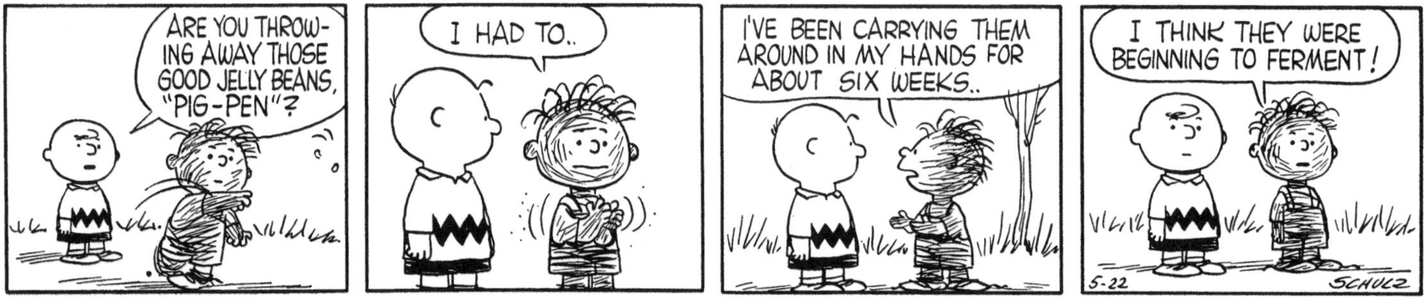
ARE YOU THROWING AWAY THOSE GOOD JELLY BEANS, "PIG-PEN"?
I HAD TO..
I'VE BEEN CARRYING THEM AROUND IN MY HANDS FOR ABOUT SIX WEEKS..
I THINK THEY WERE BEGINNING TO FERMENT!
5-22
SCHULZ

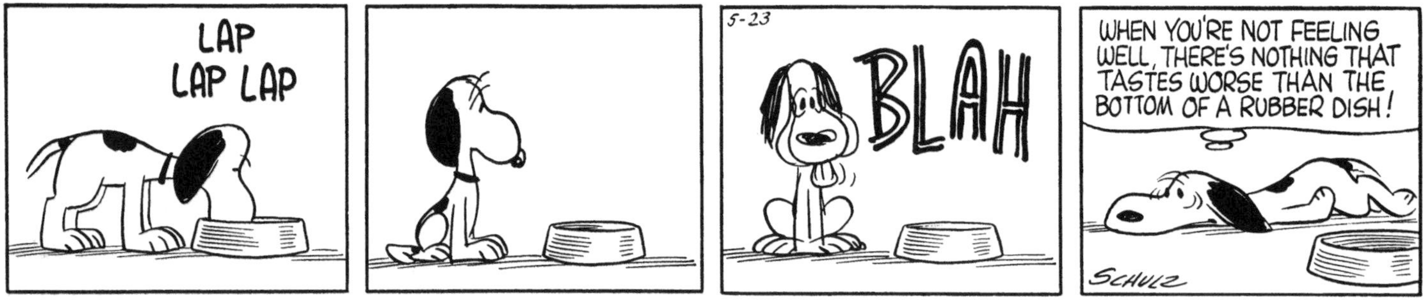
LAP
LAP LAP
5-23
BLAH
WHEN YOU'RE NOT FEELING WELL, THERE'S NOTHING THAT TASTES WORSE THAN THE BOTTOM OF A RUBBER DISH!
SCHULZ

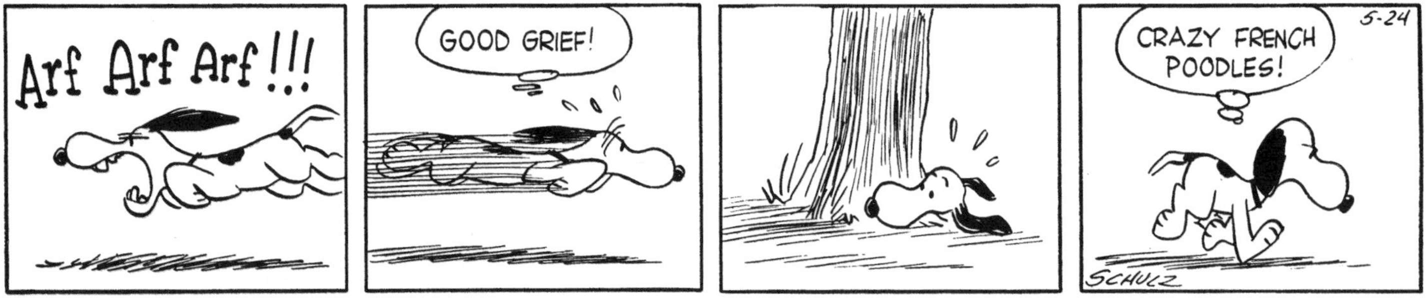
Arf Arf Arf!!!
GOOD GRIEF!
5-24
CRAZY FRENCH POODLES!
SCHULZ

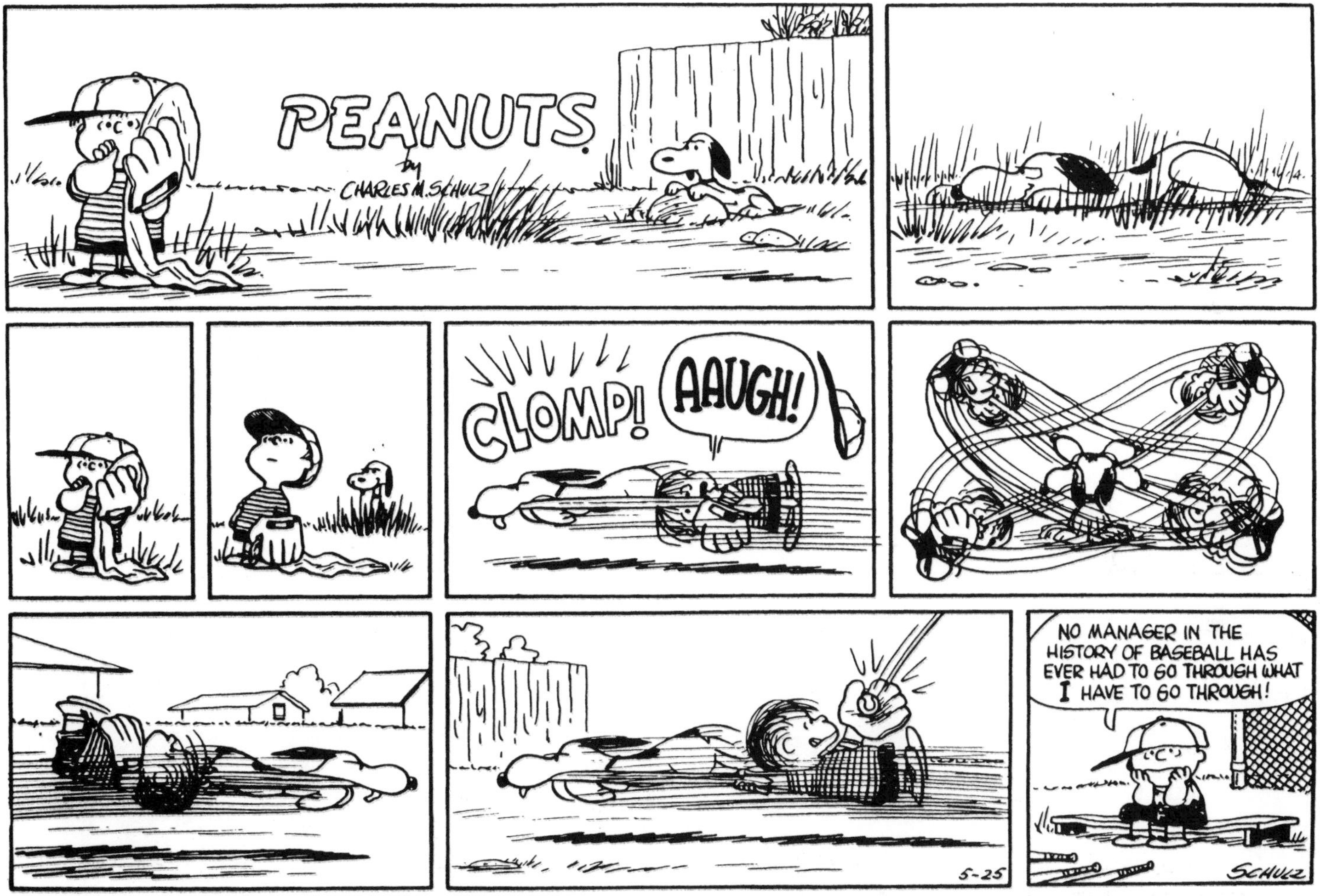
PEANUTS
by
CHARLES M. SCHULZ
CLOMP!
AAUGH!
5-25
NO MANAGER IN THE HISTORY OF BASEBALL HAS EVER HAD TO GO THROUGH WHAT I HAVE TO GO THROUGH!
SCHULZ

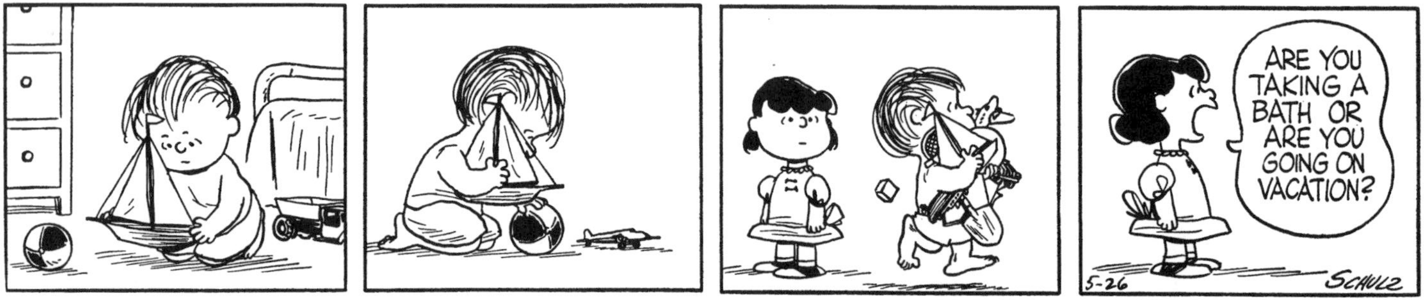
ARE YOU TAKING A BATH OR ARE YOU GOING ON VACATION?
5-26
SCHULZ

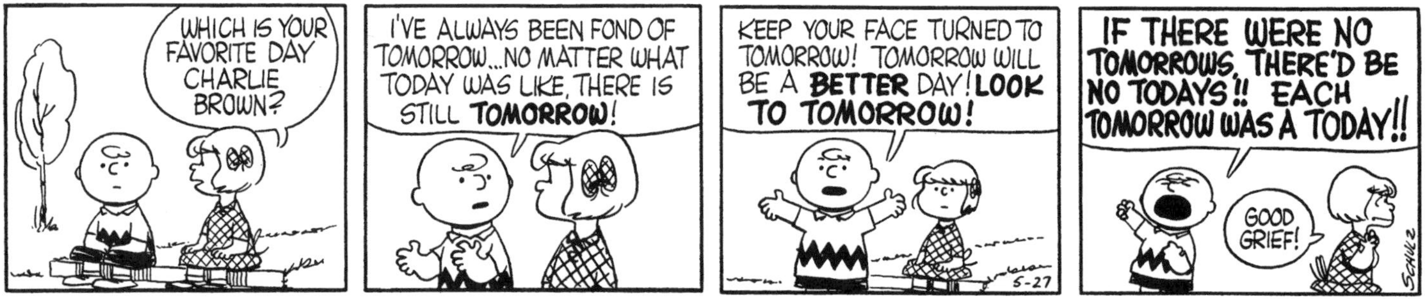
WHICH IS YOUR FAVORITE DAY CHARLIE BROWN?
I'VE ALWAYS BEEN FOND OF TOMORROW...NO MATTER WHAT TODAY WAS LIKE, THERE IS STILL TOMORROW!
KEEP YOUR FACE TURNED TO TOMORROW! TOMORROW WILL BE A BETTER DAY! LOOK TO TOMORROW!
5-27
IF THERE WERE NO TOMORROWS, THERE'D BE NO TODAYS!! EACH TOMORROW WAS A TODAY!!
GOOD GRIEF!
SCHULZ

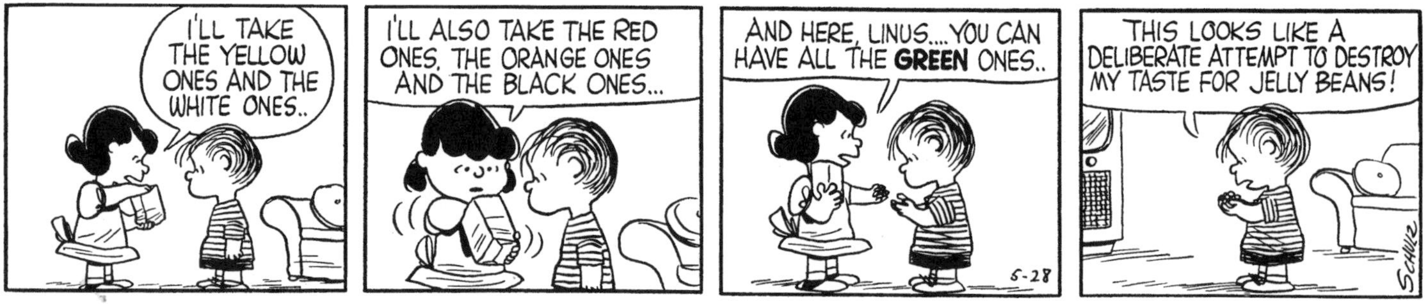
I'LL TAKE THE YELLOW ONES AND THE WHITE ONES..
I'LL ALSO TAKE THE RED ONES, THE ORANGE ONES AND THE BLACK ONES...
AND HERE, LINUS....YOU CAN HAVE ALL THE GREEN ONES..
5-28
THIS LOOKS LIKE A DELIBERATE ATTEMPT TO DESTROY MY TASTE FOR JELLY BEANS!
SCHULZ

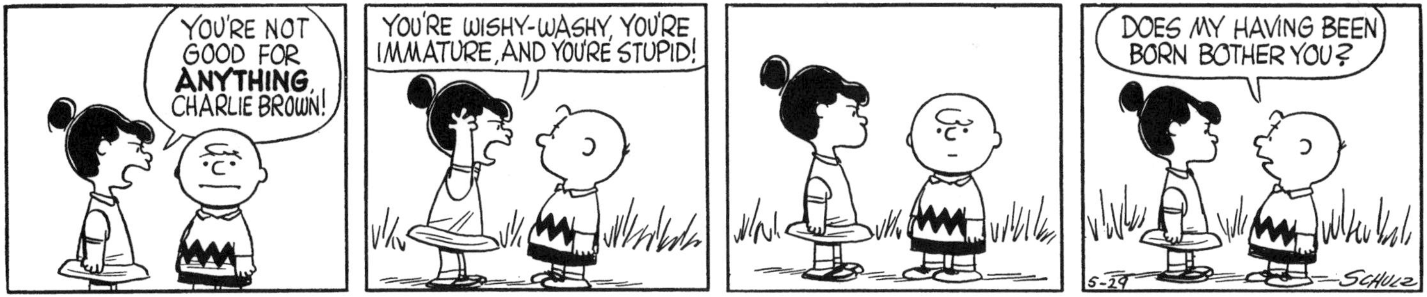
YOU'RE NOT GOOD FOR **ANYTHING**, CHARLIE BROWN!
YOU'RE WISHY-WASHY, YOU'RE IMMATURE, AND YOU'RE STUPID!
DOES MY HAVING BEEN BORN BOTHER YOU?
5-29
SCHULZ

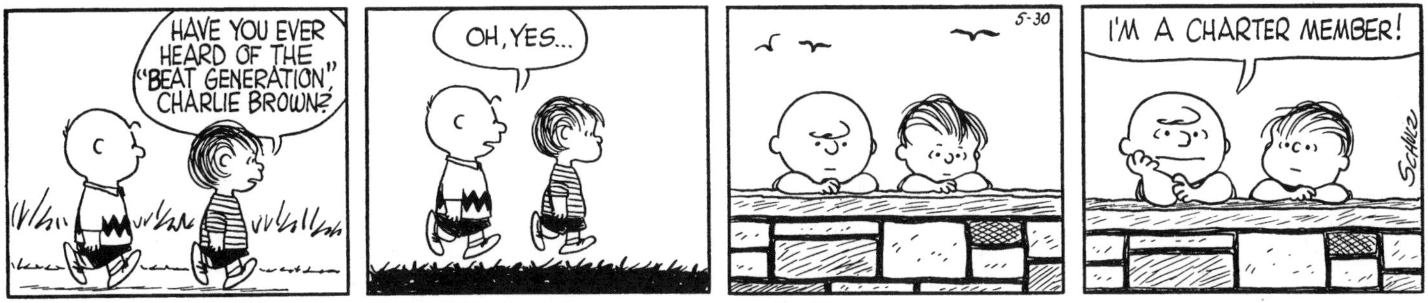
HAVE YOU EVER HEARD OF THE "BEAT GENERATION," CHARLIE BROWN?
OH, YES...
5-30
I'M A CHARTER MEMBER!
SCHULZ

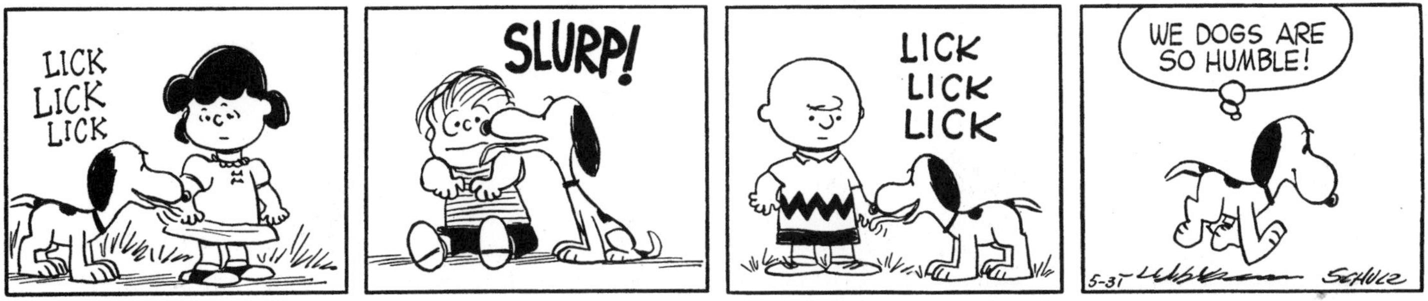
LICK LICK LICK
SLURP!
LICK LICK LICK
WE DOGS ARE SO HUMBLE!
5-31
SCHULZ

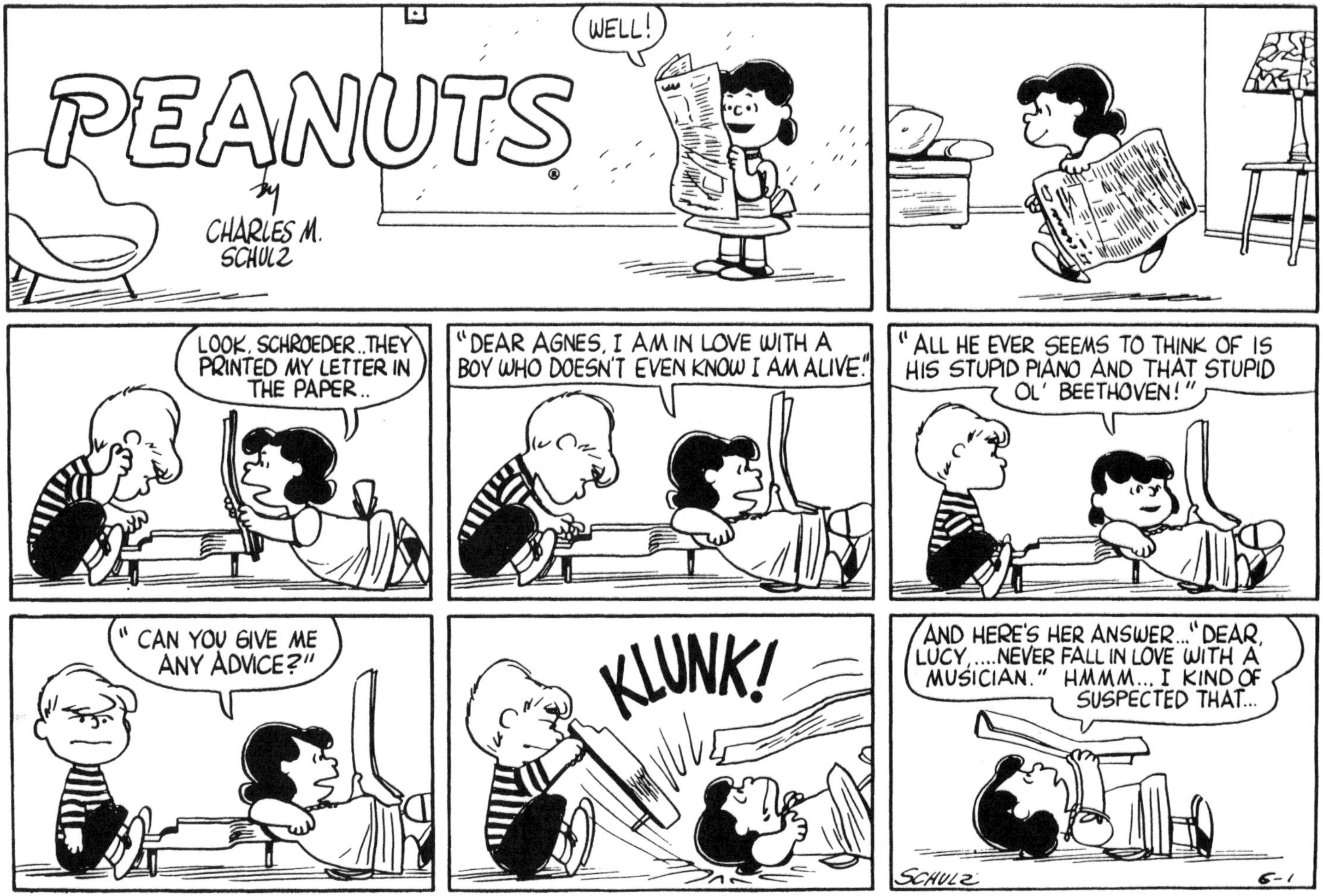
WELL!
PEANUTS
by CHARLES M. SCHULZ
LOOK, SCHROEDER..THEY PRINTED MY LETTER IN THE PAPER..
"DEAR AGNES, I AM IN LOVE WITH A BOY WHO DOESN'T EVEN KNOW I AM ALIVE."
"ALL HE EVER SEEMS TO THINK OF IS HIS STUPID PIANO AND THAT STUPID OL' BEETHOVEN!"
"CAN YOU GIVE ME ANY ADVICE?"
KLUNK!
AND HERE'S HER ANSWER..."DEAR, LUCY,....NEVER FALL IN LOVE WITH A MUSICIAN." HMMM... I KIND OF SUSPECTED THAT...
SCHULZ
6-1

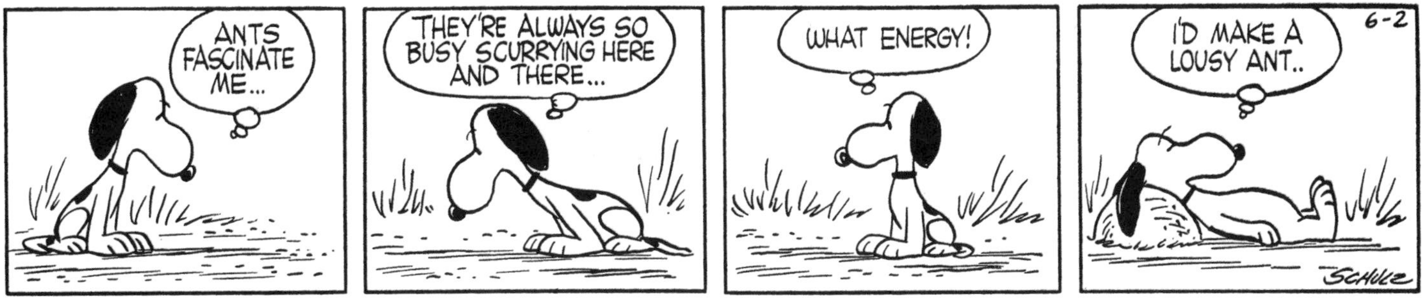
ANTS FASCINATE ME...
THEY'RE ALWAYS SO BUSY SCURRYING HERE AND THERE...
WHAT ENERGY!
I'D MAKE A LOUSY ANT..
6-2
SCHULZ

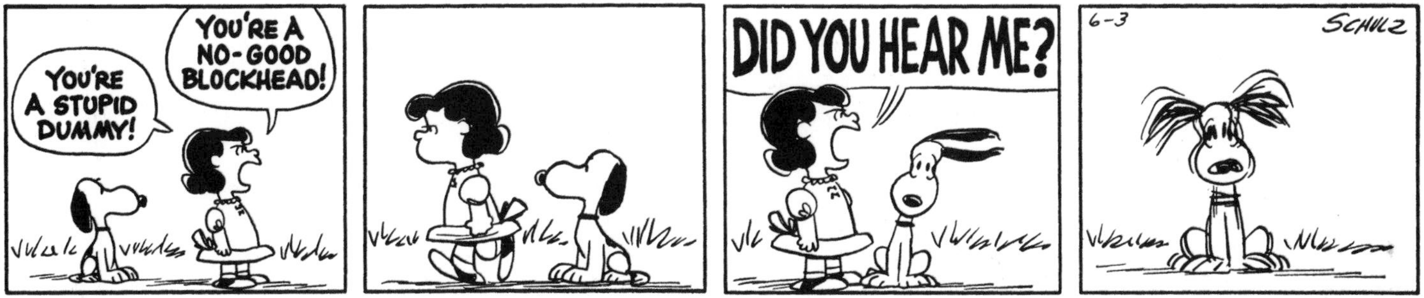
YOU'RE A STUPID DUMMY!
YOU'RE A NO-GOOD BLOCKHEAD!
DID YOU HEAR ME?
6-3
SCHULZ

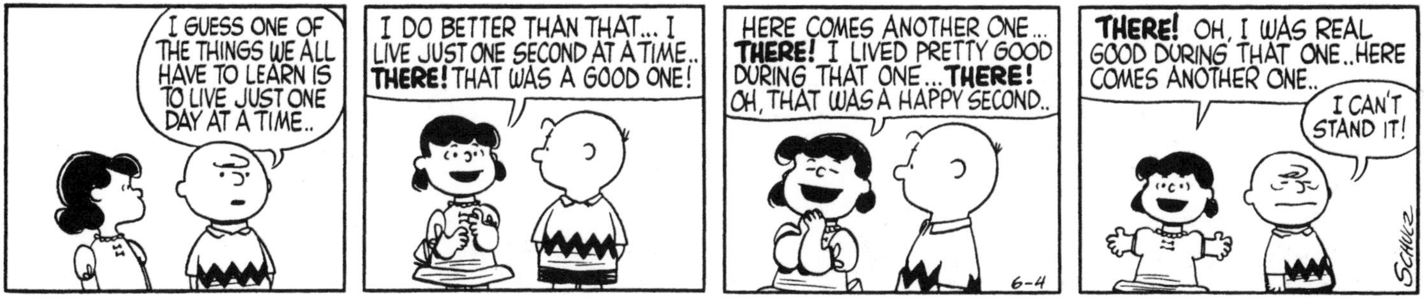
I GUESS ONE OF THE THINGS WE ALL HAVE TO LEARN IS TO LIVE JUST ONE DAY AT A TIME..
I DO BETTER THAN THAT... I LIVE JUST ONE SECOND AT A TIME.. THERE! THAT WAS A GOOD ONE!
HERE COMES ANOTHER ONE... THERE! I LIVED PRETTY GOOD DURING THAT ONE... THERE! OH, THAT WAS A HAPPY SECOND..
6-4
THERE! OH, I WAS REAL GOOD DURING THAT ONE..HERE COMES ANOTHER ONE..
I CAN'T STAND IT!
SCHULZ

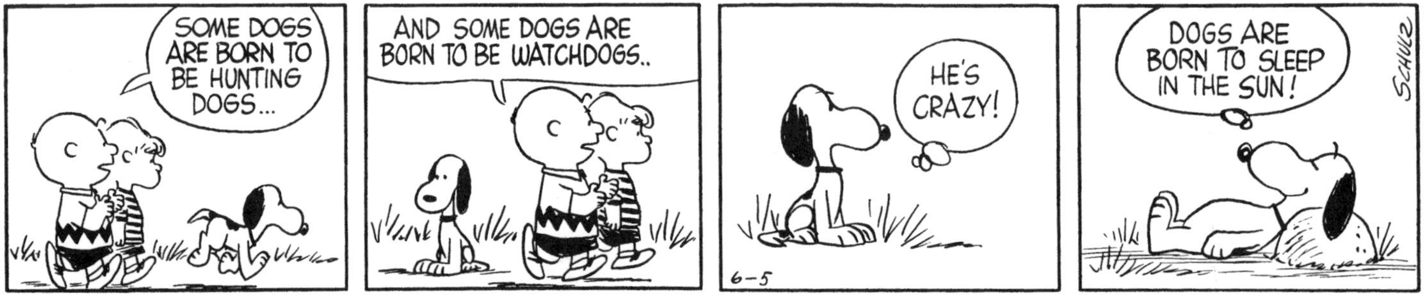
SOME DOGS ARE BORN TO BE HUNTING DOGS...
AND SOME DOGS ARE BORN TO BE WATCHDOGS..
HE'S CRAZY!
DOGS ARE BORN TO SLEEP IN THE SUN!
SCHULZ
6-5

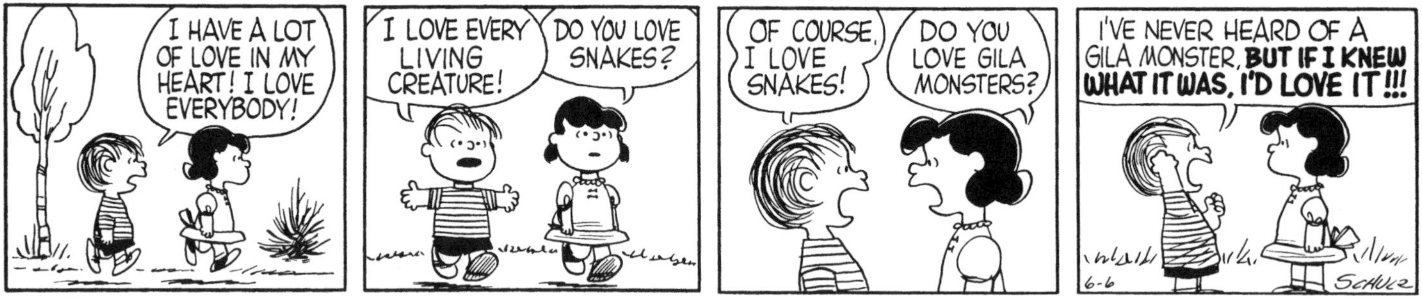
I HAVE A LOT OF LOVE IN MY HEART! I LOVE EVERYBODY!
I LOVE EVERY LIVING CREATURE!
DO YOU LOVE SNAKES?
OF COURSE, I LOVE SNAKES!
DO YOU LOVE GILA MONSTERS?
I'VE NEVER HEARD OF A GILA MONSTER, **BUT IF I KNEW WHAT IT WAS, I'D LOVE IT!!!**
6-6
SCHULZ

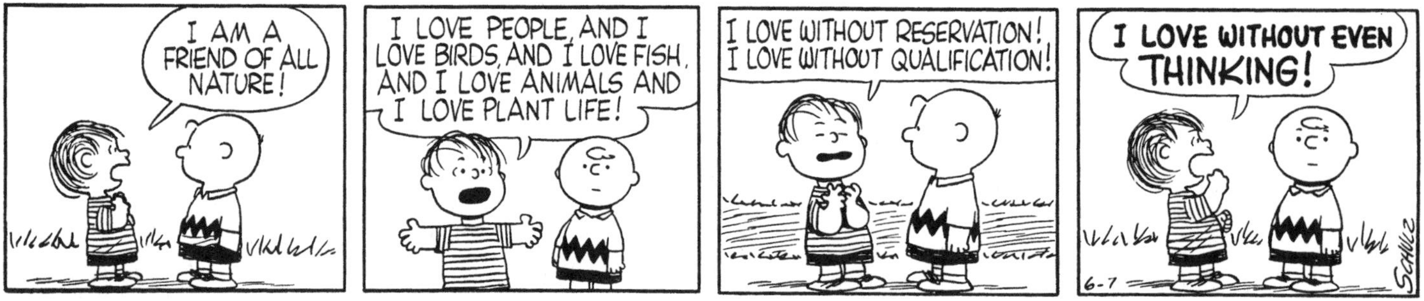
I AM A FRIEND OF ALL NATURE!
I LOVE PEOPLE, AND I LOVE BIRDS, AND I LOVE FISH, AND I LOVE ANIMALS AND I LOVE PLANT LIFE!
I LOVE WITHOUT RESERVATION! I LOVE WITHOUT QUALIFICATION!
I LOVE WITHOUT EVEN THINKING!
6-7
SCHULZ

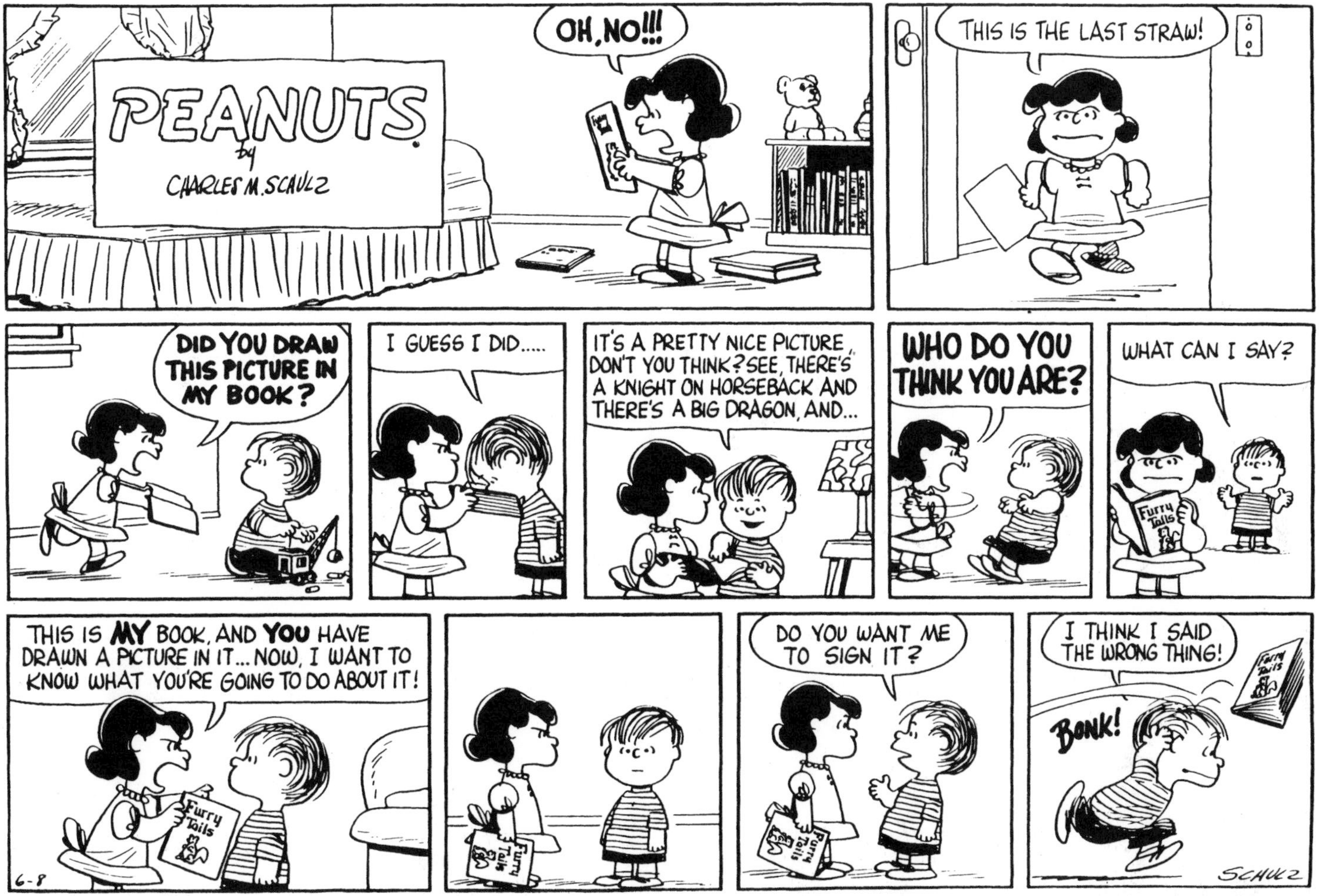
PEANUTS
by
CHARLES M. SCHULZ
OH, NO!!!
THIS IS THE LAST STRAW!
DID YOU DRAW THIS PICTURE IN MY BOOK?
I GUESS I DID.....
IT'S A PRETTY NICE PICTURE, DON'T YOU THINK? SEE, THERE'S A KNIGHT ON HORSEBACK AND THERE'S A BIG DRAGON, AND...
WHO DO YOU THINK YOU ARE?
WHAT CAN I SAY?
Furry Tails
THIS IS MY BOOK, AND YOU HAVE DRAWN A PICTURE IN IT... NOW, I WANT TO KNOW WHAT YOU'RE GOING TO DO ABOUT IT!
Furry Tails
6-8
Furry Tails
DO YOU WANT ME TO SIGN IT?
Furry Tails
I THINK I SAID THE WRONG THING!
BONK!
Furry Tails
SCHULZ

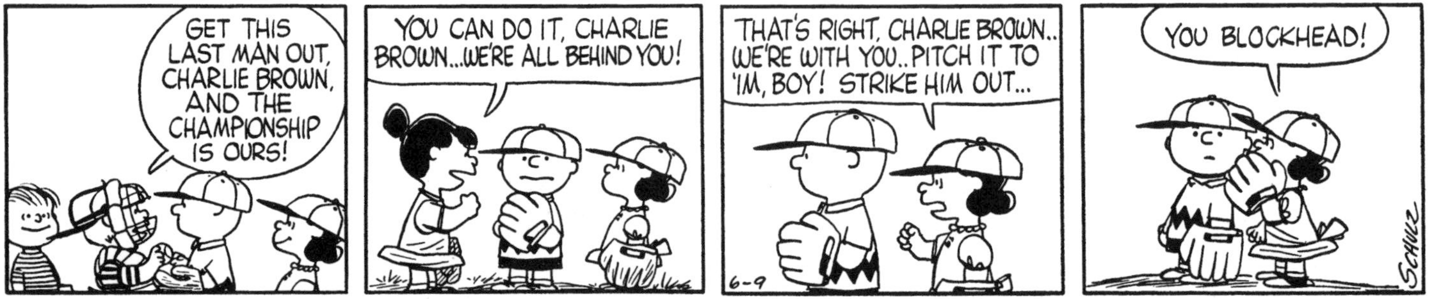
GET THIS LAST MAN OUT, CHARLIE BROWN, AND THE CHAMPIONSHIP IS OURS!
YOU CAN DO IT, CHARLIE BROWN...WE'RE ALL BEHIND YOU!
THAT'S RIGHT, CHARLIE BROWN.. WE'RE WITH YOU.. PITCH IT TO 'IM, BOY! STRIKE HIM OUT...
6-9
YOU BLOCKHEAD!
SCHULZ

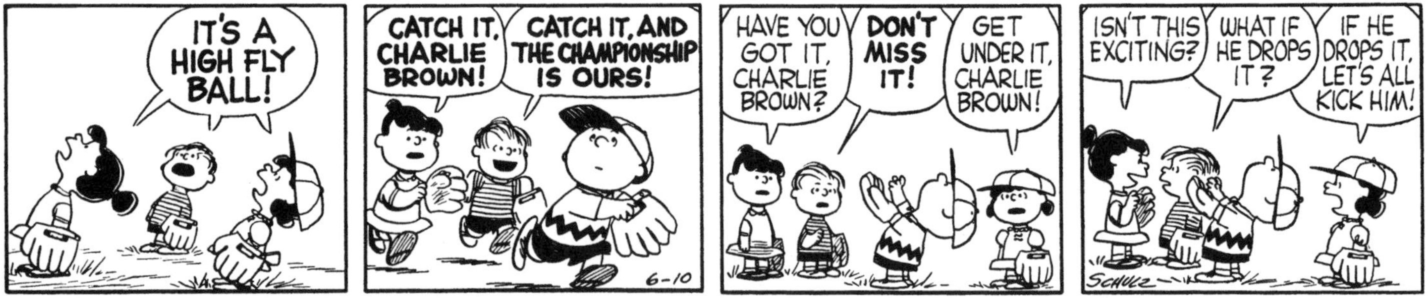
IT'S A HIGH FLY BALL!
CATCH IT, CHARLIE BROWN!
CATCH IT, AND THE CHAMPIONSHIP IS OURS!
6-10
HAVE YOU GOT IT, CHARLIE BROWN?
DON'T MISS IT!
GET UNDER IT, CHARLIE BROWN!
ISN'T THIS EXCITING?
WHAT IF HE DROPS IT?
IF HE DROPS IT, LET'S ALL KICK HIM!
SCHULZ

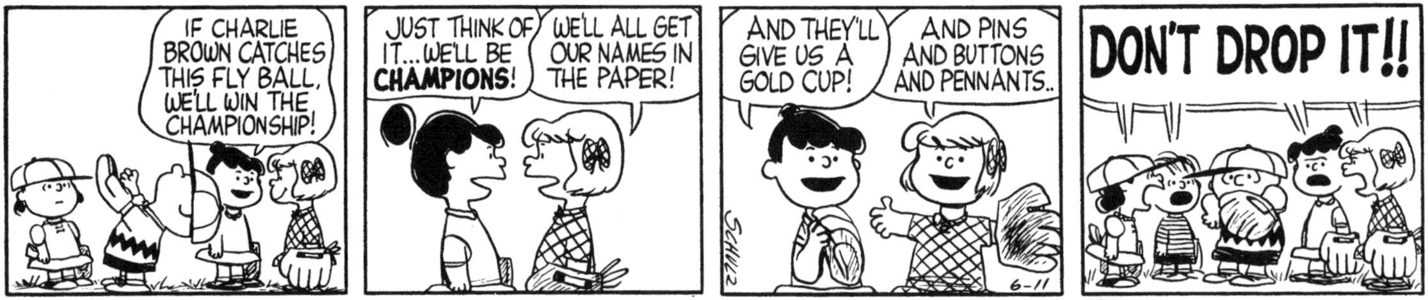
IF CHARLIE BROWN CATCHES THIS FLY BALL, WE'LL WIN THE CHAMPIONSHIP!
JUST THINK OF IT... WE'LL BE CHAMPIONS!
WE'LL ALL GET OUR NAMES IN THE PAPER!
AND THEY'LL GIVE US A GOLD CUP!
AND PINS AND BUTTONS AND PENNANTS..
SCHULZ
6-11
DON'T DROP IT!!

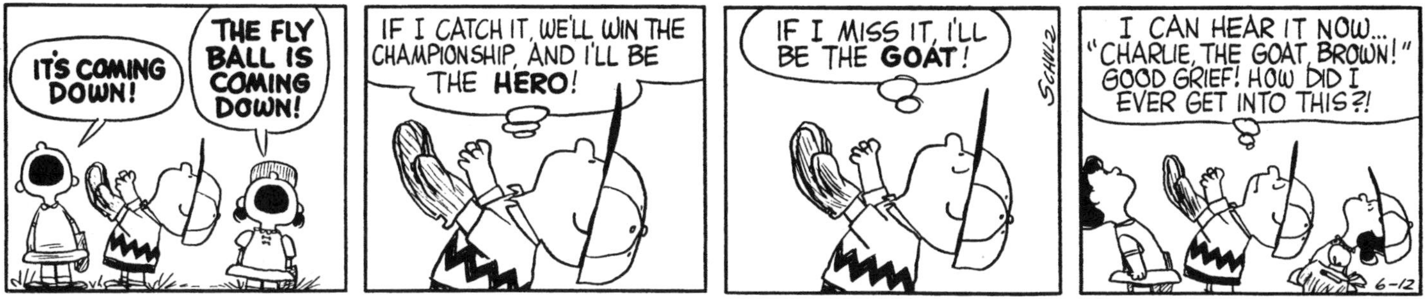
IT'S COMING DOWN!
THE FLY BALL IS COMING DOWN!
IF I CATCH IT, WE'LL WIN THE CHAMPIONSHIP, AND I'LL BE THE HERO!
IF I MISS IT, I'LL BE THE GOAT!
SCHULZ
I CAN HEAR IT NOW... "CHARLIE, THE GOAT, BROWN!" GOOD GRIEF! HOW DID I EVER GET INTO THIS?!
6-12

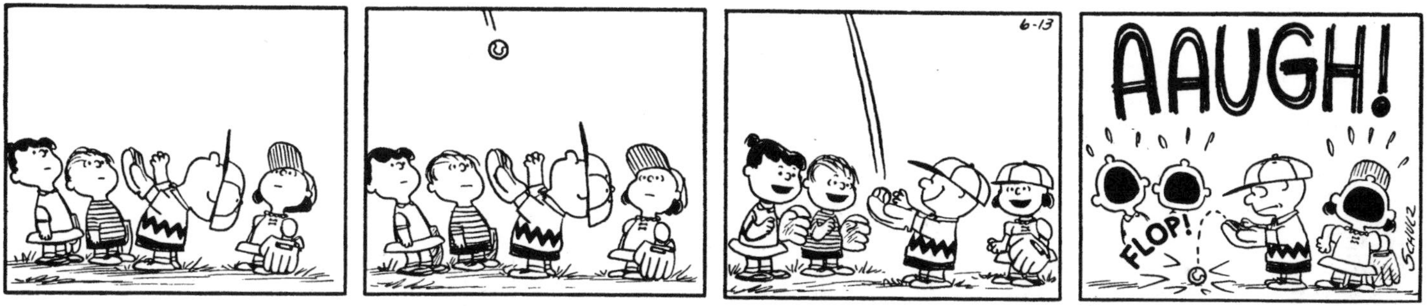
6-13
AAUGH!
FLOP!
SCHULZ

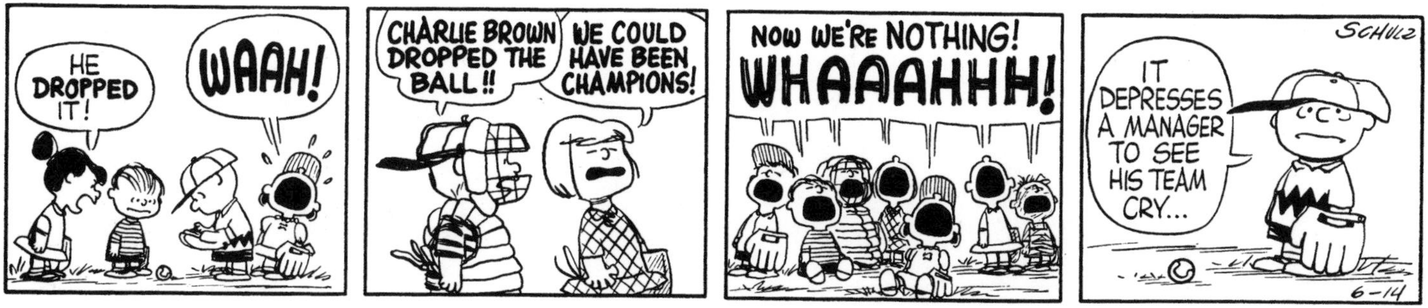
HE DROPPED IT!
WAAH!
CHARLIE BROWN DROPPED THE BALL!!
WE COULD HAVE BEEN CHAMPIONS!
NOW WE'RE NOTHING! WHAAAAHHH!
SCHULZ
IT DEPRESSES A MANAGER TO SEE HIS TEAM CRY...
6-14

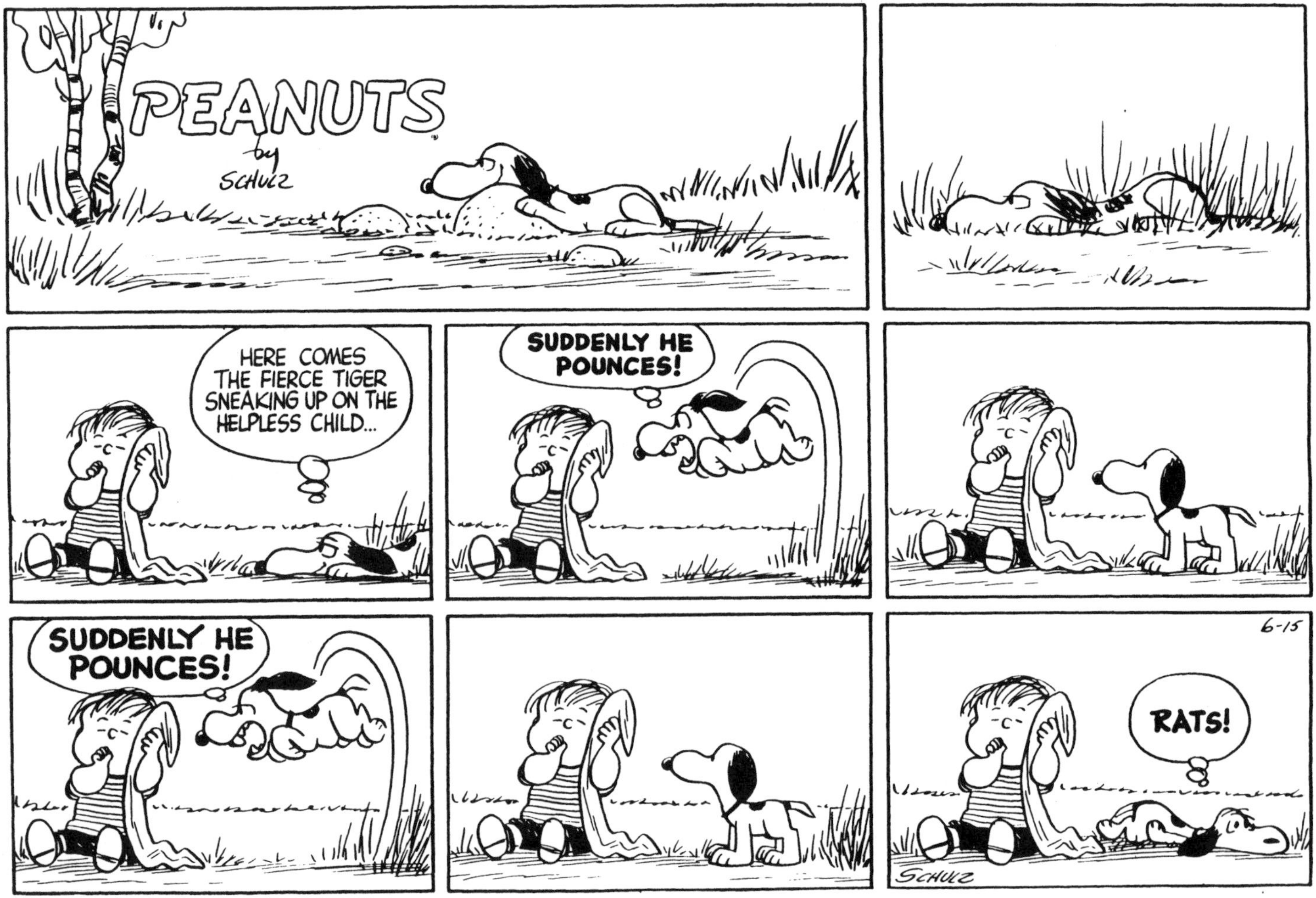
PEANUTS
by
SCHULZ
HERE COMES THE FIERCE TIGER SNEAKING UP ON THE HELPLESS CHILD...
SUDDENLY HE POUNCES!
SUDDENLY HE POUNCES!
6-15
RATS!
SCHULZ

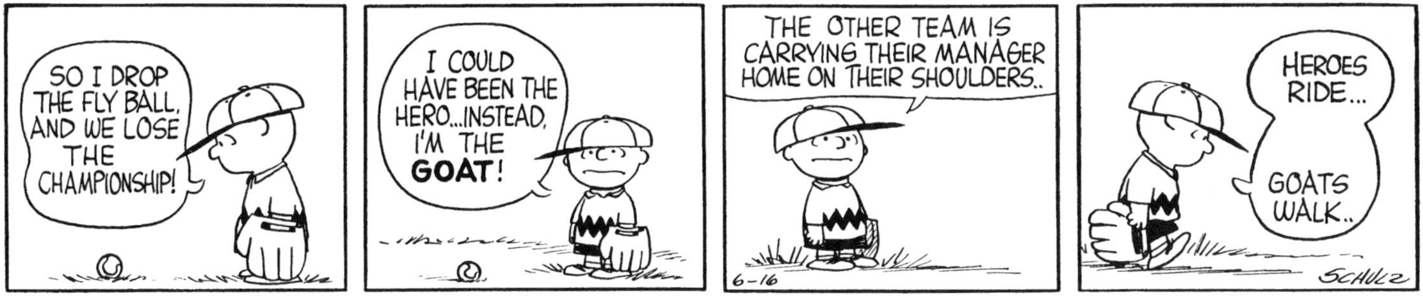
SO I DROP THE FLY BALL, AND WE LOSE THE CHAMPIONSHIP!
I COULD HAVE BEEN THE HERO...INSTEAD, I'M THE GOAT!
THE OTHER TEAM IS CARRYING THEIR MANAGER HOME ON THEIR SHOULDERS..
HEROES RIDE...
GOATS WALK..

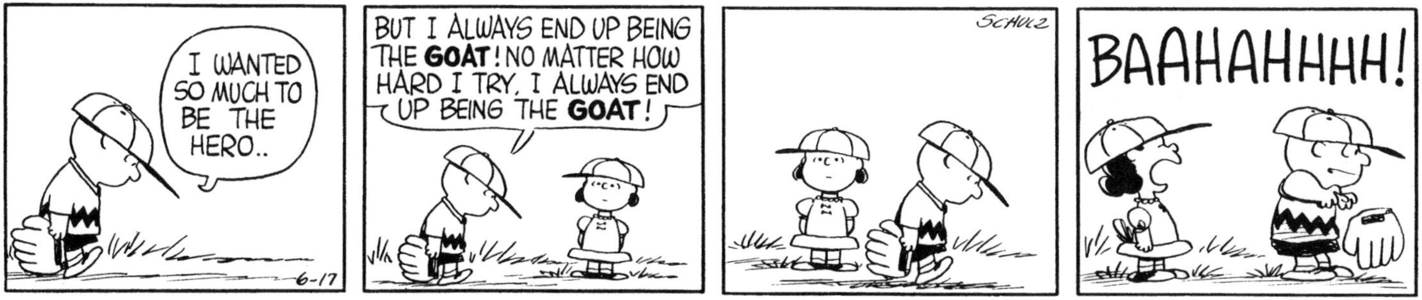
I WANTED SO MUCH TO BE THE HERO..
BUT I ALWAYS END UP BEING THE GOAT! NO MATTER HOW HARD I TRY, I ALWAYS END UP BEING THE GOAT!
BAAHAHHHH!

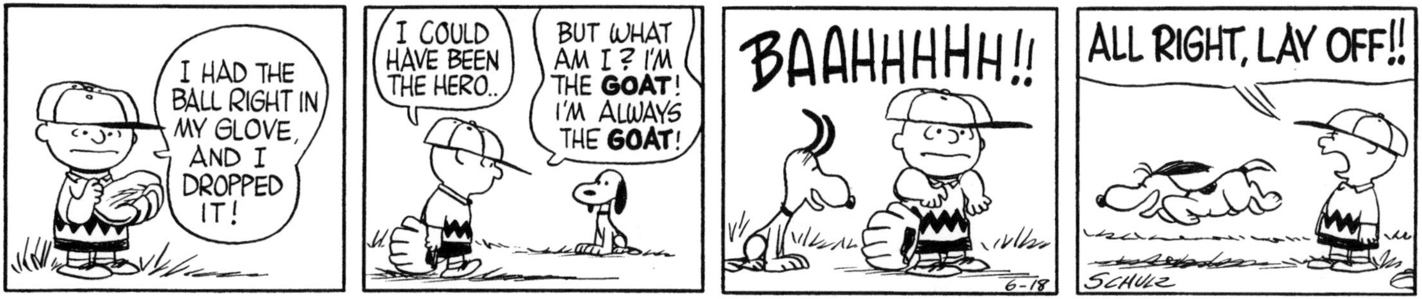
I HAD THE BALL RIGHT IN MY GLOVE, AND I DROPPED IT!
I COULD HAVE BEEN THE HERO..
BUT WHAT AM I? I'M THE GOAT! I'M ALWAYS THE GOAT!
BAAHHHHH!!
ALL RIGHT, LAY OFF!!

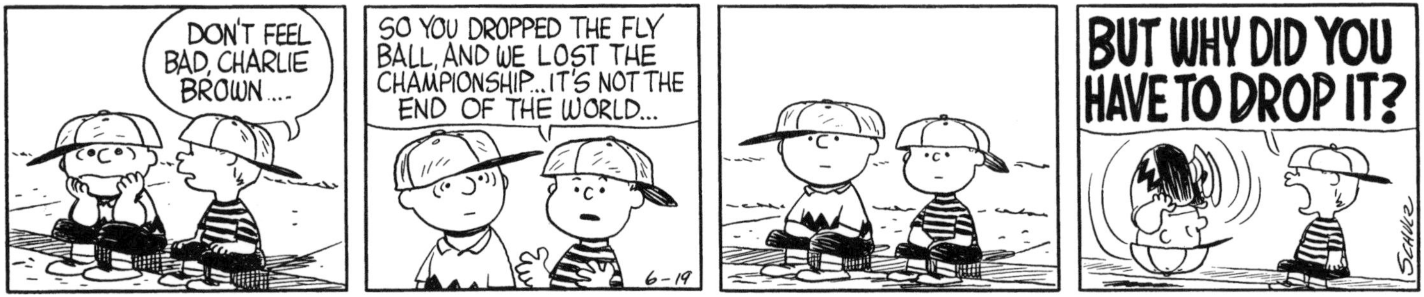
DON'T FEEL BAD, CHARLIE BROWN....
SO YOU DROPPED THE FLY BALL, AND WE LOST THE CHAMPIONSHIP...IT'S NOT THE END OF THE WORLD...
6-19
BUT WHY DID YOU HAVE TO DROP IT?
SCHULZ

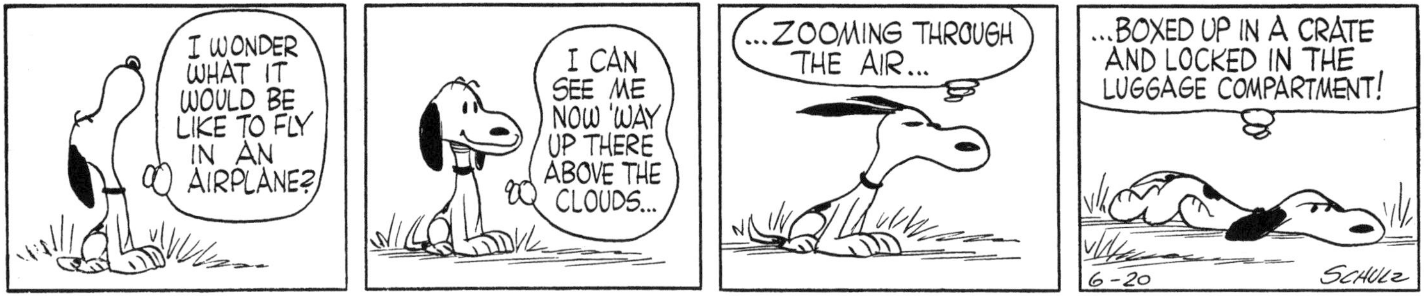
I WONDER WHAT IT WOULD BE LIKE TO FLY IN AN AIRPLANE?
I CAN SEE ME NOW 'WAY UP THERE ABOVE THE CLOUDS...
...ZOOMING THROUGH THE AIR...
...BOXED UP IN A CRATE AND LOCKED IN THE LUGGAGE COMPARTMENT!
6-20
SCHULZ

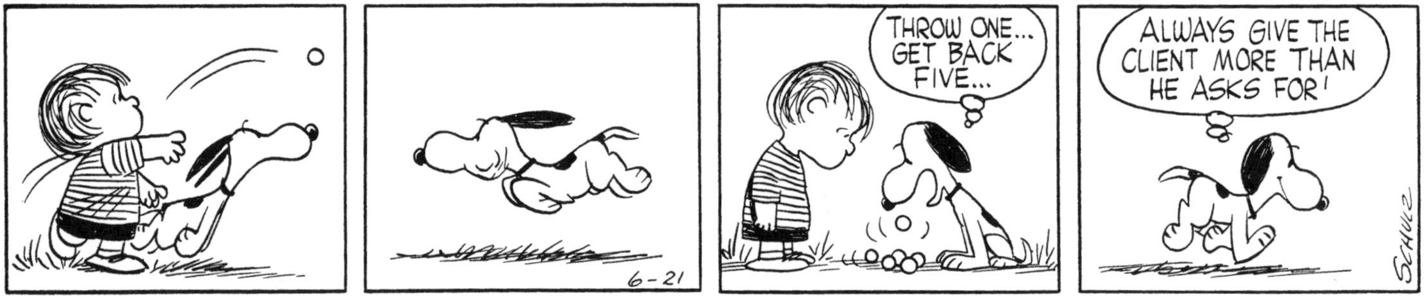
6-21
THROW ONE... GET BACK FIVE...
ALWAYS GIVE THE CLIENT MORE THAN HE ASKS FOR!
SCHULZ

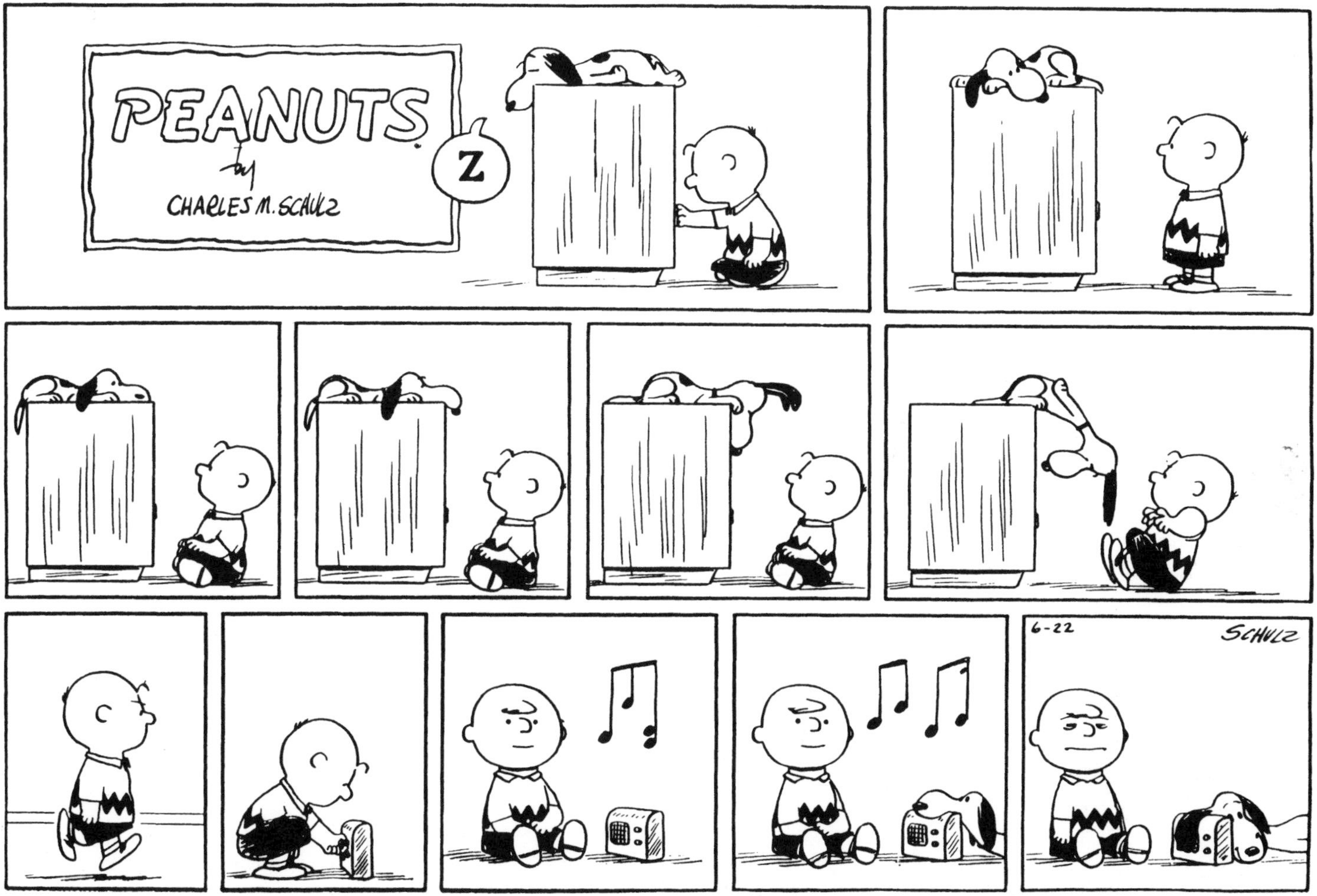
PEANUTS
by
CHARLES M. SCHULZ
Z
6-22
SCHULZ

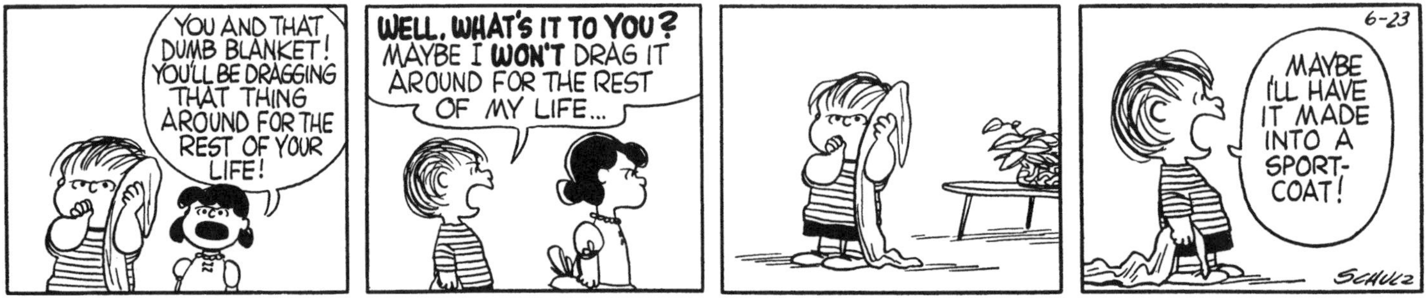
YOU AND THAT DUMB BLANKET! YOU'LL BE DRAGGING THAT THING AROUND FOR THE REST OF YOUR LIFE!
WELL, WHAT'S IT TO YOU? MAYBE I WON'T DRAG IT AROUND FOR THE REST OF MY LIFE...
6-23
MAYBE I'LL HAVE IT MADE INTO A SPORT-COAT!
SCHULZ

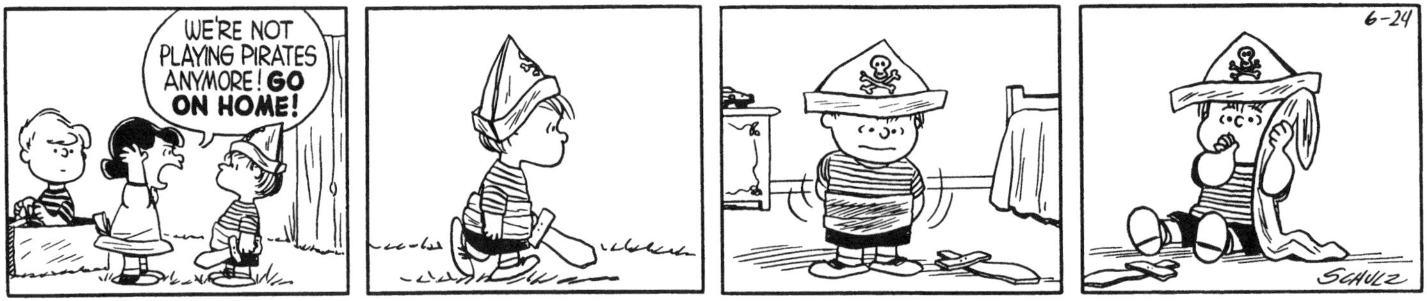
WE'RE NOT PLAYING PIRATES ANYMORE! GO ON HOME!
6-24
SCHULZ

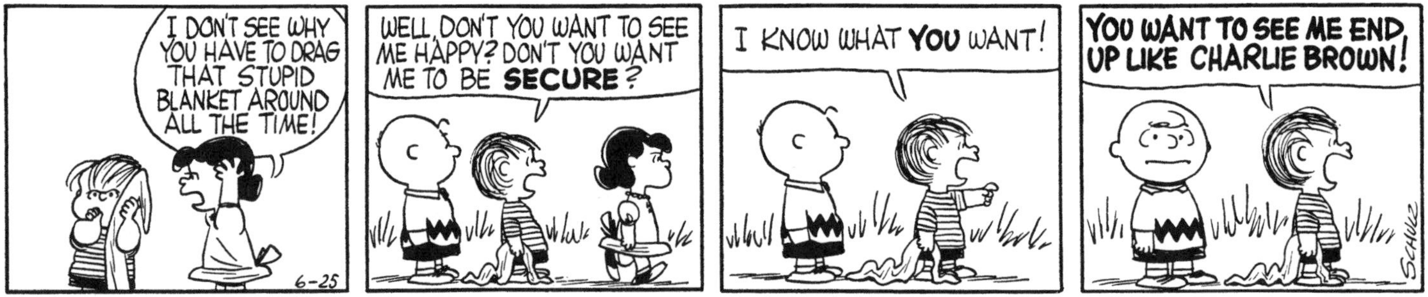
I DON'T SEE WHY YOU HAVE TO DRAG THAT STUPID BLANKET AROUND ALL THE TIME!
6-25
WELL, DON'T YOU WANT TO SEE ME HAPPY? DON'T YOU WANT ME TO BE SECURE?
I KNOW WHAT YOU WANT!
YOU WANT TO SEE ME END UP LIKE CHARLIE BROWN!
SCHULZ

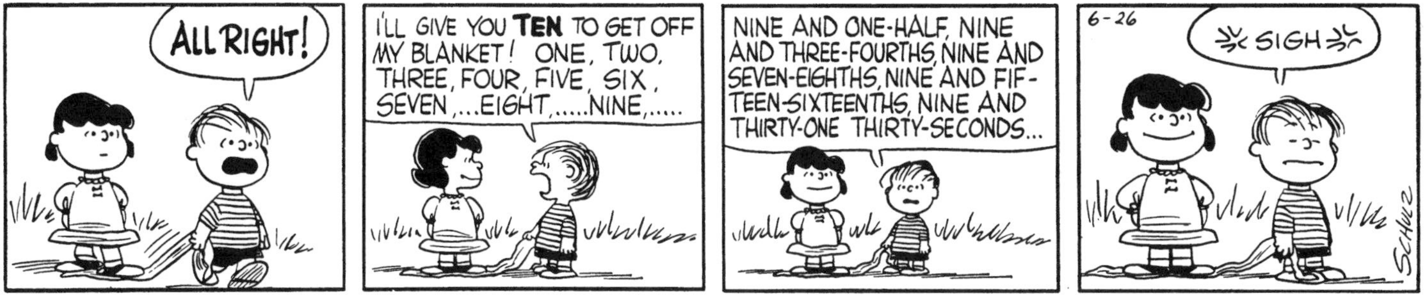
ALL RIGHT!
I'LL GIVE YOU TEN TO GET OFF MY BLANKET! ONE, TWO, THREE, FOUR, FIVE, SIX, SEVEN,...EIGHT,.....NINE,.....
NINE AND ONE-HALF, NINE AND THREE-FOURTHS, NINE AND SEVEN-EIGHTHS, NINE AND FIF-TEEN-SIXTEENTHS, NINE AND THIRTY-ONE THIRTY-SECONDS...
6-26
SIGH
SCHULZ

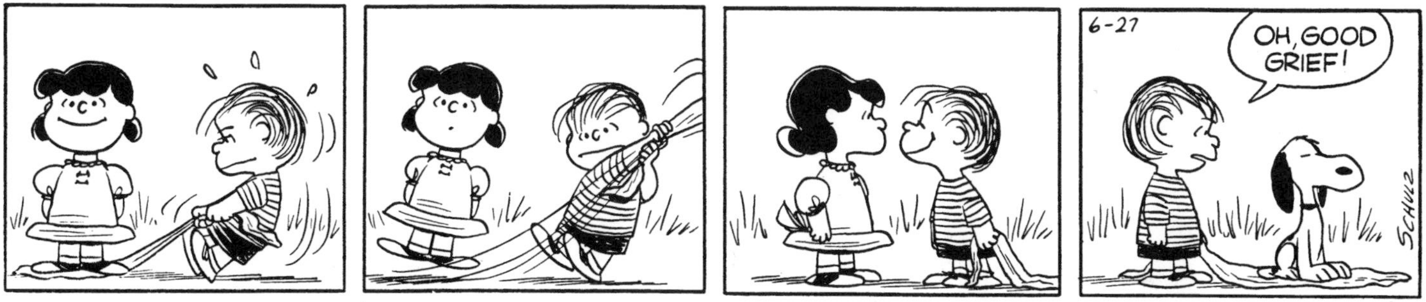
6-27
OH, GOOD GRIEF!
SCHULZ

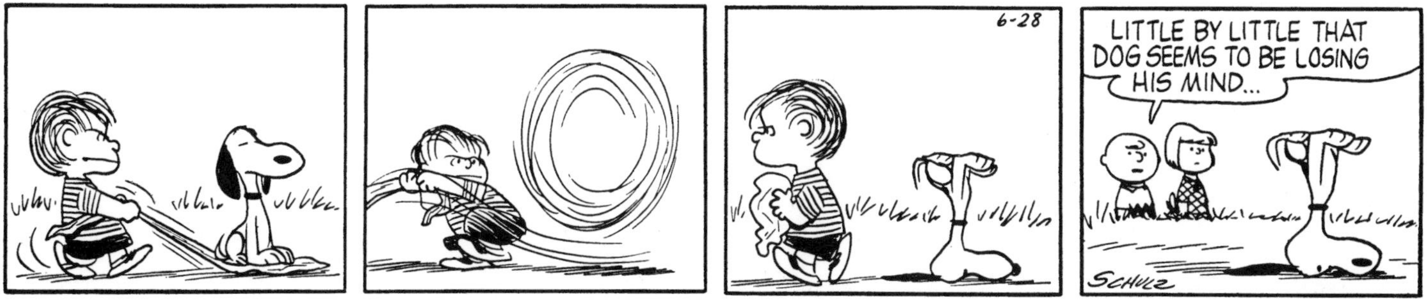
6-28
LITTLE BY LITTLE THAT DOG SEEMS TO BE LOSING HIS MIND...
SCHULZ

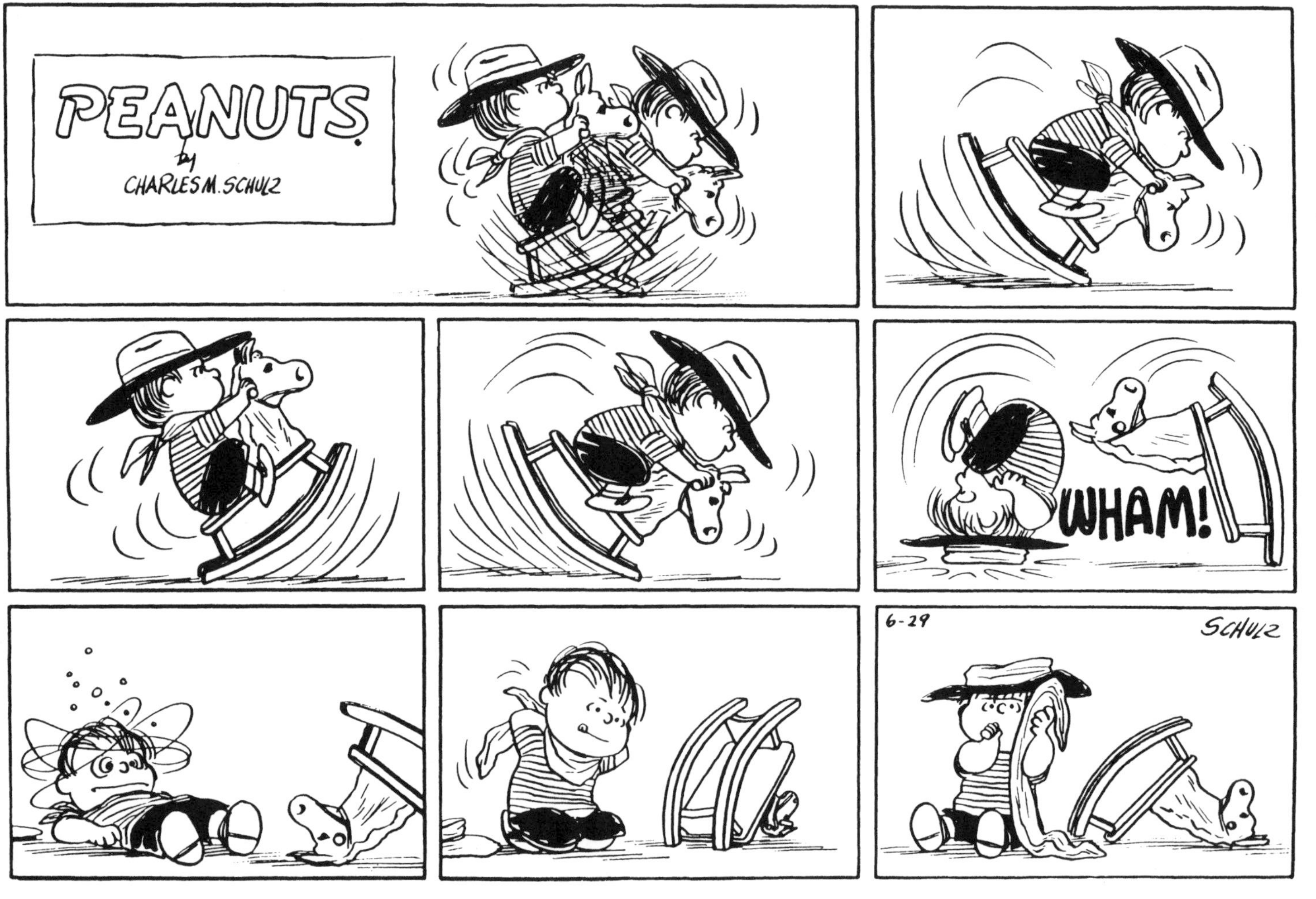
PEANUTS
by
CHARLES M. SCHULZ
WHAM!
6-29
SCHULZ

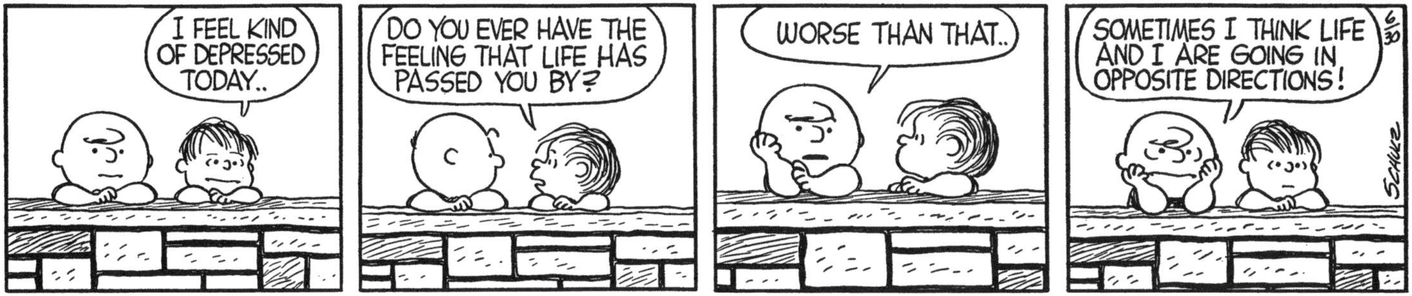
I FEEL KIND OF DEPRESSED TODAY..
DO YOU EVER HAVE THE FEELING THAT LIFE HAS PASSED YOU BY?
WORSE THAN THAT..
SOMETIMES I THINK LIFE AND I ARE GOING IN OPPOSITE DIRECTIONS!
6/30
SCHULZ

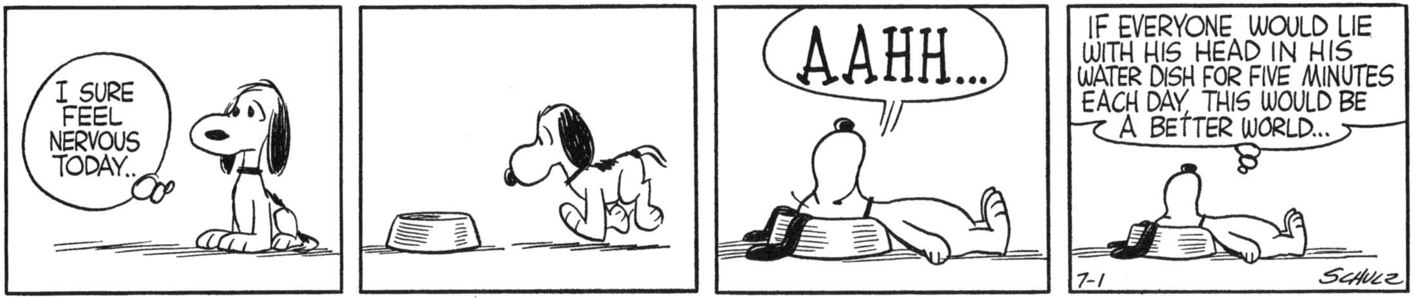
I SURE FEEL NERVOUS TODAY..
AAHH...
IF EVERYONE WOULD LIE WITH HIS HEAD IN HIS WATER DISH FOR FIVE MINUTES EACH DAY, THIS WOULD BE A BETTER WORLD...
7-1
SCHULZ

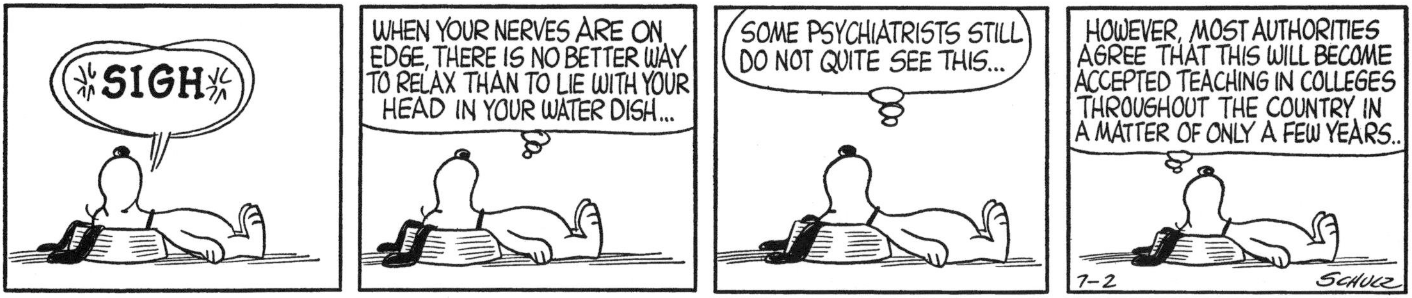
SIGH
WHEN YOUR NERVES ARE ON EDGE, THERE IS NO BETTER WAY TO RELAX THAN TO LIE WITH YOUR HEAD IN YOUR WATER DISH...
SOME PSYCHIATRISTS STILL DO NOT QUITE SEE THIS...
HOWEVER, MOST AUTHORITIES AGREE THAT THIS WILL BECOME ACCEPTED TEACHING IN COLLEGES THROUGHOUT THE COUNTRY IN A MATTER OF ONLY A FEW YEARS..
7-2
SCHULZ

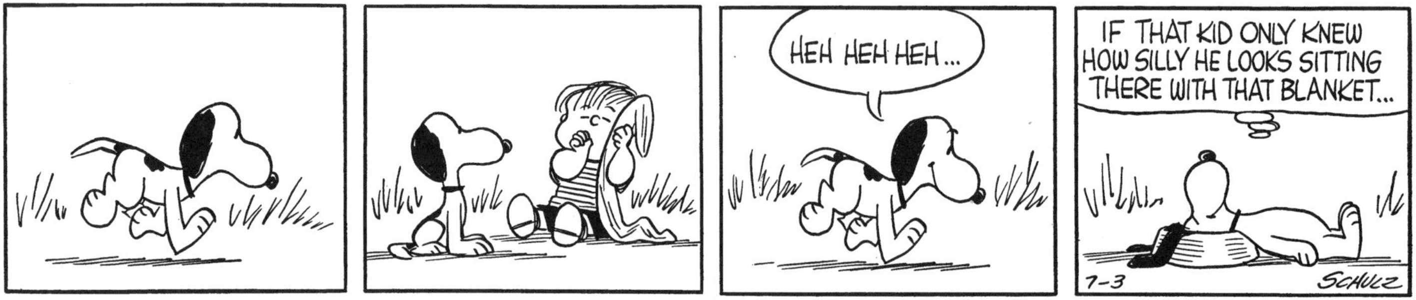
HEH HEH HEH...
IF THAT KID ONLY KNEW HOW SILLY HE LOOKS SITTING THERE WITH THAT BLANKET...
7-3
SCHULZ

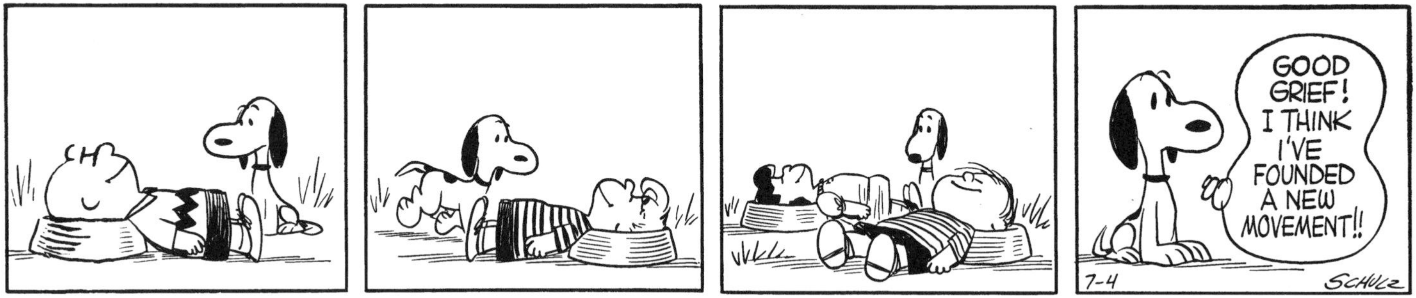
GOOD GRIEF! I THINK I'VE FOUNDED A NEW MOVEMENT!!
7-4
SCHULZ

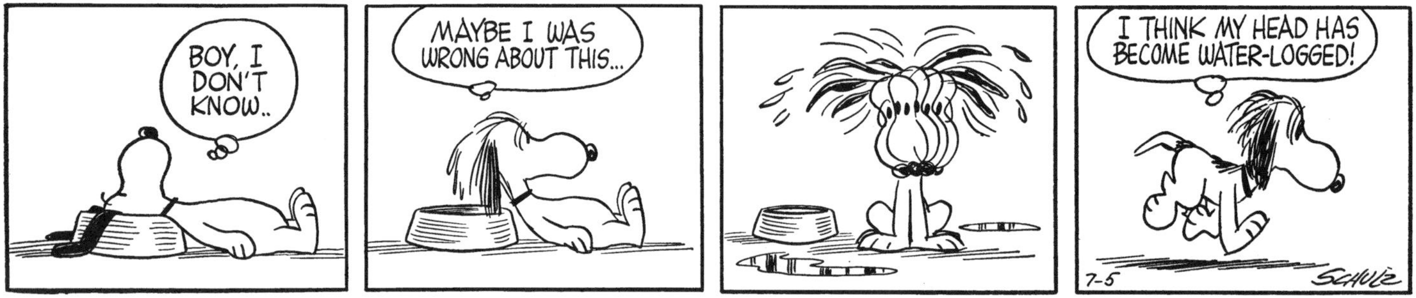
BOY, I DON'T KNOW..
MAYBE I WAS WRONG ABOUT THIS...
I THINK MY HEAD HAS BECOME WATER-LOGGED!
7-5
SCHULZ

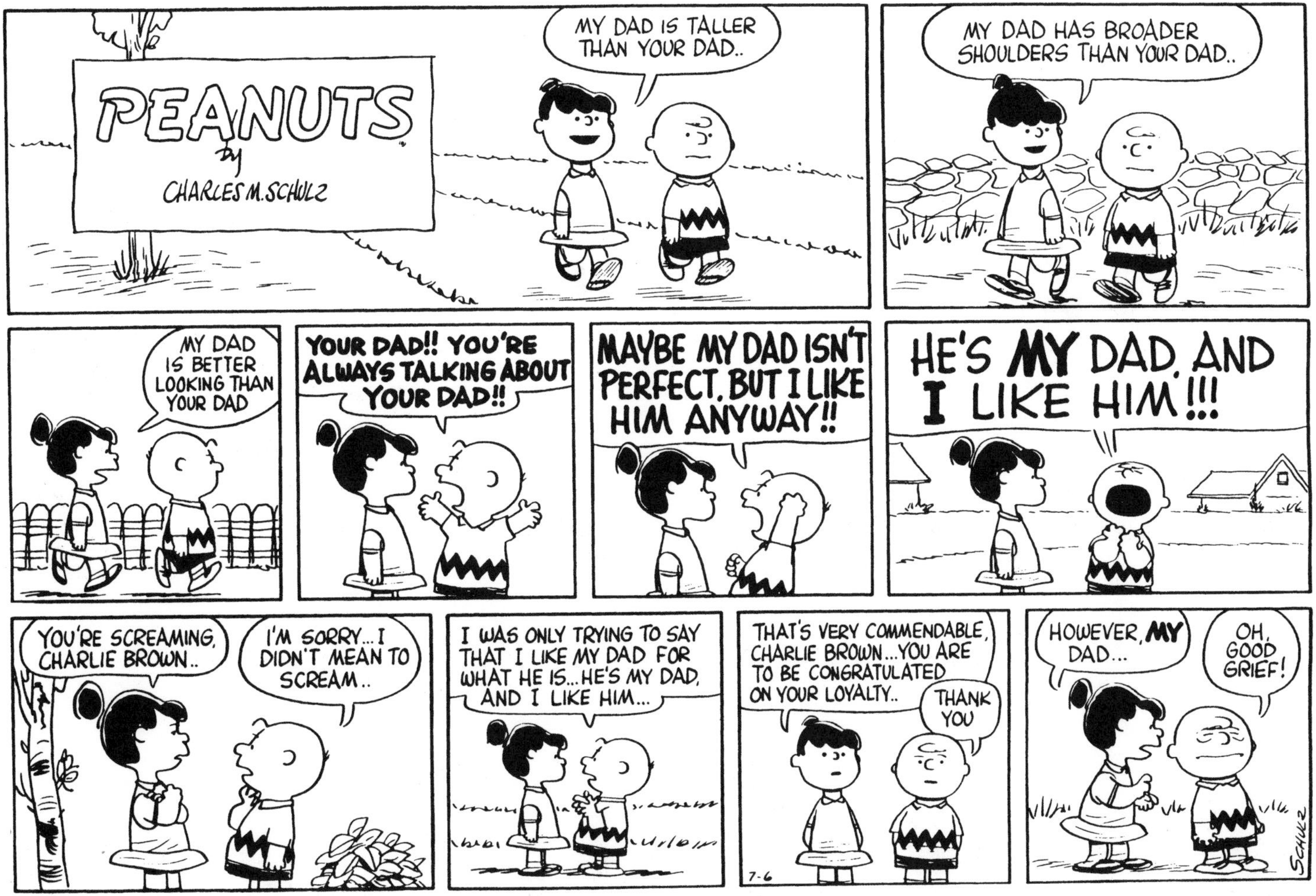
PEANUTS
by
CHARLES M. SCHULZ
MY DAD IS TALLER THAN YOUR DAD..
MY DAD HAS BROADER SHOULDERS THAN YOUR DAD..
MY DAD IS BETTER LOOKING THAN YOUR DAD
YOUR DAD!! YOU'RE ALWAYS TALKING ABOUT YOUR DAD!!
MAYBE MY DAD ISN'T PERFECT, BUT I LIKE HIM ANYWAY!!
HE'S MY DAD, AND I LIKE HIM!!!
YOU'RE SCREAMING, CHARLIE BROWN..
I'M SORRY... I DIDN'T MEAN TO SCREAM..
I WAS ONLY TRYING TO SAY THAT I LIKE MY DAD FOR WHAT HE IS... HE'S MY DAD, AND I LIKE HIM...
THAT'S VERY COMMENDABLE, CHARLIE BROWN... YOU ARE TO BE CONGRATULATED ON YOUR LOYALTY..
THANK YOU
7-6
HOWEVER, MY DAD...
OH, GOOD GRIEF!
SCHULZ

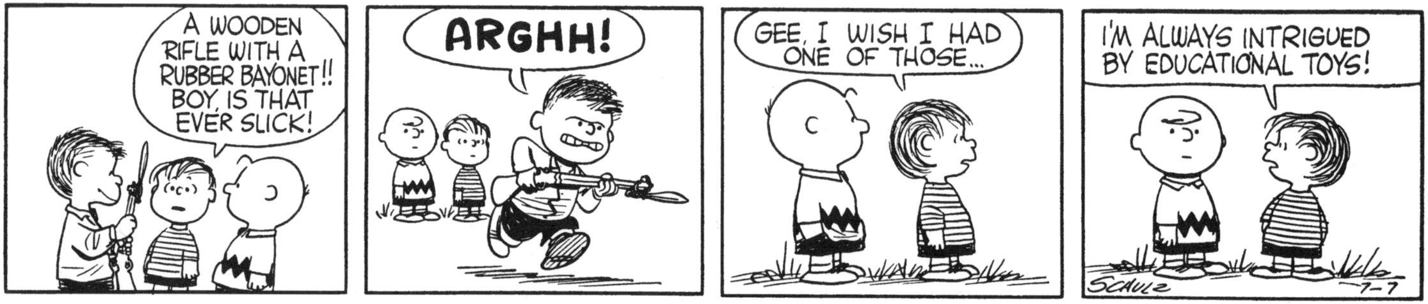
A WOODEN RIFLE WITH A RUBBER BAYONET!! BOY, IS THAT EVER SLICK!
ARGHH!
GEE, I WISH I HAD ONE OF THOSE...
I'M ALWAYS INTRIGUED BY EDUCATIONAL TOYS!
SCHULZ
7-7

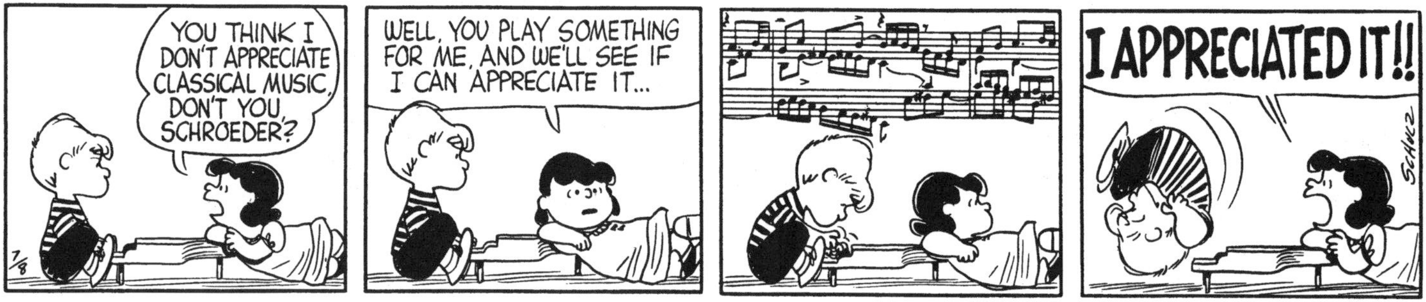
YOU THINK I DON'T APPRECIATE CLASSICAL MUSIC, DON'T YOU, SCHROEDER?
7/8
WELL, YOU PLAY SOMETHING FOR ME, AND WE'LL SEE IF I CAN APPRECIATE IT...
I APPRECIATED IT!!
SCHULZ

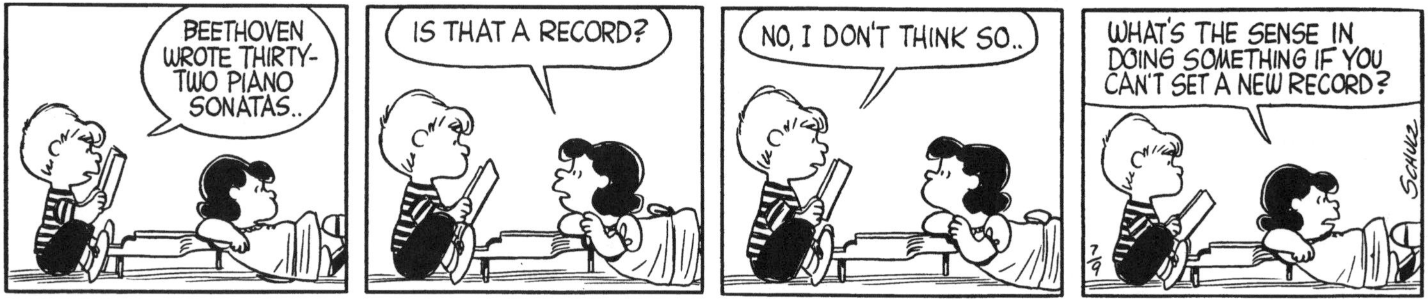
BEETHOVEN WROTE THIRTY-TWO PIANO SONATAS..
IS THAT A RECORD?
NO, I DON'T THINK SO..
WHAT'S THE SENSE IN DOING SOMETHING IF YOU CAN'T SET A NEW RECORD?
SCHULZ
7/9

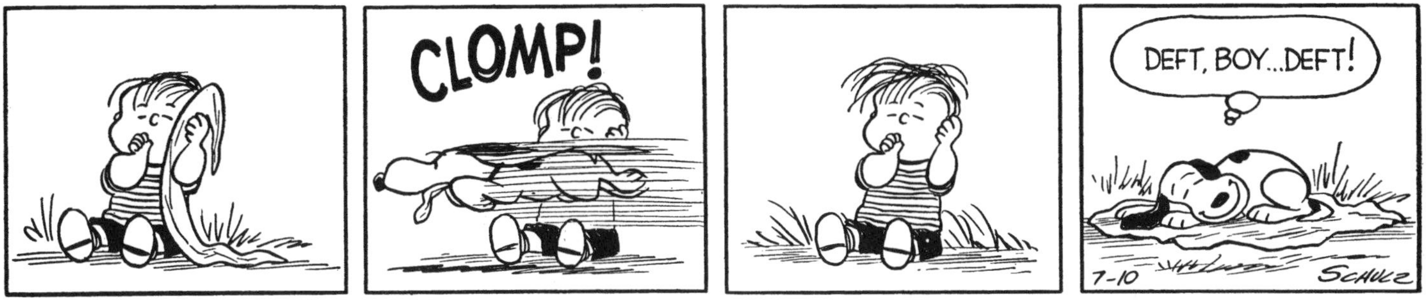
CLOMP!
DEFT, BOY...DEFT!
7-10
SCHULZ

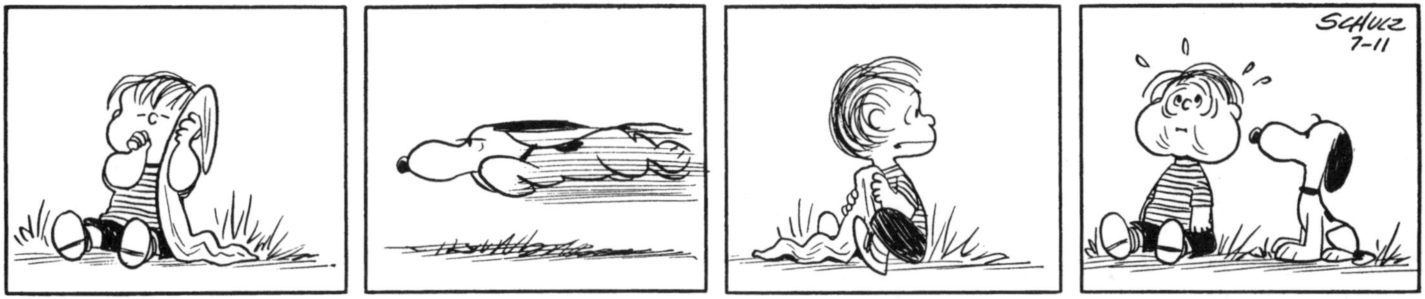
SCHULZ
7-11

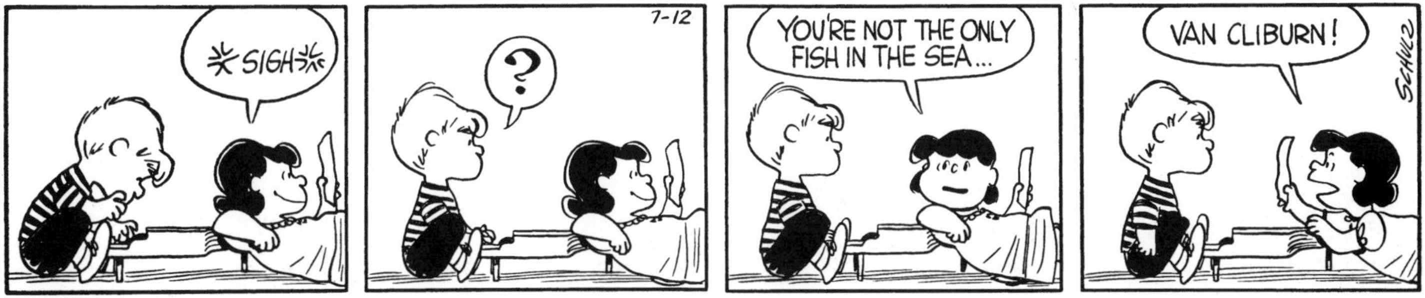
SIGH
7-12
?
YOU'RE NOT THE ONLY FISH IN THE SEA...
VAN CLIBURN!
SCHULZ

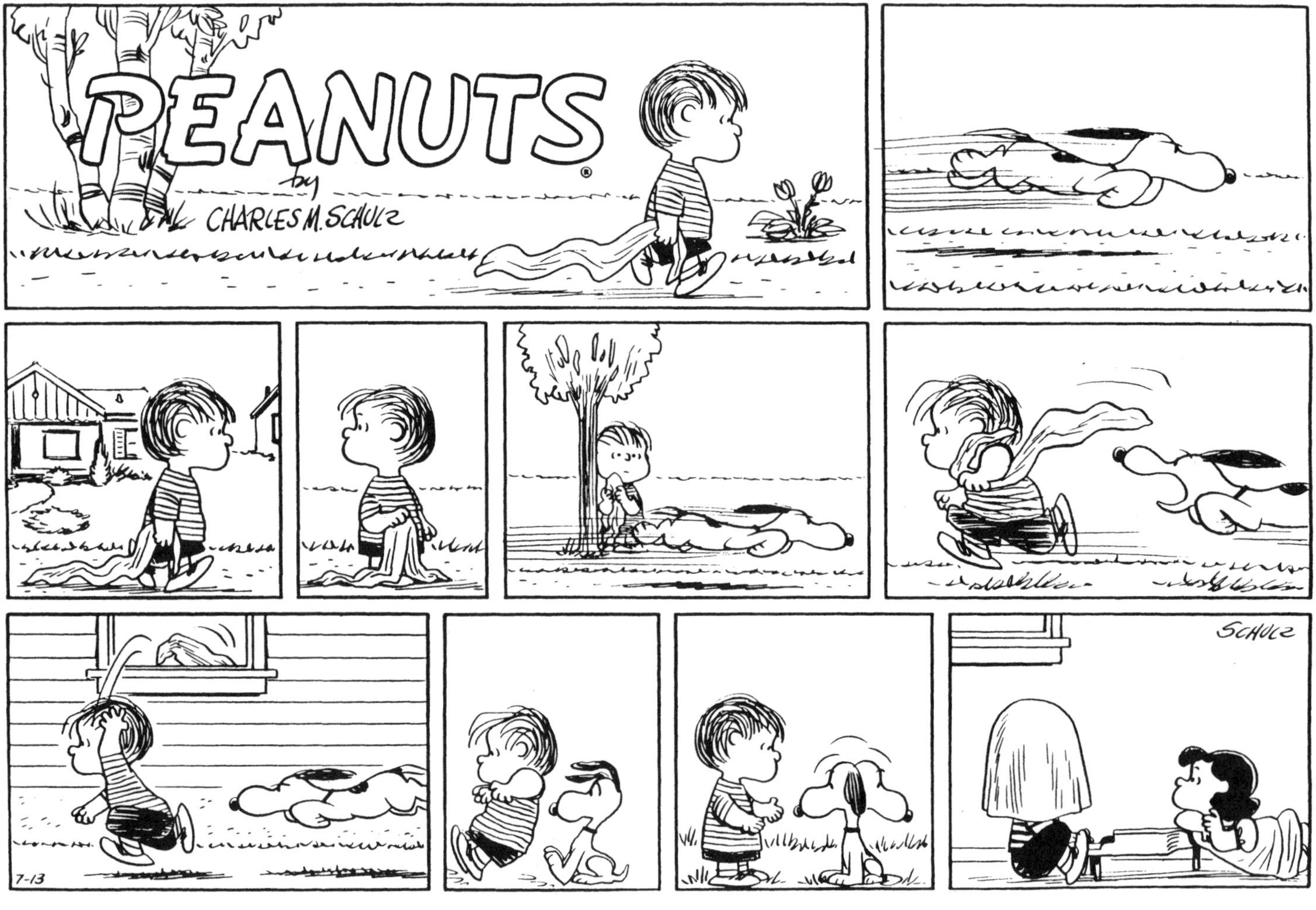
PEANUTS
by
CHARLES M. SCHULZ
7-13
SCHULZ

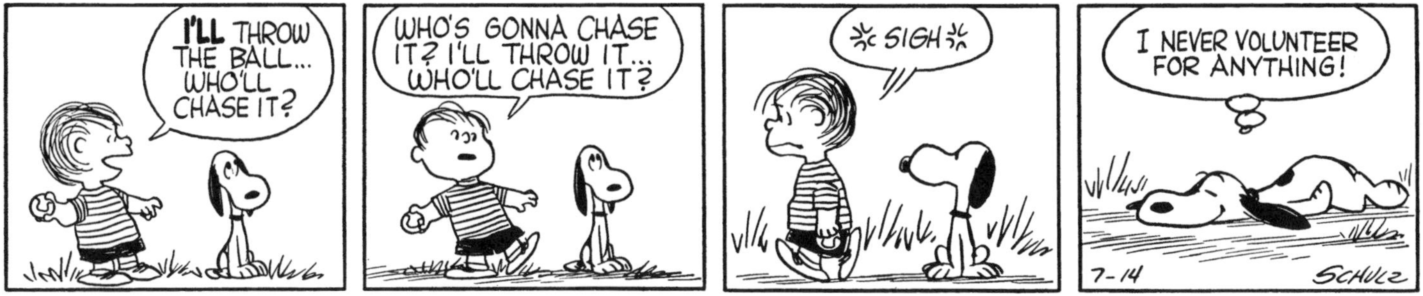
I'LL THROW THE BALL... WHO'LL CHASE IT?
WHO'S GONNA CHASE IT? I'LL THROW IT... WHO'LL CHASE IT?
SIGH
I NEVER VOLUNTEER FOR ANYTHING!
7-14
SCHULZ

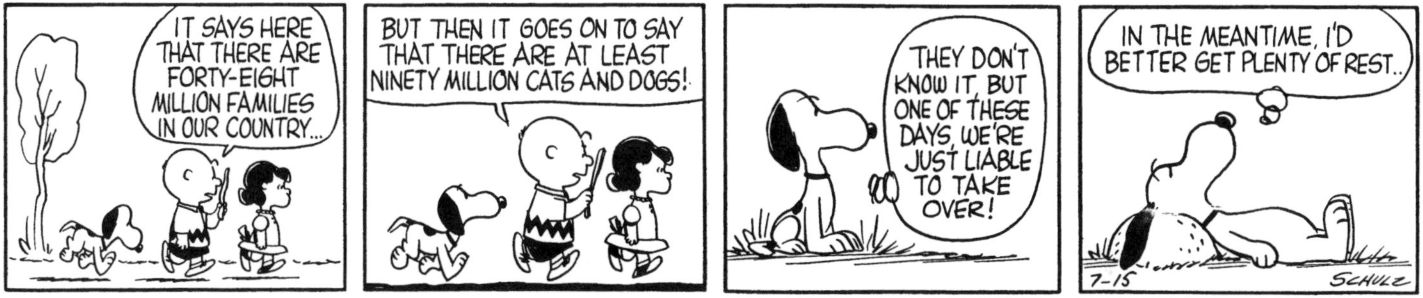
IT SAYS HERE THAT THERE ARE FORTY-EIGHT MILLION FAMILIES IN OUR COUNTRY...
BUT THEN IT GOES ON TO SAY THAT THERE ARE AT LEAST NINETY MILLION CATS AND DOGS!
THEY DON'T KNOW IT, BUT ONE OF THESE DAYS, WE'RE JUST LIABLE TO TAKE OVER!
IN THE MEANTIME, I'D BETTER GET PLENTY OF REST..
7-15
SCHULZ

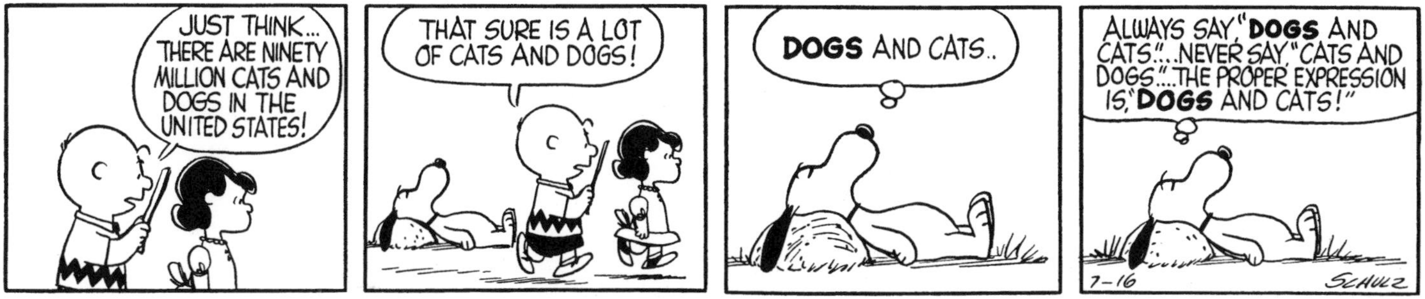
JUST THINK... THERE ARE NINETY MILLION CATS AND DOGS IN THE UNITED STATES!
THAT SURE IS A LOT OF CATS AND DOGS!
DOGS AND CATS..
ALWAYS SAY, "DOGS AND CATS."...NEVER SAY, "CATS AND DOGS."...THE PROPER EXPRESSION IS, "DOGS AND CATS!"
7-16
SCHULZ

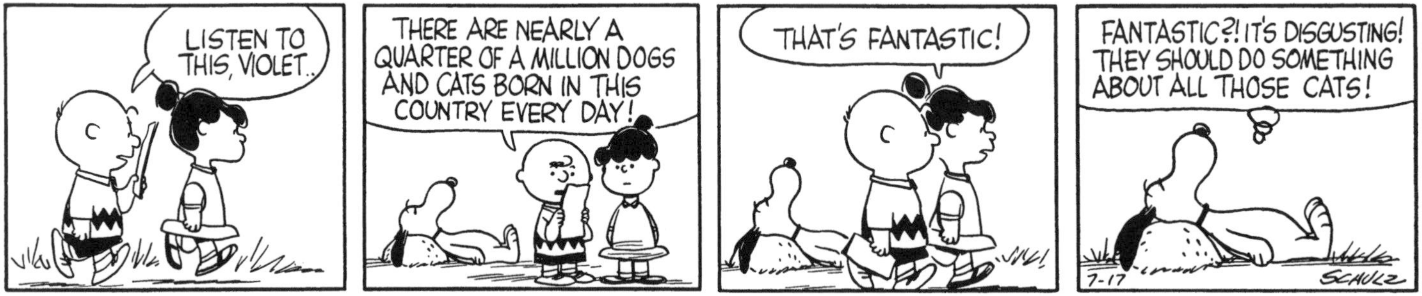
LISTEN TO THIS, VIOLET..
THERE ARE NEARLY A QUARTER OF A MILLION DOGS AND CATS BORN IN THIS COUNTRY EVERY DAY!
THAT'S FANTASTIC!
FANTASTIC?! IT'S DISGUSTING! THEY SHOULD DO SOMETHING ABOUT ALL THOSE CATS!
7-17
SCHULZ

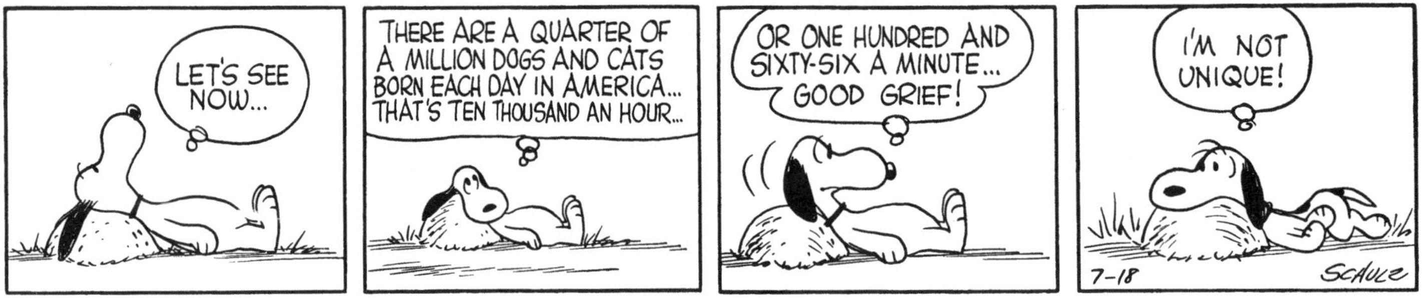
LET'S SEE NOW...
THERE ARE A QUARTER OF A MILLION DOGS AND CATS BORN EACH DAY IN AMERICA... THAT'S TEN THOUSAND AN HOUR...
OR ONE HUNDRED AND SIXTY-SIX A MINUTE... GOOD GRIEF!
I'M NOT UNIQUE!
7-18
SCHULZ

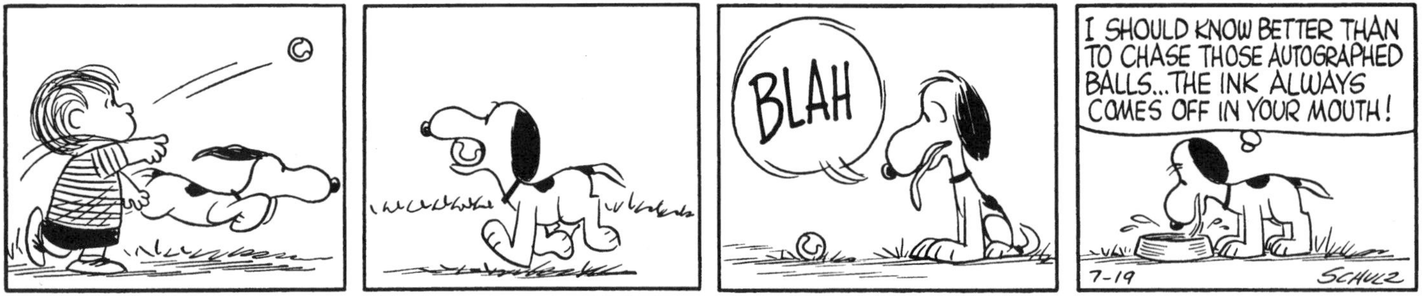
BLAH
I SHOULD KNOW BETTER THAN TO CHASE THOSE AUTOGRAPHED BALLS...THE INK ALWAYS COMES OFF IN YOUR MOUTH!
7-19
SCHULZ

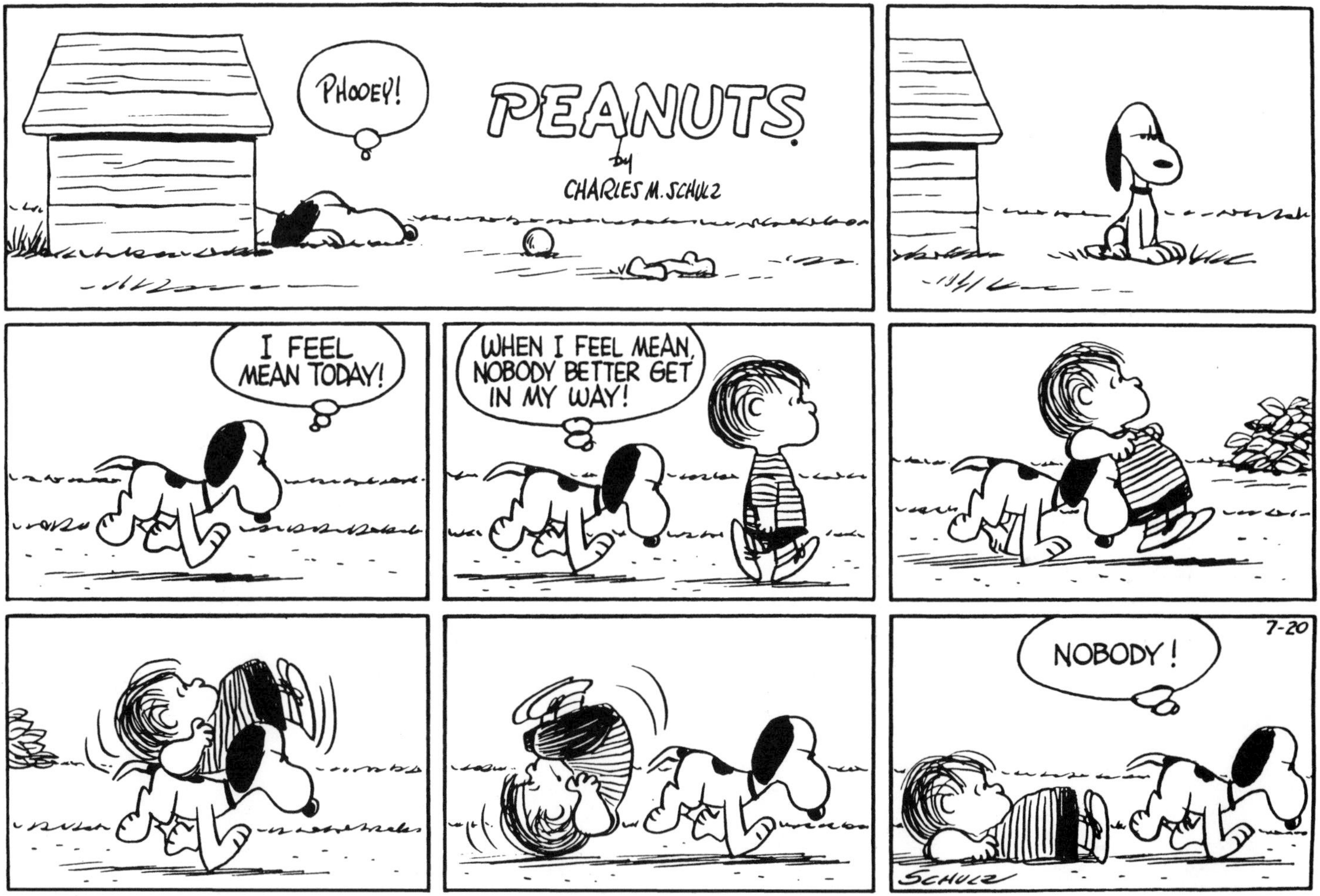
PHOOEY!
PEANUTS
by
CHARLES M. SCHULZ
I FEEL MEAN TODAY!
WHEN I FEEL MEAN, NOBODY BETTER GET IN MY WAY!
7-20
NOBODY!
SCHULZ

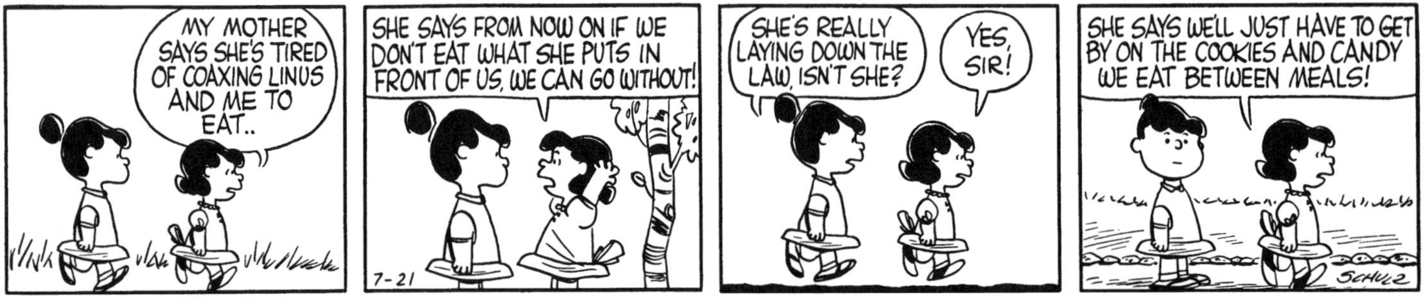
MY MOTHER SAYS SHE'S TIRED OF COAXING LINUS AND ME TO EAT..
SHE SAYS FROM NOW ON IF WE DON'T EAT WHAT SHE PUTS IN FRONT OF US, WE CAN GO WITHOUT!
SHE'S REALLY LAYING DOWN THE LAW, ISN'T SHE?
YES, SIR!
SHE SAYS WE'LL JUST HAVE TO GET BY ON THE COOKIES AND CANDY WE EAT BETWEEN MEALS!

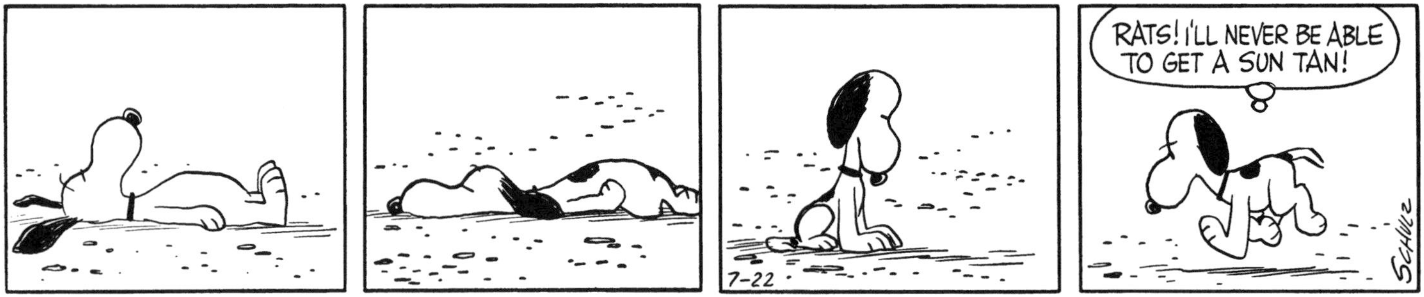
RATS! I'LL NEVER BE ABLE TO GET A SUN TAN!

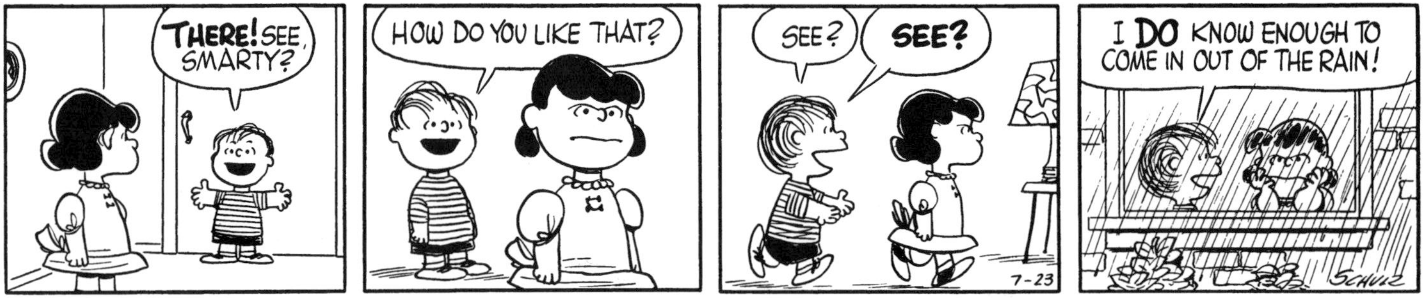
THERE! SEE, SMARTY?
HOW DO YOU LIKE THAT?
SEE?
SEE?
I DO KNOW ENOUGH TO COME IN OUT OF THE RAIN!

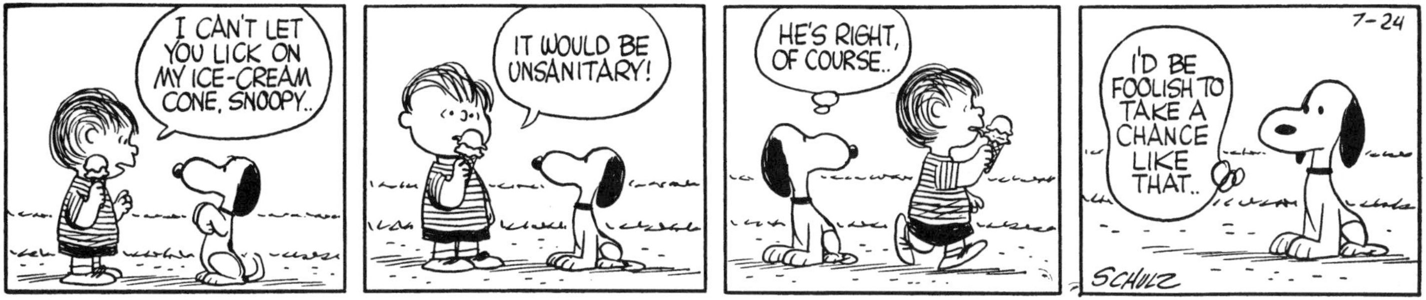
I CAN'T LET YOU LICK ON MY ICE-CREAM CONE, SNOOPY..
IT WOULD BE UNSANITARY!
HE'S RIGHT, OF COURSE..
7-24
I'D BE FOOLISH TO TAKE A CHANCE LIKE THAT..
SCHULZ

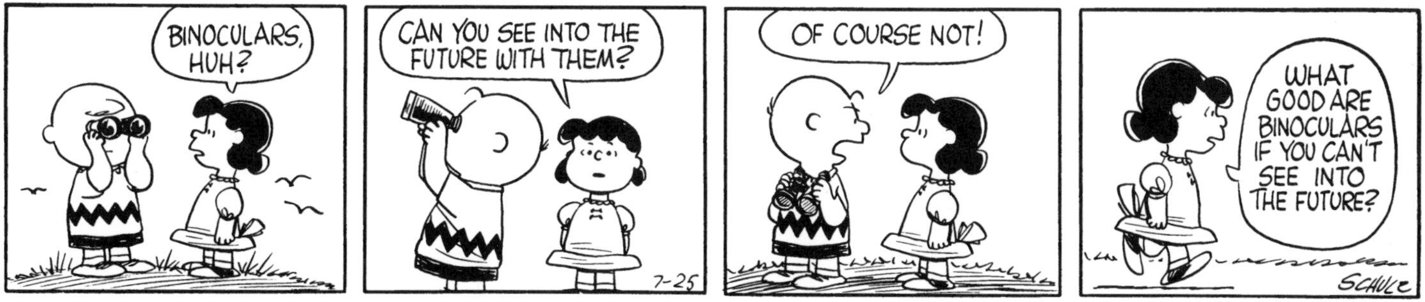
BINOCULARS, HUH?
CAN YOU SEE INTO THE FUTURE WITH THEM?
7-25
OF COURSE NOT!
WHAT GOOD ARE BINOCULARS IF YOU CAN'T SEE INTO THE FUTURE?
SCHULZ

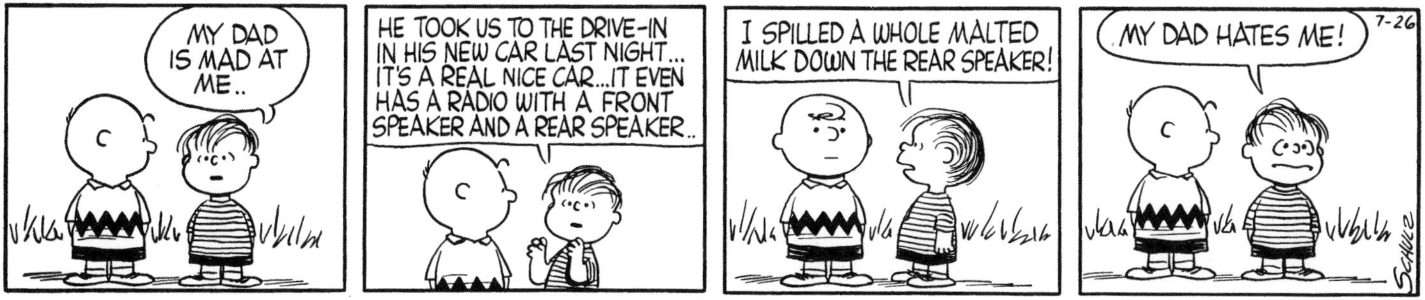
MY DAD IS MAD AT ME..
HE TOOK US TO THE DRIVE-IN IN HIS NEW CAR LAST NIGHT... IT'S A REAL NICE CAR...IT EVEN HAS A RADIO WITH A FRONT SPEAKER AND A REAR SPEAKER..
I SPILLED A WHOLE MALTED MILK DOWN THE REAR SPEAKER!
MY DAD HATES ME!
7-26
SCHULZ

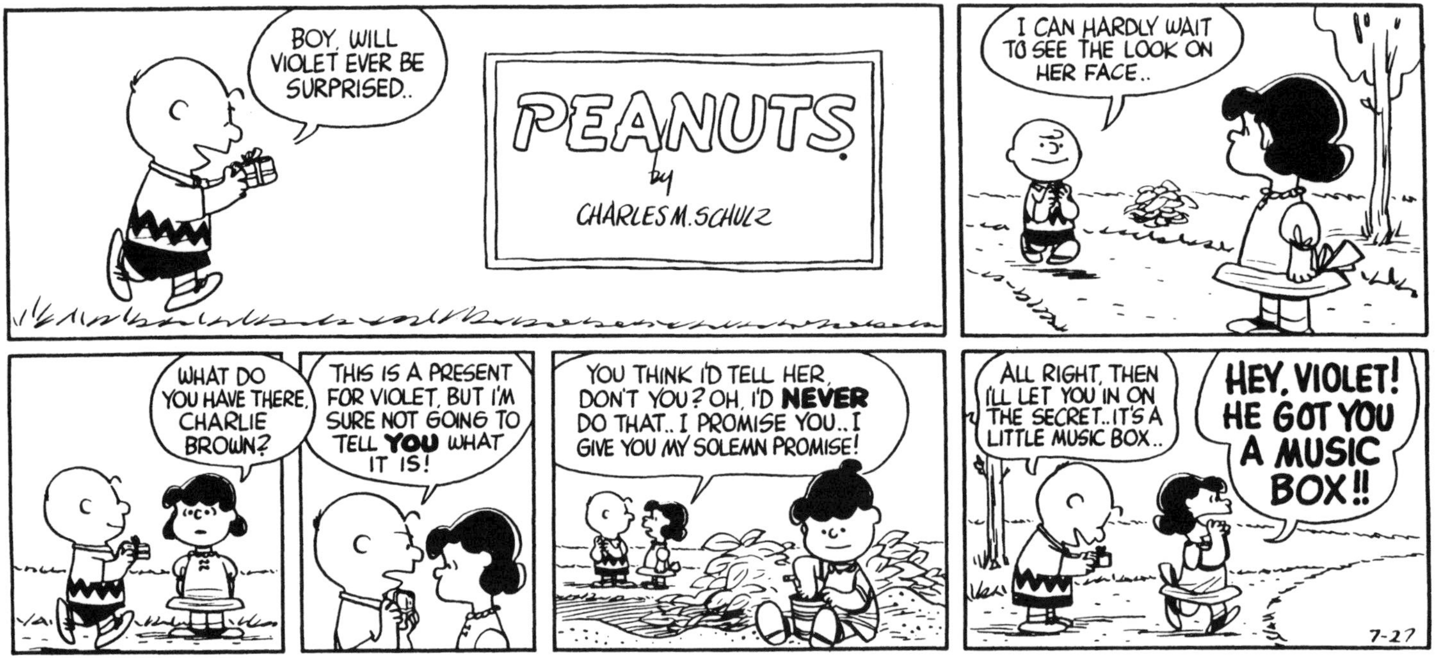
BOY, WILL VIOLET EVER BE SURPRISED..
PEANUTS by CHARLES M. SCHULZ
I CAN HARDLY WAIT TO SEE THE LOOK ON HER FACE..
WHAT DO YOU HAVE THERE, CHARLIE BROWN?
THIS IS A PRESENT FOR VIOLET, BUT I'M SURE NOT GOING TO TELL YOU WHAT IT IS!
YOU THINK I'D TELL HER, DON'T YOU? OH, I'D NEVER DO THAT.. I PROMISE YOU.. I GIVE YOU MY SOLEMN PROMISE!
ALL RIGHT, THEN I'LL LET YOU IN ON THE SECRET.. IT'S A LITTLE MUSIC BOX..
HEY, VIOLET! HE GOT YOU A MUSIC BOX!!
7-27

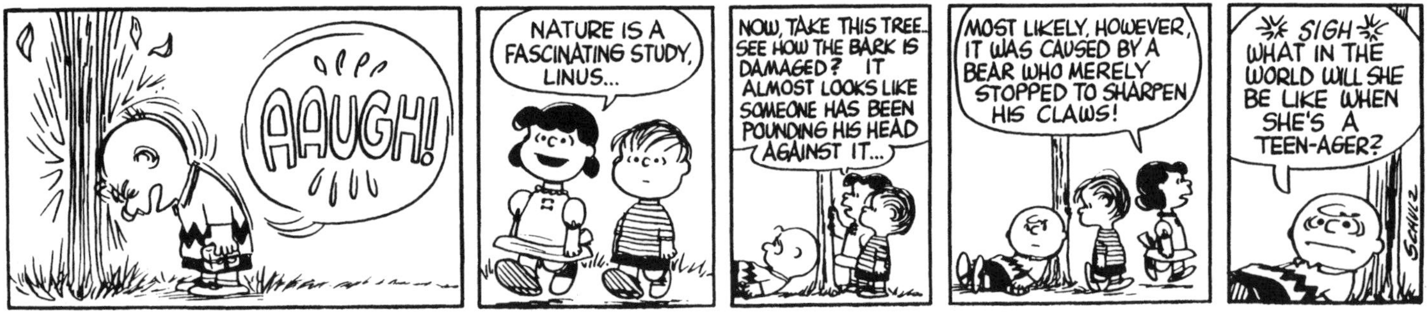
AAUGH!
NATURE IS A FASCINATING STUDY, LINUS...
NOW, TAKE THIS TREE.. SEE HOW THE BARK IS DAMAGED? IT ALMOST LOOKS LIKE SOMEONE HAS BEEN POUNDING HIS HEAD AGAINST IT...
MOST LIKELY, HOWEVER, IT WAS CAUSED BY A BEAR WHO MERELY STOPPED TO SHARPEN HIS CLAWS!
SIGH
WHAT IN THE WORLD WILL SHE BE LIKE WHEN SHE'S A TEEN-AGER?
SCHULZ

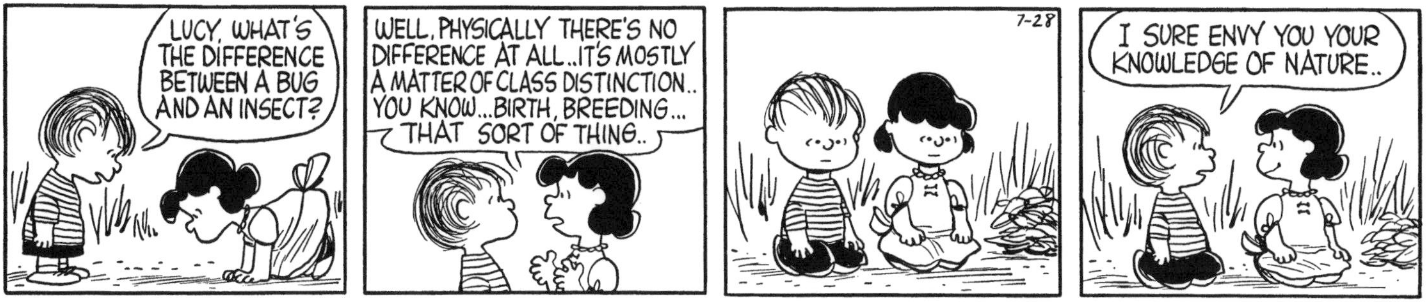
LUCY, WHAT'S THE DIFFERENCE BETWEEN A BUG AND AN INSECT?
WELL, PHYSICALLY THERE'S NO DIFFERENCE AT ALL..IT'S MOSTLY A MATTER OF CLASS DISTINCTION.. YOU KNOW...BIRTH, BREEDING... THAT SORT OF THING..
7-28
I SURE ENVY YOU YOUR KNOWLEDGE OF NATURE..

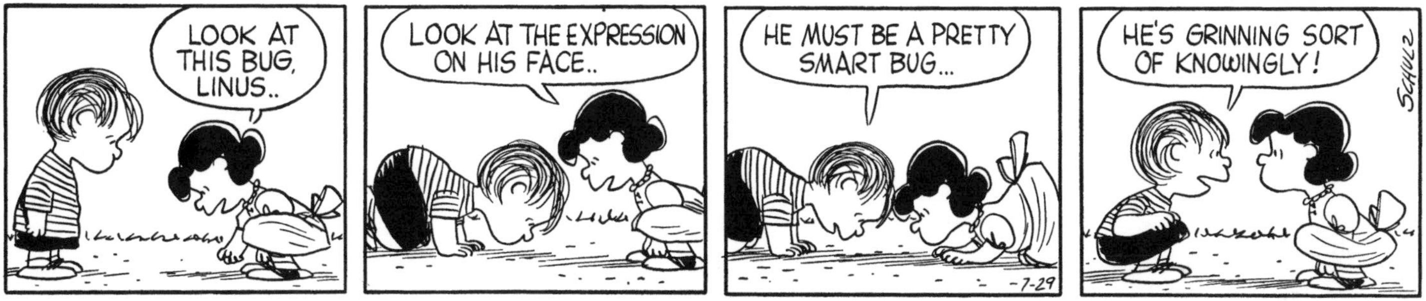
LOOK AT THIS BUG, LINUS..
LOOK AT THE EXPRESSION ON HIS FACE..
HE MUST BE A PRETTY SMART BUG...
7-29
HE'S GRINNING SORT OF KNOWINGLY!
SCHULZ

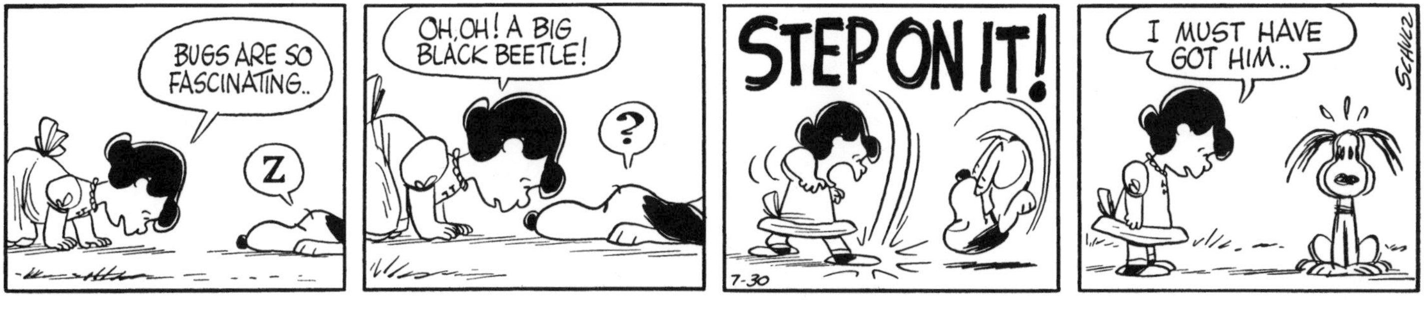
BUGS ARE SO FASCINATING..
Z
OH, OH! A BIG BLACK BEETLE!
?
STEP ON IT!
7-30
I MUST HAVE GOT HIM..
SCHULZ

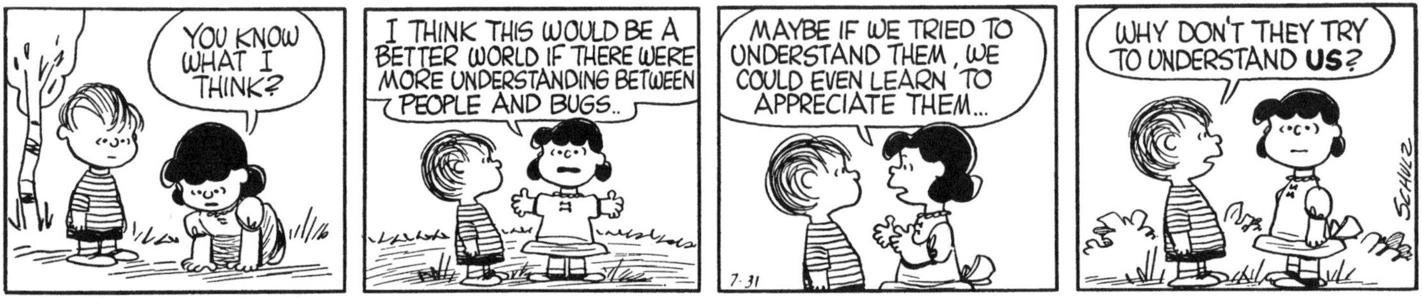
YOU KNOW WHAT I THINK?
I THINK THIS WOULD BE A BETTER WORLD IF THERE WERE MORE UNDERSTANDING BETWEEN PEOPLE AND BUGS..
MAYBE IF WE TRIED TO UNDERSTAND THEM, WE COULD EVEN LEARN TO APPRECIATE THEM...
7-31
WHY DON'T THEY TRY TO UNDERSTAND **US**?
SCHULZ

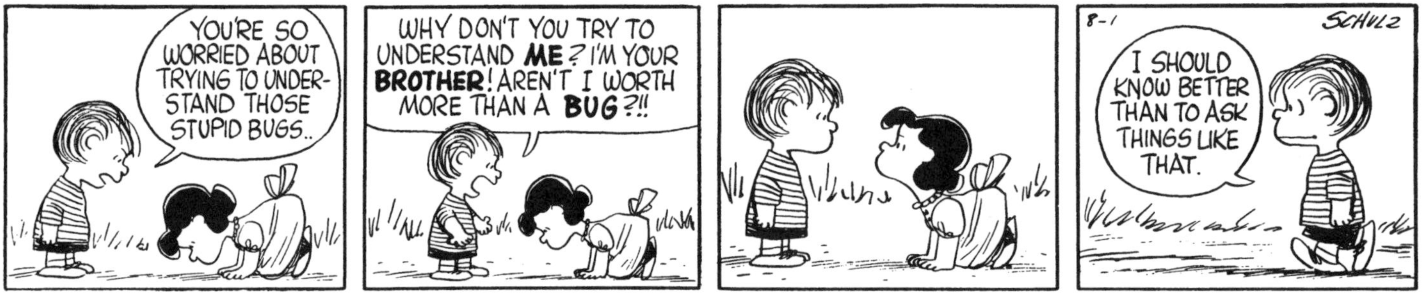
YOU'RE SO WORRIED ABOUT TRYING TO UNDERSTAND THOSE STUPID BUGS..
WHY DON'T YOU TRY TO UNDERSTAND **ME**? I'M YOUR **BROTHER**! AREN'T I WORTH MORE THAN A **BUG**?!!
8-1
SCHULZ
I SHOULD KNOW BETTER THAN TO ASK THINGS LIKE THAT.

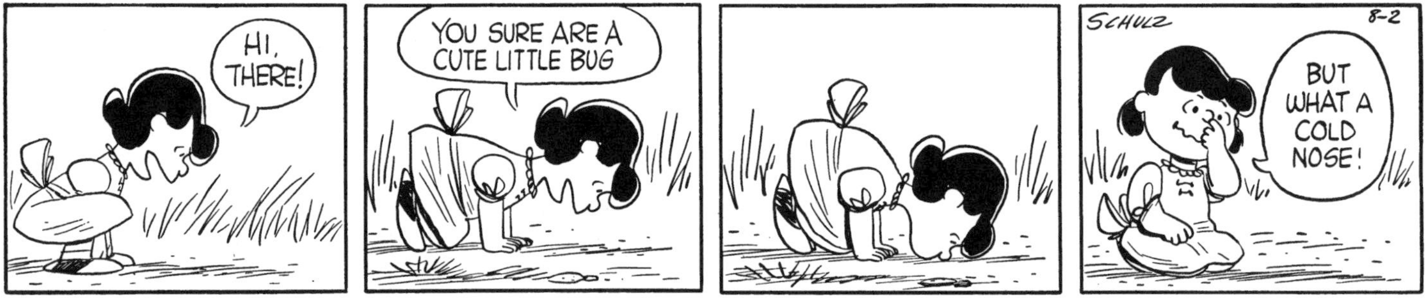
HI, THERE!
YOU SURE ARE A CUTE LITTLE BUG
SCHULZ
8-2
BUT WHAT A COLD NOSE!

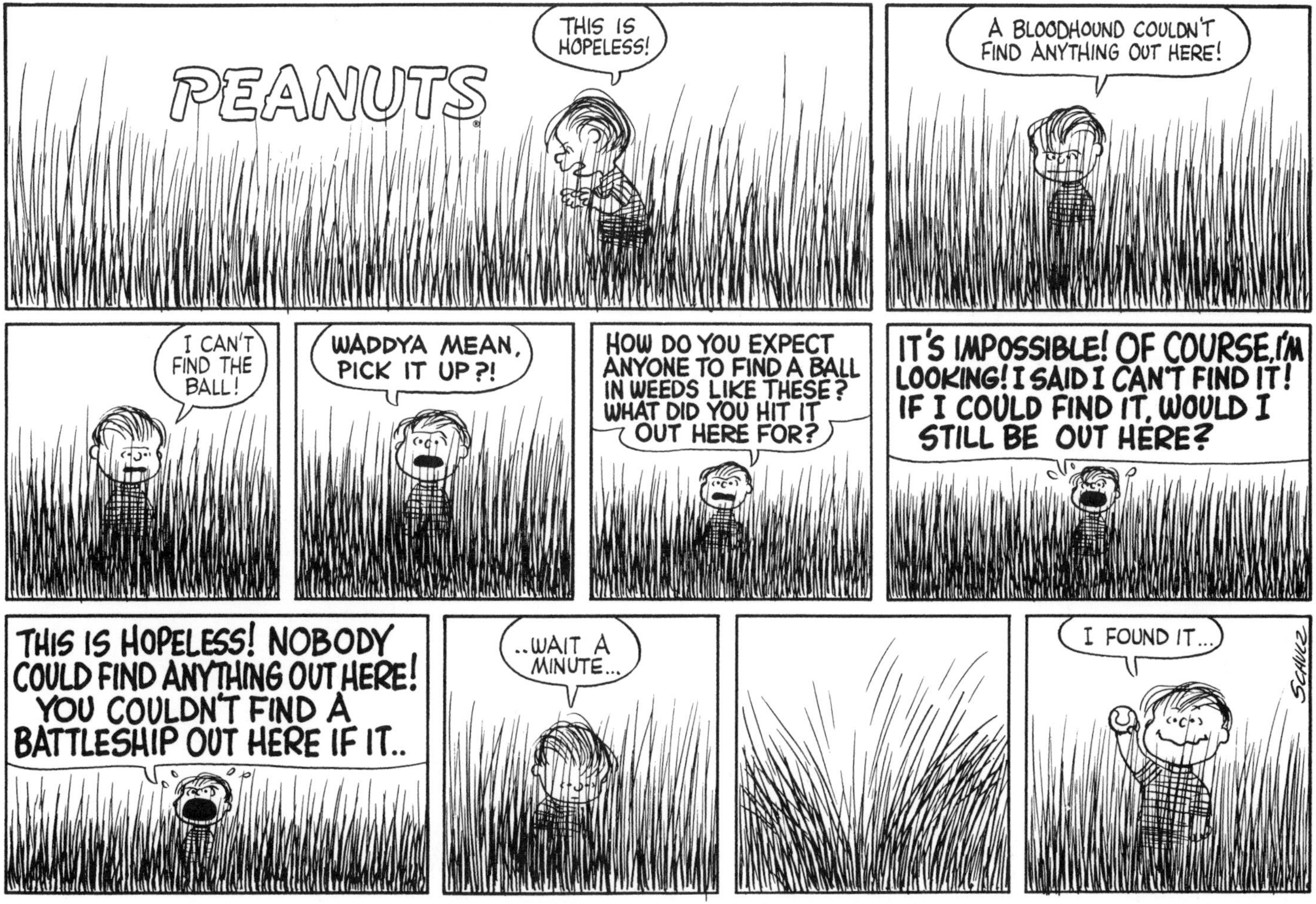
PEANUTS
THIS IS HOPELESS!
A BLOODHOUND COULDN'T FIND ANYTHING OUT HERE!
I CAN'T FIND THE BALL!
WADDYA MEAN, PICK IT UP?!
HOW DO YOU EXPECT ANYONE TO FIND A BALL IN WEEDS LIKE THESE? WHAT DID YOU HIT IT OUT HERE FOR?
IT'S IMPOSSIBLE! OF COURSE, I'M LOOKING! I SAID I CAN'T FIND IT! IF I COULD FIND IT, WOULD I STILL BE OUT HERE?
THIS IS HOPELESS! NOBODY COULD FIND ANYTHING OUT HERE! YOU COULDN'T FIND A BATTLESHIP OUT HERE IF IT..
..WAIT A MINUTE...
I FOUND IT...
SCHULZ

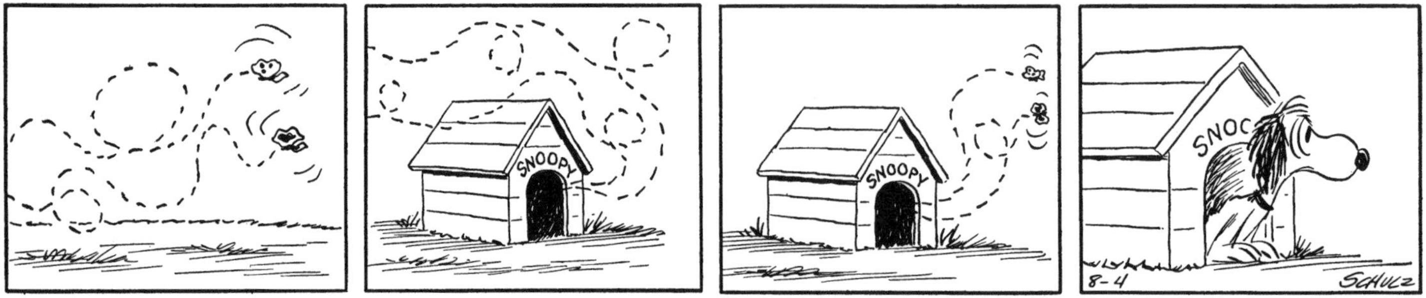
SNOOPY
SNOOPY
SNOO
8-4
SCHULZ

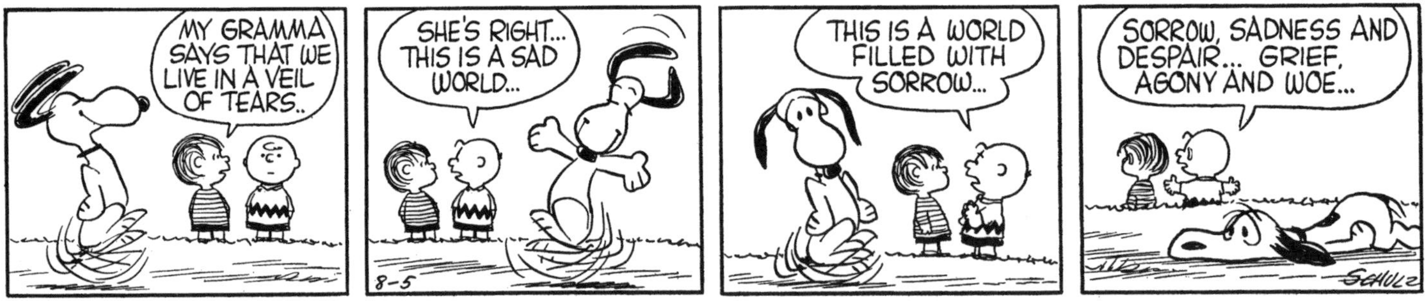
MY GRAMMA SAYS THAT WE LIVE IN A VEIL OF TEARS..
SHE'S RIGHT... THIS IS A SAD WORLD...
8-5
THIS IS A WORLD FILLED WITH SORROW...
SORROW, SADNESS AND DESPAIR... GRIEF, AGONY AND WOE...
SCHULZ

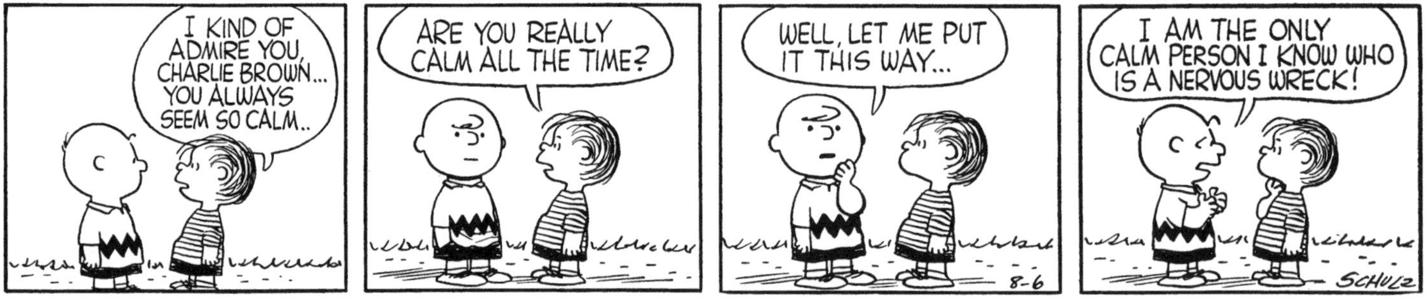
I KIND OF ADMIRE YOU, CHARLIE BROWN... YOU ALWAYS SEEM SO CALM..
ARE YOU REALLY CALM ALL THE TIME?
WELL, LET ME PUT IT THIS WAY...
8-6
I AM THE ONLY CALM PERSON I KNOW WHO IS A NERVOUS WRECK!
SCHULZ

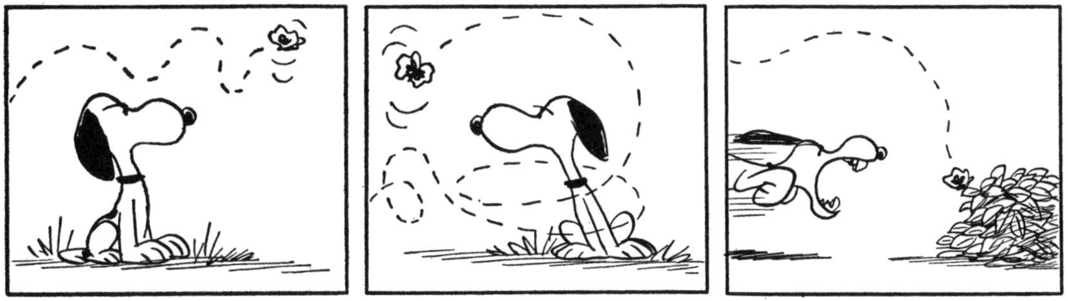
8-7
SCHULZ

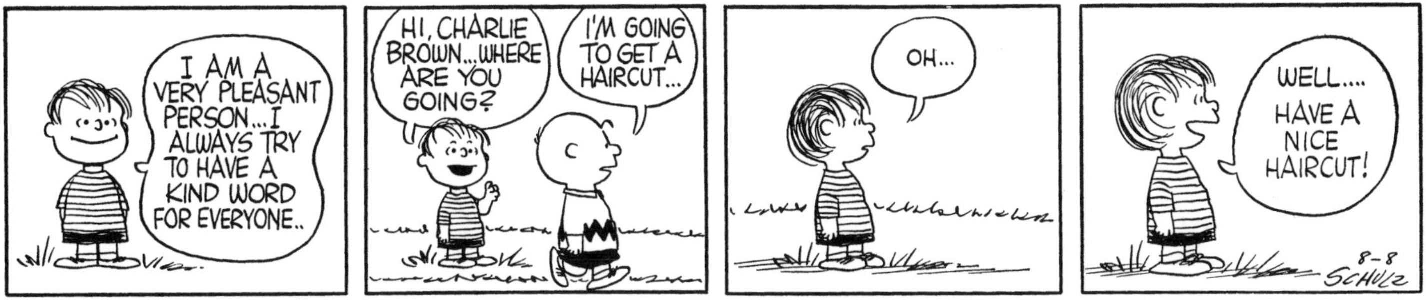
I AM A VERY PLEASANT PERSON...I ALWAYS TRY TO HAVE A KIND WORD FOR EVERYONE..
HI, CHARLIE BROWN...WHERE ARE YOU GOING?
I'M GOING TO GET A HAIRCUT...
OH...
WELL.... HAVE A NICE HAIRCUT!
8-8
SCHULZ

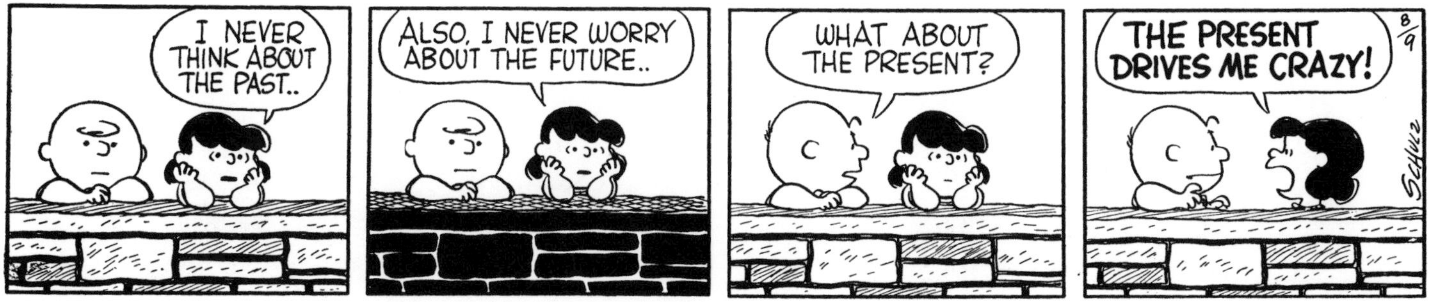
I NEVER THINK ABOUT THE PAST..
ALSO, I NEVER WORRY ABOUT THE FUTURE..
WHAT ABOUT THE PRESENT?
THE PRESENT DRIVES ME CRAZY!
8/9
SCHULZ

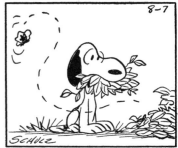

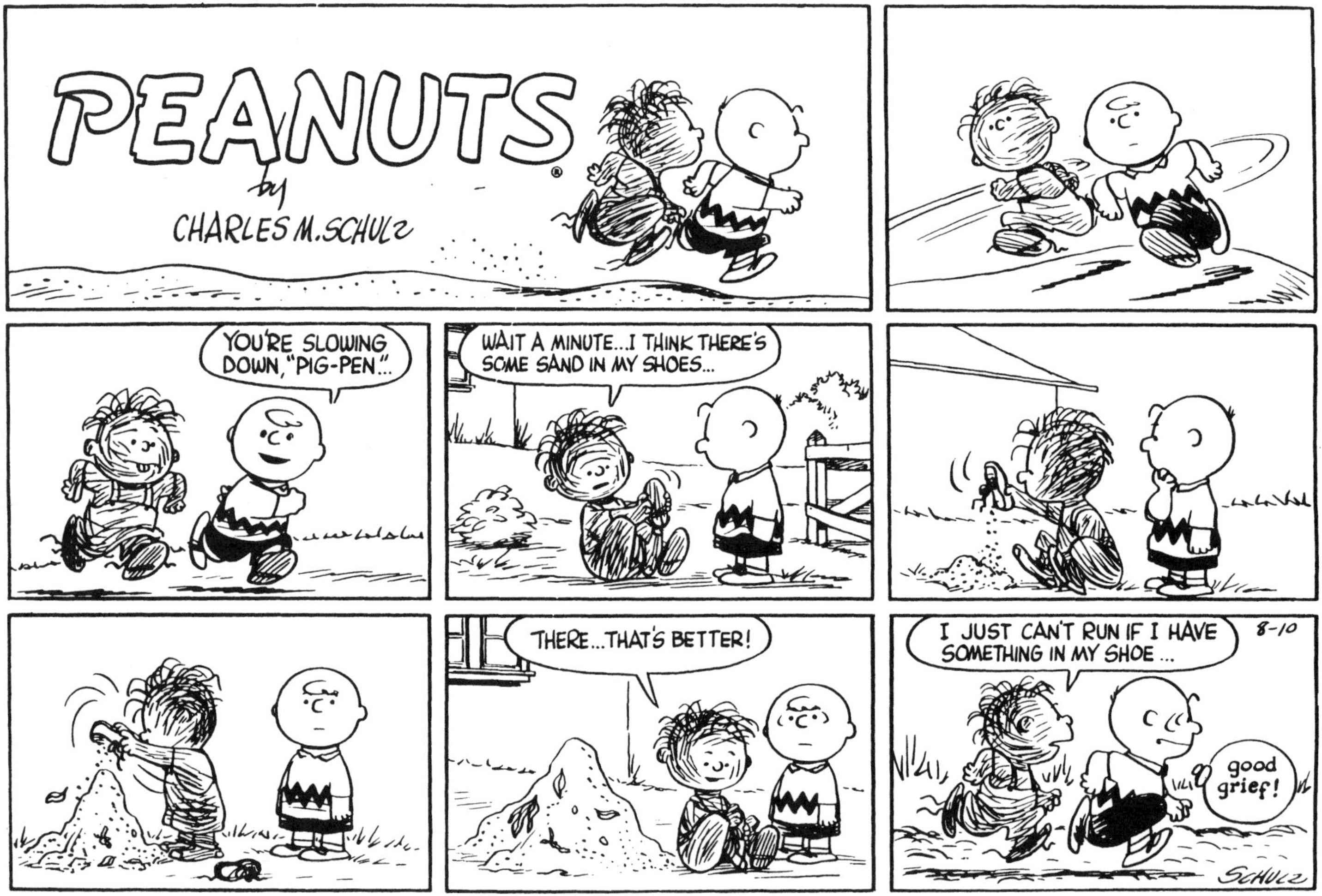
PEANUTS
by
CHARLES M. SCHULZ
YOU'RE SLOWING DOWN, "PIG-PEN."
WAIT A MINUTE...I THINK THERE'S SOME SAND IN MY SHOES...
THERE...THAT'S BETTER!
I JUST CAN'T RUN IF I HAVE SOMETHING IN MY SHOE ...
8-10
good grief!
SCHULZ

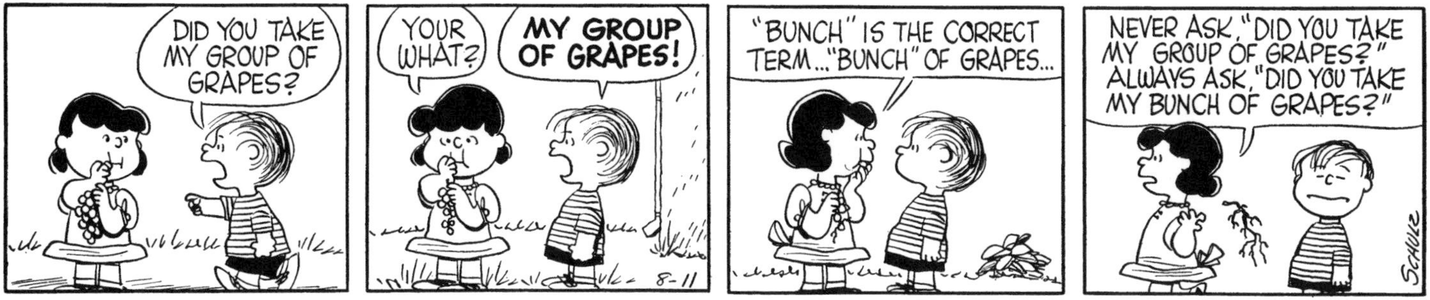
DID YOU TAKE MY GROUP OF GRAPES?
YOUR WHAT?
MY GROUP OF GRAPES!
8-11
"BUNCH" IS THE CORRECT TERM..."BUNCH" OF GRAPES...
NEVER ASK, "DID YOU TAKE MY GROUP OF GRAPES?" ALWAYS ASK, "DID YOU TAKE MY BUNCH OF GRAPES?"
SCHULZ

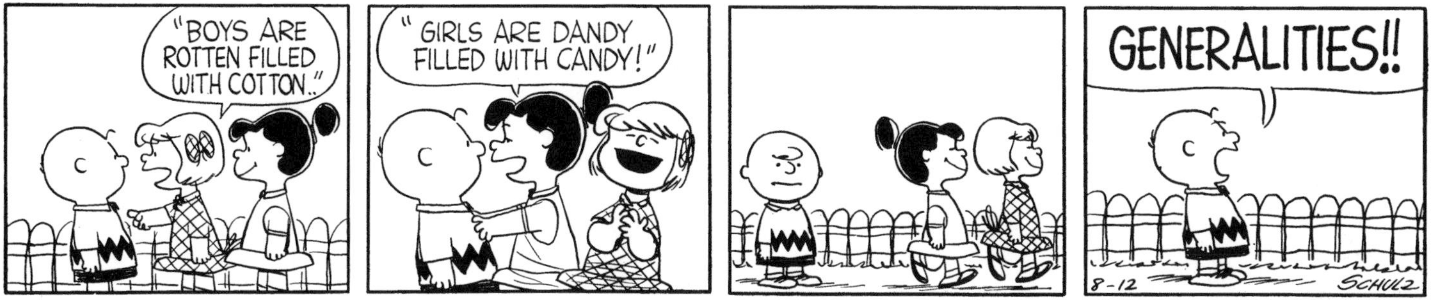
"BOYS ARE ROTTEN FILLED WITH COTTON."
"GIRLS ARE DANDY FILLED WITH CANDY!"
GENERALITIES!!
8-12
SCHULZ

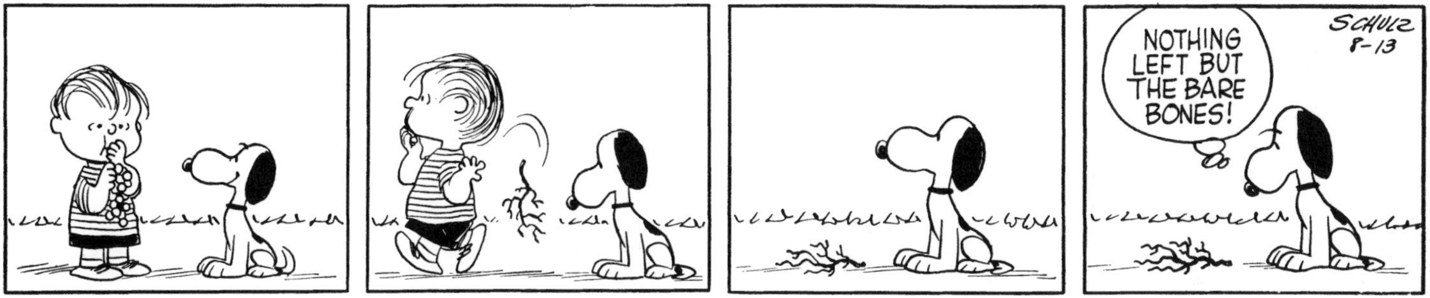
SCHULZ
8-13
NOTHING LEFT BUT THE BARE BONES!

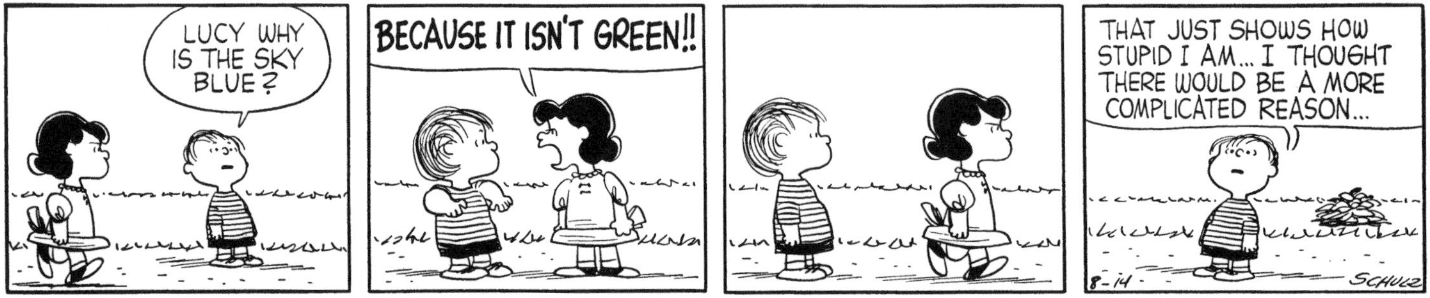
LUCY WHY IS THE SKY BLUE?
BECAUSE IT ISN'T GREEN!!
THAT JUST SHOWS HOW STUPID I AM... I THOUGHT THERE WOULD BE A MORE COMPLICATED REASON...

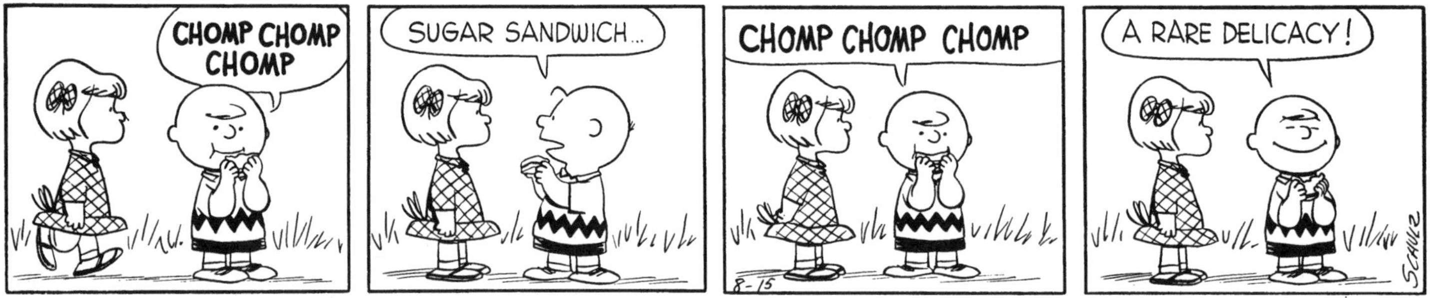
CHOMP CHOMP CHOMP
SUGAR SANDWICH...
CHOMP CHOMP CHOMP
A RARE DELICACY!

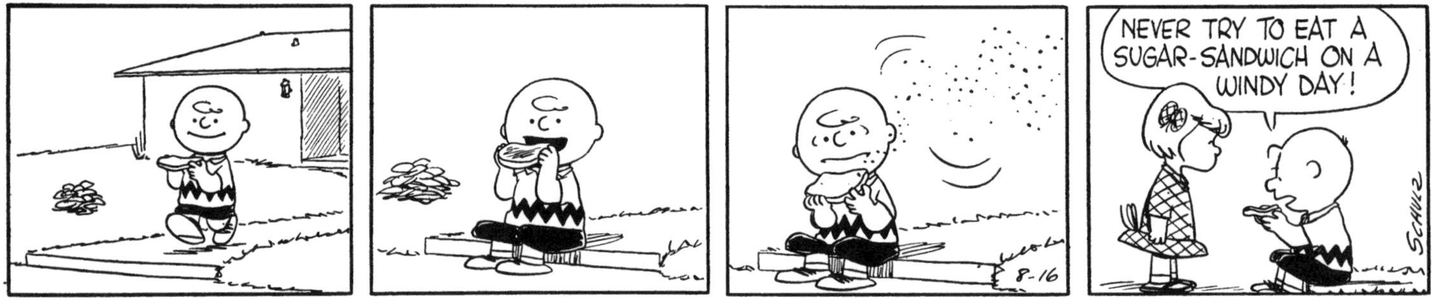
NEVER TRY TO EAT A SUGAR-SANDWICH ON A WINDY DAY!

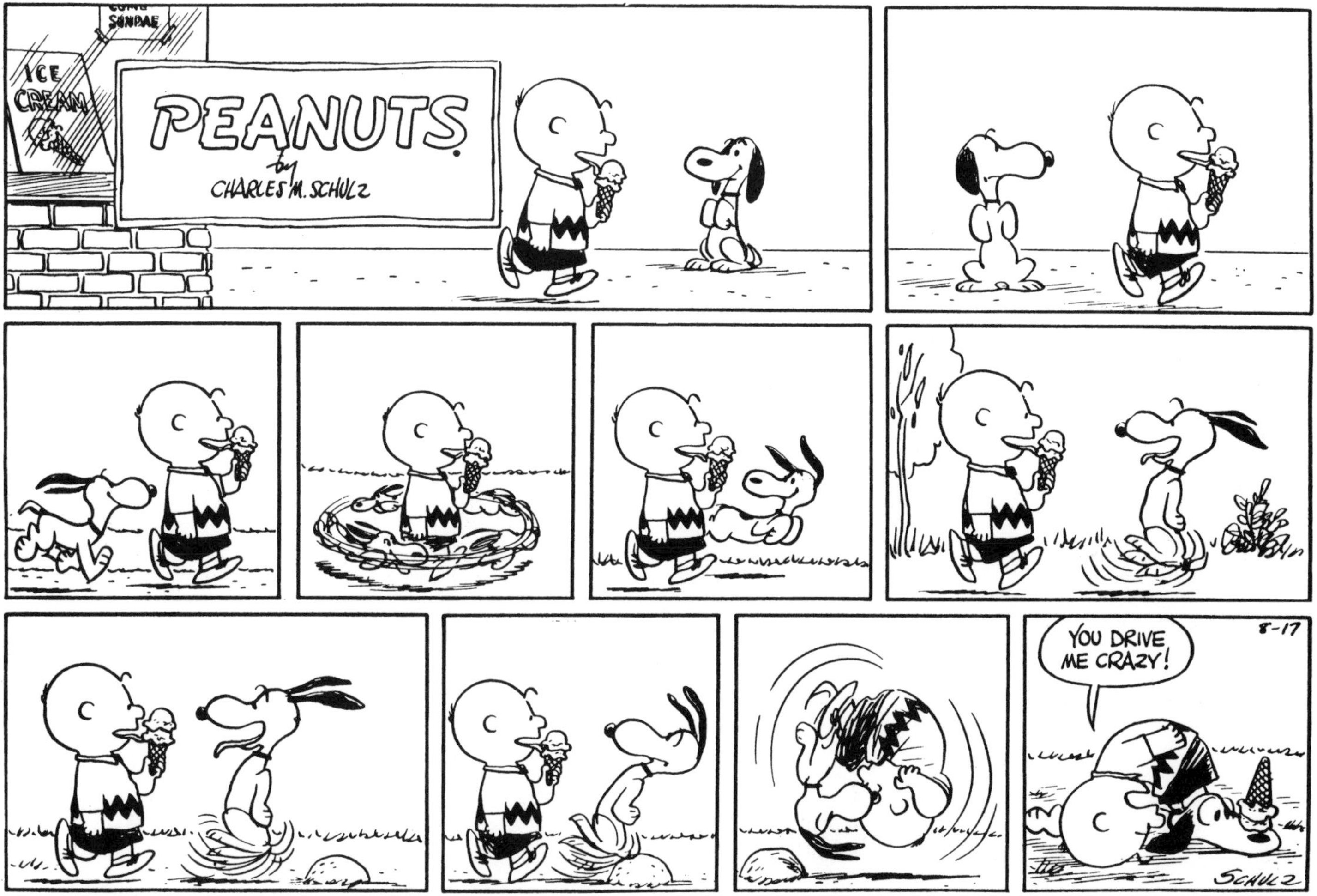
CONE SUNDAE
ICE CREAM
PEANUTS
by CHARLES M. SCHULZ
YOU DRIVE ME CRAZY!
8-17
SCHULZ

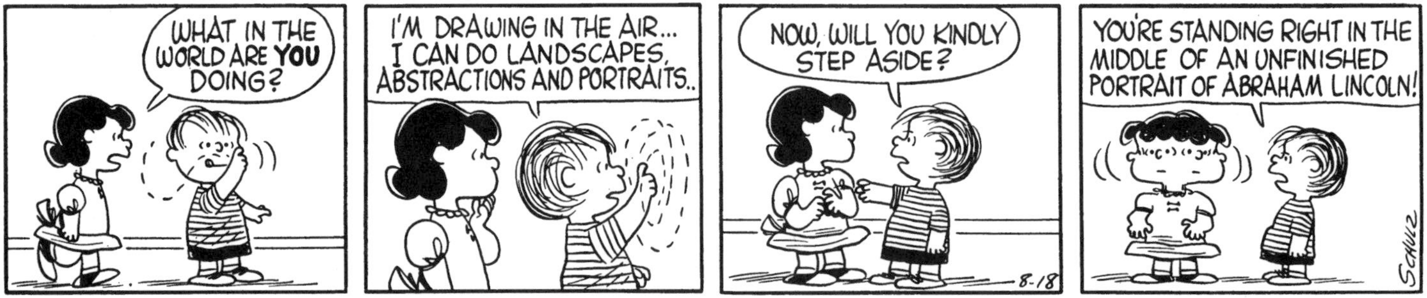
WHAT IN THE WORLD ARE **YOU** DOING?
I'M DRAWING IN THE AIR... I CAN DO LANDSCAPES, ABSTRACTIONS AND PORTRAITS..
NOW, WILL YOU KINDLY STEP ASIDE?
YOU'RE STANDING RIGHT IN THE MIDDLE OF AN UNFINISHED PORTRAIT OF ABRAHAM LINCOLN!
8-18
SCHULZ

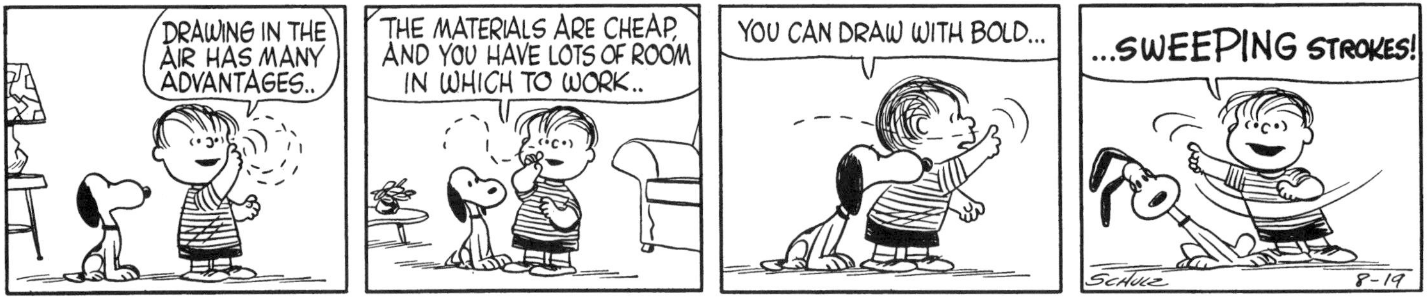
DRAWING IN THE AIR HAS MANY ADVANTAGES..
THE MATERIALS ARE CHEAP, AND YOU HAVE LOTS OF ROOM IN WHICH TO WORK..
YOU CAN DRAW WITH BOLD...
...SWEEPING STROKES!
SCHULZ
8-19

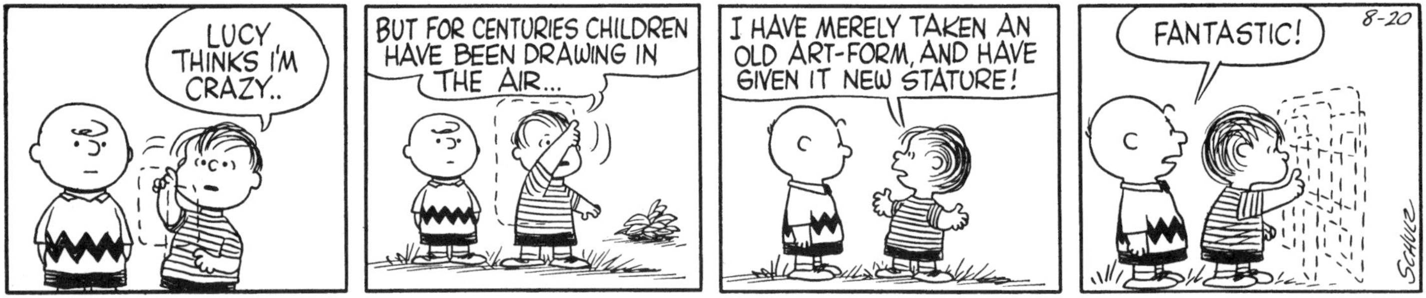
LUCY THINKS I'M CRAZY..
BUT FOR CENTURIES CHILDREN HAVE BEEN DRAWING IN THE AIR...
I HAVE MERELY TAKEN AN OLD ART-FORM, AND HAVE GIVEN IT NEW STATURE!
FANTASTIC!
8-20
SCHULZ

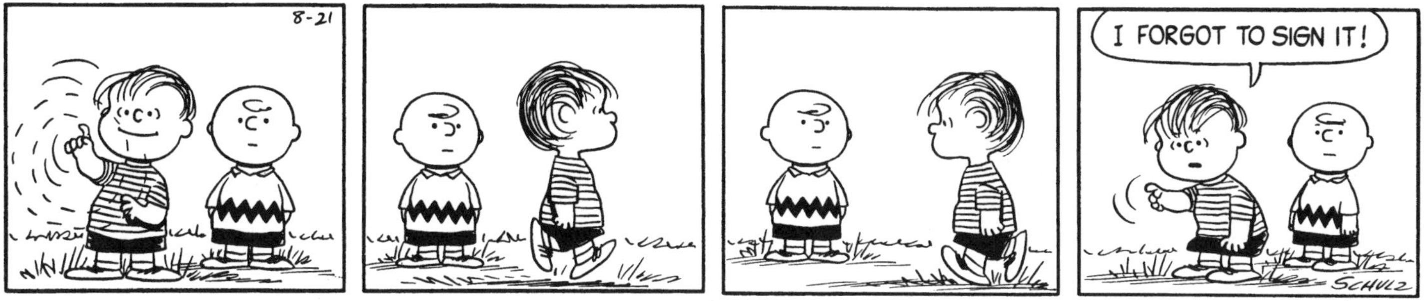
8-21
I FORGOT TO SIGN IT!
SCHULZ

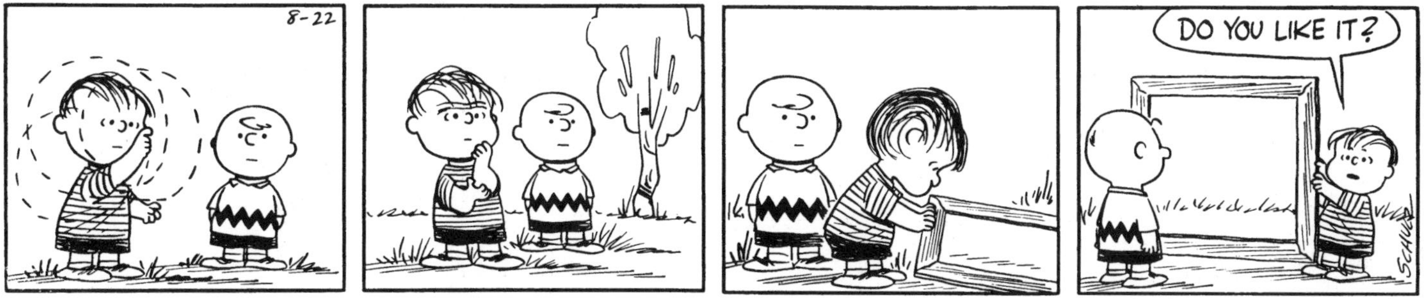
8-22
DO YOU LIKE IT?
SCHULZ

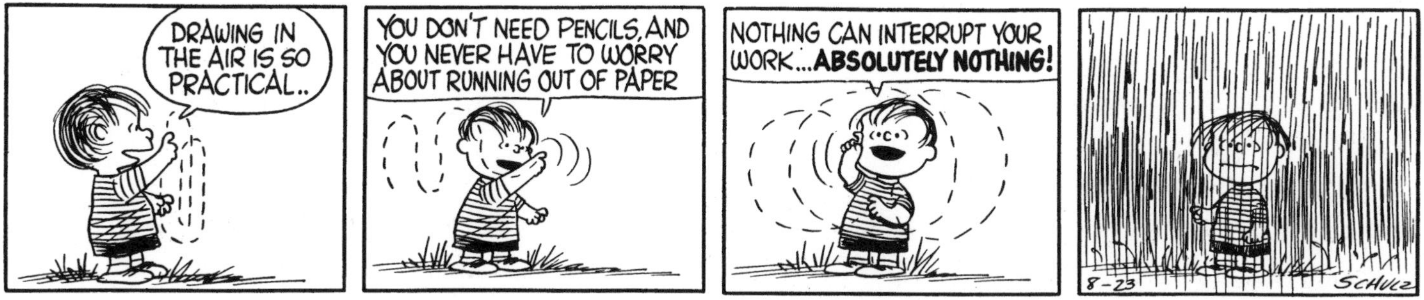
DRAWING IN THE AIR IS SO PRACTICAL..
YOU DON'T NEED PENCILS, AND YOU NEVER HAVE TO WORRY ABOUT RUNNING OUT OF PAPER
NOTHING CAN INTERRUPT YOUR WORK...**ABSOLUTELY NOTHING!**
8-23
SCHULZ

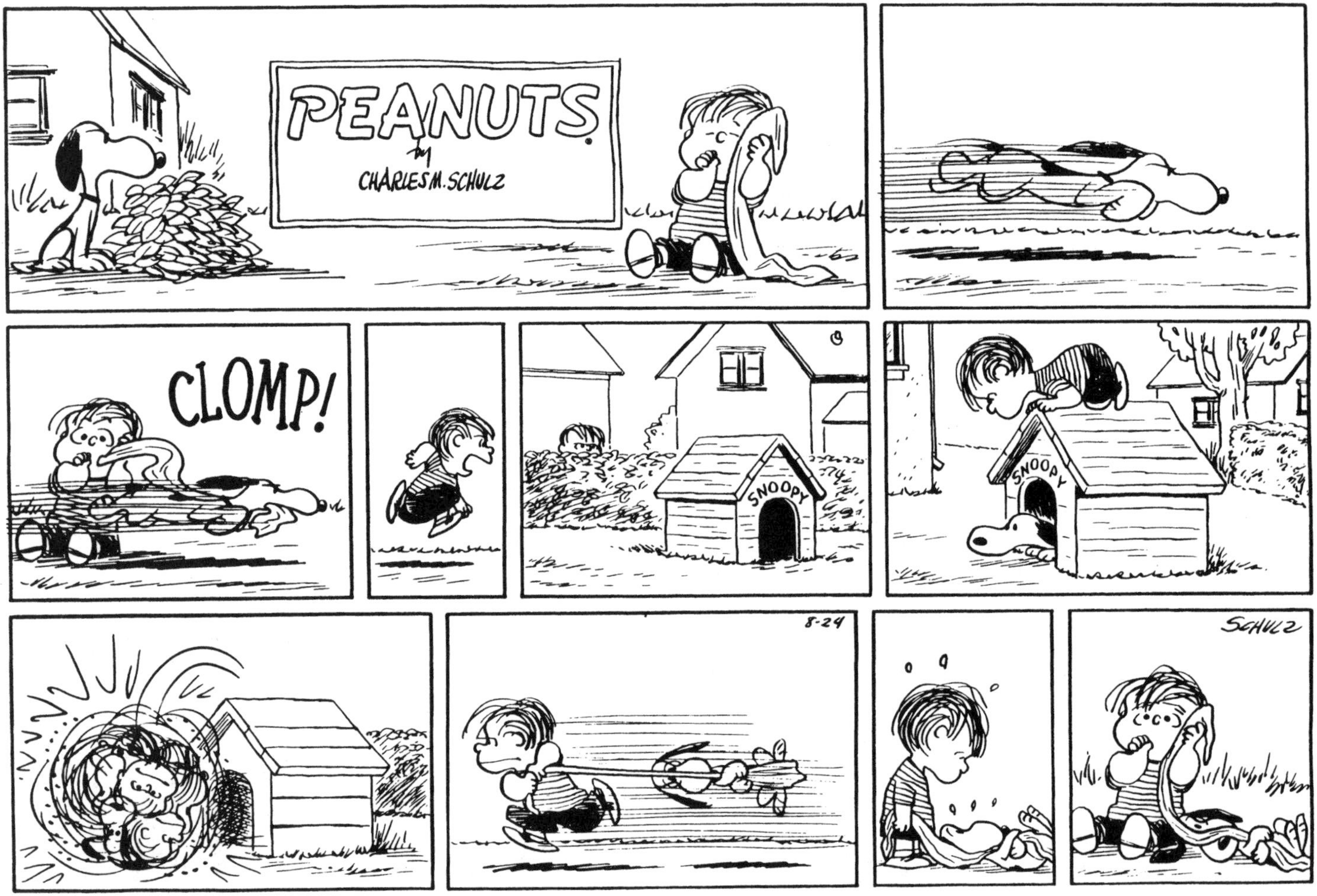
PEANUTS
by
CHARLES M. SCHULZ
CLOMP!
SNOOPY
SNOOPY
8-24
SCHULZ

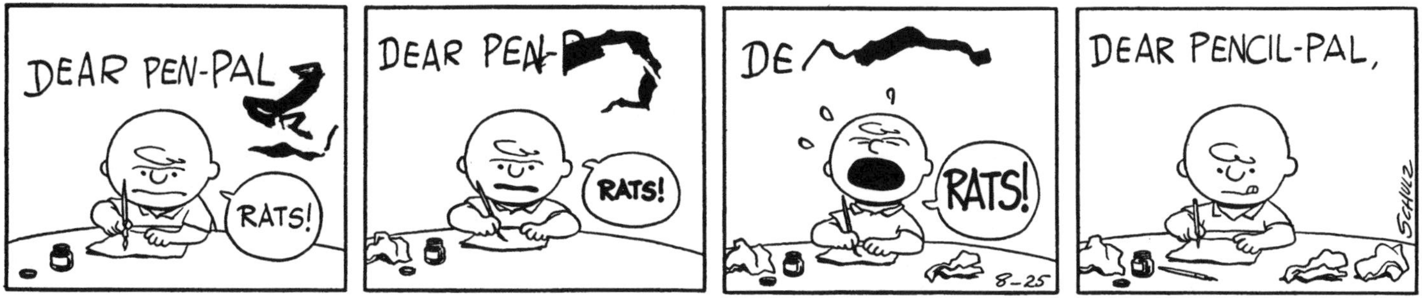
DEAR PEN-PAL
RATS!
DEAR PEN-
RATS!
DE
RATS!
8-25
DEAR PENCIL-PAL,
SCHULZ

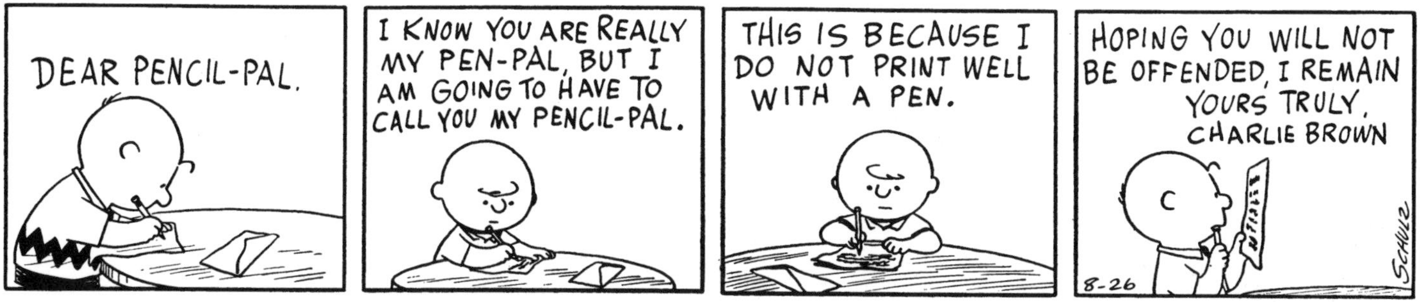
DEAR PENCIL-PAL.
I KNOW YOU ARE REALLY MY PEN-PAL, BUT I AM GOING TO HAVE TO CALL YOU MY PENCIL-PAL.
THIS IS BECAUSE I DO NOT PRINT WELL WITH A PEN.
HOPING YOU WILL NOT BE OFFENDED, I REMAIN YOURS TRULY, CHARLIE BROWN
8-26
SCHULZ

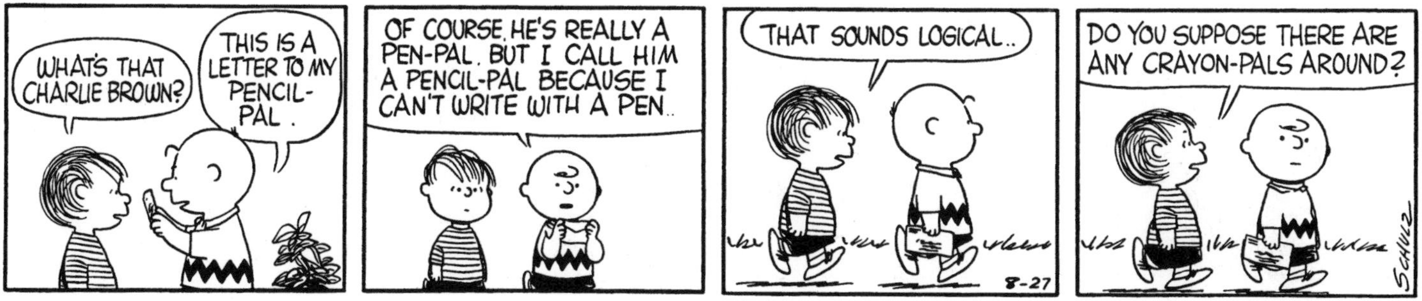
WHAT'S THAT CHARLIE BROWN?
THIS IS A LETTER TO MY PENCIL-PAL.
OF COURSE, HE'S REALLY A PEN-PAL. BUT I CALL HIM A PENCIL-PAL BECAUSE I CAN'T WRITE WITH A PEN..
THAT SOUNDS LOGICAL..
8-27
DO YOU SUPPOSE THERE ARE ANY CRAYON-PALS AROUND?
SCHULZ

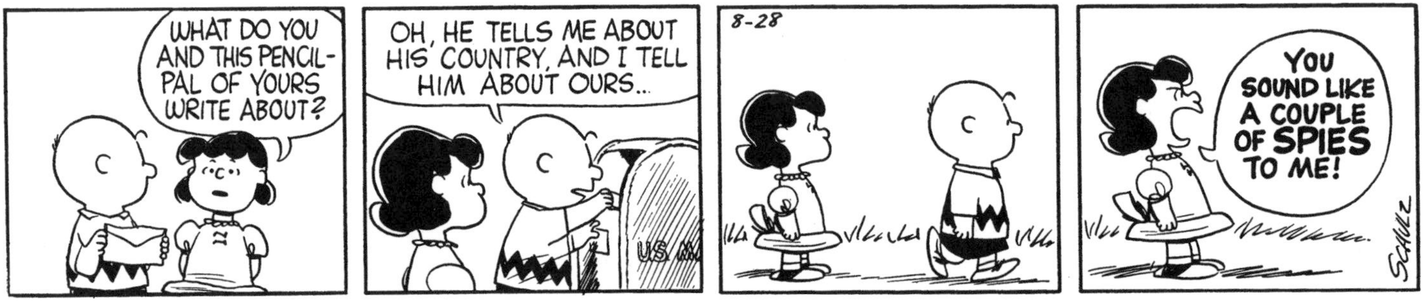
WHAT DO YOU AND THIS PENCIL-PAL OF YOURS WRITE ABOUT?
OH, HE TELLS ME ABOUT HIS COUNTRY, AND I TELL HIM ABOUT OURS...
US MA
8-28
YOU SOUND LIKE A COUPLE OF SPIES TO ME!
SCHULZ

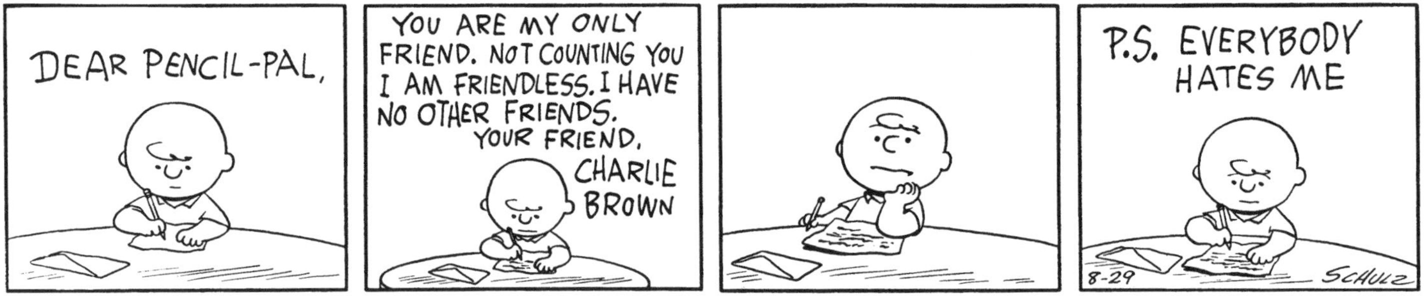
DEAR PENCIL-PAL,
YOU ARE MY ONLY FRIEND. NOT COUNTING YOU I AM FRIENDLESS. I HAVE NO OTHER FRIENDS.
YOUR FRIEND,
CHARLIE BROWN
P.S. EVERYBODY HATES ME
8-29
SCHULZ

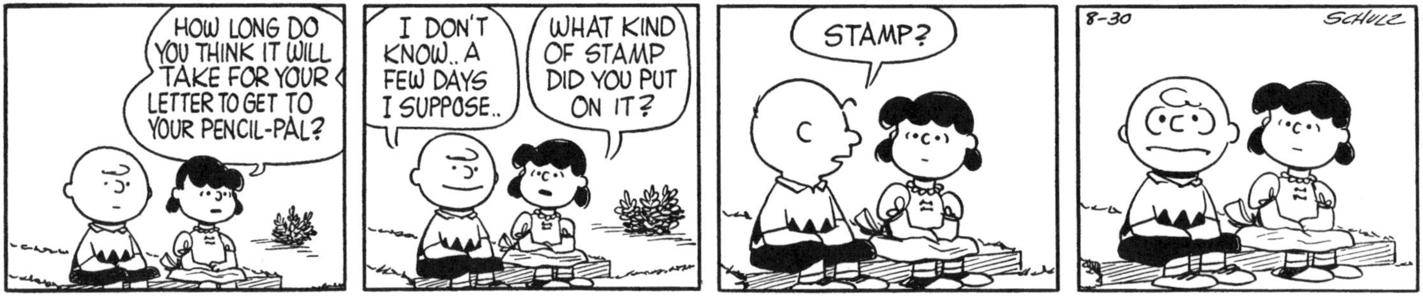
HOW LONG DO YOU THINK IT WILL TAKE FOR YOUR LETTER TO GET TO YOUR PENCIL-PAL?
I DON'T KNOW.. A FEW DAYS I SUPPOSE..
WHAT KIND OF STAMP DID YOU PUT ON IT?
STAMP?
8-30
SCHULZ

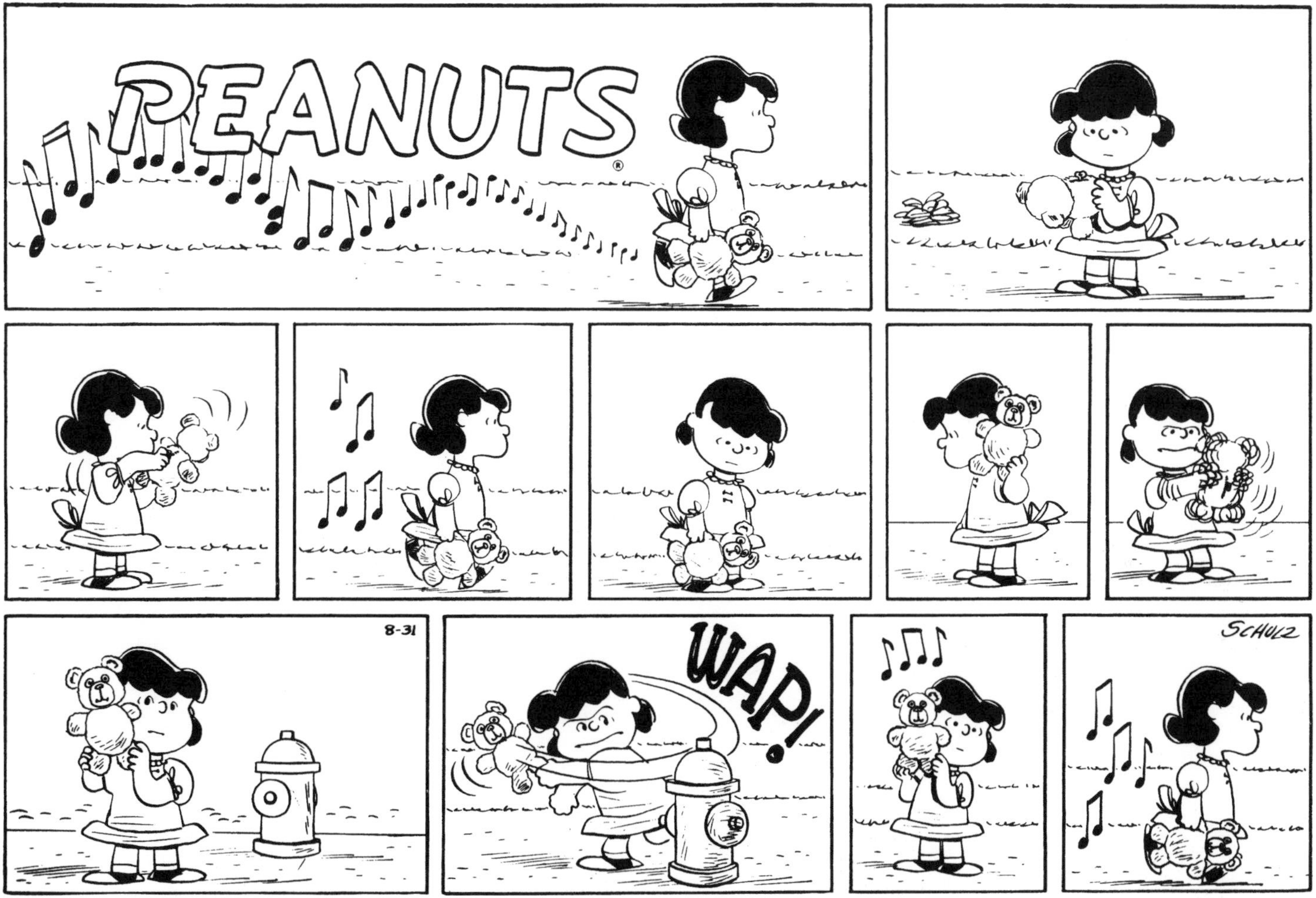
PEANUTS
8-31
WAP!
SCHULZ

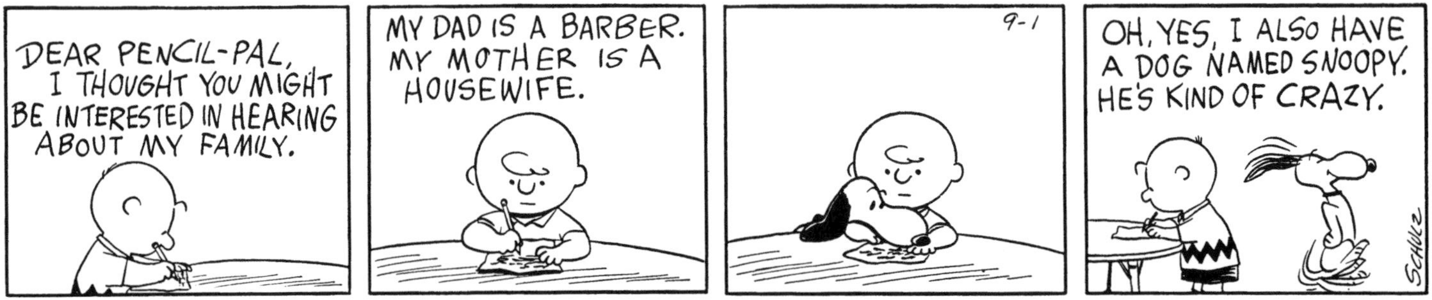
DEAR PENCIL-PAL,
I THOUGHT YOU MIGHT BE INTERESTED IN HEARING ABOUT MY FAMILY.
MY DAD IS A BARBER. MY MOTHER IS A HOUSEWIFE.
9-1
OH, YES, I ALSO HAVE A DOG NAMED SNOOPY. HE'S KIND OF CRAZY.
SCHULZ

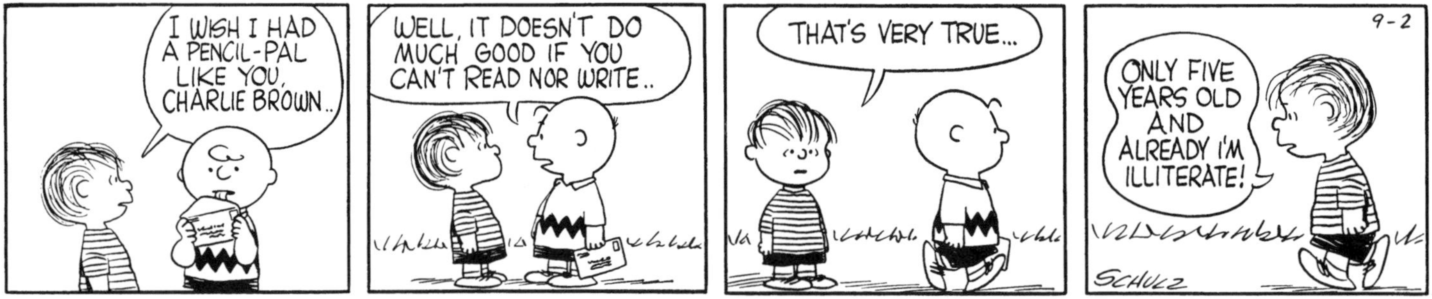
I WISH I HAD A PENCIL-PAL LIKE YOU, CHARLIE BROWN..
WELL, IT DOESN'T DO MUCH GOOD IF YOU CAN'T READ NOR WRITE..
THAT'S VERY TRUE...
9-2
ONLY FIVE YEARS OLD AND ALREADY I'M ILLITERATE!
SCHULZ

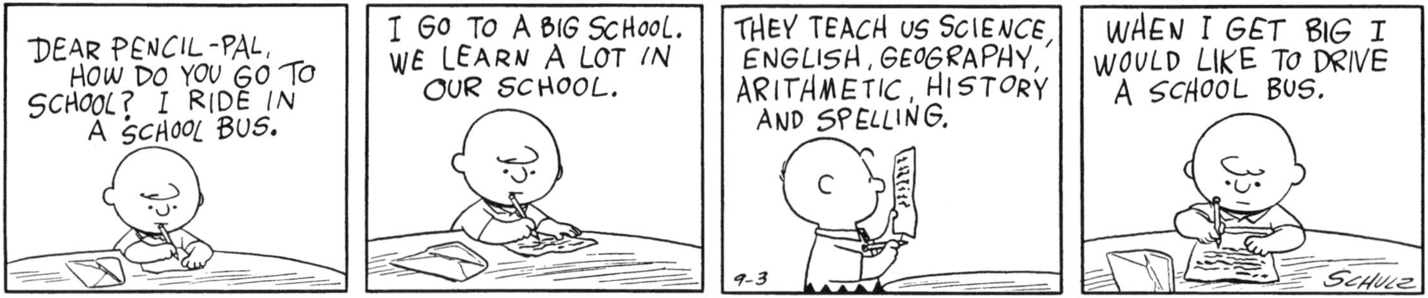
DEAR PENCIL-PAL,
HOW DO YOU GO TO SCHOOL? I RIDE IN A SCHOOL BUS.
I GO TO A BIG SCHOOL. WE LEARN A LOT IN OUR SCHOOL.
THEY TEACH US SCIENCE, ENGLISH, GEOGRAPHY, ARITHMETIC, HISTORY AND SPELLING.
9-3
WHEN I GET BIG I WOULD LIKE TO DRIVE A SCHOOL BUS.
SCHULZ

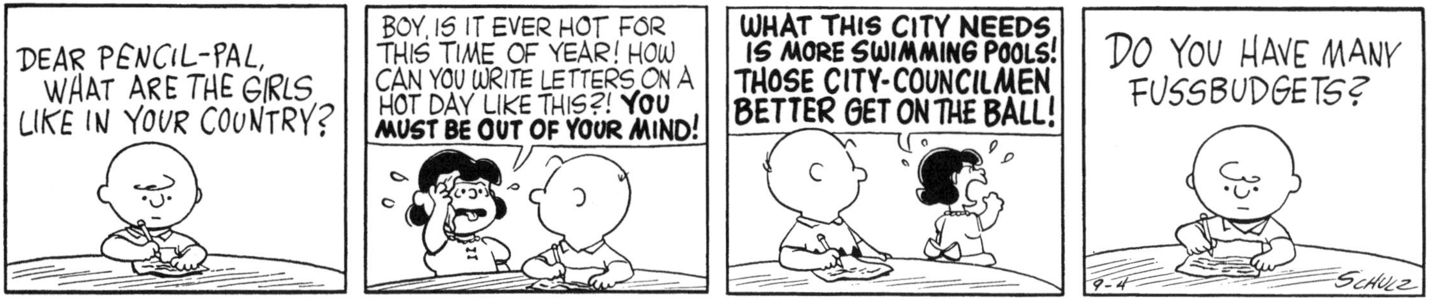
DEAR PENCIL-PAL, WHAT ARE THE GIRLS LIKE IN YOUR COUNTRY?
BOY, IS IT EVER HOT FOR THIS TIME OF YEAR! HOW CAN YOU WRITE LETTERS ON A HOT DAY LIKE THIS?! YOU MUST BE OUT OF YOUR MIND!
WHAT THIS CITY NEEDS IS MORE SWIMMING POOLS! THOSE CITY-COUNCILMEN BETTER GET ON THE BALL!
DO YOU HAVE MANY FUSSBUDGETS?
9-4
SCHULZ

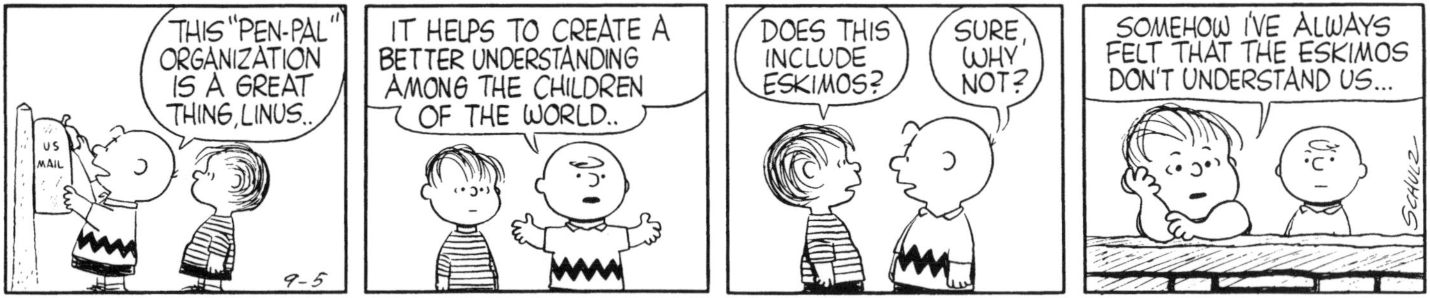
US MAIL
THIS "PEN-PAL" ORGANIZATION IS A GREAT THING, LINUS..
9-5
IT HELPS TO CREATE A BETTER UNDERSTANDING AMONG THE CHILDREN OF THE WORLD..
DOES THIS INCLUDE ESKIMOS?
SURE, WHY NOT?
SOMEHOW I'VE ALWAYS FELT THAT THE ESKIMOS DON'T UNDERSTAND US...
SCHULZ

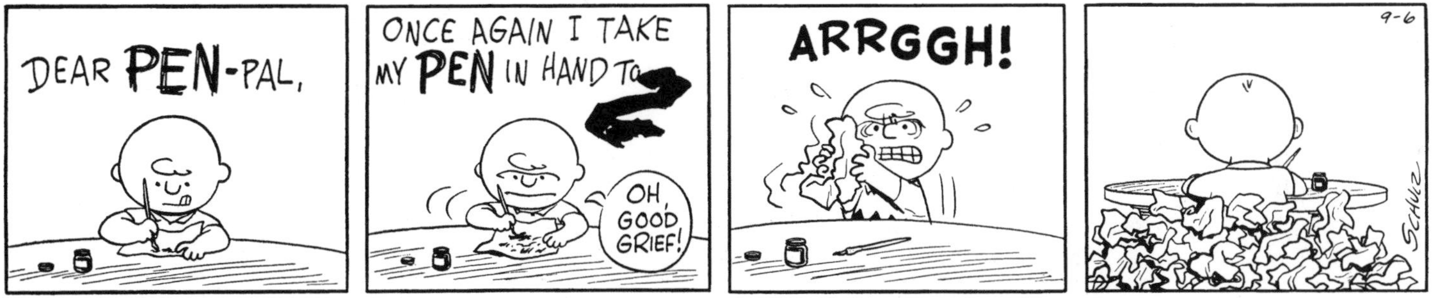
DEAR PEN-PAL,
ONCE AGAIN I TAKE MY PEN IN HAND TO
OH, GOOD GRIEF!
ARRGGH!
9-6
SCHULZ

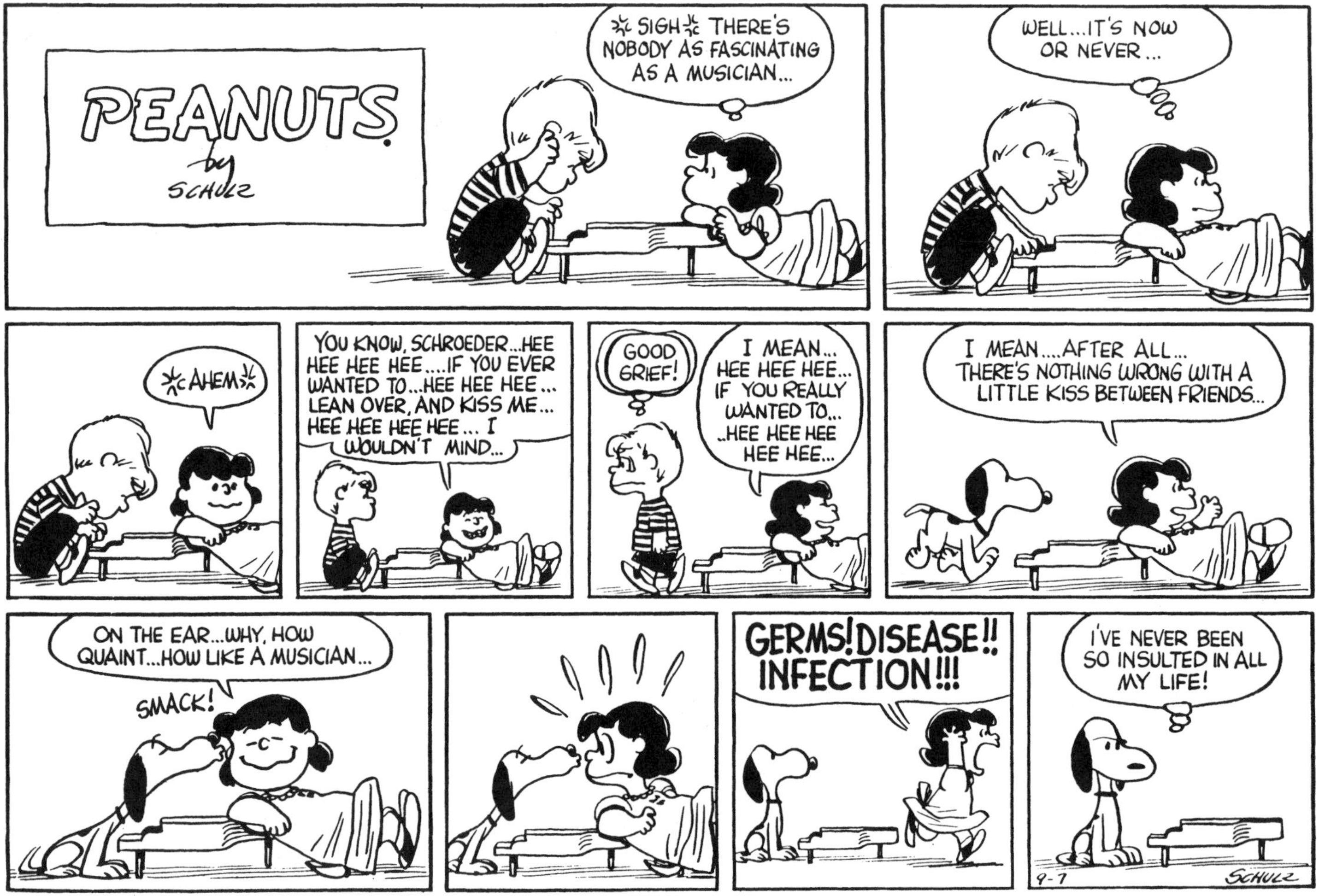
PEANUTS
by SCHULZ
SIGH THERE'S NOBODY AS FASCINATING AS A MUSICIAN...
WELL...IT'S NOW OR NEVER...
AHEM
YOU KNOW, SCHROEDER...HEE HEE HEE HEE....IF YOU EVER WANTED TO...HEE HEE HEE... LEAN OVER, AND KISS ME... HEE HEE HEE HEE... I WOULDN'T MIND...
GOOD GRIEF!
I MEAN... HEE HEE HEE... IF YOU REALLY WANTED TO... ..HEE HEE HEE HEE HEE...
I MEAN....AFTER ALL... THERE'S NOTHING WRONG WITH A LITTLE KISS BETWEEN FRIENDS...
ON THE EAR...WHY, HOW QUAINT...HOW LIKE A MUSICIAN...
SMACK!
GERMS! DISEASE!! INFECTION!!!
I'VE NEVER BEEN SO INSULTED IN ALL MY LIFE!
9-7
SCHULZ

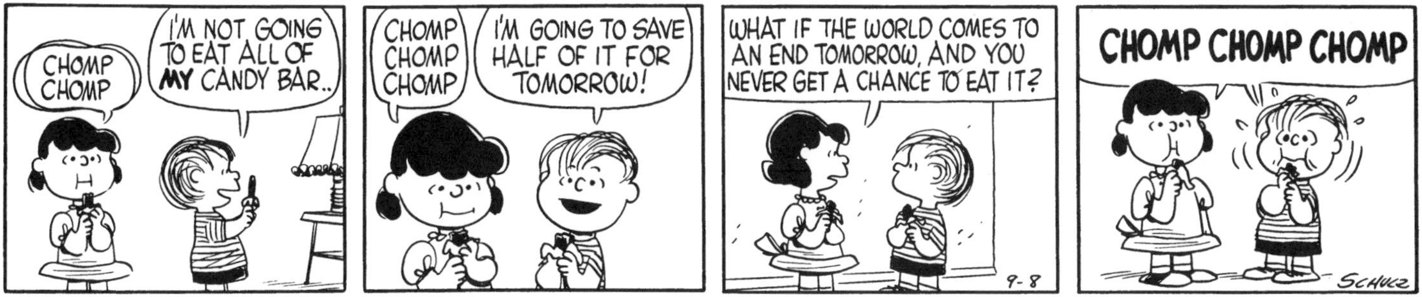
CHOMP CHOMP
I'M NOT GOING TO EAT ALL OF MY CANDY BAR..
CHOMP CHOMP CHOMP
I'M GOING TO SAVE HALF OF IT FOR TOMORROW!
WHAT IF THE WORLD COMES TO AN END TOMORROW, AND YOU NEVER GET A CHANCE TO EAT IT?
CHOMP CHOMP CHOMP

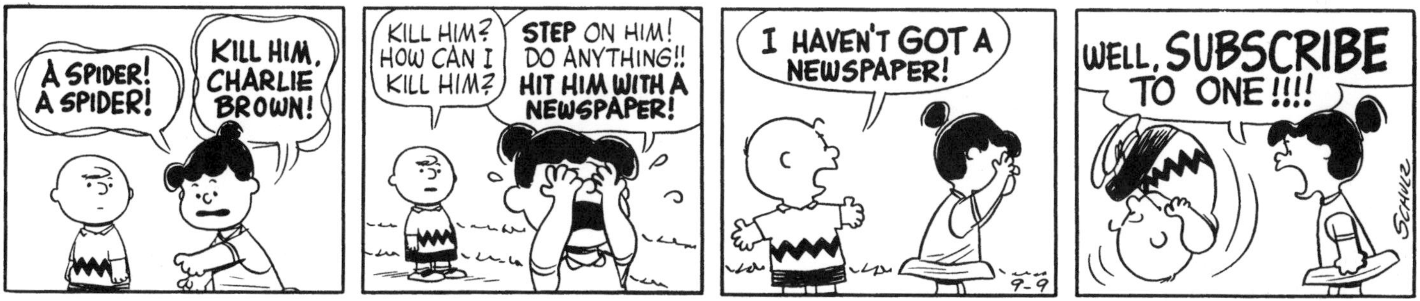
A SPIDER! A SPIDER!
KILL HIM, CHARLIE BROWN!
KILL HIM? HOW CAN I KILL HIM?
STEP ON HIM! DO ANYTHING!! HIT HIM WITH A NEWSPAPER!
I HAVEN'T GOT A NEWSPAPER!
WELL, SUBSCRIBE TO ONE!!!!

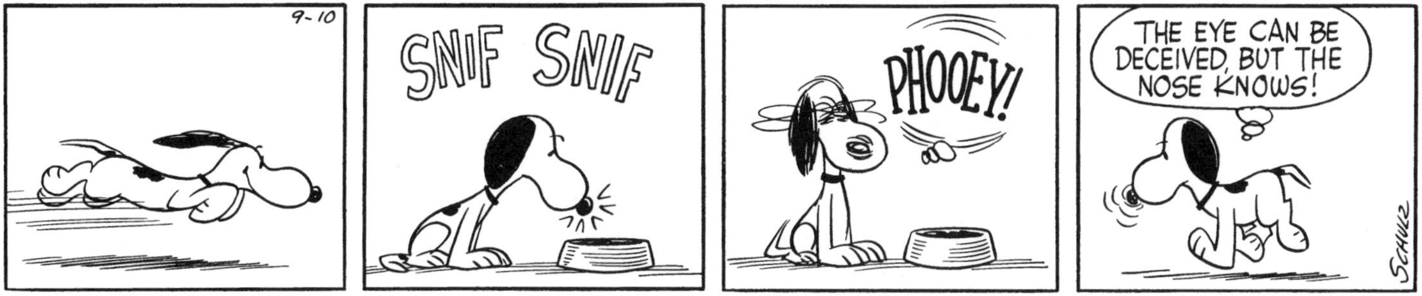
SNIF SNIF
PHOOEY!
THE EYE CAN BE DECEIVED, BUT THE NOSE KNOWS!

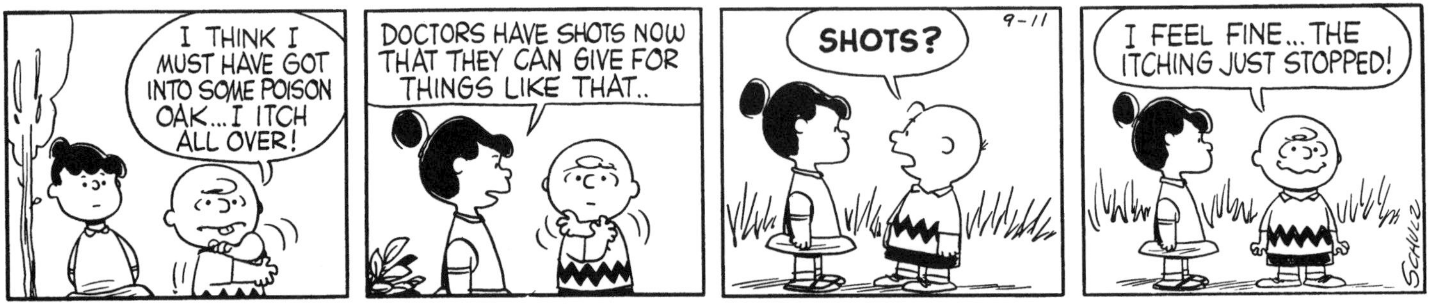
I THINK I MUST HAVE GOT INTO SOME POISON OAK...I ITCH ALL OVER!
DOCTORS HAVE SHOTS NOW THAT THEY CAN GIVE FOR THINGS LIKE THAT..
SHOTS?
9-11
I FEEL FINE...THE ITCHING JUST STOPPED!
SCHULZ

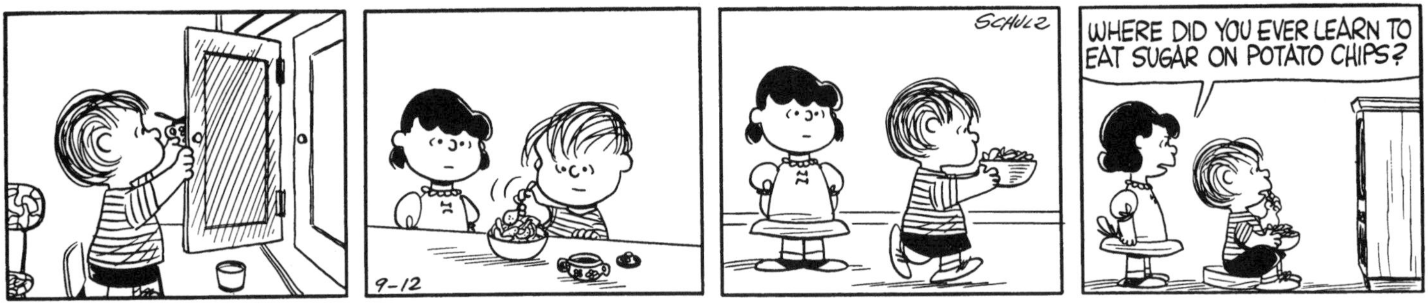
9-12
SCHULZ
WHERE DID YOU EVER LEARN TO EAT SUGAR ON POTATO CHIPS?

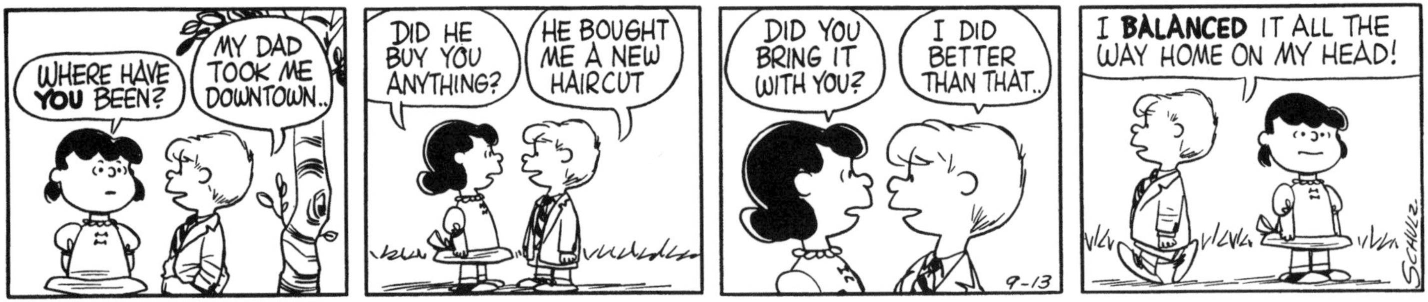
WHERE HAVE **YOU** BEEN?
MY DAD TOOK ME DOWNTOWN..
DID HE BUY YOU ANYTHING?
HE BOUGHT ME A NEW HAIRCUT
DID YOU BRING IT WITH YOU?
I DID BETTER THAN THAT..
9-13
I **BALANCED** IT ALL THE WAY HOME ON MY HEAD!
SCHULZ

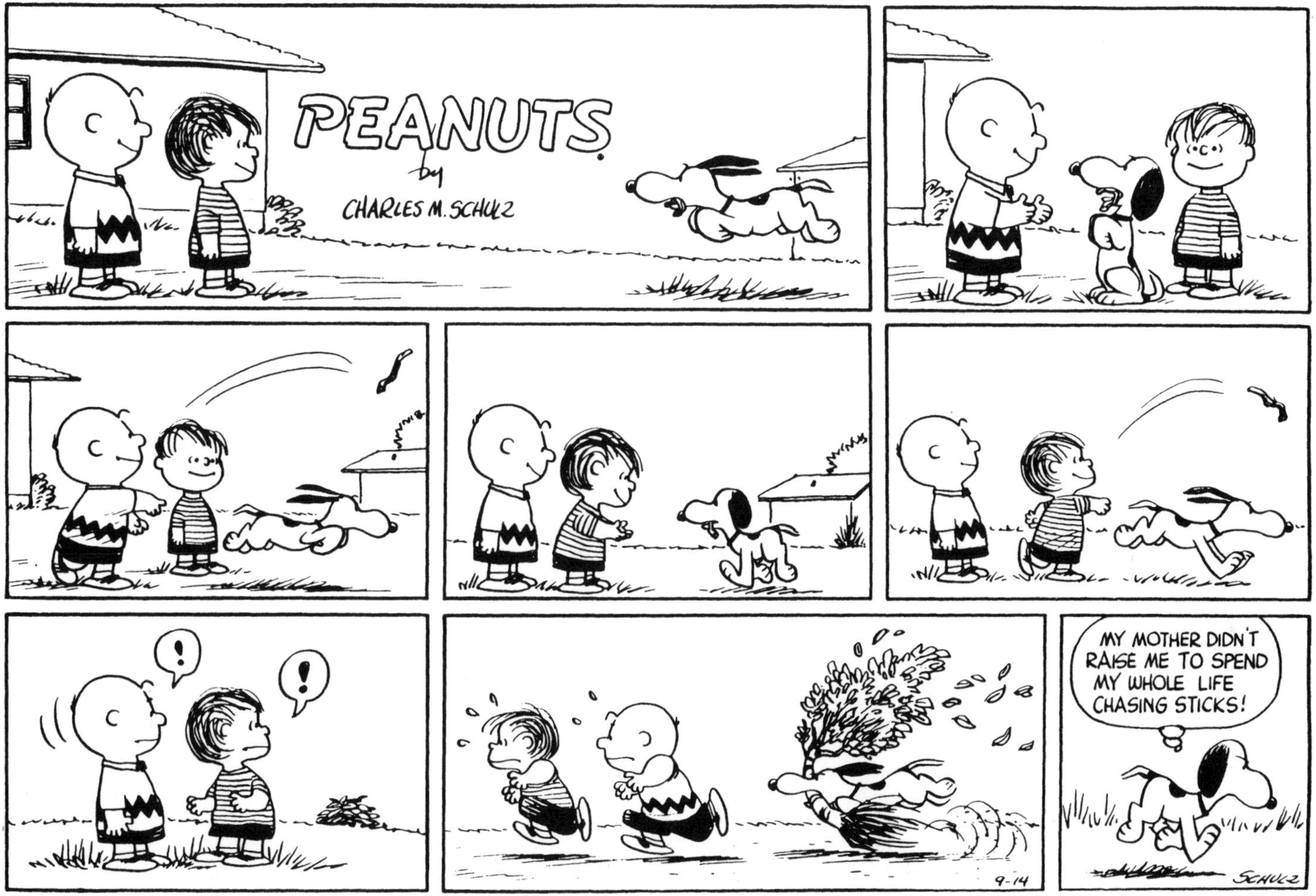
PEANUTS
by
CHARLES M. SCHULZ
!
!
9-14
MY MOTHER DIDN'T RAISE ME TO SPEND MY WHOLE LIFE CHASING STICKS!
SCHULZ

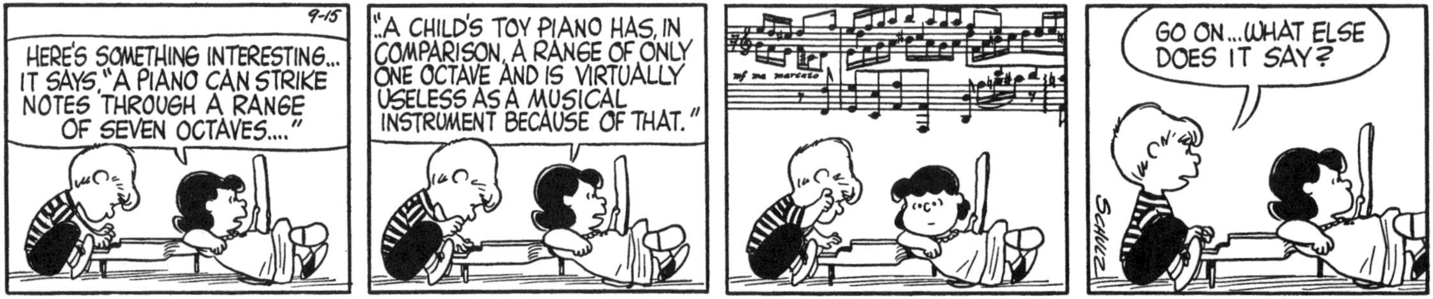
9-15
HERE'S SOMETHING INTERESTING... IT SAYS, "A PIANO CAN STRIKE NOTES THROUGH A RANGE OF SEVEN OCTAVES...."
"...A CHILD'S TOY PIANO HAS, IN COMPARISON, A RANGE OF ONLY ONE OCTAVE AND IS VIRTUALLY USELESS AS A MUSICAL INSTRUMENT BECAUSE OF THAT."
GO ON...WHAT ELSE DOES IT SAY?
SCHULZ

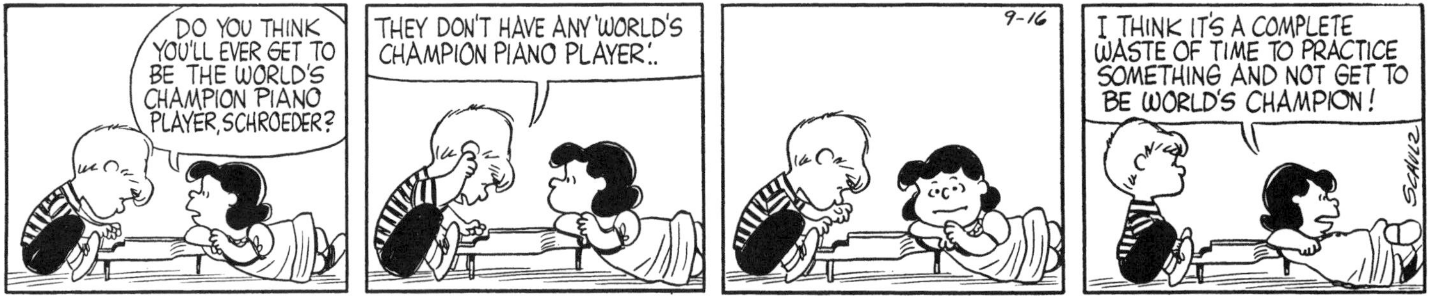
DO YOU THINK YOU'LL EVER GET TO BE THE WORLD'S CHAMPION PIANO PLAYER, SCHROEDER?
THEY DON'T HAVE ANY 'WORLD'S CHAMPION PIANO PLAYER'..
9-16
I THINK IT'S A COMPLETE WASTE OF TIME TO PRACTICE SOMETHING AND NOT GET TO BE WORLD'S CHAMPION!
SCHULZ

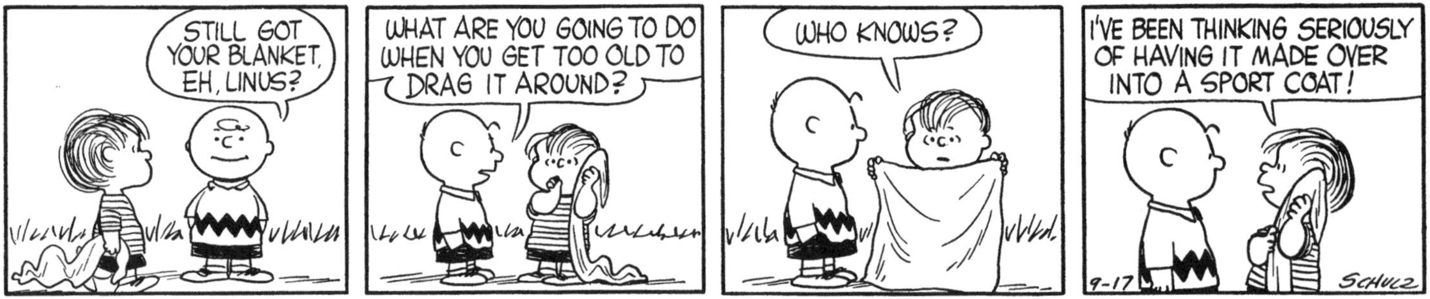
STILL GOT YOUR BLANKET, EH, LINUS?
WHAT ARE YOU GOING TO DO WHEN YOU GET TOO OLD TO DRAG IT AROUND?
WHO KNOWS?
I'VE BEEN THINKING SERIOUSLY OF HAVING IT MADE OVER INTO A SPORT COAT!
9-17
SCHULZ

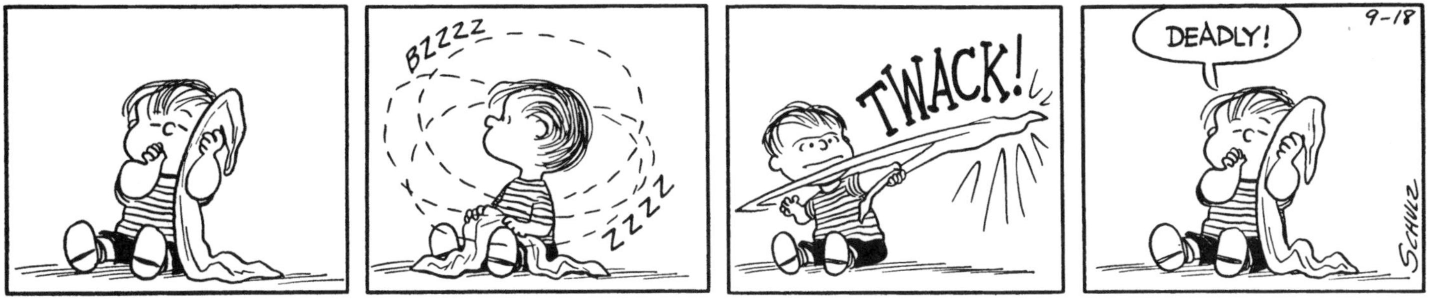
BZZZZ
ZZZZ
TWACK!
DEADLY!
9-18
SCHULZ

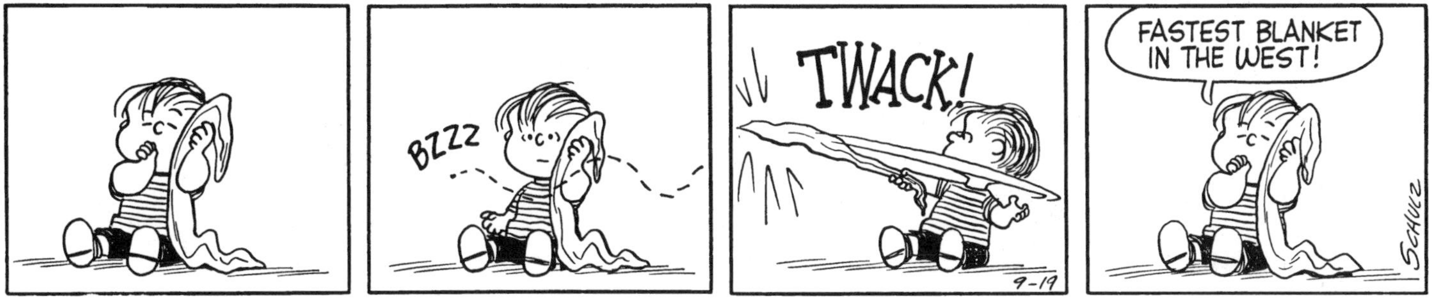
BZZZ
TWACK!
9-19
FASTEST BLANKET IN THE WEST!
SCHULZ

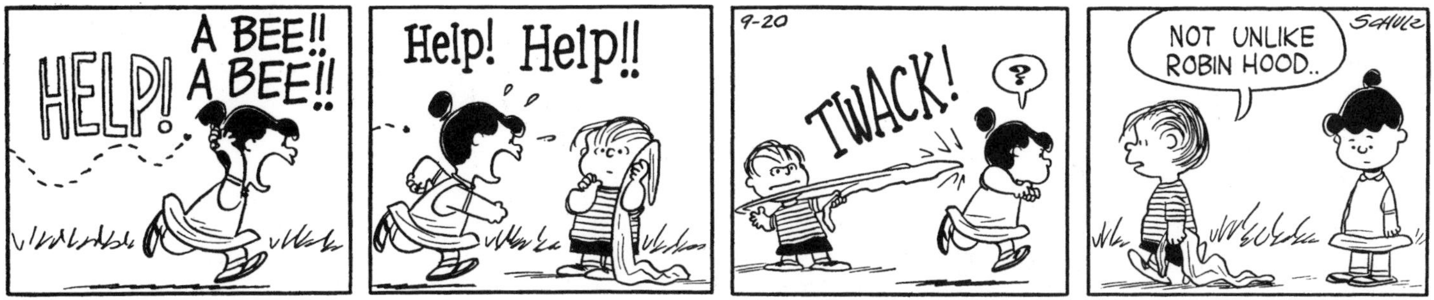
HELP!
A BEE!! A BEE!!
Help! Help!!
9-20
TWACK!
?
NOT UNLIKE ROBIN HOOD..
SCHULZ

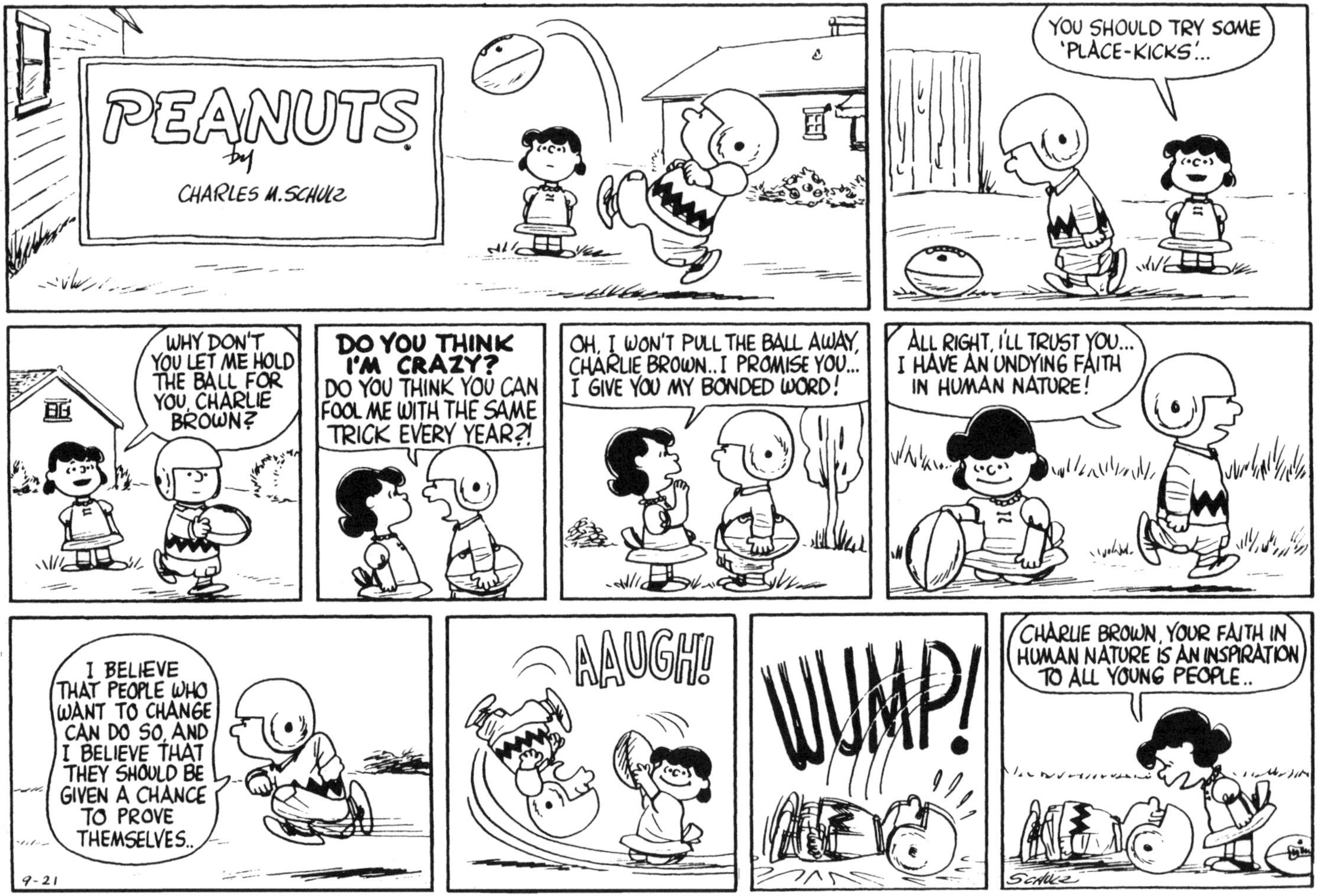
PEANUTS
by
CHARLES M. SCHULZ
YOU SHOULD TRY SOME 'PLACE-KICKS'...
WHY DON'T YOU LET ME HOLD THE BALL FOR YOU, CHARLIE BROWN?
DO YOU THINK I'M CRAZY? DO YOU THINK YOU CAN FOOL ME WITH THE SAME TRICK EVERY YEAR?!
OH, I WON'T PULL THE BALL AWAY, CHARLIE BROWN..I PROMISE YOU... I GIVE YOU MY BONDED WORD!
ALL RIGHT, I'LL TRUST YOU... I HAVE AN UNDYING FAITH IN HUMAN NATURE!
I BELIEVE THAT PEOPLE WHO WANT TO CHANGE CAN DO SO, AND I BELIEVE THAT THEY SHOULD BE GIVEN A CHANCE TO PROVE THEMSELVES..
9-21
AAUGH!
WUMP!
CHARLIE BROWN, YOUR FAITH IN HUMAN NATURE IS AN INSPIRATION TO ALL YOUNG PEOPLE..
SCHULZ

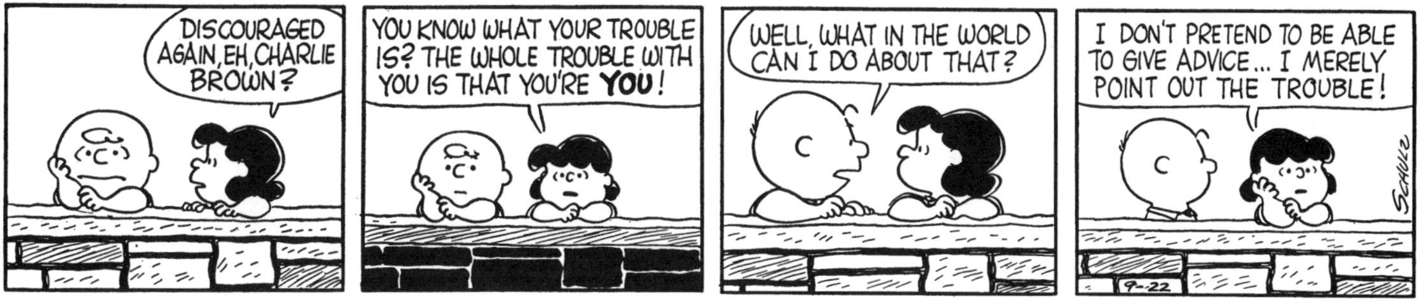
DISCOURAGED AGAIN, EH, CHARLIE BROWN?
YOU KNOW WHAT YOUR TROUBLE IS? THE WHOLE TROUBLE WITH YOU IS THAT YOU'RE **YOU**!
WELL, WHAT IN THE WORLD CAN I DO ABOUT THAT?
I DON'T PRETEND TO BE ABLE TO GIVE ADVICE... I MERELY POINT OUT THE TROUBLE!
SCHULZ
9-22

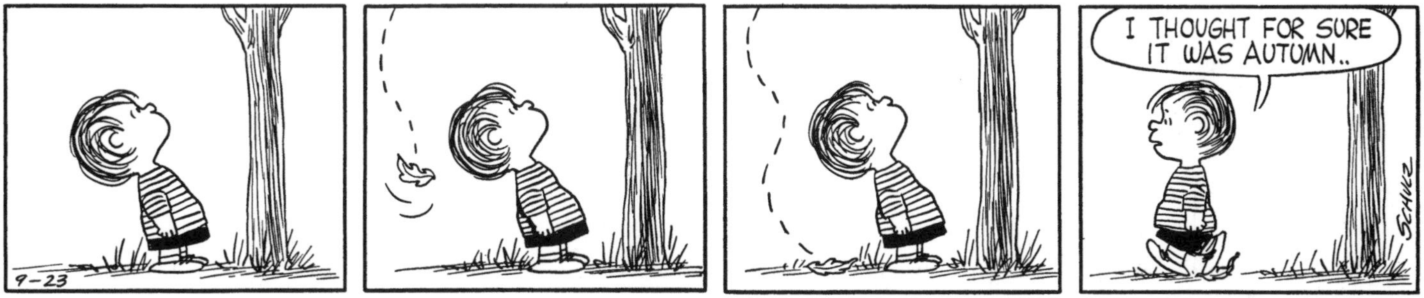
9-23
I THOUGHT FOR SURE IT WAS AUTUMN..
SCHULZ

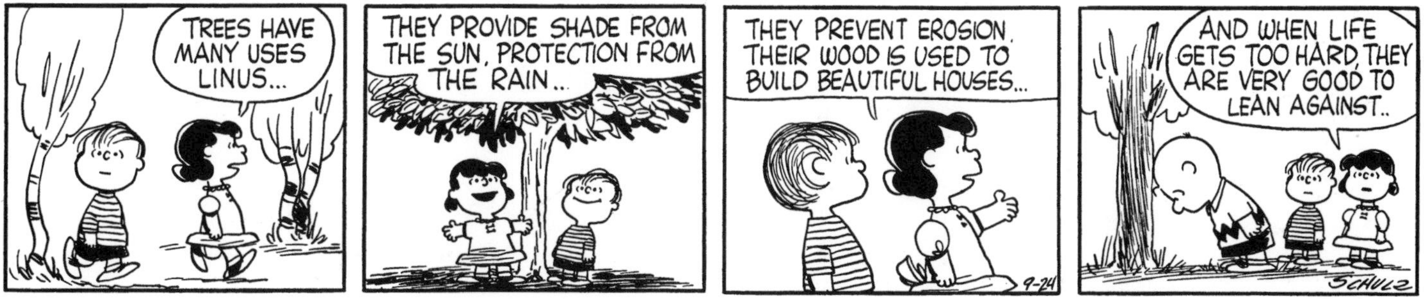
TREES HAVE MANY USES LINUS...
THEY PROVIDE SHADE FROM THE SUN, PROTECTION FROM THE RAIN...
THEY PREVENT EROSION. THEIR WOOD IS USED TO BUILD BEAUTIFUL HOUSES...
9-24
AND WHEN LIFE GETS TOO HARD, THEY ARE VERY GOOD TO LEAN AGAINST..
SCHULZ

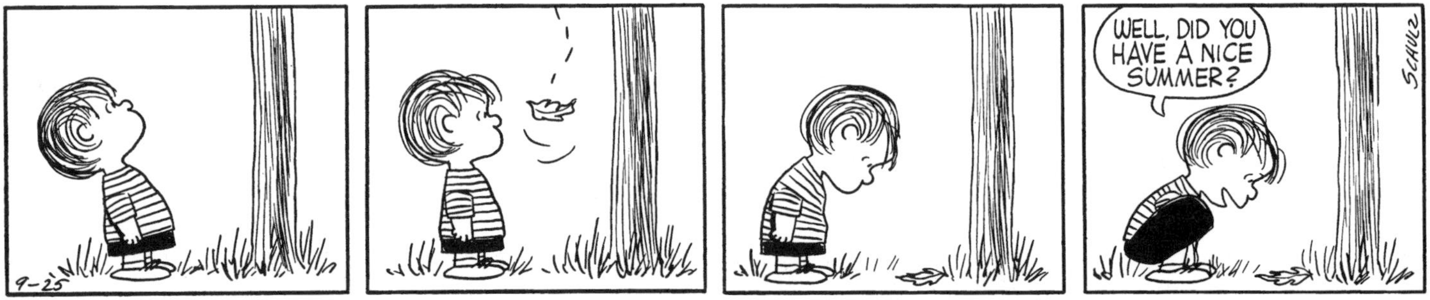

9-25
WELL, DID YOU HAVE A NICE SUMMER?
SCHULZ

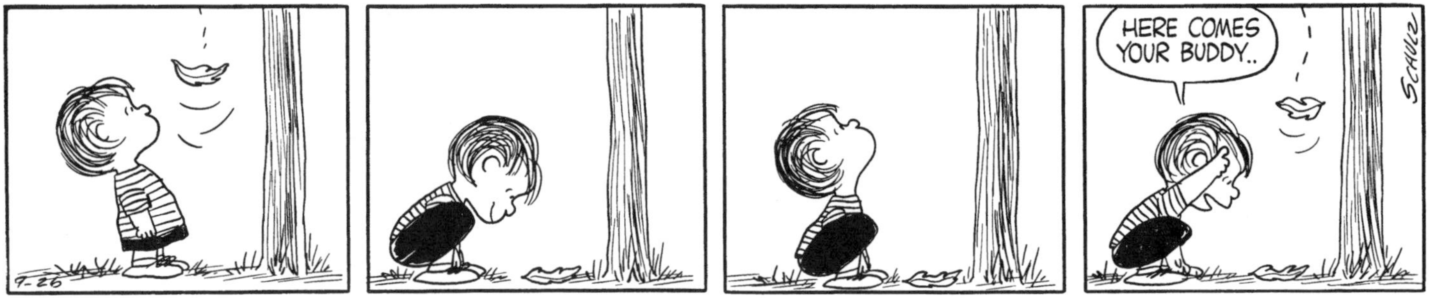

9-26
HERE COMES YOUR BUDDY..
SCHULZ

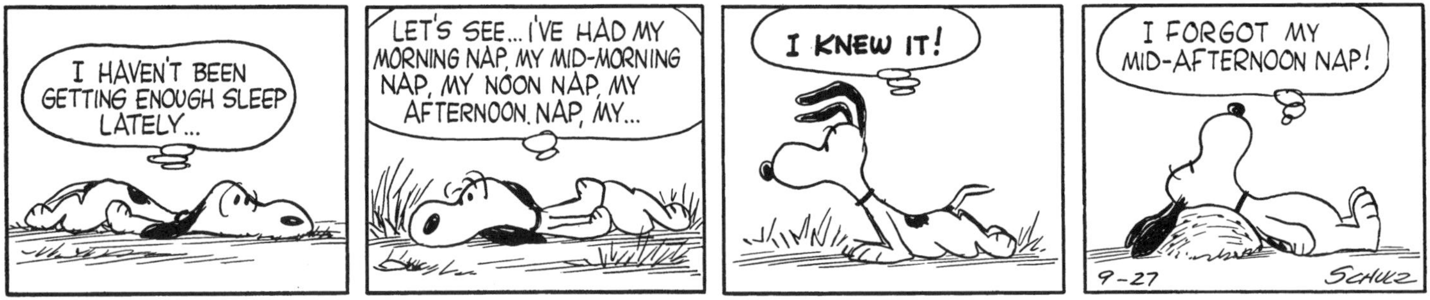

I HAVEN'T BEEN GETTING ENOUGH SLEEP LATELY...
LET'S SEE... I'VE HAD MY MORNING NAP, MY MID-MORNING NAP, MY NOON NAP, MY AFTERNOON NAP, MY...
I KNEW IT!
I FORGOT MY MID-AFTERNOON NAP!
9-27
SCHULZ

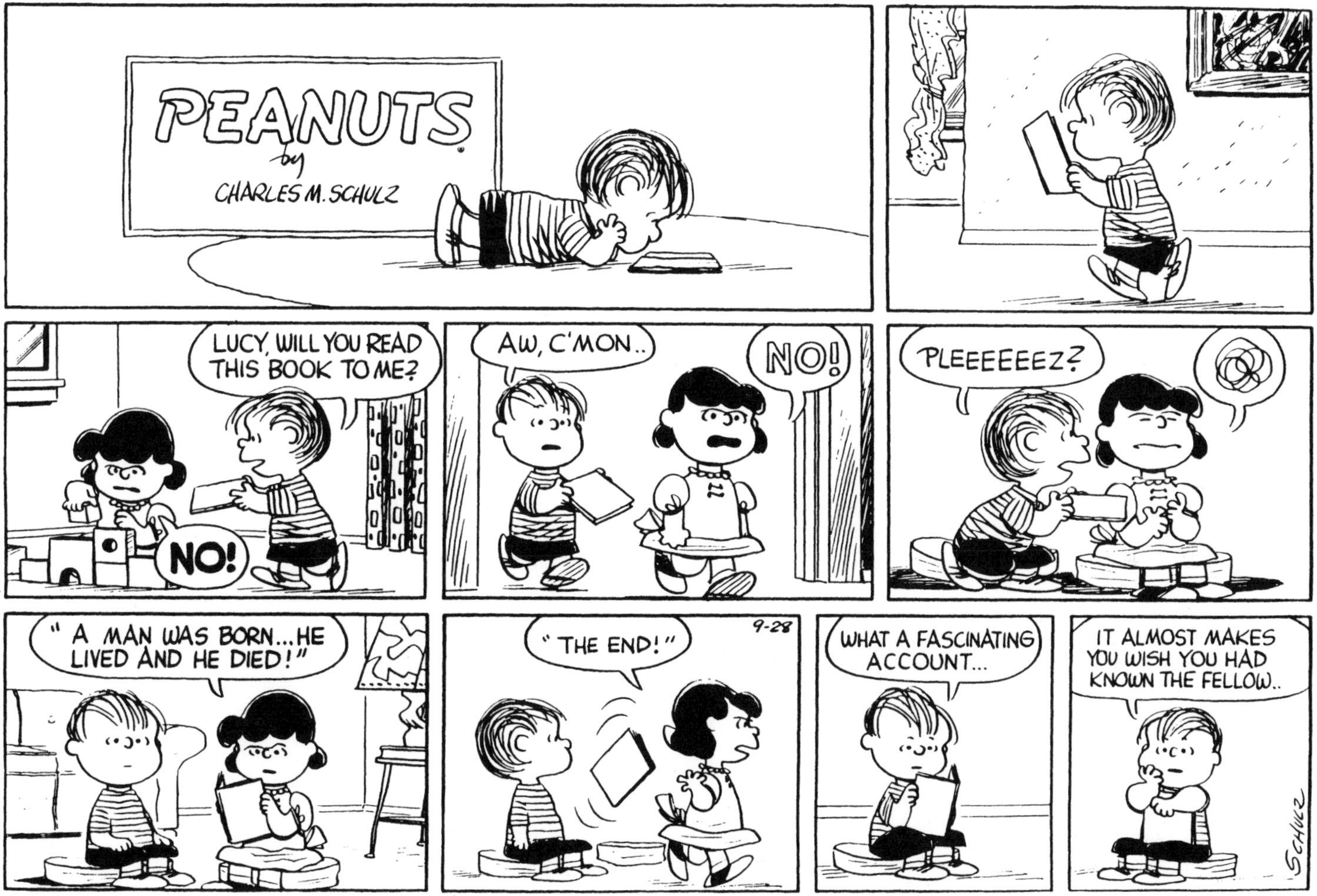
PEANUTS
by
CHARLES M. SCHULZ
LUCY, WILL YOU READ THIS BOOK TO ME?
NO!
AW, C'MON..
NO!
PLEEEEEEZ?
" A MAN WAS BORN...HE LIVED AND HE DIED!"
9-28
" THE END!"
WHAT A FASCINATING ACCOUNT...
IT ALMOST MAKES YOU WISH YOU HAD KNOWN THE FELLOW..
SCHULZ

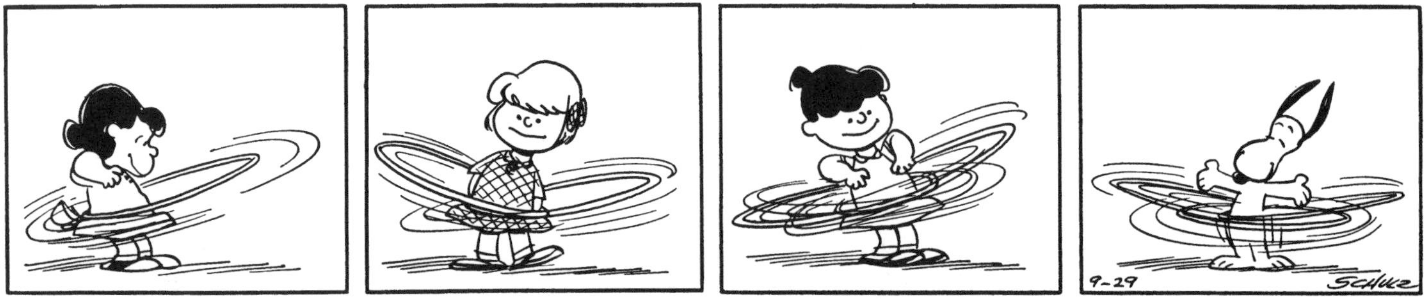
9-29
SCHULZ

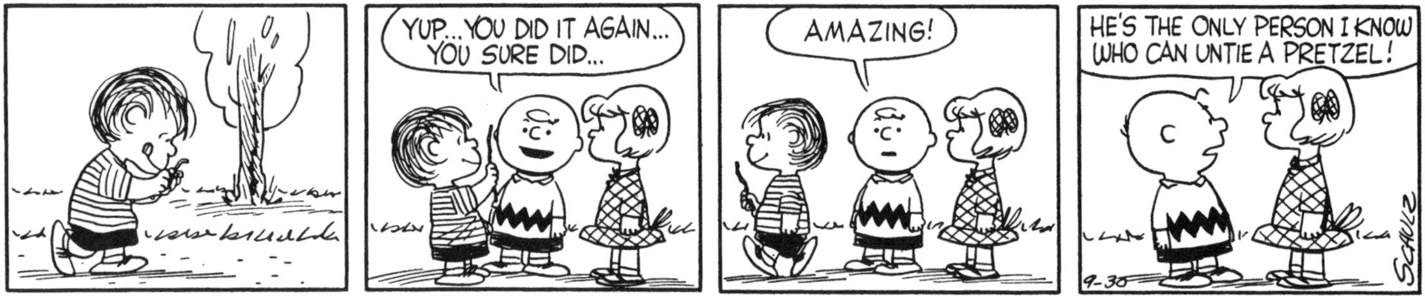
YUP... YOU DID IT AGAIN... YOU SURE DID...
AMAZING!
HE'S THE ONLY PERSON I KNOW WHO CAN UNTIE A PRETZEL!
9-30
SCHULZ

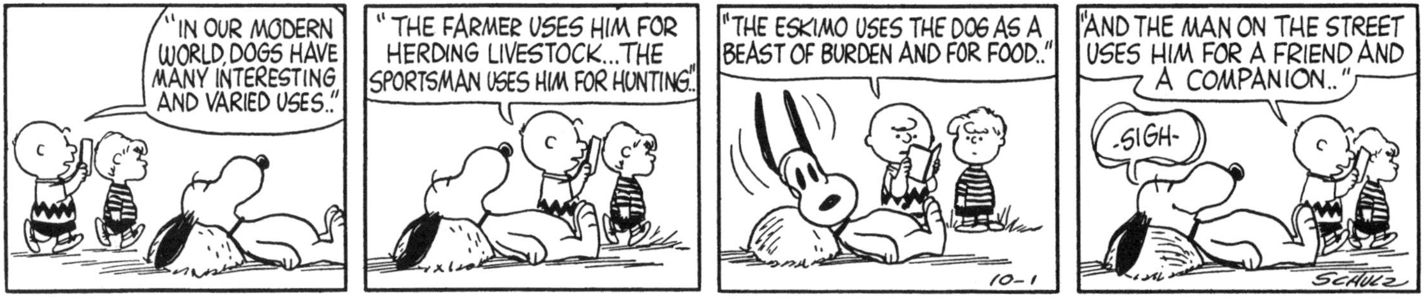
"IN OUR MODERN WORLD, DOGS HAVE MANY INTERESTING AND VARIED USES.."
"THE FARMER USES HIM FOR HERDING LIVESTOCK...THE SPORTSMAN USES HIM FOR HUNTING.."
"THE ESKIMO USES THE DOG AS A BEAST OF BURDEN AND FOR FOOD.."
"AND THE MAN ON THE STREET USES HIM FOR A FRIEND AND A COMPANION.."
-SIGH-
10-1
SCHULZ

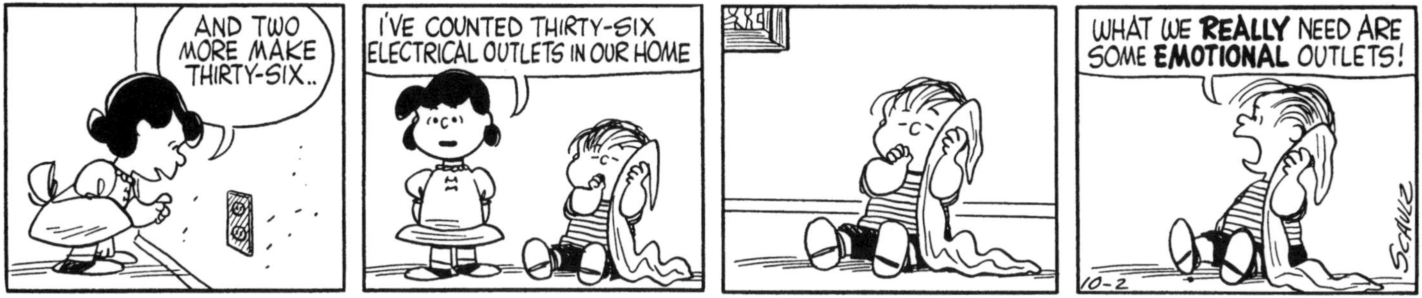
AND TWO MORE MAKE THIRTY-SIX..
I'VE COUNTED THIRTY-SIX ELECTRICAL OUTLETS IN OUR HOME
WHAT WE **REALLY** NEED ARE SOME **EMOTIONAL** OUTLETS!
10-2
SCHULZ

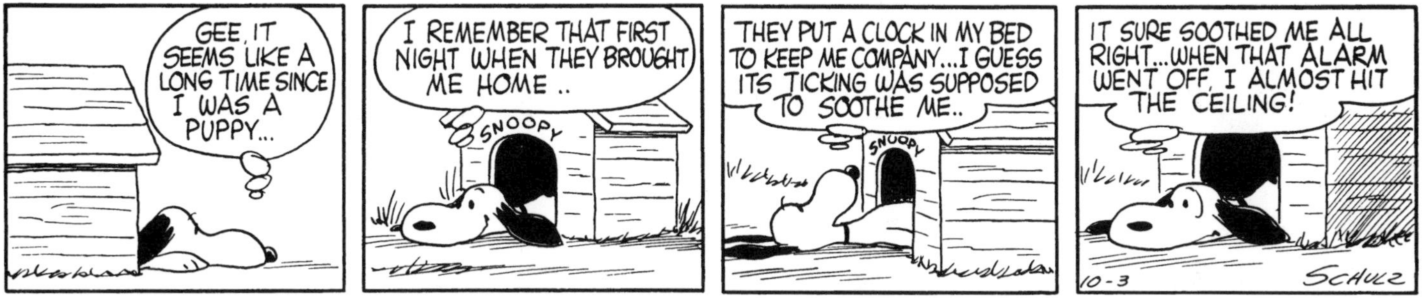
GEE, IT SEEMS LIKE A LONG TIME SINCE I WAS A PUPPY...
I REMEMBER THAT FIRST NIGHT WHEN THEY BROUGHT ME HOME ..
SNOOPY
THEY PUT A CLOCK IN MY BED TO KEEP ME COMPANY...I GUESS ITS TICKING WAS SUPPOSED TO SOOTHE ME..
SNOOPY
IT SURE SOOTHED ME ALL RIGHT...WHEN THAT ALARM WENT OFF, I ALMOST HIT THE CEILING!
10-3
SCHULZ

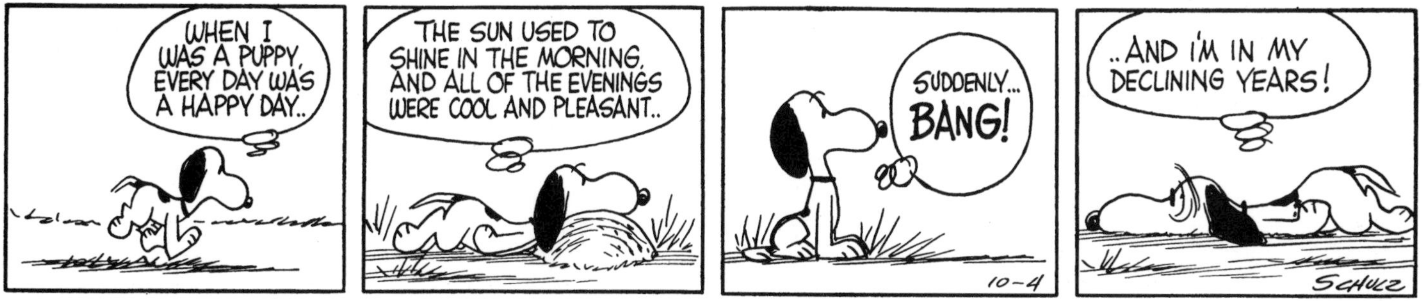
WHEN I WAS A PUPPY, EVERY DAY WAS A HAPPY DAY..
THE SUN USED TO SHINE IN THE MORNING, AND ALL OF THE EVENINGS WERE COOL AND PLEASANT..
SUDDENLY... BANG!
10-4
..AND I'M IN MY DECLINING YEARS!
SCHULZ

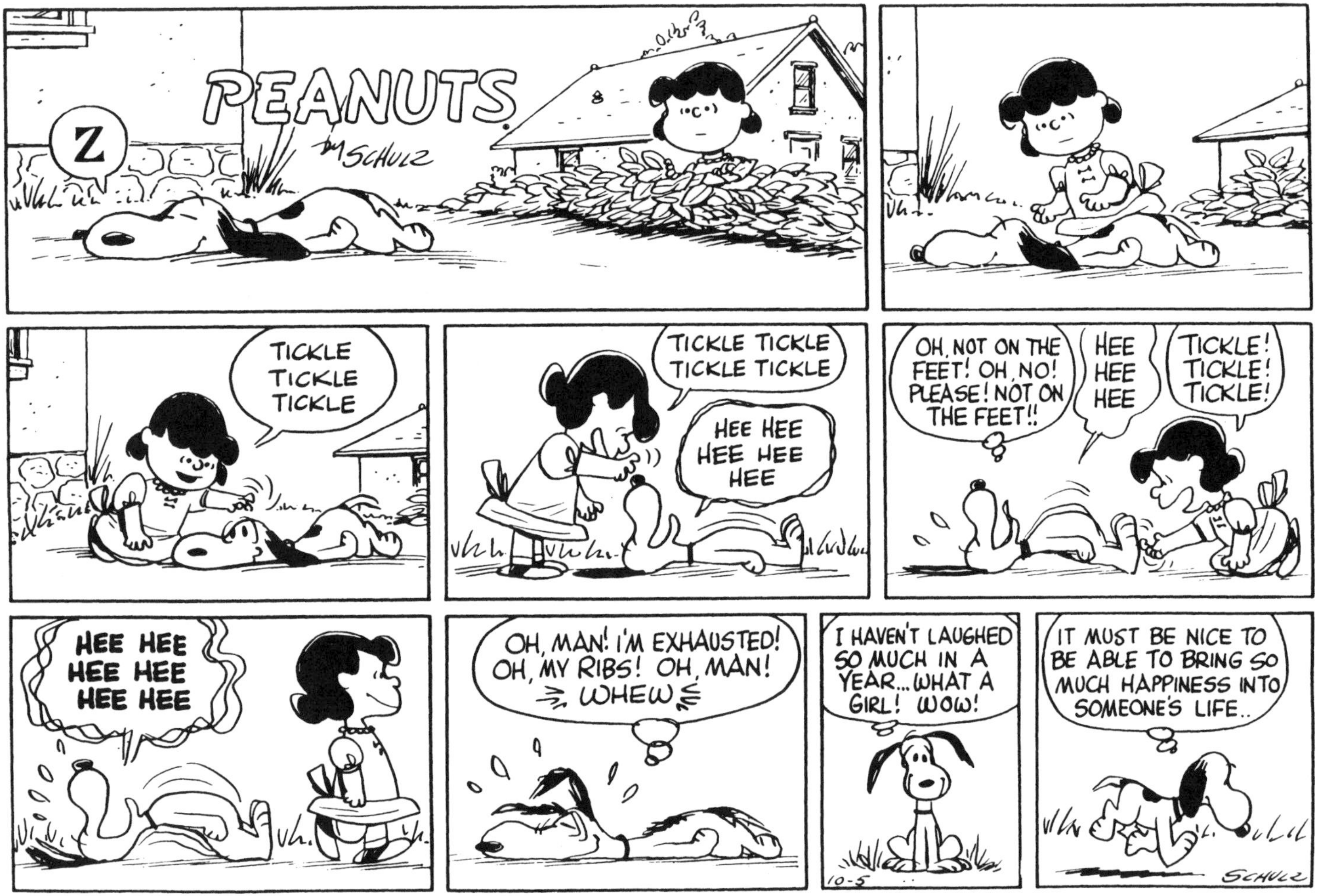
PEANUTS
by SCHULZ
Z
TICKLE TICKLE TICKLE
TICKLE TICKLE TICKLE TICKLE
HEE HEE HEE HEE HEE
OH, NOT ON THE FEET! OH, NO! PLEASE! NOT ON THE FEET!!
HEE HEE HEE
TICKLE! TICKLE! TICKLE!
HEE HEE HEE HEE HEE HEE
OH, MAN! I'M EXHAUSTED! OH, MY RIBS! OH, MAN! WHEW
I HAVEN'T LAUGHED SO MUCH IN A YEAR... WHAT A GIRL! WOW!
IT MUST BE NICE TO BE ABLE TO BRING SO MUCH HAPPINESS INTO SOMEONE'S LIFE..
10-5
SCHULZ

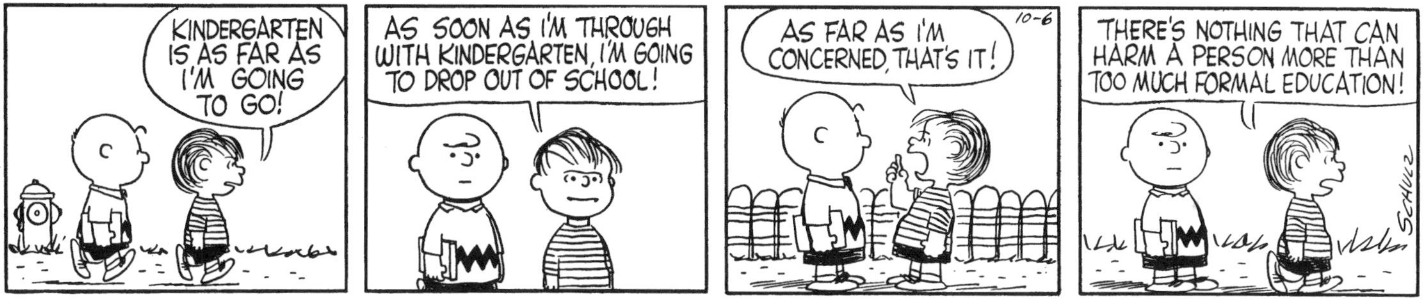
KINDERGARTEN IS AS FAR AS I'M GOING TO GO!
AS SOON AS I'M THROUGH WITH KINDERGARTEN, I'M GOING TO DROP OUT OF SCHOOL!
AS FAR AS I'M CONCERNED, THAT'S IT!
10-6
THERE'S NOTHING THAT CAN HARM A PERSON MORE THAN TOO MUCH FORMAL EDUCATION!
SCHULZ

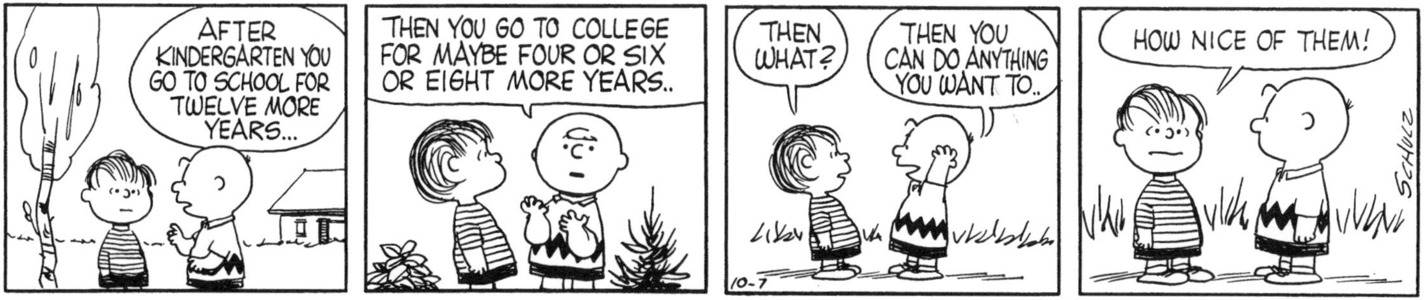
AFTER KINDERGARTEN YOU GO TO SCHOOL FOR TWELVE MORE YEARS...
THEN YOU GO TO COLLEGE FOR MAYBE FOUR OR SIX OR EIGHT MORE YEARS..
THEN WHAT?
THEN YOU CAN DO ANYTHING YOU WANT TO..
10-7
HOW NICE OF THEM!
SCHULZ

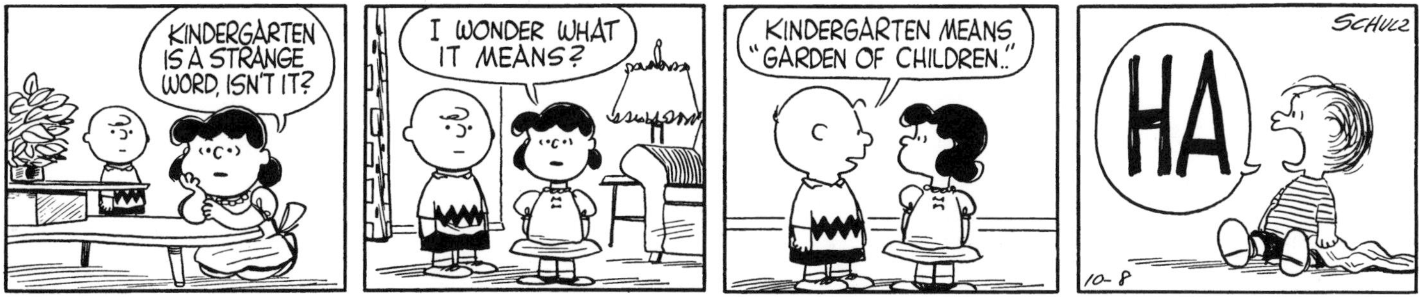
KINDERGARTEN IS A STRANGE WORD, ISN'T IT?
I WONDER WHAT IT MEANS?
KINDERGARTEN MEANS "GARDEN OF CHILDREN."
SCHULZ
HA
10-8

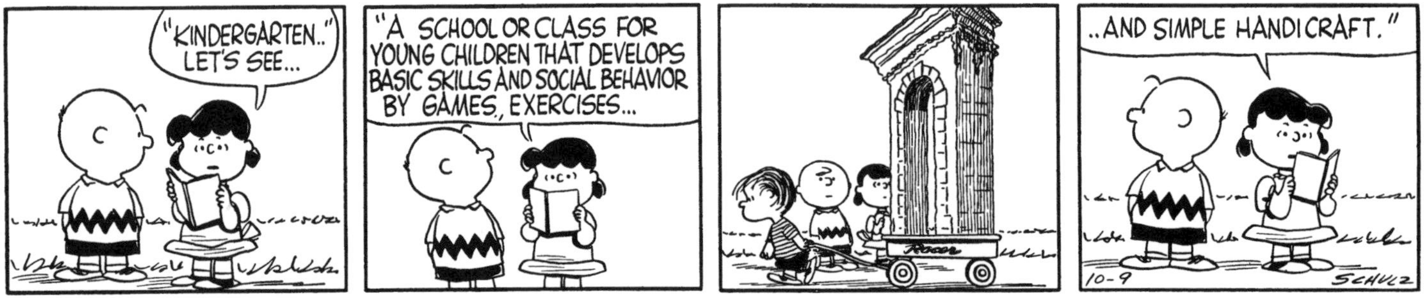
"KINDERGARTEN.." LET'S SEE...
"A SCHOOL OR CLASS FOR YOUNG CHILDREN THAT DEVELOPS BASIC SKILLS AND SOCIAL BEHAVIOR BY GAMES, EXERCISES...
..AND SIMPLE HANDICRAFT."
10-9
SCHULZ

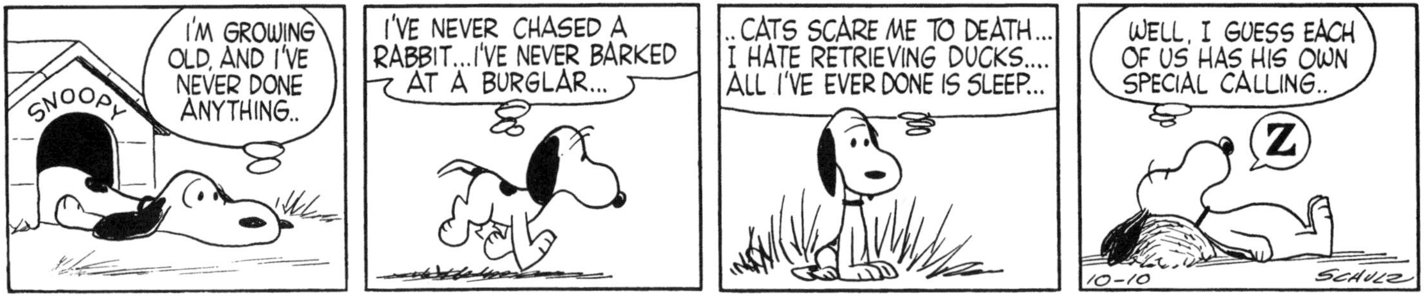
SNOOPY
I'M GROWING OLD, AND I'VE NEVER DONE ANYTHING..
I'VE NEVER CHASED A RABBIT...I'VE NEVER BARKED AT A BURGLAR...
..CATS SCARE ME TO DEATH... I HATE RETRIEVING DUCKS.... ALL I'VE EVER DONE IS SLEEP...
WELL, I GUESS EACH OF US HAS HIS OWN SPECIAL CALLING..
Z
10-10
SCHULZ

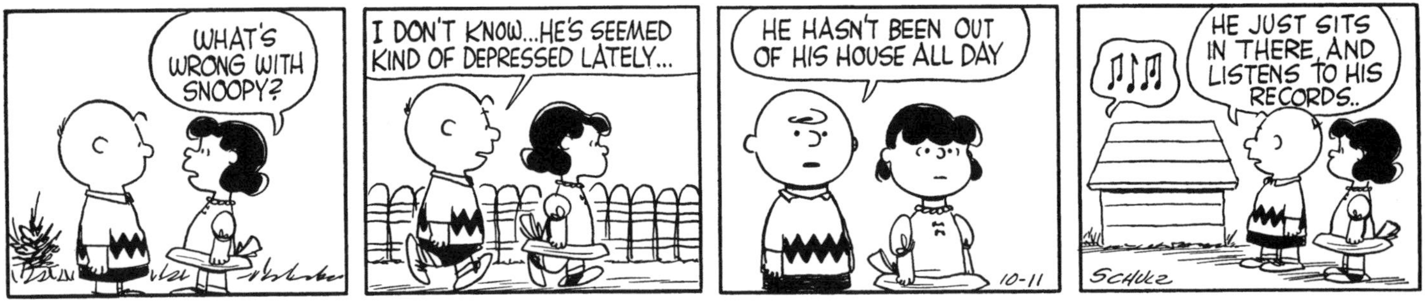
WHAT'S WRONG WITH SNOOPY?
I DON'T KNOW...HE'S SEEMED KIND OF DEPRESSED LATELY...
HE HASN'T BEEN OUT OF HIS HOUSE ALL DAY
10-11
HE JUST SITS IN THERE AND LISTENS TO HIS RECORDS..
SCHULZ

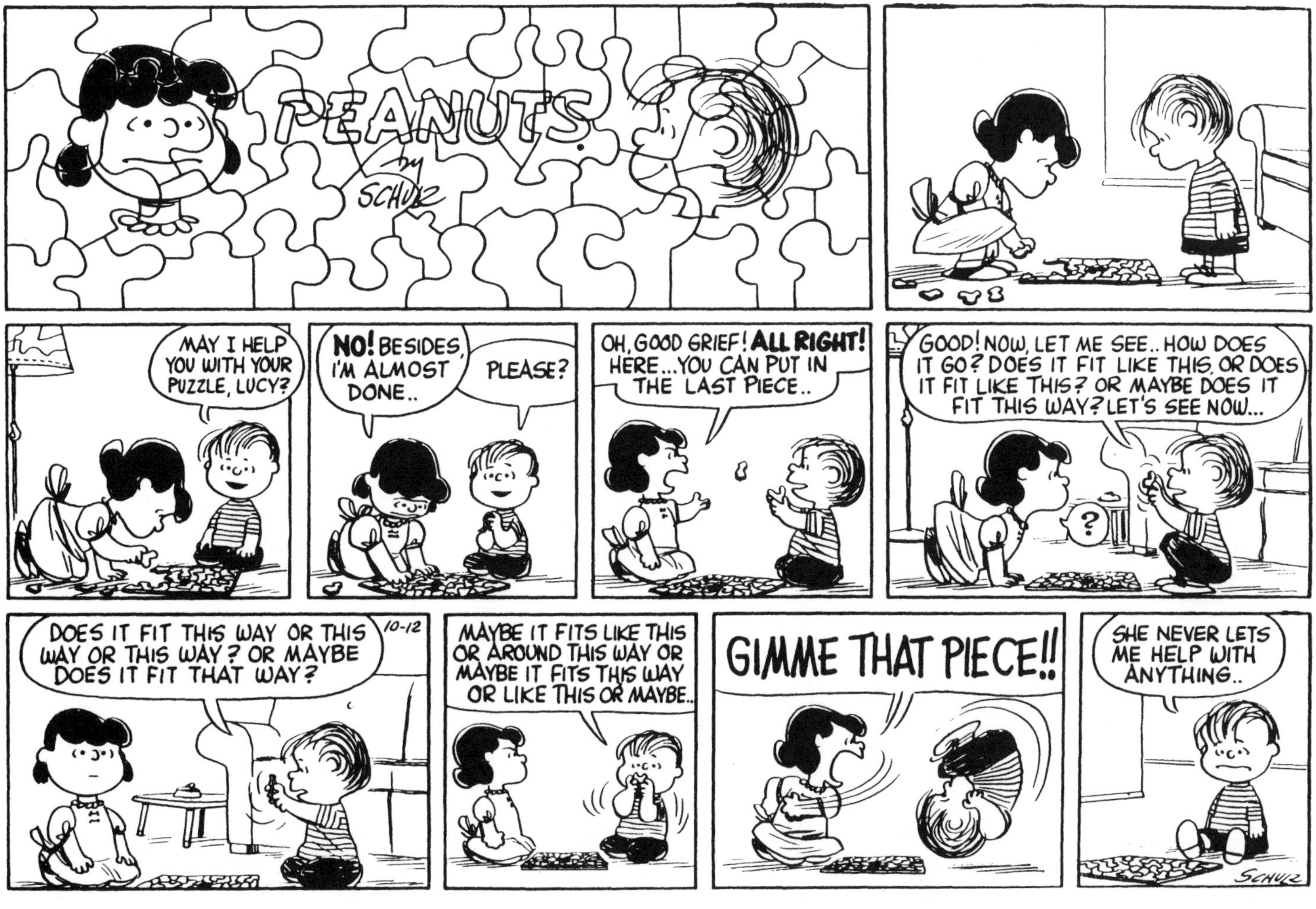
PEANUTS
by SCHULZ
MAY I HELP YOU WITH YOUR PUZZLE, LUCY?
NO! BESIDES, I'M ALMOST DONE..
PLEASE?
OH, GOOD GRIEF! ALL RIGHT! HERE...YOU CAN PUT IN THE LAST PIECE..
GOOD! NOW, LET ME SEE.. HOW DOES IT GO? DOES IT FIT LIKE THIS, OR DOES IT FIT LIKE THIS? OR MAYBE DOES IT FIT THIS WAY? LET'S SEE NOW...
?
DOES IT FIT THIS WAY OR THIS WAY OR THIS WAY? OR MAYBE DOES IT FIT THAT WAY?
10-12
MAYBE IT FITS LIKE THIS OR AROUND THIS WAY OR MAYBE IT FITS THIS WAY OR LIKE THIS OR MAYBE..
GIMME THAT PIECE!!
SHE NEVER LETS ME HELP WITH ANYTHING..
SCHULZ

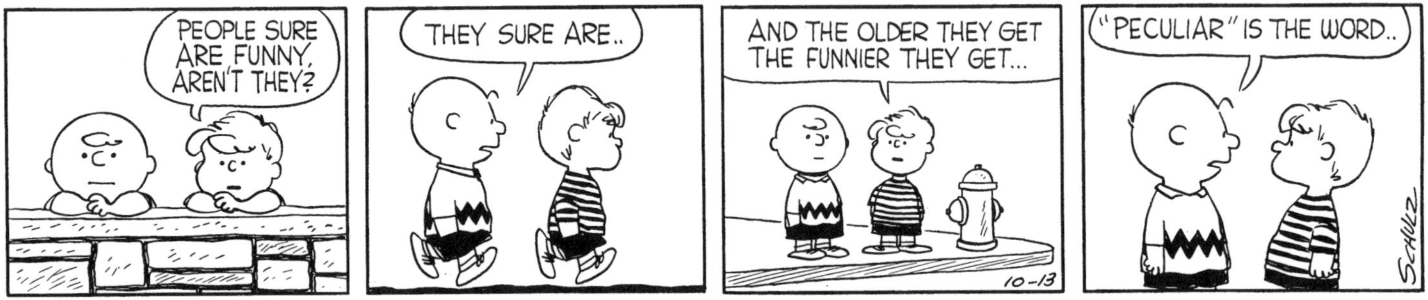
PEOPLE SURE ARE FUNNY, AREN'T THEY?
THEY SURE ARE..
AND THE OLDER THEY GET THE FUNNIER THEY GET...
10-13
"PECULIAR" IS THE WORD..
SCHULZ

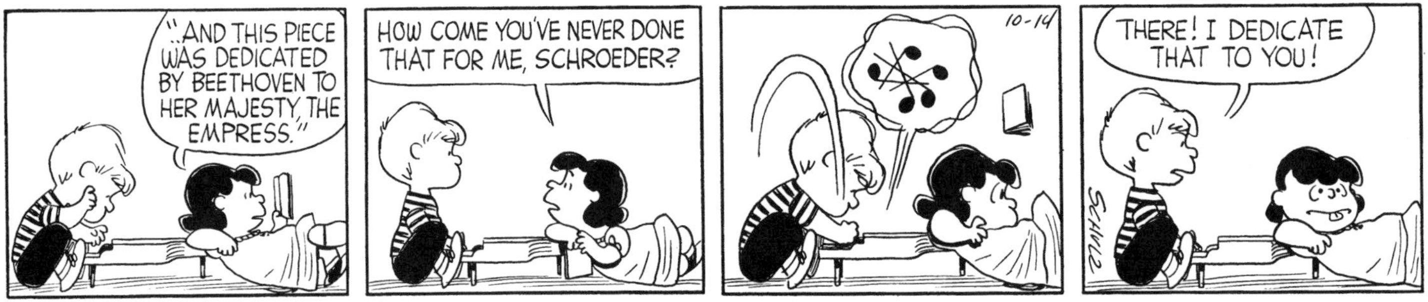
"..AND THIS PIECE WAS DEDICATED BY BEETHOVEN TO HER MAJESTY, THE EMPRESS."
HOW COME YOU'VE NEVER DONE THAT FOR ME, SCHROEDER?
10-14
SCHULZ
THERE! I DEDICATE THAT TO YOU!

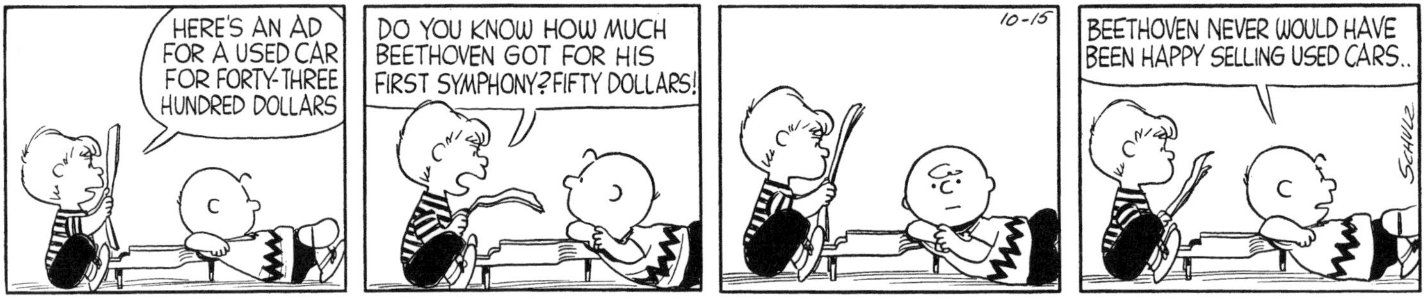
HERE'S AN AD FOR A USED CAR FOR FORTY-THREE HUNDRED DOLLARS
DO YOU KNOW HOW MUCH BEETHOVEN GOT FOR HIS FIRST SYMPHONY? FIFTY DOLLARS!
10-15
BEETHOVEN NEVER WOULD HAVE BEEN HAPPY SELLING USED CARS..
SCHULZ

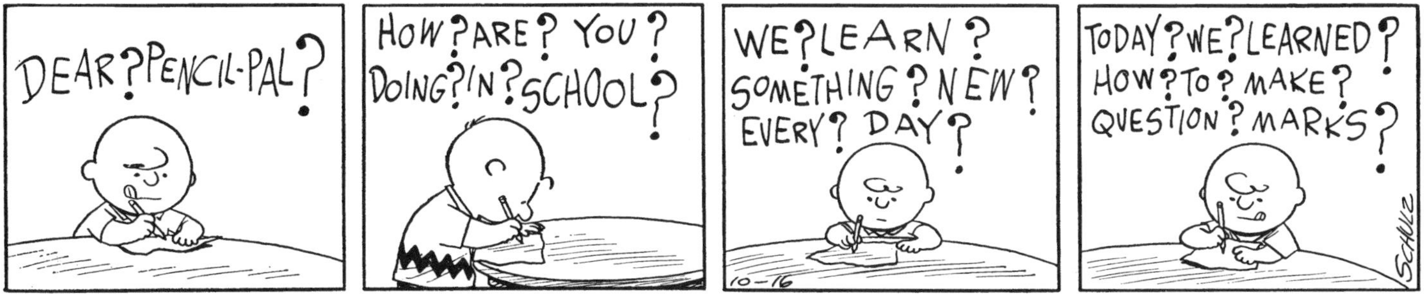
DEAR?PENCIL-PAL?
HOW?ARE? YOU? DOING?IN?SCHOOL?
WE?LEARN? SOMETHING?NEW? EVERY? DAY?
10-16
TODAY?WE?LEARNED? HOW?TO?MAKE? QUESTION?MARKS?
SCHULZ

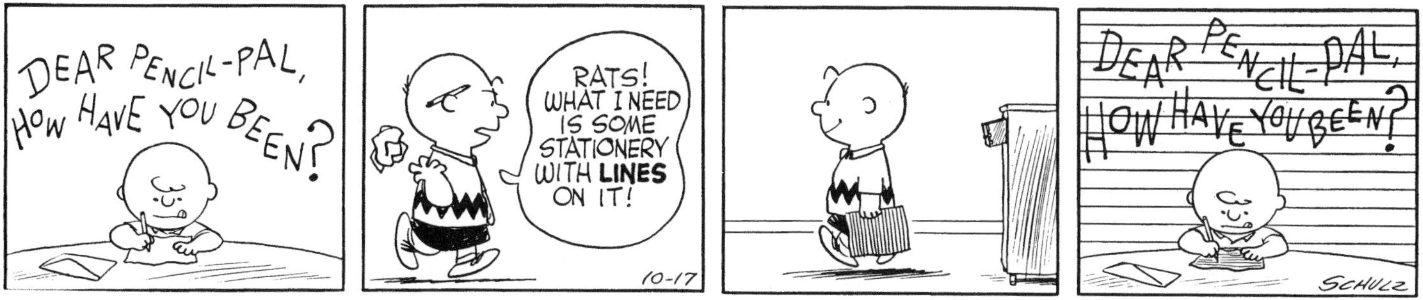
DEAR PENCIL-PAL, HOW HAVE YOU BEEN?
RATS! WHAT I NEED IS SOME STATIONERY WITH **LINES** ON IT!
10-17
DEAR PENCIL-PAL, HOW HAVE YOU BEEN?
SCHULZ

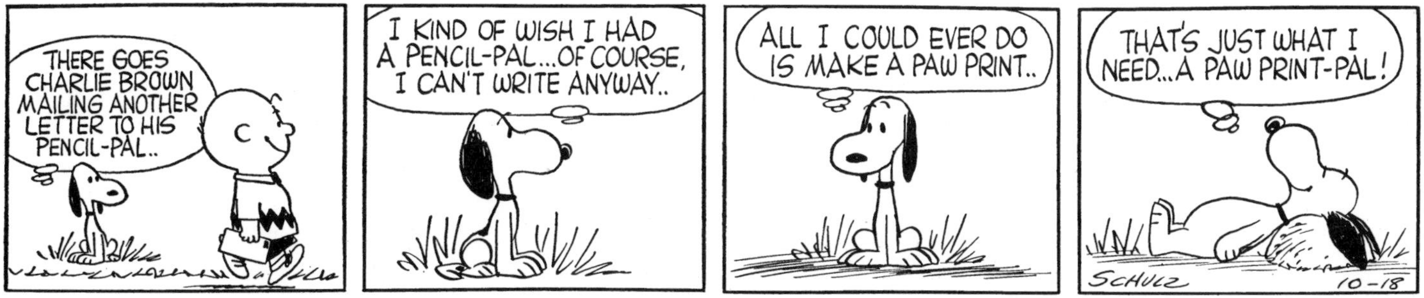
THERE GOES CHARLIE BROWN MAILING ANOTHER LETTER TO HIS PENCIL-PAL..
I KIND OF WISH I HAD A PENCIL-PAL...OF COURSE, I CAN'T WRITE ANYWAY..
ALL I COULD EVER DO IS MAKE A PAW PRINT..
THAT'S JUST WHAT I NEED...A PAW PRINT-PAL!
SCHULZ
10-18

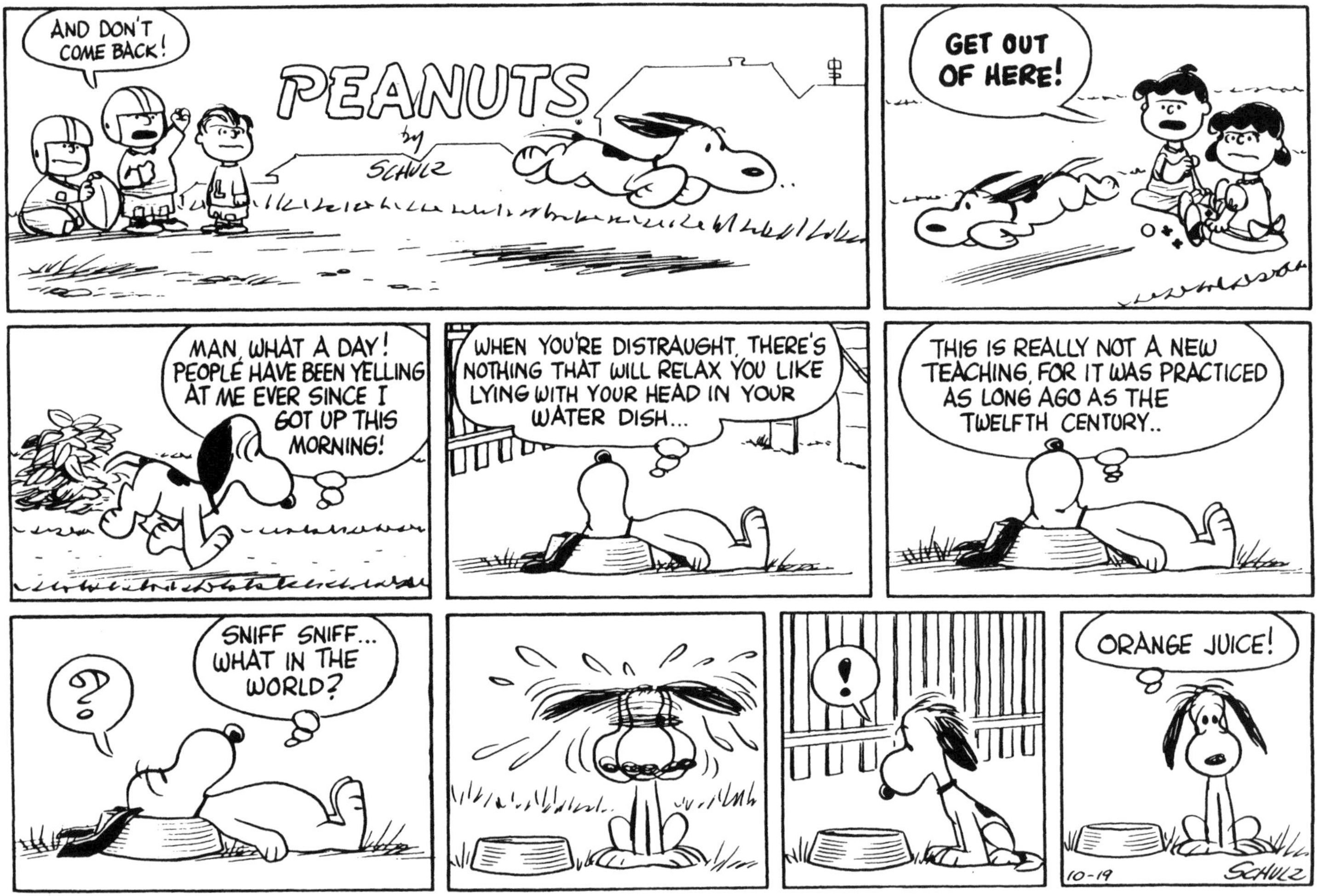
AND DON'T COME BACK!
PEANUTS
by SCHULZ
GET OUT OF HERE!
MAN, WHAT A DAY! PEOPLE HAVE BEEN YELLING AT ME EVER SINCE I GOT UP THIS MORNING!
WHEN YOU'RE DISTRAUGHT, THERE'S NOTHING THAT WILL RELAX YOU LIKE LYING WITH YOUR HEAD IN YOUR WATER DISH...
THIS IS REALLY NOT A NEW TEACHING, FOR IT WAS PRACTICED AS LONG AGO AS THE TWELFTH CENTURY..
?
SNIFF SNIFF... WHAT IN THE WORLD?
!
ORANGE JUICE!
10-19
SCHULZ

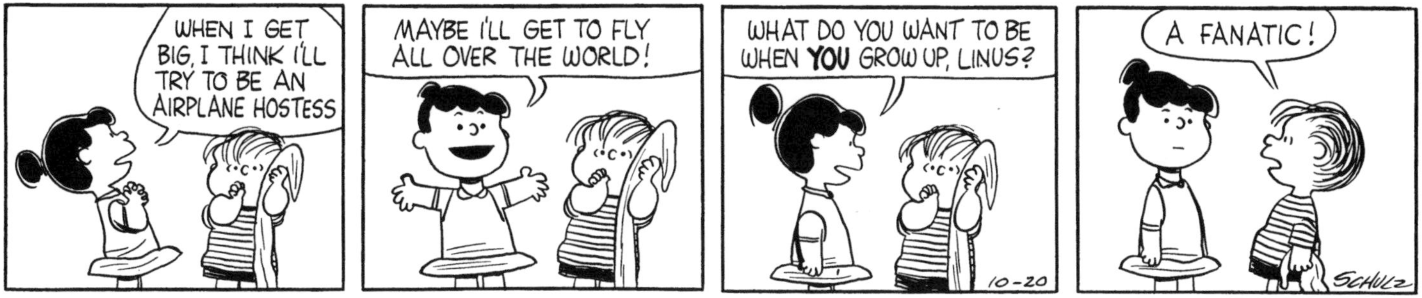
WHEN I GET BIG, I THINK I'LL TRY TO BE AN AIRPLANE HOSTESS
MAYBE I'LL GET TO FLY ALL OVER THE WORLD!
WHAT DO YOU WANT TO BE WHEN YOU GROW UP, LINUS?
A FANATIC!
10-20
SCHULZ

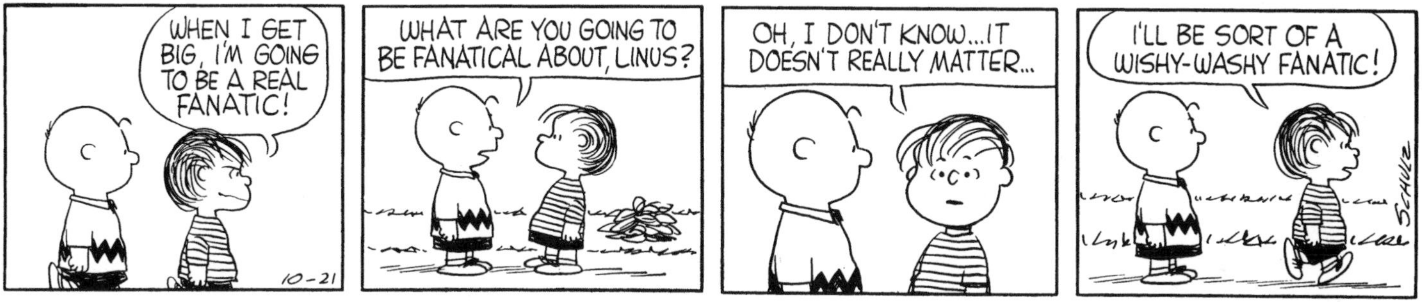
WHEN I GET BIG, I'M GOING TO BE A REAL FANATIC!
10-21
WHAT ARE YOU GOING TO BE FANATICAL ABOUT, LINUS?
OH, I DON'T KNOW...IT DOESN'T REALLY MATTER...
I'LL BE SORT OF A WISHY-WASHY FANATIC!
SCHULZ

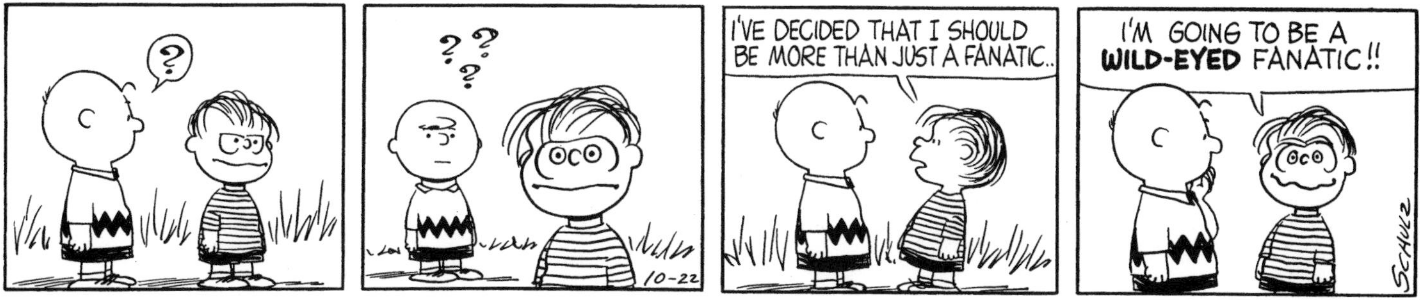
?
? ? ?
10-22
I'VE DECIDED THAT I SHOULD BE MORE THAN JUST A FANATIC..
I'M GOING TO BE A WILD-EYED FANATIC!!
SCHULZ

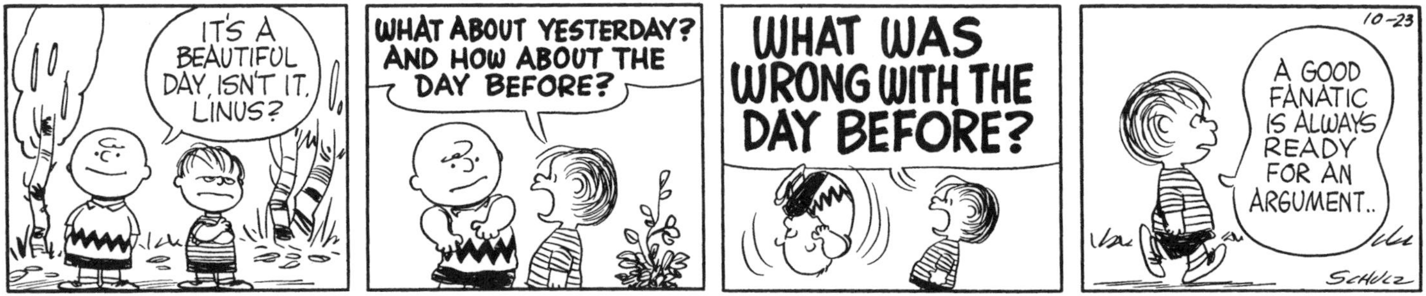
IT'S A BEAUTIFUL DAY, ISN'T IT, LINUS?
WHAT ABOUT YESTERDAY? AND HOW ABOUT THE DAY BEFORE?
WHAT WAS WRONG WITH THE DAY BEFORE?
10-23
A GOOD FANATIC IS ALWAYS READY FOR AN ARGUMENT..
SCHULZ

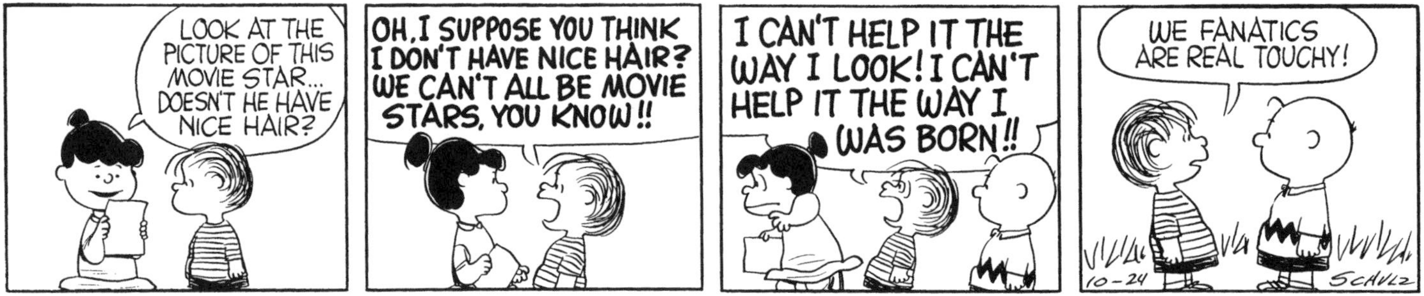
LOOK AT THE PICTURE OF THIS MOVIE STAR... DOESN'T HE HAVE NICE HAIR?
OH, I SUPPOSE YOU THINK I DON'T HAVE NICE HAIR? WE CAN'T ALL BE MOVIE STARS, YOU KNOW!!
I CAN'T HELP IT THE WAY I LOOK! I CAN'T HELP IT THE WAY I WAS BORN!!
WE FANATICS ARE REAL TOUCHY!
10-24
SCHULZ

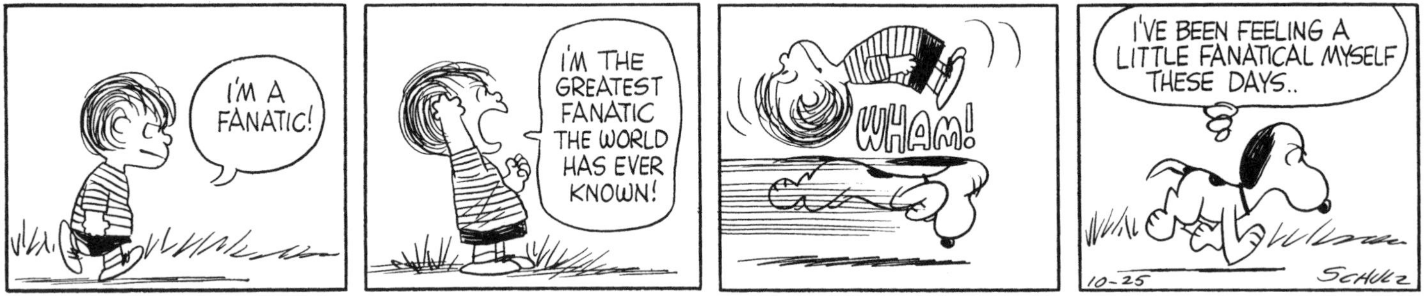
I'M A FANATIC!
I'M THE GREATEST FANATIC THE WORLD HAS EVER KNOWN!
WHAM!
I'VE BEEN FEELING A LITTLE FANATICAL MYSELF THESE DAYS..
10-25
SCHULZ

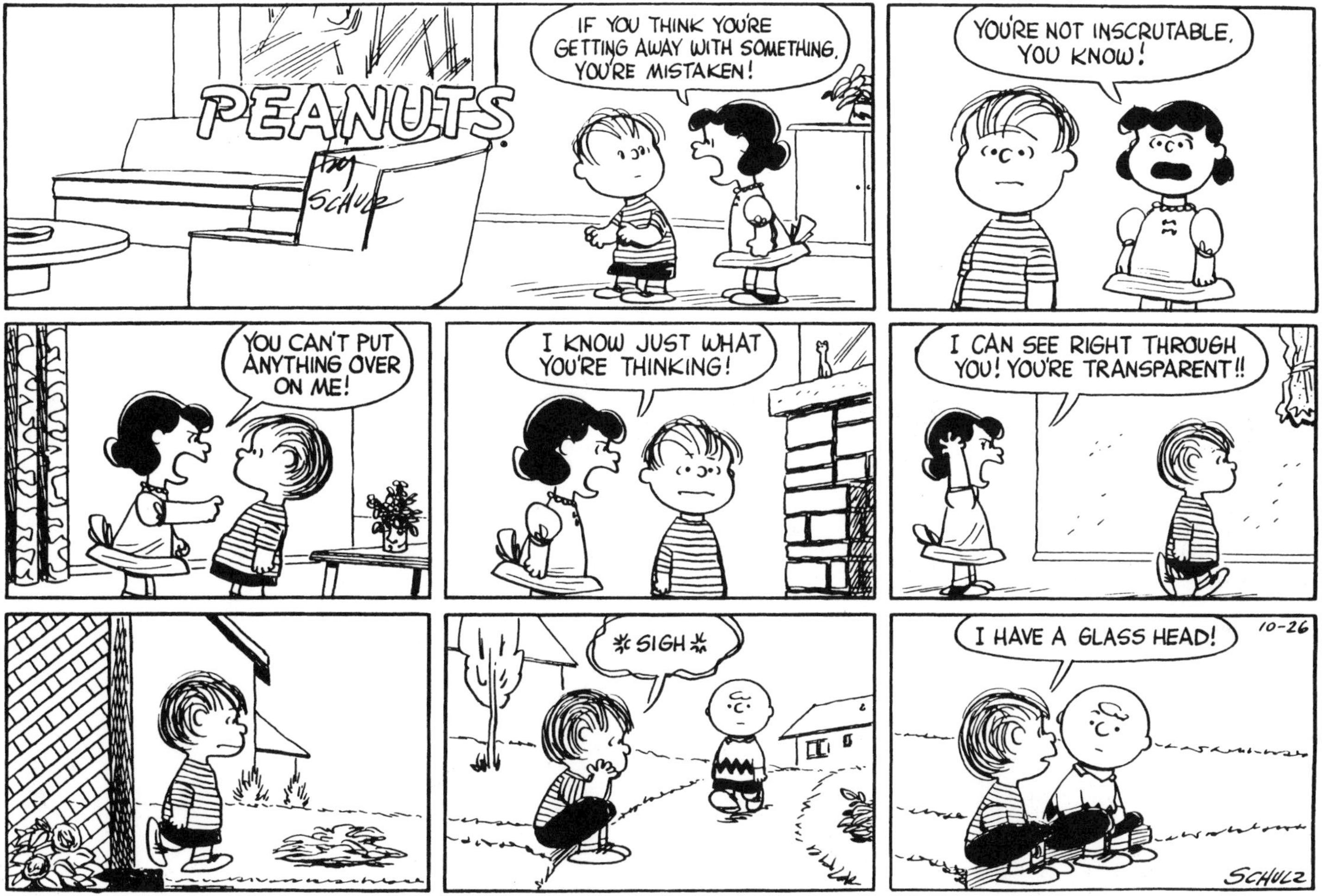
PEANUTS
by SCHULZ
IF YOU THINK YOU'RE GETTING AWAY WITH SOMETHING, YOU'RE MISTAKEN!
YOU'RE NOT INSCRUTABLE, YOU KNOW!
YOU CAN'T PUT ANYTHING OVER ON ME!
I KNOW JUST WHAT YOU'RE THINKING!
I CAN SEE RIGHT THROUGH YOU! YOU'RE TRANSPARENT!!
SIGH
10-26
I HAVE A GLASS HEAD!
SCHULZ

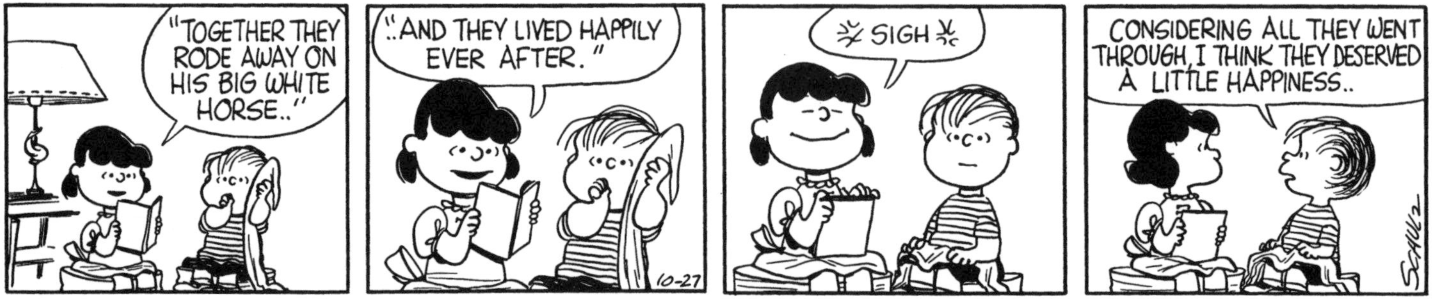
"TOGETHER THEY RODE AWAY ON HIS BIG WHITE HORSE.."
"..AND THEY LIVED HAPPILY EVER AFTER."
SIGH
CONSIDERING ALL THEY WENT THROUGH, I THINK THEY DESERVED A LITTLE HAPPINESS..
10-27
SCHULZ

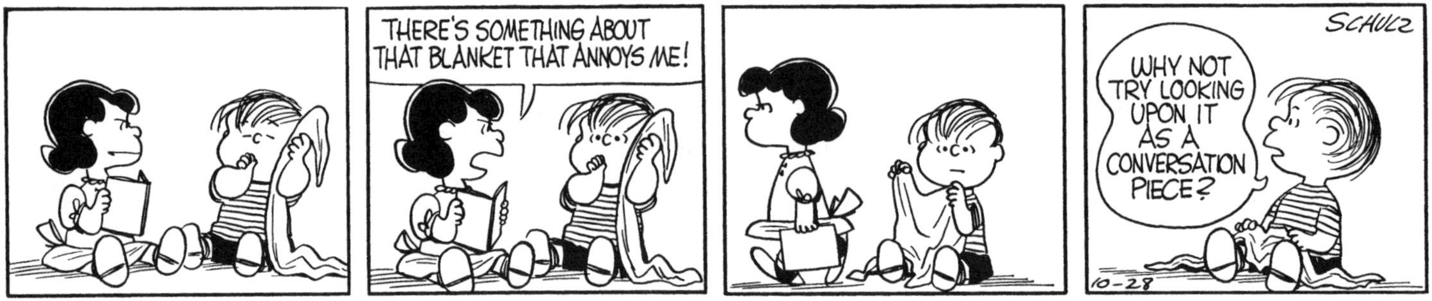
THERE'S SOMETHING ABOUT THAT BLANKET THAT ANNOYS ME!
SCHULZ
WHY NOT TRY LOOKING UPON IT AS A CONVERSATION PIECE?
10-28

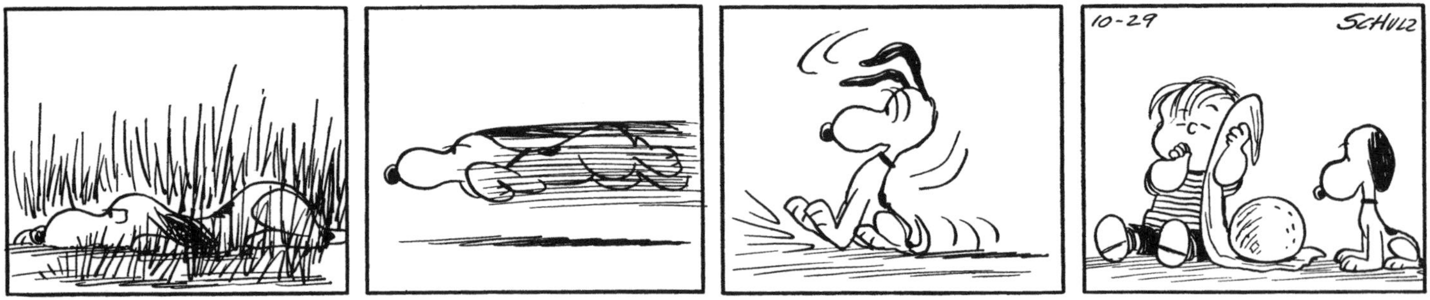
10-29
SCHULZ

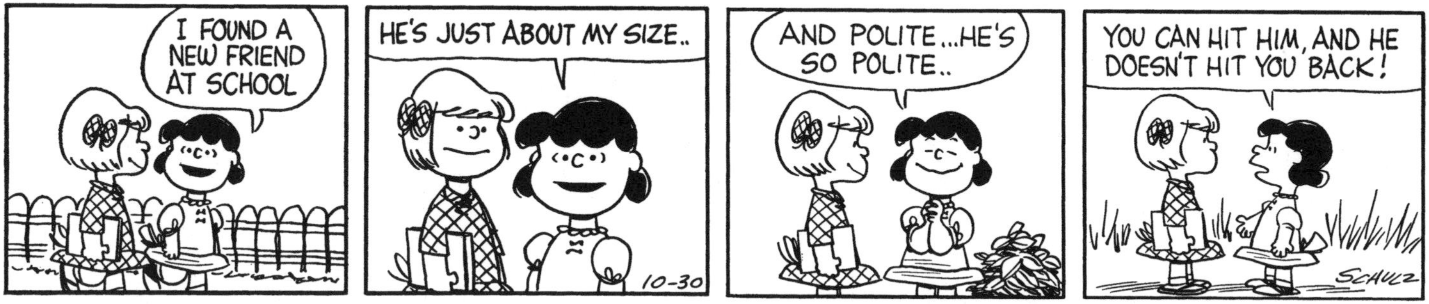
I FOUND A NEW FRIEND AT SCHOOL
HE'S JUST ABOUT MY SIZE..
10-30
AND POLITE...HE'S SO POLITE..
YOU CAN HIT HIM, AND HE DOESN'T HIT YOU BACK!

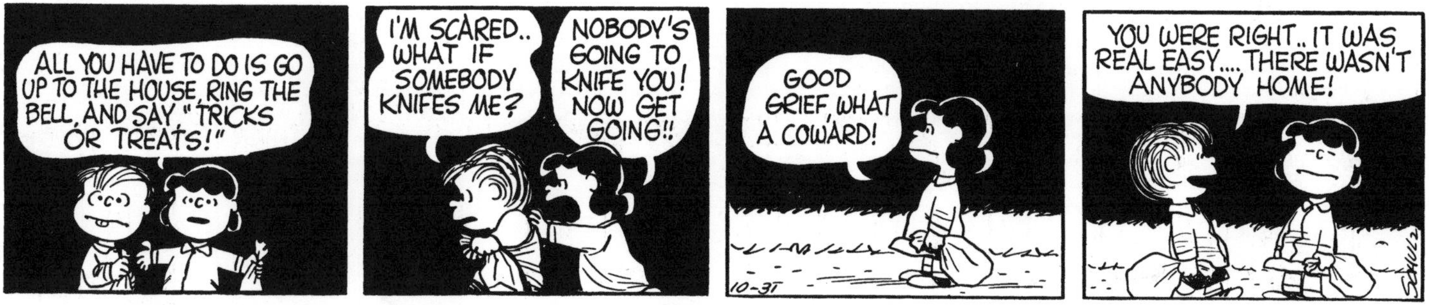
ALL YOU HAVE TO DO IS GO UP TO THE HOUSE, RING THE BELL, AND SAY, "TRICKS OR TREATS!"
I'M SCARED.. WHAT IF SOMEBODY KNIFES ME?
NOBODY'S GOING TO KNIFE YOU! NOW GET GOING!!
GOOD GRIEF, WHAT A COWARD!
10-31
YOU WERE RIGHT.. IT WAS REAL EASY.... THERE WASN'T ANYBODY HOME!

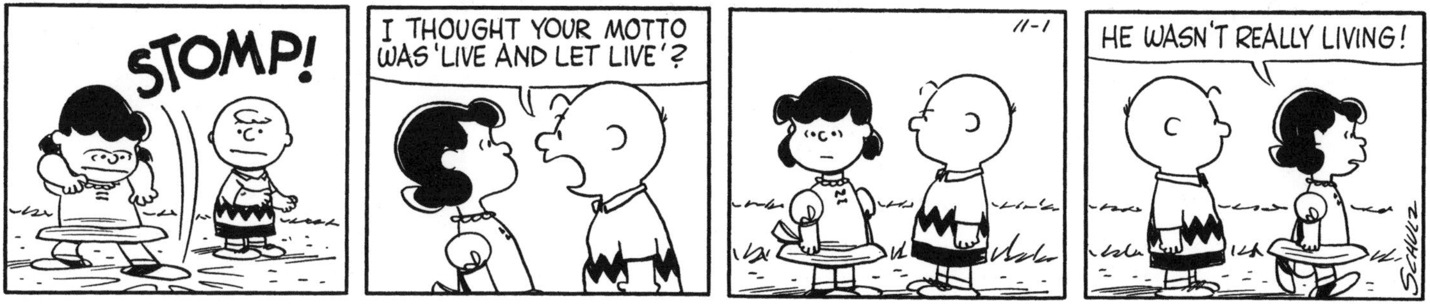
STOMP!
I THOUGHT YOUR MOTTO WAS 'LIVE AND LET LIVE'?
11-1
HE WASN'T REALLY LIVING!

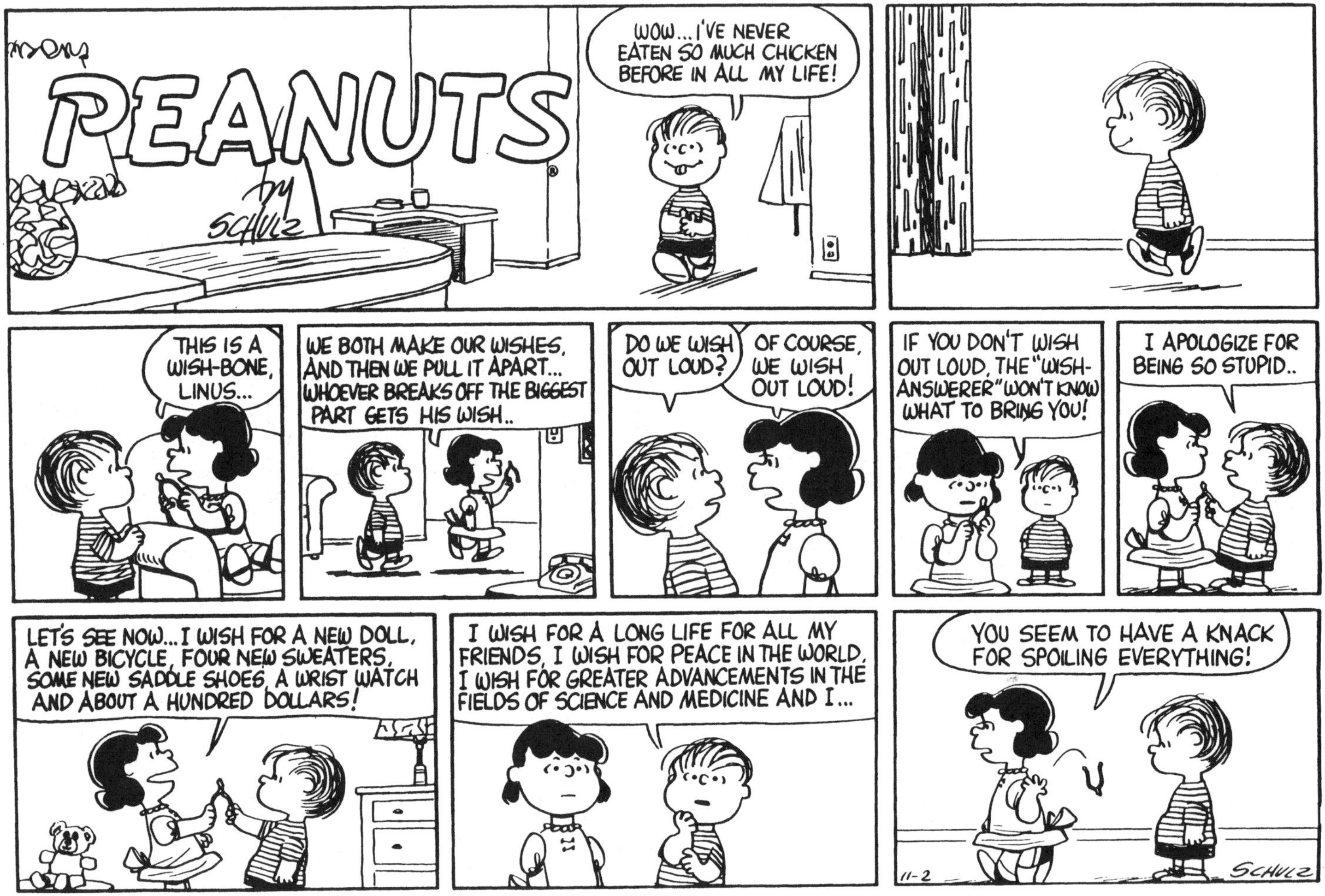
PEANUTS
BY SCHULZ
WOW... I'VE NEVER EATEN SO MUCH CHICKEN BEFORE IN ALL MY LIFE!
THIS IS A WISH-BONE, LINUS...
WE BOTH MAKE OUR WISHES, AND THEN WE PULL IT APART... WHOEVER BREAKS OFF THE BIGGEST PART GETS HIS WISH..
DO WE WISH OUT LOUD?
OF COURSE, WE WISH OUT LOUD!
IF YOU DON'T WISH OUT LOUD, THE "WISH-ANSWERER" WON'T KNOW WHAT TO BRING YOU!
I APOLOGIZE FOR BEING SO STUPID..
LET'S SEE NOW... I WISH FOR A NEW DOLL, A NEW BICYCLE, FOUR NEW SWEATERS, SOME NEW SADDLE SHOES, A WRIST WATCH AND ABOUT A HUNDRED DOLLARS!
I WISH FOR A LONG LIFE FOR ALL MY FRIENDS, I WISH FOR PEACE IN THE WORLD, I WISH FOR GREATER ADVANCEMENTS IN THE FIELDS OF SCIENCE AND MEDICINE AND I...
YOU SEEM TO HAVE A KNACK FOR SPOILING EVERYTHING!
11-2
SCHULZ

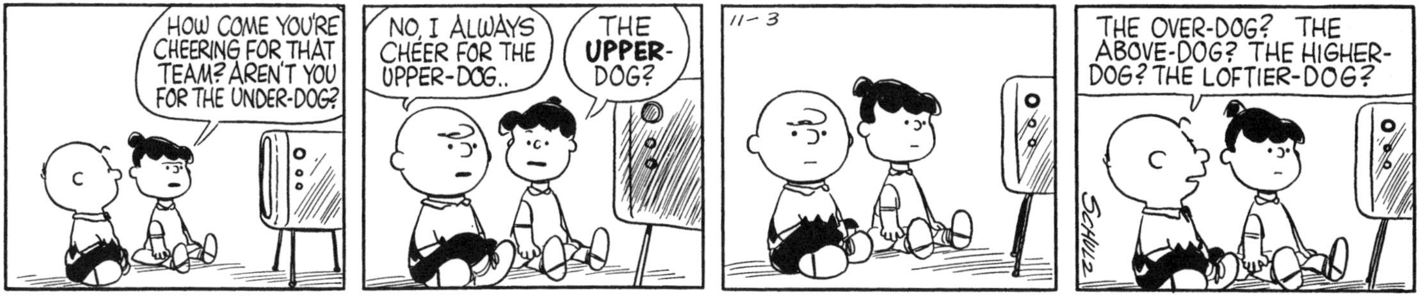
HOW COME YOU'RE CHEERING FOR THAT TEAM? AREN'T YOU FOR THE UNDER-DOG?
NO, I ALWAYS CHEER FOR THE UPPER-DOG..
THE **UPPER**-DOG?
11-3
THE OVER-DOG? THE ABOVE-DOG? THE HIGHER-DOG? THE LOFTIER-DOG?
SCHULZ

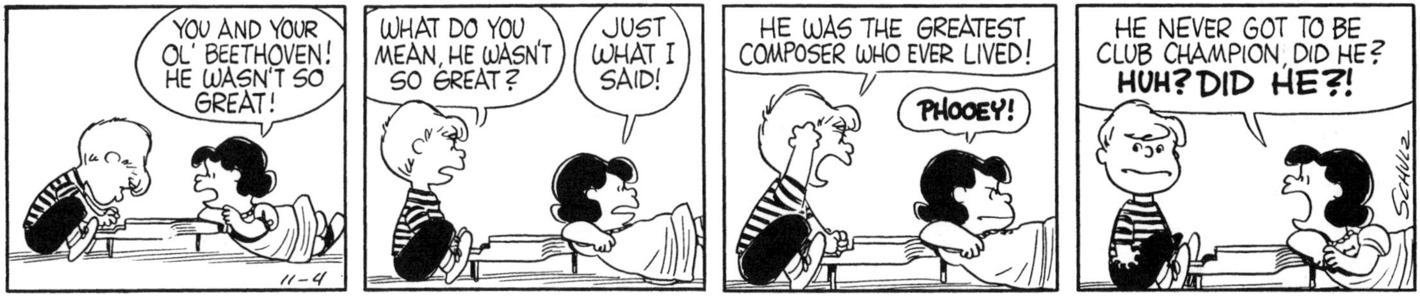
YOU AND YOUR OL' BEETHOVEN! HE WASN'T SO GREAT!
11-4
WHAT DO YOU MEAN, HE WASN'T SO GREAT?
JUST WHAT I SAID!
HE WAS THE GREATEST COMPOSER WHO EVER LIVED!
PHOOEY!
HE NEVER GOT TO BE CLUB CHAMPION, DID HE? **HUH? DID HE?!**
SCHULZ

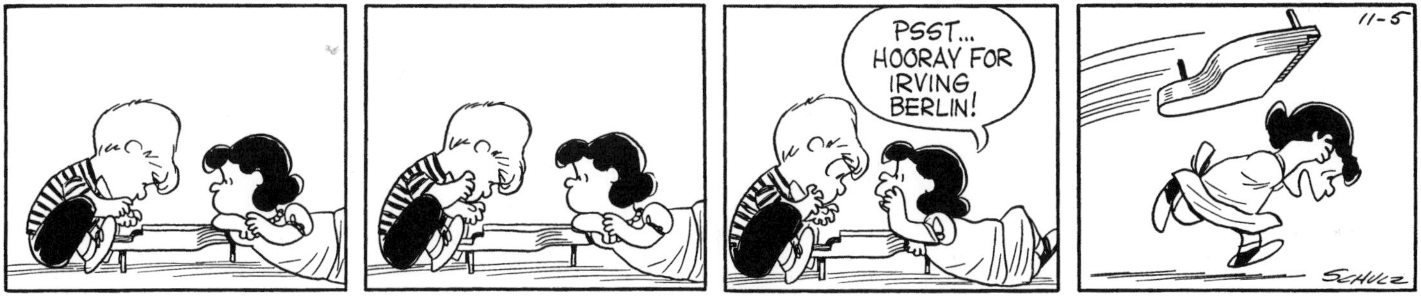
PSST... HOORAY FOR IRVING BERLIN!
11-5
SCHULZ

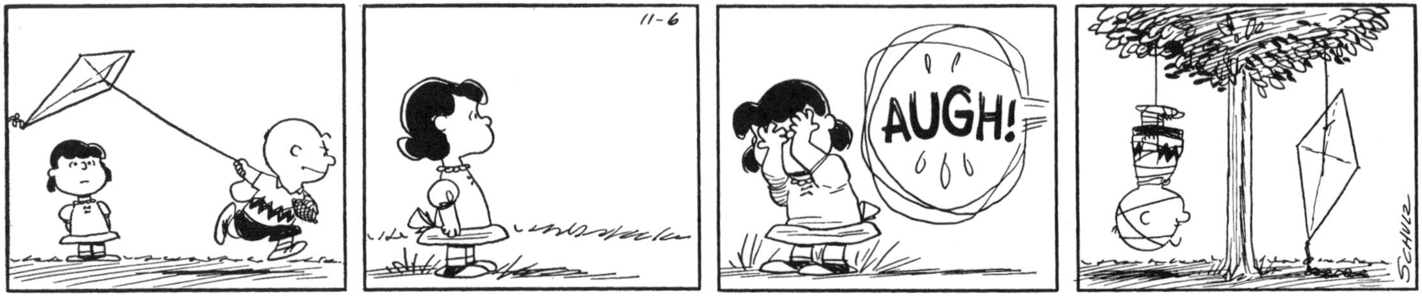
11-6
AUGH!
SCHULZ

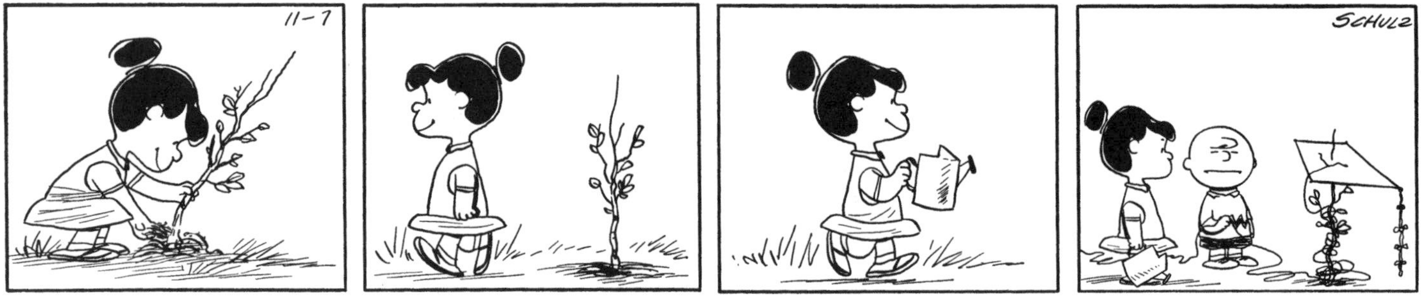
11-7
SCHULZ

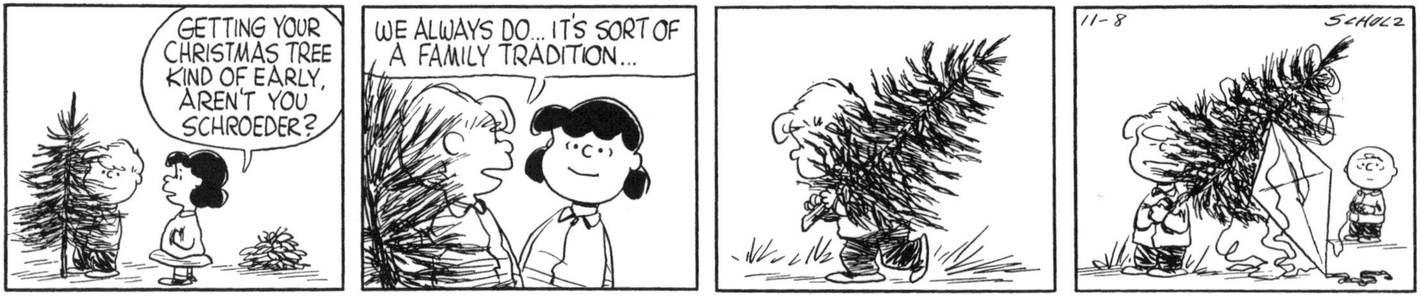
GETTING YOUR CHRISTMAS TREE KIND OF EARLY, AREN'T YOU SCHROEDER?
WE ALWAYS DO... IT'S SORT OF A FAMILY TRADITION...
11-8
SCHULZ

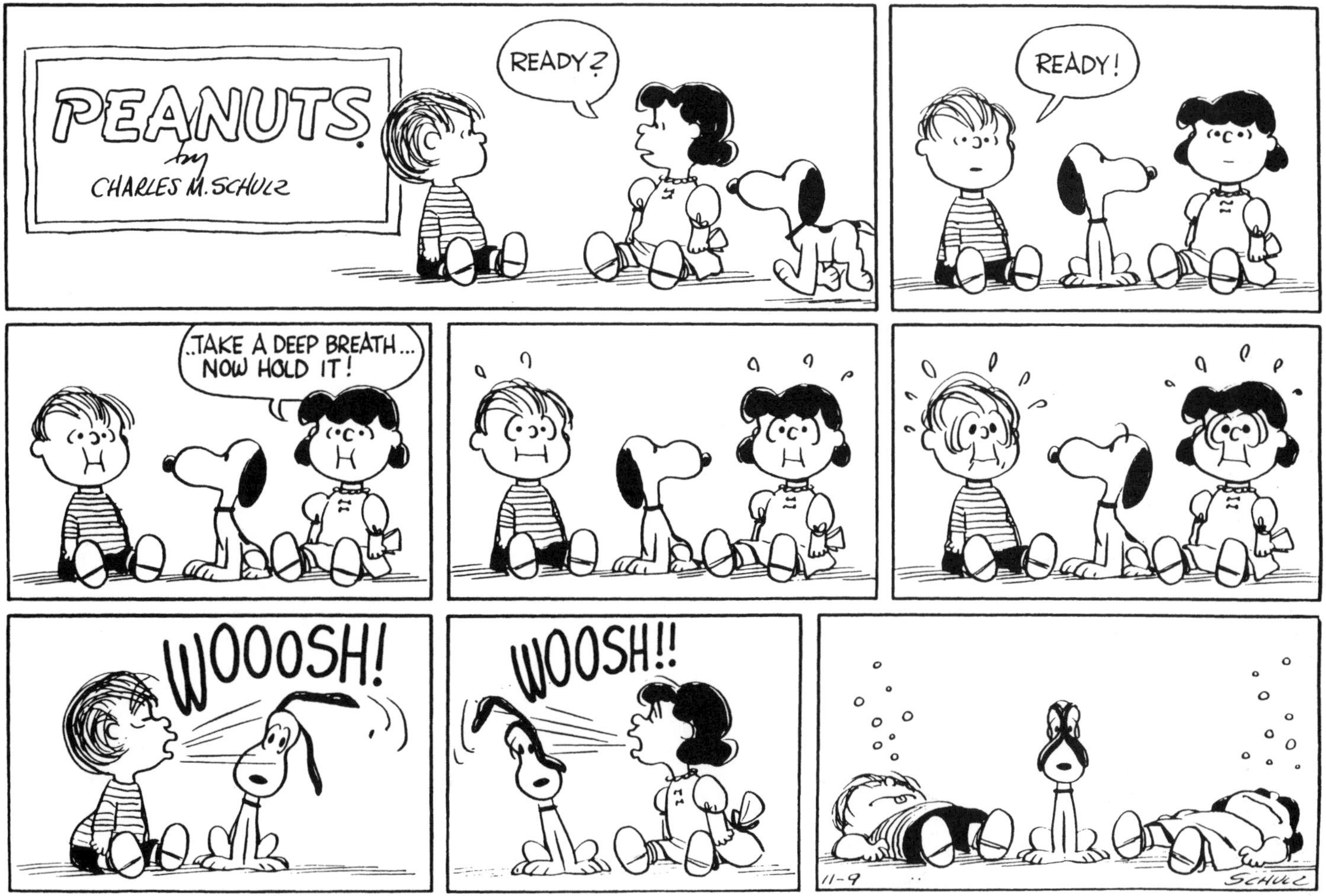
PEANUTS
by
CHARLES M. SCHULZ
READY?
READY!
..TAKE A DEEP BREATH... NOW HOLD IT!
WOOOSH!
WOOSH!!
11-9
SCHULZ

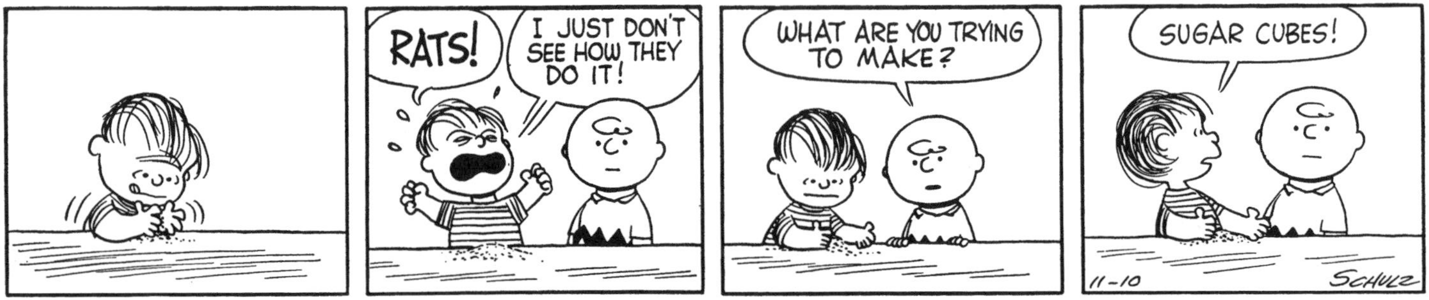
RATS!
I JUST DON'T SEE HOW THEY DO IT!
WHAT ARE YOU TRYING TO MAKE?
SUGAR CUBES!
11-10
SCHULZ

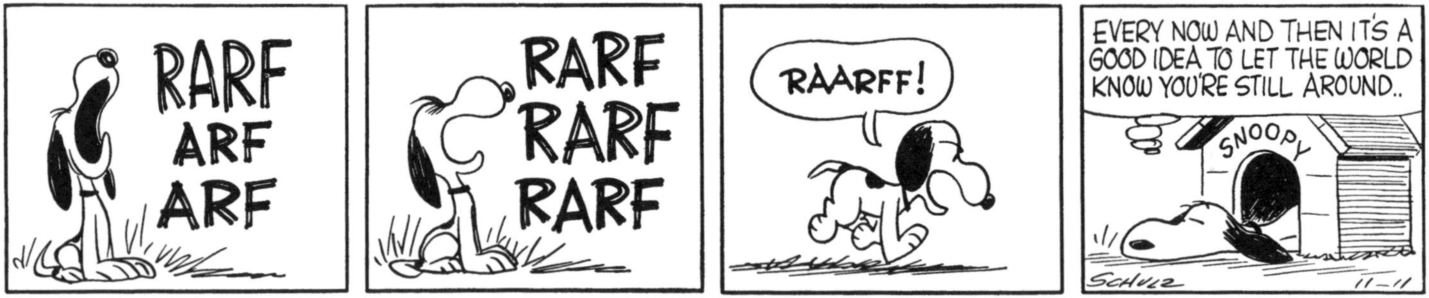
RARF
ARF
ARF
RARF
RARF
RARF
RAARFF!
EVERY NOW AND THEN IT'S A GOOD IDEA TO LET THE WORLD KNOW YOU'RE STILL AROUND..
SNOOPY
SCHULZ
11-11

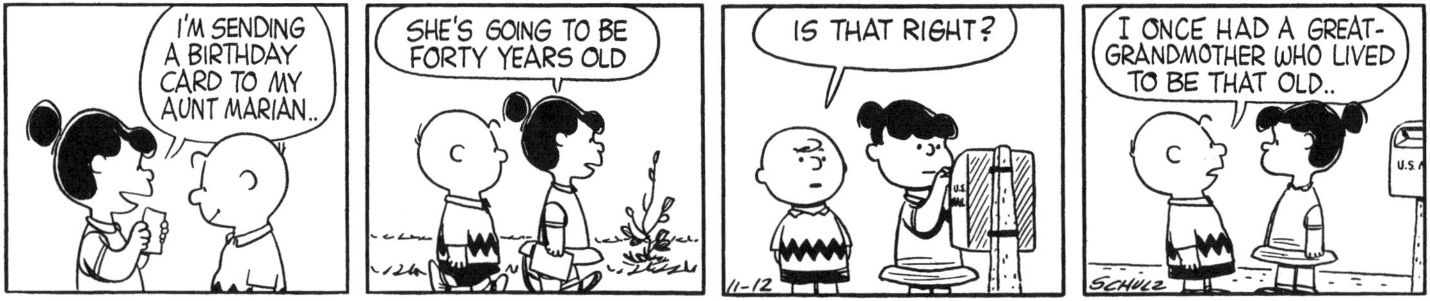
I'M SENDING A BIRTHDAY CARD TO MY AUNT MARIAN..
SHE'S GOING TO BE FORTY YEARS OLD
IS THAT RIGHT?
11-12
I ONCE HAD A GREAT-GRANDMOTHER WHO LIVED TO BE THAT OLD..
SCHULZ

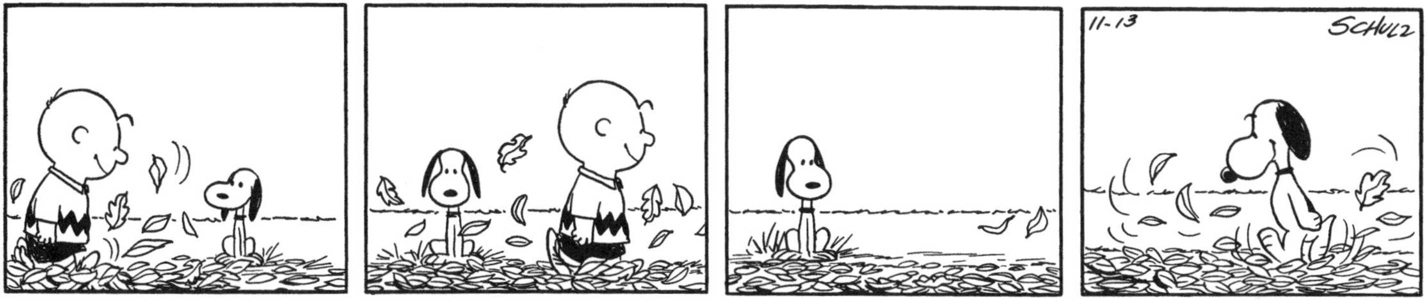
11-13
SCHULZ

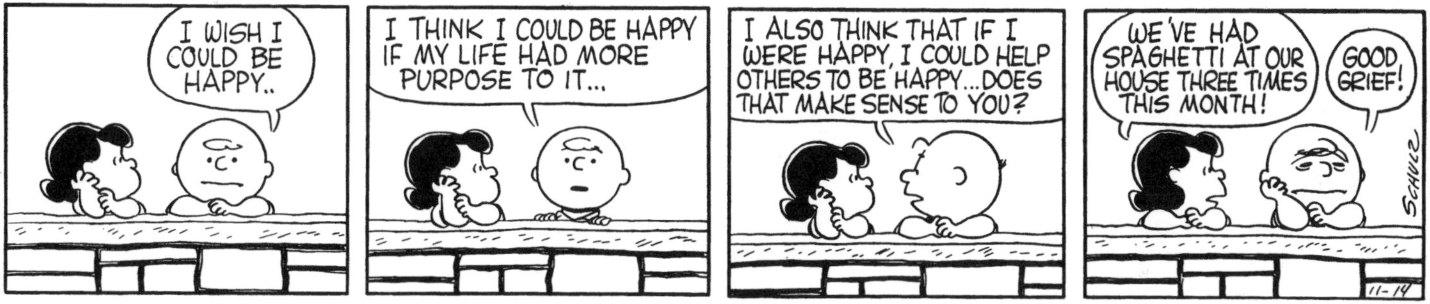
I WISH I COULD BE HAPPY..
I THINK I COULD BE HAPPY IF MY LIFE HAD MORE PURPOSE TO IT...
I ALSO THINK THAT IF I WERE HAPPY, I COULD HELP OTHERS TO BE HAPPY...DOES THAT MAKE SENSE TO YOU?
WE'VE HAD SPAGHETTI AT OUR HOUSE THREE TIMES THIS MONTH!
GOOD GRIEF!
SCHULZ
11-14

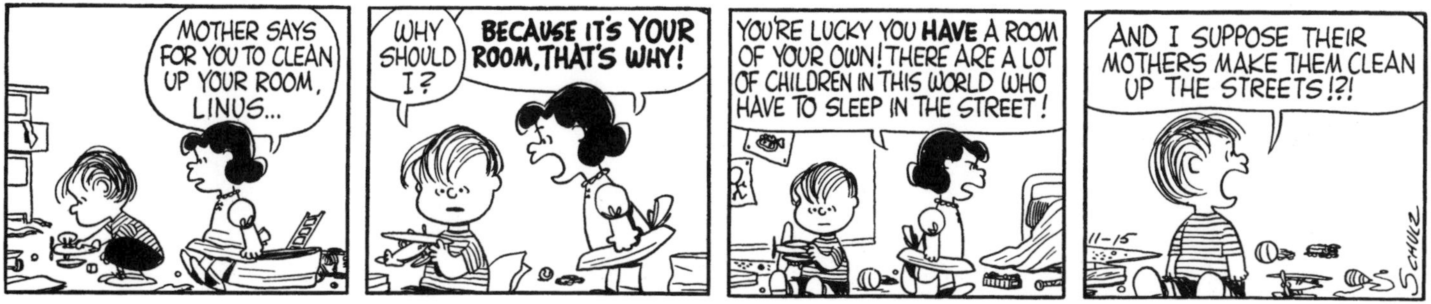
MOTHER SAYS FOR YOU TO CLEAN UP YOUR ROOM, LINUS...
WHY SHOULD I?
BECAUSE IT'S YOUR ROOM, THAT'S WHY!
YOU'RE LUCKY YOU HAVE A ROOM OF YOUR OWN! THERE ARE A LOT OF CHILDREN IN THIS WORLD WHO HAVE TO SLEEP IN THE STREET!
AND I SUPPOSE THEIR MOTHERS MAKE THEM CLEAN UP THE STREETS!?!
11-15
SCHULZ

THERE IT IS! YES, SIR... WOW!

PEANUTS
by CHARLES M. SCHULZ

HOW ABOUT THAT?

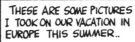

THESE ARE SOME PICTURES I TOOK ON OUR VACATION IN EUROPE THIS SUMMER..

HERE'S ONE OF BEETHOVEN'S HOUSE IN "BONN AM RHEIN"...

THIS IS A SCULPTURE WHICH STANDS IN THE LITTLE GARDEN JUST BEHIND THE HOUSE..

HERE I AM AGAIN POSING BY THE HOUSE

11-16

WILL THESE PICTURES BE WORTH A LOT OF MONEY SOMEDAY?

I DOUBT IT..

I DON'T SEE HOW ANYBODY CAN SAVE SOMETHING THAT WON'T BE WORTH A LOT OF MONEY SOMEDAY..

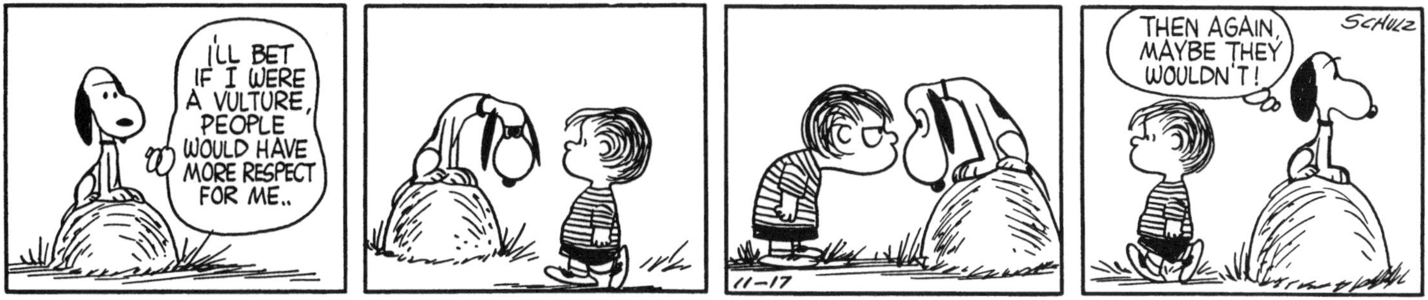
I'LL BET IF I WERE A VULTURE, PEOPLE WOULD HAVE MORE RESPECT FOR ME..
11-17
SCHULZ
THEN AGAIN, MAYBE THEY WOULDN'T!

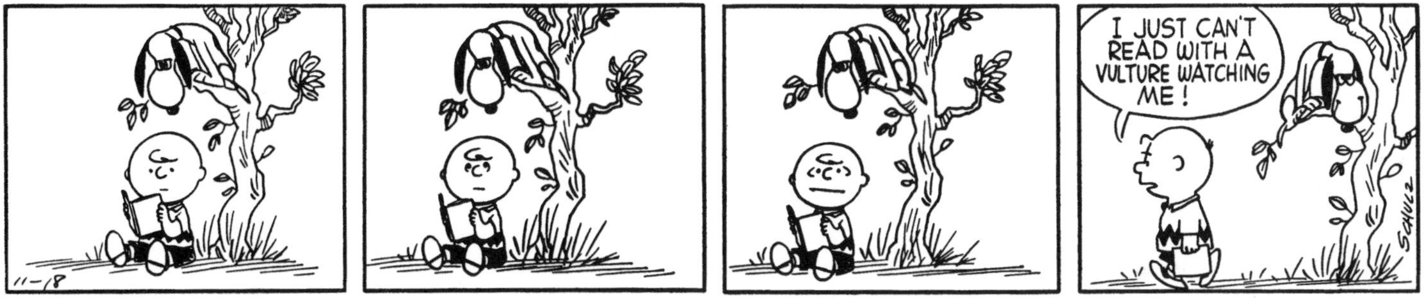
11-18
I JUST CAN'T READ WITH A VULTURE WATCHING ME!
SCHULZ

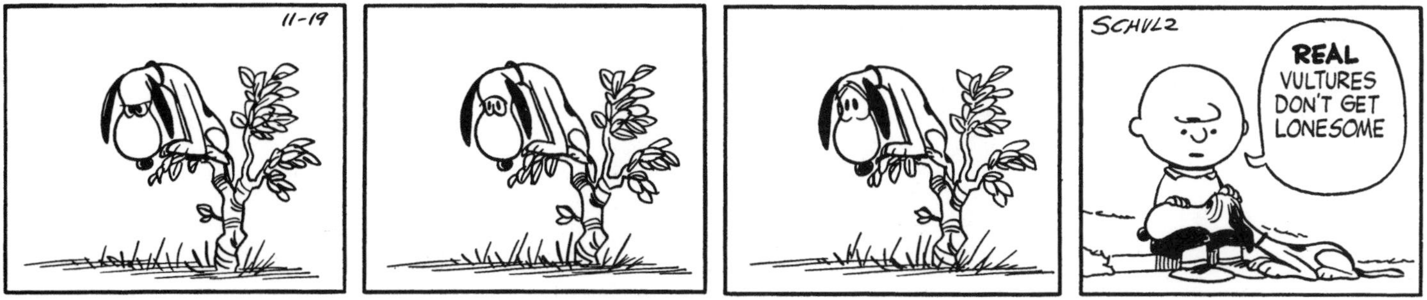
11-19
SCHULZ
REAL VULTURES DON'T GET LONESOME

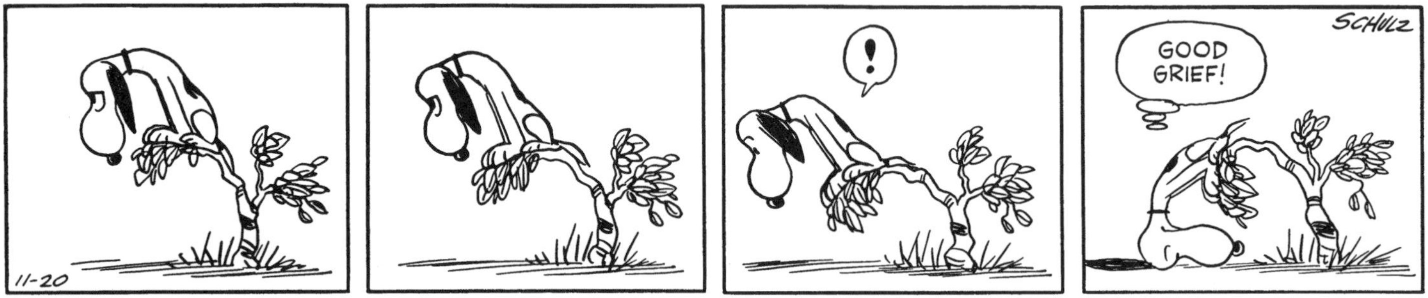
11-20
!
SCHULZ
GOOD GRIEF!

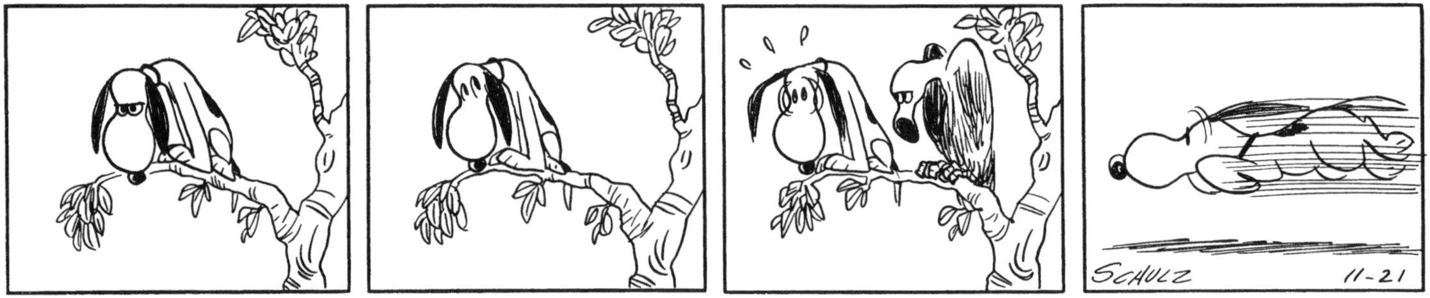
SCHULZ
11-21

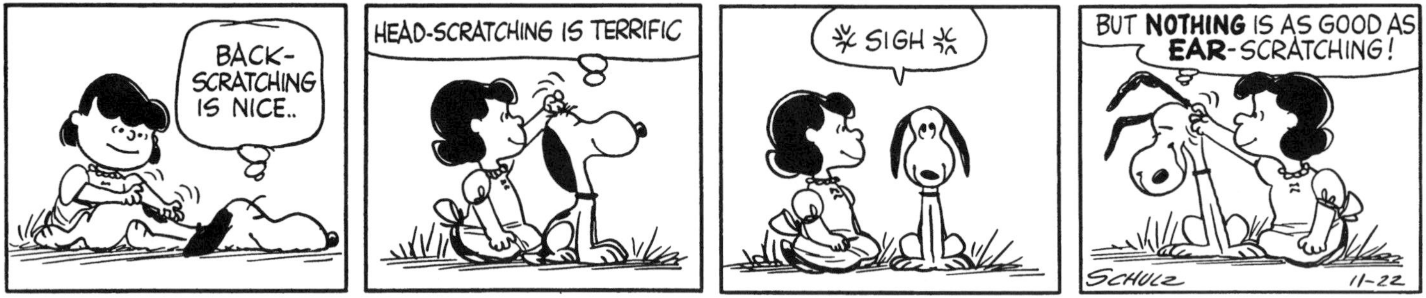
BACK-SCRATCHING IS NICE..
HEAD-SCRATCHING IS TERRIFIC
SIGH
BUT **NOTHING** IS AS GOOD AS **EAR**-SCRATCHING!
SCHULZ
11-22

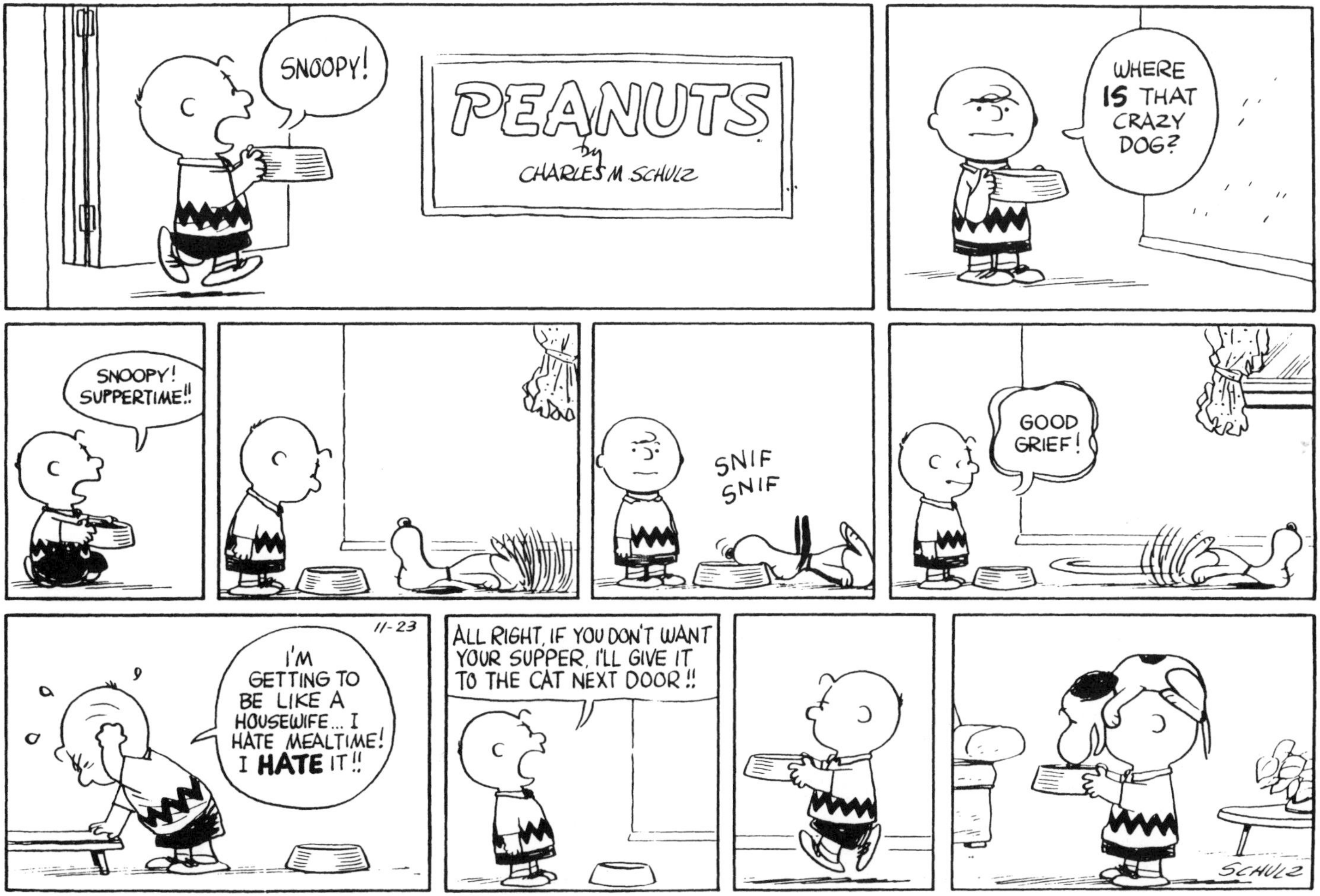
SNOOPY!
PEANUTS
by CHARLES M. SCHULZ
WHERE IS THAT CRAZY DOG?
SNOOPY! SUPPERTIME!!
SNIF SNIF
GOOD GRIEF!
11-23
I'M GETTING TO BE LIKE A HOUSEWIFE... I HATE MEALTIME! I HATE IT!!
ALL RIGHT, IF YOU DON'T WANT YOUR SUPPER, I'LL GIVE IT TO THE CAT NEXT DOOR!!
SCHULZ

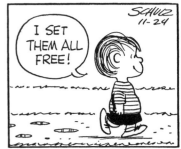

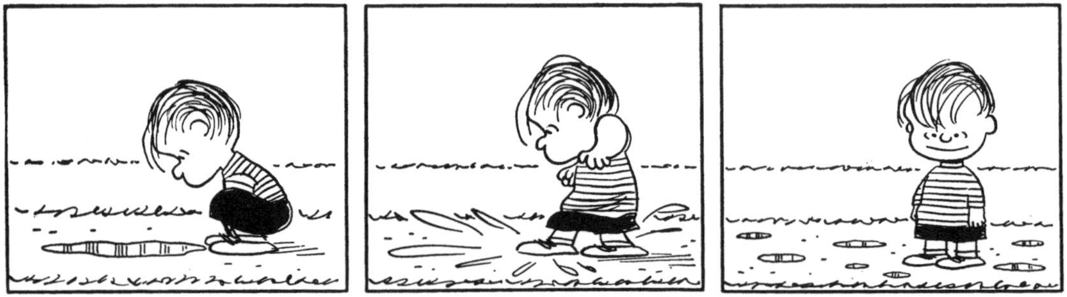
SCHULZ 11-24
I SET THEM ALL FREE!

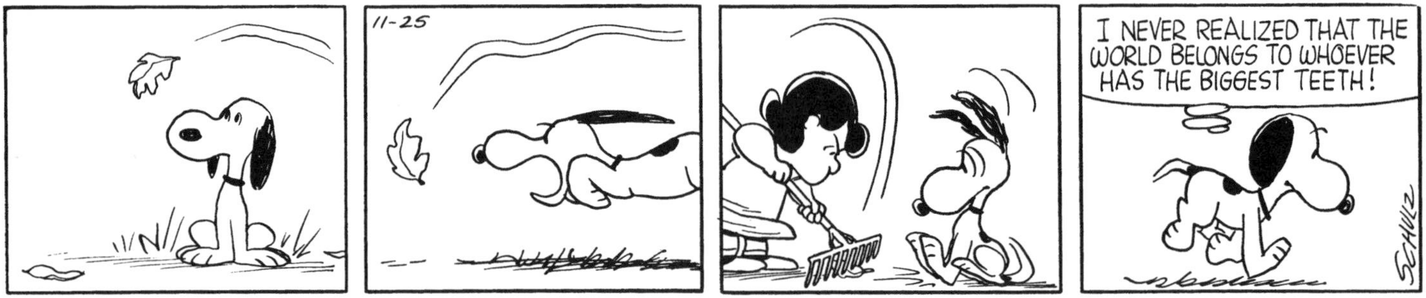
11-25
I NEVER REALIZED THAT THE WORLD BELONGS TO WHOEVER HAS THE BIGGEST TEETH!
SCHULZ

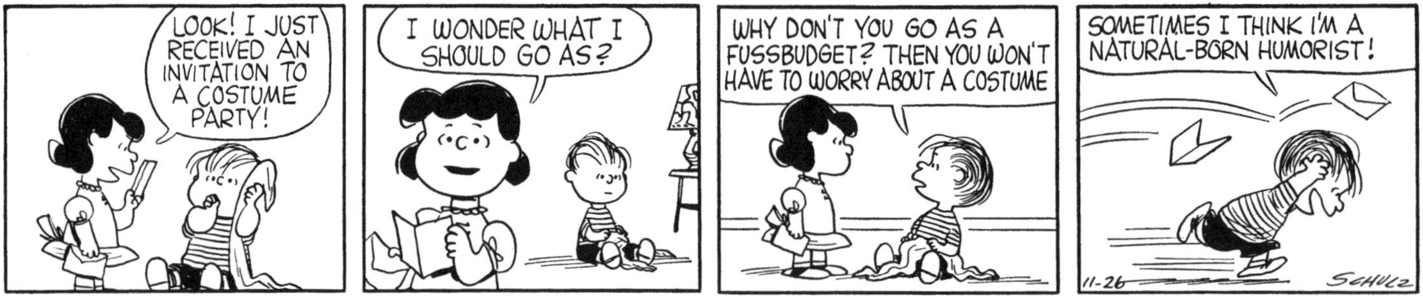
LOOK! I JUST RECEIVED AN INVITATION TO A COSTUME PARTY!
I WONDER WHAT I SHOULD GO AS?
WHY DON'T YOU GO AS A FUSSBUDGET? THEN YOU WON'T HAVE TO WORRY ABOUT A COSTUME
SOMETIMES I THINK I'M A NATURAL-BORN HUMORIST!
11-26
SCHULZ

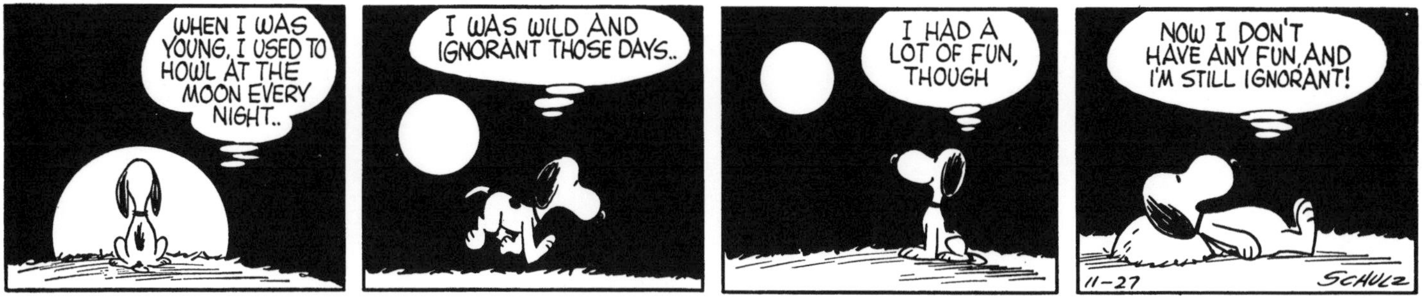
WHEN I WAS YOUNG, I USED TO HOWL AT THE MOON EVERY NIGHT..
I WAS WILD AND IGNORANT THOSE DAYS..
I HAD A LOT OF FUN, THOUGH
NOW I DON'T HAVE ANY FUN, AND I'M STILL IGNORANT!
11-27
SCHULZ

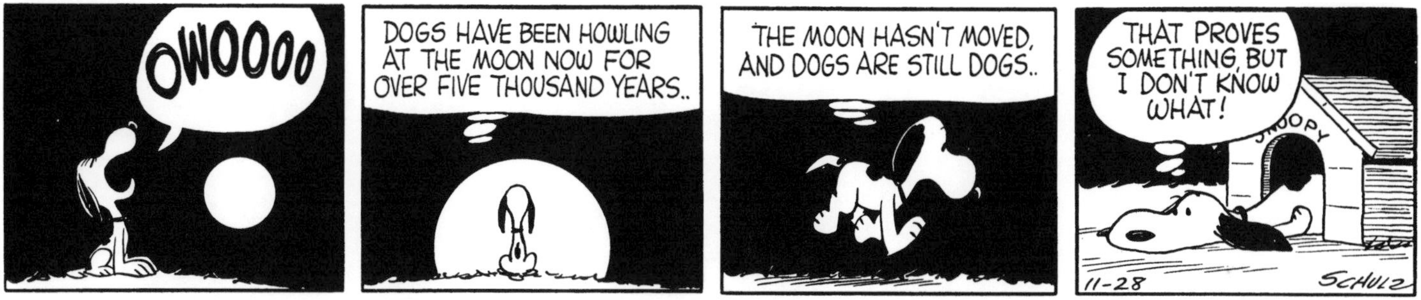
OWOOOO
DOGS HAVE BEEN HOWLING AT THE MOON NOW FOR OVER FIVE THOUSAND YEARS..
THE MOON HASN'T MOVED, AND DOGS ARE STILL DOGS..
THAT PROVES SOMETHING, BUT I DON'T KNOW WHAT!
SNOOPY
11-28
SCHULZ

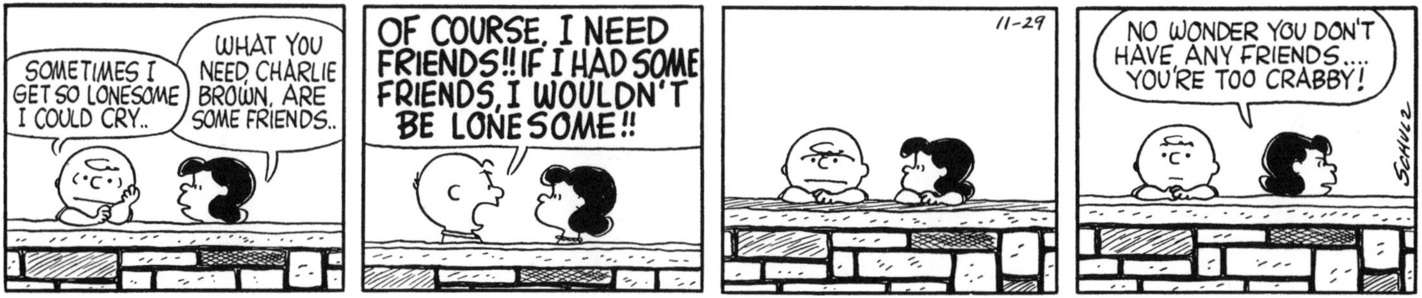
SOMETIMES I GET SO LONESOME I COULD CRY..
WHAT YOU NEED, CHARLIE BROWN, ARE SOME FRIENDS..
OF COURSE, I NEED FRIENDS!! IF I HAD SOME FRIENDS, I WOULDN'T BE LONESOME!!
11-29
NO WONDER YOU DON'T HAVE ANY FRIENDS.... YOU'RE TOO CRABBY!
SCHULZ

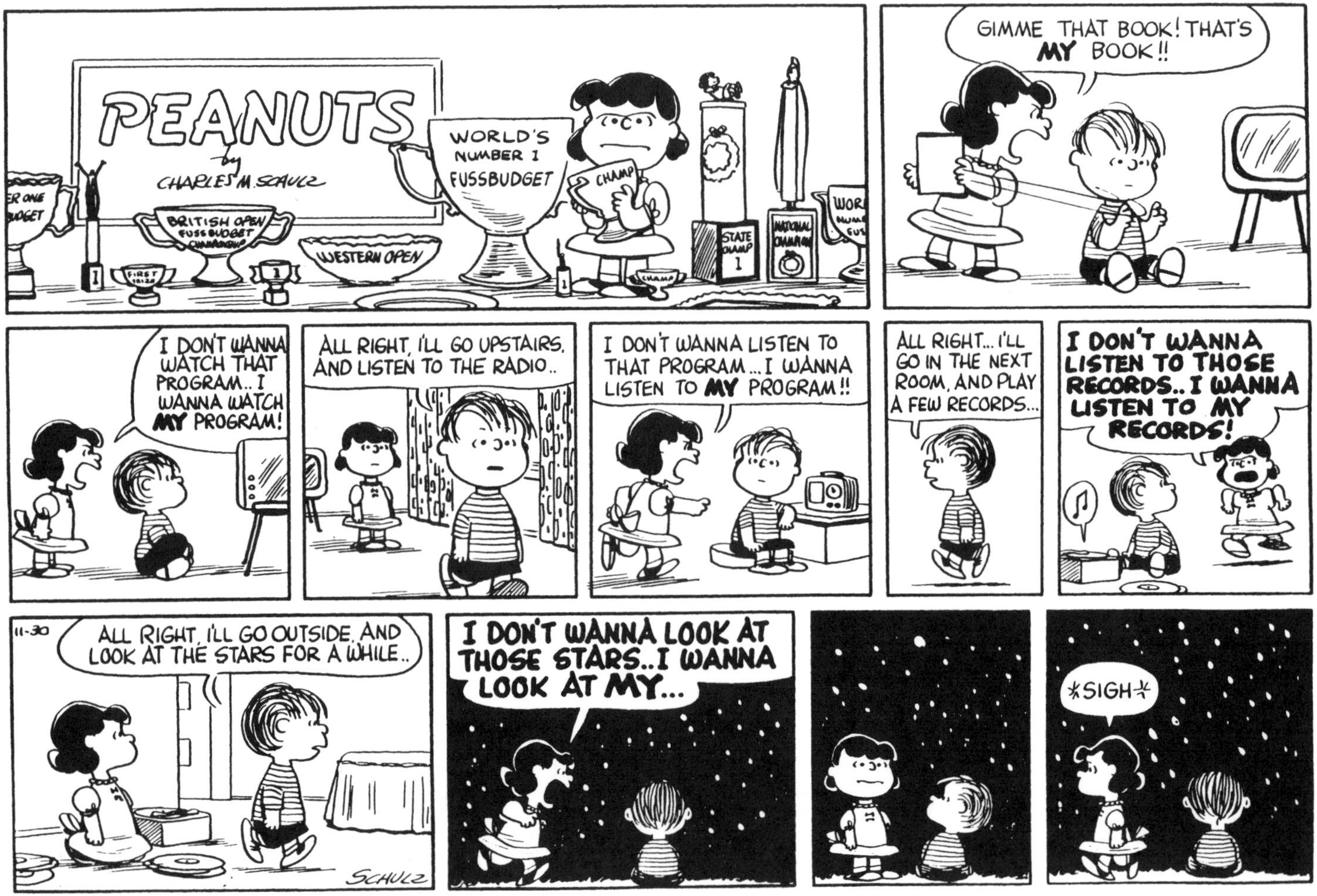
PEANUTS
by CHARLES M. SCHULZ
WORLD'S NUMBER 1 FUSSBUDGET
BRITISH OPEN FUSSBUDGET CHAMPIONSHIP
WESTERN OPEN
CHAMP
STATE CHAMP 1
NATIONAL CHAMPION
GIMME THAT BOOK! THAT'S MY BOOK!!
I DON'T WANNA WATCH THAT PROGRAM.. I WANNA WATCH MY PROGRAM!
ALL RIGHT, I'LL GO UPSTAIRS, AND LISTEN TO THE RADIO..
I DON'T WANNA LISTEN TO THAT PROGRAM... I WANNA LISTEN TO MY PROGRAM!!
ALL RIGHT... I'LL GO IN THE NEXT ROOM, AND PLAY A FEW RECORDS...
I DON'T WANNA LISTEN TO THOSE RECORDS.. I WANNA LISTEN TO MY RECORDS!
11-30
ALL RIGHT, I'LL GO OUTSIDE, AND LOOK AT THE STARS FOR A WHILE..
SCHULZ
I DON'T WANNA LOOK AT THOSE STARS..I WANNA LOOK AT MY...
SIGH

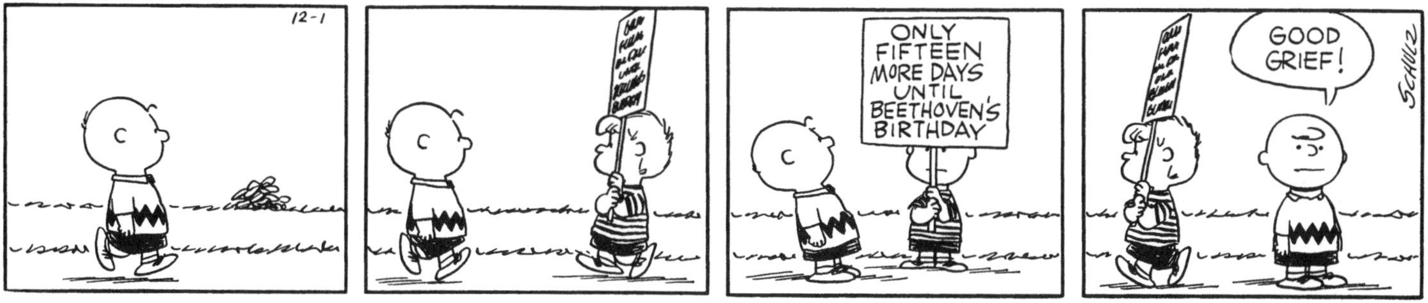
12-1
ONLY FIFTEEN MORE DAYS UNTIL BEETHOVEN'S BIRTHDAY
GOOD GRIEF!
SCHULZ

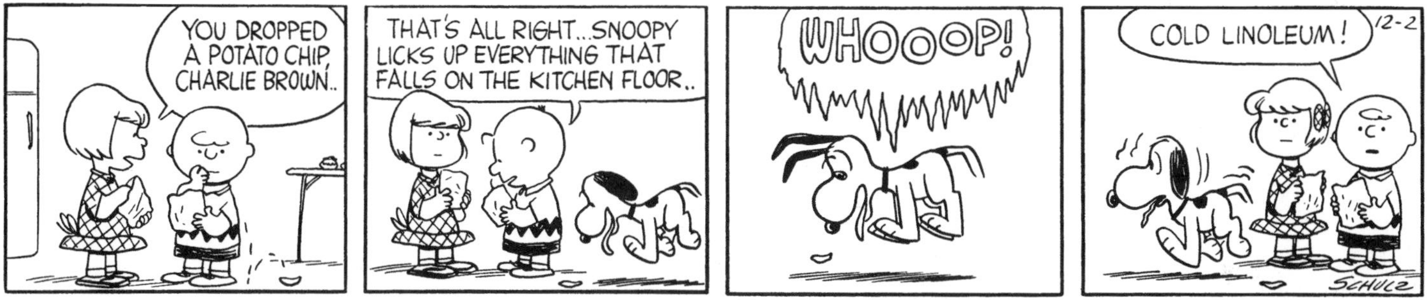
YOU DROPPED A POTATO CHIP, CHARLIE BROWN..
THAT'S ALL RIGHT...SNOOPY LICKS UP EVERYTHING THAT FALLS ON THE KITCHEN FLOOR..
WHOOOP!
COLD LINOLEUM!
12-2
SCHULZ

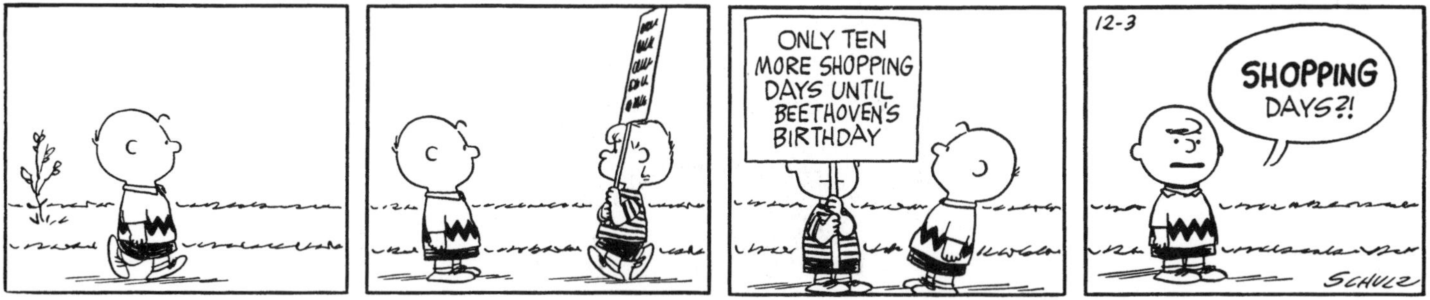
ONLY TEN MORE SHOPPING DAYS UNTIL BEETHOVEN'S BIRTHDAY
12-3
SHOPPING DAYS?!
SCHULZ

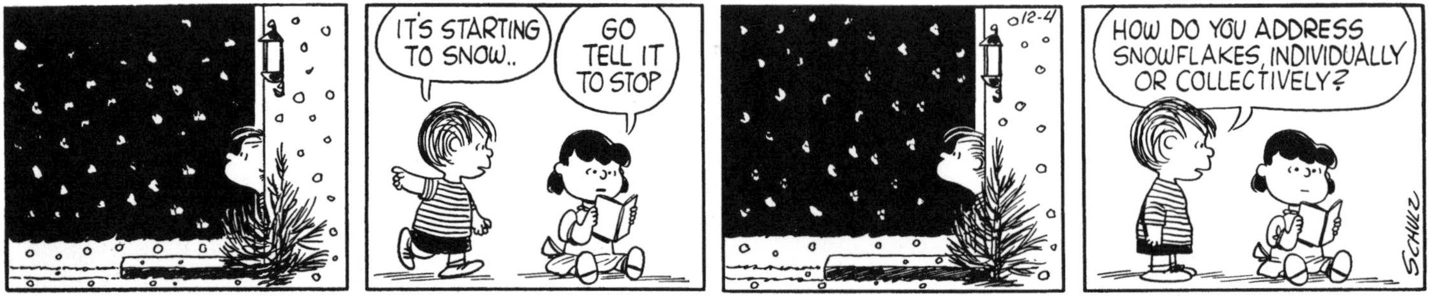
12-4
IT'S STARTING TO SNOW..
GO TELL IT TO STOP
HOW DO YOU ADDRESS SNOWFLAKES, INDIVIDUALLY OR COLLECTIVELY?

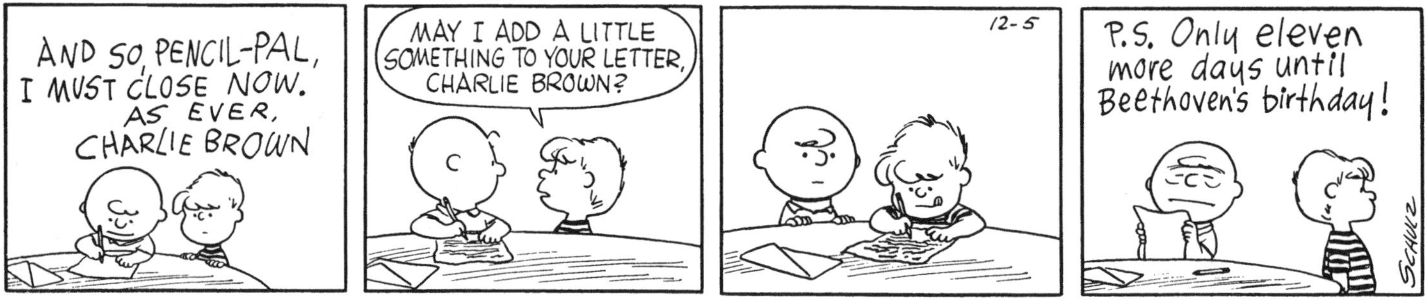
AND SO, PENCIL-PAL, I MUST CLOSE NOW. AS EVER, CHARLIE BROWN
MAY I ADD A LITTLE SOMETHING TO YOUR LETTER, CHARLIE BROWN?
12-5
P.S. Only eleven more days until Beethoven's birthday!

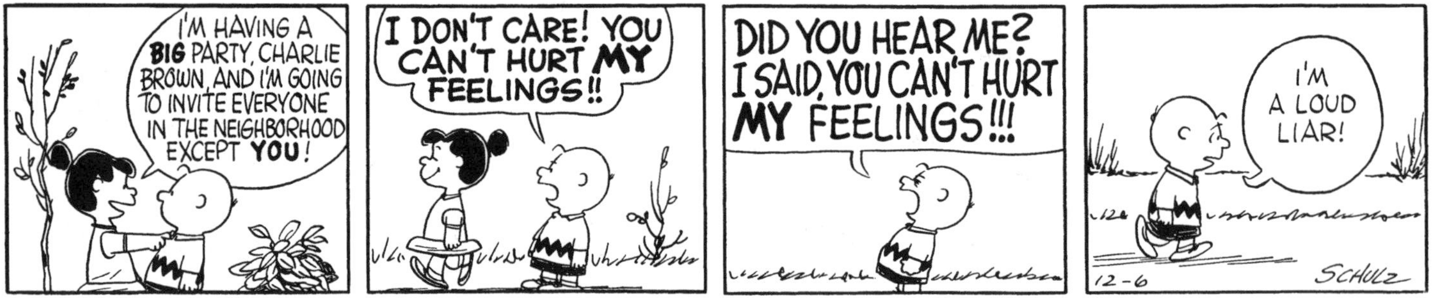
I'M HAVING A BIG PARTY, CHARLIE BROWN, AND I'M GOING TO INVITE EVERYONE IN THE NEIGHBORHOOD EXCEPT YOU!
I DON'T CARE! YOU CAN'T HURT MY FEELINGS!!
DID YOU HEAR ME? I SAID, YOU CAN'T HURT MY FEELINGS!!!
I'M A LOUD LIAR!
12-6

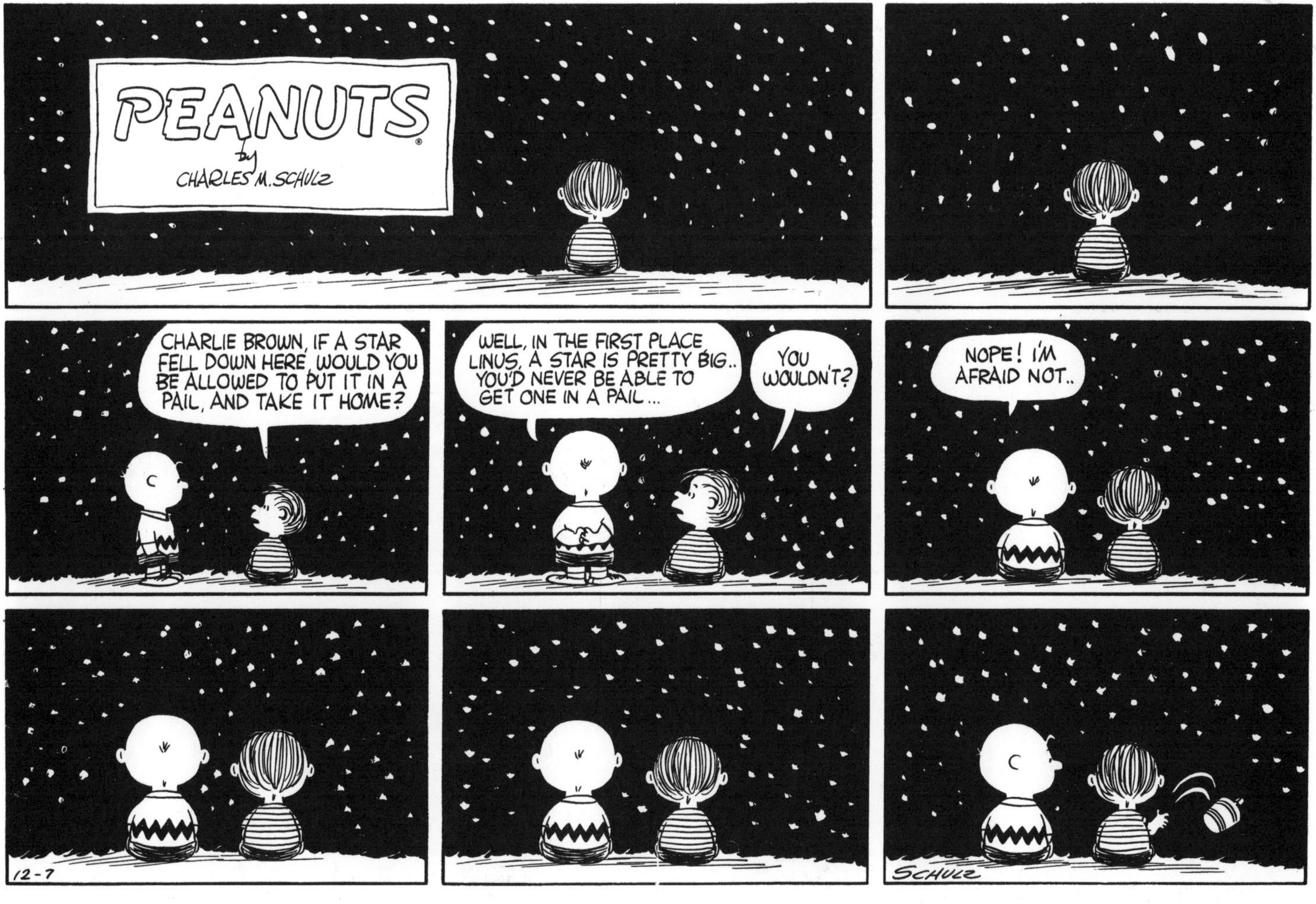
PEANUTS
by
CHARLES M. SCHULZ
CHARLIE BROWN, IF A STAR FELL DOWN HERE, WOULD YOU BE ALLOWED TO PUT IT IN A PAIL, AND TAKE IT HOME?
WELL, IN THE FIRST PLACE LINUS, A STAR IS PRETTY BIG.. YOU'D NEVER BE ABLE TO GET ONE IN A PAIL...
YOU WOULDN'T?
NOPE! I'M AFRAID NOT..
12-7
SCHULZ

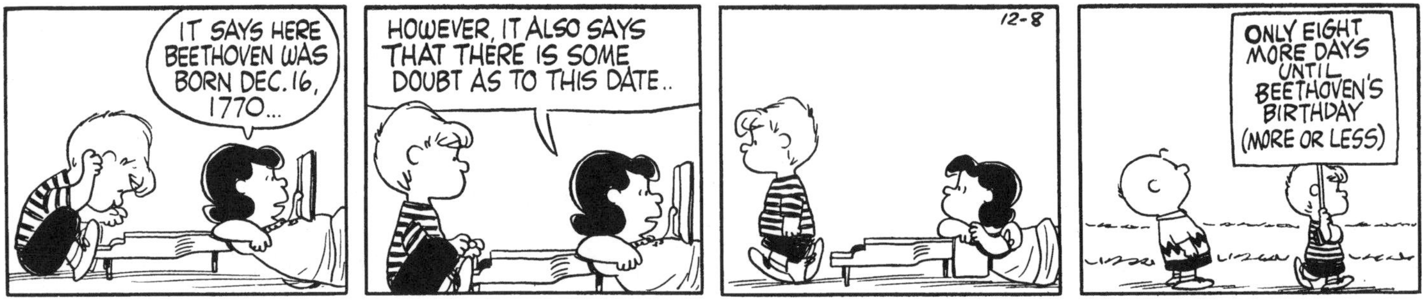
IT SAYS HERE BEETHOVEN WAS BORN DEC. 16, 1770...
HOWEVER, IT ALSO SAYS THAT THERE IS SOME DOUBT AS TO THIS DATE..
12-8
ONLY EIGHT MORE DAYS UNTIL BEETHOVEN'S BIRTHDAY (MORE OR LESS)

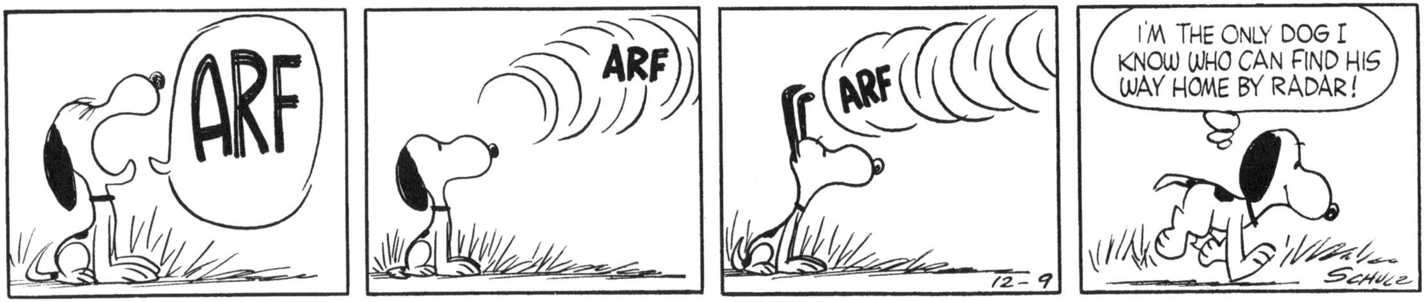
ARF
ARF
ARF
12-9
I'M THE ONLY DOG I KNOW WHO CAN FIND HIS WAY HOME BY RADAR!
SCHULZ

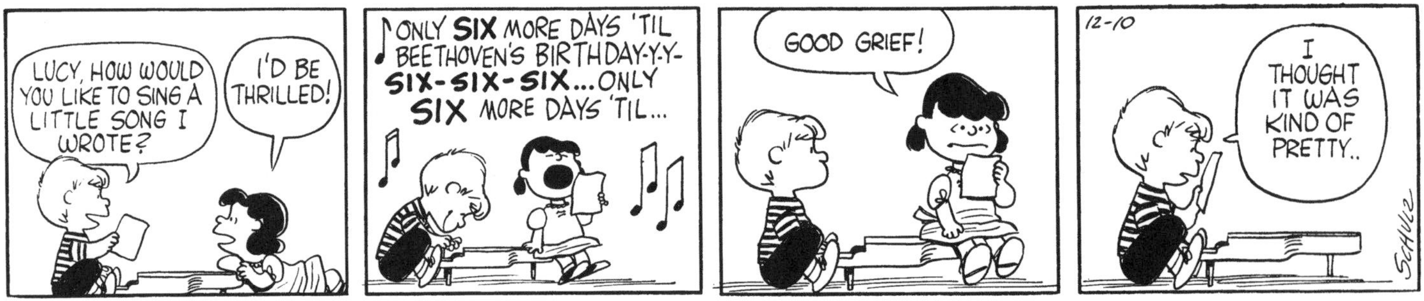
LUCY, HOW WOULD YOU LIKE TO SING A LITTLE SONG I WROTE?
I'D BE THRILLED!
ONLY SIX MORE DAYS 'TIL BEETHOVEN'S BIRTHDAY-Y-Y-SIX-SIX-SIX...ONLY SIX MORE DAYS 'TIL...
GOOD GRIEF!
12-10
I THOUGHT IT WAS KIND OF PRETTY..
SCHULZ

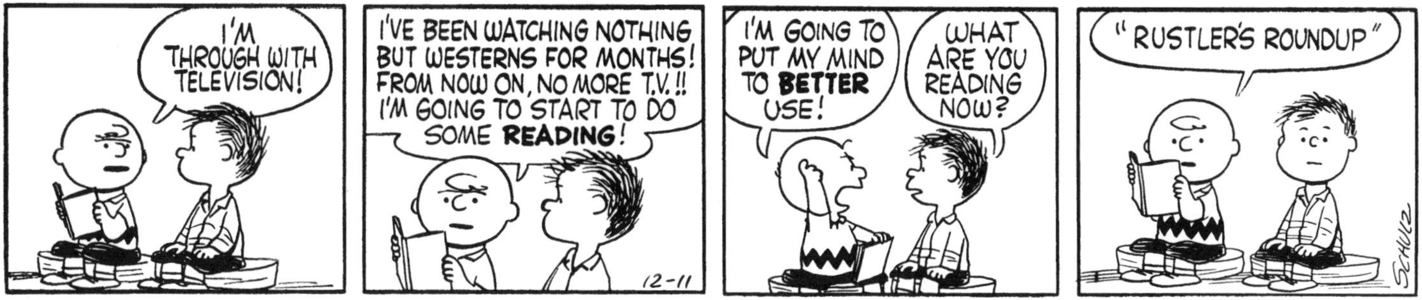
I'M THROUGH WITH TELEVISION!
I'VE BEEN WATCHING NOTHING BUT WESTERNS FOR MONTHS! FROM NOW ON, NO MORE T.V.!! I'M GOING TO START TO DO SOME **READING**!
12-11
I'M GOING TO PUT MY MIND TO **BETTER** USE!
WHAT ARE YOU READING NOW?
"RUSTLER'S ROUNDUP"
SCHULZ

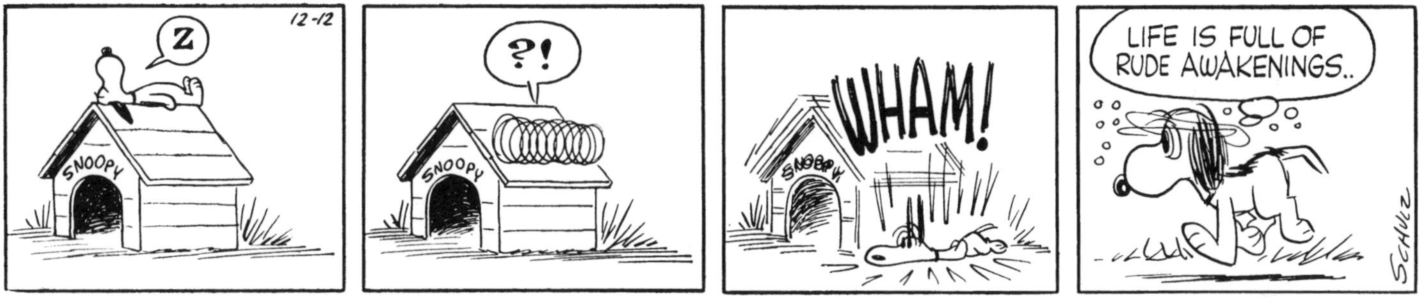
12-12
Z
SNOOPY
?!
SNOOPY
WHAM!
LIFE IS FULL OF RUDE AWAKENINGS..
SCHULZ

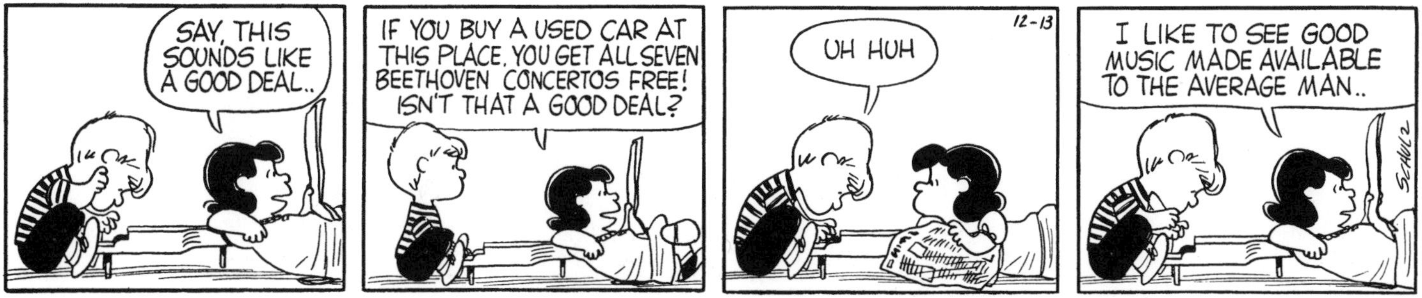
SAY, THIS SOUNDS LIKE A GOOD DEAL..
IF YOU BUY A USED CAR AT THIS PLACE, YOU GET ALL SEVEN BEETHOVEN CONCERTOS FREE! ISN'T THAT A GOOD DEAL?
12-13
UH HUH
I LIKE TO SEE GOOD MUSIC MADE AVAILABLE TO THE AVERAGE MAN..
SCHULZ

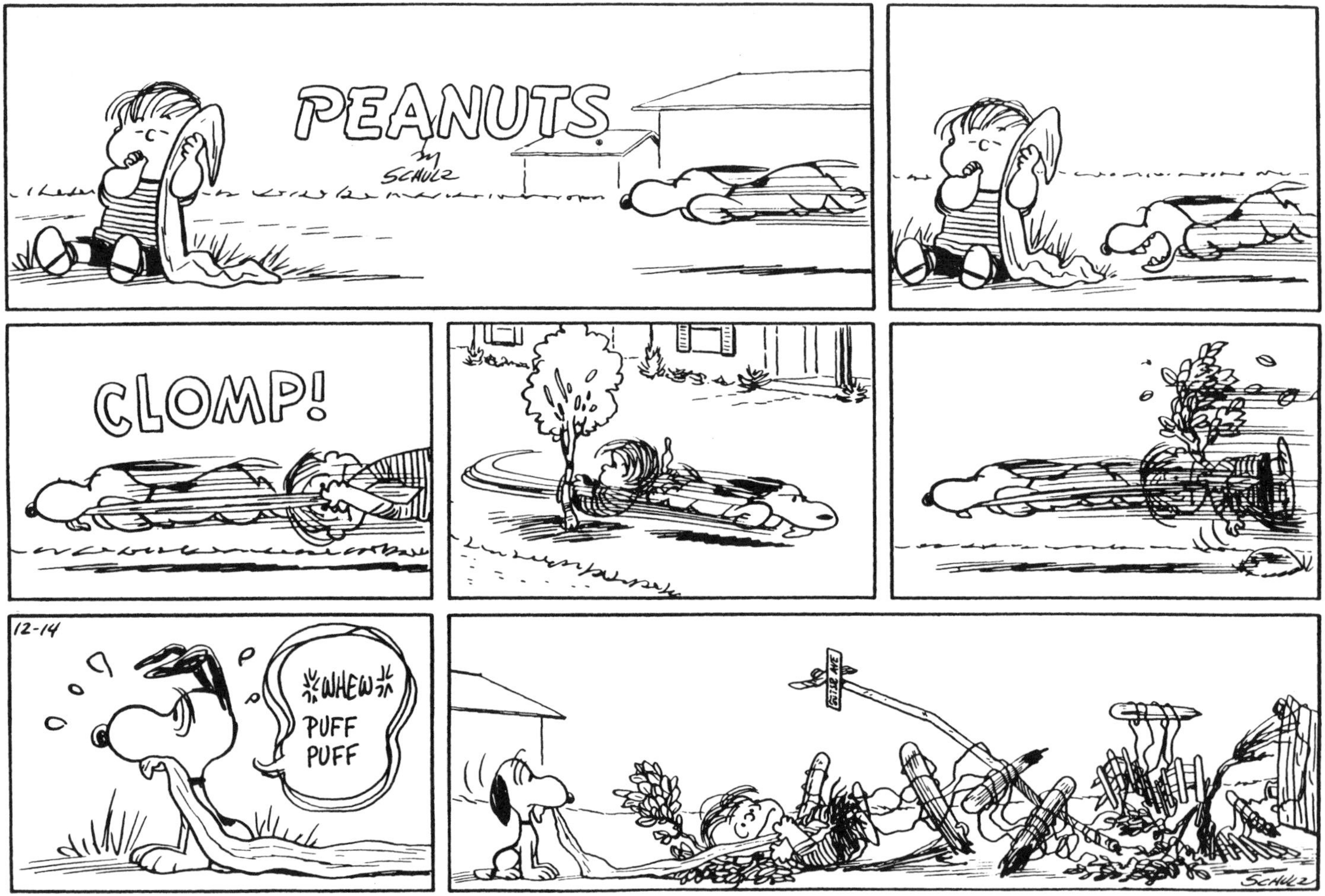
PEANUTS
by SCHULZ
CLOMP!
12-14
WHEW
PUFF
PUFF
SCHULZ

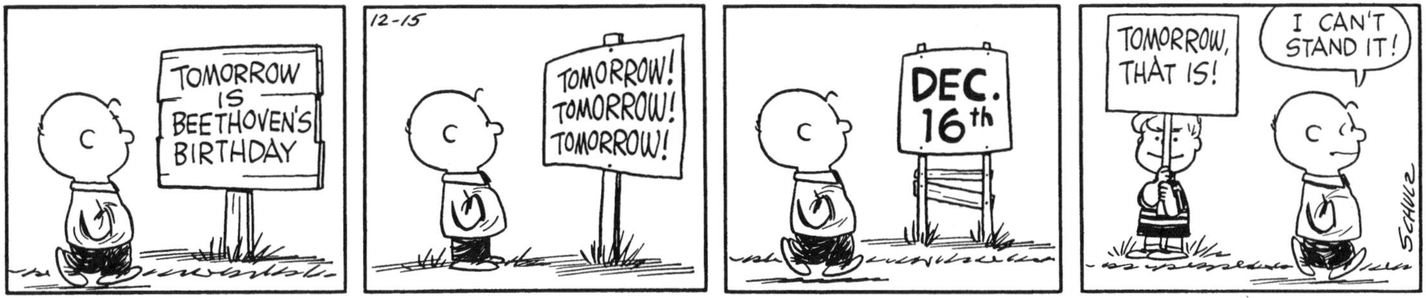
12-15
TOMORROW IS BEETHOVEN'S BIRTHDAY
TOMORROW! TOMORROW! TOMORROW!
DEC. 16th
TOMORROW, THAT IS!
I CAN'T STAND IT!
SCHULZ

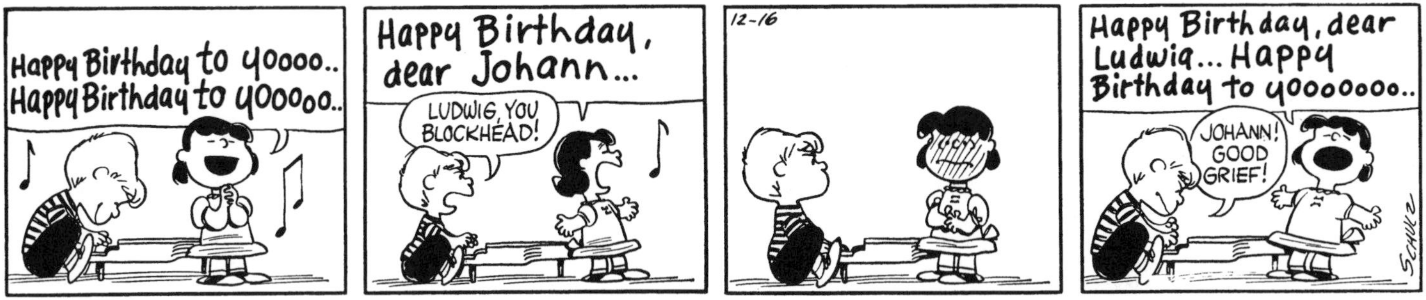
Happy Birthday to yoooo.. Happy Birthday to yooooo..
Happy Birthday, dear Johann...
LUDWIG, YOU BLOCKHEAD!
12-16
Happy Birthday, dear Ludwig... Happy Birthday to yooooooo..
JOHANN! GOOD GRIEF!
SCHULZ

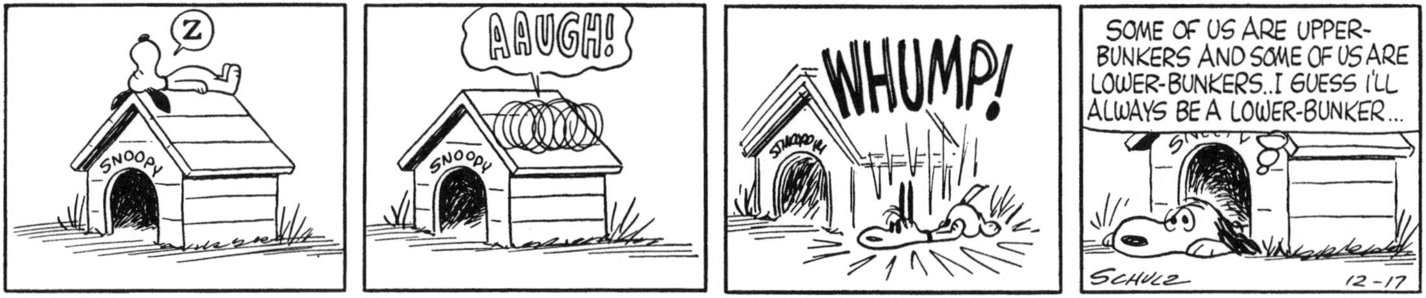
Z
SNOOPY
AAUGH!
SNOOPY
WHUMP!
SOME OF US ARE UPPER-BUNKERS AND SOME OF US ARE LOWER-BUNKERS..I GUESS I'LL ALWAYS BE A LOWER-BUNKER...
SCHULZ
12-17

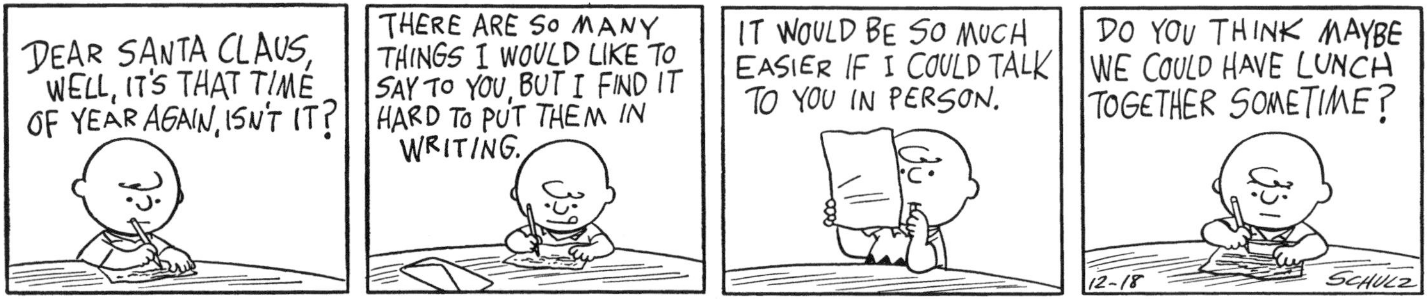
DEAR SANTA CLAUS, WELL, IT'S THAT TIME OF YEAR AGAIN, ISN'T IT?
THERE ARE SO MANY THINGS I WOULD LIKE TO SAY TO YOU, BUT I FIND IT HARD TO PUT THEM IN WRITING.
IT WOULD BE SO MUCH EASIER IF I COULD TALK TO YOU IN PERSON.
DO YOU THINK MAYBE WE COULD HAVE LUNCH TOGETHER SOMETIME?
12-18
SCHULZ

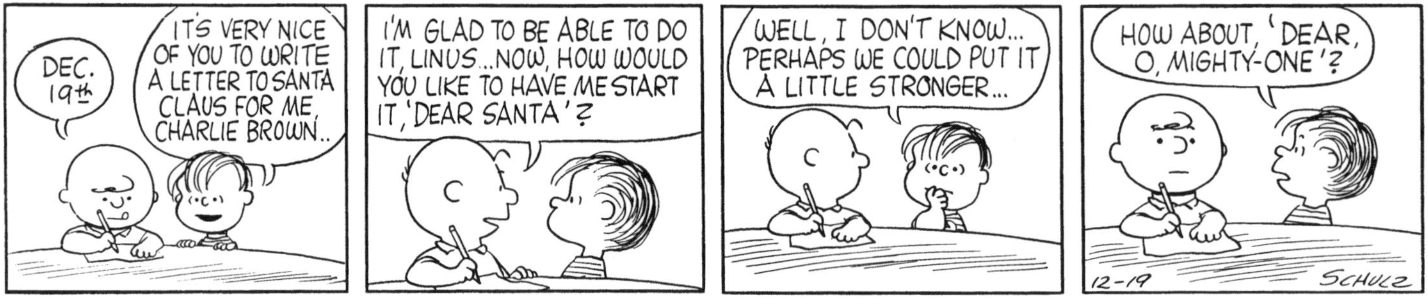
DEC. 19th
IT'S VERY NICE OF YOU TO WRITE A LETTER TO SANTA CLAUS FOR ME, CHARLIE BROWN..
I'M GLAD TO BE ABLE TO DO IT, LINUS...NOW, HOW WOULD YOU LIKE TO HAVE ME START IT, 'DEAR SANTA'?
WELL, I DON'T KNOW... PERHAPS WE COULD PUT IT A LITTLE STRONGER...
HOW ABOUT, 'DEAR, O, MIGHTY-ONE'?
12-19
SCHULZ

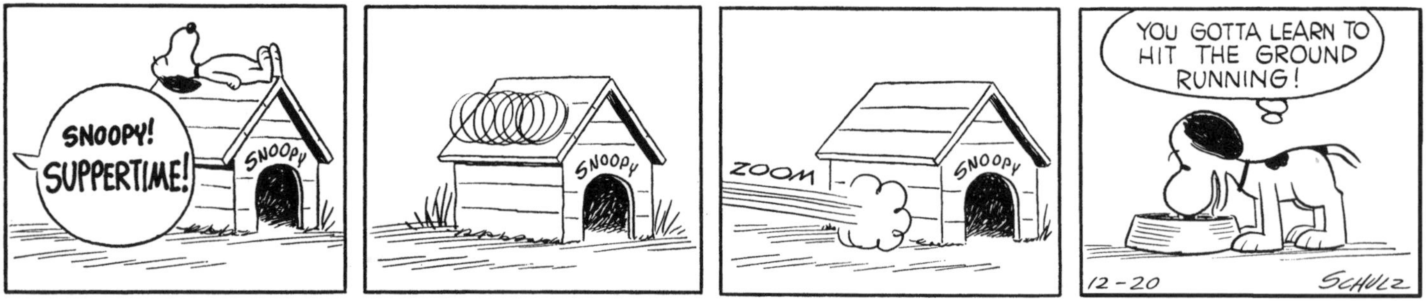
SNOOPY! SUPPERTIME!
SNOOPY
SNOOPY
ZOOM
SNOOPY
YOU GOTTA LEARN TO HIT THE GROUND RUNNING!
12-20
SCHULZ

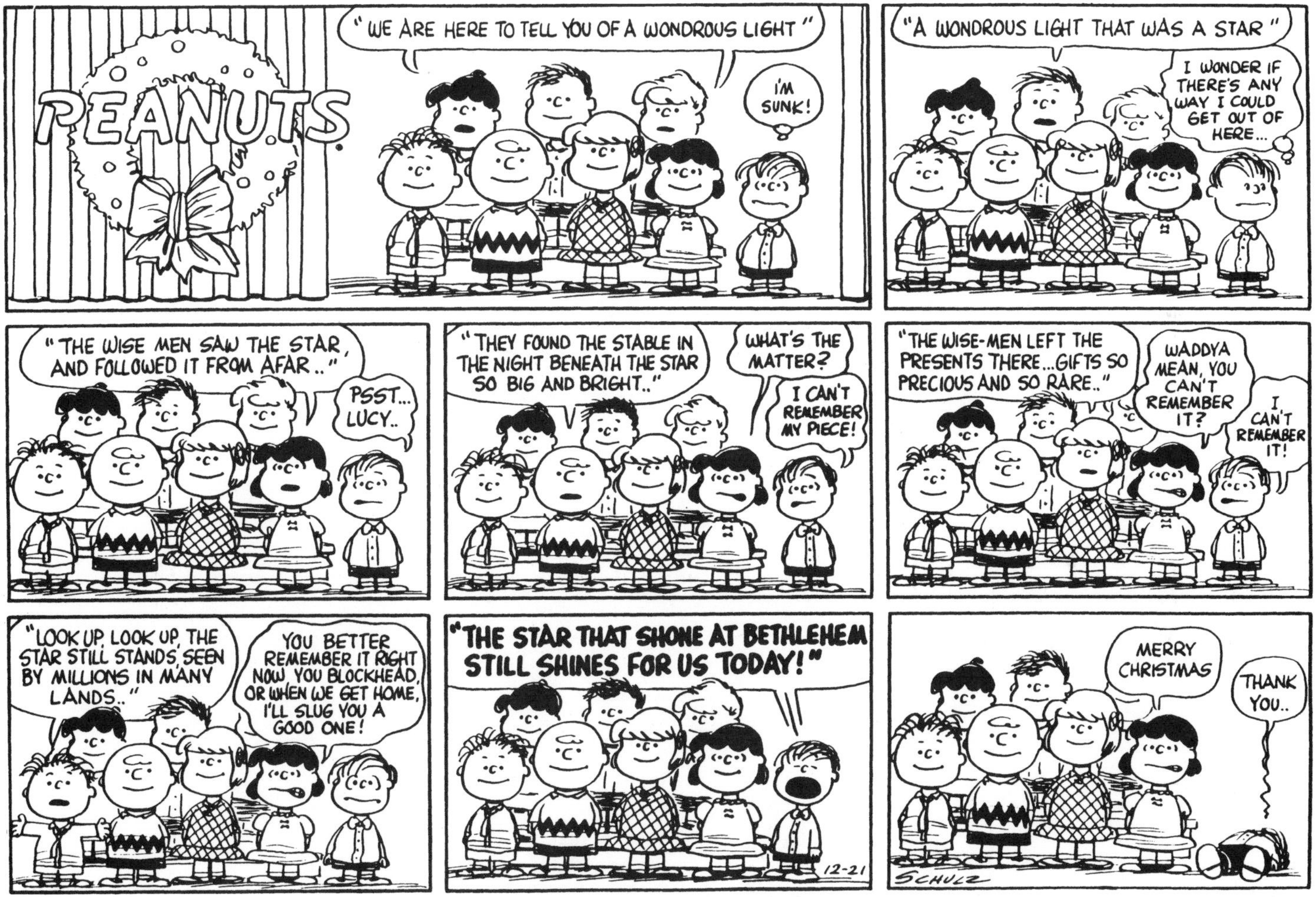
PEANUTS
"WE ARE HERE TO TELL YOU OF A WONDROUS LIGHT"
I'M SUNK!
"A WONDROUS LIGHT THAT WAS A STAR"
I WONDER IF THERE'S ANY WAY I COULD GET OUT OF HERE...
"THE WISE MEN SAW THE STAR, AND FOLLOWED IT FROM AFAR.."
PSST... LUCY..
"THEY FOUND THE STABLE IN THE NIGHT BENEATH THE STAR SO BIG AND BRIGHT.."
WHAT'S THE MATTER?
I CAN'T REMEMBER MY PIECE!
"THE WISE-MEN LEFT THE PRESENTS THERE...GIFTS SO PRECIOUS AND SO RARE.."
WADDYA MEAN, YOU CAN'T REMEMBER IT?
I CAN'T REMEMBER IT!
"LOOK UP, LOOK UP, THE STAR STILL STANDS, SEEN BY MILLIONS IN MANY LANDS.."
YOU BETTER REMEMBER IT RIGHT NOW, YOU BLOCKHEAD, OR WHEN WE GET HOME, I'LL SLUG YOU A GOOD ONE!
"THE STAR THAT SHONE AT BETHLEHEM STILL SHINES FOR US TODAY!"
12-21
MERRY CHRISTMAS
THANK YOU..
SCHULZ

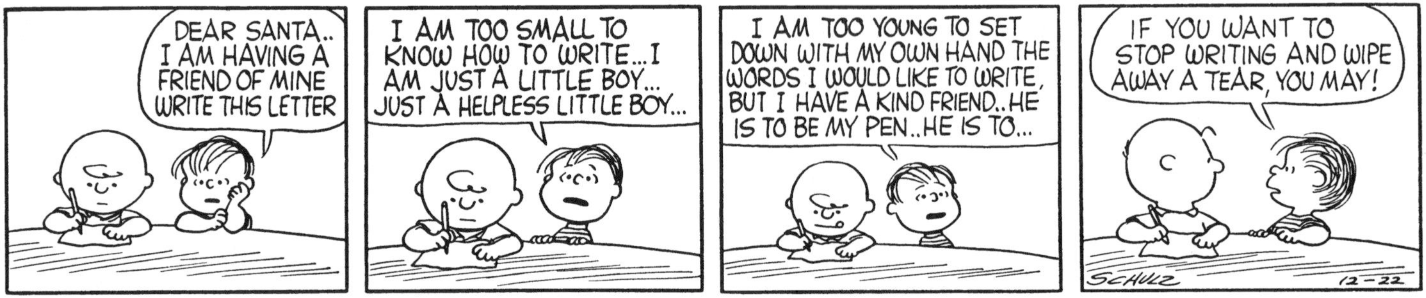
DEAR SANTA.. I AM HAVING A FRIEND OF MINE WRITE THIS LETTER
I AM TOO SMALL TO KNOW HOW TO WRITE...I AM JUST A LITTLE BOY... JUST A HELPLESS LITTLE BOY...
I AM TOO YOUNG TO SET DOWN WITH MY OWN HAND THE WORDS I WOULD LIKE TO WRITE, BUT I HAVE A KIND FRIEND..HE IS TO BE MY PEN..HE IS TO...
IF YOU WANT TO STOP WRITING AND WIPE AWAY A TEAR, YOU MAY!
SCHULZ
12-22

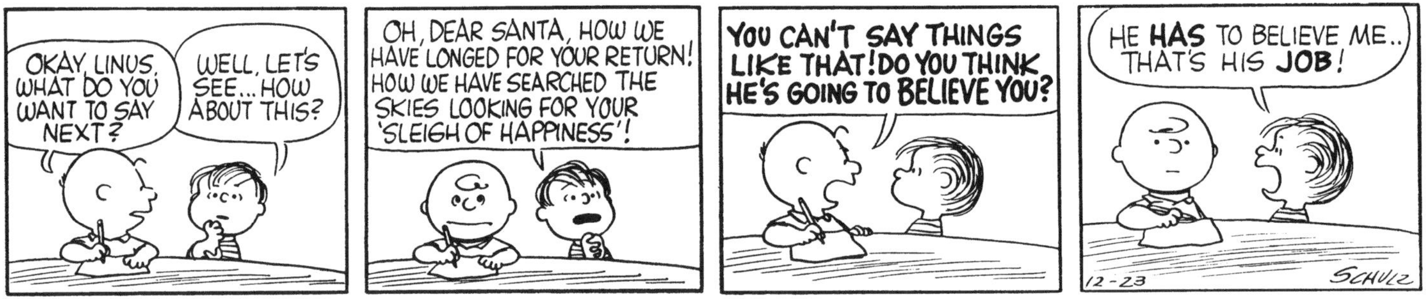
OKAY, LINUS, WHAT DO YOU WANT TO SAY NEXT?
WELL, LET'S SEE...HOW ABOUT THIS?
OH, DEAR SANTA, HOW WE HAVE LONGED FOR YOUR RETURN! HOW WE HAVE SEARCHED THE SKIES LOOKING FOR YOUR 'SLEIGH OF HAPPINESS'!
YOU CAN'T SAY THINGS LIKE THAT! DO YOU THINK HE'S GOING TO BELIEVE YOU?
HE HAS TO BELIEVE ME.. THAT'S HIS JOB!
12-23
SCHULZ

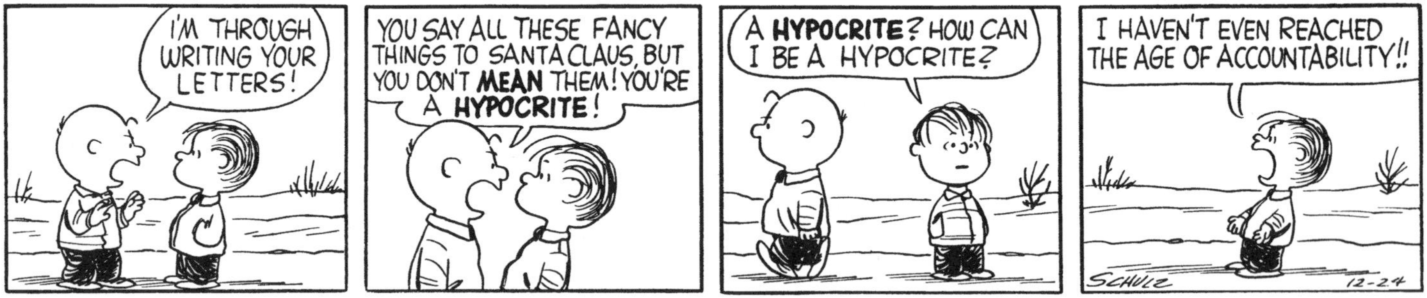
I'M THROUGH WRITING YOUR LETTERS!
YOU SAY ALL THESE FANCY THINGS TO SANTA CLAUS, BUT YOU DON'T MEAN THEM! YOU'RE A HYPOCRITE!
A HYPOCRITE? HOW CAN I BE A HYPOCRITE?
I HAVEN'T EVEN REACHED THE AGE OF ACCOUNTABILITY!!
SCHULZ
12-24

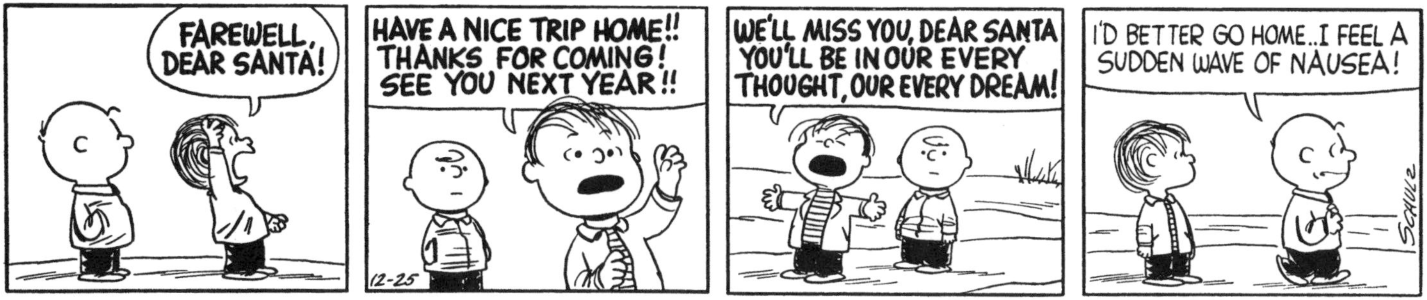
FAREWELL, DEAR SANTA!
HAVE A NICE TRIP HOME!! THANKS FOR COMING! SEE YOU NEXT YEAR!!
12-25
WE'LL MISS YOU, DEAR SANTA YOU'LL BE IN OUR EVERY THOUGHT, OUR EVERY DREAM!
I'D BETTER GO HOME..I FEEL A SUDDEN WAVE OF NAUSEA!
SCHULZ

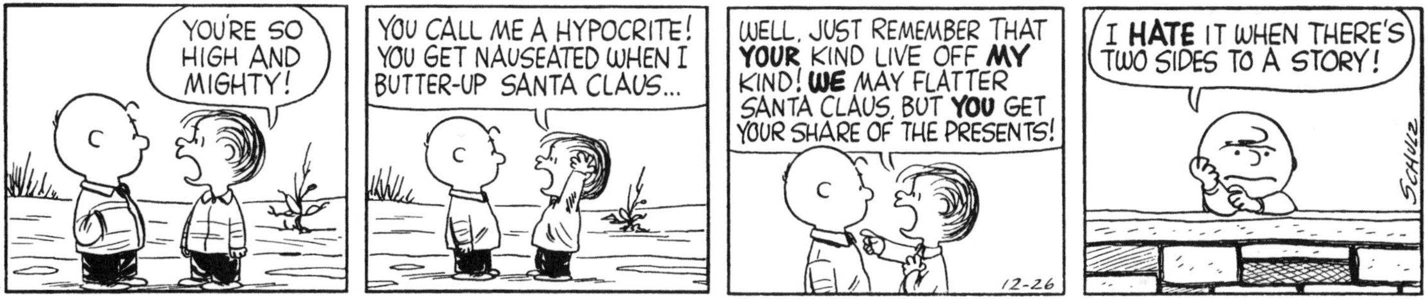
YOU'RE SO HIGH AND MIGHTY!
YOU CALL ME A HYPOCRITE! YOU GET NAUSEATED WHEN I BUTTER-UP SANTA CLAUS...
WELL, JUST REMEMBER THAT YOUR KIND LIVE OFF MY KIND! WE MAY FLATTER SANTA CLAUS, BUT YOU GET YOUR SHARE OF THE PRESENTS!
12-26
I HATE IT WHEN THERE'S TWO SIDES TO A STORY!
SCHULZ

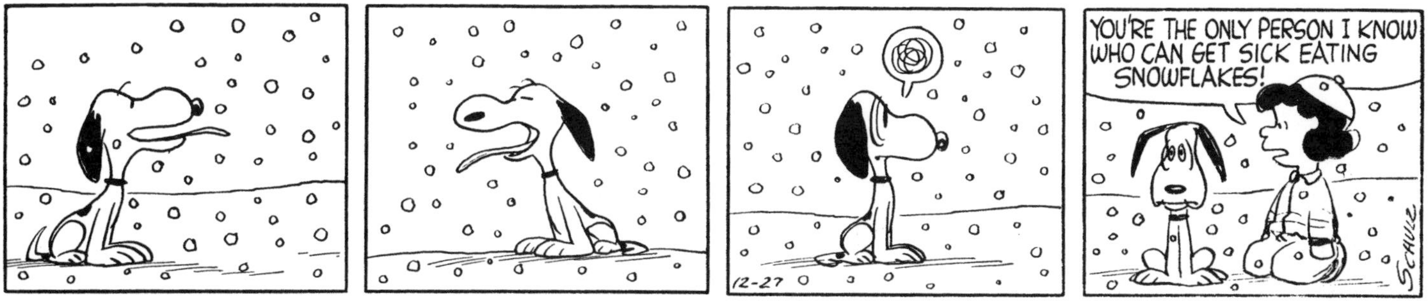
12-27
YOU'RE THE ONLY PERSON I KNOW WHO CAN GET SICK EATING SNOWFLAKES!
SCHULZ

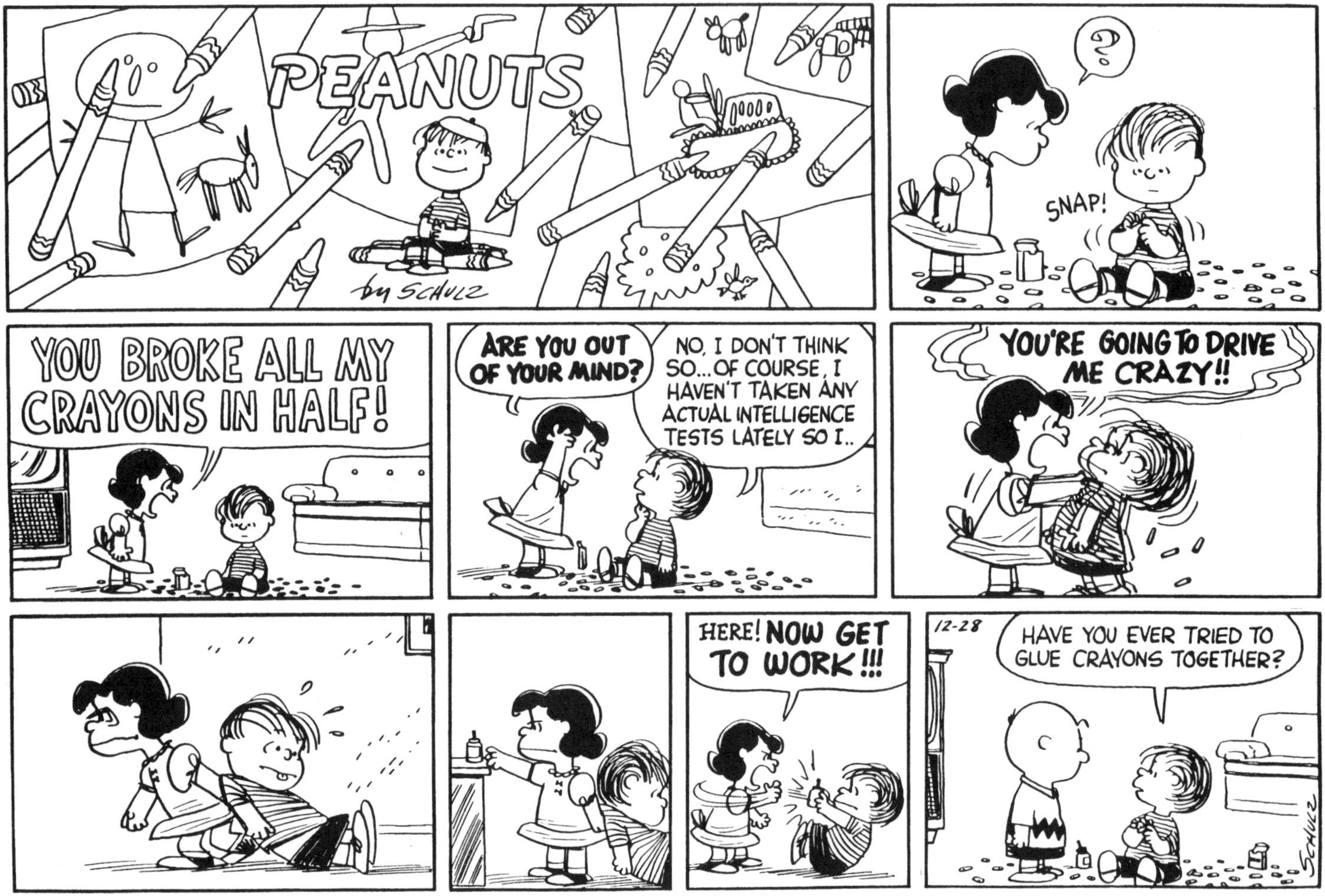
PEANUTS
by SCHULZ
?
SNAP!
YOU BROKE ALL MY CRAYONS IN HALF!
ARE YOU OUT OF YOUR MIND?
NO, I DON'T THINK SO...OF COURSE, I HAVEN'T TAKEN ANY ACTUAL INTELLIGENCE TESTS LATELY SO I..
YOU'RE GOING TO DRIVE ME CRAZY!!
HERE! NOW GET TO WORK!!!
12-28
HAVE YOU EVER TRIED TO GLUE CRAYONS TOGETHER?
SCHULZ

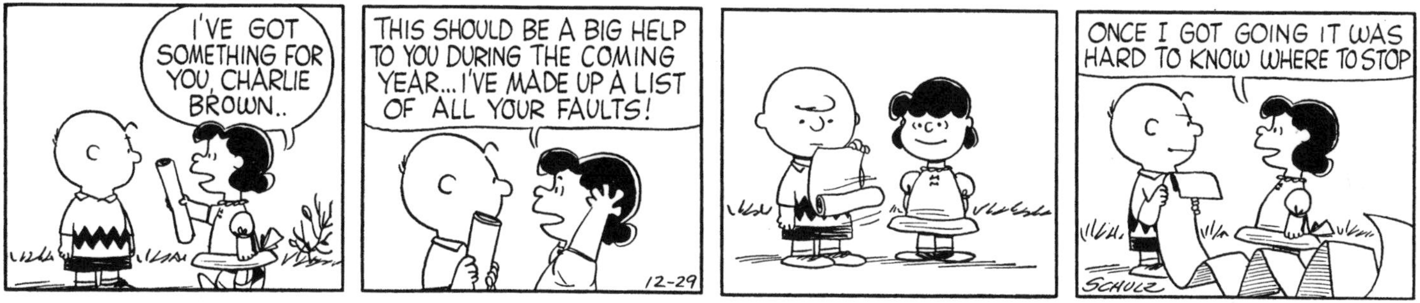
I'VE GOT SOMETHING FOR YOU, CHARLIE BROWN..
THIS SHOULD BE A BIG HELP TO YOU DURING THE COMING YEAR... I'VE MADE UP A LIST OF ALL YOUR FAULTS!
12-29
ONCE I GOT GOING IT WAS HARD TO KNOW WHERE TO STOP
SCHULZ

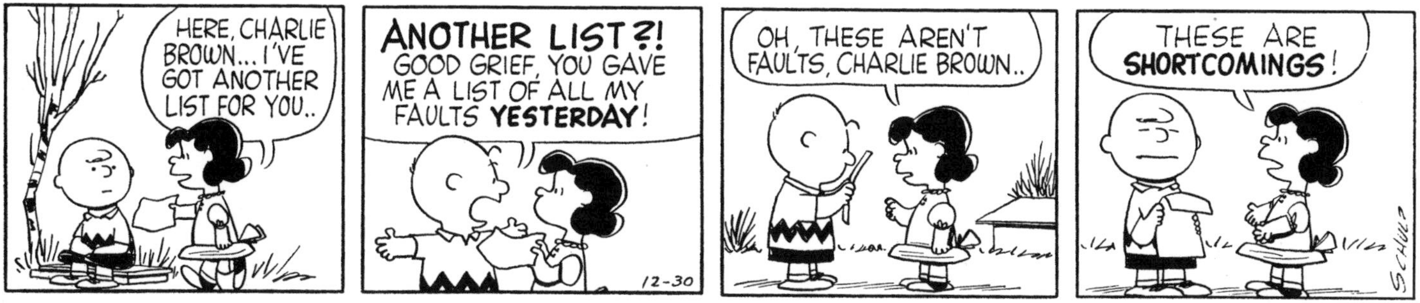
HERE, CHARLIE BROWN... I'VE GOT ANOTHER LIST FOR YOU..
ANOTHER LIST?! GOOD GRIEF, YOU GAVE ME A LIST OF ALL MY FAULTS YESTERDAY!
12-30
OH, THESE AREN'T FAULTS, CHARLIE BROWN..
THESE ARE SHORTCOMINGS!
SCHULZ

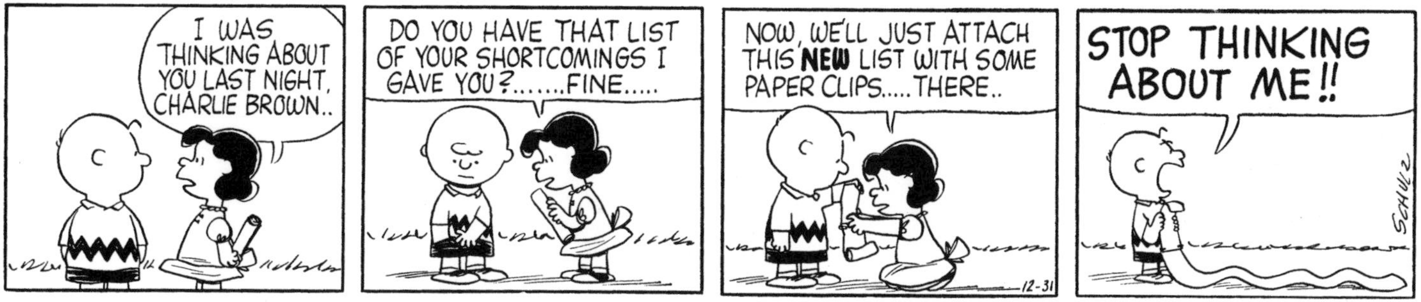
I WAS THINKING ABOUT YOU LAST NIGHT, CHARLIE BROWN..
DO YOU HAVE THAT LIST OF YOUR SHORTCOMINGS I GAVE YOU?.......FINE.....
NOW, WE'LL JUST ATTACH THIS NEW LIST WITH SOME PAPER CLIPS..... THERE..
12-31
STOP THINKING ABOUT ME!!
SCHULZ

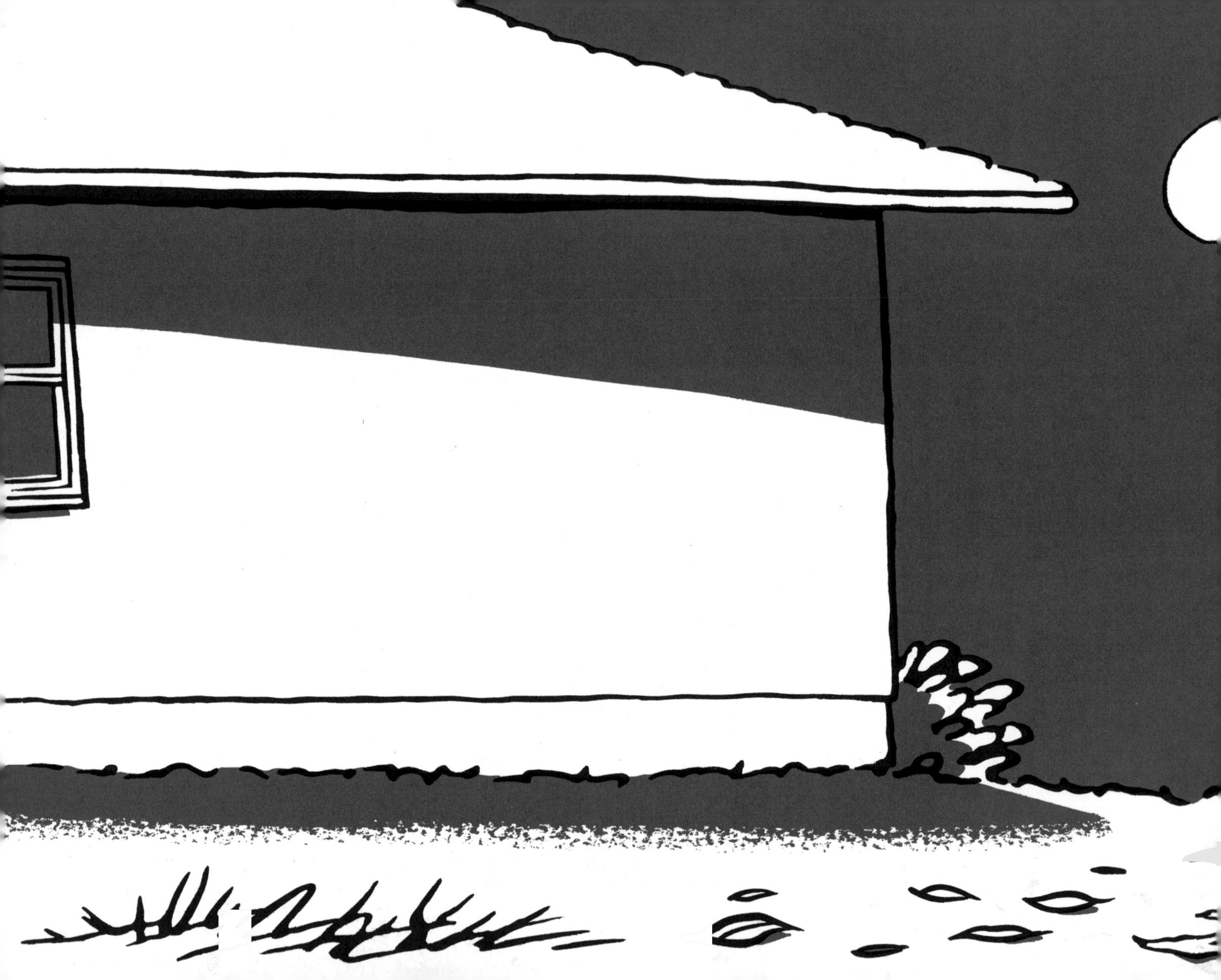

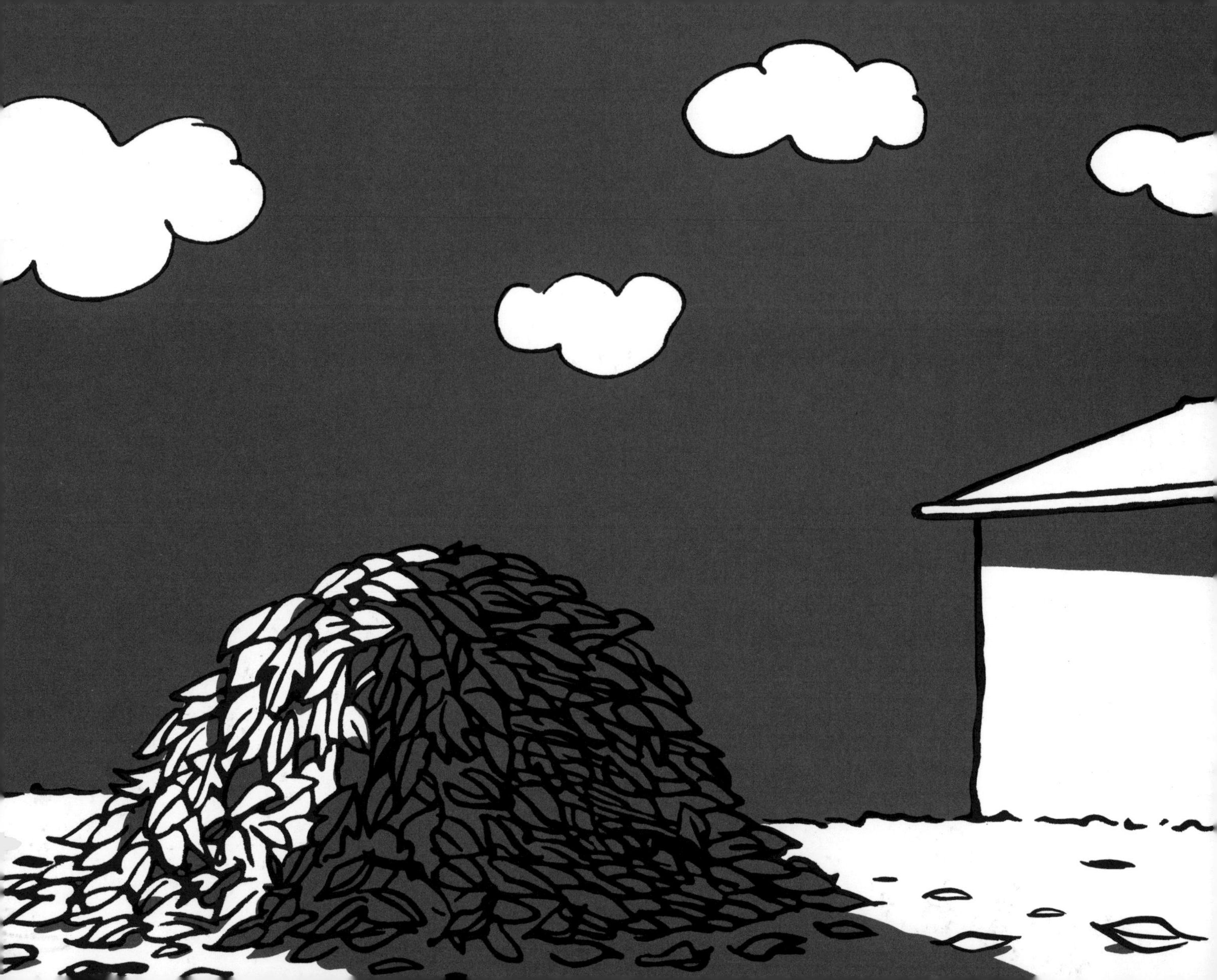

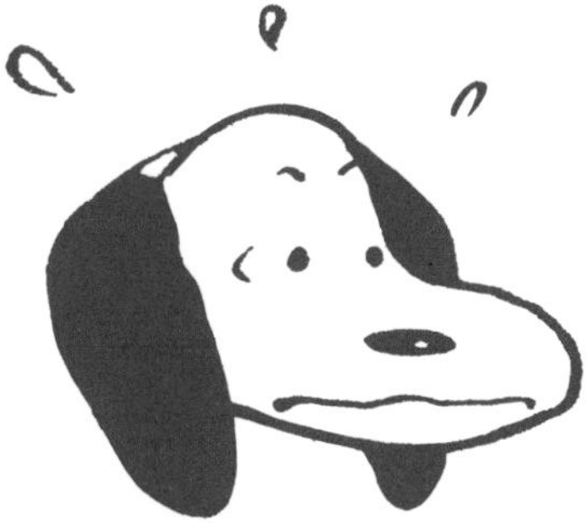

INDEX

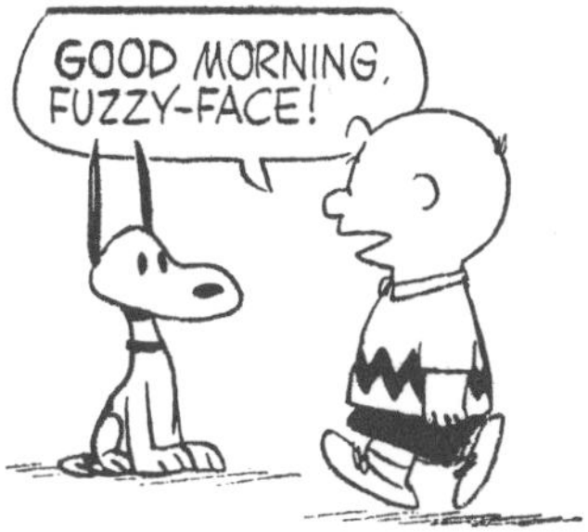

GOOD MORNING, FUZZY-FACE!

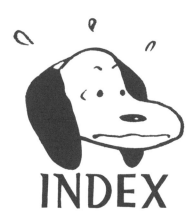

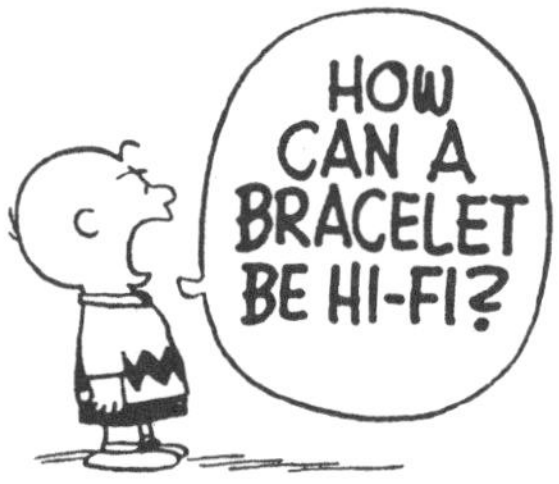
HOW CAN A BRACELET BE HI-FI?

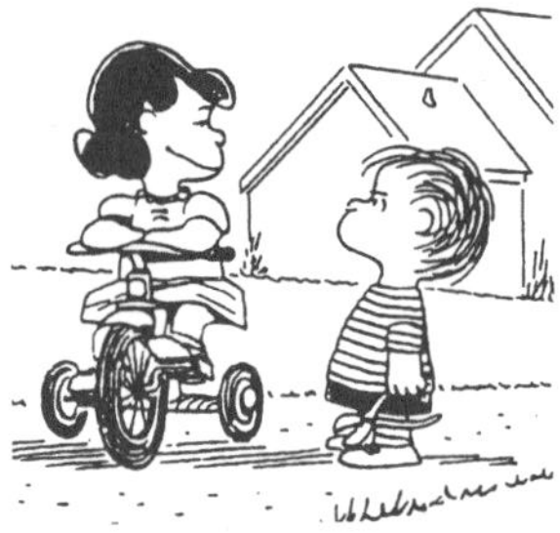

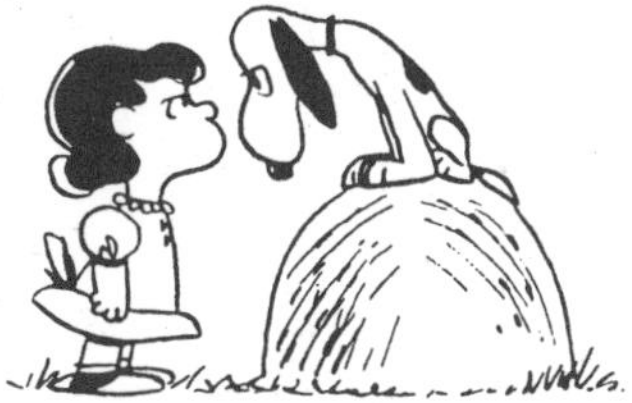

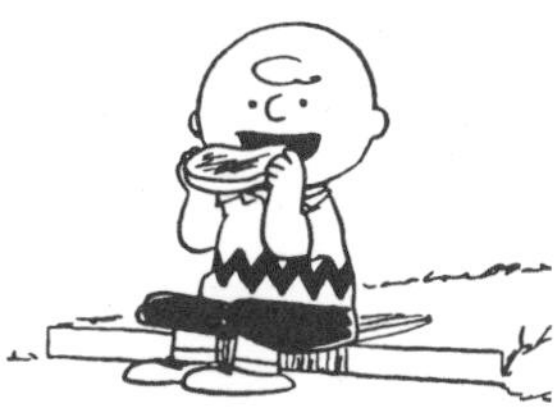

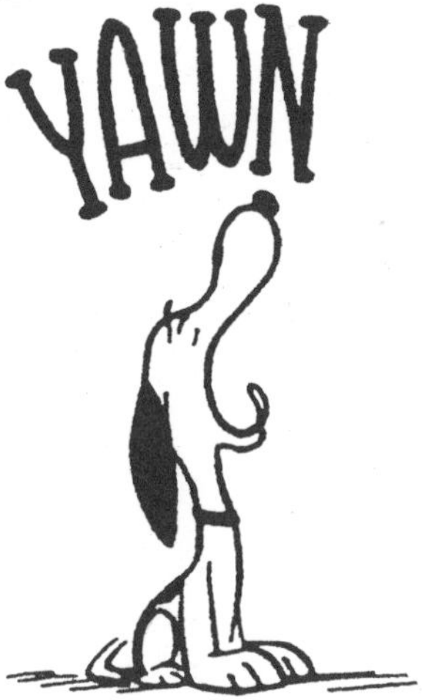
YAWN

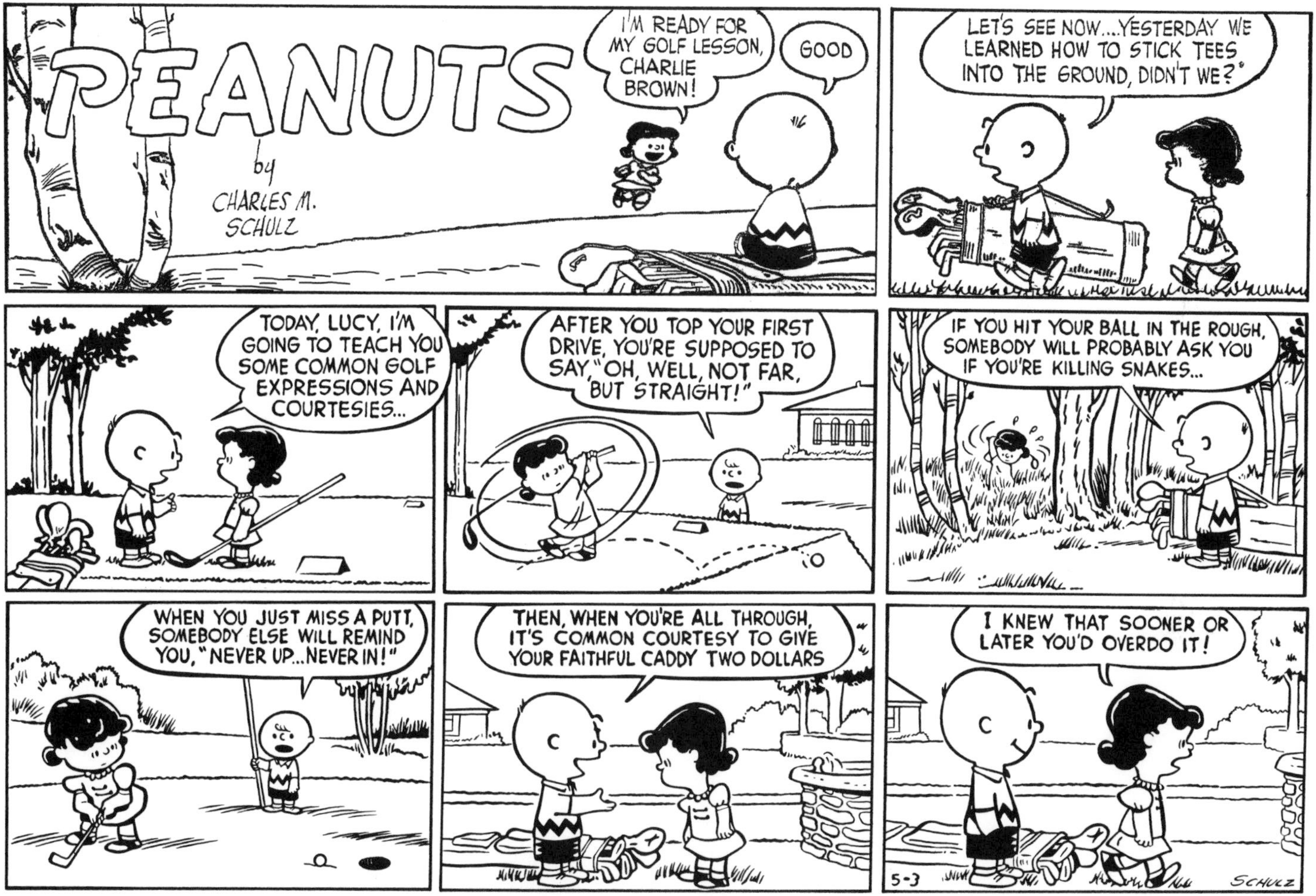
PEANUTS
by CHARLES M. SCHULZ
I'M READY FOR MY GOLF LESSON, CHARLIE BROWN!
GOOD
LET'S SEE NOW....YESTERDAY WE LEARNED HOW TO STICK TEES INTO THE GROUND, DIDN'T WE?
TODAY, LUCY, I'M GOING TO TEACH YOU SOME COMMON GOLF EXPRESSIONS AND COURTESIES...
AFTER YOU TOP YOUR FIRST DRIVE, YOU'RE SUPPOSED TO SAY, "OH, WELL, NOT FAR, BUT STRAIGHT!"
IF YOU HIT YOUR BALL IN THE ROUGH, SOMEBODY WILL PROBABLY ASK YOU IF YOU'RE KILLING SNAKES...
WHEN YOU JUST MISS A PUTT, SOMEBODY ELSE WILL REMIND YOU, "NEVER UP...NEVER IN!"
THEN, WHEN YOU'RE ALL THROUGH, IT'S COMMON COURTESY TO GIVE YOUR FAITHFUL CADDY TWO DOLLARS
I KNEW THAT SOONER OR LATER YOU'D OVERDO IT!
5-3
SCHULZ

EDITOR'S NOTE: We were unable to recover a copy of the full 5/3/1953 Sunday strip in time to publish it in *The Complete Peanuts 1953-1954* a year ago, and therefore ran it with a "mock" top strip provided by series designer Seth instead. Thanks to Peanuts megafan and tireless researcher Alan Ratliff, we've secured that missing top strip and present it here... in print for the first time in over 50 years! (Future printings of *The Complete Peanuts 1953-1954* will include this "correct" version, of course.)

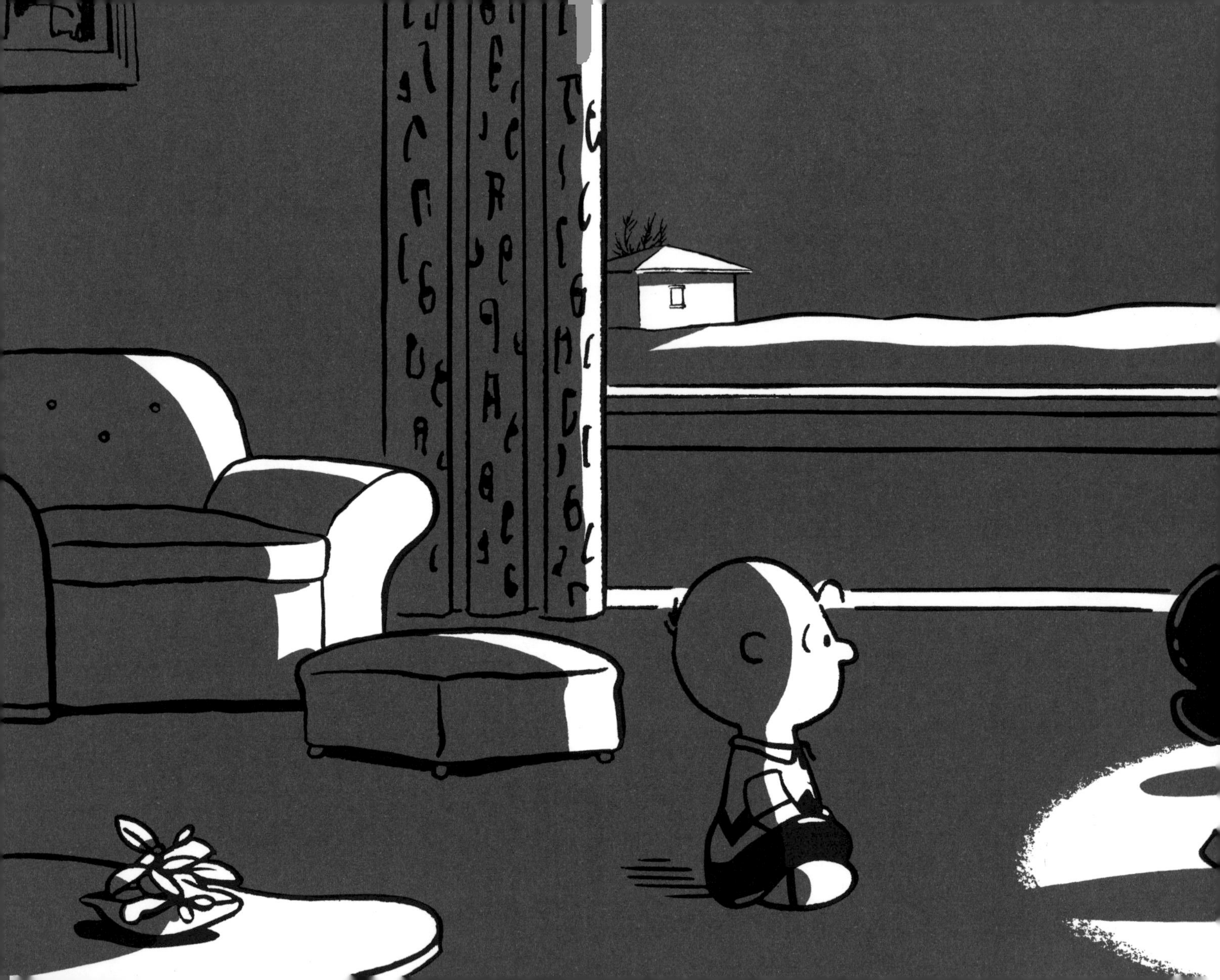

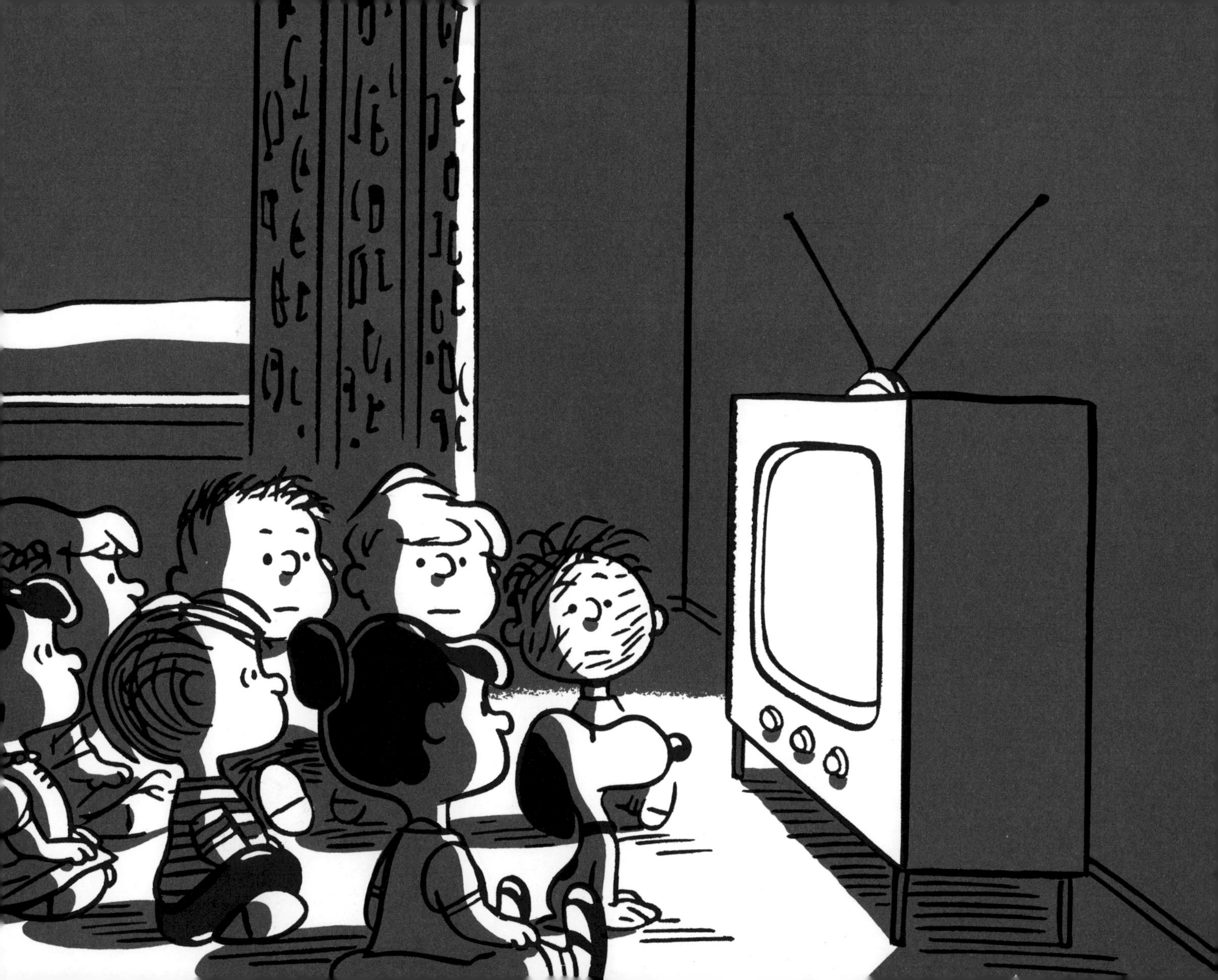

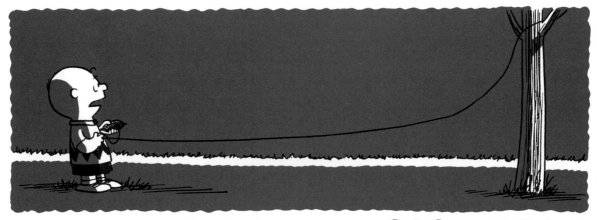

CHARLES M. SCHULZ · 1922 To 2000

Charles M. Schulz was born November 25, 1922 in Minneapolis. His destiny was foreshadowed when an uncle gave him, at the age of two days, the nickname Sparky (after the racehorse Spark Plug in the newspaper strip *Barney Google*).

Schulz grew up in St. Paul. By all accounts, he led an unremarkable, albeit sheltered, childhood. He was an only child, close to both parents, his eventual career path nurtured by his father, who bought four Sunday papers every week — just for the comics.

An outstanding student, he skipped two grades early on, but began to flounder in high school — perhaps not so coincidentally at the same time kids are going through their cruelest, most status-conscious period of socialization. The pain, bitterness, insecurity, and failures chronicled in *Peanuts* appear to have originated from this period of Schulz's life.

Although Schulz enjoyed sports, he also found refuge in solitary activities: reading, drawing, and watching movies. He bought comic books and Big Little Books, pored over the newspaper strips, and copied his favorites — *Buck Rogers*, the Walt Disney characters, *Popeye, Tim Tyler's Luck*. He quickly became a connoisseur; his heroes were Milton Caniff, Roy Crane, Hal Foster, and Alex Raymond.

In his senior year in high school, his mother noticed an ad in a local newspaper for a correspondence school, Federal Schools (later called Art

Instruction Schools). Schulz passed the talent test, completed the course and began trying, unsuccessfully, to sell gag cartoons to magazines. (His first published drawing was of his dog, Spike, and appeared in a 1937 *Ripley's Believe It Or Not!* installment.)

After World War II had ended and Schulz was discharged from the army, he started submitting gag cartoons to the various magazines of the time; his first breakthrough, however, came when an editor at *Timeless Topix* hired him to letter adventure comics. Soon after that, he was hired by his alma mater, Art Instruction, to correct student lessons returned by mail.

Between 1948 and 1950, he succeeded in selling 17 cartoons to the *Saturday Evening Post* — as well as, to the local *St. Paul Pioneer Press*, a weekly comic feature called *Li'l Folks*. It was run in the women's section and paid $10 a week. After writing and drawing the feature for two years, Schulz asked for a better location in the paper or for daily exposure, as well as a raise. When he was turned down on all three counts, he quit.

He started submitting strips to the newspaper syndicates. In the Spring of 1950, he received a letter from the United Feature Syndicate, announcing their interest in his submission, *Li'l Folks*. Schulz boarded a train in June for New York City; more interested in doing a strip than a panel, he also brought along the first installments of what would become *Peanuts* — and that was what sold. (The title, which Schulz loathed to his dying day, was imposed by the syndicate). The first *Peanuts* daily appeared October 2, 1950; the first Sunday, January 6, 1952.

Prior to *Peanuts*, the province of the comics page had been that of gags, social and political observation, domestic comedy, soap opera, and various adventure genres. Although *Peanuts* changed, or evolved, during the 50 years Schulz wrote and drew it, it remained, as it began, an anomaly on the comics page — a comic strip about the interior crises of the cartoonist himself. After a painful divorce in 1973 from which he had not yet recovered, Schulz told a reporter, "Strangely, I've drawn better cartoons in the last six months — or as good as I've ever drawn. I don't know how the human mind works." Surely, it was this kind of humility in the face of profoundly irreducible human questions that makes *Peanuts* as universally moving as it is.

Diagnosed with cancer, Schulz retired from *Peanuts* at the end of 1999. He died on February 12th 2000, just two days before Valentine's day — and the day before his last strip was published — having completed 17,897 daily and Sunday strips, each and every one fully written, drawn, and lettered entirely by his own hand — an unmatched achievement in comics.

—Gary Groth

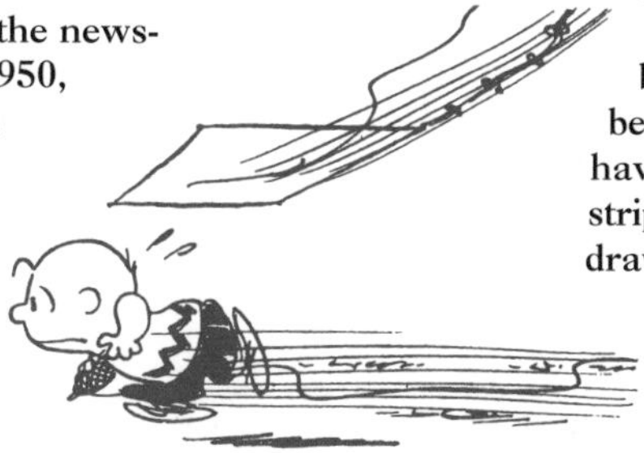

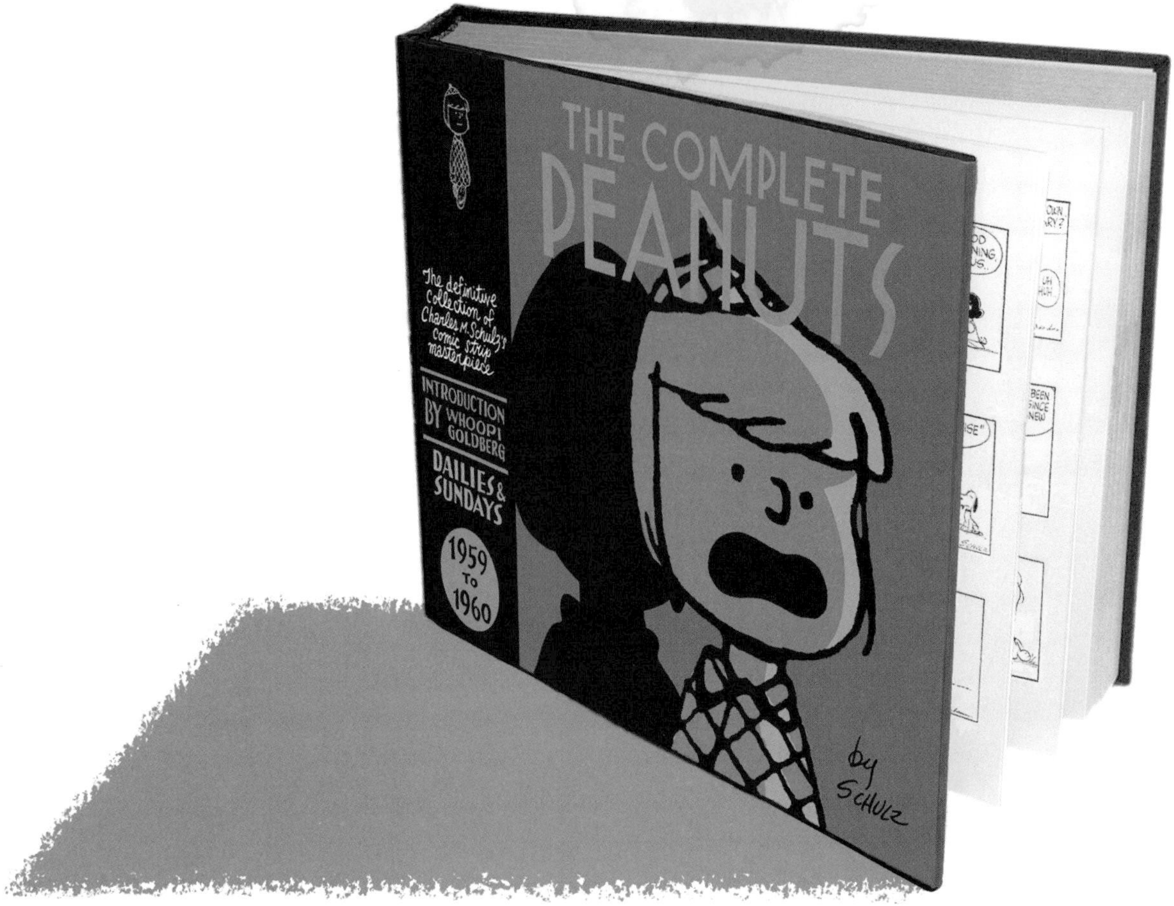
THE COMPLETE PEANUTS
The definitive collection of Charles M. Schulz's comic strip masterpiece
INTRODUCTION BY WHOOPI GOLDBERG
DAILIES & SUNDAYS
1959 TO 1960
by SCHULZ

COMING IN *THE COMPLETE PEANUTS: 1959-1960*

The very first "Great Pumpkin" sequence... the introduction of Linus's beloved teacher Miss Othmar... the "Happiness is a warm puppy" strip... the gang loses a baseball game 600 to nothing... a highway threatens Snoopys doghouse... the very first psychiatrist-booth gag... Linus's blanket-hating gramma debuts... and not only is Sally is born, but she swiftly matures enough to get her crush on Linus! All this plus an introduction by Whoopi Goldberg!

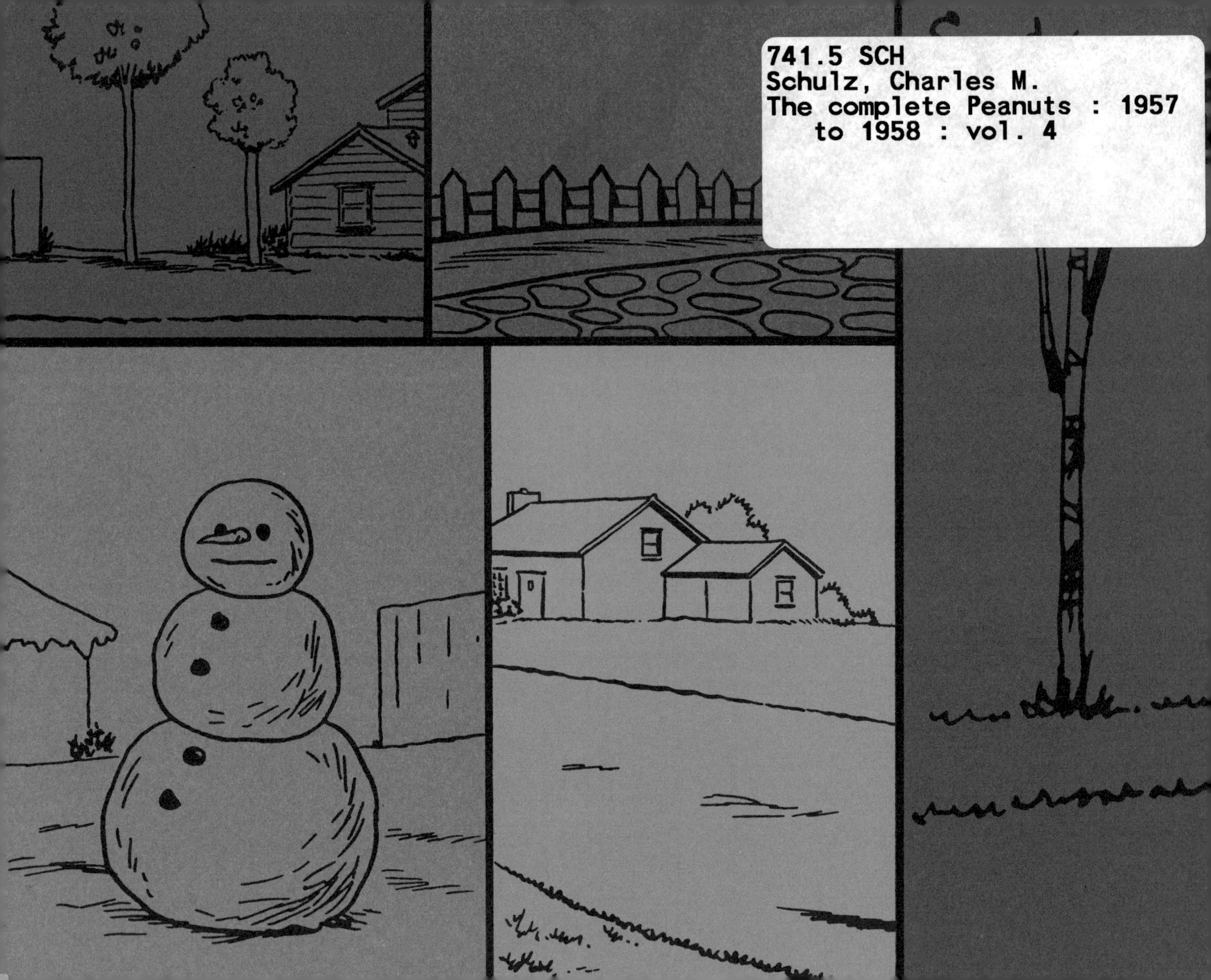